To Amy

with love and gratitude

in the year of our golden anniversary (D.V.)

and in memory of my mother-in-law

Mamie Tong (1918-2016)

聖經研究叢書

提多書註釋

馮蔭坤 著

基道出版社

▼

聖經研究叢書

提多書註釋

A Commentary on the Epistle to Titus

作者

馮蔭坤 Ronald Y. K. Fung

責任編輯

沈靜筠

裝幀設計

奇文雲海 · 設計顧問

■

出版 / 發行

基道出版社

香港沙田火炭坳背灣街 26 號富騰工業中心 1011 室

LOGOS PUBLISHERS

Unit 1011, Fo Tan Ind. Centre, 26 Au Pui Wan St., Shatin, Hong Kong

電話：(852) 2687-0331 傳真：(852) 2687-0281

網址：http://www.logos.com.hk

承印

陽光(彩美)印刷有限公司

●

3/2018 初版

Cat. No. LP1100

ISBN: 978-962-457-552-1

刷次	10	9	8	7	6	5	4	3	2	1
年份	2027	2026	2025	2024	2023	2022	2021	2020	2019	2018

目　錄

註 釋

自　序

二〇一五年四月下旬《以弗所書註釋》付梓後，筆者完成了第八卷保羅書信的註釋，但保羅書信餘下還有五卷：哥林多前書、哥林多後書，和教牧書信（提前、提後、提多書）。前兩卷在新約較長的書信中排第二和第三（最長的是羅馬書），而教牧書信三卷加起來共有十三章，像哥林多後書一樣，總共的節數（242 節）亦接近哥林多後書（256 節）。當時筆者已七十七歲，自忖沒有足夠的心力，也未必還有足夠的年日，去寫作哥林多前書或後書或教牧書信（視為一個單元）那麼長的書卷的註釋。曾一度考慮重拾路加獨有的比喻的研究，[1] 但最後覺得仍是留在保羅書信的範疇較為穩妥！這樣決定後，鎖定「目標」（下一個努力的對象）便輕易做到了——提多書，因它是教牧書信中最短的，只有三章，不像寫給提摩太的兩卷共有十章。

雖然選擇單獨處理提多書主要是基於個人的考量，但這選擇既非創新之舉，[2] 亦與教牧書信研究新近的一種趨勢相符。長久以來，教牧書信[3] 的三封信被視為一個單元。[4] 但是，就如馬歇爾所指出，新

---

1 見《比喻》i。此小書曾絕版多年，但於二〇一六年二月獲出版社以「隨量印刷」（POD [print-on-demand]）的形式延續它的生命！

2 見簡寫表之（四），尤其是其中的 Banker, Genade, Jeon I, 和 Quinn（下面 xxxix-xl）。

3 Quinn 1 這樣解釋此統稱：'These three letters are "pastoral" because they are *practical*, in other words, they are ordered to a Christian *praxis*, to the activities of believers.' 較好的解釋是，'They have been given the title "Pastoral" . . . because they are addressed to chief pastors and are largely concerned with their duties'（Kelly 1）。無論如何，此統稱其實並非完全合適：'First Timothy is the most truly pastoral, and Second Timothy least so, with Titus occupying an intermediate position'（Harrison, *INT* 347）。

4 Schnelle, 'Pastoral Letters' 327: 'This designation, to be sure, fits 2 Timothy in only a restricted sense, but nonetheless in modern times the three letters are always regarded as a unity.' 鄧雅各也認為，'In view of the degree of cohesion between the letters, it does

近的一些研究刻意將這三封信分開來（而不是作為具有共同特色的一組）獨立地研究，這種進路正在穩步發展中。採取這種進路的作者強調三封信的個別性：[5] 儘管它們具有共同的特色，且是有別於保羅信集其餘十卷的一組書信，但它們仍是單獨的三封信，各有自己的特色和神學發展，因此它們的獨特之處應受到注意，成為關注的重點。承認這一點的學者有認為三封信是出自同一位作者手筆的，亦有認為它們是由不止一位作者寫成的。[6]

---

continue to make sense to treat them as a loose unit, sufficiently distinct as such within the NT / New Testament canon'（Dunn 777 / Dunn, 'Titus' 275*a*）。See also Fatum, 'Christ' 180.

5 E.g., P. H. Towner, *NDBT* 335*b*: 'In spite of the overlap of themes and language, it is clear that each letter is unique' (see 335*b*-36*a* for details); Witherington 98 n.31: 'Without neglecting the common features these three documents share, we should study each letter as an individual unit, having its own situation in life.' See also Towner, 'Method' 302: 'there are no internal clues to suggest that they originated from the same place or time, or that they are to be read as one literary unit. Is it, therefore, justified to interpret the three letters as if they are one literary unit? . . . each letter possibly addresses a unique historical situation'; Towner III 30:「現代範例強加給它們的文集地位〔the corpus status thrust upon them by the modern paradigm〕是不當的，也是過度簡化的理解。三者的相互關係比較微妙〔are more subtle [than that]〕；若要公平解讀其信息，每一封書信的個別性與獨立性是更基本的」（唐書禮 43）。Johnson II 33 表示，'in order to sharpen the perception of the letters as separate and distinct compositions, I will deal with 2 Timothy first, and then 1 Timothy and Titus.'

6 See Marshall, 'Recent Study' 304-8; 308: 'This is recognized both by scholars who believe in one author (Fuchs, Towner, and Wieland) and by those who believe in more than one author (Aageson, Richards)*.'「正在穩步發展中」英文原作 'is developing in momentum'（304）。（*Murphy-O'Connor ['2 Timothy'] 辯證，提前和提多書二者跟提後有超過三十點不同之處，這使三封信極不可能是出自同一作者的手筆。但是鄧雅各認為莫氏 'overstates the disagreements' [Dunn 776 n.5].）（**1**）Cf. **Van Neste**, 'Structure' 120: 'A growing trend in Pastorals research suggests that the individual letters must be studied first <u>on their own terms</u> before they are compared with each other. Otherwise the distinctive nuances of each letter can be missed'; **idem**, Review of Montague [2008] 417: 'In keeping with the current (and, I believe, correct) trend, Montague argues that each of these letters must be understood <u>in its own terms</u> before being combined with one another'; **Jeon** II xii: 'a careful study of the letter [Titus] should begin by treating the letter <u>on its own</u>, without undue reliance on what Saint Paul wrote in 1 and 2 Timothy'; **Sumney**, *Opponents* 302: 'We have found a separate group of opponents in each of these letters. . . . Since these three letters each address different opponents, each letter addresses a somewhat different occasion. This provides some confirmation that they are indeed letters. . . . This being the case, our study of the opponents of the Pastoral Epistles also confirms that these letters must be read <u>on their own</u> before looking for similarities and connections'; **Wieland**, 'Function' 167 (after a

部分由於本書只是提多書的註釋，因此筆者沒有詳細討論「教牧書信的作者」這個十分複雜的問題，[7] 只提供了簡單的導論[8] 交代自

---

study of salvation language in the PE): 'There is sufficient specificity about the application of soteriological material in each letter to support the view that each represents a distinct response to a particular occasion. . . . Clearly there are implications here for the study of the PE. If each of these letters offers its own distinctive soteriological presentation, it must be asked whether each may not also have a unique contribution to make in other areas. The voice of each should be heard.' See also **Genade** 3 n.8: 'The call is for scholars to consider the three letters individually rather than as a corpus'; **C. Martin** 412*a*: 'Each letter must be studied individually, even if there are common themes'; **Hagner**, 'Titus' 546: 'Planners of the Theology of the Disputed Paulines Group decided that it would be a sound procedure to treat each of the Pastoral Epistles individually rather than to deal with the corpus as a whole. . . . The current paper attempts to explore Titus along similar lines, reading it as a Pauline document.'（But note 558: 'In my opinion, however, these letters need ultimately to be considered together.' 見下面之〔**4**〕。）（**2**）**Johnson** I 4 也認為，三封信是 'quite different letters'. 'Wherever it started, the habit of treating all three letters as one fundamentally inhibits our ability to hear each text on its own terms'（I 5; 7-9 列出三封信之間的種種分別）。他指出有關教牧書信作者問題的爭議中的一種趨勢：'Characterizations of "the Pastorals" are typically drawn from all three letters coalesced into a whole, while the individual characteristics of the respective letters are overlooked'（Johnson, 'Titus' 376*a*）。See also **Hempelmann**, Review of Oden [1989] 161: 'the topical approach to the Pastorals, Oden's attempt to make them "more accessible for preaching and teaching," may not be the best if, in fact, these books are three separate letters from Paul. Taken separately, they are not one document and should not be treated as though they were.'
（**3**）Towner III 88-89（唐書禮 122-23）甚至倡議告別「教牧書信（Pastoral Epistles）」這總稱。唐書禮將提前、提後、提多書改稱為 'letters to coworkers'（其餘十卷則稱為 'letters to churches'），藉此表明 'both the individuality of the letters and their cluster relationship.'（**4**）不過，哈格拿認為，'because the letters display a similar perspective and sufficient commonality and are ostensibly the only letters addressed to Paul's individual co-workers, they warrant consideration as a group. This approach need not close our eyes to the distinctives of the three letters'（Hagner, *New Testament* 635）。

7 Metzger, 'Reconsideration' 94*b*: 'The problems which are involved in this question are complex and bear upon not only style and vocabulary, but also such diverse matters as the organization of the Church reflected in these Epistles, their theological thought-forms, the nature of the errorists who are combatted, and the personal history of the Apostle.'「教牧書信的作者」這問題，在以下註釋書的「導論」部分都佔了很大／不少的篇幅：Knight II 13-52（out of 3-54 = 40 out of 52 pages = 76.9%）；Marshall 57-92（out of 1-108 = 35 out of 108 pages = 32.4%〔這卻不是 'Almost half of [his] introduction' [Belleville, 'Christology' 317]〕）。在古特立的《新約導論》第十七章裏（Guthrie, *NTI* 607-59），'The Authenticity of the Epistles'（607-49）的討論（43 out of 53 pages）更高達全章篇幅的 81.1%.

8 孟威廉的註釋之導論部分為 91 頁（Mounce xlvi-cxxxvi; 連書目則為 96 頁），然而他稱之為 'this brief introduction'（xlvii）！（希伯來書的作者也稱他那長達十三章的講章為這簡短的規勸〔來十三 22，新普；參《來》2.489-90，1.24-26〕！）本

己的立場。本註釋的重點仍然在於根據原文對經文作出的詳細闡釋。適逢今年是宗教改革五百週年，[9] 最近讀到關於法國宗教改革神學家加爾文的一段話，頗適合在此引述。加爾文認為，

> 「呈現聖經作者的思想〔mens scriptoris〕幾乎是註釋者惟一的任務，故此他帶領讀者離開作者的意思越遠，他就越是偏離自己的目標，起碼是離開了正題。*
> 換言之，註釋者不應令讀者或聽眾把注意力放在註釋者自己身上，而是應該運用他一切的知識和語文能力，引領他們進入聖經作者的原意之中。……他一切的知識，不論是對文法、修辭、歷史、文化以至教會傳統的認識，皆不過是聖道的僕役，幫助普羅信徒跨越障礙進入聖經作者的原意。」[10]

這位宗教改革家對聖經作者原意的著重，仍然值得今天的釋經者奉為圭臬。[11]

註釋相對地簡單的導論（僅 36 頁）比較名副其實。

9 「1517 年 10 月 31 日，〔馬丁・路德〕針對教廷售賣贖罪券，提出〈九十五條論綱〉（*Ninety-Five Theses*）反對，掀起宗教改革運動」（《聖神》334*b*-35*a*）。

10 李耀坤：《加爾文》25。（*此句是加爾文著作的直接引句〔六角括號是原來的〕；隨後一段則是李氏對加爾文的闡述。）這裏的四重強調令人印象深刻！必須補充的是，「加爾文並不反對從註釋中引伸〔原文照錄〕出適切當代處境的教導和應用，……他所提倡的，是在經文與釋義之間保持一種主從的區別」（26）。參《加》001 註 3 之（3）。梁薇則建議，「華人教會及神學界當考慮的詮釋模式」，是「『兩個中心』（two-centred model）的詮釋策略，即『文本』與『讀者』同為中心（text-centred and reader-oriented）的模式」（〈詮釋方向〉63，詳見 64-66）。Cf. Lai, 'Hermeneutical Prospects' 150: 'Toward a Proposal of a Two-Centre [*sic*] Model: Text-Centred and Folder [*sic*] Reader-Oriented'; see 150-54.

11 參以下學者的見解：（**1**）Dunn, 'Romans 13.1-7' 63: 'hearing the text with the meaning and force which Paul intended his first readers to hear [is] the primary task of exegesis'（參《羅》4.10）；（**2**）Vanhoozer, 'Reader' 317-18:「釋經者的首要興趣應該是，讓聖經文本表達它的意見（'have its say'），亦即是說，以謙卑和尊敬的態度專心聆聽並注意經文」（《加》001 註 3 之〔3〕）；（**3**）Hagner, 'New Testament' 9*b*-*c*:

每一本書的稿件完成，都是感恩和鳴謝的召喚。一如既往，上帝是應當稱頌的（詩六十六 20，六十八 35）；祂讓筆者以望八之年完成此註釋，使筆者也許可以在這意義上置身於詩人口中的義人的行列中：他們髮白的時候仍結果子（詩九十二 12、14）。由於上帝的恩典和保守，此註釋出版之年，將會是（主若許可）筆者的結婚五十週歲；衷心感激內子碧薇經年累月的堅定支持。也是由於上帝的恩典，「中大」於二〇〇三年開始對筆者發出的委任（三年一任），已在「崇神」前任院長及原推薦人（盧龍光牧師）和現任院長（邢福增教授）的任內先後更新了四次；如果筆者只能在茅舍的小書房寫作，過去十四年（＝在「中神」任職年期的一半！）所完成的著作（包括本註釋）是不可能出現的。對筆者而言，中神發出的「退休教授證」和中大發出的「（名譽）職員證」都是珍貴的證件，它們讓筆者可以從兩所圖書館借書。最後，本註釋由基道出版社出版，可說更新了闊別二十七年的合作關係，[12] 這也是值得高興的事。

提多書這信函雖然比較簡短，但其主要課題的論述——使徒保羅的身分和信息（一 1～3）、教會領袖的資格和職能（一 5～9）、與福音相符的生活及其神學基礎（二 1～三 8），以及真理與謬誤的區分和對立（一 10～16，三 9～

前瞻二十一世紀，'New Testament scholars will continue to stress the importance of grammatical-historical *exegesis*, the determination of the meaning of texts in the light of their respective historical contexts and of the intended meaning of the author. And they will continue to protest the misuse of texts by those who seem to have no appreciation of the importance of exegesis. . . . If it is finally an author's intention that determines our understanding of a passage, there is simply no other way to proceed.'（參《羅》3.13 註 16，附中譯。）筆者知道，聖經作者的「意指意義（intended meaning）」是否存在或是否可以確定備受爭議；在這方面，筆者再次（參同上）大力推薦這篇文章——余達心：〈閱讀、詮釋的道德責任〉，《中國神學研究院期刊》27（1999）41-56。

12 見註 1（上面 ix）。

11）——仍然對今天的教會和信徒提供清晰的教導，是我們不應忽視的。

馮蔭坤　謹誌

香港中文大學崇基學院神學院

二〇一七年六月六日

附錄：一名「筆耕文兵」的分享[1]

我在英皇書院唸大學預科時信主，就讀於香港大學期間獻身，畢業前蒙召，畢業後立即加入全職事奉的行列。第一份工作是在宣道書局任編輯助理（1960-62 年），同時兼任國際基督徒學生福音團契[2] 遠東區的英文學生季刊《道路》[3] 的創刊編輯（1961-62 年）。因此，我的第一本護照上，在「職業」一欄填寫的是 'Christian Literature Worker'。這樣樸實的描寫竟然在重要的意義上預示了我的一生！

在英國倫敦聖經學院完成了初步的神學訓練（1962-65 年），回港後成為國際基督徒學生福音團契的遠東區幹事（1965-67 年），主要工作仍是編輯《道路》雜誌。但在這崗位上常感捉襟見肘，部分原因是稿源不足；於是改往播道神學院任教（1967-69 年），期間深感必須進修。上帝也開路供應，遂於美國福樂神學院和英國曼徹斯特大學度過了六年的研究生生涯（1969-75 年）。在美國兩年的進修時期，被當時正籌備於香港設立具研究院水準的神學院的數位華人神學生招募入伍，其後於一九七二年加入了「中國神學研究院儲備師資」（faculty-in-preparation）的行列，一九七五年回港後開始在中神事奉，自至二〇〇三年正式退休。

「正式退休」暗示「非正式」的退休。因為在一九八三年，我離開了專任講師的行列，一九八八年起不再授課，為要專心閱讀和寫作。在此之前，曾與陳濟民合編《初熟之果：聖經與本色神學》（中神、天道聯合出版，1979），又和余達心合編《事奉的人生》（滕近輝院長賀壽文集；宣道，1982）。我的第一本書（《恩賜與事奉：保羅神學點滴》

---

1 編按：本文轉載自第七屆金書獎頒獎典禮場刊（2015 年，作者獲頒金筆獎），頁 20-21，承蒙基督教出版聯會蒙允轉載。

2 International Fellowship of Evangelical Students (IFES).

3 *The Way*. *Way* = Witnessing to Asian Youth 的首字母組合字（acronym）。對象是亞洲的大專學生。

〔天道，1980〕）和第一本註釋書（《真理與自由——加拉太書註釋》〔證道，1982〕），以及其後收集成為《擘開生命之餅——路加五個獨有的比喻》（基道，1990）的文章，也是在我「非正式」退休前出版的。

一九八三至二〇〇三年這二十年之內，先後完成了我惟一的一本英文註釋書、[4] 天道聖經註釋叢書的《腓立比書》、《帖撒羅尼迦前書》、《帖撒羅尼迦後書》和《希伯來書（卷上）（卷下）》（1987-95 年），以及四卷的《羅馬書註釋》（台灣：校園書房，1997-2003）。從中神正式退休後，上帝的奇妙恩典讓我可以在香港中文大學崇基學院神學組（2004 年升格為「神學院」）繼續我的文字事奉，在過去的十二年（2003-15 年），先後完成了重新寫作的《加拉太書註釋》（兩卷；台灣：校園，2008）、《歌羅西書‧腓利門書註釋》（兩卷；明道，2013）和《以弗所書註釋》（兩卷；明道，2016）。如果把早年的翻譯之作[5] 也計算在內，可以說我和基督教文字工作結下不解之緣已超過五十五個寒暑。

以上像流水帳一般的分享，一方面是對邀稿的回應，同時也召喚我再次（在書本的序言以外）感恩和鳴謝。我衷心向上帝感恩，祂讓我在基督教文字事工、尤其是在解釋聖經的園地上，有許多機會努力耕耘；特別感激在這過程中內子碧薇堅定的支持，以及中神和崇神不嫌我白佔地土（因對學院的工作並無貢獻）而多年提供大有幫助的寫作環境。也感謝以其他方式（例如為拙著寫推薦序或推薦文）給予鼓勵的基督徒同道，還有相關的出版社及有關的編輯；沒有後者相助，含辛茹苦才孕育出來的作品，就不能以可拿在手裏的書本的形式面世。最後的但非最不重要的，我感謝基督教出版聯會頒給我這個獎項；儘管它不像網上投票的兩個獎項那麼具「真普選」的成分，它所代表的專業肯定仍是我所欣然接受的。

4　*The Epistle to the Galatians* (NICNT; Grand Rapids: Eerdmans, 1988).

5　何金斯著：《從今以後》（證道，1959）；麥加夫著：《在基督裏的生命》（宣道，1961）；《基督徒校園生活指南》（三冊；香港：國際基督徒學生福音團契，1967）；（與李思潔合譯）金候華著：《活祭》（證道，1968）。

簡寫表

簡寫表（之一）：中文的

甲部：聖經譯本（按最早的出版年份排列）

呂譯	呂振中譯：《聖經》（香港：聖經公會，1970；新約 1952）。新約部分載《新約聖經並排版》（聯合聖經公會，1997）
思高	《聖經》（香港：思高聖經學會，1968）。新約部分載《新約聖經並排版》（聯合聖經公會，1997）
當代	《當代福音》（香港：香港新力出版社，1978 第九版）
新譯	《聖經新譯本》（香港：天道書樓，1992；新約 1976）〔本註釋引用的是網上「徒‧書館」的《聖經新譯本－新約（神字版）》2016 環球天道機構〕
新和	《聖經——新標點和合本》（香港：聖經公會，1988）。新約部分載《新約聖經並排版》（聯合聖經公會，1997）

現修	《現代中文譯本修訂版》（1995）之新約部分，載《新約聖經並排版》（聯合聖經公會，1997）
和修	《聖經——和合本修訂版（上帝版）》（香港：香港聖經公會，2010〔網上版〕）〔除非另外註明，這是本註釋引用的中譯本〕
新普	《聖經・新約全書——中英對照（新普及譯本・NLT）》（香港：漢語聖經協會，2006）
馮譯	馮象譯注：《新約》（Hong Kong: OUP (China), 2010）

乙部：字典、辭典、文法書

《牛津》	張芳杰主編：《牛津現代高級英漢雙解詞典》（第三版；香港：啟思出版有限公司，1984；第 24 刷 1992）
《成語》	西北師範學院中文系《漢語成語詞典》編寫組編著：《漢語成語詞典》（香港：中華書局香港分局／上海教

	育出版社，1987）[1]
《宗教》	鄧肇明編：《英漢宗教字典》（增修版；香港：道聲，2001）
《國語》	《學生國語辭典》（第七版；台北：遠東圖書公司，中華民國七十七年〔1988〕）
《聖神》	盧龍光主編：《基督教聖經與神學詞典》（香港：漢語聖經協會，2003）
《新希》	黃根春主編：《新約希臘文詞典》（香港：香港聖經公會，2015）
《新雅》	《新雅中文字典》（香港：新雅文化事業，1985；第五刷 1989）
《輔讀》	黃錫木著：《原文新約輔讀》（新約希臘文研究系列，3；香港：崇真會救恩堂、基道出版社聯合出版，1994）
《簡明》	《新約希漢簡明字典》（聯合聖經公會，1989）

1 原著用簡體中文；本註釋引用時一律化為繁體中文。

《辭典》	霍桑、馬挺主編，里德副編，楊長慧譯，郭秀娟審校：《21 世紀保羅書信辭典》（兩冊；台北：校園，2009）

丙部：教牧書信 / 提多書註釋及研究（按姓氏的英文字母序排列）

陳（Chan）	陳終道著：〈提多書〉， 載《提摩太前後書・提多書》（新約書信讀經講義；台北：校園，1982 四版增修〔初版 1971〕）[2]
張（Cheung）	張永信著：《教牧書信》（天道聖經註釋；香港：天道，2005）〔尤其是 305-389〕
周（Chow）	周天和著：〈教牧書信〉，載石清州、周天和合著：《帖撒羅尼迦前後書・提摩太前後書・提多書・腓利門書》（中文聖經註釋第 38 卷；香港：基督教文藝，1997〔初版 1988〕）117-448（尤其是 405-448）

2 三卷教牧書信的註釋皆各以頁 1 開始：提前 = 1-216；提後 = 1-161；多 = 1-53。

古特立（Guthrie）	古特立著，李信毅、徐成德譯：《教牧書信》（丁道爾新約聖經註釋；台北：校園，2004）[3]〔尤其是 191-224〕
黃（Huang）編	黃迦勒主編：《提摩太前後書註解；提多書註解；腓利門書註解＝提I多I門》（解經系列；香港：基督徒文摘社／天道，2007）1-242（尤其是185-232）
侯嘉文（Hultgren）	侯嘉文著：〈提摩太前後、提多書〉，載侯嘉文、奧斯著，陸秀雲譯：《提摩太前後、提多、帖撒羅尼迦後書》（道聲新約神學註釋；香港：道聲，1989）7-181（尤其是 139-167）
Keegan II	Terence J. Keegan 著，活水編輯小組編譯：《保祿牧靈書信詮釋》（台北：光啟文化事業，2015）[4]〔尤其是85-105〕
利斐特（Liefeld）	利斐特著，黃宜嫻譯：《提摩太前書、提摩太後書、提多書》（國際釋經應用系列 • 54-56；香港：漢語聖經

3 英文原著見簡寫表（之五）：Guthrie II（下面 xlviii）。
4 英文原著見簡寫表（之五）：Keegan I（下面 li）。

	協會，2005）[5]〔尤其是 13-36、325-377〕
馬唐納（MacDonald）	馬唐納著，角石翻譯組翻譯：《新約聖經註釋（中冊——保羅書信）》（香港：角石出版社，1997）〔尤其是 551-569〕
彭（Peng）編	彭國瑋總編輯：《提摩太前後書、提多書研讀本》（台北：台灣聖經公會，2011）〔尤其是 90-109〕
曾（Tsang）	曾思瀚著：《教牧書信神學——牧養職志傳承》（聖經神學系列 1；香港：香港浸信會神學院，2014）〔尤其是 1-155〕
唐（Towner）	唐書禮著，潘秋松、陳志文、李忠晉、梁永勝譯：《提摩太與提多書註釋（上）（下）》（South Pasadena, CA: 美國麥種傳道會，2008）〔尤其是 953-1181〕

5 此書為簡體版；本註釋引用時一律化為繁體中文。**(1)** 此書的繁體版為：利斐特著，黃宜嫻譯：《提前、提後、提多書》（國際釋經應用系列 54-56；香港：漢語聖經協會，2004）。「利斐特」這譯名值得商榷，因為 Liefeld 的首個讀音是 'lie'（如在多一 2 的 'God . . . does not lie' [NIV, NJB]）而不是 'lee'（as in 'Mr. Lee'）。**(2)** 英文原著見簡寫表（之五）：Liefeld（下面 liii-iv）。

丁部：其他

《串釋（增簡）》	《聖經——串珠‧註釋本（增訂簡體版）》（香港：中國神學研究院編撰，證道出版社出版；中國基督教協會印發，2000）[6]
《羅》1	馮蔭坤著：《羅馬書註釋（卷壹）》（台北：校園，二版二刷 2003〔初版 1997〕）
《羅》2	馮蔭坤著：《羅馬書註釋（卷貳）》（台北：校園，二版 2001〔1999〕）
《羅》3	馮蔭坤著：《羅馬書註釋（卷叁）》（台北：校園，2001）
《羅》4	馮蔭坤著：《羅馬書註釋（卷肆）》（台北：校園，2003）
《加》	馮蔭坤著：《加拉太書註釋》（兩冊；台北：校園，三刷 2011〔初版 2008〕）
《弗》	馮蔭坤著：《以弗所書註釋》（聖經註釋叢書；兩卷；香港：明道社，2016）
《腓》	馮蔭坤著：《腓立比書》（天道聖經註釋；

6 原著用簡體中文；本註釋引用時一律化為繁體中文。

香港：天道，八刷 2015〔初版 1987〕）

《西・門》 馮蔭坤著：《歌羅西書・腓利門書註釋》（聖經註釋叢書；兩冊；香港：明道社，2013）

《帖前》 馮蔭坤著：《帖撒羅尼迦前書》（天道聖經註釋；香港：天道，六刷 2016〔初版 1989〕）

《帖後》 馮蔭坤著：《帖撒羅尼迦後書》（天道聖經註釋；香港：天道，六刷 2015〔初版 1990〕）

《來》1 馮蔭坤著：《希伯來書（卷上）》（天道聖經註釋；香港：天道，六刷 2013〔初版 1995〕）

《來》2 馮蔭坤著：《希伯來書（卷下）》（天道聖經註釋；香港：天道，七刷 2016〔初版 1995〕）

《恩賜》 馮蔭坤著：《恩賜與事奉：保羅神學點滴》（增訂版；香港：天道，1988〔初版 1980〕）

《比喻》 馮蔭坤著：《擘開生命之餅：路加五個獨有的比喻》（香港：基道，1990；隨量印刷 2016）

簡寫表（之二）：外文一般性的

AB	Anchor Bible
ABD	*The Anchor Bible Dictionary*, ed. David Noel Freedman (6 vols; New York: Doubleday, 1992)
AGJU	Arbeiten zur Geschichte des antiken Judentums und des Urchristentum (Ancient Judaism and Early Christianity)
AshTJ	*Ashland Theological Journal*
Aune	David E. Aune, *The Westminster Dictionary of New Testament and Early Christian Literature and Rhetoric* (Louisville: WJK, 2003)
AUSS	*Andrews University Seminary Studies*
BAGD	*A Greek-English Lexicon of the New Testament and other Early Christian Literature* (2nd ed.), revised and augmented by F. Wilbur Gingrich & Frederick W. Danker from Walter Bauer's Fifth Edition, 1958 (Chicago and London: UCP, 1979)
BBR	*Bulletin for Biblical Research*

BDAG	*A Greek-English Lexicon of the New Testament and Other Early Christian Literature* (3rd ed.), revised and edited by Frederick William Danker (Chicago and London: UCP, 2000)
BDF	F. Blass, A. Debrunner & Robert W. Funk, *A Greek Grammar of the New Testament and Other Early Christian Literature* (Chicago: UCP, 1967 [1961])
BibInt	*Biblical Interpretation*
BibTr	*The Bible Translator*
BJRL	*Bulletin of the John Rylands (University) Library (of Manchester)*
BNTC	Black's New Testament Commentary
BS	*Bibliotheca Sacra*
BV	The Berkeley Version (1959)
BZNW	Beihefte zur Zeitschrift für die neutestamentliche Wissenschaft
CBQ	*Catholic Biblical Quarterly*
CGEDNT	Barclay M. Newman Jr., *A Concise Greek-English Dictionary of the New Testament* (London: United Bible Societies, 1971)
CJ	*Concordia Journal*
Concordance	*Concordance to the Novum Testamentum Graece* [= *Konkordanz*

	zum Novum Testamentum Graece] (3rd ed.; Berlin and New York: de Gruyter, 1987)
CTR	*Criswell Theological Review*
CUP	Cambridge University Press
CurTM	*Currents in Theology and Mission*
DBI	*A Dictionary of Biblical Interpretation*, ed. R. J. Coggins & J. L. Houlden (London: SCM / Philadelphia: TPI, 1990)
Discourse Analysis	Stanley E. Porter & Jeffrey T. Reed (ed.), *Discourse Analysis and the New Testament* (JSNTSS 170; Sheffield: Sheffield Academic, 1999)
DM	Dana, H. E., & Julius R. Mantey, *A Manual Grammar of the Greek New Testament* (New York: Macmillan, 1955 [1927])
DNTB	*Dictionary of New Testament Background*, ed. Craig A. Evans & Stanley E. Porter (Downers Grove, IL / Leicester, England: IVP, 2000)
DNTT	*The New International Dictionary of New Testament Theology*, ed. Colin Brown (E.T.; 3 vols; Exeter: Paternoster, 1975-1978)

DPL	*Dictionary of Paul and His Letters*, ed. Gerald F. Hawthorne, Ralph P. Martin & Daniel G. Reid (Downers Grove / Leicester: IVP, 1993)[1]
DTIB	*Dictionary for Theological Interpretation of the Bible*, ed. Kevin J. Vanhoozer et al. (Grand Rapids: Baker / London: SPCK, 2005)
EDNT	*Exegetical Dictionary of the New Testament*, ed. Horst Balz & Gerhard Schneider (E.T.; 3 vols; Grand Rapids: Eerdmans, 1990-1993)
e.g.	*exempli gratia*, for example
EQ	*Evangelical Quarterly*
ERT	*Evangelical Review of Theology*
esp.	especially
ESV	English Standard Version (2001)
E.T.	English Translation
et al.	*et alii*, and others
EurJTh	*European Journal of Theology*
ExpT	*Expository Times*
FilNeot	*Filología Neotestamentaria*
HBT	*Horizons in Biblical Theology*
IBD	*Illustrated Bible Dictionary*, rev. ed. N. Hillyer (3 parts; Leicester: IVP, 1980)

1 此辭典之中譯本為《辭典》；見簡寫表（之一）乙部（上面 xxi）。

ICC	International Critical Commentary
Idiom	C. F. D. Moule, *An Idiom-Book of New Testament Greek* (2nd ed.; Cambridge: CUP, 1968 [1959])
Int	*Interpretation*
ISBE	*The International Standard Bible Encyclopedia*, ed. Geoffrey W. Bromily et al. (fully revised, 4 vols; Grand Rapids: Eerdmans, 1979-88)
IVP	Inter-Varsity / Inter Varsity Press (England / U.S.A.)
JBL	*Journal of Biblical Literature*
JETS	*Journal of the Evangelical Theological Society*
JSNT	*Journal for the Study of the New Testament*
JSNTSS	Journal for the Study of the New Testament Supplement Series (now LNTS)
JTS	*Journal of Theological Studies*
KJV	King James (Authorized) Version (1611)
LN	Johannes P. Louw & Eugene A. Nida (ed.), *Greek-English Lexicon of the New Testament Based on Semantic Domains* (2 vols; United Bible Societies, 1989 [1988])

LNTS	Library of New Testament Studies (formerly JSNTSS)
LXE	LXX English Translation (Brenton)
LXX	The Septuagint
MGM	*Moulton & Geden Concordance to the Greek New Testament* (6th edition fully revised), ed. I. Howard Marshall (Edinburgh: TTC, 2002)
MHT	James Hope Moulton, Wilbert Francis Howard & Nigel Turner, *A Grammar of New Testament Greek* (4 vols; Edinburgh: TTC, 1906-1976)
MM	James Hope Moulton & George Milligan, *The Vocabulary of the Greek Testament* (London: Hodder & Stoughton, 1972 [1930])
NAU	New American Standard Bible with Codes (1995)
NDBT	*New Dictionary of Biblical Theology*, ed. T. Desmond Alexander et al. (Leicester / Downers Grove: IVP, 2000)
NEB	The New English Bible (1970, NT 1961)
Neot	*Neotestamentica*
Nestle-Aland	*Novum Testamentum Graece*, in the tradition of Eberhard Nestle and Erwin Nestle, ed. Barbara & Kurt Aland et al. (27th ed.), incorporated in *Greek-English*

	New Testament (9th rev. ed.; Stuttgart: Deutsche Bibelgesellschaft, 2001)
NIB	*The New Interpreter's Bible*, ed. Leander E. Keck et al. (12 vols; Nashville: Abingdon, 1994-2002)
NICNT	The New International Commentary on the New Testament
NIV	The New International Version (1984)
NIV2011	The New International Version (2011)
NJB	The New Jerusalem Bible (1985)
NKJV	New King James Version (1982, NT 1979)
NLT	New Living Translation (2004)
NovT	*Novum Testamentum*
NovTSup	Supplements to *Novum Testamentum*
NRSV	New Revised Standard Version (1989)
n.s. / NS	new series / New Series
NTS	*New Testament Studies*
OUP	Oxford University Press
Pace	with or by the leave (= permission) of
Paraphrase	F. F. Bruce, *An Expanded Paraphrase of the Epistles of Paul* (Exeter: Paternoster, 1965)
Paul and Pseudepigraphy	Stanley E. Porter & Gregory E. Fewster (ed.), *Paul and Pseudepigraphy* (Leiden and Boston: Brill, 2013)

Phillips	J. B. Phillips, 'The New Testament in Modern English' (rev. ed.), in *Eight Translation New Testament* (Wheaton: Tyndale House Publishers, 1974)
Pseudepigrapha	James Hamilton Charlesworth (ed.), *The Old Testament Pseudepigrapha* (2 vols; Garden City: Doubleday, 1983-1985)
RB	*Revue biblique*
REB	The Revised English Bible (1989)
RestQ	*Restoration Quarterly*
rev. ed.	revised edition; revision editor
RSR	*Religious Studies Review*
RSV	Revised Standard Version (1952, NT 1946)
RV	Revised Version (1898)
SAP	Sheffield Academic Press
SBJT	*Southern Baptist Journal of Theology*
SCJ	*Stone-Campbell Journal*
sic	thus; as it appears in the original
SNTSMS	Society of New Testament Study Monograph Series
Stern	*Jewish New Testament*, translation by David H. Stern (Jerusalem, Israel / Clarksville, MD: Jewish New Testament Publications, 1994 [1989])
s.v.	sub verbo / voce [under the word / heading]; sub verbis / vocibus [under

	the words / headings]
SWJT	*Southwestern Journal of Theology*
TDNT	*Theological Dictionary of the New Testament*, ed. Geoffrey W. Bromiley (E.T.; 9 vols; Grand Rapids: Eerdmans, 1964-1974), with index (10th) volume compiled by Ronald E. Pitkin (1976)
TDNTA	*Theological Dictionary of the New Testament*, abridged in one volume by Geoffrey W. Bromiley (Grand Rapids: Eerdmans, 1985)
TEV	Today's English Version (1976)
TextC	Bruce M. Metzger, *A Textual Commentary on the Greek New Testament* (2nd ed.; United Bible Socities, 1994)
Thayer	Joseph Henry Thayer, *A Greek-English Lexicon of the New Testament*, translated, revised and enlarged from Grimm's Wilke's *Clavis Novi Testamenti* (New York: American Book Company, no date)
ThEd	*Theological Educator*
TINT	*Theological Interpretation of the New Testament: A Book-by-Book Survey*, ed. Kevin Vanhoozer et al. (Grand Rapids,

	MI: Baker Academic / London: SPCK, 2008)
TNTC	Tyndale New Testament Commentaries
TNIV	Today's New International Version (2005, NT 2002)
TPI	Trinity Press International
Trench	Richard Chenevix Trench, *Synonyms of the New Testament* (1880; reprint, Grand Rapids: Eerdmans, 1966)
TTC / TTCI	T. & T. Clark / T. & T. Clark International
TynB	*Tyndale Bulletin*
UCP	The University of Chicago Press
Vine	W. E. Vine, *An Expository Dictionary of New Testament Words* (London and Edinburgh: Oliphants, 1963 [13th impression; originally in 4 volumes, 1940])
Wallace	Daniel B. Wallace, *Greek Grammar beyond the Basics: An Exegetical Syntax of the New Testament* (Grand Rapids: Zondervan, 1996)
WBC	Word Biblical Commentary
WJK	Westminster John Knox (Press)
WTJ	*Westminster Theological Journal*
WUNT	Wissenschaftliche Untersuchungen zum Neuen Testament

Zerwick	Maximillian Zerwick, *Biblical Greek* (E.T.; Rome: Pontifical Biblical Institue, 1963)

簡寫表（之三）: 外文的祝賀文集

F. F. **Bruce** *FS*(2)	*Pauline Studies*, ed. Donald A. Hagner & Murray J. Harris (Exeter: Paternoster / Grand Rapids: Eerdmans, 1980)
James D. G. **Dunn** *FS*(1)	*The Holy Spirit and Christian Origins*, ed. Graham N. Stanton, Bruce W. Longenecker & Stephen C. Barton (Grand Rapids, MI / Cambridge, U.K.: Eerdmans, 2004)
Michael D. **Goulder** *FS*	*Crossing the Boundaries*, ed. Stanley E. Porter, Paul Joyce & David E. Orton (Leiden: Brill, 1994)
Morna D. **Hooker** *FS*	*Early Christian Thought in its Jewish Context*, ed. John Barclay & John Sweet (Cambridge: CUP, 1996)
Grant R. **Osborne** *FS*	*On the Writing of New Testament Commentaries*, ed. Stanley E. Porter & Eckhard J. Schnabel (Texts and Editions for New Testament Study 8; Leiden and Boston: Brill, 2013)

Calvin J. **Roetzel** *FS*	*Pauline Conversations in Context*, ed. Janice Capel Anderson, Phillip Sellew & Claudia Setzer (JSNTSS 221; London and New York: Sheffield Academic, 2002)
Max **Turner** *FS*	*The Spirit and Christ in the New Testament and Christian Theology*, ed. I. Howard Marshall, Volker Rabens & Cornelis Bennema (Grand Rapids, MI / Cambridge, U.K.: Eerdmans, 2012)
Pieter Willem **van der Horst** *FS*	Empsychoi Logoi—*Religious Innovations in Antiquity*, ed. Alberdina Houtman, Albert de Jong & Magda Misset-van der Weg (AGJU 73; Leiden and Boston: Brill, 2008)
Bruce W. **Winter** *FS*	*The New Testament in Its First Century Setting: Essays on Context and Background*, ed. P. J. Williams, Andrew D. Clarke, Peter M. Head & David Instone-Brewer (Grand Rapids / Cambridge: Eerdmans, 2004)

簡寫表（之四）：外文的提多書註釋及研究

Banker	John Banker, *A Semantic and Structural Analysis of Titus* (rev. ed.; Dallas, TX: Summer Institute of Linguistics, 1994)
Baugh	S. M. Baugh, 'Titus', in Clinton E. Arnold (ed.), *Zondervan Illustrated Bible Backgrounds Commentary*, Vol. 3 (Grand Rapids: Zondervan, 2002) 498-511
Bouwman	Clarence Bouwman, *Leadership for Growing Churches: Paul's Recipe for Prospering the Church in Crete* (Eugene, OR: Wipf & Stock, 2016)
Chapell	Bryan Chapell, 'Titus', in R. Kent Hughes & Bryan Chapell, *1 & 2 Timothy and Titus* (Preaching the Word; Wheaton, IL: Crossway Books, 2000) 273-365, 392 [endnotes]
Genade	Alfred A. Genade, *Persuading the Cretans: A Text-Generated Persuasion*

	Analysis of the Letter to Titus (Eugene, OR: Wipf & Stock, 2011)[1]
Goodwin	Mark Goodwin, 'Titus', in William R. Farmer et al. (ed.), *The International Bible Commentary: A Catholic and Ecumenical Commentary for the Twenty-First Century* (Collegeville: Liturgical, 1998) 1752*a*-1758*b*
Griffin	Hayne P. Griffin Jr., 'Titus', in Thomas D. Lea & Hayne P. Griffin Jr., *1,2 Timothy, Titus* (New American Commentary 34; Nashville: Broadman, 1992)[2] 263-333（The introductory material [19-60] is written jointly by Griffin and Lea, cited as **Griffin－Lea**）
Hiebert	D. Edmond Hiebert, 'Titus', in Frank E. Gaebelein (ed.), *The Expositor's*

1 Review: Neil Marius, *Neot* 46.1 (2012) 212-214. 簡內德對所用的方法的名稱解釋如下（Genade 13）：'The basic premise is the centrality of *persuasive intent* on the part of the author of an epistle. The second premise is *textual sufficiency* for analyzing and reconstructing persuasive intent. Hence, the name that I attribute to this method is *text-generated persuasion analysis*.' 意即，這方法有兩個作為先決條件的前提：基本的前提是，書信作者的遊說意圖是最重要的；第二個前提是，要分析和重構作者的遊說意圖，倚靠文本便足夠。因此，這方法稱為「根據文本而產生的、作者的遊說意圖之分析」。

2 Reviews: Greg Couser, *CTR* 7 (Fall 1993) 130-132; Erich H. Kiehl, *CJ* 19.4 (1993) 415; Thomas L. Constable, *BS* 151.604 (1994) 499-500; Anthony D. Hopkins, *Perspectives in Religious Studies* 21.3 (1994) 261-263; James E. Rosscup, *Master' Seminary Journal* [*MSJ*] 5.1 (1994) 107-109; David E. Lanier, *Faith and Mission* 12.2 (1995) 73-74; Austin B. Tucker, *ThEd* No. 52 (1995) 136*b*-137*b*.

	Bible Commentary, Vol. 11（Grand Rapids: Zondervan, 1978）419-449
Jeon I	Paul S. Jeon, *To Exhort and Reprove: Audience Response to the Chiastic Structures of Paul's Letter to Titus* (Eugene, OR: Pickwick, 2012)[3]
Jeon II	Paul S. Jeon, *True Faith: Reflections on Paul's Letter to Titus* (Eugene, OR: Wipf & Stock, 2012)[4]
Keener	Craig S. Keener, 'Titus', *The IVP Bible Background Commentary. New Testament* (2nd ed.; Downers Grove: IVP Academic, 2014) 625-631
Krause I	Deborah Krause, 'Titus', in Gail R. O'Day & David L. Petersen (ed.), *Theological Bible Commentary* (Louisville: WJK, 2009) 443-444
Krause II	Deborah Krause, 'Titus', in Margaret Aymer, Cynthia Briggs Kittredge & David A. Sánchez (ed.), *Fortress Commentary on the Bible. Vol. 2: The*

3 Review: Benjamin Fiore, *CBQ* 76.3 (2014) 556-557.
4 Review: Jennifer L. Koosed, *CBQ* 76.2 (2014) 144-145.

	New Testament (Minneapolis: Fortress, 2014) 607-611
Neyrey	Jerome H. Neyrey, 'Titus', in Robert J. Karris (ed.), *The Collegeville Bible Commentary. Vol. 2: New Testament* (Collegeville: Liturgical, 1995 [1992]) 1215-1218
Quinn	Jerome D. Quinn, *The Letter to Titus* (Anchor Yale Bible 35; New Haven and London: Yale University Press, 2008 [originally AB 35; New York: Doubleday, 1990])
Sadler	M. F. Sadler, *The Epistles of St. Paul to Titus, Philemon and the Hebrews* (Church Commentary of the New Testament; Eugene, OR: Wipf & Stock, 2014 [previously published in 1890 by G. Bell & Sons, London]) v-viii, 1-29
Stern, *Comm.*	David H. Stern, 'Titus', *Jewish New Testament Commentary* (6th ed.; Clarksville, MD: Jewish New Testament Publications, 1999) 654-657
Titus	Eric Lane Titus, 'The Letter of Paul to Titus', in *The Interpreter's One-Volume*

Commentary on the Bible, ed. Charles M. Laymon (Nashville and New York: Abingdon, 1971) 892*a*-893*b*

簡寫表（之五）: 外文的教牧書信註釋及研究

Aageson	James W. Aageson, *Paul, the Pastoral Epistles, and the Early Church* (Library of Pauline Studies; Peabody, MA: Hendrickson, 2008)[1]
Arichea－Hatton	Daniel C. Arichea & Howard A. Hatton, *A Handbook on Paul's Letters to Timothy and to Titus* (New York: United Bible Societies, 1995)[2] 260-315
Barclay	William Barclay, *The Letters to Timothy, Titus, and Philemon* (Daily Study Bible; rev. ed.; Philadelphia: Westminster, 1975) [esp. 227-266]
Barrett	C. K. Barrett, *The Pastoral Epistles in the New English Bible* (Oxford: Clarendon, 1963) [esp. 126-148]

1 Reviews: Jack Barentsen, *CTR* 6.1 (2008) 103-105; Joan C. Campbell, *Toronto Journal of Theology* 24.2 (2008) 247-248; Greg Couser, *JETS* 51.4 (2008) 860-861; I. Howard Marshall, *Themelios* n.s. 33.3 (2008) 85-87; Frank Ramirez, *Brethren Life and Thought* 53.2 (2008) 45*b*-47*b*.

2 Reviews: Panayotis Coutsoumpos, *AUSS* 35.1 (1997) 103-104; James P. Grimshaw, *Encounter* 58.1 (1997) 112-113; Robert Holst, *CJ* 23.2 (1997) 161-162.

Bassler	Jouette M. Bassler, *1 Timothy, 2 Timothy, Titus* (Abingdon New Testament Commentaries; Nashville: Abingdon, 1996) [esp. 181-214]
Blaiklock	E. M. Blaiklock, *The Pastoral Epistles* (Grand Rapids: Zondervan, 1972) [esp. 69-92]
Calvin	Jean Calvin, *The Second Epistle of Paul the Apostle to the Corinthians and the Epistles to Timothy, Titus and Philemon* (E.T.; Calvin's Commentaries; Grand Rapids: Eerdmans, 1976 [1964]) 345-389
Collins	Raymond F. Collins, *I & II Timothy and Titus: A Commentary* (New Testament Library; Louisville: WJK, 2002)[3] [esp. 295-375]
Davies I	Margaret Davies, *The Pastoral Epistles: I and II Timothy and Titus* (Epworth

3 Reviews: Greg A. Couser, *JETS* 46.3 (**2003**) 562-564; Judith Lieu, *ExpT* 114.12 (2003) 426*b*; Patricia M. McDonald, *CBQ* 65.2 (2003) 276-278; C. K. Barrett, *JTS* 55.2 (**2004**) 655-656; Craig A. Evans, *BBR* 14.1 (2004) 133-134; I. Howard Marshall, *BBR* 14.1 (2004) 136-137; Frances Young, *Theology Today* 61.1 (2004) 97-98; Deborah Krause, *Int* 59.1 (**2005**) 74-76; Edgar Krentz, *CurTM* 32.4 (2005) 300*a-b*; Larry J. Walters, *BS* 162.646 (2005) 247-249; Nijay Gupta, *AshTJ* 40 (**2008**) 46-47. See also Marshall, 'Recent Study' [2010] 277-78.

	Commentaries; London: Epworth, 1996) [esp. 91-112]
Davies II	Margaret Davies, *The Pastoral Epistles* (New Testament Guides; Sheffield: SAP, 1996)
DC	Martin Dibelius & Hans Conzelmann, *The Pastoral Epistles* (E.T.; Hermeneia; Philadelphia: Fortress, 1972) [esp. 129-155]
Donelson I	Lewis R. Donelson, *Pseudepigraphy and Ethical Argument in the Pastoral Epistles* (Hermeneutische Untersuchungen zur Theologie 22; Tübingen: J. C. B. Mohr, 1986)
Donelson II	Lewis R. Donelson, *Colossians, Ephesians, 1 and 2 Timothy, and Titus* (Westminster Bible Companion; Louisville: WJK, 1996) [4] [esp. 170-181, 187-189]
Drury	Clare Drury, 'The Pastoral Epistles', in John Barton & John Muddiman (ed.),

4 Reviews: Jeffrey S. Lamp, *AshTJ* 30 (1998) 138-140; Ralph P. Martin, *Int* 52.1 (1998) 92*b*, 93*a*, 94*a*; Joel C. Elowsky, *CJ* 26.4 (2000) 375.

	The Oxford Bible Commentary (Oxford and New York: OUP, 2001) 1220-1233 [esp. 1231-1233]
Dunn	James D. G. Dunn, 'The First and Second Letters to Timothy and the Letter to Titus', in *The New Interpreter's Bible*, ed. Leander E. Keck et al., Volume 11 (Nashville: Abingdon, 2000) 773-880 [esp. 775-787, 861-880]
Fairbairn	Patrick Fairbairn, *Commentary on the Pastoral Epistles: I and II Timothy, Titus* (Grand Rapids: Zondervan, 1956 reprint [1874]) [esp. 255-305]
Fee	Gordon D. Fee, *1 and 2 Timothy, Titus* (New International Biblical Commentary; Peabody, MA: Hendrickson, 1988) [5] [esp. 1-14, 167-216]
Fiore I	Benjamin Fiore, *The Function of Personal Example in the Socratic and*

5 此書是作者的 *1 and 2 Timothy, Titus* (Good News Commentary; San Francisco: Harper & Row, 1984) 之修訂版；該書以 Good News Bible 為其經文，此書則採用 NIV. 作者在修訂版的序言中指出，'this edition is intended to be basically the same commentary as before' [xi]. 故此，筆者沒有參閱該書。

	Pastoral Epistles (Analecta biblica 105; Rome: Biblical Institute, 1986)
Fiore II	Benjamin Fiore, *The Pastoral Epistles: First Timothy, Second Timothy, Titus* (Sacra Pagina Series Volume 12; Collegeville: Liturgical, 2007)[6] [esp. 5-24, 191-228]
Gorday	Peter J. Gorday (ed.), *Colossians, 1-2 Thessalonians, 1-2 Timothy, Titus, Philemon* (Ancient Christian Commentary on Scripture: New Testament 9; Downers Grove: IVP, 2000)[7] 129-308 [esp. 281-308]
Guthrie I	Donald Guthrie, *The Pastoral Epistles* (TNTC; London: Tyndale, 1957) [esp. 180-211]
Guthrie II	Donald Guthrie, *The Pastoral Epistles* (TNTC; 2nd ed.; Leicester, England: IVP / Grand Rapids, MI: Eerdmans, 1990)[8] [esp. 192-223]

6 See Marshall, 'Recent Study' [2010] 279.

7 Reviews: Robert E. Cogswell, *American Theological Library Association Newsletter* 48.3 (2001) 22-24; David A. deSilva, *AshTJ* 36 (2004) 163-164; idem, *AshTJ* 37 (2005) 141-142.

8 中譯本見簡寫表（之一）丙部：古特立（Guthrie）= 上面 xxii。

Hanson I	Anthony Tyrrell Hanson, *The Pastoral Letters* (The Cambridge Bible Commentary; Cambridge: CUP, 1966) [esp. 105-123]
Hanson II	Anthony Tyrrell Hanson, *Studies in the Pastoral Epistles* (London: SPCK, 1968)
Hanson III	Anthony Tyrrell Hanson, *The Pastoral Epistles* (New Century Bible Commentary; Grand Rapids, MI: Eerdmans / London: Marshall, Morgan & Scott, 1982) [esp. 167-197]
Harding I	Mark Harding, *Tradition and Rhetoric in the Pastoral Epistles* (Studies in Biblical Literature 3; New York: Peter Lang, 1998)[9]
Harding II	Mark Harding, *What Are They Saying About the Pastoral Epistles?* (New York: Paulist, 2001)[10]

9 'This book is about the Pastor as a user of persuasive techniques derived from the traditions of epistolary moral exhortation and the rhetoric of persuasive speech. My contention is that the Pastor drew on rhetorical and epistolary conventions, as well as on the Pauline heritage, in order to commend his actualization [*Vergegenwärtigung*] of Pauline tradition for the needs of his own day' (Harding I 54). Reviews: Veronika Koperski, *AshTJ* 32 (2000) 132-133; Stanley E. Porter, *JSNT* 81 (2001) 126.

10 Reviews: David Hunter, *St Mark's Review* 187 (2001) 40; Mary Lynnette Delbridge, *Int*

Hendriksen	William Hendriksen, *A Commentary on I & II Timothy and Titus* (London: Banner of Truth Trust, 1964 [1960]) [esp. 335-400]
Hinson	E. Glenn Hinson, 'First and Second Timothy and Titus', in Watson E. Mills, Richard F. Wilson et al., *Acts and Pauline Writings* (Mercer Commentary on the Bible, Vol. 7; Macon GA: Mercer University Press, 1997) 269-284 [esp. 269-270, 282-284]
Houlden	J. L. Houlden, *The Pastoral Epistles* (London: SCM / Philadelphia: TPI, 1989) [esp. 139-156]
Johnson I	Luke Timothy Johnson, *1 Timothy, 2 Timothy, Titus* (Knox Preaching Guides; Atlanta: John Knox, 1987) [esp. 111-139]
Johnson II	Luke Timothy Johnson, *Letters to Paul's Delegates: 1 Timothy, 2 Timothy, Titus* (The New Testament in

56.4 (2002) 440; Bonnie Bowman Thurston, *CBQ* 64.2 (2002) 376-377.

	Context; Valley Forge, PA: TPI, 1996)[11] [esp. 211-254]
Karris	Robert J. Karris, *The Pastoral Epistles* (New Testament Message 17; Wilmington, DE: Michael Glazier, 1984 [1979]) [esp. 105-124]
Kartzow	Marianne Pjelland Kartzow, *Gossip and Gender: Othering of Speech in the Pastoral Epistles* (BZNW 164; Berlin and New York: Walter de Gruyter, 2009)
Keegan I	Terence J. Keegan, *First and Second Timothy, Titus, Philemon* (New Collegeville Bible Commentary; Collegeville: Liturgical, 2006)[12] [esp. 54-66]
Kelly	J. N. D. Kelly, *A Commentary on the Pastoral Epistles* (BNTC; London: Black, 1963) [esp. 225-259]
Knight I	George W. Knight III, *The Faithful Sayings in the Pastoral Letters*

11 Reviews: Erwin Buck, *Int* 52.3 (1998) 314*a-b*; Thomas Scott Caulley, *SCJ* 1.1 (1998) 136-138; E. Earle Ellis, *SWJT* 40-2 (1998) 116-117.

12 中譯本見簡寫表（之一）丙部：Keegan II（上面 xxii）。

	(Kampen: J. H. Kok, 1965)
Knight II	George W. Knight III, *The Pastoral Epistles* (New International Greek Testament Commentary; Grand Rapids: Eerdmans / Carlisle, England: Paternoster, 1992) [13] [esp. 281-360]
Köstenberger	Andreas J. Köstenberger, '1 Timothy, 2 Timothy, Titus', in Tremper Longman III & David E. Garland (ed.), *The Expositor's Bible Commentary*, Vol. 12 (rev. ed.; Grand Rapids: Zondervan, 2006) 487-625 [14] [esp. 601-625]
Köstenberger－Wilder	Andreas J. Köstenberger & Terry L. Wilder (ed.), *Entrusted with the Gospel: Paul's Theology in the Pastoral Epistles* (Nashville: B&H Academic, 2010)
Laansma	Jon C. Laansma, '2 Timothy, Titus', in Linda Belleville, Jon C. Laansma & J. Ramsay Michaels, *1 Timothy, 2*

13 Reviews: Alistair V. Campbell, *Anvil* 10.2 (**1993**) 161-162; John E. Dent Jr., *ThEd* 48 (Fall, 1993) 129*a*-130*b*; Paul Ellingworth, *Themelios* n.s. 19.3 (**1994**) 22-23; Frank Bellizzi, *RestQ* 37.2 (**1995**) 124-126; Cyril S. Rodd, *ExpT* 106.4 (1995) 122; David J. Valleskey, *Wisconsin Lutheran Quarterly* 92.2 (1995) 148-149.

14 See Marshall, 'Recent Study' [2010] 280.

	Timothy, Titus, Hebrews (Cornerstone Biblical Commentary 17; Carol Stream, IL: Tyndale House Publishers, 2009) 125-302 [esp. 221-302]
Larson	Knute Larson, *I & II Thessalonians, I & II Timothy, Titus, Philemon* (Holman New Testament Commentary 9; Nashville: Broadman & Holman, 2000) [esp. 335-394]
Lau	Andrew Y. Lau, *Manifest in Flesh: The Epiphany Christology of the Pastoral Epistles* (WUNT 2/86; Tübingen: J. C. B. Mohr [Paul Siebeck], 1996)[15]
Leaney	A. R. C. Leaney, *The Epistles to Timothy, Titus and Philemon* (London: SCM, 1960) [esp. 111-132]
Liefeld	Walter L. Liefeld, *1 & 2 Timothy, Titus* (The NIV Application Commentary 54-56; Grand Rapids: Zondervan, 1999) [16] [esp. 19-41,

15 Review: Lewis R. Donelson, *Review of Biblical Literature* 1 (1999) 378-380.

16 中譯本見簡寫表（之一）丙部：利斐特（Liefeld）= 上面 xxii。Reviews: Stephen Drey, *Evangel* 20.3 (2002) 88*c*-89*a*; Buist M. Fanning, *BS* 159.634 (2002) 251-252. See also Marshall, 'Recent Study' [2010] 280.

	308-360]
Lock	Walter Lock, *The Pastoral Epistles* (ICC; Edinburgh: TTC, 1966 [1924]) [esp. 121-159]
Long	Thomas G. Long, *1 & 2 Timothy and Titus* (Belief: A Theological Commentary on the Bible; Louisville: WJK, 2016) [esp. 249-282]
Maloney	Linda M. Maloney, 'The Pastoral Epistles', in Elisabeth Schüssler Fiorenza (ed.), *Searching the Scriptures. Vol. 2: A Feminist Commentary* (New York: Crossroad, 1994) 361-380
Marshall	I. Howard Marshall, in collaboration with Philip H. Towner, *The Pastoral Epistles* (ICC; Edinburgh: TTC, 1999)[17] [esp. 111-350]
Martin, C.	Clarice J. Martin, '1-2 Timothy and Titus (The Pastoral Epistles)', in Brian K. Blount et al. (ed.), *True to Our*

17 Reviews: C. K. Barrett, *JTS* 52.2 (2001) 824-827; Andreas J. Köstenberger, *JETS* 44.3 (2001) 550-553; Stephen Drey, *Evangel* 20.3 (2002) 88*c*-89*a*; Buist M. Fanning, *BS* 159.634 (2002) 251-252.

	Native Land: An African American New Testament Commentary (Minneapolis: Fortress, 2007) 409-436 [esp. 432*b*-434*a*]
Martin, S.	Seán Charles Martin, *Pauli Testamentum: 2 Timothy and the Last Words of Moses* (Roma: Pontificia Università Gregoriana, 1997)
Miller	James D. Miller, *The Pastoral Letters as Composite Documents* (SNTSMS 93; Cambridge and New York: CUP, 1997)[18] [esp. 124-137, 187-191]
Montague	George T. Montague, *First and Second Timothy, Titus* (Catholic Commentary on Sacred Scripture; Grand Rapids: Baker Academic, 2008)[19] [esp. 211-256]

18 Review: Philip H. Towner, *JBL* 118 (1999) 374. See also Marshall 16-18 ('Miller's case is unconvincing' [17]). 亦參註 36（下面 lxiii）。

19 Reviews: Patrick Gray, *RSR* 35.3 (2009) 191*a*; Mary Ann Beavis, *CBQ* 72.3 (2010) 604-605; Ray van Neste, *JETS* 53.2 (2010) 417-418. See also Marshall, 'Recent Study' [2010] 281.

Mounce	William D. Mounce, *Pastoral Epistles* (WBC 46; Nashville: Thomas Nelson, 2000)[20] [esp. 375-460]
Ngewa	Samuel M. Ngewa, *1 & 2 Timothy and Titus* (Africa Bible Commentary Series; Grand Rapids: Zondervan / Africa: Hippo Books, 2009)[21] [esp. 321-414, 457-464 (endnotes)]
Oden	Thomas C. Oden, *First and Second Timothy and Titus* (Interpretation; Louisville: John Knox, 1989)[22]
Perkins	Pheme Perkins, 'The Pastoral Epistles', in James D. G. Dunn & John W. Rogerson (ed.), *Eerdmans Commentary on the Bible* (Grand Rapids, MI / Cambridge, U.K.: Eerdmans, 2003) 1428-1446 [esp. 1442-1446]
Pietersen	Lloyd K. Pietersen, *The Polemic of the Pastorals: A Sociological Examination*

20 Reviews: Stephen Drey, *Evangel* 20.3 (2002) 88*c*-89*a*; Andreas J. Köstenberger, *JETS* 45.2 (2002) 365-366. See also Marshall, 'Recent Study' [2010] 270-71.

21 Reviews: Rob Howell, *Detroit Baptist Seminary Journal* 15 (2010) 127-128; Arland J. Hultgren, *CBQ* 72.3 (2010) 607-609; Robert W. Yarbrough, *JETS* 53.2 (2010) 418-420; Lloyd K. Pietersen, *JSNT* 33.5 (2011) 112.

22 Review: L. Dean Hempelmann, *Concordia Theological Quarterly* 68.2 (2004) 160-161.

	of the Development of Pauline Christianity (JSNTSS 264; London and New York: TTCI, 2004)[23]
Ramsay	William M. Ramsay, *Historical Commentary on the Pastoral Epistles*, ed. Mark Wilson (Grand Rapids: Kregel Publications, 1996 reprint)
Richards	William A. Richards, *Difference and Distance in Post-Pauline Christianity: An Epistolary Analysis of the Pastorals* (Studies in Biblical Literature 44; New York: Peter Lang, 2002)[24] [esp. 67-99, 212-220]
Saarinen	Risto Saarinen, *The Pastoral Epistles with Philemon and Jude* (Brazos Theological Commentary on the Bible; Grand Rapids: Brazos, 2008)[25] 19-196 [esp. 19-28, 169-196]
Scott	E. F. Scott, *The Pastoral Epistles* (Moffatt New Testament Commentary;

23 See Marshall, 'Recent Study' 307 n.70.

24 See the (largely negative) comments of Marshall ('Recent Study' 284-85) on its main thesis.

25 Review: Patrick Gray, *RSR* 35.3 (2009) 191*a*. See also Marshall, 'Recent Study' [2010] 280-81.

	London: Hodder & Stoughton, 1939 [1936]) [esp. 147-183]
Simpson	E. K. Simpson, *The Pastoral Epistles* (Grand Rapids: Eerdmans, 1954) [esp. 94-119]
Smith	Claire S. Smith, *Pauline Communities as "Scholastic Communities": A Study of the Vocabulary of "Teaching" in 1 Corinthians, 1 and 2 Timothy and Titus* (WUNT 2/335; Tübingen: Mohr Siebeck, 2012)
Spencer	Aída Besançon Spencer, *2 Timothy and Titus* (New Covenant Commentary Series; Eugene, OR: Cascade Books, 2014) [esp. 3-74]
Stepp	Phillip L. Stepp, *Leadership Succession in the World of the Pauline Circle* (New Testament Monographs 5; Sheffield: Sheffield Phoenix, 2005)[26]
Stott	John R. W. Stott, *The Message of Timothy & Titus* (The Bible Speaks

26 Review: Robert J. Karris, *CBQ* 68.3 (2006) 554-555; 555: 'what S. has done is to give a historical basis and understanding to the conception of succession that a number of commentators had previously seen in the Pastorals.'

	Today; Leicester, England: IVP, 1997) [esp. 165-213]
Taylor	Walter F. Taylor Jr., '1-2 Timothy, Titus', in Gerhard Krodel (ed.), *The Deutero-Pauline Letters: Ephesians, Colossians, 2 Thessalonians, 1-2 Timothy, Titus* (Minneapolis: Fortress, 1993)[27] [esp. 59-93]
Towner I	Philip H. Towner, *The Goal of Our Instruction: The Structure of Theology and Ethics in the Pastoral Epistles* (JSNTSS 34; Sheffield: SAP, 1989)[28]
Towner II	Philip H. Towner, *1-2 Timothy & Titus* (IVP New Testament Commentary; Downers Grove, IL / Leicester, England: IVP, 1994)[29] [esp. 216-264]
Towner III	Philip H. Towner, *The Letters to Timothy and Titus* (NICNT; Grand Rapids: Eerdmans, 2006)[30] [esp. 657-805]

27 Reviews: Edgar Krentz, *CurTM* 21.4 (1994) 298*b*-299*a*; Jim Wilson, *Trinity Seminary Review* 17.2 (1995) 81.

28 Review: Neil Elliott, *Int* 45.2 (1991) 202*a*-203*a*.

29 Review: Charles B. Stephenson, *JETS* 39.4 (1996) 673-674.

30 中譯本見簡寫表(之一)丙部：唐(Towner)= 上面 xxiii。Reviews: Jouette M. Bassler,

Towner IV — Philip H. Towner, '1-2 Timothy and Titus', in G. K. Beale & D. A. Carson (ed.), *Commentary on the New Testament Use of the Old Testament* (Grand Rapids, MI: Baker Academic / Nottingham, U.K.: Apollos, 2007) 891-918 [esp. 913*a*-917*a*]

Twomey — Jay Twomey, *The Pastoral Epistles through the Centuries* (Black Bible Commentaries; Chichester, U.K. / Malden, MA: Wiley-Blackwell, 2009)[31] [esp. 189-225]

Van Neste — Ray Van Neste, *Cohesion and Structure in the Pastoral Epistles* (JSNTSS 280; London and New York: TTCI, 2004)[32] [esp. 234-282, 311-315]

Verner — David C. Verner, *The Household of God: The Social World of the*

CBQ 69.3 (**2007**) 598-599; Michael F. Bird, *Colloquium* 39.1 (2007) 114-116; Allan Chapple, *ExpT* 118.9 (2007) 466*a-b*; Peter H. Davids, *BBR* 17.2 (2007) 349-350; Jeremy Duff, *JSNT* 29.5 (2007) 106; Neil Richardson, *Epworth Review* 34.3 (2007) 68-69; Chris L. de Wet, *Neot* 42.2 (**2008**) 409-411; Buist M. Fanning III, *BS* 165.659 (2008) 380-381; Bart J. Koet, *Bijdragen* 69.2 (2008) 227-228; Perry L. Stepp, *SCJ* 11.1 (2008) 155-157; Stephen H. Travis, *JTS* 59.1 (2008) 293-295; Terry L. Wilder, *JETS* 51.3 (2008) 656-659. See also Marshall, 'Recent Study' [2010] 275-277.

31 See Marshall, 'Recent Study' [2010] 281-82.

32 '[This] is a comprehensive response to Miller [1997]' (Van Neste, 'Structure' 88 n.37). Review: *Religious Studies Review* 32.1 (2006) 47*c*. See also Marshall, 'Recent Study' [2010] 282: 'the study confirms that there is a coherence in each of the letters and offers a more refined analysis of it than in any previous investigations.'

	Pastoral Epistles (Society of Biblical Literature Dissertation Series 71; Chico, CA: Scholars, 1983)
Wall	Robert W. Wall with Richard B. Steele, *1 & 2 Timothy and Titus* (The Two Horizons New Testament Commentary; Grand Rapids, MI / Cambridge, U.K.: Eerdmans, 2012)[33] [esp. 331-401]
Ward	Ronald A. Ward, *Commentary on 1 & 2 Timothy & Titus* (Waco, TX: Word, 1978 [1974]) [esp. 227-279]
White	Newport J. D. White, 'The First and Second Epistles to Timothy and the Epistle to Titus', in W. Robertson Nicoll (ed.), *The Expositor's Greek Testament* (5 vols; Grand Rapids: Eerdmans, 1961 reprint [1897-1910]) 4.55-202 [esp. 185-202]
Wieland	George M. Wieland, *The Significance of Salvation: A Study of Salvation Language in the Pastoral Epistles* (Paternoster Biblical Monographs;

33 Reviews: Dillon T. Thornton, JETS 56.4 (2013) 882-884; Peter R. Rodgers, *RSR* 40.1 (2014) 45*a-b*.

	Milton Keynes, U.K.: Paternoster, 2006) [34] [esp. 181-238, 261-263]
Wild	Robert A. Wild, 'The Pastoral Letters', in Raymond E. Brown et al. (ed.), *The New Jerome Biblical Commentary* (London: Chapman, 2000 [1989]), 891-901 [esp. 891-895]
Wilson	Stephen G. Wilson, *Luke and the Pastoral Epistles* (London: SPCK, 1979)
Witherington	Ben Witherington III, *A Socio-Rhetorical Commentary on Titus, 1-2 Timothy and 1-3 John*, Volume 1 of *Letters and Homilies for Hellenized Christians* (Downers Grove, IL: IVP Academic / Nottingham, England: Apollos, 2006)[35] 47-390 [esp. 86-167]
Young	Frances Young, *The Theology of the Pastoral Letters* (New Testament Theology; Cambridge: CUP, 1994)

34 See Marshall, 'Recent Study' [2010] 295-96.

35 Reviews: Gerald L. Bray, *Churchman* 121.4 (2007) 363-365; Will Rutherford, *ExpT* 119.9 (2008) 463*a*-464*a*; Duane F. Watson, *CBQ* 70.1 (2008) 178-179. See also Marshall, 'Recent Study' [2010] 279; Genade [2011] 8-9 n.37: 'Vernon Robbins is the originator of socio-rhetorical criticism. Witherington does not adhere to the strictures and categories of the discipline but employs socio-rhetorical criticism in a more generic manner so that it cannot *strictu sensu* be considered as socio-historical.'

Zamfir	Korinna Zamfir, *Men and Women in the Household of God: A Contextual Approach to Roles and Ministries in the Pastoral Epistles* (Göttingen: Vandenhoeck & Ruprecht, 2013)[36]
Zehr	Paul M. Zehr, *1 & 2 Timothy, Titus* (Believers Church Bible Commentary; Waterloo, ON and Scottdale, PA: Herald, 2010)[37] [esp. 233-318, 323-324]

36 Reviews: Dillon T. Thornton, *BBR* 24.1 (2014) 123-125; Kai Akagi, *RSR* 41.3 (2015) 119*a-b*.

37 Review: Dan Nighswander, *Direction* 42.1 (2013) 104-105.

導　論

A Commentary on the Book of Titus

導論（壹）: 教牧書信的作者

卷首語清楚表示，保羅是提多書的作者，因為一章 1 至 4a 節這一小段的基本結構就是這一句：保羅（1 節）……寫信給……提多（4a 節）。[1] 同樣，提摩太前書和後書，也是保羅寫給提摩太的：保羅……寫信給……提摩太（提前一 1～2；提後一 1～2）。來自早期教會的外證與教牧書信的內證一致，即是指向教牧書信是保羅的作品；[2] 例如，第二世紀的〈穆拉多利經目〉將這三封書信與腓利門書一起放在使徒保羅給教會的信之後，並無提到對保羅是這三卷書的作者有任何質疑。[3] 事實上，教牧書信是保羅所寫的這傳統看法，直到十九

---

1 （**1**）有釋經者不討論作者問題，他說：'I do not take a position regarding historical authorship because it is impossible to "prove" the authenticity of the letter. Moreover, my concern is for the implied author* who is to be understood by the implied audience* as the historical apostle'（Jeon I 5）。*「隱含的作者」是讀者根據經文而建構出來對作者的描繪（見《弗》15 註 11）;「隱含的聽眾」可作同樣理解。參較《羅》1.69 註 6。（**2**）Merz（'Self-Exposition' 123）認為：'The most important literary element in the composition of a pseudo-Pauline letter is its fictitious authorship. In literary terms, this consists above all of a veiled onomastic reference to Pauline prescripts in the opening verse: for example "Paul, servant of God" (Titus).' 她稱之為 'fictitious self-reference'（124）。（**3**）Murphy-O'Connor（'Pastoral Epistles' 631; cf. '2 Timothy'）認為，提多書和提前皆為冒名之作，提後則是保羅寫的。但見 Towner III 27（唐 39）所提出的反對理由。Harding II 23-24 也認為，'it is difficult to see how any of the differences he [Murphy-O'Connor] isolates necessarily rules out common authorship.'

2 Dunn 779（= Dunn, 'Titus' 276*a*）談到 'the universal acceptance of them from the earliest attributions as written by Paul himself (from at least 200 CE).' Similarly, Harding II 10: 'the early fathers, beginning from Irenaeus, unfailingly acknowledge them as Pauline.' Riesner（'Once More' 257）指出，'Contrary to other New Testament letters (Hebrews, 2 Peter, etc.) the ascription of the Pastoral Epistles to Paul was never disputed in orthodox churches.' 詳見（例如）Guthrie, *NTI* 608-12; Marshall 2-8; Mounce lxiv-lxix; Witherington 52-54; Ellis, 'Pastoral Letters' 659*a*（《辭典》953*b*）。

3 Guthrie II 19.〈穆拉多利經目〉即 'Muratorian Canon',「是現存最早的新約正典綱目」(《聖神》372*a*)。古特立 16 的翻譯有兩點值得商榷：（**i**）「將這三本書信放在使徒保羅給教會的信之後，並與腓利門書放在一起」英文原作 'these three Epistles are placed after the church epistles of Paul, together with Philemon',「並」字卻使隨後的意思變成與之前的意思同等重要；（**ii**）「編者……對保羅是這三封信的原作者，

世紀才開始受到質疑。[4]

到了近代，極多釋經者認為，教牧書信是託名之作。[5] 按這種理解，這些書信其實是雙重的託名之作：真正的作者並非保羅，真正的收信人也不是提多或提摩太。[6] 多勞臣這樣表達他的立場：「反

沒有任何質疑」，但原文（'There is no mention of any doubts about their Pauline origin'）的 'any doubts' 所指的較可能不是來自「編者（the compiler）」的，而是他人的。

4 詳見 Guthrie I 15-16; Guthrie II 21-22（古特立 17-19）; Ellis, 'Pastoral Letters' 659*a*-60*b*（《辭典》953*b*-55*b*）。

5 E.g., **(i)** Barrett 4-12; Bassler 17-21; Davies II 105-117; DC 1*a*-5*a*; Donelson I 66; Fiore II 6, 16; Hanson III 2-11; Harding I 2; Harding II 81; Houlden 18-35; Karris xi-xii; Long 1, 4, 11-12; Maloney 363-65; C. Martin 410*a*; Wall ix, 1, 5; Wild 892*a-b*; Young 22-23, 136; Zamfir xviii; **(ii)** Aune, 'Pastoral Letters' 563; Barrett, Review of Collins [2002] 655; Bassler, Review of Towner III [2006] 598; Carter－Levine, 'Pastorals' 238-40; Classen, 'Titus' 429, 'Epistle to Titus' 47; Ehrman, 'Pastoral Epistles' 452*b*-457*b*; Goulder, 'Wolves' 242; Hanson, 'Domestication of Paul' 402; Hultgren, 'Pastoral Epistles' 142-44; Kaestli, 'Luke-Acts' 111 with n.2; Malherbe, 'Paulus Senex' 199; Meade, 'Pseudonymity' 118-22（139 聲稱，'in the Pastorals, attribution [of the letters to Paul] is primarily an assertion of authoritative [Pauline] tradition, not of literary origins' [endorsed by Harding I 2]）; Merz, 'Self-Exposition' 123-30; Nardoni, 'Pastoral Epistles' 1731*a-b*; Schnelle, 'Pastoral Letters' 328-32; Tamez, 'Pastoral Epistles'; Ziesler, 'Pastoral Epistles' 519*b*-20*a*; **(iii)** Burkett, *INT* 436-39; Conzelmann－Lindemann, *INT* 211-12; Hagner, *New Testament* 614-622; Kümmel, *INT* 370-84; Martin, *Foundations* 298-307.（**1**）Marshall [1999] 58 寫道：'The reigning hypothesis is that they are pseudonymous documents in the sense that they were written to deceive readers into believing that they contain the actual wording and teaching of Paul and therefore bear Paul's authority. This hypothesis is in danger of uncritical acceptance.' Cf. 80: 'The reigning . . . hypothesis is that the letters were written much later than Paul by some unknown person who was using Paul's authority to say what he believed that the church of his day needed to know.'（**2**）Krause I 443*a* 稱提多書為 'the pseudepigraphical and pseudo-epistolary fiction'.

6 Fiore II 21: 'As the author of the Pastoral Epistles is not Paul, so too the addressees Timothy and Titus might well be fictitious'; Aune, 'Pastoral Letters' 561: 'since these letters are pseudepigraphical, they were never actually sent to the named recipients, but in all likelihood rather circulated, at least initially, as a small collection of Pauline letters'. Cf. Aune 475*b*: '[Titus is] a doubly pseudonymous letter in that both sender and receiver are fictitious'; Collins, 'Theology' 57: 'On the working assumption that the text [of Titus] is pseudepigraphical, it is most likely that it is doubly pseudonymous. Not only is the designation of the author of the epistle a literary fiction, so too is the designated recipient.' See also Meade, 'Pseudonymity' 127, Fatum, 'Christ' 176-77: 'double pseudonymity'; Harding I 233: 'he [the Pastor] summons them [the leaders] to perseverance through the fiction created by the technique of double pseudonymity.' 後一個詞指「作者是偽保羅，而受書人是偽提摩太或偽提多」（張 9 註 23）。

對保羅是教牧書信作者的論據，與反對保羅是歌羅西書和以弗所書作者的論據，在思維上是相同的。若有分別的話，所有反對保羅為作者的論據，針對教牧書信而言更具說服力。這些書信在語言、文法和風格上都明顯地偏離了保羅書信⋯⋯。然而，最重要的論據是神學方面的，如在歌羅西書和以弗所書一樣。教牧書信的神學顯然有別於保羅的神學⋯⋯。最簡單和最令人滿意的解決辦法就是，這些書信不是保羅寫的。」[7]

不過，就如反對保羅是歌羅西書或以弗所書的作者的理據不足以推翻傳統的看法，即二書皆為保羅所寫，[8] 照樣，反對教牧書信是保羅所寫的各種理由（關乎作者的歷史處境、假教師的描繪、書信中的教會組織、詞彙和風格，尤其是神學母題）也不是駁不倒的。[9] 就筆

---

7 Donelson II 187-88, 189. 'The arguments against Pauline authorship of the Pastoral Epistles follow the same lines as those of Colossians and Ephesians. If anything, all the arguments against Pauline authorship are more persuasive regarding the Pastoral Epistles. . . .'

8 參《西・門》8-28；《弗》12-41。

9 Cf. Stott 33: 'The arguments adduced . . . can all be answered. They are not sufficient to overthrow the case for the Pauline authorship.' Wilder（'Pastoral Epistles' 29-34）將學者典型地用來表示教牧書信並非真確的保羅書信的那些準則，應用到腓立比書，為要表明若用這種方法，公認為保羅所寫的腓立比書，其真確性亦可被質疑（28）。**Hagner**（*New Testament*）對這些問題提供了簡要的、正反雙方的論證：（**1**）'Language and Style'（615-18）；（**2**）'Church Organization'（618）；（**3**）'Theology and Ethics'（618-19）；（**4**）'Nature of Opposition'（619-20）；（**5**）'The Picture of Paul'（620）；（**6**）'The Personal History of Paul'（620-21）。他在每個題目之下，先提出託名著作的觀點，然後是持傳統看法者的回應（615）；這做法對讀者甚有幫助。**Harding** II 11-15 將反對保羅為作者的理據綜合為五方面；**Mounce** lxxxiv 則把基本的問題歸納為三類：歷史方面的（'the PE do not fit into the historical framework of Acts'）、神學方面的（'the PE omit some themes that are central to Paul's theology and develop some in ways unlike Paul, or, it is argued, in ways that contradict Pauline thinking'），和文學風格方面的（'the vocabulary and style of writing in the PE are different from the "acknowledged" Paulines'）。Similarly, **Massey**, 'Cicero' 69: 'Reasons for rejecting Pauline authorship . . . can be boiled down to three principal arguments: 1) theological ideas, 2) historical background, and 3) the issue of language and style.' 他的文章所探討的是第 3) 點。
關於（**3**），Porter（'Implications' 113）同意，'the theological data are the only – or at least the strongest – evidence that raises justifiable doubt regarding Pauline authorship of the Pastorals'. 關於（**2**），留意 Johnson II 14-16 的八點觀察。See also Fung, 'Charismatic'

者的涉獵所及，為教牧書信之真確性提出最詳細和有力辯護的，[10] 是古特立、基里、費歌頓、卡森和穆爾、勵佐治，和孟威廉等新約學者。[11] 其他接受教牧書信之真確性的釋經者也為數不少。[12]

206-10（=《恩賜》153-59）。關於（**1**），（**i**）Marshall 63 認為：'despite the lack of precision that is inevitable when handling matters of style, there should be no room for doubt that the PE are distinctive in the Pauline corpus in that the three letters share a common shape of vocabulary, style and method of argument which is somehow different from that of the other ten letters in it.' 另一方面，（**ii**）Van Nes（'Problem' 169）說：'What this [his] survey does want to question is whether the work of [P. N.] Harrison can still be used by scholars to support the (semi-)pseudonymous authorship of the PE. For if both its statistical argument and its proposed theory of authorship have been shown to be fallacious, why would one still rely on it?' 統計學家一般都同意，教牧書信整體的長度不足以構成一個令人滿意的、可以進行統計的樣本（see, e.g., Metzger, 'Reconsideration' 94*a*: 他引 Yule 的意見指出，一萬字的論述才足以構成穩固的統計基礎；但是教牧書信的字數遠不及此。Porter ['Implications' 110 with n.17] 指出，提多書只有 659 字，提前 1,591 字，提後 1,238 字〔合共 3,488 字〕)。(**iii**)Metzger（art. cit. 94*b* n.2）稱 Guthrie I 212-28 的「附錄」(= Guthrie II 224-40 = 古特立 225-243）為 'a penetrating critique of Harrison's linguistic argument'.（**iv**）古特立 53 批評「哈里生完全不考慮作者心理上的變化，對作品造成的影響。如果他能更全面的觀察到：差異是由於主題的不同，多樣化是因為時代的進步〔這是 'variations due to advancing age' [Guthrie I 47, Guthrie II 54] 的誤譯〕」，增加的字彙是因為環境的改變，還有收信的對象與其他書信的不同，那麼教牧書信裏特殊的語言現象，就能在更大的範圍裏，做出最合理的解釋〔'can in large measure be satisfactorily explained [ibid.]〕。」古特立 243 重申，「年歲增長〔'Variations due to advancing age' [Guthrie I 228, Guthrie II 240]〕影響了語言差異的程度，這往往是風格與字彙多樣化的原因，必須要納入考量。」（Malherbe ['Paulus Senex'] 辯證，'the Pastoral Epistles portray their author as an old man' [198].）不過，對於年齡增長引起風格變化這一點，Marshall 64 斷言：'This theory should be abandoned from further consideration. It is based on a false assumption. . . . There simply is no evidence that old age does have these effects in general or the specific effect seen in the PE.'（**v**）另見註 49（下面 21）。

10 Guthrie（*NTI* 622）指出，舉證的責任是在挑戰傳統看法者的一方，支持保羅為作者的一方只需提出辯護：'The case for Pauline authorship must of necessity be presented largely on the defensive since the onus of proof rests with the challengers. If each objection can be answered in a satisfactory way in agreement with the self-claims of the epistles to be written by Paul, the authenticity may be regarded as established. Only if in the course of investigations facts come to light which appear conclusive for non-authenticity will the onus of proof pass to the defenders.' 參註 35、36（下面 17）。

11 （1）Guthrie I 11-52, 212-28; Guthrie II 11-61（古特立 13-62，225-43）; Guthrie, *NTI* 607-49; also Guthrie, 'Pastoral Epistles' 681*a*-85*a*;（2）Kelly 4-34;（3）Fee 1-31;（4）卡森－穆爾：〈教牧書信〉539-52；（5）Knight II 13-52;（6）Mounce xcvi-cxxix. 因此，'it is now a common academic assumption – a consensus – that the PE were not authored by Paul'（Massey, 'Cicero' [2014] 66）這話（筆者加上底線的字），應當受到質疑。

12 E.g., **(i)** Banker 10*a*-11*a*; Genade ix; Griffin－Lea 23-40; Johnson II 1-33; Liefeld 24-28

關於教牧書信的作者是誰這問題，哈格拿強調兩點：第一，反對教牧書信出自保羅手筆的論據是累積性的。沒有單一的論據具有完全的說服力，但這些論據的數目增加時，其力度也增加，要辯護保羅是作者亦成為愈來愈難應付的挑戰。第二，雙方的論據的性質皆不足以證明其立場是對的；我們處於可能性的範疇中，任何一方的結論都不應被漫不經心地摒棄。[13] 哈格拿的結論是：「雖然它們有可能是保羅寫的（也許提後最有資格作此聲稱），但稍微較大的可能是，作者是保羅的一位或多位門徒，他們可能使用了源自保羅的一些殘篇。」[14] 費

（利斐特 18-22）；Oden 10-15; Stott 21-34; Towner II 30-35; Towner III 3, 83-84, 88（唐 5，115-16，121）；張 5-34; **(ii)** E. E. Ellis, 'Pastoral Letters' 659*a*-61*a*（《辭典》953*b*-56*b*）；Klinker-De Klerck, 'Pastoral Epistles' 103*a*-6*a*; Köstenberger, 'Pastoral Epistles' 1-8; Köstenberger－Kellum－Quarles, 'Titus' 268-71; Lea, 'Pseudonymity' 553-55; McDonald－Porter, 'Pastoral Letters' 488*b*-97*b*; Van Neste, 'Message' 27 n.1; Review of Montague [2008] 417; Wendland, 'Discourse' 334 n.1; Wilder, 'Pastoral Epistles' 34-37; Witherington, 'Pastoral Epistles', 248, 252-53; **(iii)** Harrison, *INT* 351-363; Robinson, *Redating* 70; **(iv)** Couser, Review of Collins [2002] 564; Fanning, Review of Marshall [1999] 251. 古特立 18（Guthrie II 22）舉出一整列支持傳統看法的學者後，說（以下提供英文原作以補中譯之不足）：「事實上〔The fact that〕，可以舉出為數令人驚訝〔so impressive a list〕的學者仍然支持保羅為原著者的說法〔in favour of Pauline authorship〕，可以給那些認為〔the tacit assumption〕，沒有空間留給堅持傳統想法的人，以及傳統想法〔all who maintain it〕需要求助於特別理由〔are obliged to resort to special pleading*〕的人，一些警訊。」（*'Special pleading' =「只講有利之點而迴避不利之點的詭辯法」。）

13 Hagner, *New Testament* 621-22: 'Two points should be stressed. First, the arguments against the Pauline authorship of the Pastorals are cumulative. No single argument is totally persuasive, but as the number of arguments against Pauline authorship increase, they grow in strength, and the defense of Pauline authorship becomes an increasingly difficult challenge. Second, the nature of the evidence and arguments falls short of proof or demonstration. We are in a realm of probabilities, where the conclusions of either side cannot be cavalierly dismissed.' Cf. 625: 'the question persists concerning whether the cumulative arguments against Pauline authorship have been successfully answered.' 有趣的是，Kelly 34 同樣指著某些支持傳統看法的論據說：'The cumulative effect of these arguments is impressive'！

14 Hagner, *New Testament* [2012] 615: 'Although quite possibly by Paul (2 Timothy perhaps having the best claim), a slight probability favors a disciple or disciples of Paul, possibly making use of fragments stemming from Paul.'（**1**）這有別於哈格拿早十多年前所表達的立場，那時他是這樣說的（'Titus' [1998] 556）：'The position taken here is that the new and unusual can be explained by the following: (1) in contrast to the undisputed letters, Paul here writes towards the end of his career; (2) he writes primarily (but not exclusively) to his lieutenant [Titus], who has the task of establishing the churches of Crete for the future, against heresy and unacceptable conduct; (3) he

歌頓則表示，雖然他十分清楚保羅是教牧書信作者之說所涉及的許多困難，但是他深信，以教牧書信為冒名作品的種種理論，所涉及在歷史方面的困難是更大的。[15] 孟威廉正確指出，要回答的問題是：「哪一種重構整體而論看來是可信的呢？」認為保羅在他的生命末期在一獨特的歷史處境中寫了教牧書信（甲），抑或認為一位愛慕保羅之人，或在保羅死後不久，或在接近第一世紀的末期，也許借助於一些零碎的真確資料，為要使保羅的信息能夠切實對應那個世代所出現的具體問題，而寫了這三封書信（乙），何者較為可信呢？[16]

筆者認為（甲）比（乙）可信，理由如下：**(一)** 託名之作的倡議者未能令人滿意地解釋，為何作者需要寫三封書信；[17] 但若視之為

---

employed an amanuensis who had considerable liberty in formulating the letter.' **(2)** Johnson（'Titus' 382*b*）則認為，'In the final analysis, it is difficult to make any assured claims about either the authenticity or the inauthenticity of the Pastorals as a whole or as individual letters.'

15 Fee 1.

16 Mounce xlvii: 'The question is, "Which reconstruction is generally plausible?" Is it more credible to see Paul writing the PE at the end of his life in a unique historical situation or to see an admirer of Paul, either shortly after his death or toward the end of the first century, perhaps with scraps of authentic material, writing the three letters in an attempt to make Paul's message relevant to the specific issues that arose in that generation?'

17 **Fee** 6: 'it never adequately answers the question, Why *three* letters? For example, why write Titus or 1 Timothy, given one or the other, and why from such a considerably different perspective and historical context? And why 2 Timothy at all, since it fails so badly to fit the proposed reconstruction?'; 25: 最大的困難是 'to find an adequate reason for such an author to have written these letters and, most significantly, to have written *three* letters.'（亦見下註上半部分。）同樣地，**Mounce** cxix-cxx: 'If a forger were writing in the second century, using the name of the apostle Paul to add validity, why would this person write three forgeries, tripling the possibility of detection? Why write three documents that are significantly different in content and, in the case of Titus and 2 Timothy, add so little to the forger's argument?'; lxxxiii: 'The question still stands even if one believes pseudepigraphy was accepted and recognized as such by the early church.' **Hopkins**（Review of Lea－Griffin [1992] 262）就批評作者們沒有提及 'what may be the most problematic issue for their opponents:* why *three* letters unless they were in fact written by Paul'（*= the opponents of 'those who support Pauline authorship'）。如卡森－穆爾（〈教牧書信〉551）所言：「學者對那位冒名作者的確切處境眾說紛紜，對他所面對的問題，或是他面對這些問題的時間，或是他面對這些問題的教會處境，都完全不清楚。那麼，我們怎能發掘出作者所寫的內容的真正含意呢？」（cf. Carson－Moo－Morris, *INT* 366）。

真正的保羅書信，則可重構其歷史背景，所得出的圖畫更為具體明確，書信的寫作原因和目的亦更為清晰。[18]（二）如果認為教牧書信不是保羅寫的，則其中一些關於個人的細節（例：提前三 14～15，四 13；多三 12；尤其是提後四 9～21）是很難解釋的。如卡森和穆爾所指出，「那些認為這幾封書信是託名著作的學者，也應當把教牧書信裏面的個人資料，套進他們所想像的架構裏，來面對有關的困難。書信為何提及保羅的外衣和書卷呢（提後四 13）？[19] 又或他提到自己往馬其頓

（1）Quinn 19 將教牧書信視為一信集：'why are there three letters? One might have sufficed. The genre of letter collections suggests the answer. Various churches in the second generation knew they had received letters from Paul. This correspondence as a whole was yet to be collected . . . . The PE as a collection would have been received and read not as individual letters from the Paul of history but as a "characterization" of the great apostle and his teaching for the new generation.'（2）但是 Guthrie（*NTI* 638-39）早已指出這種理論的破綻，他說：'At best, we are in the realm of conjecture here, but the advocates of the theory cannot produce any parallels for such a fictitious corpus production from the early period, and in the absence of such evidence cannot reasonably claim that the pseudo-Paulinist's activities were in full accord with the literary conventions of his own time. If these epistles are inventions of a pious author they stand, as a group, unique in early Christian literature.'

18 Fee 7 認為，'In the final analysis this is the strongest argument for their authenticity.' 詳參 Fee 5-14.（1）費歌頓表示，以上兩點就是他為何深信教牧書信至終是出自保羅手筆的（主要）原因：'Although fully aware of the difficulties I am convinced that the PE are ultimately Pauline because, *inter alia*, (1) one can make such good sense of them as fitting the historical situation of the mid-60s; (2) I have yet to have anyone give a good answer to the question: Why three letters? That is, given 1 Timothy, why did a pseudepigrapher write Titus, and given 1 Timothy and Titus and their concerns, why 2 Timothy at all?'（Fee, 'Reflections' 141 n.2）。（亦見上註開首部分。）（2）Wilder（*Pseudonymity* 251）指出「託名」這問題對釋經的含意：'the authority that an apostle's letters assert cannot be separated from the authority of the apostle himself. The impact of pseudo-apostolicity upon exegesis is further compounded when one realizes that this seems to demand that the letter also contains pseudo-recipients and circumstances. So, the interpretation of a deceptive non-Pauline letter, for example, must differ from one that is genuinely Pauline. Consequently, the exegesis of such "pseudo-Pauline" letters cannot be used to form a Pauline theology.'

19 Cf. **Moule**, 'Problem' 128: 'in II Tim. iv. 6 ff. where there is indeed a "last words" setting, perfectly suited to a pseudepigraph, the effect is gratuitously ruined by the introduction of those extraordinary snippets of trivial detail, about the cloak and the books. It is hard enough to understand what Paul would want with them if he really thought that he was soon going to be executed. But it is still harder, in my opinion, to see why a pseudepigrapher should invent details so little consistent with an idealized scene of martyrdom. Surely, of the two, it is easier to believe that Paul really did send a message to Timothy . . . to this effect, either because he had a secret hope he might be reprieved and outlast the winter, or because he did not know that there would not be a

的時候，留下提摩太在以弗所（提前一 3）？又或他指望快到提摩太那裏去，卻不肯定自己是否會耽延（提前三 14～15）？[20] 信中為何要提及阿尼色弗一直在羅馬找保羅，最終找到了（提後一 16～17）？為何要吩咐提多幫助律師西納和亞波羅（多三 13）？若然認定這幾封信是在第一世紀末至第二世紀初，由一位不認識保羅處境的作者託名寫成的，我們就很難理解他信中提及這一切的用意了。作者若真是託保羅之名寫作，便顯然會將敘事的部分，套進已知的保羅年表資料中。提出這理論的學者，沒有為作者為何捏造這類假設性的處境，提出令人信服的解釋。」[21]

（三）託名著作的一個版本（或變體）說，雖然三封書信整體而論皆為託名之作，但作者將一些真確的保羅書信的殘篇納入這些信函內，為要使後者顯得更為逼真。[22] 可是，這種理論涉及好些困難：第

---

long delay before the execution, even if he were condemned.' **Kaestli**（'Luke-Acts' 116）則認為，'referring to concrete data and personal details is part of the common literary techniques in the Greco-Roman pseudepigraphical letters. Frugality and simple clothing habits are typical of the philosophical way of life, and such features are often illustrated by some practical advice or personal detail which the philosopher gives to the addressee of his letter. . . . In 2 Tim. 4.13, the author of the Pastorals illustrates this ideal of soberness in the use of material goods [1 Tim. 6.8] through the personal example of Paul: nearing his death, the apostle recalls his belongings; <u>all he owns</u> and all he needs, <u>is one single cloak</u>.'（這是否等於說，保羅當時身上或身邊連一件外衣也沒有——因他把自己僅有的一件留給了加布？！）但就算接受這解釋，其他的細節（見正文）有類似的解釋嗎？

20 Cf. Moule, 'Problem' 128: '. . . I find it harder to conceive of an apostle's disciple pretending, after his master's death, that he was still shortly coming to visit his addressee. Twice in I Timothy this note is struck: iii. 14 f.: "I am hoping to come to you before long, but I write this in case I am delayed . . ."; iv. 13 [*sic*] "until I arrive . . .". . . . Some may say that this is an obvious device to lend verisimilitude, and I know that judgements of this sort are difficult to assess objectively. I can only say that to me it seems a piece of gratuitous irony and in bad taste.'

21 卡森－穆爾：〈教牧書信〉547（cf. Carson－Moo－Morris, *INT* 363）。Guthrie（'Pastoral Epistles' 685*a*）指出，'the difficulty that many have found with a fiction theory is that the result in some parts (e.g., 2 Tim. 4) is so realistic as to be improbable. . . . Indeed, the strength of support for the fragment theory〔見下文之（三）〕is a sufficient indication of the difficulties of a fiction theory.'

22 **（1）**最著名的例子是 P. N. Harrison 的「五殘篇」，其後修正為「三殘篇」（詳見 Marshall 73）。這三塊殘篇是：（1）多三 12～15，由馬其頓發出；（2）提後四 9～

一，作者的做法是奇怪的。為甚麼他把絕大部分的資料放在提摩後書，提多書只有一短篇，提摩太前書則一點真確資料都沒有呢？第二，這些真確的殘篇是如何被保存下來的呢？如果它們是以完整的單元被保存下來的，則為何它們是以被解體的形式分置於教牧書信的不同地方呢？但若它們被保存下來的時候已經不是完整的單元，則它們被保存的過程是無法解釋的，因它們並非人們通常會保存的碎片。[23] 如此難以置信的理論竟然廣為流傳，使慕爾大為驚奇。[24]**（四）**託名之說和

15、20、21a、22b，由尼哥坡里發出；（3）提後一 16～18，三 10～11，四 1、2a、5b～8、16～19、21b～22a，由羅馬發出。這理論其中一點困難是 'to understand the reason why the compiler interwove his two genuine notes in 2 Timothy in the way he did. . . . There is certainly no parallel where genuine notes are mixed in with fictitious personal allusions* as must be the case in the fragment theory of 2 Timothy'（Guthrie, *NTI* 637）。*提後一 5（你外祖母羅以和你母親友妮基）、15（所有在亞細亞的人……其中有腓吉路和黑摩其尼），二 17（許米乃和腓理徒）。'Since these allusions are not in the "genuine" sections, they must have been invented by the Paulinist to create a greater impression of verisimilitude, but why was this necessary if the genuine notes were self-evidently Pauline? And how can we be certain that the compiler did not also compose the "genuine" notes since he was prone to do this sort of thing?'（Guthrie, *NTI* 638）。**（2）**另一例子見 Martin, *Foundations* 302-3, 306: 'The compiler . . . had access to materials that go back to Paul's own statements of his faith and life . . . . These he incorporated to display Paul's deep concern for the churches'（306）。Mounce cxxi 評論說，'Martin [303] uses the phrase "let us imagine," and the major critique of this [*sic*, not "his"] position is that it requires too much imagination. Not one point in the hypothetical reconstruction is based on fact. There is only supposition; there are no textual indications'.

23 Guthrie, *NTI* 637, 638. See also Guthrie, 'Pastoral Epistles' 684*a-b*; Kümmel, *INT* 385. 亦參卡森－穆爾：〈教牧書信〉550（cf. Carson－Moo－Morris, *INT* 366）。

24 Moule, 'Problem' 129: 'I must confess that it amazes me that such a solution has gained wide currency, for it presupposes (what, to the best of my knowledge there is not a shred of evidence to support) that Paul wrote these little scraps on separate, detached papyri; and, even if that could be established, it requires us to believe that they were kept by the recipients – another improbable assumption; and finally, it asks us to picture an imitator going round and collecting them and copying them into the letter he has fabricated at points so captiously* selected that they have puzzled commentators ever since. . . . What seems to me fatal to the scrap theory . . . is that it requires so much credulity on all sides.'（Also cited [minus the last sentence] in Harrison, *INT* 365 and in Mounce cxxi.）Cf. Kelly 29: 'The whole theory . . . is a tissue of improbabilities, and it is impossible to find an exact parallel in ancient literature.'（*'Captious' here apparently = 'tending to raise objections'?）'Because of the fragment theory's many problems, most scholars no longer consider the hypothesis a plausible explanation' (Wilder, *Pseudonymity* 225).

殘篇論皆與教牧書信本身的倫理教導不符。[25]「當我們想到那幾卷教牧書信，均提醒信徒要防備說謊之人的哄騙（提前四 1；提後三 3；多一 10），以及作者還在其中一節經文指出，他從前也是受迷惑的，但如今因得救而完全改變了（多三 3），問題就變得更難解了。一個刻意寫信提醒信徒要小心受人哄騙的人，自己卻怎會假冒保羅的名義來寫信呢？他會否堅定的說：『我說的是真話，不是謊言』（提前二 7）？」[26]

---

25 Davies II 116 對這 'ethical dilemma' 的解釋是蒼白無力的，她說：'I have no evidence . . . to explain how the author reconciled his theological ethics and his actual fraud. All I can do is to appeal to the common human failing of contradiction. I think that it is bad to tell lies, but this understanding has not always prevented my doing so. Moreover, reflection is often necessary to recognize something as a lie. The author of the Pastorals may have noticed and deplored many instances of lying <u>without recognizing his own activity as such an instance</u>.'

26 卡森－穆爾：〈新約書信〉326。（不過，關於多三 3，見該節註釋註 2 之〔1〕= 下面 369。）Cf. **Banker** 10*a-b*: 'The pseudonymous view . . . renders the discourse itself incoherent in the sense that the discourse condemns the very thing that the pseudonymous writer would be practicing – untruthfulness (cf. references to truth and falsehood in [Titus] 1:1, 2, 4, 12, 14; 2:7; 3:3)'; **Liefeld** 28（利斐特 22）：'It would be strange indeed if an author who intended to teach such [ethical] standards would himself go beyond honesty and truth by attempting to deceive the readership into thinking that not he but Paul was the author.' See also **Marshall** 82: 'The weakness of this argument is that it measures the morality of pseudonymity by the standards of the non-Christian ancient world rather than by the standards of Christian teaching. It is a simple and incontrovertible fact that second-century orthodox Christianity objected strongly to it, as practiced by heretics or even by the presbyter who wrote "out of love for Paul" (Tertullian, *De Baptismo* 17 . . .).' 亦參卡森－穆爾：〈新約書信〉327：「總的而言，我們無法找出一些相應的例子，來證明部分新約書卷的原初讀者，早已知悉該書卷是託名著作，所以並不存在欺騙的意圖。反之，我們擁有的證據，卻只能驅使我們得出以下的結論：一就是部分新約書卷屬於託名著作，它們的真正作者意圖欺騙讀者；一就是新約書卷的所有作者都只想說真話，所以並不能夠證明新約當中有託名經書。」

（1）以下作者都指出、承認，甚或強調託名著作存有欺騙性質：**Harding** II 4: 'Since writing in his own name would not command the attention of the addressees, the author wrote in Paul's name even if that meant <u>deceiving</u> the faithful'; **Marshall**, 'Deception' 789: 'the writer of the Pastoral Epistles, whether well-intentioned or not, undertook a <u>deceitful</u> writing strategy in falsifying the authorship of letters and risked rejection of his writing'; n.27**:** 'Even allowing that Pseudo-Paul might have thought that the Pastoral Epistles are exactly what Paul would have written in Pseudo-Paul's situation does not remove the <u>deception</u>'; **Meade**, 'Pseudonymity' 121: '"I am not lying" [1 Tim 2:7] illustrates the difficulty of affirming the truth of Paul's authority and teaching by using a technique that involves <u>deception</u>'; **Merz**, 'Self-Exposition' 115 n.7: 'the idea, proposed

（五）雖然馬歇爾試圖以「化名寫作」之說來代替「託名之作」，為要排除作者有欺騙成分，[27] 但是他的試圖並不成功。馬氏的理論是這樣的：教牧書信（尤其是提摩太後書）是基於真確的保羅資料，很可能是一組人（包括提摩太和提多）的集體創作。促成這些書信的因素是在提摩太後書背後的一封真確的保羅書信，此書信已開始正視反對者所造成的問題，這就導致提摩太前書和提多書的寫作，為要更明確和充分地處理在以弗所和克里特的反對陣營和異端所引起的問題。這些書信的目的是要給予提摩太、提多及相關的教會領袖（他們的工作是召喚眾教會從假教義和錯誤的行徑返回正道）保羅的支持。「它們不是託名之作的例子，而是化名寫作的例子。」這些書信完全沒有欺騙的意圖，因為人們知道它們是「考慮到改變中的處境而對保羅的教導作出新的表述」。只不過，隨著時間的流逝，書信的起源被忘記了，它們遂被視為保羅自己的作品。[28] 可是：

---

by some scholars, that there was an "open" pseudepigraphy in early Christianity . . . is exceedingly improbable on historical grounds'; 131 提到 'the . . . deceit which is inherent in the composition and divulgation of pseudepigrapha (despite all the subjectively good intentions of their authors)'; **Donelson** I 16: 'We are forced to admit that in Christian circles pseudonymity was considered a dishonorable device and, if discovered, the document was rejected and the author, if known, was excoriated' (cited in Marshall, 'Deception' 786). （**2**）Marshall（'Recent Study' 288-92, section on 'Pseudepigraphy and Authorship'）討論了 'contributions from the conservative side of scholarship'.

27 Marshall 84: 'Since the nuance of deceit seems to be inseparable from the use of the terms "pseudonymity" and "pseudepigraphy" and gives them a pejorative sense, we need another term that will refer more positively to the activity of writing in another person's name without intent to deceive: perhaps "allonymity" and "allepigraphy" may be suggested as suitable alternatives.' 唐 36、37、38 將 'allonymity'（Towner III 25, 26）翻譯為「化名寫作」。

28 Marshall 92. 兩個引句英文依次原作 'They are examples not of pseudonymity but of allonymity' 和 'fresh formulations of Pauline teaching to take account of the changing situation'. 馬歇爾的理論另見於 Marshall, 'Recent Study' 274：'the letters are put together on the basis of Pauline materials and traditions by a later compiler without any intention to deceive the audience'; idem, 'Timothy and Titus' 185*a*: 'It claims that the letters were written by a colleague of Paul not long after his death to make available to the next generation of Christian leaders the kind of instructions that he gave to Timothy and Titus because these were still relevant and necessary. There was no intention to deceive, and the first readers were aware what was going on'; 198*b*-99*a*.

「這個理論若然正確，那麼，撰寫提摩太前書和提多書的那個人，縱然是為了某個崇高的動機而借用保羅的名義，但實際上仍屬於託名經書了；這兩卷書之所以被納入正典之中，只能歸咎於初期教會沒有審視清楚，未能認出它們是偽名著作了。這個重構的理論似乎不太可信。而且，信中還有不少地方，是使徒保羅談及他本人的；因此，要不去指控那位託名作者帶有欺騙意圖，便極為困難。」[29]

（六）早期教會並不承認或接受他們知道是託名的著作。[30]「從來沒

---

29 卡森－穆爾：〈新約書信〉326。作者們甚至認為，「這個見解似乎是支持某些新約書卷是託名著作的古老論據，只是沒有勇氣把它直接說出來。」（**1**）Towner III 26（唐 37-38）對馬歇爾的理論提出質疑：'there remains a rather undeniable "if" in this whole proposition. This solution explains the dissimilarities with Pauline style and theology and retains for the letters an unsullied (if slightly derivative) apostolic authority *if* the procedure, code-named "allonymity," was in fact regarded as acceptable in the early church that first received the "allonymous" letters.' 唐氏的最後評語是：'the jury continues to deliberate'（唐 38：「仍有待學者們繼續探討」）。Wilder（Review of Towner III [2006] 657）的評估較為肯定：'My own deliberation on allonymity is that the proverbial jury will likely come back with the [Scottish] verdict: "not proven"'（方括號是原來的）。（**2**）Köstenberger（'Pastoral Epistles' [2010] 4）這樣說明馬歇爾的見解之性質：'If Marshall's line of reasoning is applied to his own commentary (which Marshall acknowledges to have been written "in collaboration with" Philip Towner), perhaps several hundred years from now, some might claim that the commentary was actually not written by Marshall himself but compiled subsequent to his death by Towner based on Marshall's notes and perhaps also based on some of his previous publications — not to mention oral interchanges and conversations or informal notes, such as e-mail messages, and so on, during Marshall's lifetime. With the passing of time, doubtless a plausible case could be construed along those lines. While plausible, however, such a theory would obviously not square with the facts, since Howard Marshall is demonstrably still alive* and did publish his commentary during his lifetime and is the person responsible for his work (the degree of collaboration by Towner is another issue). Marshall would therefore rightly protest any such attribution of his work to a posthumous author. One wonders whether Marshall's attribution of the Pastorals' authorship to an "allonymous" writer similarly gives short shrift to the apostle and his role in writing these letters.'（*馬氏於 2015 年去世。）

30 See, e.g., **Witherington** 26-36, 63; **Wilder**, 'Pseudonymity' 157: 'the available evidence from the early church . . . (e.g. Tertullian's comments in *de Baptismo* 17 on the *Acts of Paul*; Serapion's remarks recorded in Eusebius' *Ecclesiastical History* 6.12.2ff. on the *Gospel of Peter* [see Wilder, *Pseudonymity* 128-32, 135-39 respectively; also 132-35, which deals with 'a reference in the Muratorian Fragment to the epistles to the

有一本是教父明知的託名作品——任何文體也不例外——被接受為正典的。」[31] 如唐書禮所指出的，多數派的解釋假定了，「適用在某些

Laodiceans and the *Alexandrians*' (126)]) indicates that the early church (second century onwards) generally did not accept apostolic pseudepigrapha and suggests that it regarded such writings as deceptive.' 參《弗》36-37；《西‧門》14-15。See also **Wilder**, 'Pastoral Epistles' 42: 'Any theory of pseudonymity or unauthorized allonymity [Marshall] in the New Testament must assume that the early Christians tolerated the practice. However . . . the available documentary evidence shows that the early church soundly rejected pseudo-apostolic works upon their discovery. Thus, the view that pseudepigraphic or allepigraphic [Marshall] writings in the names of the apostles were gladly accepted by the early church is not secure'; **Wilder**, *Pseudonymity* 146-47: 'This chapter [Chapter 4: 'Responses of Early Christian Leaders to Apostolic Pseudepigrapha', 123-63] showed that the early church did not readily accept pseudonymity. Generally . . . where a work was known to be pseudonymous, the early church rejected and excluded it from the writings they recognized as normative. . . . *both* the authorship of writings *and* their content were important criteria for the early church when determining which books were to be recognized or rejected as having normative status. . . . If a writing was heretical, it was considered inauthentic, and if inauthentic, then the work was not used publicly in the churches. Only where a writing appeared to meet both of these criteria was it ever recognized as normative and accepted for public reading in the churches. In other words, the early church did not *knowingly* allow either pseudo-apostolic or heretical works to be read publicly in the churches along with the apostolic writings. . . . evidence is lacking for a convention of pseudonymity which existed amongst orthodox Christians.' **Duff**（'Pseudepigraphy' 309）的專題研究的核心是早期基督徒對冒名寫作的態度，他的結論同樣是：'despite the limitations of the evidence, it is most likely to have been that the value of a text was closely connected to its true authorship; that pseudonymity was known about and generally seen as a deceitful practice to be condemned; and that texts which were thought to be pseudonymous were marginalized – if they were not it was because they were seen mistakenly as authentic.'

31 卡森－穆爾：〈教牧書信〉552。詳參同作者的〈新約書信〉314-27「託名寫作及託名經書」之下的「教父的立場」（319-21）；Carson－Moo－Morris, *INT* 367-71. See also **Guthrie**, *NTI* 1011-28 (appendix on 'Epistolary Pseudepigraphy'; 1028: 'The history of the canon does not lead to the conclusion that works under assumed names would have been accepted into the New Testament collection. It is a fatal objection to all attempts to make pseudepigraphy respectable in early Christianity that the external evidence from our extant sources can supply no positive support for it'); **Marshall** 83: 'it can be argued on the basis of the early church's attitude to truth that the practice of deceptive pseudonymity in the first century by defenders of orthodox Christianity is extremely improbable'; 91: 'Theories of deliberate deceit assume far too easily that the practice was acceptable in the early church'; **Porter**, 'Implications' 114: 'The general if not invariable pattern in Christian circles [in the early church] was that if a work was known to be pseudonymous it was excluded from the canon of authoritative writings'; 'Response to R. W. Wall's Response' 136: 'So far as our limited evidence in the early church indicates, there is no known pseudepigraph that was knowingly accepted into the New Testament canon.' 坡特又指出，'Many have argued that these pseudonymous writings are transparent fictions, and no one would have thought them actually to have been written by Paul. This encounters the severe problem of why they were accepted into the canon in the light of the apparently universal response by the early church to known

情況的一種已知的作法」也適用於教牧書信；可是，「這個假設不僅遠未獲得證明，而且事實上仍舊頗有問題。」[32]（七）教牧書信並不是匿名的書信（像希伯來書），作者自稱為使徒保羅。因此，它們不是真確的保羅書信，就是託名的書信，只是早期教會沒有認出來。但若是後者，便引起教牧書信在今天教會中的地位這嚴肅的問題，[33] 因為早期教會不會把託名著作納入正典內；對早期教會而言，教牧書信是使徒保羅的書信，因而具有權威，因此被納入正典之內，但若它們是託名著作，它們就不應具有正典的地位和權威。[34]

---

pseudepigrapha: they were rejected carte blanche'（Porter, 'Implications' 119）。

32 Towner III 21（引句出自唐 31）。作者繼續說：'Yet in much of NT scholarship it has passed into the realm of the unassailable, reliable "facts" upon which the consensus view is founded.'

33 Thornton, Review of Wall [2012] 884. Cf. Ellis, 'Authorship' 57: 'Any final conclusion that the Pastorals are pseudonymous must face anew the propriety of their canonicity.'

34 參《弗》36-37 註 114 之（3）（4）。**（1）** *Pace* Hagner, *New Testament* 433-34: 'there is no need to think that the acceptance of pseudonymity in the NT – at least of the kind discussed above* – in any sense threatens or undermines the authority and canonicity of such writings.' *615: 'That the pseudonymity involved, if these letters are not by Paul himself, is of a harmless kind has been argued above (see chap. 24 [pp. 426-35]).' **（2）** 威爾達探討「託名書信」之正典地位的問題（252-55）：'The early church clearly would have excluded such [pseudonymous] works, had they known about them.' 但在今天又如何呢？'Should deceptive pseudepigrapha be dropped from the canon if they exist in the NT?'（252）。威爾達指出，研究人員對聖經和倫理的看法會斷定他們對這問題的答案；他以圖表列出數種可能的合併如下（254）：

KEY

A = deceptive pseudonymous letter
B = consequentialist view of ethics ['which holds that what makes an action right or wrong is determined by its foreseen consequences', 253]
B' = deontological view of ethics ['which holds that "a right action is one whose maxim can be universalized consistently, whereas its opposite cannot be", 252]
C = Scripture is about divine revelation and events.
C' = Scripture is divine revelation.

A + B + C = canon（即持這三種看法，有關的書信可保留在正典中）
A + B' + C = canon
A + B + C' = canon
A + B' + C' = no canon（持這三種看法，有關的書信不應保留在正典中）

總結以上的討論，舉證的責任是在反對的一方：[35] 認為教牧書信是託名著作者必須證明，它們確是冒名的著作，又不帶著欺騙的意圖，而早期教會亦會將明知是託名的作品納入正典內。[36] 但是他們並不成功。[37] 不但如此，不論是「杜撰論」或「殘篇論」都牽涉到難以解釋的疑問。[38] 因此筆者認為，接受教牧書信作者的自我宣稱，以及

威爾達的結論如下（254-55）：'In the light of this discussion [252-54], the question posed earlier – *"Should pseudonymous works, if written with the intention to deceive and present in the NT, be retained in the canon?"* – is provided with an answer. If scholars desire to preserve the traditional concept of canon and believe, as this researcher does, that the following views are those closest to the positions held by the early church: (1) apostolic pseudepigrapha were written to deceive; (2) a deontological view of ethics; (3) Scripture is divine revelation; and (4) the canon of Scripture is a binding norm of truth, then they should either drop any pseudonymous letters from the canon, or seriously reconsider that such works indeed do not exist in the NT.'

35 Mounce lxix: 'The authenticity of the PE was not questioned until the nineteenth century. This does not make the raising of this question wrong; but it must be admitted that it is a modern concern. The external evidence for the authenticity of the PE is strong and consistent with the self-witness of the PE. This places the burden of proof on those denying authenticity.' See also Stott 33: 'Both the internal claims and the external witness are strong, substantial and stubborn. The burden of proof rests on those who deny them.' 參註 10（上面 6）。

36 Knight II 47: 'the burden of proof is on those who advocate pseudonymity for letters that claim to be from the apostle Paul and that were accepted as canonical by the early church: It must be demonstrated not only that these letters are pseudonymous and not deceptive but also that the early church would accept letters known to be pseudonymous into the canon.' 在更廣（涉及整本新約）的層面上，Wilder（*Pseudonymity* 250-51）指出，'scholars who formulate hypotheses promoting the view that pseudo-apostolic letters – which many believe to be present in the NT – were acceptably written with no intention to deceive, *are embracing argumentation which generally lacks the support of surviving documentary evidence. . . . Thus, the burden of proof is upon those scholars who claim that pseudo-apostolic works were accepted by the church and not written with the intention to deceive their readers*.'

37 參 Johnson II 2-3 的自述：'For many years . . . I shared the majority position that I had learned from earlier scholars. Only when I tried to communicate to students the logic underlying the majority position, and found that I could not make it convincing, did I adopt – with considerable hesitation – the traditional position as the more elegant and reasonable hypothesis.'

38 (1)唐書禮解釋，他沒有跟隨主流意見的原因是：'the majority view (pseudonymity in one permutation or another)* assumes a historical reconstruction . . . that remains largely hypothetical at numerous critical junctures and has yet to address adequately numerous methodological questions'（Towner III 84. *唐 116 作「用種種替換作法的託名寫作」。但 'in one permutation or another' 在這裏應該是指「託名之作」以不同的「組合形式」出現。）(2) Johnson II 21 甚至這樣質疑，說：'The majority opinion . . . is not without serious difficulties. In fact, these difficulties [see 21-26] are so real that it makes one wonder whether so many hold the position because they are convinced by its

大公教會（尤其是早期教會）堅實的見證，[39] 以這些書信為使徒保羅寫給他的副手提摩太和提多的真確信函，比起其他的理論可取。[40]

在這大前提下，（一）慕爾認為，教牧書信是保羅在世時路加按照保羅的指示，並在某程度上（只是某程度）由保羅口授而寫成的。[41] 但這看法受到嚴重的質疑。[42]（二）威瑟靈頓深信，教牧書信（尤其

---

arguments, or because it is simply more convenient.'

39 Johnson II 23: 'the Pastorals appear in *all* the canonical lists of antiquity, whereas other productions attributed to Paul (*Third Corinthians*, *Letter to Laodiceans*, *Letters of Paul and Seneca*) or dealing with him (*Acts of Paul and Thecla*) were just as universally rejected.'

40 Cf. Guthrie, *NTI* 646: 'In spite of the acknowledged differences between the pastorals and Paul's other epistles, the traditional view that they are authentic writings of the apostle cannot be said to be impossible, and since there are greater problems attached to the alternative theories it is most reasonable to suppose that the early church was right in accepting them as such'; Porter, 'Response to R. W. Wall's Response' 138 n.13: 'On the basis of my historical-critical investigation of the Pastoral Epistles, I remain unconvinced that there is at present a better explanation of their origin than Pauline authorship.'

41 Moule, 'Problem' 117: 'My suggestion is . . . that Luke wrote all three Pastoral epistles. But he wrote them during Paul's lifetime, at Paul's behest, and, in part (but only in part), at Paul's dictation.' Cf. Witherington 58: 'This, I think, gets the balance right.'（**1**）Wilson（*Luke*）則以教牧書信為託名著作，真正的作者是路加（see esp. 136-43; 137-38: 'The combination of linguistic, theological, and historical parallels [between Luke-Acts and the Pastorals] seems to me to point . . . to . . . common authorship'; 139: 'False teachers were becoming increasingly influential . . . . To counter this Luke wrote three epistles in the name of Paul giving what he imagined Paul's response would have been under the circumstances'; 141: 'The close parallels with Luke and the differences from Paul show that a far stronger case can be made for Lucan than for Pauline authorship [of the Pastorals]）。（**2**）Zehr 239 稱提多書為「保羅和路加合著」的。他的意思是：'Many of the main ideas likely came from Paul and were put into writing at a later time by Luke. In doing so, Luke adapted Paul's thought to fit the immediate post-Pauline period of the church in the Hellenized world while retaining Paul's name (Titus 1:1).' 這其實是以提多書為託名著作。

42 （**1**）Strecker（'Sound Doctrine' 577）認為，這種理論 'merely confirms that we are not dealing with letters composed by Paul himself'; 哈格拿問道：'if a secretary were virtually given carte blanche in terms of content and style, how fair is it to call it a letter by Paul and not a pseudonymous document?'（Hagner, *New Testament* 623）。Cf. Davies II 111: 'if the secretary wrote the Pastorals from his own resources, or even from a Pauline outline, but not at the dictation of Paul, then the letters are pseudonymous.'（**2**）Harding II 17-18 提出此理論至少三點困難：教牧書信並無提到代筆人；路加不願稱保羅為使徒，但教牧書信五次這樣稱他；作者似乎認識其他的保羅書信，路加則似乎並不。（**3**）Marshall 87 認為，'Despite the advocacy of this view [author of PE = Luke] by a number of scholars, it is indefensible on grounds of style and theology'

是提摩太前書和提多書）混合了保羅和路加的風格。[43] 勵佐治認為，鑑於路加長期和保羅在一起，尤其是在保羅第一次羅馬監禁之時和之後（參：使徒行傳的「我們」段落〔十六 10～17，二十 5～15，二十一 1～8，二十七 1～二十八 16〕；西四 14；門 24 節；提後四 11〔只有路加在我這裏〕[44]），保羅在教牧書信的用詞與風格可能受了路加的

（referring to his 'Review of Wilson [1979]'）。例如，（**i**）路－徒（路加福音和使徒行傳）與教牧書信這兩組著作共有的字是 554 個，其中只是這兩組著作共有的是 34 字（即 6.137%）。教牧書信與其他十卷保羅書信共有的字是 574 個，其中只是這兩組著作共有的是 55 字（即 9.582%）；路－徒的詞彙量比保羅信集的更大，這使第二組數字更形重要。第二組數字顯示，Wilson 5-10 所引的數據 'are quite inadequate to give reason for preferring Lucan authorship of the Pastorals to Pauline authorship'（Marshall, Review 72; cf. Knight II 49）。（**ii**）在神學方面，馬歇爾 'find[s] nothing here to "encourage the notion of common authorship" of L-A/Past. as compared with the Pauline authorship of Past.'（Review 73）。馬歇爾的結論是（74），'In short, time and again one fails to find anything that really *demands* common authorship. . . . [Wilson's] assessment of the significance of the evidence has failed to convince this reader.' Marshall 88 直言，'The hypothesis of a Lucan origin for the PE should be dropped from consideration.' See also Kaestli, 'Luke-Acts' 117-20; 他認為 '[Wilson's] thesis of a common authorship is not convincing'（120）。（**4**）Riesner（'Once More' 246）則辯證，'It seems that the arguments of I. H. Marshall against the Lucan authorship of the Pastoral Epistles are not irrefutable [243-46] and one can add to the reasons favouring such a contention [246-57].' 他的結論是，'There are many similarities in language and theological expression between the Pastoral Epistles and Luke-Acts'（258, point (6)）。見 Marshall（'Recent Study' 290-91）的撮要及評估。（**5**）Johnson II 11-12 認為，比起以路加為教牧書信的作者，'It would be more accurate to say that the Pastorals and Luke-Acts share a broader sample of koine Greek than is attested in the undisputed letters.'

43 （**i**）Witherington, 'Pastoral Epistles' 241: 'In the case of the pastoral epistles [*sic*], I would argue that the "voice is the voice of Paul, but the hands are the hands of Luke.' Witherington 60: 'These letters, then [based on the evidence given in 57-60], reflect a combination of Pauline and Lukan style. . . . To borrow a Biblical metaphor, the voice is the voice of Paul, but the hand is the hand of Luke'; 61-62: 'All and [*sic*, in] all, a good case can be made that these documents reflect both Pauline and Lukan diction and ways of putting things.'（**ii**）Witherington 102: 'we have good reason for saying about Titus and 1 Timothy that the voice is that of Paul, but the hand and the diction often are those of Luke.' 參一 8 註釋註 49 之（3）= 下面 139。（**iii**）Witherington 92-93: 'Luke, the most knowledgable [*sic*] of Paul's companions about the Greco-Roman world and its social and political customs and correspondences, is the one who chose to shape these letters [1 Tim and Titus] like a *mandatum principiis* [*sic*].' 後一個詞見一 5 註釋註 38 之（3）= 下面 98。

44 Riesner（'Once More' 254）指出，'According to 2 Tim. 4:11, Luke, and at such a crucial time, was nearer to the apostle than all his other companions – and this makes Luke a person of deep insight and personal trust.' 作者（253）接受基里對只有路加在我這裏

影響；路加亦有可能是保羅寫作教牧書信時的抄寫員。[45] 孟威廉同樣認為，鑑於保羅所處的困境以及他和路加的友誼，他會給予路加比另一位代筆人更大的自由度。[46] 這些看法試圖以路加的參與來解釋，教牧書信的詞彙和風格為甚麼跟其他的保羅書信有所分別。[47]（三）費歌頓承認，鑑於教牧書信與路加福音－使徒行傳的詞彙大量相似，路加為教牧書信的代筆人之說具吸引力，但是他隨即加上一句，說：「但在這事上，我們只能臆測。」[48]（四）孟威廉指出，並無記

的解釋：'This does not imply, as is often assumed, that the Apostle is literally alone, but that Luke is the only member of his intimate circle who is with him'（Kelly 213-14）。

45 Knight II 50-51. 勵佐治早前就認為（Knight I 150-51），那些「可信的話」（參三 8a 註釋註 6 及所屬正文〔下面 422-23〕）只在教牧書信出現，可能與路加是這幾封信的抄寫員（amanuensis）有關，因路加是個會收集並使用這種項目的人（參路一 1～4；一 46～55，一 67～79，二 29～32〔馬利亞的「尊主頌」，撒迦利亞的「以色列頌」，西面的「求主頌」；參鮑維均：《路加（上）》99、114、146〕；徒二十 17～35）。換一個講法，那些「可信的話」似乎指向路加是保羅的抄寫員（Knight I 3）。

46 Mounce lxiv: 'Regardless of how much freedom Paul would have given to another amanuensis, Paul's serious predicament and Luke's friendship suggest that Paul would have given Luke more freedom as an amanuensis than he would have given to others'; cxxvii-ix.

47 （**1**）Harrison（*INT* 363）也認為保羅寫教牧書信時有抄寫員的協助，該名抄寫員就是路加。Ellis（'Pastorals' 45*b*）認為，'in antiquity a trusted and gifted amanuensis customarily shaped the vocabulary, style and composition of an author's work.' Stott 34 認為最可能的場景是，'Paul the apostle wrote the three Pastorals, towards the end of his life, addressing contemporary issues, and communicating through a trusted amanuensis'; 他同時強調，'the amanuensis must not be allowed to oust the author, nor the author be robbed of his leadership role [in the composition of the letters] and apostolic authority.' （**2**）Porter（'Implications' 106）則反對代筆人之說：'Although we know quite a bit about the widespread use of scribes of various sorts in the ancient world, we do not know very much of direct relevance concerning how Paul used his scribes. It is dubious to posit scribal independence as a means of accounting for supposed discrepancies when we have two such letters as Romans, which has a direct claim to scribal intervention (Rom 16:22), and Galatians, with the strong implication of use of a scribe (Gal 6:11-17). In theology, as well as language, they are very similar, even though we do not know if the same scribe was used for both. This may well indicate the force of the Pauline personality, but makes it difficult to prove much regarding the use of a scribe. The issue of co-authorship is similar. This solution to the difficulties, therefore, looks too much like special pleading*.'（*參上面 7 註 12 末尾。）

48 Fee 26: 'But on this matter, one can only conjecture.' Guthrie（*NTI* 648）認為，'The major problem is the degree of liberty which a man like Paul would have been prepared to grant.' 他又說（'Pastoral Epistles' 684*a*）：'It is easier to suppose an amanuensis theory for official church epistles than for semipersonal letters. Nevertheless, knowledge

錄表示早期教會因教牧書信的文學特色、詞彙或風格而煩惱；基於教會的鑑別和評估，教牧書信被接納為保羅所寫。既然說希臘語的早期教會對於教牧書信是如何寫成的並無顯示任何掛慮的跡象，那麼在今天的學術討論中，風格和詞彙的問題顯得這麼突出，是使人感到驚訝的。[49]

鑑於（三）（四）兩點，即我們不能確定路加在教牧書信寫作上的參與及其程度，筆者認為費歌頓和唐書禮的結論值得接納。費歌頓說：「保羅是教牧書信的作者」這話的意思是，這三封書信至終來自保羅，他當時的處境就如信上所描述的。這話並不告訴我們，這三封

---

of Paul's literary habits is not sufficient to exclude the possibility that many of the peculiarities of these Epistles are due to his secretary.'

49 Mounce cxvi: 'there is no record that the church struggled with the literary features of the PE, vocabulary or style; based on the church's critical assessment, the PE were accepted as Pauline. If the Greek-speaking church showed no sign of concern about how the PE were written, one wonders why today the issue of style and vocabulary looms so large on the scholarly horizon.' See also Johnson II 12: 'It may be worth noting that no one in the ancient church challenged the authenticity of the Pastorals on the basis of style, a point more worth noting because criticism on this issue was not lacking when it came to the attribution of Hebrews, and because we might suppose the sense of Greek style to be better among those who continued to be schooled in the same system of *paideia* than among those who learned their Greek in a German gymnasium or American prep school or seminary.'（**1**）Towner III 23 指出，「一個古代希臘化時代的作者的行文風格是會因時制宜的」；「保羅的行文風格是由他的個性塑造的」（一個現代的觀念）這個理據並不適用。「場合或需要決定所採取的行文風格。關於提摩太前後書與提多書，必須問的是：甚麼『行文風格』最適合保羅設法要處理的情況，而他可能有甚麼可以選擇的行文風格，不管他是否曾經在給教會的書信中選擇它們」（唐 34）。（**2**）Massey（'Cicero' 73-82）藉著比較「羅馬政治家、演說家和學者」西塞羅（公元前106-43〔《聖神》136*b*〕）的兩封信（74: Letter 75 ['to his friend Atticus about political turmoil in Rome'] and Letter 24 ['to another friend, Marius, about Pompey's magnificent games']）來說明，以一個作者的風格來決定其作品是託名之作是困難的。在遣詞用字方面，兩封信的分別極大；'Consequently, it is hard to imagine the same individual writing both Letter 24 and Letter 75'（78）。在提供人名、日期、時間、地點方面，'Once again, it is hard to imagine the same individual writing both Letter 24 and Letter 75'（81）。同一作者所寫的兩封信卻在風格上迥然不同，可見 'This difference is not an argument for pseudonymity. Therefore, this study concludes that the attempt to prove pseudonymity on the basis of style alone can be a literary slippery slope'（82），即是極不穩妥。'The thesis of this article concludes that terms such as "colorless" and "monotonous" [Quinn 6] are really inadequate and ineffectual as an aid to settle the matter [of authorship]. Therefore, they should not be employed to undermine or overthrow genuineness of authorship'（84）。亦參註 9 第三段（上面 5～6）。

書信是如何來自保羅；我們並沒有這問題的最終答案。[50] 唐書禮說：「這三封書信的寫作過程問題必然仍舊是懸而未決的〔我們對此問題必須繼續維持開放的態度〕，這是我的觀點。事實上，作者寫這三封書信的環境可能也是彼此不同。由於寫作保羅文集的過程的複雜性，為這三封給同工的書信堅持主張任何特別的寫作理論，是不會得到甚麼好處的。本註釋的觀點是：正如保羅其他書信，保羅是這三封書信的作者，不管其他人對其信息與內容有多少貢獻。」[51]

50 Fee 26: 'To say that Paul is the author of the PE means that the letters ultimately come from him in the historical settings contained within them. It does not say *how* they came from him; the final answer to that question is not available to us.' 曾 31-32 則認為：「保羅有可能口述了大綱，由他其中一個門徒編輯並把文本與傳統合併，然後由保羅核對內容，表達他對以弗所和克里特教會的關注。……即使是保羅的書記用『傳統』(παραθήκη) * 來填補那大綱，但只要是保羅親筆署名，** 那封信就等於是保羅的作品。」(*παραθήκη 在教牧書信所指的是保羅受託傳揚、如今交付給提摩太〔提前六 20；提後一 14〕亦交託給上帝〔提後一 12〕的福音〔so Towner III 55, 431, 476, 478 = 唐 78，615，686，689〕。**參三 15 註釋引言〔下面 469〕。)

51 唐 121。英文原作(Towner III 88)：'it is my view that the question of the authorship process in the case of these letters must remain open. In fact, the circumstances of the authorship of these three letters may well differ from letter to letter. Given the complex nature of the authorship process that gave us the Pauline corpus, there is nothing to be gained by insisting on a particular theory of composition for the three letters to coworkers. The view of this commentary is that, just as with the remainder of the Pauline letters, Paul is the author of these three letters however much or little others contributed to their messages and composition.' Cf. Johnson II 32-33: 'the premise that these are real letters places them in the same category of the occasional and contingent as the rest of the Pauline Epistles.' 因此莊臣表示，'I will use the rest of the Pauline corpus as the appropriate comparative context for the analysis of these letters' (32). 筆者贊同這種做法。

導論（貳）：提多書的收信人

提多書的收信人是保羅稱為**在共同的信仰上作我真兒子的提多**（一 4a）。**提多**的名字[1] 在新約一共出現十二次，全部都是在保羅的書信中。雖然使徒行傳並無記載關於提多的事，連他的名字也沒有提及，[2] 但是從保羅的書信可知，**(i)** 保羅歸主後第二次訪問耶路撒冷時（加二 1～10），[3] 提多以從屬者的地位隨行（1 節：**帶了提多一起去**），一方面充當「展覽品甲」或「證物甲」——展示了上帝在外邦人當中所做的工作，同時作為保羅提供的「判例案件」，藉以逼使耶城教會的領袖正視「外邦信徒在教會中的地位，他們如何可以跟猶太信徒一樣完全地有分於基督的身體」的問題（參 3 節）。[4] **(ii)** 後來，保羅稱為**我的弟兄**的提多（林後二 13）成了保羅的親密同工，有時還擔

---

1 Τίτος. 陳 7 說「這名字的意思即『號角』」，未知有何根據。

2 Ward 237 認為，這可能是由於提多是路加（使徒行傳作者）的親戚。

3 按筆者的理解，這是徒十一章的賑災之訪（十一 30 ＝ 十二 25），不是徒十五章的使徒會議之訪（十五 2～29）；詳見《加》71-100，尤其是 74-76、89-100。

4 詳參《加》382-83（「判例案件」即 'test case'）。**(1)** 馬特羅聲稱，提多書的（冒名）作者選擇以提多為（虛構的）收信人，這選擇暗示提多書代表著 'a strand of Christianity that champions Paul's apostleship and resists the subordination of Paul's gospel to "the gospel of the circumcision."' 這兩種立場（維護保羅的使徒身分；拒絕將保羅的福音置於**受割禮的福音**〔加二 7，呂譯〕之下）成為二世紀上半的「馬吉安主義（Marcionism）*」的獨特標誌（Martin, 'Titus' 11）。（*「指馬吉安的主張，反對舊約，另編以路加福音大部分及保羅書信十封組成之正典」〔《宗教》195*b*〕；參《聖神》346*a*。）**(2)** 馬文的主旨在於辯證，提多書所描寫的對手與提前所主張的看法相符，反之亦然；'Titus represents a Marcionite understanding of Christianity that rejects a judaizing Christianity while 1 Timothy asserts the connection of Christianity with its Jewish roots'; 這兩封信顯示基督徒之間對於何為「基督教的正確理解」的辯論，各自駁斥對方的基督徒觀點（'Titus' 21; cf. 23: 'these letters stand on opposite sides of a second century intrachurch struggle over the correct understanding of Christianity'; n.63: 因而二書並非出自同一作者）。筆者對馬氏（根據經文而建構出來的）這種「隱含的修辭處境（implied rhetorical situations）**」存疑。（**參較《弗》15 註 11。）

任了保羅的個人代表（多一 5），[5] 特別在處理保羅與哥林多教會的關係（參：林後二 12～13，七 5～16）[6] 以及該教會參與耶路撒冷教會的賑災籌款（林後八 6～九 5，[7] 參十二 18a、b）二事上（二者都是需要小心和技巧處理的），提多作為保羅的「特使」[8] 獲得令保羅欣慰的成功。**(iii)** 除了提摩太，[9] 提多就是保羅最信任的夥伴和同工（林後八 23）。事實上，當保羅憤怒地否認在自己為教會集資一事上有任何追逐私利的企圖時，他把提多和自己相提並論，指出二人都充滿同樣的無私精神：我所差遣到你們那裏去的人，我何曾藉著他們中的任何人佔過你們的便宜呢？我勸提多到你們那裏去，又差遣那位弟兄與他同去，提多佔過你們的便宜嗎？我們的行事為人不是同一心靈嗎？不是同一步伐嗎？（林後十二 17～18）。[10] **(iv)** 在寫作提多書之前，保羅曾把提多留在克里特（多一 5），信末則囑咐提多要往尼哥坡里去見保羅（三 12）。再後來，提多去了達馬太（提後四 10，新譯）。[11]

雖然這封書信是寫給提多的，但是信上有好些線索提示，此信也是寫給克里特的教會的。信末的祝福說，願恩惠與你們眾人同在！（三 15c）。眾人顯然是指克里特的信徒；他們可說是這封信的「背景聽眾」。[12] 卷首對寫信人的描述強調他的身分和信息（一 1a～2a，2b～

5 關於保羅差派使者替他辦事這一點，可參《羅》4.554-55。

6 提多的名字在這兩段出現四次：二 13（已在正文提及），七 6、13、14。

7 提多的名字在這一段出現三次：八 6、16、23。

8 See Mitchell, 'Envoys', esp. 641-43, 661-662. 'Some fondly refer to him as Paul's "spiritual hit-man" because of his propensity to send Titus to deal with difficult situations (e.g., Corinth)' (Akin, 'Mystery' 141-42).

9 關於提摩太與保羅的關係，可參《西‧門》104-5；《羅》4.787；《帖前》47-48。特別留意腓二 20：我沒有別人與我同心，真正關懷你們的事（參《腓》301-4）。

10 Sadler vii. Scott 151-52 認為，可能正是由於保羅在加、林後二書提到提多，致使提多書的作者（不是保羅）覺得，保羅可能會給提多寫一封像提多書那樣的書信。

11 如果提多書是早於提摩太後書寫成的，我們便可以假定，提多在克里特島工作之後（多一 5）就去了撻馬太（Marshall 816），「很可能為要完成保羅指派給他的另一項任務」（利斐特 14〔Liefeld 20〕; cf. Fee 3: 'presumably for ministry'）。參三 12 註釋註 10（下面 455）。

12 Laansma 296: 'Though the letter had been [*sic*] to Titus, the church has been the

3），這種資料對作為保羅代表的提多是不需要的，但是對提多和克里特的信徒都具有重要的功能。[13] 信上給予提多的指示，尤其是關於「與福音相符的生活」的兩大段（二 1～15，三 1～8），其實是對克里特信徒的教導：保羅透過指導提多來教導信徒。[14] 總言之，提多書是保羅為著克里特教會的好處而寫給他的代表提多的。[15]

---

background audience for the whole.' 亦參一 3b 註釋註 5 之（3）= 下面 73-74。*Pace* Witherington 50: 'No one is standing in the background and meant to be hearing these documents other than the named addressees, it would appear'.

13 詳見一 3b 註釋首段，連註 5 之（1）= 下面 73-74。

14 'The letter is private in form but public in intent'; '1 Timothy and Titus, while private in form, are public in intention, speaking through Paul's delegates to the churches'（Mounce lx, xcvi）。參張 316：「此信的內容，絕大部分是為革哩底* 教會而寫的。」（*和合；新和、和修：克里特。）亦參一 11 註釋末段末尾（下面 171）。

15 如果提多書不是保羅寫的，收信人是誰便可以有很多（由釋經者提供）不同的（但都缺乏說服力的）答案。例如：**（1）** Quinn 21: 'If the PE appeared after Paul's death, not only Titus and Timothy but also the places to which the letters are addressed may have a typical or representative function. Thus the many small congregations on "Crete" seem to be conceived of as comparatively new Jewish-Christian churches, and accordingly "Titus" transmits and represents what Paul has to contribute to the organization and formation of such congregations.' **（2）** Marshall, 'Deception' 784: 'The Pastoral Epistles were written as a unit, and it is unlikely that any of them ever had an independent existence. It is not sufficient to say that they are pseudonymous letters. Conceived in their original situation, they are not letters at all. Only by practicing an initial deception do they even sneak into the letter genre and appropriate the functions of a letter. Thus, the original audience of the letter to Titus is probably the audience of the letters to Timothy. The identity of the intended audience is likely a congregation in Asia Minor, perhaps Ephesus.'

導論（叁）：寫作的原因和目的

提多書一章 5 節表示，保羅曾與提多在克里特島一起宣教（**我從前把你留在克里特**），且在多個城鎮（**在各城**）建立了教會；由於這事很難放在使徒行傳的年表裏，[1] 它最可能是在使徒行傳二十八章 16 至 31 節所記載的事（保羅第一次的羅馬監禁）和他寫提摩太後書（第二次的羅馬監禁）之間發生的。[2]

以下的事實提示，克里特教會的年日尚淺：（1）保羅指示提多要在各城**設立長老**（一 5），但是沒有提到也要設立**執事**（提前三 8、10、12）。（2）保羅列出長老／監督的資格時，並沒有包括**剛信主的**，

---

1 （**1**）Robinson（*Redating* 67-85）的研究將教牧書信置於使徒行傳所載事件的框架中：提前（55 年秋）是寫於林前與林後之間；提多書（57 年春末）是寫於羅馬書與腓立比書之間；提後（58 年秋）則寫於監獄書信（腓、門、西、弗）之後，* 是十三卷保羅書信的最後一卷（見 84 之總結）。但這種試圖並不成功：費歌頓認為它 'founders on the fact of their homogeneity with one another and their dishomogeneity with the other letters'（Fee 27 n.6 [cf. Kelly 24: 'The homogeneity of the Pastorals with one another and their dishomogeneity with the other Paulines must be regarded as an established fact', cited in Fee 24]）。*羅便臣認為提後和四卷監獄書信都是保羅在該撒利亞坐牢時寫的，他把阿尼色弗**一到羅馬就急切尋找我，並且找到了**（提後四 17）解釋為，阿尼色弗在羅馬找不到保羅，然後 'made it his business to go out of his way to Caesarea to visit him before returning to Ephesus'（76）。但如馬歇爾所說，'This exegesis is quite unconvincing and its failure makes this part of the hypothesis untenable'（Marshall 72）。（**2**）Reicke（*Paul's Letters* 141）認為，提前（56 年夏／秋）是寫於林前與林後之間，提多書（58 年）是寫於羅馬書與腓利門書之間，提後（60 年）則寫於以弗所書與腓立比書（保羅書信的最後一卷）之間。（**3**）van Bruggen 將提前和提多書歸入保羅的第三次宣教旅程（徒十八 23～二十一 15）時期，提後則寫於保羅在羅馬坐牢（徒二十八）的時期。見 Marshall 71-72; 詳見 Towner III 13-14（唐書禮 19-21）。（**4**）Hagner（*New Testament* 621）指出，'The fatal flaw in these hypotheses [Robinson, Reicke], however, is that they separate the Pastorals from one another and thereby require Paul's style and perspective to change back and forth, in what would be a most strange oscillation.' 另見（例如）Mounce lxxxv-lxxxvi 所提出的質疑。Marshall 72 認為，'it would seem that for defenders of the substantial authenticity of the PE, the theory of the second imprisonment affords less difficulties than attempting to place 1 Tim and Tit earlier in his career.'

2 Mounce lix. 參一 5 註釋首段，連註 6（下面 88-89）。

不可作監督（提前三 6）這項限制。（3）信上有關「與福音相符的生活」（二 1～10，三 1～2）的部分，是一些尤其適合初信者的基本教導，這些教導指出了上帝的救贖（二 11～14，三 3～7）對信徒日常生活的含意。[3]

保羅寫這封書信的目的主要有兩方面：[4] **第一**，保羅告訴提多要照我所吩咐你的，在各城設立長老（一 5，6～9），並且針對教會的一些缺陷進行改革（一 5，將那沒有辦完的事都辦妥）。[5] 具體而言，提多要教導克里特的信徒如何過「與福音相符的生活」（在教會中〔二 1～10〕及在社會上〔三 1～2〕，見上段）；保羅亦指示提多如何對付反對的人（一 10～16，三 9～11）。[6] **第二**，保羅告訴提多要給〔送信人〕西納律師和亞波羅送行（三 13），並且在接替他的亞提馬或推基古抵達之後，即前往尼哥坡里與保羅會合（三 12）。

---

3 Cf. Mounce lx.
4 Cf. Mounce lxi.
5 見一 5 註釋第二段之（**甲**）= 下面 91-93。
6 參導論第伍節末後兩段（下面 36-38）。Fee 11 認為，'The letter . . . may be termed both *prophylactic* (serving to warn against false teaching) and *evangelistic* (serving to encourage behavior that will be attractive to the world) in its thrust.'

導論（肆）：寫作的地點和日期

如果教牧書信是託名之作，它們的寫作時期就一定是在保羅死後，但在保羅死後多久則有多種看法。[1]

但本註釋的立場是，教牧書信是真確的保羅書信。「對於他在愛琴海岸第二次的事工旅程，我們所知不多，大部分只能靠推想，因為保羅書信及其他來源並沒有透露這方面的資料。」[2] 相對於提摩太前書，提多書所反映的假教師危害教會的情況不是那麼緊迫，故此提多書可能是寫於提摩太前書之後。保羅把提多留在克里特去執行他的任務（一 5）之後，就和提摩太到了以弗所，發現該處的教會正受到假教師（教會本身的一些長老！）的誤導，於是把提摩太留在以弗所，為要恢復教會的秩序（提前一 3～4）。保羅自己繼續前往馬其頓，在該處寫信給提摩太，在教會面前賦予權柄去處理以弗所教會的危機；與此同時，保羅也寫信給提多，同樣地賦予他權柄去履行他在克里特島的任務。[3] 如此，提多書（和提摩太前書）可能是寫於六〇年代的早中期，即是在保羅寫了監獄書信的最後

1 例如：（**1**）Nardoni（'Pastoral Epistles' 1731*b*）認為，教牧書信所反映的教會體制是 'something in between'《革利免一書》（96 年）和《伊格那丟書信》（113 年），因此教牧書信的成書日期是介乎 96 年與 113 年之間。Fiore II 19-20 更明確地將這日期定於約 80-90 年間。（**2**）Aune 338*a* 認為它們是 'probably written early in the 2nd cent. to solve the competing forms of Christianity.'（**3**）Wilson（*Luke* 140）認為，同一位作者寫了路－徒和教牧書信，'I would guess at 85-90 A.D. for Acts and 90-95 for the Pastorals, but it is little more than a guess.'

2 Ellis, 'Pastoral Letters' 661*b*（引句出自《辭典》957*b*）。Wilson（*Luke* 141）認為，'The Pastorals . . . give so few indications of their place of composition that they could be located almost anywhere.'

3 Fee 12, cf. 10. Witherington 65 則認為提多書是教牧書信中最早的一卷。

一卷（腓立比書，寫於保羅第一次羅馬監禁獲釋之前[4]）之後的兩三年之內。[5]

4 保羅在非斯都面前受審、往羅馬的旅程，在羅馬被監禁（至少）兩年——這些事發生在 59 至 62 年（so L. C. A. Alexander, *DPL* 122*b*-23*a*〔《辭典》179*a*-80*a*〕）。

5 參《腓》57-58。Witherington 66 認為是 64-65 年，'1 Timothy was written in Macedonia, while the letter to Titus was still rather fresh in Paul's mind.' Guthrie（'Pastoral Epistles' 685*a*）則認為，三封教牧書信都是寫於 63-64 年間。F. F. Bruce（*ISBE* 3.699*b*）的意見是：提多書和提前皆寫於 62 年（？）之後，前者發自以弗所，後者發自馬其頓；提後寫於 65 年（？）之後，發自羅馬（問號是原來的）。

導論（伍）：本書的結構和大綱

甲部：開首的話（一 1～4）

壹　卷首問安（一 1～4）

1.1　寫信人（一 1～3）

1.1.1 寫信人的身分（一 1～2a）

1.1.2 寫信人的信息（一 2b～3）

1.2　收信人（一 4a）

1.3　問安語（一 4b）

乙部：書信本體（一 5～三 11）[1]

貳　長老的設立．他們的職責（一 5～9）

2.1　提多在島上的責任（一 5～6）[2]

1　以一 5～三 11 為書信本體的釋經者包括：Arichea－Hatton 267; Bassler 184; Marshall 24, 145; Towner III 76, 676（唐 105、985）; Aune, 'Pastoral Letters' 564; Marshall, 'Timothy and Titus' 187*a*; Schnelle, 'Pastoral Letters' 338; 侯嘉文 141、146。**(1)** Clark（'Structure' 106）則以 一 13b～三 8a 為 'the main body of the letter'. 但是以一 13b（對提多的命令）為新段落的開始，這做法打斷了 'the link with the description of the opponents in vs. 10-12'（Marshall, 'Recent Study' 283）。**(2)** Van Neste（'Message' 19*a*）的「書信本體（Body of the Letter）」延伸至三 14（一 5～9 = 'Body Opening'; 三 12～14 = 'Body Closing'），即是將「結束的話」視為只有最後一節（三 15〔thus already Banker 12-14, 15; Achtemeier－Green－Thompson, *INT* 459〕）。有趣的是，范尼斯稍後又說（19*b*），'1:10-16 and 3:9-11 discuss the problem of false teaching (bracketing the rest of the letter body)'. 括號內的話可被理解為，書信本體以一 10 開始（筆者不同意），以三 11 結束（筆者同意）！事實上，范尼斯對信上四個主要問題的分析，所牽涉的正是一 5～三 11 這一大段（詳見本節倒數第二段〔下面 36-37〕）。同樣地，班約翰扼要陳述書信本體（一 5～三 14）的內容時，並無觸及三 12～14（Banker 15）；他解釋書信本體的交叉配置模式時，同樣只涉及一 5b～三 11（27*a*-*b*; 見下註首段）。他以一 5～三 11 為 'the major Head [= Head$_1$] of the body', 三 12～14 則稱為 'Head$_2$'（28*b*, see also 13, 14）。**(3)** Thurston（'Titus' 175-76）以一 5～三 15a 為書信本體，「結束的話」只有半節（三 15b）。

2　Banker 27*a*-28*b* 認為，'1.5b' 和 '1.5c' 總結了書信本體的其餘部分，書信本體則呈

2.2　監督的資格和職能（一 7～9）

叁　如何對付反對的人：之一（一 10～16）[3]

3.1　假教師的描述（一 10～13a）

3.2　對他們的回應（一 13b～14）

3.3　假教師的定罪（一 15～16）

現交叉配置模式，如下：

（甲）　提多要改正那沒有辦完的事（一 5b）
（乙）　又要在各城設立長老（一 5c）
（乙'）　長老的設立和職能（一 6～9）
（甲'）　改正克里特教會的情況（一 10～三 11）

班約翰將一 5b 的動詞「改正（ἐπιδιοθώσῃ）」視為 'introducing not only the correcting of those who are following false doctrine, but also the positive side of teaching sound doctrine.'
按此分析，（甲）+（乙）只是一節的三分之二，（乙'）+（甲'）則合共 37 節，* 因而這種交叉配置模式嚴重地失衡！單此一點足以表示，作者的結構分析值得商榷。詳細的評論見 Van Neste 278-80.（*Van Neste 280 談到 'a' and b' covering the rest of the letter body (42 verses)!' 這似乎是由於他錯誤地把一 1～5 也計算在內！）See also Marshall 21: 'Since in general NT writers do not offer headings within their writings, I am tempted to argue that 1.5 is not intended to function as a heading for the body, as Banker takes it, but is rather the introduction to the section about appointing elders'. 亦參一 5 註釋註 10（下面 90-91）。

3　**(1)** 有兩點表示，10 節是新一段的開始：第一，這裏的題目從長老的資格轉到敵對者的問題；第二，動詞的主詞從監督（7a 節）轉到許多人，第三人稱複數的動詞在這裏首次出現，並在隨後數節繼續出現。從論述分析的角度，這些轉變稱為 'shifts in cohesion fields'（Van Neste, 'Structure' 123；see also Van Neste 239）。**(2)** 另外，一 9 的健全的教導（τῇ διδασκαλίᾳ τῇ ὑγιαινούσῃ）和二 1 的那健全的教導（τῇ ὑγιαινούσῃ διδασκαλίᾳ）在一 10～16 的前後出現，將本段區分出來；換言之，這重要的概念 'demarcates externally, that is, by enclosure (*exclusio*), the preceding segment (i.e. 1.10-16)'（Wendland, 'Discourse' 340）。在一 10～16 本身，10 節（不受約束……欺哄人）和 16 節（否認〔上帝〕……是悖逆的）對假教師的描寫，構成 'another sectional inclusio'（ibid.; 參下面註 5）。**(3)** Banker 45*a* 從本段看出比正文大綱（「叁」）更詳細的交叉配置模式，如下：

'A	Description of those who oppose sound doctrine	1:10-11
B	Quote (from Cretan prophet)	1:12-13a
C	Exhortation1:	13b-14
B'	Quote/Saying (of Jesus or Christian teaching) and statements based upon it	1:15
A'	Description of those who oppose sound doctrine	1:16'

肆 與福音相符的生活：之一（二 1～15）[4]

4.1 健全的行為（二 1～10）[5]

4.1.1 籠統的序言（二 1）

4.1.2 年老的男人（二 2）

4.1.3 年長的婦女（二 3～4a）

4.1.4 年輕的婦女（二 4b～5）[6]

4.1.5 年輕的男子（二 6）[7]

4.1.6 提多的教導（二 7～8）[8]

---

4 Van Neste 274: 'the section flows as exhortation [2:1-10], doctrinal grounding [2:11-14], summary exhortation [2:15].' 以二 1～15 為一大段的釋經者還包括：Bassler 191-92; Knight II 305; Lock 137; Marshall 24.

5 第 1 節的**那健全的教導**（τῇ ὑγιαινούσῃ διδασκαλίᾳ）和 10c 節的**我們救主上帝的教導**（τὴν διδασκαλίαν τὴν τοῦ σωτῆρος ἡμῶν θεοῦ）首尾呼應（*inclusio*: Wendland, 'Discourse' 340），將本段劃分為一個單元。另有三點將本段和上一段（一 10～16）分開（Banker 45*b*）：第一，主要的人物從提多及反對健全的教導的人，轉為提多及教會內的不同組別；第二，主要人物的描述從（實在的）反面的品質，轉到（理想的）正面的品質；第三，就兩段的類型而論，上一段以描述為主，勸勉為次，本段則純是勸勉。

6 將原文一氣呵成的二 3～5 分為兩小段，理由見二 4a 註釋註 1 之(2)= 下面 237。

7 以上四組呈現交叉配置模式：（甲）年老的<u>男性</u>（乙）年長的<u>婦女</u>（乙'）年輕的<u>婦女</u>（甲'）年輕的<u>男性</u>。See Hendriksen 363 n.196; Genade 44. 第二、三兩組各含有一 ἵνα-clause（4a、5b 節）。

8 **(1)** Collins 339 對二 1～10 的分析只提到五組人物：'He [Titus] is the *tradens* * of the common ethical tradition, providing instruction for five groups in the community: seniors, both male and female, youth, both male and female, and slaves.'（*拉丁文 *tradens* 是分詞 = 'delivering'; 寇雷蒙似乎把它用作名詞。）Clark（'Structure' 109）認為，就本段的結構而論，'Titus himself is subordinate to the younger men.' 即是作者將提摩太視為**年輕人**的一部分（'a subset of younger men'）。早前，他也把**年輕的婦女**（4 節）視為婦女的一部分（'a subset of women'）。留意兩種做法並非完全一樣：祈勒克沒有說，也不能說，「作者把**年輕的婦女**（4 節）視為<u>**年長的婦女**</u>的一部分（a subset of <u>elderly</u> <u>women</u>）！」不過，**(2)** 雖然 7 節的**顯出**在原文是個分詞（παρεχόμενος），附屬於 6 節的動詞**勸**字（παρακάλει），但是，7～8 節所談及的主要是提多本身的教導，而非一般年輕人應有怎麼樣的行為；**自己**在原文居於**顯出**之前（<u>σεαυτὸν</u> παρεχόμενος），表示提多本身受到強調；而且末後的目的子句（8c 節）不是說「使年輕人知道怎樣行」，而是說**使那反對的人……自覺羞愧**。因此，這兩節不應視為（只是）對年輕人所說的話的一部分（as in Zehr 263, 266-67），而是和 6 節分開的另一個單元（Banker 69*a-b*）。韓遜給予這兩節的分題是 'Titus himself / the church leader (7-8)'（Hanson I 105 / III 168, 181）。

4.1.7 家裏的奴僕（二 9～10）[9]

4.2 教義性基礎（二 11～14）[10]

4.2.1 上帝恩典的顯明（二 11～13）[11]

4.2.2 基督救贖之目的（二 14）[12]

4.3 要旨的重述（二 15）[13]

---

9 Wieland（'Crete' 341）也將二 2～10 分析如上（六組）。「此處的格式類似希臘羅馬社會的『治家格言』〔household codes〕，應與教牧書信以教會為 神的家有關」（彭編 98〔底線和空格都是原來的〕）。曾 107 卻認為，「提多書第二章裏的歸類是雜亂無章的」，理由是這裏「沒有〔弗五 22～六 9〕那麼條理分明的歸類」！其實，曾氏自己認為「提多書二章中的家庭守則的次序是羅馬人的傳統次序」（147）。但見二 1～10 註釋引言註 4（下面 216）。

10 二 10 和二 11 之間的 'shifts in cohesion fields'（見上面註 3 之〔1〕）包括：主題轉到上帝的恩典和救恩；這裏不再是勸勉，而是教義的闡釋；時間的框架從現在轉到過去；動詞的時態從幾乎全是現在時態（20/22）轉到大部分（6/8）是過去不定時時態。因此，二 11 是新一段的開始（Van Neste, 'Structure' 123; Van Neste 243〔括號內的數字是筆者得自 Banker 61*a* 的〕）。故此，把對僕人的勸勉視為「第 9～14 節」（張 343）這做法是奇怪的。

11 以下的事實將這三節連結為一個單元（Van Neste 244）：在語言方面，首尾兩節都（i）使用**顯明／顯現**（ἐπιφαίνω/ἐπιφάνεια）的詞彙（在信上不再使用），（ii）使用以 σωτηρ- 為字根的字（σωρήριος, **救**／σωτῆρ, **救主**），以及（iii）明確地提到 θεός（**上帝**）；在思想方面，這幾節從救恩在過去的顯明（11 節），進到這救恩在現今的果效（12 節，**在今世**），再進到救主在將來的顯現（13 節）。

12 第 11 節開首的動詞 ἐπεφάνη（**顯明**）是 11～14 節這一小段內惟一的非從屬（non-subordinated）限定動詞，從文法的角度，全段都是從屬於（governed by）這動詞。這小段惟一的另一個限定動詞，是 14 節的 ἔδωκεν（**捨**），雖然它是在一個關係子句中出現，但 14 節其餘的內容都是從屬於（governed by）它，而 14 節的內容，與較直接地從屬於動詞**顯明**（11 節）的 11～13 節的內容，二者的關係較像是同位（in apposition）的（Banker 75*a*-*b*）。是項觀察支持正文的做法，就是將 11～14 節分拆為 11～13 節和 14 節同等的兩段；14 節的內容大致上與 11、12 節平行（參二 14 註釋註 1 及所屬正文〔下面 329-30〕）。

13 以下理由支持本節應視為單獨地構成一個單元（see Van Neste 245, 274）：（甲）本節從上一段的教義性闡釋（11～14 節）回到勸勉，主詞亦從第三人稱的基督轉為**你**（提多）；這表示本節應與上一段分開（Wendland, 'Discourse' 339 n.11），本節的主要聯繫是與再上一段（1～10 節；本節的**講明**和**勸勉**重複了該段的兩個主要動詞**講**和**勸**〔1、6 節〕）。（乙）與此同時，本節不應連於下文，因為（**i**）本節屬摘要性質，而且 ταῦτα（**這些事**）在教牧書信另外出現十二次，幾乎全部都是指向上文的（三 8；提前三 14，四 6、11、15，五 7、21，六 2、11；提後二 2、14），惟一的例外是提後一 12（**這些苦難**）；（**ii**）本節的重點在於提多要怎樣教導，但三 1～2 的重點在於教導的明確內容（第〔ii〕點早見於 Banker 57*b*）。

伍 與福音相符的生活：之二（三 1～8）[14]

5.1 做公民的義務（三 1～2）[15]

5.2 教義性的動機（三 3～7）[16]

5.2.1 信徒從前的景況（三 3）

5.2.2 如今享受的救恩（三 4～7）

5.3 總結性的勸勉（三 8）[17]

---

14 三 1 的**提醒**（ὑπομίμνησκε）和 8b 節的**堅持**（διαβεβαιοῦσθαι），又 1 節的**善事**（ἔργον ἀγαθόν）和 8c 節的**善**（καλῶν ἔργων），分別構成首尾呼應（*inclusio*: Wendland, 'Discourse' 340-41, 342），將本段劃分為一個單元。

15 Hiebert 442: 'the duties of believers as citizens (vv.1, 2)'.

16 以三 3～7 為一段的釋經者包括：Banker 13, 14; Marshall 298, 304. 三 3 的 γάρ 字（因為）表示，§5.2 提出了 §5.1 的動機，就如 二 11 的 γάρ 字表示，§4.2 是 §4.1 的基礎。如此，從本書結構的角度而言，§5.1 和 §5.2 是與 §4.1 和 §4.2 平行的（see Clark, 'Structure' 113-14）。

17 （**1**）以下的改變表示，三 8 是新的單元：（i）本節從上文的神學闡釋轉為勸勉；（ii）其中的動詞從 3～7 節的過去未完時態和過去不定時時態，轉為現在時態；（iii）單數第一人稱的動詞再次出現（上一次是在一 5）；（iv）在 3～7 節沒有出現的單數的你字和會眾（**那些已信上帝的人**）在這裏出現（Van Neste 248-49）。See also Levinsohn, *Discourse Features* 126: 'Asyndeton is commonly found between paragraphs with different topics, so the presence of asyndeton in Titus 3:8a is consistent with a paragraph break at the beginning of v. 8.'（**2**）范尼斯把 8a 節視為引入改變的過渡性字句，因而以三 3～7 為一段／以三 8 為另一段（Van Neste 246-47 / 248-49）。如此，'in this section [3:1-8], as in the previous one [2:1-15], there is exhortation [3:1-2, cf. 2:1-10], doctrinal grounding [3:3-7, cf. 2:11-14], and a summary exhortation [3:8, cf. 2:15]'（275）。See also Van Neste, 'Structure' 129: '3.1-8 has several parallels to 2.1-15. . . . Thus we have two parallel sections calling for proper behavior based on proper doctrine.'
（**3**）Smith（'Structure' 107）批評一些譯本（包括 NIV, NKJV）將三 3～11 分為三 3～8 和三 9～11 兩段，認為這做法 'awkwardly groups the asyndetic 3:8 with the preceding paragraph.' 他認為較好的做法是將三 3～11 分為三 3～7 和三 8～11（或三 3～8a 和三 8b～11）兩段。但見下一點。（**4**）Clark（'Structure' 115）以 8a 節為三 1～8a 這一段的結束，下一小段為三 8b～11（see 114: 'a period after 3.8a seems essential'）。持此立場的譯本包括：NRSV, TEV, 新和、現修；釋經者還包括：DC 147*b*, 151*b*; Sumney, *Opponents* 295. 但是 8b 節以 καί 字開始，因此不宜將 8b 節和 8a 節分開，把二者視為分屬於兩個不同的小段（so, correctly, Van Neste 261-62; Levinsohn, *Discourse Features* 126）。καί 字表示 8b 節是 8a～c 節的一部分，'3:8a-c forms a coherent logical unit of

陸　如何對付反對的人：之二（三 9～11）[18]

丙部：結束的話（三 12～15）

柒　個人的指示（三 12～14）[19]

---

grounds-exhortation-purpose'（Banker 91*a*）。（**5**）Wendland（'Discourse' 341）則以 '3.8c'（筆者的三 8d = 由「ταῦτα（這些事）」開始的一句）為 'the contrastive beginning of a second paragraph [about the false teachers]'（第一段是一 10～16），即是以三 8c（筆者的 8d）～11 為一段（thus already Banker 13, 14, 42*b*, 91*b*, 110, 111*a*, 111*b*）。不過，Wendland 同樣指出三 1～8b（= 筆者的 8c）和二 1～12 之間在結構上的平行：二 1～10 ‖ 三 1～2；二 11～14 ‖ 三 3～7；二 15 ‖ 三 8a～b（= 筆者的 8 a～c）。但見三 8b～d 註釋註 31（下面 430）。

18 以 9～11 節為本小段的中英譯本包括：TNIV, NIV2011, NLT, BV, Phillips, Stern, 當代、新普。（**1**）雖然三 9～11 延續了三 8 的勸勉、現在時態的動詞，以及單數的你字，但（i）本段的題目從提多的教導（這些事）轉到敵對的人；（ii）上一節的動詞都是正面的，所牽涉的事情也是正面的，但本段的動詞皆指向避免一些負面的事和人。因此，本段較宜看為與三 8 分開（so Van Neste 249, 250），而不是與三 8 連起來成為一段（如在思高，Nestle－Aland; Genade 99-100; Marshall 22 n.34, 24; see also Classen, 'Titus' 444: 三 8～11 是一 5～三 7 的總結〔'summary'〕）。
（**2**）如范尼斯所指出，「叁」「肆」「伍」「陸」這四段呈現交叉配置模式（thus also Fee 210〔但省略了二 15 一節〕）：

甲　如何對待反對的人（一 10～16）
　　乙　與福音相符的生活（二 1～15）
　　乙'　與福音相符的生活（三 1～8）
甲'　如何對待反對的人（三 9～11）

對教會的勸勉和對反對者的描寫二者之間的對比* 提示，這種模式和對稱是作者的刻意安排，並且他對教會的勸勉，是刻意地與敵對者的描寫構成對比的。如此，一 10～三 11 這一整部分（= 書信本體的全部，減去一 5～9），是緊密地連結起來的（Van Neste 277）。（*參二 1～10 註釋引言第二、三兩段〔下面 216-17〕，三 1 註釋第三段，三 2 註釋第二段〔下面 354，359〕。）由此看來，「一些主題似乎沒有事先安排，重複的出現在同一封書信中」（古特立 14）這評語就顯得與事實不符了。

19 Banker 27*a*（see also 28*b*）認為這三節並非「結束的話」的一部分，'since 3:12 and 13 deal with specific instructions for Titus while 3:14 returns to the theme of the body.' 不過，根據魏馬的研究，一封典型的保羅書信的結束部分可包括勸勉的話（見《羅》4.666；《加》1370）；而三 14 的性質正是勸勉。

捌　問安和祝福（三 15）[20]

8.1　個人的問安（三 15a～b）

8.2　最後的祝福（三 15c）[21]

范尼斯指出，[22] 保羅在信上所討論並要提多（和克里特的信徒）留意的四個問題，對於教會的健康是重要的。這四個問題就是：

第一、建立正當的領導班子（一 5～9〔＝大綱之「貳」〕）。這一段結束時提到，監督必須**堅守合乎教義的可靠之道**，為要能夠〔**以**〕**健全的教導勸勉人，又能駁倒爭辯的人**（9 節）。**駁倒爭辯的人**就像「鈎狀鑰字」般使作者的思想過渡到下一段有關反對的人的討論（一 10～16〔＝大綱之

---

20 Levinsohn（'Constraints' 331 with n.71）以三 15（僅此一節）為本書的結束。他指出，從書信本體過渡至結束時，一個特色就是「無連詞（asyndeton）」現象，即是 15 節並無 γάρ, δέ, καί 或 οὖν 等字。（參一 5 註釋註 1 之〔3〕＝ 下面 88。）但三 12 同樣呈現這現象。

21 **(1)** Jeon II 3 (cf. vii, 43) 聲稱，提多書 'can be summarized under five themes, which are covered by the acronym* "TITUS": (1) *T*rue Faith (1:1-4); (2) *I*rreproachable Leaders (1:5-16); (3) *T*heocentric Household (2:1-15); (4) *U*pright Citizens (3:1-8a); and (5) *S*teadfast Devotion to Good Works (3:8b-15).'（*= 首字母組合字。）可是，作者的（2）（3）（4）（5）各點的標題將部分的主題掩蓋了，這就是說，這裏的五個主題沒有反映（甲）「如何對待反對的人」（一 10～16，三 9～11）和（乙）基督徒的行為標準之「教義性基礎／動機」（二 11～14／三 3～7）這兩個十分重要的主題；參下文的「第二」和「第四」兩點。Jeon II 6 較詳細的大綱才提到這些起初被掩蓋的主題：

'1:10-16	False Teachers'
'2:11-15	The Redemptive Basis for Godly Conduct [2:1-10]'
'3:3-8a	The Redemptive Basis for Such Godly Conduct [3:1-2]'
'3:10-11	Concerning the Divisive Person'

(2) Marshall 19 的圖表 5 並列了六位釋經者（Bernard, Lock, Spicq, Brox, Banker, Quinn）對提多書的結構分析。

22 Van Neste, 'Message' 19*b*.

「叁」)，**而就能〔以〕健全的教導勸勉人**，就像一個「遠距離的鈎狀鑰字」，引介二章 1 至 10 節（＝大綱的 4.1）的勸勉。[23]

第二、 認識並正當地處理謬誤（一 10～16，三 9～11〔＝大綱之「叁」「陸」〕）。這個問題由上述兩段來討論：前一段是由一章 9c 節的**又能駁倒爭辯的人**引進來的；後一段則由三章 9 節開首的「但」字所引入的、提多要**堅持這些事**（8b 節）和提多要**遠避**另一些事（9a 節）的對比引進來。[24]

第三、 與福音相符的生活方式（二 1～10，三 1～2〔＝大綱之 4.1，5.1〕）。

第四、 清楚認識福音本身（二 11～14，[25] 三 3～7〔＝大綱之 4.2，5.2〕）。

第三和第四個問題的討論，是連起來在彼此平行的兩大段進行的（二 1～14，三 1～7）；兩大段都是先描寫與福音相符的生活方式（二 1～10，三 1～2），然後提出教義性的基礎，[26] 即是福音的內容（二 11～14，三 3～7）。[27]

以上四個問題的邏輯關係就是：（i）提多要建立正當的領導班

---

23 詳見「**一章 9 節在本書結構中的獨特功能**」（下面 148-52）。

24 參三 9 註釋首段（下面 433-34）。關於「如何對待反對的人」這兩段（一 10～16，三 9～11）將關於「與福音相符的生活」的兩段（二 1～10，三 1～7）夾在中央。

25 范尼斯說 '2:11-15'. 筆者倒認為，15 節並非只屬於 11～14 節；它同時是 1～10 節和 11～14 節這兩段的摘要，因而是 1～14 的要旨重述（見大綱之 3.3）。參二 15 註釋首段開首（下面 341）。Van Neste 243/245 正確地以二 11～14 為一個單元／以二 15 為另一單元；參註 13 之（**甲**）＝ 上面 33。

26 二 11 和三 3 在原文開首都有「因為」（γάρ）一字。

27 這兩段的重要性，亦因它們與「寫信人」的描述（1b～3 節，此描述具教義性質）的關聯而受到強調；參一 1～4 註釋引言第二段（下面 43-46）。「第四」這段內的「三 3～7」英文原作 '3:3-8'; 但范尼斯較新近的論述已把它修正為 '3.3-7'（Van Neste 246-47, 275）。

子（「貳」），部分的目的是為要正當地處理謬誤（「叄」）；[28]（ii）假教師的謬誤（「叄」）與提多健全的教導（4.1）相對（留意二 1 的至於你）；（iii）而與福音相符的生活方式（4.1，5.1），是基於福音本身的性質和要求（4.2，5.2）。[29]

28 處理謬誤只能是設立長老／監督的部分目的，因為無論有或沒有假教師的出現，'we should expect the appointing of elders to be something that would need to be done in Crete anyway'. 在提摩太前書，監督的設立（三 1～7）跟對付假教師（四 1～7）並無直接的聯繫（Banker 46*b*）。

29 See Fiore II 23: 教牧書信使用雙重的策略——'teaching the true tradition and demonstrating it in virtuous action.'

註　釋

A Commentary on the Epistle to Titus

甲部

開首的話

（一1～4）

壹　卷首問安（一 1～4）

1a　上帝的僕人、耶穌基督的使徒保羅，
b　　為了使上帝的選民信從
c　　　與認識合乎敬虔的真理——
2a　　這真理是在盼望……永生，
b　　　　　　那無謊言的上帝在萬古之先所應許的
3a　　到了適當的時機，藉著傳揚福音，把他的道顯明了；
b　　這傳揚的責任是按著我們的救主上帝的命令交託給我的——
4a　我寫信給在共同的信仰上作我真兒子的提多。
b　願恩惠、平安從父上帝和我們的救主基督耶穌歸給你！

保羅有時在信上卷首問安所說的話，已預示了該信的內容；這一點最好的說明是羅馬書開首的話（一 1～7），[1] 另一個例子是加拉太書一章 4 節。[2] 在這裏，保羅一開始便提到，他的使徒職分的目的是要使上帝的選民……認識合乎敬虔的真理（一 1b），而敬虔的生活（甲）及其基礎——真理（乙），正是書信本體兩個重要段落（二 1～14，三 1～7）的主題。[3]

本段的基本結構是：保羅（1 節）……寫信給……提多（4a 節）。願恩惠、平安……歸給你！（4b 節）。[4] 在這公式以外的內容（1b～3

1　參《羅》1.159-61。
2　參《加》226-27、233-34。
3　見一 1～2a 註釋第四段（下面 55-56）。See also Hendriksen 339-40.
4　Miller 125 似乎將 δοῦλος θεοῦ 至 τοῦ σωτῆρος ἡμῶν θεοῦ（一 1a〔減去保羅〕至 3 節末）這部分視為 'a later editorial addition'. 他聲稱：'If Paul's apostolic credentials (unnecessary in a personal letter) and the preformed creedal material are removed, a

節)是信上第一段神學性質很重的段落，[5] 另二段是二章 11 至 14 節和三章 4 至 7 節(三段在原文都只是一長句)。饒有意義的是，本段

---

warm and intimate greeting from Paul to his colleague Titus remains'(參 187 之經文排列)。但此說並無任何古卷的證據支持。

5 (**1**) Quinn 7(apparently endorsed by Hagner, 'Titus' 552)認為，這「開首的話」的長度跟隨後的書信完全不成比例(thus also Scott 149: 'The salutation [1:1-4] is unduly drawn out for a brief letter')，這就是內在的證據，證明提多書是「多、提前、提後(也許還有門)」這信集之首。他稱這四節為 'The prologue to the PE'(272)。See also Quinn 19-20: 'The original order of the letters within the collection is probably that in which Titus leads off, followed by 1 Tim and then 2 Tim. The elaborate, sixty-six-word epistolary prologue of Titus 1:1-4 sounds like a preface to the collection, not only to the short letter that follows.'(Blomberg ['Titus' 351] 認為 '[this] is just possible'.) Thus already Wild 894*a*: 'This disproportionately lengthy greeting served to introduce the Pastorals as a group rather than just Titus'. 但(**i**)Marshall 112 n.3 指出，'there is nothing in Tit 1.1-4 that suggests it bears this relationship to 1 and 2 Tim.' Towner III 662 n.1(唐 963 註 1)也指出，昆謝隆的論點不能從本段的內容獲得證明。(**ii**)事實上，關於三卷書信的寫作次序，釋經者有多種看法，例如：提前、提後、多(e.g., Malherbe, 'Soteriology' 335)；提前、多、提後(Fee 12; Knight I 2; Liefeld 309〔利斐特 326〕; Simpson 94; Akin, 'Mystery' 138; Robinson, *Redating* 84; Schnelle, 'Pastoral Letters' 334)；多、提前、提後(Witherington 75)；多、提後、提前(Herzer, 'Perspective' 564)。(**iii**)侯嘉文 143 認為，「這一段上款篇幅較長，是另有原因的……是因為它包括了保羅奉命作『僕人』及『使徒』及他『受神所託』作傳道人(一 3)三項聲明。至於其他『教牧書信』，這些聲明並不包括在上款內，乃是屬書信主體的……〔參：提前一 11～14；提後一 11～12〕……因此，三封書信都有這些聲明；只是提多書篇幅最短，這些聲明就包括在上款中，使作者可以很快進入正文，由作監督應有的資格開始(一 5～9)。」(**iv**)更為重要的，這卷首問安除了申明保羅作使徒的權柄外，還具有預示信上的內容及與下文結連的功用；見下文。

(**2**) Maloney 374 說：'The introductory formula [of 1 Tim.] has been expanded into a kind of creedal statement.' 這表示她認為提多書寫於提前之後(教牧書信乃冒名之作)。(**3**) Hendriksen 339 指出，在十三封保羅書信的卷首問安中，只有羅馬書的(在原文為 93 字〔Johnson II 216, Witherington 97: 94 字〕)和加拉太書的(75 字〔Johnson II 216, Witherington 97: 76 字〕)比提多書的(65 字)更長。(**4**) Clark('Structure' 103)指出，從造句法的角度而言，正文提到的三段都是居於從屬的位置；但是，為要保留它們在語意上的重要性，翻譯時往往要避免給予它們從屬的地位：'all three are in syntactically subordinate positions. In order to retain their semantic prominence in translation, it will often be necessary to avoid syntactic subordination.' (**5**) Van Neste('Structure' 128)則指出，'These are the only sections of the letter in which God or Jesus are the actors.'

的一些重要詞彙在後兩段再次出現，這些重複出現的字詞構成一種內聚力，將這三段結連起來：[6]

一 1～4	二 11～14	三 3～7
上帝把他的道顯明了（3a 節）	上帝的恩典已經顯明出來（11 節）	上帝的恩慈和慈愛顯明（4 節）[7]
我們的救主上帝（3b 節）	我們〔的〕救主上帝（10 節）	我們〔的〕救主上帝（4 節）[8]
基督耶穌我們的救主（4b 節，原文次序）	我們的救主耶穌基督（13b 節）	耶穌基督我們的救主（6 節，原文次序）[9]
在盼望……永生（2a 節）	福樂的盼望（13a 節）	憑著永生的盼望（7b 節）[10]

除此以外，（i）顯明的詞彙（見註 7）、（ii）名詞救主（除了二 10 的一次）和動詞救字（三 5c）、（iii）名詞盼望、（iv）動詞過……生活（二 12c）和名詞「生命」（一 2a，三 7b）[11]——這些在這三段裏都有出現的字詞，在信上卻不再出現。[12] 這事實凸出了上表所顯示的平行之重要性，證實了這些重要字詞的重複出現，就是作者用以將這三段連繫

6 Wall 332 甚至認為，'These passages [1:1-3; 2:11-14; 3:4-8] supply a soteriological glossary for the entire Pauline canon.'

7 原文動詞依次是主動語態的 ἐφανέρωσεν（from φανερόω）和（後二次）被動語態的 ἐπεφάνη（from ἐπιφαίνω）。

8 原文三次都是所有格的 τοῦ σωτῆρος ἡμῶν θεοῦ.

9 原文三次都是所有格：Χριστοῦ Ἰησοῦ τοῦ σωτῆρος ἡμῶν（見上註），τοῦ . . . σωτῆρος ἡμῶν Ἰησοῦ Χριστοῦ, Ἰησοῦ Χριστοῦ τοῦ σωτῆρος ἡμῶν.

10 原文依次為：ἐπ' ἐλπίδι ζωῆς αἰωνίου, τὴν μακαρίαν ἐλπίδα, κατ' ἐλπίδα ζωῆς αἰωνίου.

11 ζάω 和 ζωή（後者見上註）。

12 See Van Neste 269: 'This table shows all the occurrences of ζωή/ζάω, σωτήρ/σῴζω, ἐλπίς, and the epiphany language (φανερόω/ἐπιφαίνω).' 尤其值得留意的是，在這三段，保羅都先提到我們的救主上帝（見註 8），隨後又提到我們的救主耶穌基督（見註 9）。Cf. Bowman, 'Jesus Christ' 749, 752 point (9).

起來的方法。[13] 不但如此，問安語這樣預示了下文兩段的主題，強調了後二段的重要性。[14]

13 Van Neste, 'Structure' 128. 作者談到 'the significant lexical cohesion between the letter opening (1.1-4) and the two doctrinal sections (2.11-14 and 3.3-7).' 事實上，這三段使提多書在教牧書信中享有獨特的位置：'Titus enjoys a unique and distinguished position among the Pastorals in that it contains three passages that are among the richest theological concentrations in the entire New Testament'（Collins 299）。因此，「很可能，在提多書裏最值得重視的是二章 11 至 14 節」（馬唐納 551*b*）這話值得商榷。

14 See Van Neste, 'Message' 29 n.31: 'The significance of these passages is underscored by the fact that the especially long expansion of the salutation anticipated the themes found in 2:11-1<u>5</u> and 3:3-<u>8</u>.'（**1**）留意作者在這裏的兩段，比在上註提到的兩段各多了一節。這是由於上註的講法較準確（特指 'doctrinal sections'）。關於二 15，參導論第伍節註 13（上面 33-34）。（**2**）Hanson II 82-86 認為，三 4～7 和二 11～14 原本 'probably formed one long item, whether an act of praise or prayer, we cannot say.' 'It was of baptismal origin'; 提多書的作者將它分為兩半來使用，把二 15～三 3 插在中間（Hanson III 183）。此說純屬臆測。

1.1 寫信人（一 1～3）

除了羅馬書一章 1 至 6 節，這裏對寫信人的描述是新約書信中最長的。[1] 在羅馬書該段，保羅對自己的描述有兩個重點：他的身分是蒙召為使徒，他的工作是奉派傳上帝的福音（1 節），而福音（2～4 節〔在原文為 37 字〕）比使徒的職分（5～6 節〔25 字〕）獲得更詳細的闡釋。提多書本段的自我描述則偏重於保羅的使徒職分（1a 節）：這職分的工作是傳揚福音（3 節），而這職分的目的是為了使上帝的選民信從與認識合乎敬虔的真理（1b～c 節），並使上帝的選民獲得永生的盼望（2 節）。保羅認識到，作為耶穌基督的使徒，自己在救恩歷史的重要時刻扮演著重要的角色。[2]

---

1 （**1**）Keegan II 88 說：「除了《羅馬書》之外（羅一 1～6），《弟鐸書》對收信人的描述是所有新約書信中最長的（鐸一 1～3）。」「收信人」是「寫信人」（Keegan I 55: 'the sender'）之誤。（**2**）Saarinen 169 認為，'One reason for this may be that Titus 1:1-4 employs Rom. 1:1-7 as its model.'（作者認為教牧書信是冒名之作〔22〕。）（**3**）Aune 475*b* 認為，「發信人」這一項長達 '48 words'（原文照錄〔筆者數得 47 字；thus also Richards 71 n.18; Spencer 6 說 '46 . . . Greek words'〕），這似乎表示 'Titus was the first letter in the collection and therefore the prescript articulates the purpose for the entire collection of Pastoral letters'.（歐大衛同樣認為教牧書信是冒名之作。）參一 1～4 註釋引言註 5 之（1）-（3）= 上面 44。

2 Cf. Collins 301: 'the salutation . . . contains a long reflection on salvation history that situates the apostle Paul at the crucial point within that history.' 寇雷蒙又認為（298），如果這封信確是保羅寫給他的親密伙伴、同工、特使，和*真兒子*（4 節）的，'there would have been no need for such a formal presentation of Paul's apostolate.' 但見一 1a 註釋註 12、15 及所屬正文（下面 50、51）。

1.1.1 寫信人的身分（一 1～2a）

一 **1a** 上帝的僕人、耶穌基督的使徒保羅，[1]
b 為了使上帝的選民信從
c 與認識合乎敬虔的真理——
2a 這真理是在盼望……永生，

寫信人自稱為「保羅、上帝的僕人，和[2] 耶穌基督的使徒」。保羅亦稱掃羅（徒十三 9）；保羅是他的羅馬名字，掃羅可能是非正式、較親暱的希伯來名字。[3] 第一個稱號在保羅書信出現僅此一次，[4] 就如「保羅、基督耶穌的僕人」也只出現一次（羅一 1）。[5] 這獨特的稱號可視為此信真確性的標記，因為很難想像，一個模仿者會有甚麼動

---

1 第 1a 節的原文呈現「同字尾（homoioteleuton）」現象（Genade 128）：Παῦλος δοῦλος θεοῦ, ἀπόστολος δὲ Ἰησοῦ Χριστοῦ. 另一個例子是羅十二 15：χαίρειν μετὰ χαιρόντων, κλαίειν μετὰ κλαιόντων（BDF §488(3); 詳見《羅》4.164 註 3）。

2 δέ = 'and' (KJV, NKJV, RSV, NRSV, NAU, NIV, TNIV, NIV2011, ESV, NLT). (**1**) Genade 18 則採納 'yet'（so Quinn 25）或 'but'（so Witherington 96）之意：這裏的對比是 'he is only a bond servant of God' 和 'his office is that of an apostle, authorized by Jesus Christ.' See also LN §89.94: 'δέ: a marker of an additive relation, but with the possible implication of some contrast'; Harold Greenlee as cited in Banker 19*a*: 'If he had said "apostle of God and apostle of Jesus Christ," he would have used *kai*.' (**2**) 筆者認為保羅不大可能將「『由耶穌基督授權的使徒』的職位」看為高過上帝的僕人的地位。See also Marshall 118: 'the next phrase is added hardly as a contrast (δέ) but as additional information ('and besides'; cf. Jude 1)'; Mounce 379: 'δέ . . . is continuative, not adversative'; Towner III 666 n.12（唐 969 註 12）：'it functions as it does in the μὲν . . . δέ construction (though here minus the initial particle; see also Jude 1)'.

3 關於保羅的名字，較詳細的討論請參《羅》1.161-62；《加》210-11；《西・門》101。

4 因此，這並不是「他書信中一貫通用的自稱」（陳 13）。參：雅一 1：上帝和主耶穌基督的僕人雅各。Martin（'Titus' 15）則聲稱，羅一 1（保羅自稱基督耶穌的僕人）支持他對多一 1 這兩個稱號的理解：上帝的僕人和耶穌基督的使徒都是描寫保羅與同一位神的關係，即是本節將耶穌和上帝等同（'equat[ing] Jesus and God'）。

5 但見：腓一 1，「保羅和提摩太，基督耶穌的僕人」。

機，要偏離保羅較常用的自稱（基督耶穌的僕人／基督的僕人：羅一 1／加一 10），而使他自稱為上帝的僕人。[6] 僕人原文直譯為「奴隸」或奴僕（新普），表示保羅是屬於上帝、完全順服上帝，並且委身事奉上帝的。[7] 另有認為，對保羅而言，上帝的僕人這稱號不但表達奴僕服侍主人這種關係，更是一種表明職位及表示尊敬的稱號，因為舊約一些特別蒙上帝揀選的人物，如摩西、大衛等，皆獲賜這稱號。[8] 不過，保羅亦稱一般信徒為上帝的奴僕（羅六 22）和基督的僕人（弗六

---

6 Fairbairn 256. See also White 185*a*; Hiebert 426; Kelly 225: 'an imitator would have taken pains to reproduce the idiom of the letters he knew.'

7 Quinn 62: 'It is basically a self-designation for articulating total commitment to another person.' 此解釋符合「奴僕（δοῦλος）」一詞在保羅其他的書信中所提出的意思：屬於主人、順服主人、甘心服侍主人、討主人喜歡（林前七 22～23〔參六 20〕；羅六 16；加一 10；弗六 5～7；西三 22～23）；參《羅》1.163 註 14。**(1)** LN §87.76 則認為，δοῦλος 可能還有正面的弦外之音：在古代近東的一些語言中，「王的奴隸」或「王的僕人」這種詞語已成為政府要員的職銜。**(2)** 在舊約，不同的人物被稱／自稱為「上帝的（θεοῦ）／我的（μου）／主的（κυρίου）／你的（σου）僕人」，例如：（**i**）摩西（尼十 29〔LXX 十 30〕：δούλου τοῦ θεοῦ；但九 11〔狄奧多田版本〕：δούλου τοῦ θεοῦ；書一 2：ὁ θεράπων μου）；（**ii**）約書亞（書二十四 29〔LXX 二十四 30〕：δούλου κυρίου）；（**iii**）大衛（撒下七 5／8：τὸν δοῦλον μου / τῷ δούλῳ μου）；（**iv**）猶太人的長老（拉五 11：δοῦλοι τοῦ θεοῦ τοῦ οὐρανοῦ）；（**v**）詩人（詩八十六 2〔LXX 八十五 2〕：τὸν δοῦλόν σου）；（**vi**）以色列（賽四十二 19：οἱ δοῦλοι τοῦ θεοῦ，四十四 1：παῖς μου）；（**vii**）先知們（耶七 25，二十五 4／摩三 7：τοὺς δούλους μου/αὐτοῦ；亞一 6：τοῖς δούλοις μου）；（**viii**）火中三子：沙得拉、米煞、亞伯尼歌（但三 26〔狄奧多田版本三 93〕：οἱ δοῦλοι τοῦ θεοῦ τοῦ ὑψίστου）；（**ix**）但以理（但六 20〔狄奧多田版本六 21〕：ὁ δοῦλος τοῦ θεοῦ τοῦ ζῶντος）。**(3)** 在新約，被稱為「上帝的僕人」的包括（**i**）耶穌（徒三 13、26：τὸν παῖδα αὐτοῦ）、（**ii**）保羅和同工（徒十六 17：δοῦλοι τοῦ θεοῦ τοῦ ὑψίστου）、（**iii**）基督徒（彼前二 16：θεοῦ δοῦλοι）、（**iv**）受印的十四萬四千人 = 屬靈的以色列，即是教會（啟七 3：τοὺς δούλους τοῦ θεοῦ〔see Ladd, *Revelation* 112-17; Mounce, *Revelation* 167-70〕）、（**v**）摩西（啟十五 3：τοῦ δούλου τοῦ θεοῦ）、（**vi**）地上的所有信徒（啟十九 5：πάντες οἱ δοῦλοι αὐτοῦ〔see Mounce, *Revelation* 338〕），以及（**vii**）整個蒙救贖的羣體（啟二十二 3：οἱ δοῦλοι αὐτοῦ〔see Ladd, *Revelation* 288〕）。

8 A. Weiser, *EDNT* 1.352*b* (s.v. δουλεύω, 5 d); see also Mounce 378; Ngewa 326; Collins, 'Theology' 60: 'Paul's ethos is established as that of a figure comparable to Moses and David.' 參較上註之（2）。亦參曾 64：「假如最初在克里特宣教的時候保羅使用這個稱號，那就是一個帶有榮耀的稱號。作者要提醒克里特信徒，保羅由最初到現在都具有權柄和榮耀。」

6），也稱並無使徒身分的提摩太（腓一 1，參：提後二 24）[9] 和以巴弗（西四 12）為基督耶穌的僕人；[10] 因此，僕人一詞在這裏所表達的意思，較可能只是保羅對上帝的謙恭順服、完全效忠，及不遺餘力的事奉。[11] 保羅在這裏自稱為上帝的僕人而不是基督的僕人，大抵是由於他在本段的論證把焦點放在上帝身上：信徒是上帝的選民；上帝應許賜予永生；救主上帝命令保羅傳揚福音（1b、2、3b 節）。藉著使用上帝的僕人這稱號，保羅把自己與在他之前那些領受上帝啟示的順命僕人連成一線，表明他所領受的權柄和對上帝的順從是不庸置疑的。[12] 第二個稱號[13] 亦見於彼得書信（彼前一 1；彼後一 1）。保羅較常自稱為基督耶穌〔的〕使徒（林前一 1；林後一 1；弗一 1；西一 1；提前一 1；提後一 1），並且（除了提前一 1）總是聲明，他作基督耶穌的使徒乃是奉上帝〔的〕旨意作的，這聲明充分顯示保羅的深切信念：他是由於上帝的旨意，而被揀選、被委派作基督耶穌的使徒的。[14] 這

9 提摩太並非使徒，此點可參《帖前》141-42。

10 在西四 12，有異文省略**耶穌**（Ἰησοῦ）一字；參《西・門》747 註 3。

11 參《羅》1.163-64。See also R. Tuente, *DNTT* 3.596 (endorsed by Knight II 282): 'here, as elsewhere, the distinctive thing about the concept of the *doulos* is the subordinate, obligatory and responsible nature of his service in his exclusive relation to his Lord.' **（1）** Johnson II 217 發出這修辭問句：在提多**要勸僕人順服自己的主人**（二 9）的同一封信上，保羅自稱為服在**上帝的命令**（一 3）之下的**上帝的僕人**，這豈是完全巧合的呢？不過，弗六 5 和西三 22 同樣要奴僕**聽從**主人，保羅卻沒有在信上自稱為上帝的僕人。因此，保羅在本節的自我描述，是否可能反而隱含了他和那些**不受約束**（一 10）的假教師的對比？**（2）** Richards 73 聲稱，**上帝的僕人**在 LXX 常是「先知」的同義詞。保羅在書信開首就自稱為**上帝的僕人**，為他稍後要提多「必須堵住那些自稱為先知的人的口」（一 11）這命令鋪路。可是，並無證據顯示克里特的假教師自稱為先知（cf. 94/214: 'the self-styled προφήται [*sic*, προφῆται]' / 'those self-styled prophets'）。

12 Towner III 666（唐 969）。Fee（*Christology* 438）作類似的解釋：'a title that could appear to be demeaning is most likely intended to force upon the Cretan believers that even though he is an apostle, Paul is first of all a "slave" under orders from God and therefore they should listen carefully to what he has to say because it comes from God his master.'

13 Calvin 351 說，保羅 'descends from the genus [servant of God] to the species [apostle of Christ]'.

14 參《西・門》103。關於**使徒**（ἀπόστολος）一詞，較詳細的討論請參《羅》

裏的兩個稱號並列，表示保羅將耶穌基督視為與上帝同等（如在第 4b 節），同時強調保羅的職事具有從上帝和基督而來的雙重授權。[15]

為了使上帝的選民信從的原文片語在新約書信中是獨一無二的，直譯作（一）「按照上帝的選民之[16] 信心／信仰」。[17] 但是「保羅的使徒職分是按照上帝選民的信心／信仰」這思想是難明的：作為使

1.165-67；《加》211-12；《西・門》102。（**1**）班約翰將 ἀπόστολος δὲ Ἰησοῦ Χριστοῦ 翻譯為（甲）'an apostle (who represents) Jesus Christ'（Banker 18*b*; see also 19*a*: 'Paul was representing Jesus Christ'），儘管（乙）'an apostle commissioned by Jesus Christ' 這意思也是可能的（19*a*）。事實上，作者稍後將兩個意思合併起來：'(I,) Paul, have been <u>sent/appointed</u> by Jesus Christ <u>to represent</u> him'. 筆者認為，單是提前二 7 和提後一 11（我為此／為這福音奉派〔ἐτέθην〕作傳道，作使徒）足以提示，**耶穌基督的使徒**的意思較可能是（乙）「被耶穌基督委派作使徒」，多過是（甲）「代表耶穌基督的使徒」。（**2**）張 312 註 10 認為，Ἰησοῦ Χριστοῦ「乃 genitive of definition 及 origin」。筆者認為它較可能是 genitive of possession（屬於耶穌基督），同時有 subjective genitive（被耶穌基督差遣〔參：徒二十六 17〕）的意味；see Wallace 82 n.30;《弗》98 註 8。（**3**）Marshall 118 則這樣解釋：'Apostles are always apostles of Christ rather than of God the Father, although the latter appoints them; they are <u>in the service of Christ</u>.'

15 Genade 15. 參曾 64：鑑於在克里特教會有假教師，「保羅因為要堅持他擁有的權柄而自稱是使徒」。如此，「前者『僕人』乃身分卑微的奴僕，後者『使徒』卻是在人面前具有權威的稱呼」（黃編 192）。耶柔米甚至認為，藉著自稱為**耶穌基督的使徒**，保羅表示 'all who believe in Christ are to be in submission to him'（Gorday 282*b*）。

16 ἐκλεκτῶν 是主詞所有格（the elect believe）。See Wallace 116 with n.121. J. Eckert（*EDNT* 1.418*a* [s.v. ἐκλεκτός, 3]）認為，這字是 'a formulaic designation for Christians.'

17 κατὰ πίστιν ἐκλεκτῶν θεοῦ, literally 'according to the faith of God's elect' (KJV, NKJV). （**1**）利斐特 327（Liefeld 310）的解釋是：「他〔保羅〕的**使命**是符合神選民的信仰（即真正的信仰），也符合真理，這真理須在克里特再次確立。」（**2**）Lock 125 認為這裏包含兩個意思：'(*a*) chosen in conformity to the faith'（保羅像其他蒙揀選的人一樣相信了）；'(*b*) preaching by that standard'.（**3**）Scott 150 這樣解釋：保羅以使徒身分所作的工 'is in keeping with the new revelation to which the elect have responded'.（**4**）Ward 234 的解釋是，保羅的傳講受到上帝選民的「承認（recognized）」（參：約壹四 6）。（**5**）R. Bultmann（*TDNT* 6.213）將本節放在 'πίστις as *fides quae creditur*' 的標題下。（*fides quae creditor* = the faith which is believed, 所信的內容，相對於 *fides qua creditor* = the faith by which it is believed, 信心本身。）布特曼隨後說：'In correspondence with the use of πίστις for Christianity we also find formal expressions in place of the as yet unused adjective "Christian": κατὰ κοινὴν πίστιν (Tt. 1:4), κατὰ πίστιν ἐκλεκτῶν (Tt. 1:1) . . .' 一 4 的 κατὰ <u>κοινὴν</u> πίστιν 尚可理解為 'according to the <u>common</u> (i.e., <u>Christian</u>) belief'; 但在本節，'Christian' 的意思是得自原文片語 κατὰ πίστιν ἐκλεκτῶν 的哪一部分的呢？答案見上註後半。

徒，保羅負有傳揚福音的責任，而這責任是按著上帝的命令交託給他的（3b 節）；既然如此，他為甚麼要強調，他所傳的福音是與上帝的選民的信仰相同的呢？上帝的選民的信仰，怎麼可能成為使徒職分的標準呢？[18] 因此，原文介系詞在這裏的意思很可能不是「按照」，如在第 1b 節（合乎敬虔的真理）和第 3b 節（按著……上帝的命令），而是為了或「為了……的緣故」。[19]（二）基里將原文介系詞理解為「關乎」，所得出的意思就是：保羅的職事是關乎上帝選民的兩方面：他們的信心（進一步解釋為「歸信」或「在信心上長進」），和他們對真理的認識。[20]（三）巴列特的解釋是，保羅的使徒職分是由上帝選民的信心／信仰、對真理的認識，以及永生的盼望此三者所構成和決

18 So, correctly, Banker 20*a*; Kelly 226.（1）以下的的回答均未能使人滿意：'God's elect are themselves possessors of a God-given faith and taught by His Spirit, and he [Paul] seeks no higher office than that of sealing their testimony'（Simpson 95）; 'Paul's calling as a "slave of God and apostle of Jesus Christ" accords with the "faith" that the "elect of God" already possess'（Jeon I 24）；保羅的使徒職分是與上帝選民所領受的信仰完全相符（'in full accord with'）的（Hiebert 426-27）；'Paul's teaching stands in continuity with the faith of all those chosen by God . . . and extends and supports that faith'（Wild 894*a*）。（2）Hanson III 169 則認為，κατά 的功用只在於把保羅的職分和正統基督教信仰鬆散地連起來。類似的見解在早前只被視為一種可能：'one must bear in mind the possibility that the author . . . is merely linking familiar phrases with the general intention of expanding the meaning of "apostleship"'（Hanson I 106-7）。

19 I.e., κατά = 'for'（'for the faith of God's elect / those chosen of God / those who are elect': NIV; Fairbairn 53, 255; Quinn 25, 53 / NAU / W. Köhler, *EDNT* 2.254*a* [s.v. 3 c 2]），'with a view thereto'（Fairbairn 257），or 'for the sake of'（NRSV, ESV: 'for the sake of the faith of God's elect'）。See also BAGD 406*b*-7*a* / BDAG 512*b* (s.v. κατά II 4 / s.v. 4): 'for the purpose of, for, to'（但此辭典認為，'in accordance with' 也是可能的）。（1）Clark（'Structure' 104）提出另一可能：將 κατὰ πίστιν ἐκλεκτῶν θεοῦ 這介詞片語視為與 4 節的 κατὰ κοινὴν πίστιν 平行，所得出的意思就是：'Paul . . . who holds the faith that God's people hold and knows the truth . . . to Titus, who is a true son in this shared faith . . .'. 筆者認為此解釋沒有說服力，因為前一個片語並非直接連於保羅一字，而是連於使徒一詞。（2）《新希》174*a-b*（s.v.）沒有提到多一 1；這是由於該詞典處理「代名詞及功能字*〔時〕，只列舉幾段較有代表性的經文作為例子」（viii）。（*「功能字」包括「冠詞、連接詞、感歎詞、疑問詞、虛詞和介詞」〔vii〕）。

20 Kelly 225 (κατά = 'concerned with'), 226. 參《串釋（增簡）》1754*a*：「關乎」，進一步解釋為「保羅的目標是要神所揀選的人相信福音」（參正文之〔三〕）。'Concerned with' 跟 'with respect to, in relation to'（BAGD 407*b* [s.v. II 6]）的意思相近。

定的。[21]（四）上引《和合本修訂版》的翻譯，表達了原文一個可能的意思：為了叫上帝揀選的人相信（呂譯）。[22]（五）另一種理解是：保羅受委派將這信仰傳給上帝所揀選的人（新普）。[23]（六）再一種翻譯是：「為要助長上帝選民的信心」；[24] 保羅受委派去鞏固上帝揀選的人的信心（新普頁邊註）。[25] 這種理解可取，因它和以下的事實相符：（i）羅馬書一章 5 節有類似的講法：保羅說他蒙恩受了使徒的

---

21 Barrett 126: 'his apostleship is constituted and determined by this *faith*, *knowledge*, and *hope*.' Houlden 140 則接受 NEB 的翻譯（'marked as such by faith and knowledge and hope'），認為此三者 'are all marks of the apostle which he shares with his people'.

22 參思高：為引天主所選的人，去信從；NJB: 'to bring those whom God has chosen to faith'; Mounce 379: 'to bring God's elect to faith'; W. Köhler, *EDNT* 2.254*a* (s.v. κατά, 3 c 2): 'in order to lead the elect to faith'; Barclay 227: 'to awaken faith in God's chosen ones'; Banker 17, 19*b*: 'in order that (I might lead) those whom God has chosen (to be his people) to (correctly) believe (in him).'

23 NLT: 'to proclaim faith to those God has chosen'. Banker 18*b* 將 1b 節的 πίστιν 理解為「健全或正確的信仰」，因全書都在談及在信仰上（一 13，二 2）和教義上（一 9，二 1）健全（see G. Barth, *EDNT* 3.97*a*: 'correct faith as opposed to false doctrine'）。但這字在二 2 較可能是指信心（參該節註釋註 36〔下面 227〕）。

24 RSV, TNIV, NIV2011, Arichea－Hatton 262, Johnson I 114, Knight II 283: 'to further the faith of God's elect'; Jeon II 43/8: 'to advance the faith of God's elect / to further their belief in God.' See also White 185*a*: 'for the confirmation of the faith of the elect . . . that it should be fostered'; Stott 169: 'to foster or nurture *the faith of God's elect*'; Towner III 667: 'for the purpose of, to bring about, or . . . to further'（唐 970）。（**1**）Hendriksen 339 將 κατά 翻譯為 'in the interest of', 但解釋為 'to further or promote'; see also Marshall 119: 'promoting and furthering the faith of God's people'; Goodwin 1754*b*: 'to promote the faith of the elect'; Hinson 282: 'to enhance the faith of God's elect'. 亦參當代：為要振奮上帝選民的信心。（**2**）Dunn 861*b* 合併（四）（六）兩個意思：'to bring about and to bring to greater maturity Christian faith and knowledge.'

25 NLT margin, Mounce, 'Titus' 105: 'to strengthen the faith of'. See also Marshall 120: 'to strengthen and develop the faith already held by Christian believers'; Couser, 'Savior' 133 / Ho, 'Mission' 243: 'to strengthen the faith of God's chosen / the elect'.（不過，何氏認為 'There is no exegetical or theological reason why "the elect" may not be taken proleptically; if so, it would stress the evangelistic goal of Paul's apostolic commission, that is, to convert and establish the faith of those whom God has already chosen.'）（**1**）按這種理解，πίστις 指主觀的信心，而不是客觀的信仰，如在現修：奉差遣去幫助上帝選民的信仰；彭編 93*a*：「建立與助長　神選民的信仰」。（**2**）藉著重複 πίστις 一字（1b、4a 節），以及藉著 paronomasia（= 'the recurrence of the same word or word stem in close proximity' [BDF §488(1)）這修辭技巧（πίστις . . . πιστεύω [3b: ἐπιστεύθην – from *pisteuō*] . . . πίστις），本小段強調信心／信仰（Genade 17）。

職分的直接目的，就是要在萬國中使人因信而順服。[26]（**ii**）耶穌多次稱某些人／門徒／彼得為小信的人（太六 30 ‖ 路十二 28／太八 26，十六 8／太十四 31），[27] 但稱讚迦南婦人說，你的信心很大！（太十五 28），可見信心有大小之分。保羅也談到哥林多人信心〔的〕增長（林後十 15），又稱讚帖撒羅尼迦人的信心格外增長（帖後一 3），可見信心是可以增長的。[28]（**iii**）上帝的揀選由選民的信心證實；只有當信心藉著敬虔的生活（見下文）表達出來，上帝的揀選才是明顯的。[29]

上帝的選民是甚麼意思呢？這詞語在舊約是指上帝的選民以色列，[30] 在新約則指上帝的新約子民，即是信徒（本節；羅八 33；西三 12；提後二 10）。[31] 按上段之（四）、（五）的理解，他們是上帝已經揀選去相信基督因而獲得救恩，但仍未相信的人。可是，並無清楚的證據顯示，選民的原文是指那些「在他們相信之前被上帝揀選去相信」的人。上帝的選民所表達的意思只是，他們實在是上帝子民的成員。[32]

---

26 εἰς ὑπακοὴν πίστεως，詳參《羅》1.188-90。

27 最後此節用呼格 ὀλιγόπιστε，其餘四節用主格 ὀλιγόπιστοι.

28 兩節的原文分詞／動詞依次為：αὐξανομένης／ὑπερ-αὐξάνει.

29 Cf. L. Coenen, *DNTT* 1.542: 'it is only if and when faith is lived out, that election is evident (cf. Tit. 1:1).' 保羅和同工知道帖撒羅尼迦人是蒙揀選的（帖前一 4），其部分原因就是前一節所提到、在禱告中記念的事：帖撒羅尼迦人在信愛望三方面的佳美表現（詳參《帖前》61-70），使保羅確知他們是蒙揀選的（73-74）。

30 例如：代上十六 13；詩一〇五〔LXX 一〇四〕6、43。參：次經《便西拉智訓》46.1; 47.22（思高德訓篇 24 節）；《所羅門智訓》3.9; 4.15.

31 前三節原文皆為 ἐκλεκτοὶ θεοῦ（本節；羅八 33）或 ἐκλεκτοὶ τοῦ θεοῦ（西三 12）；第四節是 οἱ ἐκλεκτοί 單獨使用（即並無修飾語）。（在約一 34，異文 ὁ ἐκλεκτὸς τοῦ θεοῦ 是指基督；但很可能上帝的兒子才是原來的說法。See *TextC* 172。）ἐκλεκτός 在保羅書信僅再出現兩次，分別指在主裏蒙揀選的魯孚（羅十六 13）和蒙揀選的天使（提前五 21）。

32 Marshall 121. 詳參《羅》2.765-68；《弗》122-26。如馬歇爾所指出，在上述保羅書信的五次（見上註；提前五 21 不算在內），這字所指的都是實在已蒙上帝拯救的人；保羅沒有說上帝的呼召是獨立於（'independent of'）人的回應，或使人不能不回應，也沒有說這呼召暗示有別的人被上帝「略過」，即上帝決定不拯救他們；這種雙重預定論超出了保羅所說的話，並且引起關乎上帝之公平的嚴重問題（Marshall, *Theology* 442, 443 with n.33）。參《羅》3.160 註 16，3.203-5 關於第（1）個答案之評語（尤其是 3.205 註 51 之〔2〕）；亦參《羅》3.127-36（尤其是 133-34 之〔五〕），在福音書裏，被選有別於被召：被召的人多，被選的人少（太二十二 14，思高）。[33] 被召的是所有被邀請（當代、現修、新普）接受福音及其福澤的人，被選的是那些回應這邀請而成為上帝子民之成員的人（參：太七 13～14）。[34] 但在保羅書信裏，這種區別並不存在；「被選」的意思就如前述，而「被召」的意思亦相若：那些蒙召的人（林前一 24，新譯）[35] 就是按〔上帝的〕旨意被召（羅八 28）、蒙召歸屬耶穌基督（羅一 6，新普）、蒙召為聖徒的人（羅一 7，思高）；上帝呼召他們作祂的子民，他們亦回應了這呼召而成為上帝的子民。[36]

保羅作使徒的目的，除了鞏固上帝揀選的人的信心（新普頁邊註）之外，還有使他們認識合乎敬虔的真理。有認為複合名詞認識是指加強的認識或較圓滿的知識。[37] 但這字的意思不必有別於其同字根的簡

3.158-63（尤其是 161-63），3.178-80，3.422-23，3.478-80。**（2）ἐκλεκτός** 在新約另外出現十六次（即新約全部 22 次），其中三次是指基督（路二十三 35；彼前二 4、6）。

33 πολλοὶ γάρ εἰσιν κλητοί, ὀλίγοι δὲ ἐκλεκτοί = 'For many are called/invited, but few are chosen' (KJV, NKJV, RSV, NRSV, NAU, ESV, NLT / NIV, TNIV, NIV2011).

34 Cf. Marshall, *Theology* 477, 699 n.19.

35 τοῖς κλητοῖς. 參：猶 1 節（τοῖς . . . κλητοῖς）；啟十七 14（κλητοὶ καὶ ἐκλεκτοί）。

36 See Marshall, *Theology* 698-99. 參《西・門》584-86。See also Wall 336: 'His use of this familiar OT idiom of the covenant community ["God's elect ones"] for the church does not suggest God's predestination of its membership "before time began" [1:2b] but refers to those whose act of "faith" in Christ Jesus marks them out as a people belonging to God'.

37 ἐπίγνωσις = 'full knowledge'（Collins 311; cf. 304, 311: 'the full knowledge of truth'），'fullness of understanding'（Mounce 379），'knowledge intensified, or in the fuller sense'（Fairbairn 113），指上帝子民對真理的特殊的認識。Jeon II 8 認為，保羅想到的是 'an embrace－a full recognition and acceptance－of the truth'. ἀληθείας [*alētheias*] 是受詞所有格（the truth is known）。**（1）** ἐπίγνωσιν ἀληθείας 這片語亦見於提前二 4；提後二 25，三 7（之前的介系詞都是 εἰς）；W. Hackenberg（*EDNT* 2.25*b* [s.v. ἐπίγνωσις, 2 b]）認為，這片語幾乎是指歸向基督信仰的專門術語。有冠詞的 τὴν ἐπίγνωσιν τῆς ἀληθείας 見於來十 26。兩種格式都符合 'the canon of Apollonius' 的要求，即是在這種結構（一個名詞附屬於另一個）裏面，或是兩個名詞都有冠詞，或是兩個名詞都沒有冠詞，不能一個有而另一個沒有。See *Idiom* 114-15; MHT 3.180；參《西・門》128 註 2。**（2）** 這「準則」的重要例外是，先行的名詞可以沒有冠詞，附屬的名詞才有冠詞（*Idiom* 115〔反之則不容許〕），例如：εἰς ἐπίγνωσιν τοῦ μυστηρίου（西二 2〔參《西・門》328 註 32〕），ἅ ἐστιν σκιὰ τῶν μελλόντων（西二 17〔參 436 註 6 之(1)〕），

單名詞，因而翻譯為知識／認識（新和／呂譯、思高、現修）[38] 便已足夠。[39] 認識……真理與以弗所的假教師所教導的所謂〔的〕「知識」（提前六 20，現修）相對。[40] 文理提示，真理就是藉著傳揚福音而顯明的上帝的道（一 3a），即是使徒所傳的信息。[41]

（一）合乎敬虔的真理（同思高；新譯略去的字）是原文的一種主要翻譯。[42]（二）《新普及譯本》的翻譯表示，這真理能使他們知道

ἐν δεξιᾷ τοῦ θεοῦ（西三 1〔參 507 註 24 之（3）〕），εἰς ἔπαινον δόξης τῆς χάριτος αὐτοῦ / εἰς ἔπαινον τῆς δόξης αὐτοῦ（弗一 6／14〔參《弗》141 註 3〕），εἰς οἰκοδομὴν τοῦ σώματος（弗四 12〔參《弗》586-87 註 20 之（2）〕），ἀνέμῳ τῆς διδασκαλίας（弗四 14〔參《弗》594-95 註 7〕）。

38 多數英譯本作 'knowledge'（RSV, NRSV, NAU, NIV, TNIV, NIV2011, NJB, ESV）。亦參《輔讀》524（第一解釋）：「知識」。KJV/NKJV 則翻譯為 'acknowledging/acknowledgment', 即是承認真理之意。

39 詳參《西・門》147-48。

40 Wild 894*a*. See also Zamfir 173: 'ψευδωνύμος γνῶσις [falsely-called knowledge] can easily be the foil of ἐπίγνωσις ἀληθείας, i.e. of sound teaching.'

41 'Evidently he conceives of the Church's faith as a formulated body of truths which must at all costs be preserved intact and which stands in sharp antithesis to every heretical system' (Kelly 17). **ἀλήθεια** 在本書僅再出現一次（一 14），教牧書信另外十二次，保羅書信另外 33 次（新約全部 109 次）。詳參 BDAG 42*a*-43*a* (s.v.);《新希》15*b*（s.v.）;《帖後》229-30。較特別的詞組有：（**i**）**ἐπ' ἀληθείας**: 誠誠實實（可十二 14 ‖ 路二十 21），（說的）很對（可十二 32，新譯），（說）實話（路四 25），實在（路二十二 59），真的（徒四 27〔新譯〕，十 34）;（**ii**）**ἡ ἀλήθεια τοῦ θεοῦ**: 神的真理（羅一 25〔新譯，參《羅》1.305-6〕），上帝的真實（羅三 7），上帝的信實（羅十五 8〔現修，參《羅》4.513-14〕）;（**iii**）**(τὴν) ἀλήθειαν λέγειν/λαλεῖν**: 講真理（約八 45、46），說真話（羅九 1），說實話（林後十二 6；提前二 7〔呂譯〕），將實情……告訴（可五 33），把真情……告訴（約十六 7）／把真理……告訴（約八 40），說誠實話（弗四 25）。Cf. MGM 39*b* (s.v.).

42 亦參利斐特 327：「大概是指 "那跟敬虔相稱的真理"〔'truth that is appropriate to godliness' [Liefeld 310]〕，而非 "那導致敬虔的真理"」（但 339 說，「這真理的知識引向 "敬虔"」〔'knowledge of this truth "leads to godliness" [Liefeld 321]〕= 正文之〔三〕）。I.e., τῆς κατ' εὐσέβειαν = 'which accords with godliness' (RSV, NKJV, ESV; Banker 18*b*), 'which is according to godliness' (NAU; Fee 168), 'that is in accordance with godliness' (NRSV). See also KJV: 'which is after godliness'; Banker 17, 20*b*, 21*a*: 'which [the true teachings about God] (teach them) to behave in a godly manner'（但見下面註 44）。κατ' εὐσέβειαν 這介詞片語亦見於提前六 3（τῇ κατ' εὐσέβειαν διδασκαλίᾳ, 合乎敬虔的教導）；認識合乎敬虔的真理（多一 1）的方法，就是接受合乎敬虔的教導（cf. Ward 235）。(**1**) Fairbairn 257 將原文片語連於認識一詞，從而得出 'knowledge that has respect to, or tends in the direction of, godliness'（「關乎敬虔，或趨向敬虔」的知識）這種意思（see also Johnson

怎樣過敬虔的生活。[43]（三）另一種主要翻譯則提供「導致敬虔的真理」之意；[44]《當代福音》更明確地翻譯為那使人有敬虔生活的

I 114: 'This "knowledge" (or "recognition") of the truth . . . must "accord with godliness (*eusebeia*)")。但所屬格的冠詞 τῆς 清楚表示，此片語所形容的是所屬格的 ἀληθείας（真理），不是直接受格的 ἐπίγνωσιν（知識）。**(2)** 同理，此片語也不能同時連於直接受格的 πίστιν（信心）和 ἐπίγνωσιν 而得以下的意思：'Faith and knowledge of the truth are said to accord with godliness or *eusebeia*'（Drury 1231*a*）。參下面註 44 之（1）。

(3) 名詞 **εὐσέβεια** 在本書出現僅此一次，但同字根的副詞 εὐσεβῶς 在二 12 出現，其意思肯定是**虔敬地**（思高），因而名詞在本節的意思可能也是**敬虔**而不是「宗教」（《新希》140*a* [s.v. I. 1]; NJB: 'true religion'; cf. Neyrey 1215*a*: ἐπίγνωσιν ἀληθείας τῆς κατ' εὐσέβειαν = 'the recognition of religious truth'; Martin, *Foundations* 388: 'In the Pastorals . . . εὐσέβεια carries more the nuance of "religion" than the possession of a personal and moral quality'）或**信仰**（現修，見下面註 45 之〔2〕）。這名詞（εὐσέβεια）在保羅書信另外出現九次（都是在教牧書信），* 新約另外五次，其意思都是 'awesome respect accorded to God, *devoutness, piety, godliness*'（BDAG 412*b*, s.v.）：**虔誠**（徒三 12）、**敬虔**（提前二 2，三 16，四 7、8，六 3、5、6、11；提後三 5；彼後三 11）、**虔敬**（彼後一 3、6、7）。Wild 894*a* 則定義為 'right behavior toward God and human society'.（*留意 Johnson II 31 的觀察：'For fellow workers of Greek education [Titus was of Greek background, Gal. 2:3; Timothy had a Greek father, Acts 16:1], we might well expect a shaping of the gospel that emphasized its godliness/piety (*eusebeia*)'.）**(4)** D'Angelo（'Family Values'）聲稱，在教牧書信和偽經《馬加比四書》（她接受兩者皆為二世紀初段的作品〔140〕），'εὐσέβεια [*eusebeia*] appears to carry the implications of *pietas*, the Roman and imperial virtue that best approximates "family values" combined with religious observance. Εὐσέβεια is thus manifested in appropriate familial relations'（141）；她認為兩者都把 *eusebeia* 這美德演繹為後奧古斯都的 *pietas*：'. . . construction of that virtue as / constructing that virtue along the lines of the Roman virtue *pietas*, that is, as duty and devotion not only to the divine, but also to those of one's household and family'（163/165）。

43 NLT: 'the truth that shows them how to live godly lives'.

44 NIV, TNIV, NIV2011, Young 58 / Mounce, 'Titus' 105 / NJB: 'the truth that leads to godliness / godly living / true religion'. See also Banker 18*a*: 'the truth that has reference to / leads to godliness'（但見上面註 42）; Marshall 123: 'the truth is commended because (among other things) it leads to godliness'; 曾 65：「很可能是指在耶穌裏的真理，引領人邁向敬虔」；黃編 192：「正確的真理〔原文照錄〕能使人產生敬虔的生活表現」。Cf. Bassler 182: 'fostering a life of piety and obedience'. **(1)** Genade 16-17 則認為 κατά 也包含目的之意：'Faith and knowledge have as their goal or outcome the godliness of the elect.' 不過，原文的結構清楚表示，**合乎敬虔**（τῆς [genitive] κατ' εὐσέβειαν）是形容**真理**（ἀληθείας [genitive]）而不是形容「信心和知識」（πίστιν . . . καὶ ἐπίγνωσιν [both accusative]）的。同理，'Knowledge of the truth leads to εὐσέβεια'（Belleville, 'Piety' 227, 243）這話（若視為原文的翻譯）也值得商榷。參上面註 42 之（1）。**(2)** 另有認為 κατά 在此表達目標：'[κατά is used] of the end aimed at; the goal to which anything tends'; κατ'

真理。[45] 鑑於下文提到那些假教師背棄真理（14b 節）、在行為上（10～11 節）否認上帝（16b 節），第（一）種翻譯可能最可取：真理是用敬虔來量度的。[46] 這真理就是福音，特指構成福音的客觀真理，[47] 即是上帝的真確啟示，這啟示帶來救恩。[48] 值得特別留意的是，雖然認識／明白真理一詞在教牧書信另外出現三次（提前二 4／提後二 25，三 7），[49] 但只有在本節，這詞才與敬虔連著出現。[50] 在教牧書信裏，名詞敬虔描寫真正的基督教，副詞敬虔地（二 12，思高）描寫真正基督教的生活方式，[51] 即是過……委身於上帝的生活（新普）。

εὐσέβειαν = 'tending to godliness'（Thayer 329*a* [s.v. κατά, II 3 d]），'with a view to godliness'（Robertson, *Pictures* 4.597）。

45 See also Banker 15*a*: 'sound doctrine motivates and produces godly living'（但見上面註 42、44）；Mounce 377, 379: '. . . that produces godliness'. Cf. Wieland 195: 'an attitudinal and behavioural outcome of teaching truth'.（**1**）REB 譯作 'the truth enshrined in our religion'.（**2**）現修則把 ἀληθείας τῆς κατ' εὐσέβειαν 翻譯成**我們的信仰所教導的**（τῆς κατ' εὐσέβειαν）**真理**（ἀληθείας）。但見上面註 42 之（3）。

46 Towner III 668（唐 972）：'the sense of "godliness" (the balance of faith and conduct) as the authentic measurement of truth is probably uppermost in mind.' 唐書禮同時認為，'the alternative is also true: the authentic gospel is intended to produce godliness' =（三）。

47 Genade 17.（**1**）在 ἐπίγνωσιν ἀληθείας τῆς κατ' εὐσέβειαν 這片語內，冠詞 τῆς 使 ἀληθείας 相當於 τῆς ἀληθείας. 另一個例子是弗一 6：εἰς ἔπαινον δόξης τῆς χάριτος αὐτοῦ.（**2**）ἐπίγνωσιν ἀληθείας（二字皆無冠詞，像弗一 6 的 ἔπαινον δόξης 一樣）符合 Apollonius' canon 的要求。詳見《弗》141 註 3；亦參《羅》2.590 註 12 之（1）（2）。

48 Marshall 122: 'In the PE [Pastoral Epistles] ἀλήθεια refers to the authentic revelation of God bringing salvation.'

49 三次原文皆為 [εἰς] ἐπίγνωσιν ἀληθείας.

50 Faber, 'Titus' 142.

51 Marshall 142-43. 馬歇爾指出，提前二 10 的**敬畏上帝**（θεοσέβεια）是**敬虔**（εὐσέβεια）的同義詞。Twomey 190 同樣以**敬虔**為 'a synonym for ideal Christian behavior'. Εὐσέβεια 是希臘倫理的主要美德之一（see Mott, 'Ethics' 23-26; 參二 12 註釋註 2 之〔1〕〔2〕= 下面 290），但教牧書信傾向於把 εὐσέβεια 視為整個在基督裏之生命的標誌（see Marshall 143）。詳見 Marshall 135-44（'εὐσέβεια in the Pastoral Epistles'），尤其是 142-44（此字在教牧書信的用法）。See also Towner II 30 (cf. 219): 'Paul's favorite term in the Pastorals for genuine Christian life, "godliness" . . . envisions Christianity as the combination of faith in God and the observable conduct that faith produces'; Towner III 57（唐 80）：'This term conceptualizes Christian existence as a balance of faith in God/Christ and the appropriate response of love and service toward others'; D'Angelo, 'Family Values' 159: 'Εὐσέβεια designates both the content and the

保羅一開始就強調敬虔的生活，簡內德認為這提示克里特的信徒所面對的問題，就是敬虔生活的崇高標準受到威脅，要他們在此事上妥協。[52] 較可能的解釋是，敬虔與真理直接相關：真理是用敬虔來量度的，沒有敬虔生活伴隨的「真理」只能稱為「所謂的真理」（參較提前六 20：所謂〔的〕「知識」〔現修〕）。[53] 饒有意義的是，敬虔的生活和真理這樣緊密相連，將本段和佔了書信本體很多篇幅的兩個重要段落（二 1～14，三 1～7）結合起來：二章 1 至 10 節有關敬虔生活的教導，就是以 11 至 14 節的教義為其基礎的；同樣地，三章 3 至 7 節為 1 至 2 節有關敬虔生活的勸勉，提供了教義性的動機。[54]

這真理是在盼望……永生（2a 節）這翻譯，將原文片語[55] 視為形容第 1 節的真理一詞；按這種理解（一），較清晰的翻譯是：這真理是以盼望永恆的生命為根據的（現修），或這真理……使他們確信自己有永生（新普）。[56]（二）《思高譯本》將這片語視為形容第 1 節的敬虔一詞，所得出的意思就是：這虔敬是本於永生的希望。[57] 另有認

practice of Christian life (Tit. 1:1)'; 侯嘉文 144：「『教牧書信』中的『敬虔』……是純正信仰及正確行為的結合。」Cf. Witherington 102: 'in Greco-Roman, Jewish and Christian discussion, the term *eusebeia* and its cognates are used to refer to both belief and behavior, both reverence and action, including ritual action. It is not an either-or matter.'（**1**）Köstenberger 604*b* 則解釋為 'mature Christian character'.（**2**）加爾文認為，「真正的敬虔……在於那種單純真摯的熱忱，它愛上帝如同父親，真摯地敬重祂為主，擁抱祂的公義，並且懼怕得罪祂更甚於死亡」（引於李耀坤：《加爾文》33〔引句來源見 46 註 5〕）。

52 Genade 115-16.

53 以弗所的假教師有敬虔的外貌，卻背棄了敬虔的實質（提後三 5）。

54 See Banker 15*a*. 亦參導論第伍節倒數第二段（上面 36-37）。Faber（'Titus' 141-45）審視了 'true doctrine is accompanied by sound living' 這主題在書中如何發展。

55 ἐπ' ἐλπίδι ζωῆς αἰωνίου, 'in hope / the hope of eternal life' (KJV, NKJV, RSV, ESV / NRSV, NAU, TNIV, NIV2011). Cf. M. J. Harris, *DNTT* 3.1193: '[ἐπί expresses] circumstance'.

56 NLT: 'This truth gives them confidence that they have eternal life'. See also Arichea－Hatton 263.

57 See also Montague 214: 'This godliness . . . rests upon the **hope of eternal life**'; Johnson I 114: 'This "godliness" . . . is governed by the "hope of eternal life"'; Genade 17: 'godliness . . . is motivated by, or premised upon, the hope of eternal life'; 25: 'the εὐσέβεια ἐπ' ἐλπίδι ζωῆς αἰωνίου'.

為，（三）永生的盼望是第 1 節的信心和知識的基礎；[58]（四）永生的盼望就是上帝選民之信心與知識至終的目標。[59]（五）原文片語是第 1 節全節的修飾語，所得出的意思就是：保羅的服事和使徒職分是為了上帝選民的信心，以及他們對合乎敬虔的真理之承認，這一切都是以永生的盼望為基礎**或**目標的。[60] 較可能的看法是，（六）這片語和第 1 節的為著神選民的信心（新譯）是平行的，它同樣是形容使徒的修飾語；在這前提下，這片語可能（六 A）指保羅作使徒的第二個目的[61]（第一個是為著神選民的信心），就是使上帝的選民獲得永生的盼望，[62] 或更可能（六 B）指保羅的使徒職事是基於永生的盼望：就

---

58 NIV: 'a faith and knowledge [v. 1] resting on the hope of eternal life'; similarly Fairbairn 257-58; Griffin 268; Larson 341; Stott 169; White 185*b*; Liefeld 311, 318（利斐特 328、335）。Arichea－Hatton 263 對這種看法提出 'an objection that is theologically based, and that is, the hope of eternal life is at best a result rather than the foundation or basis of the Christian life.' 筆者倒認為，加上底線的一句本身是有疑問的。

59 Fee 169.

60 Hendriksen 340: '*all* that has been said so far . . . rests **on the hope of life everlasting**'; Wieland 196: 'eternal life sums up the goal of both Paul's ministry and the faith and life that he taught.'

61 Kelley 225, 227, Mounce 377, 380: 'for the sake of the hope of eternal life'; Knight II 284: '[it] gives an additional reason for Paul's apostleship'.

62 See NJB: 'and to give them the hope of eternal life'; Zehr 242: 'a second purpose [of] Paul's apostolic ministry'.（**1**）Banker 17 則認為，2a 節這一句表達了 1b 節的結果（詳見 21*b*-23*b* 的討論）。參呂譯：保羅……做耶穌基督的使徒，是為了叫上帝揀選的人相信……而有永生之盼望的。班約翰認為，將 ἐπι- 片語視為表達結果或表達目的，在意思上的分別不大（23*b*）。（**2**）Clark（'Structure' 104）認為，ἐπ' ἐλπίδι ζωῆς αἰωνίου 這片語，在意思上是從屬於 κατὰ πίστιν ἐκλεκτῶν θεοῦ 的。他的理論如下：1b～2a 節呈現交叉配置模式：

κατὰ πίστιν ἐκλεκτῶν θεοῦ	according to faith of God's elect
καὶ ἐπίγνωσιν ἀληθείας	and knowledge of truth
τῆς κατ' εὐσέβειαν	according to godliness
ἐπ' ἐλπίδι ζωῆς αἰωνίου	in* hope of eternal life

他認為這可以翻譯成 '. . . to encourage God's chosen people to know the truth that leads them to godly living, and to hold the faith that gives them hope of eternal life.' **可是**，從造句法的角度來看，雖然（筆者加上底線的）第一個不定詞片語是原文（第二、三行）自然的意思，但第二個不定詞片語卻不能自然地從第一和第四行看出來，因為 ἐπ' ἐλπίδι ζωῆς αἰωνίου（第四行）不大可能是直接地連於（屬於）第一行的 πίστιν 一字的。（*DM 106 也認為，ἐπί 在這裏的意思是 'in' [as one of

如提摩太後書一章 1 節說，保羅作使徒是照著在基督耶穌裏生命的應許（新和），[63] 意即保羅受委派向人傳講〔上帝〕曾許諾藉著相信基督耶穌而得的生命（新普），照樣在這裏，保羅的使徒職事是以永生的盼望為基礎的；[64] 他自己期待所盼望的永生之實現，他所宣講的信息也邀請人接受這永生。[65] 盼望在這裏的意思是「懷著信心，對一件美好的事有期望」；[66] 這種盼望是不會落空的，因為它是基於無謊言的上帝之應許（2b 節）。永生的盼望一詞表示，這裏的永生是所盼望之事，[67] 因而所指的是在將來才實現的（而不是現今就開始享有的）永恆生命。[68] 形容詞「永遠的」亦用來描寫上帝（羅十六 26：永生〔的〕上帝）以及祂的屬性，例如祂永遠的權能（提前六 16）、祂與其子民

---

its 'remote meanings'].）

63 κατ' ἐπαγγελίαν ζωῆς <u>τῆς</u> ἐν Χριστῷ Ἰησοῦ = 'according to the promise of life which/that is in Christ Jesus' (KJV, NKJV / NIV). 冠詞表示，隨後的**在基督耶穌裏**是形容**生命**而不是形容**應許**的。

64 Spencer 6: 'the second <u>basis</u> of his apostleship'. BDAG 364*b*（s.v. ἐπί, 6 a）也認為，ἐπ' ἐλπίδι 的意思是 'on the basis of hope'. See also Barclay 227: 'whose whole work is founded on the hope of eternal life'; Couser, 'Savior' 134: 'he carries out his service "based on the hope of eternal life"'; 彭編 93*a*：「<u>保羅</u>作使徒的基礎，為永恆生命的盼望（參徒 23:6）。」Cf. Towner III 664: 'the *basis* <u>or</u> *reason* for Paul's apostolate', 669: 'it is the reason behind his calling and the promise that motivates his mission'（唐 967，974）；B. Mayer（*EDNT* 1.440*a* [s.v. ἐλπίς, 3 d]）：'The work of the apostle . . . is determined by this hope for eternal life which God has promised (1:2).' 但作者沒有進一步解釋 'determined by' 是甚麼意思。

65 See Marshall 123-24.《新希》174*a-b*（s.v. ἐπί）沒有提到多一 2；解釋見一 1a～2a 註釋註 19 之（2）= 上面 52。

66 《新希》110*a*（s.v. ἐλπίς, I.1）。See also BDAG 320*a* (s.v. 1 b α). **ἐλπίς**（盼望）在下文再出現兩次（二 13，三 7），保羅書信另外出現 33 次（參《帖後》277-79），新約全部 53 次；詳見 BDAG 319*b*-20*b* (s.v.);《新希》110*a*（s.v.）。

67 Ngewa 457 n.12 將 ἐπ' ἐλπίδι ζωῆς αἰωνίου 的末後二字視為 'an epexegetical genitive'; 但 ζωῆς 較可能是受詞所有格。Cf. Wallace 117 n.126: 'τῇ προσευχῇ τοῦ θεοῦ [Luke 6:12] means "prayer to God" (the gen. is thus objective, but after an intransitive verbal noun).' 同理，ἐλπίδι ζωῆς αἰωνίου means 'hope for eternal life'; 'the gen. is thus objective, but after an intransitive verbal noun'.

68 Cf. Ladd, *Theology* 492 n.61: 'The phrase usually designates life in the eschatological consummation'. 形容詞 **αἰώνιος**（永遠的）在保羅書信另外出現二十次（參《帖後》96-97），新約全部七十次（可十六 8 不算在內）；詳參 BDAG 33*a-b* (s.v.);《新希》12*a*（s.v.）。

分享的永遠的榮耀（提後二 10）；透過這種與上帝及來世的聯繫，這形容詞獲得了更強的意思：永生不僅是永恆的生命（現修），並且分享了上帝本身的生命之特質，它的不能毀滅和它的喜樂。[69] 永生一詞在三章 7 節再次出現，兩者首尾相應，將書信本體（一 5～三 11）的絕大部分內容夾在中間。[70]

---

69 Marshall 125. 參：彼前一 3～5；彼後一 4。
70 類似的現象亦見於提前一 16，六 12。See Collins 305 with n.9.

1.1.2 寫信人的信息（一 2b～3）

一 2b ……那無謊言的上帝在萬古之先所應許的

3a 到了適當的時機，藉著傳揚福音，把他的道顯明了；[1]

上帝……所應許的前述詞可能是第 2a 節中的盼望或永生。但是鑑於提摩太後書一章 1 節提到在基督耶穌裡的生命的應許（新譯；參：約壹二 25：基督所應許我們的就是永生），即是上帝……曾許諾藉著相信基督耶穌而得的生命（新普），這裏第 2b 節的所應許應理解為上帝所應許的永生。[2]

（一）無謊言的（同新和）[3] 原文形容詞在新約出現僅此一次。另二種主要翻譯是（二）不撒謊的（呂譯、現修）、[4] 不

---

1 一 2b～3a 的原文提供了 'an example of less than perfect structure'（Clark, 'Structure' 104）：

ἣν <u>ἐπηγγείλατο</u> ὁ ἀψευδὴς θεὸς πρὸ χρόνων αἰωνίων
<u>ἐφανέρωσεν</u> δὲ καιροῖς ἰδίοις **τὸν λόγον αὐτοῦ** ἐν κηρύγματι

這就是說，兩個動詞的主詞都是上帝，但前一個動詞的賓詞是<u>關係代名詞</u> ἥν, 後一個動詞的賓詞則為<u>直接受詞</u>他的道。BDF §469 稱之為 'Anacoluthon following a relative clause' 的例子：'Another clause in which the relative cannot take the same form is sometimes joined to a relative clause by a co-ordinating particle (καί etc.)'

2 So, e.g., Banker 23*b*; Clark, 'Structure' 104; Marshall 125; Towner III 669（唐 974）。See also Classen, 'Epistle to Titus' 49 n.9: 'Commentators and translators seem to agree that ἥν refers to ζωὴ αἰωνιος'. 呂譯、當代、新和、新譯、新普（像和修）皆以永生（現修：永恆的生命）為應許的前述詞。Beale（*Theology* 290-91）更明確地認為，'this presumably is to be identified with the promise of eternal <u>resurrection</u> life.'（**1**）周 408 則以「永生的<u>盼望</u>」為上帝……所應許的前述詞。（**2**）思高卻把應許連於 1b 節末的敬虔一詞，從而得出這虔敬是……天主……所預許的這翻譯。

3 See also H. Balz, *EDNT* 1.187*b* (s.v. ἀψευδής): 'God . . . is *without lies*'.

4 《輔讀》524（第一解釋）同。參以下英譯：'He does not lie'（NJB）；'who does not lie'（REB, NIV, TNIV, NIV2011, NLT; U. Becker, H.-G. Link, *DNTT* 2.472; Mounce cix, 377, 380; Hagner, 'Titus' 553）；'who never lies'（RSV, NRSV, ESV; Davies II 60）；'the undeceiving/unlying/not-lying/never-lying God'（Wieland, 'Function' 161 / Banker 23*b*; Jeon II 8 / Köstenberger 605*a* / Hendriksen 339, 340）。（**1**）辛普遜認為，保羅一定是在回望民二十三 19：上帝非人，必不致說謊（Simpson 95）。不過，多一 2 的用詞

會說謊的（新普）、絕對不說謊的（當代），[5] 和（三）不能說謊的（思高）。[6] 也許第一種翻譯最可取；沒有謊言的（新譯）表示上帝是完全沒有欺詐，是真實可靠的。[7] 事實上，希伯來書的作者這樣描寫上帝：在兩件不可更改的事上（來六 18），上帝絕不可能說謊（新普）。[8] 無謊言的上帝和那些欺騙人的人（10 節〔呂譯〕，參提前一 10 那些說謊話的人）[9] 和常說謊話的克里特人（12b 節）構成鮮明的對比，[10] 亦與克里特人

（無謊言、應許）沒有在 LXX 該節出現；該節的講法是：'shall he say [λέγω] and not perform [ποιέω]? Shall he speak [λαλέω] and not keep [ἐμμένω] *to his word*?' (LXE). （2）Oden 15 問得好：'How could a deceiver, however well-intentioned, write so movingly of "God, who never lies" (Titus 1:2)?'

5 參較詩八十九 35：我僅此一次指著自己的神聖起誓，我絕不向大衛說謊（LXX 八十八 36：εἰ τῷ Δαυιδ ψεύσομαι = 'I will not lie to David' [NKJV, RSV, NRSV, NAU, NIV, TNIV, NIV2011]）。

6 See KJV / NKJV, NAU; E. Hoffmann, *DNTT* 3.71; Jeon II 8: 'that/who cannot lie'; Fairbairn 258: 'incapable of lying'; Mounce, 'Titus' 105: 'its' impossible for him to lie.' 羅馬的革利免說，'nothing is impossible with God, except to lie'（Gorday 283*b*）。

7 BDAG 161*a-b* (s.v. ἀψευδής): '**free fr. all deceit**, *truthful*, *trustworthy*'; Fiore II 195, 196: 'free of all deceit'; Lock 124: 'the God who cannot deceive'; Quinn 25, 54, 64, 69, 70, 232 / Witherington 96: 'without deceit/falsehood'; LN §88.40, Spencer 6: 'truthful'; Hanson III 169: 'unerring'; Classen, 'Epistle to Titus' 49: 'trustworthy';《新希》54*a*（s.v.）：「真實的；沒有撒謊的」。（1）原文是複合形容詞（from ψευδής + α-privative [Vine 2.334]）；形容詞 ψευδής 在新約出現三次，分別指假證人（徒六 13，現修）、假的使徒（啟二 2），和說謊話的人（二十一 8）。（2）此字（ἀψευδής）在 LXX 也只出現一次，用來形容「所有事物的正確知識（γνῶσιν ἀψευδῆ）」（次經《所羅門智訓》〔思高智慧篇〕7.17）。

8 ἀδύνατον ψεύσασθαι [τὸν] θεόν = 'it is impossible for God to lie' (NKJV, NIV, TNIV, NIV2011, NAU, ESV, NLT). 那兩件……不能改變的事（現修），就是上帝對亞伯拉罕的應許和誓言（來六 17：在應許上面加上誓言〔現修〕）；參《來》1.398-400。

9 參：民二十三 19：上帝非人，必不致說謊；撒上十五 29：以色列的大能者必不說謊，也不後悔，因為他不是世人，絕不後悔。兩節都把上帝和人作對比。Marshall（'Deception' 789）聲稱，教牧書信的作者（不是保羅）知道，如果他的作品被發現為偽冒之作，他的作品會被棄絕，他自己亦會受到嚴厲譴責；這足以部分解釋為何他力圖使教牧書信看似真品（'why the Pastoral Epistles struggle so desperately to appear authentic'）。他在這裏援引那無謊言的上帝，又在提前二 7 申明我說的是真話，不是說謊，都是這種「絕望的掙扎」的例子！

10 Towner III 670-71（唐 976）認為，無謊言的上帝同樣（見下註）針對克里特人本身：他們狂妄自大地聲稱，宙斯的墳墓在克里特島上。參一 12 註釋註 5 之（2）= 下面 173。

所信奉偉大的神宙斯構成對比。[11] 當然，與**無謊言的上帝**成為最強烈對比的，是耶穌所描繪的魔鬼：**他心裏沒有真理。他說謊是出於自己的本性，因為他是撒謊者，又是撒謊者的父親**(約八 44，新普)。[12]

在萬古之先（同新和）原文介詞片語（亦見於提後一 9）[13] 另有多種翻譯：**在萬世以前**（新譯、現修），[14] **在亙古以前**（當

---

11 Wieland, 'Crete' 347. 'Not only the Cretans . . . but Zeus himself was notorious for deception and trickery' (346); 作者從（相傳為荷馬所撰的）希臘史詩《伊利亞特》提供證據。See also Towner III 660: 'In light of all this [evidence from Diodorus], Zeus (one who lacks *sophrosynē* [*sic*, *sōphrosynē*] and is a liar) forms the perfect backdrop to the characterization of the Christian God ("unlying" [*apseustēs*];* source of the virtues) in Titus.'（*這個方括號是原來的。*Apseustēs* 是 *apseudēs* 之誤〔重複於唐 958〕。）Towner III 670 認為，保羅提到**那無謊言的上帝**很可能是對克里特傳說中的宙斯之品格的諷刺，此宙斯 'did in fact lie to have sexual relations with a human woman (taking the form of her husband)'（唐 975「確實曾經渴想」誤譯了英文的 'lie' 字）。唐書禮甚至聲稱，「解讀提多書的神學策略，關鍵在於認出開頭提到的『無謊言的神』……是對革哩底* 故事發出的辯證挑戰〔a polemical challenge to the Cretan story〕」（唐 103〔Towner III 74〕）。（*和合；新和、和修：克里特。）

12 至於誰是撒謊者，約翰文獻提供了一些具定義性（definitive）的例子（見一 12 註釋註 9 之〔1〕= 下面 174-75）。

13 πρὸ χρόνων αἰωνίων, literally 'before times eternal/everlasting' (Banker 24*a*; Griffin 270; Guthrie I 182; Hiebert 427; Laansma 226; Mounce 377, 380; Ridderbos, *Paul* 51 / Hendriksen 339, 340, 341), 'before eternal time/times' (Spencer 6; Witherington 96 / Bassler 182; Jeon I 27, 28; Jeon II 9; Köstenberger 605*a*; Towner III 470). **(1)** 彭編 93*a* 謂「希臘文作『諸世諸時之前』」。但「諸世」應為名詞 αἰώνων（πρὸ αἰώνων 才可譯作「諸世之前」），原文卻是形容詞 ἀιωνίων（αἰώνιος 的複數所有格）。**(2)** MHT 3.27 認為 χρόνος 在這裏的意思是 'period'（整個片語意即 'before eternal periods'？）。其實，'times eternal' 和 'eternal periods' 兩種講法都有點奇怪，因為 time/periods 和 eternity 是相對的（參下面註 15）。如 H. Sasse（*TDNT* 1.199）所言，'eternal times is strictly a contradiction in terms.' 不過，也許亨捷晨的解釋可以自圓其說：'before times everlasting' = 'Before the ages began to roll along in their never-ending course' (Hendriksen 341; see also 358: 'before the never-ending time-process began'; see also Hiebert 427: 'before the ages of time, begun at creation, began to roll'), 即 'times everlasting' = 'the ages . . . in their never-ending course'. 如此，'*before* times everlasting' = '*from* eternity' (Hendriksen 342 n.190 [2]).

14 See also NRSV, ESV, Saarinen 170, Emerson, 'Outlook' 93: 'before the ages began';《新希》12*a*（s.v. αἰώνιος, II）：「歷世以前；萬古以前」。H. Sasse（*TDNT* 1.209）也認為，在本節（及提後一 9；羅十六 25），'The concept of eternity is weakened in χρόνοι αἰώνιοι . . . This expression is simply a variant of αἰῶνες in the eternity formulae.'

代），[15] **在創造世界之前**（新普），[16]「在時間的開始之先」。[17] 由於這詞所指的是上帝給予永生之應許的時間，這時間似乎不可能是在創世之先；故此，也許這詞旨在於表達上帝的應許是很久之前，**在久遠的時代以前**（思高）就賜下的。[18] 不過，以下的考量支持本段開首所引的那些翻譯：（1）上帝的揀選（作為祂恩慈的決定）是**在創造世界以前**就發生的事（弗一 4，新普）。[19] 這表示聖經有「上帝在人的存在以先就為人採取行動」這種觀念。（2）討論中的原文片語也在提摩太後書一章 9 節出現，該處提到上帝的恩典是**他在萬世以前就藉着基督耶穌……賜給了我們**的（現修）；[20] 類似的介詞片語[21] 形容上帝**在創造世界之前……就已為我們永恆的榮耀而定下〔一〕個計劃**（林前二 7，新普）。[22] 上帝拯救和呼召的恩典是**萬古之先在基督耶穌裏賜**

---

15 See also Simpson 95: 'from eternity'; Kelly 225, 227: 'from all eternity'. 但 'before the eternal ages'（Collins 304, 305）、'before all eternity'（B. Reicke, *TDNT* 6.685）或 'before time / eternity'（Wallace 379 n.67）這種講法則有點奇怪；問題不在於 'before time'（時間是有起始點的），而在 'before eternity / the eternal ages'（永恆有起始點的嗎？）。參上面註 13 之（2）。無論如何，'The narrative framework of the epistolary salutation is as broad as it can possibly be. It goes from eternity to eternity [eternal life, 2a]'（Collins, 'Theology' 62）。

16 See also KJV, NLT, Mounce, 'Titus' 105 / Jeon II 43: 'before the world began / was formed'; Banker 17: 'before he created the world'; Denton, 'Hope' 22*b* n.24. Wieland 190（cf. 261）則認為，'the purpose of the expression πρὸ χρόνων αἰωνίων is not to distinguish a time period pre- as opposed to post-creation, but to indicate that sphere outside human experience, known only to God and to human beings insofar as God reveals it.'

17 參以下英譯：（**i**）'before time began'（NKJV; BDAG 33*b* [s.v. αἰώνιος, 1]; Aageson 46, 49; Arichea－Hatton 264; Collins 304; Donelson I 141; Jeon II 8; Marshall 115, 126; Simpson 95; Towner I 61; Wall 335, 337, 338, 363, 374; Wall, 'Salvation's Bath' 205），（**ii**）'before the beginning of time'（NIV, TNIV, NIV2011; Smith 211; Towner III 671）。

18 參以下英譯：'ages ago'（RSV; H.-C. Hahn, *DNTT* 844），'long ages ago/past '（NEB, REB, NAU / Lock 126），'so long ago'（NJB），'in the distant past'（Scott 150）。

19 參《弗》126-27。

20 See Quinn 65: 'the phrase *pro chronōn aiōniōn* of Titus 1:2 and 2 Tim 1:9 . . . refers to the timeless order in which God himself lives in contrast to the *chronoi aiōnioi*, the countless ages through which his creatures have come and gone'.

21 πρὸ τῶν αἰώνων.

22 以上兩點見 Banker 24*a*. Hanson III 170 說，'salvation belongs to the timeless eternal

給我們的（提後一 9），但那時我們尚未存在，因此合理的推論就是，基督耶穌代我們領受了這恩典；**上帝在萬古之先……應許**（多一 2）可同樣理解為上帝對基督作出應許（**許諾賜下〔永生〕**，新普），這應許由基督代我們領受了。[23] 既然**永生……是那不會說謊的上帝在創造世界之前已許諾賜下的**（新普），這表示永生純粹是上帝所賜的禮物，並且永生的應許是絕對可靠的。

上帝的應許是**在萬古之先**就賜下的。**到了適當時機／的時期／時候**（一 3a，呂譯／思高／新譯），[24] 意即**到了**祂**認為適當的時候**（當代），[25] 則有另一件事情發生。[26] 原文

---

world; only revelation belongs to time.' Mounce 381 對前一句評為 '[a] foreign idea'.

23 Ward 235, followed by Ngewa 330. See also Bassler 182: 'probably in God's preexistent will'; 侯嘉文 145：「這是一個先存的基督裏的先存應許。」Marshall 126 則認為，'the promise is more a statement of intent by God for his own sake. All the stress lies on the fact that God's purpose is eternal and unchangeable.' Cf. Saarinen 170: 'no particular promise is meant in the phrase, but rather the salvific intent of God in its totality'.

24 参以下英譯：'in due time'（NKJV, NRSV, NJB; Quinn 25, 56），'at the proper time'（RSV, NAU, ESV），'in its proper time'（NIV），'at just the right time/moment'（NLT / Wallace 157）。

25 See NIV, TNIV, NIV2011: 'at his appointed season'; NEB, REB: 'in his own good time'; *Paraphrase* 289 / C. Brown, *DNTT* 3.198: 'in His/God's own appointed time'; Mounce 381: 'the time when God deemed it best'; Scott 150: 'at the time which He Himself had appointed'; G. Delling, *TDNT* 3.461: 'the time which God has ordained and filled with content'. J. Baumgarten 的翻譯（*EDNT* 2.234*b* [s.v. καιρός, 8]: 'the revelation of his word to his time (καιροῖς ἰδίοις)'）不大可能是正確的。

26 一 3a 在原文呈現破格文體（anacolouthon: MHT 3.325）：承接著 2b 節形容**永生**的關係子句（ἣν ἐπηγγείλατο ὁ ἀψευδὴς θεὸς πρὸ χρόνων αἰωνίων: **那無謊言的上帝在萬古之先所應許的**），3a 節應為另一形容子句（由轉折語氣的 δέ [*de*] 字引入），描寫永生如何在歷史的範疇中顯明。事實卻是，3a 節相當於獨立句子（NRSV 在 2 節末用了破折號，表示 3 節相當於新的句子），這句子將**到了適當的時機**與 2b 節的**在萬古之先**作比較，前兩節於是被懸於半空。See Quinn 67. Cf. Marshall 127: 'the relative clause has been unconsciously replaced by a main clause at this point'.（**1**）Lock 126 對原文結構提供另一種（他認為是可能的）解釋：關係子句從 2b 節的 ἣν ἐπηγγείλατο 延伸至 3a 節上的 καιροῖς ἰδίοις，而 3a 節下的 τὸν λόγον ἐν κηρύγματι 是 'in loose apposition to the whole sentence'. See also Ngewa 332: 'hope of eternal life is what was manifested at the proper time; the method of the manifestation is the word of God [458 n.19: τὸν λόγον 'is taken as an adverbial accusative of manner, translatable as "by way of his word"']; and the sphere of the manifestation is proclamation . . . or preaching'. 筆者認為兩種解釋都流於牽強。（**2**）Ward 236 問道：保羅原本要說的 '[eternal life] which God promised and manifested [ἣν

片語[27]在新約僅再出現兩次，分別與基督的工作和顯現有關：**他捨了自己作萬人的贖價，到了適當的時候，這事就**

ἐπηγγείλατο . . . καὶ ἐφανέρωσεν' 為何變成 'which God promised, and manifested his word [ἣν ἐπηγγείλατο, . . . ἐφανέρωσεν δὲ . . . τὸν λόγον αὐτου]'（即是**他的道**取代了*永生）呢？華德的答案是：這是由於保羅想到他的使徒職事，就是傳揚基督，而傳揚基督一方面是傳講基督所賜的生命，同時也是宣講真道（提後四 2，思高）。畢竟，耶穌基督就是他〔上帝〕的道。**(3)** 張 315 聲稱，「保羅把『永生』等同於*『他的道』；『他的道』，即福音的信息，而福音信息的核心，是人因着相信耶穌基督而得着所應許的永生」。**(4)** 亨捷晨的解釋是：由於**永生**是指將來才可以實現的永恆生命（參一 1～2a 註釋註 68 所屬正文〔上面 61〕），它（'life everlasting itself in its glorious heavenly phase'）是不可能對地上的人顯明的，能顯明的只是上帝的話如何論及這永生（或：上帝的話宣告，祂已實現了祂的應許〔Marshall 128〕）；因此，**顯明**的賓詞就從**永生**改為***他的道**（Hendriksen 342, endorsed by Banker 25*a*）。**(5)** Towner III 672（唐 978）認為，保羅思想的方向要求他把焦點從應許轉移到傳揚，因此他引進新的賓詞**道**字，這字一方面回望所應許的永生（就是福音〔道〕所顯明的），同時指向應許如今獲得實現的方法（這方法就是**道**的傳揚）。筆者認為，(4)(5) 可並存不悖。
(6) 周 409 這樣問和答：

> 保羅為甚麼不說，「把他的應許顯明了」，而說，**把他的道顯明了**呢？原因大概是，當我們說到「應許」時，通常都採用「宣告」這動詞，而不是採用「傳揚」這動詞。如今保羅既然說，**藉着傳揚的工夫**〔新和〕，因此在下一句便自然會說**把他的道顯明了**。

筆者從原文釋經的角度對這話有三點回應：**(i)** 2b 節的**應許**原文是動詞，所應許的是 2a 節的**永生**，而這才是 3a 節的動詞**顯明**原應以之為賓詞的。因此，應該問的問題是：保羅為甚麼不說，「把他所應許的永生顯明了」，而說，**把他的道顯明了**呢？**(ii)** **應許**在原文是動詞而非名詞，因此應當使用哪一個動詞（「宣告」抑或「傳揚」）與之配合的問題並不存在。故此，周氏看為「自然」的邏輯（「既然說……便自然會說……」）其實並不存在。**(iii)**「如今保羅既然說……因此在下一句便自然會說……」這話，完全忽視了原文的次序；原文的次序是**把他的道顯明了**（ἐφανέρωσεν . . . τὸν λόγον αὐτου）在先，**藉著傳揚福音**（ἐν κηρύγματι）在後。

27 καιροῖς ἰδίοις. **(1)** 單數的 καιρῷ ἰδίῳ 在希臘文聖經只出現一次（加六 9：**到了適當的時候**），指上帝所指定的終末收割之時（參《加》1361，連註 20-22）。**(2)** 名詞 **καιρός** 在本書出現僅此一次，在保羅書信另外 28 次（羅十二 11 的異文不算在內〔參《羅》4.143-46〕；新約全部 85 次），呈現幾種略為不同的意思：**(i)** 指一般意義的「時間」（**時間／時期**：羅五 6〔新普／思高；參《羅》2.56-57〕；**時候**：羅九 9，十三 11；林後六 2a、2b；弗二 12；提後四 3；弗六 18〔**隨時**〕；**日子**：提後三 1），這用法包括 ὁ νῦν καιρός（羅八 18：**現今**）／ἐν τῷ νῦν καιρῷ（羅三 26／十一 5／林後八 14：**今時／現在這時刻／現在**）和 πρὸς καιρὸν ὥρας / πρὸς καιρόν（帖前二 17／林前七 5：**暫時**）等介詞片語。**(ii)** 指**機會**（加六 10；弗五 16〔現修、新普〕；西四 5〔現修〕）；**(iii)** 指某些特別的時

證實了（提前二 6，新譯）；到了恰當的時候，上帝會使基督從天上顯現（六 15，新普）。同一個原文片語將這三節串連起來，讓我們看見這樣的圖畫：在上帝認為適當的時候，（i）基督降世成就救贖（提前二 6）；（ii）上帝的道——就是福音——被廣傳（多一 3a：藉著傳揚福音，[28] 把他

候，如舉行慶筵的節期（加四 10〔複數〕）、保羅離世的時候（提後四 6）、不法者要出現的時辰（帖後二 6，思高），以及在到了／在適當的時候（加六 9〔καιρῷ ἰδίῳ〕；提前六 15〔複數 καιροῖς ἰδίοις, 如在多一 3〕／提前二 6〔複數〕）和上帝所定的時刻一到（弗一 10〔當聖〕，τὸ πλήρωμα τῶν καιρῶν〔參《弗》165-66、173〕）這些片語中所指的時候；（**iv**）指末期，即是最後的時期（林前四 5〔時候未到〕，七 29；〔複數〕弗一 10）。See BDAG 497*b*-98*b* (s.v. καιρός);《新希》169*b*-70*a*（s.v.）。（**3**）形容詞 **ἴδιος** 在下文出現三次，意思都是自己的（一 12〔呂譯、思高〕，二 5、9）；在保羅書信另外出現 40 次（新約全部 114 次）。較特別的組合有（**i**）κατ' ἰδίαν（私下，例如：加二 2；太十四 13 ‖ 可六 31；太十七 19 ‖ 可九 28〔對觀福音另 11 次〕；徒二十三 19）和（**ii**）τὰ ἴδια（自己的事〔帖前四 11〕，自己所有的〔路十八 28〕，自己的地方〔約一 11（新普作自己的百姓），十六 32〕，自己的羊〔約十 3、4〕，本性〔約八 44，呂譯、現修、新譯〕，屬於自己的人〔約十五 19，思高〕），自己家裏（約十九 27，參徒二十一 6）。See BDAG 466*b*-67*a* (s.v.),《新希》159*b*-60*a*（s.v.）。

28 藉著傳揚福音原文為介詞片語：ἐν κηρύγματι = 'through preaching' (KJV, NKJV), 'through or by means of preaching' (Towner III 673 n.39), 'by means of proclamation' (Smith 174, 211). 'Here the *kērygma* is the actual act of proclamation' (L. Coenen, *DNTT* 3.53); 'the κήρυγμα is *actus praedicandi*' (G. Friedrich, *TDNT* 3.716).（**1**）昆謝隆則認為，κήρυγμα 'specif[ies] the result of the action'（BDF §109[2]; Quinn 70），即 κήρυγμα 是 κηρύσσειν 的結果（後者見提前三 16〔被傳於外邦〕；提後四 2〔務要傳道〕）。（**2**）另有認為，κήρυγμα 合併了宣講及其內容兩方面的意思：'2 Tim 4:17 and Titus 1:3 bring together the activity of proclaiming and the content of proclamation in the use of κήρυγμα'（O. Merk, *EDNT* 2.291*a* [s.v. κηρύσσω, 4 a]）；'the κήρυγμα may be understood as the activity of preaching together with its content'（Wieland 192）。（**3**）名詞 **κήρυγμα** 在保羅書信另外出現五次，也都是指關於耶穌基督之死與復活的宣講：我〔保羅〕所宣講的耶穌基督（羅十六 25，思高）；我們所傳那「愚拙」的信息（林前一 21，現修）；我的／我們的宣講（林前二 4／十五 14，思高）；福音的宣講（提後四 17，思高）。此字在新約另外出現兩次（不包括可十六 9〔短結語〕的異文；新約一共八次），指先知約拿的宣講／宣道（太十二 41 ‖ 路十一 32，思高／現修）。See BDAG 543*a* (s.v.);《新希》185*b*（s.v.）。（**4**）同字根的動詞 κηρύσσω 在新約一共出現 61 次：一次（啟五 2）指「透過傳令官或起傳令官作用的人，以正式或官方的方式宣佈」（《新希》185*b* [s.v. I 1]），其餘則指公開的宣揚（例：太十 27 ‖ 路十二 3）或宣講（例：太四 17 ‖ 可一 14；林前二 1；弗六 20；西四 3）。See also BDAG 542*b*-43*a* (s.v.).（**5**）同字根的人物名詞 κῆρυξ 在新約出現三次，分別指保羅奉派作傳道（提前二 7；提後一 11），以及挪亞是正義的報信者（彼後二 7，呂譯）。在世俗的用法裏，這字指 'an official entrusted with a proclamation, *herald*'（BDAG 543*a* [s.v. 1]）。寇雷蒙就認為，多一 3 所用的名詞（κήρυγμα）

的道顯明[29]）；（iii）基督再來（提前六 15）。這一切都是／都會在上帝自己所定、適合祂的目的之時候成就的。[30]

顯明原文是過去不定時時態。這動詞的同一時態被動語態分詞，在提摩太後書一章指上帝**萬古之先在基督耶穌裏賜給我們的**恩典（9 節）**如今藉著我們的救主基督耶穌的顯現已經表明出來**（10 節）；恩典的**表明**是藉著基督的首次降臨。在提多書本節，上帝**把他的道顯明**的方法是**藉著傳揚福音**，而福音的基本內容是基督臨世成就救贖，可見本節的**顯明**仍然指向基督的首次降臨（如在提後一 10 一樣）；不過，這裏是從福音被傳揚的角度來看基督事件：只一次發生的基督事件與

'connotes the public and official character of the content* of the message'（Collins 307）。（*但見本註開首。）

29 動詞 **φανερόω** 在本書出現僅此一次，在教牧書信另外出現兩次（提前三 16；提後一 10），在保羅書信另十九次（新約全部 49 次；在 LXX 僅一次〔耶四十 6，中英譯本三十三 6〕）。See BDAG 1048*a-b* (s.v.);《新希》344*a-b*（s.v.）。（**1**）在提前三 16，**他在肉身顯現**（新譯）指道成肉身，即是基督**以人的形體顯現**（現修）。在提後一 10，上帝那**萬古之先在基督耶穌裏賜給我們的**恩典（9 節）**藉著我們的救主基督耶穌的顯現**（διὰ τῆς ἐπιφανείας）**已經表明出來**（φανερωθεῖσαν）；祂的顯現與救贖論有關連（**他把死廢去**〔καταργήσαντος〕），亦與末世論有關連（**藉著福音，將不朽的生命彰顯出來**〔φωτίσαντος〕）——**基督粉碎了死亡的權勢，並藉著福音為我們照明了通向不朽生命的道路**（新普）。（**2**）在希羅世界裏，ἐπιφάνεια 描寫某物（例：黎明）或某人（例：敵人）的「出現」或「被看見」：神明向敬拜者「顯現」並「彰顯」神明的能力；尤其值得留意的是，ἐπιφάνεια 用來指君王加冕時或從戰事回歸時的出現。See Belleville, 'Christology' 336 (with reference to Lau).

30 Marshall 129.（**1**）Saarinen 170 認為，複數的 καιροῖς ἰδίοις 'specifies the recent and present events in which God's "word" (*logos*) was revealed.' 曾 67 聲稱，「『時候』這個字是複數的，表示有多個傳道的時期。這個複數的字表示作者在這段期間有多次分享福音的機會。」兩種看法都值得商榷，因為同一個詞語（καιροῖς ἰδίοις）在提前六 15 不能理解為基督會多次顯現。「在祂所定的日期」、「神指定的時候」（曾 68、133）才是原文片語的意思。（**2**）同理，Bassler 182 對複數的 καιροῖς 一字的理解也不可取，她說：'the intended meaning [of the plural καιροῖς] here is probably plural, for the apostolic proclamation reveals the existence and nature of God's promise of salvation on repeated occasions, each one part of God's predetermined plan.' '[At] the time determined by God'（Bassler, 'Epiphanies' 320; 參註 25〔上面 67〕）才是原文片語的意思。

傳揚福音的持續行動被視為聯合為一的一件事件。傳揚福音的持續行動將基督事件對世人的意義繼續闡明。[31]

他的道可理解為「來自他本人的信息」。[32] 他的道就是上帝的道（二 5；參：提後四 2：務要傳道），[33] 相當於上帝的福音（羅一 1，十五 16）[34] 或關於基督的福音（羅十五 19，現修）。這可靠之道（多一 9a）就是信上重複提到的健全的教導（一 9b，二 1）的基礎。而健全的教導是健全的信仰（一 13：在信仰上健全）和健全的信心（二 2：在信心……上……健全）的基礎。

31 Marshall 127: 'here the [Christ-]event is viewed from the perspective of its proclamation, through which its relevance is continued: Christ and the message concerning him are seen as one, unified event.'

32 Banker 17, 24*b*: 'the message from himself'. I.e., αὐτοῦ – genitive of origin. 另有解釋為 'the "word" . . . of God's promise'（Köstenberger 605*a*），'his promise concerning the hope of eternal life'（Smith 211），'the message about the aforementioned promise'（Wieland 191），即上帝的應許（賜永生）之言。不過，保羅奉上帝之命傳揚（3b 節）的信息之內容，一定不限於上帝賜永生的應許，因此他的道所涉及的內涵應是更廣的。

33 **(1)**「上帝的道」在使徒行傳和新約的書信裏常指基督教的福音信息，例：（**i**）主格 ὁ λόγος τοῦ θεοῦ: 二 5；徒六 7，十七 13；林前十四 36；提後二 9；來四 12（參《來》1.278）；（**ii**）直接受格 λόγον θεοῦ／τὸν λόγον τοῦ θεοῦ: 帖前二 13b／徒四 31，六 2，八 14，十一 1，十三 46，十八 11；林後二 17，四 2；西一 25；來十三 17；（**iii**）所有格 λόγου . . . θεοῦ: 彼前一 23；啟一 9，六 9，二十 4。**(2)** 留意以上的「道」字全部是單數的 λόγος, 因此以下的評論不可取：「神的信息稱為『祂的道』……這個單數的字看來有些奇怪，因為保羅傳講了神的許多話語。……這個字表示神已經全部實現了祂以往一切的應許」（曾 67）；「最合理的解釋是，把這個詞語視為概括地應驗神之前所有的應許。它是屬於單數的，因為那源頭是單數，只有單一個目標，就是表明神的心意」（133）。

34 τὸ εὐαγγέλιον τοῦ θεοῦ（羅一 1 欠冠詞）。另見於：帖前二 2、8、9；林後十一 7（後者作 τὸ τοῦ θεοῦ εὐαγγέλιον, 即是形容詞被放在冠詞和名詞中間）。

一 3b 這傳揚的責任是按著我們的救主上帝的命令交託給我的——

保羅在提摩太前書一章 1 節解釋，他作基督耶穌的使徒，是**奉我們的救主上帝……的命令**作的；照樣，他在這裏解釋，傳揚上帝的道的責任，[1] 是**按著我們的救主上帝的命令**交託給他的。[2] 他奉命作

1 （1）3b 節開首的關係代名詞（ὅ [*ho*], 中性）的前述詞，是 3a 節的最後一字（κηρύγματι, 中性）= 'preaching/proclamation'（KJV, NKJV, RSV, NIV, TNIV, NIV2011, ESV / NAU, NJB, NRSV），不是**道**字（τὸν λόγον, 陽性）。ὃ ἐπιστεύθην ἐγώ 這子句亦見於提前一 11，其關係代名詞的前述詞是 τὸ εὐαγγέλιον（**福音**）。兩次的關係代名詞都相當於 'the "retained accus[ative]" <u>after</u> a pass.'（M. J. Harris, *DNTT* 3.1211〔Marshall 130 則稱本節的關係代名詞為 'acc. of respect'〕）；這就是說，若以其前述詞取代關係代名詞，上述兩句會變成 ἐπιστεύθην ἐγὼ τὸ κήρυγμα / τὸ εὐαγγέλιον. 參帖前二 4（新譯）：保羅說，**神……考驗過我們**（δεδοκιμάσμεθα），**把福音委託給我們**（πιστευθῆναι τὸ εὐαγγέλιον = 'to be entrusted with the gospel' [NKJV, RSV, NAU, NIV, TNIV, NIV2011, NJB, ESV]）。（2）動詞「被委以（ἐπιστεύθην）」的主詞**我**字，是獨立的主格代名詞 ἐγώ, 有強調作用（Genade 15: 'emphatic use'）。（3）'Paul was "<u>considered faithful</u> according to the command of God our savior" with the "word"'（Jeon I 38 [cf. 126]）這翻譯不能成立，因為 πιστεύω 的意思並不包括 'to consider faithful'（see BDAG 816*a*-18*b* [s.v.]; LN vol. 2, p. 198*a*;《新希》267*a-b* [s.v.]）。參較彼前五 12：**我看為忠心的弟兄**原文作 τοῦ πιστοῦ ἀδελφοῦ, ὡς λογίζομαι, 即 'consider faithful' 這意思是用動詞 λογίζομαι + 形容詞 πιστός 表達的。

2 原文兩個介詞片語幾乎完全一樣：

κατ' ἐπιταγὴν <u>θεοῦ</u> σωτῆρος ἡμῶν（提前一 1）
κατ' ἐπιταγὴν <u>τοῦ</u> σωτῆρος ἡμῶν <u>θεοῦ</u>（多一 3）

只是在後一節，**上帝**一詞多了一個冠詞，並且被放在**我們的救主**之後而不是之前。（1）BDAG 512*b*（s.v. κατά, 5 a δ）認為，在這兩節，'*in accordance with* and *because of* are merged'.《新希》174*a-b*（s.v.）沒有提到多一 3；解釋見一 1a～2a 註釋註 19 之（2）= 上面 52。（2）κατ' ἐπιταγήν 這介詞片語（Mounce 381 認為可能是 'a technical term meaning "by order of"'）在保羅書信再出現三次（在新約不再出現），分別指：上帝的奧祕「藉著先知們的著作、<u>照著</u>永恆上帝的<u>命令</u>讓人知道，使人因信而順服，及於萬國」（羅十六 26b～c〔參《羅》4.807、822-26〕）；保羅對哥林多人說的某句話**是容許你們，並不是**<u>**命令**</u>（林前七 6，新譯）；另一句話也**並不是**<u>**命令**</u>**你們**（林後八 8）。（3）W. Grimm（*EDNT* 2.41*b* [s.v. ἐπιτάσσω, 3 a]）認為，在多一 3、提前一 1 和羅十六 26 這三節，ἐπιταγή 指 '[t]he *concrete command* of God

使徒和他奉命傳揚上帝的道，是一體的兩面（參：提前二 7，他說他奉派作傳道，作使徒）。我們的救主上帝這稱號在下文再出現兩次（二 10，三 4）；[3] 我們的意即「我們所有基督信徒的」。[4] 保羅這麼強調他的職事有上帝和基督的授權（這裏，1a 節），為要對提多和他的會眾（尤其是後者，他們會聽見這信被公開宣讀[5]）指出他們應當聽從他的

---

which corresponds to his will and plan for salvation in a definite point in time'. 不過，此字在羅十六 26 可能不是指一明確的命令（如在另外二節），而是指上帝「要在救恩歷史的這個時間（如今）使奧祕被人知道」的旨意；這旨意的含意就是，福音要被傳給萬邦（《羅》4.825）。**（4）**名詞 **ἐπιταγή** 在新約僅再出現兩次（即全部七次）：多二 15（要充分運用你的職權勸勉人，責備人）；林前七 25（關於未婚女子，我沒有主的命令）。

3 三次都是所有格的 τοῦ σωτῆρος ἡμῶν θεοῦ. **（1）**在這片語內，θεοῦ 與 σωτῆρος 同格，前者解釋後者（White 198*a*: 'θεοῦ . . . is epexegetical of σωτῆρος'）。**（2）**我們的救主上帝亦在提前出現兩次（一 1，二 3）；提前四 10 稱上帝為人人的救主，更是信徒的救主（在原文，σωτήρ 只出現一次）。另外，上帝我的救主（路一 47）這稱號出自馬利亞的口；我們的救主獨一的上帝則見於猶大書的信末祝福（猶 25 節）。如此，在新約聖經稱上帝為救主的八次中，六次是在教牧書信裏（多三次，提前三次）。Donelson I 135 認為，這也許就是教牧書信「最引人注目的神學特質（the most striking theological idiosyncracy）」。參較一 4b 註釋註 12 之（1）= 下面 82-83。

4 K. H. Schelkle（*EDNT* 3.326*b* [s.v. σωτήρ, 3]）聲稱，多一 3 及提前一 1 'teach the universality of salvation'; 但這聲稱難以成立。

5 See Genade 9, 23. Cf. Dunn 782: 'The plural form of the final "you" [Tit 3:15c; 1 Tim 6:21b; 2 Tim 4:22b] in each case indicates that these letters were intended to be read to the church as a whole'. **（1）**提多被譽為「處理危機的專家（crisis intervention specialist）」（Witherington 90; cf. Jeon II 2: 'an intervention-specialist'）；既是這樣，他需要信上所展現那種程度的遊說嗎（Genade 9: 'the level of persuasion evident in the text'）？此外（Genade 20），'Would someone like Titus need to be persuaded about Paul's authority? Or would he need to be taught about the content of legitimate teaching? The answer is obvious. Paul is addressing the church at Crete.' 作者不止一次表示，本書信的主要收信人（'primary recipients' [25]）是克里特的教會，提多只是次要的收信人（'It addresses Titus only secondarily' [27]）。不過，較準確的講法是 'the instruction is intended to strengthen the hand of the leaders [Titus and Timothy] as they pass it on. What they are to teach is given the stamp of Pauline authority'（Marshall 55）。**（2）**Fiore II 10（cf. 197）同樣談到以下的異常情況（'the anomaly'）：教牧書信含有給提摩太和提多的命令和責任，但這些命令和責任，應該是保羅把他們分別留下在以弗所和克里特打理教會之前，就已對他們交代過的。作者認為，在這方面，教牧書信與古代希羅的官式備忘錄（'official memoranda'）相似：這些備忘錄或委任憲章（'official memorandum letter or appointment charter'）不但總結了長官把下屬調派到新的崗位之前和他討論過的一切事情，並且要求把這些文件公佈。參一 5 註釋註 38 之（3）= 下面 98。**（3）**Quinn 51 說：'Paul's commission to one of his collaborators is intended to be "overheard" by the Cretan churches. The personal and the public aspects of this letter can be distinguished but not separated.' Cf. Richards 76: 'In

教導的理由；他的意圖似乎是要他們知道，惟有那些事奉上帝和耶穌基督的人，才可以服侍教會或使**上帝的選民**在信心**與認識合乎敬虔的真理**（1b 節）這事上長進。保羅似乎在書信的開首就處理和抗衡克里特信徒當中的一種傾向，就是他們傾向於接受並容忍不合格的教師（參 10～16 節）；他認為這種情況不應持續，因為教會的屬靈長進有賴教會領袖的素質。因此，他以自己作為一位獲得授權，因而有權對教會發言的上帝僕人的例子。[6] 他把自己的使徒職事置於上帝的拯救計劃的中心；藉著申明他有使徒的權柄去指導提多，他證實提多的職事有他（直接）和上帝（間接）的授權。[7]

到此為止，在短短三節的篇幅裏已經四次提到**上帝**（1a、1b、2b、3b 節；本小段的最後一次是在 4b 節：**父上帝**與 1a 節的**上帝**前後呼應），[8] 一起強調了一些重要的事實：(**i**)保羅是**上帝的僕人**（1a 節），他的職事的對象是**上帝的選民**（1b 節）；(**ii**)上帝是**無謊言的上帝**（2b 節），因此這樣的一位上帝的**應許**是可靠的，那宣告祂已經實現了祂的應許的**道**，已藉著福音的宣講**顯明**了（3a 節）；[9]（**iii**）上帝是救主（3b

---

this Letter Paul and Titus <u>converse</u> in public, expecting others to "overhear" the nature of the mission with which both sender and recipient have been entrusted.' See also Marshall 12 (cf. 52): '[the three letters] are implicitly overheard by the Christian believers associated wit the named recipients'. 可是，如果此信是由提多向教會宣讀的，* 則教會「無意中聽到」保羅對提多的差派這講法並不適合。在信上只有寫信人對提多說話，並無提多的回應，因而此信也不能稱為二人的「交談」。（*Richards 95: 'this correspondence is . . . the Official [*sic*] communication in which a superior authorizes a sub-ordinate for work entrusted to him or her. As an Official Letter it is necessarily public.'）

6 Genade 15-16. See also Kelly 228: 'he is tacitly glancing at the teaching of the Cretan errorists, which cannot claim equivalent authority'; Marshall 115: 'in view of the challenge posed by heresy, the stress [in 3b] is . . . on his *consequent authority* [by virtue of the divine command] and the indispensable role of the (in this context, "his") apostolic preaching ministry in the salvation plan of God (hence the emphasis on ἐν κηρύγματι).'

7 Cf. Towner III 665（唐 967）。

8 原文從 θεός（1a、1b 節）進到 ὁ ἀψευδὴς θεός（2b 節）到 ὁ σωτῆρ ἡμῶν θεός（3b 節），再回到 θεὸς πατήρ（4b 節）。

9 參一 2b～3a 註釋註 26 之（4）（5）= 上面 68。**應許**（2b 節）／**顯明**（3a 節）

節），祂是福音所宣講的救恩的來源。上帝和祂的角色布滿了這一小段：人沒有任何功勞，焦點都是在於上帝的品格和祂的作為。[10]

這模式實際上合併了應許／兌現和隱藏／顯明這兩種模式（Marshall 114）。

10 Cf. Genade 17-18.

1.2 收信人（一 4a）

一 **4a** 我寫信給在共同的信仰上作我真兒子的提多。

保羅在這裏對提多[1] 的稱呼，和他對提摩太的稱呼幾乎完全一樣：因信主作我真兒子的（提前一 2）。[2] 真字原文的字面意義是「婚生的、合法的」；[3] 但並無任何文獻表示提多是保羅的親生兒子，因此真字必須理解為比喻意義的「真正、真實」之意。[4] 在共同／共有的

---

1 關於提多，見導論第貳節首段（上面 23-24）。

2 二者的分別在於不同的介詞片語：κατὰ κοινὴν πίστιν（多一 4），ἐν πίστιν（提前一 2）。（**1**）前一個片語（κοινὴ πίστις）在新約僅見於此處；可堪比擬的是猶 3 節的 ἡ κοινὴ ἡμῶν σωτηρία（我們共享／所共享的救恩〔思高、當代、新譯／新普〕）。（**2**）Knight II 9 認為，共同的一字（κοινή）沒有在提前一 2 出現而只在本節出現，可能是由於保羅覺得有需要提醒提多、克里特的眾教會，以及那些奉割禮的（一 10）假教師，沒受割禮的希臘人提多和希伯來人所生的希伯來人（腓三 5）保羅 'share the same faith'.（**3**）名詞 **τέκνον** 在下文再出現一次（一 6），保羅書信另外 37 次（新約全部 99 次），其中五次以呼格的形式出現（加四 19：我的孩子們哪；弗六 1／西三 20：作兒女的／你們作兒女的；提前一 18／提後二 1：我兒提摩太啊／我兒啊）；常見的組合是上帝的兒女（羅八 16、21，九 8b；腓二 15）；* 比喻性用法包括應許的兒女（羅九 8c；加四 28〔呂譯；參《加》1094-95〕）、耶路撒冷……的兒女（加四 25〔參《加》1081-83〕）、可怒的兒女（弗二 3，新譯），和光明的子女（五 8）。詳見 MGM 1019*a*-20*b* (s.v.); BDAG 994*a*-95*a* (s.v.);《新希》326*a*（s.v.）。 *順帶一提，加三 26 的上帝的兒女原文作上帝的兒子（呂譯、新和），所用的 υἱός [*hyios*] 一字和 τέκνον 被保羅不加鑑別地使用於羅八 14～21（參《羅》2.641-42）。參啟十二 5：婦人生了一個男孩子（υἱόν）……她的孩子（τέκνον）被提到上帝……那裏去。

3 BDAG 202*a* (s.v. γνήσιος, 1): 'lit. of children *born in wedlock, legitimate*'. Cf. NEB, REB: 'my true-born son'.

4 Collins 316. See also BDAG 202*a-b* (s.v. 1): '***true*** . . . fig., of affective relationship, esp. as developed through sharing of value or experiences'; Richards 75: 'Paul claims Titus as his . . . true child'.（**1**）形容詞 **γνήσιος** 在保羅書信僅再出現兩次（在新約不再出現），分別指一位不具名的、保羅稱為忠誠的同負一軛的人（腓四 3〔新普頁邊註〕；參《腓》426-27），以及哥林多人愛心的真誠（林後八 8；冠詞 + 形容詞〔τὸ . . . γνήσιον〕= 名詞）。（**2**）此字在 LXX 僅出現兩次：一次指「真誠的」行為（偽經《馬加比三書》3.19〔RSV, NRSV: 'sincere'〕）；在另一次（次經《便西拉智訓》7.18），「朋友（φίλον）」與「真正的兄弟（ἀδελφὸν γνήσιον）」構成同義平

信仰上（同新譯／呂譯）[5] 意即在我們共同的信仰上（現修），[6]「在我們所分享的信仰上」。[7]（一）費歌頓將真兒子解釋為提多繼續了保羅的事工。[8] 不少釋經者認為，（二）提多是由保羅帶領歸主的，因而

行（思高《德訓篇》7.20 作「你最親愛的兄弟」）。

5 See also RSV, NAU, ESV: 'in a common faith'; 思高：在共同的信仰裏。(**1**) Collins 317 認為這裏的意思是，'Titus has been engendered by Paul according to the standard of the common faith (see 2 Tim. 2:2).' (**2**) Hendriksen 343 則把 πίστις 理解為主觀意義的「信心」。Similarly, Marshall 215: '"faith" (in Christ) is the sphere or basis of the relationship between Christians'. Mounce 382 似乎贊同這種看法：'it has the usual Pauline sense of a believing response that binds Paul the Jew and Titus the Gentile together, a significant point in light of the Jewish nature of the heresy being taught in Crete (cf. 1:10, 14 . . .).' 參上面註 1 之（2）。不過，不見得那些假教師有強調外邦信徒必須受割禮；參一 10 註釋末段之（一）（二）= 下面 162-64。

6 See also NIV, TNIV, NIV2011, NKJV: 'in our common faith'; 新普：在我們同一〔的〕信仰裏。形容詞 **κοινός** 在保羅書信僅再出現於羅十四 14，三次的意思都是禮儀上的不潔淨（參《羅》4.419-23）。此字在新約另外出現十次（即全部十四次），分別指不潔淨的手（可七 2、5）、不潔淨的人（啟二十一 27）、俗物（新譯：徒十 14，十一 8〔與不潔的東西平行〕；來十 29）；上帝指示彼得，不可把任何人當作<u>凡俗</u>（徒十 28，呂譯、新譯）；早期的信徒凡物<u>共</u>有（徒二 44，呂譯）、凡物<u>共</u>享（徒四 32，新普）；以及我們<u>同享</u>的救恩（猶 3 節）。See BDAG 551*b*-52*a* (s.v.);《新希》188*b*（s.v.）。

7 See NRSV; Kelly 225, 228 / NJB, NLT: 'in the faith we share / that we share'; LN §57.9: 'in the faith that we have in common'; Hanson III 171: 'either "common to both of us" or "common to all (orthodox) Christians".'（Hanson I 107 曾解釋為 'the faith common to Jews and Gentiles'. See also Köstenberger 605*b*: 'The expression "our common faith" may indicate unity between Paul the Jew and Titus the Gentile (so Barrett, 170).' Mounce ['Titus' 105] 的意譯也在 'my true son Titus with whom I share a common faith' 之後，加上 'even though he is Greek and I am Jewish' 這個意思。)Lock 128 以前者（'common to you, to me'）為主要，後者（'common to all Christians'）為次要的意思。F. G. Untergassmair（*EDNT* 2.302*b* [s.v. κοινός, 2]）似乎認為意思是後者，他說：'The reference to the "*common* faith" . . . corresponds to the community of Jesus.'（**1**）另一些翻譯是照着我們共信之道（新和；see also KJV: 'after the common faith'）和 'in terms of (the) common faith'（Hendriksen 339, 343）。（**2**）Quinn 25, 57, 58, 72 則翻譯為 '<u>for</u> the faith all share'（參 1b 節：'for the faith of God's elect'），即 κατὰ πίστιν 兩次皆表達目的（62）。

8 Fee 170: 'he is a legitimate child of Paul in carrying on Paul's ministry.'（但見下註末。）Similarly, Drury 1231*b*: 'Titus . . . is called "my loyal child", in other words, legitimate successor'; Goodwin 1755*a*: 'he is a "loyal child in the faith," a title that stresses his faithfulness to Paul's teaching'; Saarinen 170: 'This wording ["my loyal child in the faith"] . . . emphasizes the right succession of the apostolic faith'; Wild 894*a*: 'Titus is Paul's true <u>heir</u> because he accepts and will promote the faith proclaimed by Paul.' Cf. Van Neste 253: 真兒子這稱謂提示，提多和保羅一同參與福音事工。(**1**) Thatcher（'Matrix' 43）認為，真字表達「合法（legitimacy）」之意，尤其凸出收信人的「忠誠（loyalty）」。Cf. Taylor 63: 'loyal child'; 馮象：我忠實的孩兒。(**2**)Genade

成為保羅在信仰上(不是肉身意義上)的**真兒子**(參:門 10 節)。[9] 這種理解為猶太人「為父」的觀念所支持:如寇雷蒙所解釋的,根據拉比的教導,父親的首要責任就是兒子的「社會化」;父親必須對兒子行割禮、贖回他、教他律法、為他完婚,並教他一門手藝。人若將律法教導另一人的兒子,他就彷彿生了那個兒子;透過教導,別人的兒子成了他的兒子。保羅分享了這種「為父」的觀念,但是以福音取代律法作為生殖的媒介:他對哥林多人說**我是在基督耶穌裏用福音生了你們**(林前四 15),因他曾把福音傳給他們(林前二 1～2,十五 1～8)。

19-20 **就作我真兒子的提多**一詞作了以下三項聲稱:(**i**)**真兒子……提多**原文(Τίτῳ γνησίῳ τέκνῳ)呈現「半押韻(assonance)」現象,這現象使保羅和提多的家屬關係受到強調。(**ii**)保羅使用表示親屬關係的語言,稱呼提多為**我的真兒子**(現修),其作用是在教會面前給予尊重。作者認為這是一種修辭技巧,他稱之為 '*honorific referencing* or *classification*'. (**iii**)保羅用 'a son who stands in the service of his father' 這種講法來描寫提多在克里特的工作,這種講法使人想起忠誠和可靠的圖像,構成 'an argument of authorization based on paternal or parental validation'. 其效果就是對聽眾(包括那些不合法的教師)證實,提多是以「獲得使徒授權的代表」之身分行事的。筆者倒認為:(**i**)的聲稱欠缺說服力。同樣的現象亦見於提前一 2 的**真兒子……提摩太**原文:Τιμοθέῳ γνησίῳ τέκνῳ. 兩處的「半押韻」都是由希臘文的字尾變化規則(declension)自然地造成的。關於(**iii**),保羅對提多的授權,在 5 節才清楚地提出來。因此筆者認為,保羅以父親的身分認可提多(對父親)的服侍(留意加上底線的引句部分),這種講法可能是對**我的真兒子**一詞過度的解讀。其實,保羅之所以可以**吩咐**提多(5c 節),是由於他是**上帝的僕人**和**耶穌基督的使徒**(1a 節;so also Genade 22),多過因他是提多的「父親」。

9 See Fiore II 197; 199: 'child . . . = spiritual convert'; Dunn 862*b*; Hendriksen 343; Hiebert 428; Kelly 1; Long 257; Montague 215; Oden 5; Towner II 221, 222; Witherington 105(Timothy and Titus 'were his dearly beloved converts' [74]);Zehr 235; Brindle, 'Titus' 248, 251; Hagner, 'Titus' 546; Meade, 'Pseudonymity' 127; Strecker, 'Sound Doctrine' 578: 'Titus was converted or ordained by Paul'; 周 124;張 39、316;當代:**提多……是因為相信我所傳的福音,成為我真兒子的**。換一個講法,'The apostle is regarded as "father" of those Christians who owe their faith to his preaching'(O. Hofius, *DNTT* 1.619)。(**1**) Martin－Wu('Galatians' 274*a*)認為,提多可能住在安提阿,通過保羅在該地的福音工作而成為基督徒。(**2**) Quinn 72 的解釋似乎合併了(二)和(一):'They [Titus and Timothy] are really his children because they have believed in and acted on the message that the apostle proclaimed'; 二人**真**是保羅的兒子,因他們參與了他的使徒工作('sharing in his apostolic work')。Similarly, Fee 3: 'Paul calls him [Titus] his "true [legitimate] son," which at least means that his ministry is a legitimate expression of Paul's; most likely it also indicates that he is Paul's convert'(後一個方括號是原來的)。

提多稱為保羅的**真兒子**，就是由於保羅曾透過傳福音將提多「社會化」，使他成為基督羣體的成員。[10] 不過，（三）解釋的關鍵可能在於隨後（原文次序）的介詞片語**在共同的信仰上**：這片語指出了就哪一方面保羅和提多的關係可比喻為親子關係；由於他們分享了同一信仰，他們就像一家人，而對年長的保羅而言，年輕的提多就像他的**真兒子**。[11] 對於收信人或聽到此信被讀出的人而言，保羅稱提多為**真兒子**的主要含意就是，提多可以代表使徒保羅。[12] 這裏的**信仰**和第 1b 節的**信從**在原文是同一個字，二者前後呼應，有助於將第 1 至 4 節連結起來。

---

10 Collins 316-17.「為父」英文原作 'paternity';「社會化」兩次英文依次原作 'socialization / socialized', 指一個人獲得自己的身分，並學到與自己的社會地位相稱的常規、價值、行為、社交技巧等。Cf. Wall 338: 'the adjective "true" . . . connotes someone whose apprenticeship is completed and whose right to assume the family's trade is proven.'

11 Marshall 133: 'The whole phrase . . . expresses that in respect of which the metaphorical [parent-child] relationship exists.' See also Banker 17, 26*a*; Arichea – Hatton 266: 'because we both believe in Christ, you are like a son to me'; Laansma 229: 'their bond consisted in their shared faith'; F. Büchsel, *TDNT* 1.727: 'Timothy [1 Tim. 1:2] and Titus are genuine sons of Paul because they have a true faith'（cf. *TDNTA* 125: 'because of their faith'）。**（1）**洛窩特則把**真兒子**意譯為 'a son whom he [Paul] knows he can trust'（Lock 124）。Cf. Murphy-O'Connor, '2 Timothy' 405: γνήσιος 在一世紀的 'dominant connotation . . . was that of authorized interpretation particularly in the sphere of religion. . . . The effect of the address is to identify Timothy and Titus as teachers in whom the communities may put their trust.' **（2）** Thurston（'Titus' 171）認為**真兒子**暗示 'there might be "false children" outside this faith'.

12 Towner III 674（唐 981）。Cf. Jeon I 30: 'The figurative application to Titus calls the audience to recognize Titus as Paul's legitimate representative'; Jeon II 9: 'What is subtly implied is that Titus . . . is Paul's true representative.' 唐書禮進一步認為，在這種屬靈的家庭關係中，提多有責任像忠心的兒子服事父親一樣服事保羅；這種含意為即將提到的「提多在克里特的工作」（和修一 5 前的標題）鋪路（Towner III 675〔唐 982〕）。有趣的是，在腓二 22 保羅說提摩太**與我為了福音一同服事，待我像兒子待父親一樣**（ὡς πατρὶ τέκνον σὺν ἐμοὶ ἐδούλευσεν εἰς τὸ εὐαγγέλιον），原文的結構似乎提示，保羅以「就如兒子（服事）父親」開始，但是他並沒有以「他為了福音服事我」完成句子，而是改為「他和我……一同服事」（參《腓》307-8）。

1.3 問安語（一 4b）

一 4b 願恩惠、平安從父上帝和我們的救主基督耶穌歸給你！

原文並無你字（提前一 2 和提後一 2 也沒有）。昆謝隆認為，若在這裏提到祝福的領受者，便得使用單數的「你」字，而這會使人獲得這樣的印象，即此信只是兩個人之間的個人通信，但是信末的祝福（三 15c：願恩惠與你們眾人同在〔提前六 21b 及提後四 22b 缺「眾人」〕）提示，此信其實是要讓全體信眾聽到的；因此省略祝福的領受者較為合宜，而欠少「你」字亦不會使問安語的意思有所改變。[1] 與提摩太前後書的問安語相比（願恩惠、憐憫、平安〔提前一 2；提後一 2〕）相比，這裏缺少了憐憫一字。[2] 辛普遜猜想，這是由於使徒保羅細緻優雅的分辨力，使他的問安語「因人而異」：比起提摩太，提多是身心都較為強壯的。[3] 但是馬歇爾認為，很難看出這裏缺少了憐

---

1 Quinn 74.

2 （1）有古卷在 χάρις（恩惠）和 εἰρήνη（平安）之間有 ἔλεος（憐憫）一字；這似乎是有抄寫員根據提前一 2 和提後一 2 而把它加進經文裏的結果（*TextC* 584; Fairbairn 260）。（2）Quinn 75 聲稱：'The phrase [χάρις καὶ εἰρήνη] is practically a hendiadys, a single reality designated by terms in a bound phrase.' 按哈理斯的解釋，'the καί used in hendiadys points to a relation, not to an identity'，意即在「重言法」裏，由「和」字連起來的兩個意思不是相同的，而是主從關係，或是先主後從（例如西二 5 的 χαίρων καὶ βλέπων = 'rejoicing to see'），或是先從後主（同上，翻譯為 'viewing with joy'）（Harris, *Colossians* 300）。按這種解釋，若以「恩惠和平安」（χάρις καὶ εἰρήνη）為「重言法」，所得出的意思就是（甲）「來自恩典（從）的平安（主）」或（乙）「平安（從）的恩典（主）= the grace of peace」。鑑於信末祝福只提到恩惠（三 15c〔見正文上文〕），而且恩惠在信上再出現兩次（二 11，三 7），且都是在重要的神學論述中，因此（乙）比（甲）可取。不過，「恩惠和平安」根本不必視為重言法，將兩個名詞分開來解釋是較自然的做法。參二 13 註釋註 34 之（2）= 下面 312。

3 Simpson 96; 'Titus represents a robuster type of character than his Ephesian colleague.'

憫一字的任何確切理由。[4] 恩惠是上帝對不配得的人所施予的仁慈；平安包括與上帝和好的平安。在舊約，以色列人獲得「平安」的方法是藉著獻祭；對保羅而言，來自上帝的平安是透過基督獻己為祭的工作而臨到信徒的。舊約的祭牲只能成就暫時和局部的平安，但基督的祭獻成就了完全的平安[5]（參：弗二 14：他自己是我們的和平）。

恩惠和平安的共同來源是父上帝和我們的救主基督耶穌。在其餘的兩卷教牧書信，這來源是父上帝和我們的主基督耶穌（提前一 2；提後一 2）。在另八卷保羅書信，這來源是我們的父上帝和主耶穌基督（羅一 7；林前一 3〔並〕；林後一 2；加一 3；弗一 2；腓一 2；帖後一 2；[6] 門 13 節）。帖撒羅尼迦前書一章 1b 節沒有指明恩惠、平安的來源；不過，該節上文已把收信人描寫為在父上帝和主耶穌基督裏的教會（1a 節），故此問安語所提及的恩惠、平安可自然地理解為從父上帝和主耶穌基督臨到他們。[7] 歌羅西書的卷首問安則只提到我們的父上帝為恩惠、平安的來源，沒有包括「主耶穌基督」（西一 2b）；這獨特的現象似乎未有令人滿意的解釋。[8]

回到提多書本節，(一) 洛窩特認為也許應從我們的救主補充我們的來形容父上帝，從而得出「我們的父上帝」之意；若不是這樣，

---

4 Marshall 134. Collins（'Theology' 66 n.60）認為，'That "mercy" is found in 1 Tim 1,2 and 2 Tim 1,2, as the central element in a triad, might be cited as a potential argument for the view that the epistle to Titus is the earliest of the Pastoral Epistles.'

5 Beale, *Theology* 546, with reference to Stanley E. Porter, 'Peace', *NDBT* 682-83.「祭獻」一詞取自思高聖經（參〔例如〕來十章的標題〔「舊約的祭獻不能赦罪」〕，十 2、3、10）。相對於我們所熟悉的「獻祭」，「祭獻」這詞較不常見，但採用此詞的好處是，它使我們可方便地表達以下的區別：「獻（祭）」是動詞，「祭獻」是名詞，後者可指獻祭的行動，亦可指所獻之祭（《羅》1.502 註 2）。

6 如果該節的 ἡμῶν 是原來的（see *TextC* 567）。

7 以上十一卷書信的證據，有力地否定馬特羅對多一 4 的解釋（Martin, 'Titus' 15）：他聲稱和字在這裏具解釋作用（καί = 'namely'），父上帝就是我們的救主基督耶穌。「父上帝」是指 'the father-god, who could be Zeus, Osirus, or any number of deities'; 提多書的作者隨即解釋，這位 'father-god' 就是基督徒所信奉的神——我們的救主基督耶穌。

8 參《西‧門》109 連註 3。

父上帝可視為最廣義的用法，指上帝是萬人之父，**各家都是從他得名的**（弗三 15）。[9] 筆者倒認為，即使不補充**我們的**，這裏的**父**字仍然不是指萬人的父，也不是指耶穌基督的父，而是指信徒的父；因為**父上帝**和**我們的救主耶穌基督**是平行的；就如**我們的救主**表示基督與信徒的關係，照樣，**父**也是表示上帝與信徒的關係。[10]（二）本節以**我們的救主基督耶穌**[11] 代替較常見的**主耶穌基督**，也許是由於前者在這裏拾起上一節**我們的救主**（3b 節，指**上帝**）一詞，將**我們的救主**應用到基督身上；[12] 如此，保羅一方面將基督與上帝視為同等（如在 1a

---

9 Lock 128.

10 按筆者的理解，弗三 15 並不是說上帝是 'Father of all'（Lock 128），而是說「上帝的整個家庭都是**從他得名**，是祂所認識及承認為祂的兒女的」（詳見《弗》468-72）。

11 這稱號（亦見於提後一 10）在下文再出現兩次（二 13，三 6），三次（皆為所有格）的字序略有分別：<u>Χριστοῦ</u> Ἰησοῦ / <u>Ἰησοῦ</u> Χριστοῦ τοῦ σωτῆρος ἡμῶν（一 4／三 6），σωτῆρος ἡμῶν <u>Ἰησοῦ</u> Χριστου（二 13）。一 1 的次序也是 <u>Ἰησοῦ</u> Χριστοῦ. 如此，這稱號在本書四居其三的次序是**耶穌基督**。原因不詳（Fee, *Christology* 438 n.67 [continued]: 'For reasons not at all clear'）。**（1）**Quinn 52 認為：'The preference for the order "Jesus Christ" may signal a Jewish-Christian emphasis', 因希伯來書三次使用**耶穌基督**（來十 10，十三 8、21）這次序，相反的次序則一次也沒有。**（2）** Belleville（'Christology' 322; 'Piety' 226）則認為，**耶穌基督**的意思是 'Jesus the "Anointed One" or "Messiah"', **基督耶穌**的意思則為 'Christ the Saving One'. 但一 4 和三 6 的平行（**我們的救主基督耶穌**，**我們的救主耶穌基督**）使這種區別成疑；按此區別，前一個片語的意思豈不變成有點累贅的 'Christ the Saving One, our Saviour'？**（3）**提前後的情況則與提多書剛好相反：**基督耶穌**是常規（24 次：提前一 1a、1b、2、12、14、15、16，二 5，三 13，四 6，五 21，六 13；提後一 1a、1b、2、9、10、13，二 1、3、10，三 12、15，四 1），**耶穌基督**只出現三次（提前六 3、14；提後二 8）。Quinn 53 再次認為，也許這表示提前後的聽眾有別於提多書，從 'predominantly Jewish-Christian congregations' 變為 'Pauline congregations containing significant numbers of converts from paganism.'

12 兩個片語在原文呈現交叉配置模式：

一 3b [A] τοῦ σωτῆρος ἡμῶν [B] θεοῦ
一 4b [B'] Χριστοῦ Ἰησοῦ [A'] τοῦ σωτῆρος ἡμῶν

相同的現象（除了 [B'] 的字序）亦見於三 4、6；參三 6 註釋註 20（下面 401）。二 10（τοῦ σωτῆρος ἡμῶν θεοῦ）和二 13（σωτῆρος ἡμῶν Ἰησοῦ Χριστου）則呈現平行模式。在新約他處，只有路加福音將 σωτήρ（救主）一字同時用於上帝（一 47）和基督（二 11）身上（Wieland 185 n.10）。**（1）**事實上，教牧書信一個特色就是將上帝的拯救行動和基督的拯救行動明顯地平排並列；上帝是救恩的啟創者，基督則是救恩的傳遞者。**我們的救主上帝**（一 3，二 10，三 4〔後二節欠**的**〕；提前

節），[13] 同時強調二者對所有信徒（尤其是收信人）的意義——是他們的**救主**。[14] 上帝是**我們的救主**（一 3），祂的「執行代理」是基督耶

一 1，二 3）**是人人的救主**（提前四 10），**他願意人人得救，並得以認識真理**（提前二 4）；上帝的願望藉著耶穌而成就——**基督耶穌到世上來〔就〕是要拯救罪人**（提前一 15）。See Belleville, 'Christology' 322. See also A. B. Luter, Jr., *DPL* 869*a* =《辭典》1245*a*. 如 Marshall 291-92 所指出的，在提前和提多書，'God is primarily a Saviour. Consequently, the concept of Jesus as Saviour is directly related to this dominant theme. Salvation is the work of God through Jesus.' 由此看來，Scott 152 的聲稱很難成立：他認為**救主**這稱謂用於上帝時只有 'a God who helps and delivers' 的意思，用於基督時才有更明確的人類拯救者之意。(**2**) Genade 19, 127 將一 3b 的片語（見本註開首）分拆為 'A－τοῦ σωτῆρος' 和 'B－<u>ἡμῶν</u> θεοῦ'. 可是，將 ἡμῶν 撥入 B 這做法不可取，因（i）它破壞了原文呈現的完全對應（complete symmetry）：[A] 和 [A'] 是完全一樣的，[B] 和 [B'] 都沒有所有格代名詞作為修飾語；（ii）從造句法的角度看，3b 節的 ἡμῶν 顯然是屬於 [A]（**我們的救主**）而非屬於 [B]（我們的上帝）的。

13 (**1**) Genade 19 認為，保羅在本段的首尾都強調基督與上帝同等，也許是為要預先制止有關基督之神性的錯誤看法：那些假教師所傳的道理是否跟一種不完全或妥協的基督論有關聯呢？(**2**) Tollefson（'Titus' 148*b*）則認為，**救主上帝**和**救主基督**這樣交換使用，提示舊約羣體（參：賽四十三 3、11，四十五 15、21，六十 16；何十三 4）和新約羣體之間的連貫性。「救主上帝」是 LXX 常見的組合：(**i**)「我的上帝、我的救主」（θεός μου καὶ σωτήρ μου: 詩六十一 3〔譯本六十二 2〕，六十一 7〔六十二 6〕；ὁ θεός μου σωτήρ μου: 賽十二 2）；(**ii**)「上帝我的救主」（ὁ θεὸς ὁ σωτήρ μου: 詩二十四〔二十五〕5，二十六〔二十七〕9；彌七 7；哈三 18）；(**iii**)「上帝你的救主」（ὁ θεὸς ὁ σωτήρ σου: 賽十七 10）；(**iv**)「上帝他的救主」（θεὸς σωτήρ αὐτοῦ: 申三十二 15；詩二十三〔二十四〕5）；(**v**)「上帝我們的救主」（ὁ θεὸς ὁ σωτὴρ ἡμῶν: 詩六十四 6〔六十五 5〕，七十八〔七十九〕9，九十四〔九十五〕1）；(**vi**)「以色列的上帝、救主」（ὁ θεὸς τοῦ Ισραηλ σωτήρ: 賽四十五 15）。(**3**) Hanson III 171 卻認為，教牧書信的作者這樣任意地（'indiscriminately'）使用**救主**一詞，暗示 'a rather muddled soteriology on [his] part'! Similarly, Hanson I 107: 'surely the mark of a not very clear mind'! 其實，這種做法是刻意的：'The repetition of the same significant word in the same context must be to enforce an intentional association. God and Christ are closely related in bringing salvation to people'（Mounce cxxxv, cf. 382）。(**4**) 綜合上面註 12 和一 3b 註釋註 3 之（2）= 上面 73，便得出「救主（σωτήρ）一字在教牧書信的用法」以下的圖畫：在提前，這稱號出現三次，皆指上帝（一 1，二 3，四 10）；在提後只出現一次，指基督（一 10）；在提多書則出現六次，指上帝（一 3，二 10，三 4）和指基督（一 4，二 13，三 6）的各半。參二 13 註釋註 39 及所屬正文（下面 313-14）。'This repetitive but diverse usage suggests that the title is a key element of the soteriology, theology, and Christology of the Pastoral Epistles'（Collins 308）。

14 See Classen, 'Titus' 432, 'Epistle to Titus' 51. 提多書沒有稱耶穌基督為「主」。（Witherington 104 聲稱，'the typical Pauline language of Jesus as "Lord" is omitted in Titus <u>and elsewhere in the Pastorals</u>.' 這話不確；見提前一 2、12，六 3、14；提後一 2。）在其餘的十二卷保羅書信的卷首問安中，八卷皆以 καὶ κυρίου Ἰησοῦ

穌我們的救主；是透過基督耶穌，上帝救恩的福澤（恩惠、平安）臨到祂的子民。[15]（三）願……歸給這翻譯正確地假定，原文沒有表達出來的動詞是祈願式語法的「是」字。[16] 恩惠、平安代表保羅的祝願，上帝會供給提多一切所需以便從事他的工作（恩惠），並保護他，使他在需要時得享平靜安寧（平安）。[17]

Χριστοῦ = 和／並主耶穌基督結束（羅一 7；林後一 2；加一 3；弗一 2；腓一 2；帖後一 2；門 3 節／林前一 3）。提前一 2 和提後一 2 則使用 καὶ Χριστοῦ Ἰησοῦ τοῦ κυρίου ἡμῶν = 和我們〔的〕主基督耶穌，即是改變了耶穌基督的次序，並加上了我們的。西一 2 無此片語，只提到我們的父上帝；帖前一 1 只作願恩惠、平安歸給你們！See Quinn 59.

15 Collin 318.（「執行代理」英文原作 'executive agent'.）See also Fee, *Christology* 440: '"God our Savior" refers to the ultimate source of salvation and "Jesus Christ our Savior" refers to the effective means of salvation'; Mounce cxxxv: 'God and Christ are closely related in bringing salvation to people'. 亦參張 317。(1) 稱基督為救主，對當時的羅馬皇帝自稱為「救主」的宣告，是「一個顛覆性打擊」(唐 984〔Towner III 676〕)。Cf. Wall 339: 'The subtext of Paul's salutation . . . is that any claim for Caesar's kingdom without end, characterized by peace and grace, is a fiction.' (2) 一 3b 稱上帝為我們的救主，一 4b 稱基督為我們的救主；Witherington 103 認為這是 'more a Lukan way of speaking' than 'a Pauline way of speaking': 在路一 47，馬利亞稱上帝為我的救主；在二 11，天使宣告今天在大衛的城裏，為你們生了救主，就是主基督。

16 εἴη, optative. 參《西・門》111 連註 9、10；《腓》77；《羅》1.201。Jeon I 31 則聲稱，'the absence of a verb in the greeting <u>allows it to be heard</u> in all three temporal dimensions: it affirms that the audience have received already [in the past] "grace and peace" when they first heard the gospel; it indicates that the letter intends to give the audience a renewed experience [in the present] of this "grace and peace" as they listen presently [= in the present] to the letter; and it prays that after, and as a result of, listening to the letter the audience may continue [in the future] to experience and grow in "grace and peace."' 這解釋是作者的「聽眾回應（audience response）」（見其書的分題）釋經法的例子。

17 Towner III 675(唐 983)。Cf. Oden 22: 'The apostolic blessing was . . . for . . . grace that would enable them [Titus, and Timothy] to continue their ministry . . . and for inward peace through whatever troubles they might face.'

乙部

書信本體

（一5～三11）

貳 長老的設立・他們的職責（一5～9）

5a 我從前把你留在克里特，

5b 是要你將那沒有辦完的事都辦妥，又……在各城設立長老。

5c 照我所吩咐你的，

6a 若有無可指責的人，只作一個婦人的丈夫，

6b 兒女也是信主的，沒有人告他們放蕩，不受約束，就可以設立。

7a 監督既然是上帝的管家，必須無可指責、

7b 不自負、不暴躁、不酗酒、不好鬥、

不貪財；

8 卻要樂意接待外人、好善、克己、正直、聖潔、節制，

9a 堅守合乎教義的可靠之道，

9b 就能將健全的教導勸勉人，

9c 又能駁倒爭辯的人。

2.1 提多在島上的責任（一5～6）

一 **5a** 我從前把你留在克里特，

5b 是要[1] 你將那沒有辦完的事都辦妥，

---

1 第 5 節以 Τούτου χάριν（'For this cause/reason': KJV / NKJV, NAU）開始，τούτου 由 5b 節的 ἵνα-clause 解釋，因此是 cataphoric/kataphoric 用法（Clark, 'Structure' 106 / Jeon I 36 n.4; Towner III 678 n.4〔唐 989 註 3 改為較常見的 'cataphoric'〕; see also Hendriksen 345: 'anticipative τούτου χάριν followed by ἵνα, as in Eph. 3:1, 14-16'〔但 Τούτου χάριν 在弗三 1、14 並非指向下文，而是指向上文；參《弗》

又⋯⋯在各城設立長老。

5c 照我所吩咐你的，

緊隨著卷首問安之後，這裏並無保羅書信常見的感恩項目，而是立即進入作者要收信人注意的事情（如在提前一 3；參：加一 6）。[2] 從前宜改為「之前」，表示「此時提多仍在克里特，而非已經離開。」[3] 留字的意思顯然不是「意外地遺留」，而是有目的的「把（某人）留在」（如在提後四 13、20）。[4] 除了本節，並無任何其他經文記載保羅曾到訪克里特，更遑論在該地建立了教會。除了本節，**克里特**在新約僅

403，465〕）。參較一 13a 的 αὕτη（下面 179 註 2）。（**1**）Ngewa 337 則認為 Τούτου χάριν 回望 4 節的**在共同的信仰上作我真兒子**：'It was because Titus was spiritually ready that Paul could assign him this task in Crete.'（**2**）介系詞 **χάριν** 在保羅書信另外出現三次（一 11；加三 19；提前五 14），新約另三次（路七 47；約壹三 12；猶 16 節）：'in contrast to *koine* [*sic*] use and unlike ἕνεκα it comes after . . . we find it before [only] at 1 Jn. 3:12'（H. Conzelmann, *TDNT* 9.391）。（**3**）如 Levinsohn（'Constraints' 331）所指出，從卷首問安過渡至書信本體時，一個特色就是「無連詞（asyndeton）」現象，即是 5 節並無 γάρ, δέ, καί 或 οὖν 等字。參導論第伍節註 20（上面 36）。

2 Classen, 'Titus' 433, 'Epistle to Titus' 51. 參《加》238-40。Genade 22 認為，這裏沒有感恩項目，可能是由於並無明確的事情要感恩，而這可以用來支持學者的臆測，即克里特教會是頗為新近才成立的。

3 彭編 95*a*。（**1**）原文並無「從前」或「之前」，因此，好些中英譯本只作**我留你在克里特**（思高），**我把你留在克里特島／克里特**（現修／新普）或 'I left you behind / I left you in Crete'（NRSV, NJB / NKJV, RSV, NAU, NIV, TNIV, NIV2011, ESV）。（**2**）「克里特為地中海五大島嶼之一，為今日希臘所屬愛琴海諸島中最南方的一個。克里特為希臘文明的搖籃之一⋯⋯主後一世紀，克里特隸屬羅馬帝國的古利奈與克里特省*（約為今日利比亞）」（彭編 95*a*〔底線是原來的〕）。*Cf. W. S. Lasor, *ISBE* 1.845*a*: 'By the provisions of the will of Ptolemy Apion, Cyrenaica passed to the Romans in 96 B.C., to form the Senatorial Province of Cyrenaica, with Cyrene as the provincial capital.'

4 See LN §85.65; BDAG 115*b* (s.v. ἀπολείπω, 1): 'to cause or permit to remain in a place upon going away, *leave behind*';《新希》39*b*（s.v. I 1）：「留下」。除了上述的三次，這字在新約僅再出現四次（來四 6、9，十 26；猶 6 節）。（**1**）Lock 129 認為，這動詞比帖前三 1 所用的 καταλείπω（留）提示更強的 'intention' 之意；Robertson（*Pictures* 4.598）則認為，也許 ἀπολείπω 提示 'a more temporary stay' 的意思。（**2**）按優西比烏的記載，提多是克里特的第一任監督（see Aitken, 'Fragments' 168 with n.7）！

再出現四次（徒二十七 7、12、13、21）；使徒行傳第二十七章記載了保羅坐船往羅馬途中的一段驚險歷程，從這段記載可見，雖然保羅所坐的船曾貼近克里特島，但沒有在那裏停留。[5] 保羅事後的抱怨表明了這一點，他說：**諸位，你們本該聽我的話不離開克里特島，就不致遭到這樣的損失和破壞**（21 節）。因此，保羅在克里特的福音工作，是在使徒行傳記載的事（即是在保羅第一次的羅馬監禁）之後，但是在他寫提摩太後書（第二次的羅馬監禁）之前發生的。[6] 按使徒行傳

---

5 Strecker（'Sound Doctrine' 579）因此斷言，'Therefore, despite Titus 1:5, there were probably no churches founded by Paul on Crete.' Baugh 499*a-b* 卻認為，'Paul's witness in Crete while on his way to Rome the first time (Acts 27) had formed an embryonic church'.

6 Mounce lix, 385. Hanson I 109（曾）認為，'there was plenty of time for Paul to have visited the island in between the two Roman captivities.' 按這種理解，保羅上訴凱撒成功（參：徒二十六 32），從第一次羅馬監禁獲釋後，就與提多和提摩太二人前往克里特島，在該處建立教會。然後，他把提多留在克里特（多一 5），自己帶著提摩太前往以弗所，發現該處的教會領袖受到異端影響而偏離了福音真道。他把提摩太留在以弗所去修補所造成的損害（提前一 3），自己則繼續前往馬其頓，提摩太前書和提多書就是寫於該處的。其後他到了尼哥坡里（多三 12）、哥林多（提後四 20）、特羅亞（提後四 13）和米利都（提後四 20）。最後他再次被囚禁於羅馬（提後一 16～17），並且深信這次必會被定罪，故此亟欲提摩太來到自己身邊（提後四 6～8、16～18、21）。So Thielman, 'Old Convictions' 230. 更詳細的背景重構見 Fee 3-5; Knight II 9-10; Witherington 65-68.
(1) Johnson I 112 認為，**把你留在克里特**不必表示保羅曾經身處克里特；其意思較可能是 'I left you in that position . . . .' Marshall 150 也認為，'it is possible that the meaning intended here is closer to "dispatched", "deployed" or "assigned"'（endorsed by Pietersen 141 n.10; 但馬歇爾早前認為，提多被保羅**留在克里特** 'means that Paul was also there with him and departed leaving him in charge' [67]）。Cf. Porter, 'Implications' 107-8: 'Titus 1:5 may not be saying that Paul actually left Titus there but left him to his task, Paul being elsewhere'（cf. idem, 'Chronology' 68）。See also Towner III 40: 'better [than "left"], "assigned"'（唐 58：「譯為『指派』較好」）; 678: '"dispatch" or "assign"〔唐 989：「『差遣』或『指派』」〕. . . may be the more important nuance here'; Quinn 25, 83: 'I let you remain on Crete'.（不過，昆謝隆明言，'the second-person address underlines a particular, historical coworker who continued what had begun <u>with the apostle present</u>'; 這就是說，昆氏的翻譯不等於他認為保羅未曾身處克里特。）可是，原文動詞（ἀπολείπω）在提後四章兩次的意思都顯然是「留下」（見上面註 4 所屬正文），而文理整體亦暗示保羅曾經到過克里特（Fee 176），三 15 的問安亦支持這假設（Laansma 231）。**(2)** Krause I 444*a* 則聲稱，'Crete likely <u>does not appear in the letter as a genuine place name</u>, but rather as a symbolic reference to the difficulty of administering the church in different contexts.' 但是 Johnson II 212 指出，'it seems . . . unlikely that a later pseudepigrapher, with the undisputed letters and Acts available to

的記載，昔日在耶路撒冷聽到彼得在五旬節講道的人當中，有**克里特人**（徒二 11）。我們不能確定他們將五旬節事件的消息帶回克里特的會堂。[7] 不過，也許保羅和提多在克里特開始他們的福音工作時，當地已經有一些基督徒，雛型的教會已經存在；[8] 但是保羅和提多把福音傳到島上更多的市鎮，以致保羅離開克里特之前，吩咐提多要在**各城**設立長老。

克里特的道德頹廢在古代是眾所周知的事。[9] 提多的任務包括兩方面：籠統地說，是要（甲）**將那沒有辦完的事都辦妥**（5b 節上）；更明確地，是要（乙）**在各城設立長老**（5b 節下～5c 節）。[10] 有釋

---

him, would have picked such an unlikely location for the posting of Paul's delegate.' See also Witherington 86: 'Of the three Pastoral Epistles, it [Titus] is in some ways the letter least likely to be a pseudepigraphon, for who would invent a missionary tour by Paul to Crete!'

7 Fee 172.

8 亦參一 7 註釋註 6 之（2）= 下面 122。**(1)** Marshall 193 n.106 (continued) 認為：'On the strength of Acts 2.11 it seems likely that some Jews had become Christians.' See also Mounce 386: 'it is perhaps because of them [the Cretans mentioned in Acts 2:11] that the gospel initially spread back to Crete'; lix: 'it is possible [that] Paul found a church in Crete when he arrived'; Spencer 10: 'most likely some Jews returned to it [Crete] from Jerusalem after Pentecost to live as disciples of the Messiah Jesus.' 侯嘉文 147 同樣認為，「革哩底〔和合；新和、和修：克里特〕教會可能是較早期的教會，由一小撮早期基督徒核心分子〔參：徒二 11〕建立」。這卻與「提多書的教導〔沒有提出提前三 6、7 的要求：**剛信主的，不可作監督……監督也必須在教外有好名聲**〕適合剛成立的宣教工場」(150) 這見解相違背。**(2)** Perkins 1443*a* 則認為，'Like other churches on busy trade routes, those on Crete must have been founded by Christians who traveled the shipping routes, probably as part of a growing Jewish community on the island.' **(3)** 無論如何，'It would be going beyond the evidence to assert that Paul and Titus founded the church in Crete'（Harrison, *INT* 349）。See also Porter, 'Chronology' 68 n.8: 'I do not believe that it is necessary . . . that Paul was the founder of the church or churches in Crete, only that there were churches in Crete to which Titus was sent.'

9 Van Neste, 'Message' 18*b*-19*a*.

10 按 Smith（'Structure' 104-5）的結構分析，這兩點就是書信本體（一 5～三 11）要討論的兩個主要題目，同時將書信本體分為兩個（不平均的）主要段落，這兩個段落按相反的次序討論那兩個題目，因而呈現交叉配置模式，如下：

（A）建立秩序（一 5b 上）＼　　／（B）設立長老（一 5b 下～5c）
×
（B'）設立長老（一 6～9）／　　＼（A'）建立秩序（一 10～三 11）

經者認為，（乙）解釋了（甲），**那沒有辦完的事**就是**在各城設立長老**。[11] 不過，**又**字較可能表明（甲）和（乙）是兩項分開的工作；信上只有四節（一 6～9）是關乎設立長老的，大部分都是論及其他的事情。[12] **（甲）辦妥**原文動詞在整本希臘文聖經只出現這一次。[13] 它的意思似乎不僅是**處理**（現修）、[14] **辦妥**[15] 或**完成**（當代、新普），[16] 而是包含了「整理＝組織起來」、[17] **整頓**（思高）、

（作者解釋，「建立秩序」是指完成工作〔參下面註 16〕，即是讓教會在健全的教義上建立起來，以及防止假教師的威脅。）按這種理解，這模式的重點便放在外面的兩項（A, A'），但交叉配置模式通常是把重點放在中間兩項的；參一 9 註釋註 59（下面 152）。亦參導論第伍節註 2（上面 31）。

11 Hendriksen 344: καί = 'namely'（345 作 '*namely* (κατά here used in that sense)'; κατά 顯然是 καί 之誤）; cf. Jeon I 37: 'The conjunction και, [*sic*] is epexegetic, expressing "particularly."' 這情況有點像徒十四 21～23：保羅和巴拿巴不是在他們首次到訪路司得、以哥念、安提阿等地建立教會時就選立長老，而是在他們回程時才這樣做；這可能提示克里特教會早前的組織是非正式的，但由於假教師的出現，較正式的程序就成為必須的（Marshall 181）。

12 Smith, 'Structure' 105. 即使把 5 節計算在內，* 設立長老的篇幅也只是 'five out of forty-six verses'（Mounce lxi）。*Hagner（'Titus' 553 [cf. 547]）就認為，'This [the appointing of elders] is the first thing that must be "set in order"'.

13 ἐπιδιορθόω. Wieland（'Crete' 351）指出，此字在基督教之前的希臘文獻（'in pre-Christian Greek literature'）也十分罕見：可考的惟一一次來自克里特，'in a second-century BCE inscription from Hierapytna', 指一位區域行政人員的活動。**(1)** ἐπιδιορθόω 是個複合動詞（from ἐπί + διά + ὀρθός [Vine 3.145]）；形容詞 ὀρθός 在新約僅出現兩次，分別指保羅叫瘸腿的人**起來！兩腳站直**（徒十四 10），以及信徒**要時常走在筆直的路上**（來十二 13，現修），即是走在成直線地引到目標的路上（參《來》2.370-71）。**(2)** 沒有前置詞 ἐπί 的 διορθόω（BDAG 251*a* [s.v.]: 'set on the right path'）不見於新約聖經，但在 LXX 出現七次，其意思包括**堅立**寶座（賽十六 5），**建立**耶路撒冷（賽六十二 7），**改正**行為（耶七 3；5 節 διορθοῦντες διορθώσητε = **實在改正**），「修直」道路（舊約次經《所羅門智訓》〔思高智慧篇〕9.18）。以上六次；餘下一次見箴十五 29：'that his steps may be rightly ordered [διορθωθῇ] of God'（LXE）。

14 《輔讀》524（第一解釋）同。

15 **辦整齊**（呂譯、新和）是甚麼意思呢？大抵是「整理妥當」（《新希》125*b* [s.v. ἐπιδιορθόω]）之意。

16 See also NLT, Fee 172: 'complete'; Smith, 'Structure' 105: 'Paul and Titus began a task while they were both in Crete; Paul commissioned Titus to complete it.' Hanson III 172 接受 'complete unfinished reforms' 這意思，並認為它暗示克里特的教會已因日久而腐敗，改革正在進行。這種情況較可能在一世紀末而非保羅時代發生。可是，'that is to put far too much weight on a dubious rendering of *ta leiponta*'（Fee 176）。

17 NJB: 'organise'; KJV, NKJV, NAU / NRSV, NIV2011: 'set/put in order'; ESV: 'put . . .

「改正」[18] 之意。也許最可能的意思是「另外要改正」：[19] 保羅離開克里特時，還有尚未改正的事情，這些事務就留待提多去處理和完成。按這種理解，**那沒有辦完的事**就不僅是**尚未完成的事**（思高），[20] 而是「所欠缺的事、缺陷」。[21] 如此，提多在克里特的主要任務，就

---

into order'. Perkins 1443*a* 認為，'As a legal expression "put in order" could imply rectifying a deficient situation'（參下註之〔iii〕）。

18 參《新希》125*b*（s.v.）：「調正；修正」。亦參以下英譯和解釋：（**i**）'amend'（RSV; Johnson I 115; Karris 108; Fitzmyer, 'Ministry' 585; Winter, *Roman Wives* 145）；（**ii**）'straighten out'（NIV, TNIV; Hendriksen 344; Hiebert 429; Köstenberger 606*a*）；（**iii**）'set/put right'（*Paraphrase* 291; G. Schneider, *EDNT* 2.26*a* [s.v. ἐπιδιορθόω]; DC 132*a*; Dunn 864*a*; Knight II 288; Quinn 25; Sewakpo, 'Titus' 8 / Mounce 384, 387）；'to put to rights'（Wall 339）；'to set to rights, rectify'（Simpson 97）；'rectifying matters'（Fiore II 199）；'to set right, to correct, to put into order'（LN §62.4）；'set matters in order'（Fee, *Presence* 776）；'to set right the shortcomings of the church there'（Robinson, *Redating* 81）；'setting right again what was defective'（Vine 3.145）；（**iv**）'***set right*** . . . Simply *correct* is also prob.'（BDAG 371*a* [s.v.]）；'correct those/the matters that need to be corrected'（Banker 12*a*/30）；'It was a work of correction, of putting right, and is in the spirit of what we call "reformation"'（Ward 238）。Calvin 356 將提多視為 'ἐπανορθωτής, "Corrector"'.

19 BDAG 371*a* (s.v.): '***correct in addition*** (to what has been corrected)'. See also Fairbairn 260: 'the ἐπί . . . expresses the idea of addition' (citing Huther); MHT 2.395: 'ἐπι- = *in addition*'; Fiore II 195, 197 / 201: 'to make the additional corrections which are left / make additional corrections'.

20 參呂譯、當代、新譯、新和、現修；NIV, TNIV, NIV2011 / NRSV: 'what was left unfinished / remained to be done'; REB: 'any outstanding matters';《新希》202*b*（s.v. I 4）：「未完成的事」。（**1**）Quinn 83 / Mounce 387 都提到 ἀπέλιπον（5a 節）和 τὰ λείποντα（5b 節）的文字遊戲：'[I let you] remain . . . [the] remaining [matters]' / 'he left him (ἀπέλιπον) in Crete to deal with the remaining things (τὰ λείποντα).' See also Montague 217; Witherington 107. 動詞和分詞是同字根（λειπ-）的。（**2**）Towner III 76（唐 106）認為：'As the emphasis [in the list of leaders' qualifications] falls on elements of personal and interpersonal character (they are to be "blameless"), on private and public reputation, it becomes clear from the language used that the "unfinished" business is that of extracting this church from the clutches of Crete's immoral value system.'

21 BDAG 590*b* (s.v. λείπω, 2): '*what is lacking, the defects*'; W. Günther, H. Krienke, *DNTT* 3.253: 'defects'; RSV, Karris 108, Johnson I 115, Winter, *Roman Wives* 145: 'what was defective'; Johnson II 220, 221: 'things that are deficient'. See also KJV/NKJV: 'the things that are wanting/lacking'; G. Schneider, *EDNT* 2.347*b* (s.v.): 'what is still lacking'; Knight II 288, Quinn 78: 'the things lacking'; Johnson I 115: 'what is now lacking';《新希》202*b*（s.v. I 4）：「有欠缺的事」。如此，τὰ λείποντα ἐπιδιορθώσῃ 就不必視為「一個不一致的組合〔a dissonant combination〕：目的子句的主要動詞需要的受詞是有待改正或修訂的事物，而此處以一分詞為受詞〔the object, here formed by a participle〕……卻需要一個表示完成

是要改正缺陷＝進行改革。[22] 這是一項頗為緊急的任務，因為保羅預期提多將會離開克里特（三 12），因此提多必須確保教會在他離開之後，可以健康地繼續運作。[23]

（乙）長老一詞的舊約背景可追溯到「以色列的長老」一詞（例如：出三 18，出二十四 9；利九 1、3）。[24]「初代教會主要是從猶太會堂承襲這詞（徒十一 30，十五 2 等）」，「它主要是指地位或聲望、而非功能的一個詞語。」[25] **在各城**原文的意思是「在每一市鎮」。[26] 長

的動詞」（唐 990〔Towner III 679〕）。Cf. Jeon I 37: 'It is probable that the apostle means to reflect two aspects of Titus's work through this dissonant construction: Titus is to complete unfinished work and bring reform where necessary.'

22 按此理解，**那沒有辦完的事**就可能並不「包括 3:12-14 所提的事」（彭編 91*b*）。**(1)** Hiebert 429 認為，原文動詞的中間語態可能暗示，提多要親力親為，而不是假手於人。**(2)** 和動詞 ἐπιδιορθόω 同字根的名詞 διόρθωμα 在新約僅出現一次（徒二十四 2：**改革**）；另一個同字根的名詞 διόρθωσις 亦僅出現一次（來九 10），其意思也是**改革／革新／更新**（現修／當聖／新譯），指舊約底下的一切不足之處都獲得**改正**（呂譯）的**新次序**（參《來》2.73）。See BDAG 251*a* (s.v.);《新希》85*b*（s.v.）。這支持正文的解釋。**(3)** 按威瑟靈頓的理解，提多 '[was] entrusted with the important charge of reviving a deteriorating situation on Crete in the mid-60s A.D.'（Witherington 90）。從另一角度看，'Titus is left there to get the fledgling church properly ordered and organized. It is formation for the first time, not later reformation, that is being referred to here'（107）。但他稍後（112）又認同昆謝隆的看法：'The Pauline paraenetic intervention on the Cretan scene is for the reformation of an existing body of believers, not for the conversion and formation of a new church from the pagans. This Pauline reform turns first to prospective leaders and their teaching, then to conduct of all classes of Christians'（Quinn 83）。然則提多在克里特的工作之性質是 'formation' 抑是 'reformation' 呢？也許答案是，兩者都是，視乎著眼點在哪裏：設立長老屬 formation; 教導信徒、塑造他們的品格與行為屬 formation（formation of Christian character）and reformation（correction of pagan conduct）。**(4)** Tollefson 則認為，提多書描寫了 'the religious revitalization process among the Cretan believers engaged in the task of perpetuating their faith in a hostile environment'（'Titus' 146*b*）。他從本書看出「宗教更新運動」的六個階段，如下：（**i**）'Mazeway Reformation Phase: Titus 1:1-3'（147*b*）；（**ii**）'Communication Phase: Titus 1:4'（148*b*）；（**iii**）'Organization Phase: Titus 1:5-9'（149*b*）；（**iv**）'Adaptation Phase: Titus 1:10-16'（150*b*）；（**v**）'Cultural Transformation Phase: Titus 2:1-3:7'（153*a*）；（**vi**）'Routinization Phase: Titus 3:8-15'（155*a*）。這些階段的名稱之解釋見 146*a*.

23 Marshall 145.

24 這詞在 LXX 依次為 ἡ γερουσία Ισραηλ（主格）、τῆς γερουσίας（所有格）、τὴν γερουσίαν Ισραηλ（直接受格），和 τῇ γερουσίᾳ Ισραηλ（間接受格）。

25 依次見：唐 991（Towner III 680），唐 346（Towner III 245）。

26 κατὰ πόλιν = 'in every city' (KJV, NKJV, NAU, *Paraphrase* 291), 'in each/every town'

老原文為複數，因而**在各城設立長老**提示每一市鎮有不止一名長老。[27] 但更多的細節則無法從「在每一市鎮設立多過一名長老」這話看出來。<u>若假定</u>每一市鎮只有一間教會，[28] 這表示每一間教會有不止一名長老；這種理解似乎為保羅（和巴拿巴）在首次宣教旅程回途中的

(NLT / RSV, NRSV, NIV, TNIV, NIV2011, NJB, ESV), 'in every single city' (Quinn 78), 'city by city' (Knight II 288; Wild 894*a*), 'town by town' (Banker 33*b*). 'The πόλεις of Crete were considered to number one hundred. During the Hellenistic period* some 40 πόλεις are known to have been viable political units. . . . This number seems to have been roughly halved by the Roman period given the evidence from cities which issued their own coinage or had their own magistrates (κόσμοι)' (Gill, 'Saviour' 222, 223). 但「在每一市鎮」的意思顯然只是指已有教會存在的每一市鎮。(*「希臘化時期」是「希臘文化思想極盛的時期，一般認為起始點是亞歷山大大帝逝世(公元前 323 年)，直至羅馬帝國開始(公元前 31 年)」〔《聖神》251*a*〕。) (**1**) 原文片語在徒十五 21、36，二十 23 也是這個意思；另見於路八 1、4。複數的 κατὰ πόλεις 見於路十三 22。(**2**) 此片語（κατὰ πόλιν）在 LXX 出現八次：(**i**) 四次用作副詞——代下十一 12（κατὰ πόλιν καὶ κατὰ πόλιν, 'in every several [= separate] city' [LXE]）；斯八 17（κατὰ πόλιν = 'in every city' [NIV, TNIV, NIV2011, NJB]）；次經《馬加比一書》1.51（κατὰ πόλιν καὶ πόλιν = 'city by city / town by town' [RSV, NJB / NRSV]）；(**ii**) 另四次用作形容詞——《馬加比二書》4.36（οἱ <u>κατὰ πόλιν</u> Ἰουδαῖοι = 'the Jews in the city' [RSV, NRSV]）；偽經《馬加比三書》3.16（τοῖς <u>κατὰ πόλιν</u> ἱεροῖς = 'the temples in the cities' [RSV, NRSV]），4.4（τῶν <u>κατὰ πόλιν</u> στρατηγῶν = 'the generals in the several cities' [RSV, NRSV]），6.41（τοὺς <u>κατὰ πόλιν</u> στρατηγούς = 'the generals in the cities' [RSV, NRSV]）。

27 See Lock 129: 'a body of "elders" in each city'; Marshall, 'Book of Titus' 809*a* / 'Titus' 180: 'It is probable that a plurality of leaders in each local situation is in mind rather than one in/for each Christian group'(〈提多書〉764*b*)；Marshall, 'Recent Study' 300: 'Titus 1:5 could be interpreted of the appointment of elders (plural) in each town or of one elder per town. The analogy of the synagogue favors the former interpretation.' Perkins 1443*a* 則認為，'The necessity of <u>a</u> reliable leader in each town is evident from the difficulty of travel from one to the next.'

28 E.g., Quinn 17: 'Crete with a congregation in each <u>large</u> town'; 16: '[these are] communities that appear to be <u>small</u>, independent house churches, dispersed throughout the many towns of the island'; Arichea－Hatton 268: '. . . Nor is it likely that there were towns where there were more than one congregation'. 另有認為，如果「教會」是個集合名詞，指某地方的數個家庭教會，* 那麼較小的單位（家庭教會）只有一名長老是可能的；單數的**監督**（一 7）亦可能暗示，每一個家庭教會由一位長老負責。So Marshall 153; see also Towner III 680（唐 992）。亦參一 7 註釋註 17（Wild 894*b*, 下面 126）。(*一些大城市有不止一所家庭教會，例如：羅馬〔羅十六 5a、14b、15c（參《羅》1.70-71，4.705-6、744-45、748-49）〕；哥林多〔林十四 23：**全教會聚在一處**；羅十六 23：**接待全教會的該猶**——這種講法暗示複數的家庭教會（see Fee, *First Corinthians* 683;《羅》4.795-96）〕；歌羅西〔西一 2；門 2 節（參《西．門》841，連註 39、40）〕。)

做法——兩人在〔南加拉太的〕各教會為他們指派了長老（徒十四 23，新譯）——所支持，[29] 亦與腓立比教會（腓一 1：諸位監督）和以弗所教會（徒二十 17／28：長老／監督原文皆為複數）的情況相符。[30] 雖然使徒行傳十四章 23 節說在各教會，本節則說在各城，但在各城的意思可能只是「在有教會在其中的每一市鎮」，[31] 因而相當於在各教會。無論如何，至少在以弗所，複數的長老構成一個長老團（提前四 14〔思高〕[32]）。

設立（同呂譯、思高、新和、現修、新譯）原文的另兩種翻譯是選立（當代）和委任（新普）、「任命」；[33] 後二者都似乎暗示，這些長老並非由選舉產生，而是由提多自己（作為獲得保羅授權的人）選立和委任的。[34] 原文動詞在使徒行傳六章 3 節指耶路撒冷教會的眾

---

29 See Van Neste, 'Message' 20*a*. 比較：

徒十四 23	χειροτονήσαντες δὲ αὐτοῖς	κατ'	<u>ἐκκλησίαν</u>	πρεσβυτέρους
多一 5	καταστήσῃς	κατὰ	<u>πόλιν</u>	πρεσβυτέρους

See also Schreiner, 'Overseeing' 106: 'It is . . . likely that there was a plurality of elders in each church, for each town in Crete likely had only one church, and Paul instructs Titus to appoint *elders* in each town. This fits with Acts 14:23'.

30 Knight II 288. 'Several elders/overseers are appointed in each church'; 馬唐納 555*b*：「聖經的方式是將幾個監督放在一家教會裏」。See also Keener 626*b*: '"In each city" meant that the different house churches in each city would each have their own leaders.'

31 Arichea－Hatton 268 (cf. 269): 'Titus is being told to appoint elders for every church in Crete, that is, for every town where there is a church.'

32 長老會（呂譯）不是指 'The Presbyterian Church'！原文名詞為 πρεσβυτέριον, 在新約僅再出現二次：民間的<u>眾長老</u>（路二十二 66）和議會的眾長老（徒二十二 5）所指的都是在耶路撒冷的、猶太人的議會（徒二十二 30；see BDAG 861*b* [s.v. a]）。參《新希》280*b*（s.v.）。

33 See NKJV, RSV, NRSV, NAU, NIV, TNIV, NIV2011, NJB, ESV, NLT: 'appoint'; A. Oepke, *TDNT* 3.444: 'instal'. 另有翻譯為「按立（ordain）」（KJV, and NIV, TNIV, NIV2011 margins），但是 Mounce 387 指出，'none of the biblical references supports "ordain" (Luke 12:14; Acts 7:10, 27, 35; Titus 1:5; Heb 5:1; 7:28; 8:3)'（詳見下註）。

34 上帝吩咐摩西要在耶和華……所賜的各城中，為各支派<u>設立</u>〔καταστήσεις〕審判官和官長（申十六 18），LXX 所用的就是多一 5b 的動詞。**(1)** 這動詞（**καθίστημι**）在保羅書信僅再出現二次，分別指所有的人因亞當一人的悖逆而成為 = 被「構成」罪人（羅五 19a），信徒則因基督一人的順從而成為 = 被「構成」義人（19b 節）（詳參《羅》2.163-68）。**(2)** 這動詞在新約另外出現十八次（在徒十七 15 以 καθιστάνω 的形式出現），呈現三種不同的意思：(**i**) 護送（徒十七 15）或送（思

門徒選出七名合資格的人士後，由使徒們派他們管理飯食；也許克里特的教會沒有耶路撒冷教會那麼成熟，因而長老的設立並非經由今天我們所理解的「選舉」產生。[35] 不過，這不是惟一可能的解釋；[36] 如

高、新和）**一次**；（**ii**）「使之成為」（如在羅五 19）**三次**：凡想要與世俗為友的，就成了上帝的敵人（雅四 4，思高）；在我們的肢體中，舌頭〔構成〕不義的世界（三 6〔參張略：《雅各書》206-7〕）；信徒在某些方面長進，會使他們在認識主這事上，不致於懶散和不結果子（彼前一 8）。（**iii**）「設立、授權、委派」（如在多一 5）**十四次**：來五 1（奉派），八 3（設立）；（動詞 + 介系詞 ἐπί + 所有格名詞〔五次〕：）太二十四 45，二十五 21、23，路十二 42，徒六 3（派⋯⋯管理）；（動詞 + ἐπί + 間接受格名詞〔兩次〕：）太二十四 47，路十二 44（派⋯⋯管理）；（動詞 + accusative and predicate accusative〔四次〕：）路十二 14（誰立我〔耶穌〕作你們的判官）；徒七 10（法老派他〔約瑟〕作埃及國的宰相）、35（誰立你〔摩西〕作我們的領袖）；來七 28（律法⋯⋯立軟弱的人為大祭司）；（動詞 + accusative and predicate accusative + ἐπί + 所有格名詞〔一次〕：）徒七 27（誰指定你作領袖、作法官來管我們呢？〔現修，參思高〕）。See BDAG 492*b* (s.v.);《新希》168*b*（s.v.）。

35 See Kelly 230-31: 'the entire responsibility for choosing the elders seems to be left with Titus, an arrangement which was probably made necessary by the immaturity of the Cretan communities'; Fee 22: 'They were to be appointed in Crete by Titus'; Witherington 107: 'we are not talking about congregations selecting their own leaders, but rather about them being appointed by the apostolic delegate.' 參：徒十四 23：二人〔保羅和巴拿巴〕在各教會中選立（χειροτονέω）了長老，同樣提示這些新成立的教會的長老是由保羅和巴拿巴選立的。早期的信徒都是在私人的家中聚集的，而這些家庭教會的主人往往由於他們的背景及才能是最適合的領袖人選；因此，看來徒十四 23 的意思就是，當保羅和巴拿巴向他們所剛建立的一個家庭教會告別時，就會把照顧教會的責任交給那個家庭的主人，這人就這樣被「選立」為長老（《恩賜》115-16）。See also Aune, 'Pastoral Letters' 559: 'This text [Titus 1:5] indicates that authorities outside the local church were responsible for appointing the primary local official who was regarded as the highest authority in each community. This coheres well with Acts 14:23 . . . individual bishops were apparently named by authorities external to the local church'; Witherington 107: 'Paul was not, nor was the early church in general, democratic about such matters.'

36 Calvin 357 就認為，保羅 'is only ordering him [Titus] to preside as moderator at elections, as is necessary.' Spencer 12 也認為，'Paul appears to allow the local Christians to select their elders.' Hendriksen 345 認為，雖然保羅說 'that *you* might appoint', 但這並不排除 'the responsible co-operation of the individual congregations'（cf. Robertson, *Pictures* 4.598: 動詞 καθίστημι 並不排除教會的選擇）。Griffin 278 說，'It is unlikely that Titus made such appointments without the advice and consent of the local Cretan congregation.' Barrett 128-29 同樣認為，'the fact that Titus is told to institute them does not mean that the congregation was to play no part.' Stott 174 也認為，長老必須無可指責這項要求 'indicates that the congregation will have a say in the selection process.' Hiebert 430 認為，可能會眾在提多的鼓勵下挑選了長老們，然後由提多正式任命他們。See also Towner III 680（唐 991）：'probably the candidates would have been selected by the communities that knew them best', 然後

果照**我所吩咐你的**（5c 節）包括「如何設立」的指示（即是設立的方式），我們卻無法從經文看出設立長老的過程是怎樣的。

這裏的動詞**吩咐**和第 3b 節的名詞**命令**提示一種「命令的等級制度」：保羅的權柄直接來自上帝，提多的權柄則間接地來自保羅的吩咐；[37] 從上帝而來的權柄透過保羅臨到提多，最後也臨到教會的領袖，[38] 後者是**上帝的管家**（7a 節）。**照我所吩咐你的**不僅指保羅

由提多憑著使徒所授予的權柄正式認可及委任。（**1**）Ramsay 69 說，'probably election played some part even in Crete, but much influence would be exercised by Titus in consultation with those whom he knew to be leading men in the congregation.' 周 412「相信，提多在挑選時也必然會與一些在信仰和生活經驗上比較成熟的信徒商討，不會獨斷獨行。」可是，這些「在信仰和生活經驗上比較成熟的信徒」（= 'leading men'）豈不正是合適的候選人嗎？（**2**）Stott 174-75 和張 324 皆認為，這裏的**設立** =「按立」（見上面註 33）牽涉「按手之禮」（參：徒六 6；提前四 14，五 22）。See also Marshall, 'Congregation' 120: 'It is most likely that the appointment of local leaders in the congregations of Ephesus and Crete was also recognized in this way (cf. 1 Tim 5:22)', i.e. with the laying on of hands (as in the case of Timothy's appointment [1 Tim 4:14; 2 Tim 1:6]); Towner II 224: 'The appointment of the elders would have been signaled by the laying on of hands . . . in the presence of the congregation'; Dunn 864*a*: 'Although the language is different ("appoint"), the thought is no doubt the same as in 1 Tim 5:22 ("laying on of hands").' 勵佐治也認為，多一 5 像徒十四 23 一樣，將整個選舉的過程（記載於徒六 3、5～6）壓縮，只提到最後的委任或按手這一步（Knight II 288）。（**3**）L. Coenen（*DNTT* 1.200）認為，提多奉保羅之名在個別教會中委任長老，這就是 'the first hints of the emergence of monarchical heads over several churches.' 可是，提多是以巡迴的「"特使" 或 "使徒的代表"」（利斐特 13〔Liefeld 19: 提摩太和提多是 '"envoys" or "apostolic delegates"'; Mounce lxxxii, xcviii / lxxxviii: 'apostolic delegates / itinerant, apostolic delegates'; cf. Knight II 23, 25, 26: 'apostolic assistants'; Kelly 14: 'the Apostle's personal emissaries'; Tomlinson, 'Purpose' 61, 82: 'Titus as an apostolic representative'〕）的身分做這事，而不是以日後出現的 monarchical bishop 的身分自居。Cf. Fee 21: 'they are itinerants on special assignment, there as Paul's apostolic delegates, not as permanent resident pastors.' 亦參一 7 註釋註 8 之（2）Coenen（下面 124）。

37 Stepp 181 指出，'He [Titus] is represented as Paul's delegate, not Paul's replacement. His work had limited scope and required limited authority.'

38 Genade 23（引句英文原作 'a hierarchy of command'）。See also Van Neste 253: 'There is then a continuous chain of authority . . . : God－Paul－Titus－local elders.' Wieland 193 認為，'While there is no explicit mention of the Moses-Joshua succession [see Josh. 1:1-2] in Titus 1:1-4, it offers a natural paradigm of delegated authority and the author is certainly concerned to establish the "chain of command" from God to his servant Paul and thence to Titus.'（**1**）Zamfir 162 則稱教牧書信（作者並非保羅）這種等級制度為 '[a] (<u>largely fictitious</u>) chain of authority and sound doctrine flowing from God through Christ down to Paul and his delegates'. 在 'Tit 1,5 elaborates the three-staged continuity that starts with Paul, passing through Timothy [*sic*] and reaching down to the

曾囑咐提多要在克里特的各城設立長老，而是特指保羅曾告訴提多要怎樣設立長老，提多要依照保羅的指示而行。[39] 這些指示的主要部分

local leaders'（Zamfir 9）這話裏面，'Timothy' 顯然是 'Titus' 之誤。（2）按 Young（'Ethics' 113-14）的理解（她認為教牧書信是冒名之作），這些書信 '[*a*] would appear to be indirectly addressed to communities in order to confirm the authoritative position of their leaders [Timothy and Titus] as inheritors of the tradition and authority of Paul. [*b*] So, the text-type slips from the surface genre of personal letter, to the implied genre of manual of instruction.' 兩種理論都是多餘的，因為：（3）提多書（和提前）大可以視為取了類似「委任信」（卡森－穆爾：〈教牧書信〉544）= 'a *mandata principis* [mandates of a ruler] letter' 的格式（Johnson II 212 (cf. 32); Johnson, 'Titus' 395*a*; see also C. Martin 412*a*; Marshall 12: 'Both Tit and 1 Tim . . . fit into the genre of mandates'; Marshall, 'Timothy and Titus' 187*b*: '[Titus] has the character of a "mandate" or letter of instruction to a delegate'; Towner III 34〔唐 49〕; Towner, 'Pastoral Epistles' 331*a*; Wall 11; Witherington 90, 92; deSilva, *INT* 745*b*-46*a*; Murphy-O'Connor, 'Pastoral Epistles' 630: 1 Tim and Titus 'are mandates'; Herzer, 'Perspective' 562: '1 Tim and Titus are mostly identified as so called *mandata principis letters*, whereas 2 Tim is usually characterized as *testamentum*' [cf. Johnson, 'Titus' 384*b*: 'Second Timothy can be read as a personal parenetic epistle, and 1 Timothy and Titus can be understood as *mandata principis* letters']）。這種書信將統治者的命令，傳達給他在某一地區或省份新委任的代表；雖然書信是寫給個人（即有關的代表）的，但信上的指示（或命令）有類似公開（'quasi-public'）的性質，其用意是要收信人以外的其他人也閱讀（Johnson II 106-7）。如此，提多書一方面確立提多是保羅的代表的身分，具有保羅所賦予他的權柄（216），同時保羅給提多的指示也（間接地）是保羅對克里特信徒的指示。See also Blomberg, 'Titus' 351: 'In terms of genre, Titus and 1 Timothy may both be thought of as *mandate letters*, analogous to epistles from Greco-Roman rulers to newly appointed delegates in districts or provinces. Formally addressed to individuals, they nevertheless were more public in character and were intended to be read widely.' 亦參一 3b 註釋註 5 之（2）= 上面 73。（4）歐大衛則指出，Margaret Mitchell* 'calls attention to the flaws in arguments that PTeb 703 is not [*sic*] in fact an example of the genre *mandata principiis* [*sic*] ("commandments of a ruler"), so that arguments that 1 Timothy is *mandatum principiis* [*sic*] on the basis of PTeb [Tebtunis Papyrus] 703 are invalid'（Aune, 'Pastoral Letters' 568; see also Towner III 34-35〔唐 49-50〕）；不過，'This does not mean that 1 Timothy cannot share common features with *mandata principiis* [*sic*], only that PTeb 703 is not a valid example of the genre'（563）。（*M. Mitchell, 'PTeb 703 and the Genre of 1 Timothy: The Curious Career of a Ptolemaic Papyrus in Pauline Scholarship', *NovT* 44 (2002) 344-370. Contra Witherington 90: 'the papyrus Tebtunis 703' is an 'especially' good example of this type of letter.）既是這樣，（3）的看法（留意筆者加上底線的幾個字）可以成立。「委任信的論點，與提摩太前書及提多書——當我們按照聲稱是屬於個人書信的類別來閱讀它們時——所內含的權威性結構和職責委任，提供了一個似乎可信的類比」（卡森－穆爾：〈教牧書信〉545）。See also Towner III 53（唐 75）：'the letters, incorporating mandate elements, served to endorse the delegates to the receiving communities as well as to set out their authoritative job descriptions for public appraisal.'

39 NJB: '. . . appoint elders in every town, in the way that I told you.'（1）主詞我字（ἐγώ）不僅是隱含於動詞之內，而是獨立代名詞，因而有強調作用。動詞被放在句末

就是隨即詳列的長老的資格。[40] 值得留意的是，在所列出的資格當中，大部分是關乎品格方面的（6～8 節〔原文為 42 字〕），只有最後的目的子句，才描述關乎職務方面的要求（9 節〔原文為 21 字〕）。如范尼斯所指出，這表示保羅要討論的問題不是「長老的工作是甚麼？」，而是「怎樣的人才有資格作長老？」保羅所要求的，就是獲得證實的道德品格，[41] 以及教導的能力。其實，下文所列出的道德品

（ὡς ἐγώ σοι διεταξάμην）似乎有同樣的作用；通常的字序是動詞、主詞、賓詞（BDF §472(1)）。保羅刻意地強調，吩咐提多的是他（see Genade 23）；這強調的我字所帶出來的，並不是保羅的自我中心，而是他帶著權柄為長老制度背書（Guthrie I 184, Guthrie II 196: 'his authoritative endorsement of the elder-system'〔古特立 199「而是他在任命長老系統中所擁有的權柄」將重點誤置於 'authoritative' 一字上〕）。**(2)** MHT 3.37 則認為，ἐγώ 在這裏並無強調之意。

40 Fairbairn 261. 留意以下譯本在 5 節末的冒號：現修：我曾經吩咐過：當長老的必須是無可指責的人；NRSV: '. . . as I directed you: someone who is blameless . . .'; REB: '. . . in accordance with the principles I have laid down: Are they men . . . ?'（REB 不尋常地將本節翻譯為一連串的三個問題〔NEB 只作一個問題〕，即是將 εἰ 視為引介直接問句。Davies I 95 認為這是可能的〔這種用法見 BDAG 278*a* [s.v. 5]〕。但翻譯為若無疑是正確的；見一 6 註釋開首〔下面 101〕。）See also Van Neste 236-37: '"as I commanded you" may serve to introduce 1.6 as a quotation or summary of what Paul said to Titus when he had left him in Crete.' Cf. Fee 172: 照我所吩咐你的一方面連於上文（5b 節，原文次序），所得出的意思就是：'I left you in Crete to complete the unfinished task, just as I instructed you, of appointing elders in all the churches'; 另一方面亦指向下文，意即「你會記得我的吩咐有以下的指標（為了眾教會的緣故，現在寫下來）」。

41 See Van Neste, 'Message' 20*b* ('proven moral character'; cf. 22*a*: 'proven, evident maturity in Christian character'). See also Witherington 73: 'what we actually find in the Pastorals in regard to overseers and elders and deacons is not so much job descriptions as character descriptions – advice on what sort of persons to look for to fill such roles.' Cf. Stepp 202: 'In the Pastorals, authority and office have more to do with the type of person the leader is than the title or office the leader possesses.' 同樣，政治領袖的品格比才能更重要。參李怡：〈世道人生：雞鳴狗盜之出其門〉：「不論一個國家，一個地區，一個機構，邪夫顯進之日，即直士幽藏之時，概莫能外。……雞年選特首〔香港特別行政區首長〕，最重要是產生一個不會是『雞鳴狗盜出其門』的特首。……求才納賢首先注重的不是才能，而是品德，是得到市民信任」（http:/hk.apple.nextmedia.com/news/art/20170203/19916491, 2017.02.03 瀏覽）。Sewakpo（'Titus' 18）'recommend[s] that every prospective leader in Africa should imbibe the aforementioned guidelines of leadership in the book of Titus'.

(1) Richards 80 卻認為，'The presbyter's virtues are not so much qualities of his "interior" character as externally "verifiable" qualifications. He . . . is married, has a family, and enjoys a good reputation in the community.' 這是由於他區別 'the short presbyter Virtue List'（6 節）和 'a much longer list for bishops'（7～9 節）。下文將

格是所有信徒都應具備的，只是人們常常沒有達到理想，而保羅對提多的指示，就是要他從那些最接近這理想的人當中，選出教會的領袖。[42]

會辯證，6～9 節是 one list for presbyters/bishops; 見一 7 註釋首段（下面 120-21）。（**2**）Zamfir 117 認為，教牧書信對教會領袖的要求 'comprise values and virtues largely corresponding to those demanded from officials in the Greco-Roman world and reflect an elite mindset centred on honourable public service.'

42 Marshall 148. Mappes 辯證，在教牧書信裏，保羅以教會領袖的資格（提前三 1～7、8～13；多一 5～9）和個人榜樣的功能（例：提後一 8～14；提前四 12；多二 7）來攻擊假教師的教導和行為，同時將健全〔的〕教義／健全的教導（提前一 10／提後四 3；多一 9，二 1）教導教會，並且指出所要求於教會領袖和所有信徒的倫理行為是怎樣的（'Virtues' 212-18）。

一 **6a** 若有無可指責的人，只作一個婦人的丈夫，

6b 兒女也是信主的，沒有人告他們放蕩，不受約束，就可以設立。

驟然看來，若有無可指責的人……是條件句子的發端子句（即「如果」句），就可以設立是它的歸結子句。[1] 其實就可以設立並不是本節原文一部分，而是譯者加上的。[2] 按原文的結構來看，本節（從若有到不受約束〔即 6 節〕）確是條件句子的「如果」句，[3] 但和它相對應的歸結子句乃是上一節的在各城設立長老（5b 節下）。[4] 這正是為甚麼本節屬於「提多在島上的責任（一 5～**6**）」這單元，[5] 而不是屬於「長老的資格和職能（一 **6**～9）」[6] 的原因。[7] 若有無可指責的人這

---

1 另有三本中譯本同樣在 5 節末使用句號，然後在本節末加上就可以設立／纔可以擔當／才可以作長老（新和／呂譯／新譯）。Cf. Mounce 388: 'we can assume an apodosis such as "let them serve"'; Laansma 230: 'This clause . . . leaves out the implied apodosis'.

2 Marshall 154 認為有此可能：從若有到不受約束（即 6 節）是條件句了的「如果」句，但是由於 7a 節（從監督到無可指責）的插入而造成破格文體*（詳見一 7 註釋第一段〔下面 120-21〕），因此被省略而應補充的，是類似就可以設立的話。（*參一 2b～3a 註釋註 26〔上面 67〕。）

3 Fee 172-73 則把 6 節視為一連串的問句 ＝ 'Is a man **blameless**?' 'Does he have only **one wife**?' 'Do his **children believe** . . . **not** being **open to the charge of being wild and disobedient**?' 參一 5 註釋註 40（上面 99）。

4 按這種理解，'the clause has been added loosely to what precedes'（Marshall 154, second alternative）。

5 思高／現修在 5 節末使用冒號（：），然後以長老應是／當長老的必須是開始 6 節，充分地表明了這一點。即使在 5 節末使用句號，也不必（不應）加上「就／纔／才」句（見上面註 1），而可以這樣開始 6 節：'An elder must be / must . . .'（NIV, TNIV, NIV2011 / NLT）或 'Appoint as elders men like this:'（Banker 35*a*）。另參以下英譯本的做法：NAU 在 6 節開首加上 '*namely*' 一字；NJB 以 'that is, each of them must be . . .' 開始 6 節。

6 如在 Hiebert 425, 429.

7 范尼斯認為，提多書有三個主要的「美德目錄」（catalogue of virtues or virtue lists）：第一段列出長老／監督的資格（一 6～8），另二段則描寫信徒應有的表現（二 1～10，三 1～2）。另見二 12（克己、正直、敬虔），三 4～5（〔上帝的〕恩慈、慈愛、憐憫）所牽涉的詞彙。See Van Neste 264-66.（**1**）更準確地說，一 6～9 'has the form of a *Pflichtenlehre* (duty code), more specifically a *Berufspflichtenlehre* (duty code for a specific occupation). This listing of qualities appropriate to a specific office or status is a specific category within the more general genre of lists of virtues and vices'（Marshall 147）。（**2**）Van Neste 把一 15，二 14，三 8、14 也歸入他的 'lists of virtue'（264）

話可能表示，哪裏有合資格的人，那裏提多才可以設立長老。[8]

（**#1**）**無可指責／指摘**（呂譯、新和、現修、新普同；另見 7 節／思高、新譯）原文在新約聖經只見於保羅書信：**無可指責**也是作執事（提前三 10：**沒有可責之處**）的資格；這詞在餘下的兩次則指信徒在主再來時的情況（林前一 8；西一 22）。[9] 費阿利引耶柔米和奧古斯丁的意見指出，若按其字面意義來理解，**無可指責**等於無罪的完全，這是一種不可能實現的期望；因此費阿利認為，這詞所表達的期望只是，候選人不會受到「公眾知道的違法行為」的指控（例如現代一些宗教人員對少年男女的性侵犯）。[10] 另有認為，原文形容詞在這

之內（265-67）。筆者不同意這做法，因為：一 15 只有一項（**潔淨**）；二 14 也只有一項（**熱心為善**），潔淨是基督的行動；三 8 其實只有兩項（**美好、有益**），而且它們並非指人的品格，「善行（καλὰ ἔργα）」是名詞；三 14 其實只有一項（**不會不結果子**），「善行（καλὰ ἔργα）」是名詞。這就是說，「無三不成幾」，一兩個項目不能構成「一列」或一個「目錄」。

8 Köstenberger 606*b*: 'Titus was to appoint elders only where qualified persons were available.'

9 參《西》267-69。原文形容詞為 ἀνέγκλητος, 在新約僅此五次。(**1**) Stott 175 強調，這裏的用詞不是 ἄμωμος（'unblemished'）而是 ἀνέγκλητος（'without blame, unaccused'）；他認為前者在新約只出現於末世的文理中，即該字 'looks forward to our final perfection'（參：弗五 27；西一 22；猶 24 節；啟十四 5）。不過，按筆者的理解，該字有兩次是指信徒現今的狀況的（弗一 4〔參《弗》129-32〕；腓二 15〔參《腓》280-82〕；在來九 14，彼前一 19，該字用於基督身上）。有趣的是，加爾文將 ἀνέγκλητος 解釋為 'he should be a man of unblemished reputation'（Calvin 358）。(**2**) 這字是複合形容詞（from ἐγκαλέω + α-privative; ἀνέγκλητος = 'that which cannot be called to account'; the *ν* is 'euphonic' [Vine 1.131], 即是 *an-enk* 比 *a-enk* 讀起來更悅耳）；動詞 ἐγκαλέω 在希臘文聖經出現七次，其意思都是**控告**（主動語態：徒十九 38，二十三 28〔思高、現修、新譯〕；羅八 33）或（被動語態：）**被告／被控**（十九 40〔呂譯／思高〕）／**被控告**（徒二十三 29〔呂譯、思高、新譯〕，二十六 2、7〔呂譯〕）。(**3**) 提前三 2 的**無可指責**（監督的一項資格）原文是另一個字：ἀνεπίλημπτος（另見五 7，六 14；在新約僅此三次）。Trench 381-82 (§103) 這樣區別二者：ἀνέγκλητος 強調沒有受到指控的客觀事實，即 '[it implies the] absence so much as of a charge or accusation brought against him of whom it is affirmed'（see also LN §33.433: 'without accusation'）；ἀνεπίληπτος (*sic*) = 'irreprehensible', 'affording nothing which an adversary could take hold of, on which he might ground a charge', 即是並無指控的根據（see also LN §33.415: 'above criticism'）。Marshall 148 則認為，二字是同義的；這裏使用 ἀνέγκλητος，也許是由於此字已在 6 節出現過（thus already, Towner I 225）。

10 Fiore II 200: 'not be subject to the accusation of a publicly known crime'; Montague 218:

裏很可能並非按其原本的意思（「沒有被指控」），而是按其口語的意思（「無可指摘、值得尊敬」）來使用。[11] 不過，「沒有被指控」仍是較自然的意思；[12] 作長老的生活行事應該沒有給人指控他有不當行為的理由。[13] 在這裏，**無可指責**是個覆蓋詞，用來引進各種品格行為方面的要求。[14]

（**#2**）**只作一個婦人／妻子的丈夫**（同新和／新譯）原文[15] 可

'The word refers primarily to the absence of any public crime or dishonor.' Cf. Spencer 13: 'not open to attack' = 'someone against whom a justifiable charge could not be brought' (14). Schreiner（'Overseeing' 106）也認為二字是同義的（見上註末），指 'There is no blatant transgression that stains his life, which causes others to wonder why this man functions as an elder'（95 [on ἀνεπίλημπτος]）。奧古斯丁認為，**若有無可指責的人**的意思是 'if anyone is "without crime", such as homicide, adultery and uncleanness of fornication, theft, fraud, sacrilege, and other things of this sort'（Gorday 286*a*）。

11 H. Währisch, *DNTT* 3.923: 'In the process the meaning underwent a change from the original sense ['not accused, innocent'] to that of respectability without reproach'; 924: 'the meaning is beyond reproach, in the ordinary sense of common respectability.' See also W. Grundmann, *TDNT* 1.356: 'blamelessness . . . in the sense of civic ethics'.

12 See Banker 35*a*: 'whom no one can justly* accuse of doing wrong'; 陳 19：「指一般而論，沒有什麼可被人指責的把柄」；周 413：「無明顯的瑕疵可供別人作把柄去攻擊」；黃編 196：「指沒有明顯的瑕疵可供別人作為攻擊的把柄」。（*參下註。）

13 Towner III 682: '[with] no grounds for an accusation of civic or domestic impropriety against him'（「不可有讓人控訴他<u>個人或家人</u>行為不檢的餘地」〔唐 995〕這翻譯，誤解了 'civic or domestic' 的意思〔=「作為公民的或對家人的」〕）; Saarinen 171: 'the person cannot be accused of clear moral or other failures'; Marshall 154: 'without fear of being denounced for misdemeanors.'（馬歇爾同時指出，「不應受到指控」和「受到無理的指控」是兩回事。）See also Wall 340: 'only "those who are without fault" in a variety of settings – social, religious, political, and financial – are to be appointed.' Chapell 293 則認為，'Paul's "blameless" standard is based upon what others <u>in the church</u> see and observe'; **無可指責**意即 'not open to <u>community</u> accusation of un-Biblical living'（294）。這看法將指控的來源似乎不必要地局限於教會內的其他信徒。

14 Fee 173: 它的功用是 'to head the list as a covering term for a variety of behavioral concerns.' Similarly, Collins 321: 'a comprehensive virtue. It introduces the list of particular qualities . . .'; 此字在提前三 10 總結了執事的資格。See also Wall 342: 'The overarching virtue is that a good elder-administrator is "without fault" or accusation . . . : he has a clean record.' 亦參彭編 95*a*：「可視為教會領袖資格的大原則。」

15 μιᾶς γυναικὸς ἀνήρ = 'husband of one wife' (NJB), 'the husband of one wife / but one wife' (KJV, NKJV, RSV, NAU, ESV / NIV).
（**1**）名詞 **γυνή** 在本書出現僅此一次，在保羅書信另外 **63** 次（新約全部 215 次），至少 **32** 次的意思是**妻子**（林前五 1〔呂譯、思高〕，七 2、3a、3b、4a、4b、10、

意譯為（**甲**）**只有一位妻子**（當代）、**只能有一個妻子**（現修）、[16]「忠於一個妻子」、[17] **對妻子忠誠**（新普），[18] 或（**乙**）**只能結一次婚**（現修頁邊註）、[19] **只做過一個婦人／妻子的丈夫**（呂譯／思高）。原文片語在提摩太前書三章 2 節是**監督**的資格之一，而提多書本節的**長老**在下一節變成**監督**，這兩點都提示長老和監督是同一個職分。這原文片語有多種解釋：（一）從未結婚的人不能擔任監督；監督不能是

11、12、14a、14b、16a、16b、27a、27b、27c〔呂譯、新和、新譯〕、29、33、39，九 5；弗五 22、23、24、25、28a、28b、31、33a、33b；西三 18、19；提前五 9）；**25** 次的意思是**女人**（羅七 2；林前七 1，十一 6a、6b、7、8a、8b、9a、9b、11a、11b、12a、12b、13、15；提前二 9、10、14）／**女子**（林前七 34；加四 4）／**婦人**（林前七 13〔呂譯、思高〕；提前三 2、12）／**婦女**（林前十四 34、35），其餘 **6** 次（林前十一 3、5、10，和提前二 11、12，三 11）的意思有爭議。(**2**) 名詞 **ἀνήρ** 在下文再出現一次（二 5：**丈夫**），在保羅書信另外 **59** 次（新約全部 216 次），至少 **35** 次的意思是**丈夫**（羅七 2a、2b、2c、3a、3c；林前七 2、3a、3b、4a、4b、10、11a、11b、13a、13b、14、16a、16b、34、39a、39b，十四 35；林後十一 2；加四 27；弗五 22、23、24、25、28、33；西三 18、19；提前三 2、12，五 9），**21** 次的意思是**人**／**男人**（羅四 8，十一 4；林前十三 11；弗四 13／林前十一 3a、4、7a、7b、8a、8b、9a、9b、11a、11b、12a、12b、14，十三 1a、11；羅七 3b、3d），其餘 **3** 次（林前十一 3b，和提前二 8、12）的意思有爭議。

16 NLT margin: 'must have only one wife'.

17 *Paraphrase* 291: 'faithful to one wife'.

18 TNIV, NIV2011, NLT, Liefeld 312: 'faithful to his wife' =「忠於他的妻子」（利斐特 329）。See also Mounce, 'Titus' 105: 'absolutely faithful to his wife.'

19 NRSV: 'married only once'; NLT margin: 'must be married only once'; Kartzow 135: 'can marry only once'; MacDonald, *Pauline Churches* 211: '[this is] intended to limit eligibility for church offices to those who had been married only once.' 參特土良：被選擔任聖職的 'must be men of one marriage'（Gorday 286*a*）；屈梭多模：'those who contracted a second marriage' 不准授予監督之職（ibid.）。(**1**) Glasscock（'Requirement' 247 [cf. 251]）說：'If Paul had stated ἔσχων μιᾶς γυναικὸς μονῆς [*sic*] ("having had only one wife"), it would be easier to argue that Paul meant possessing one wife in one's lifetime up to the point of his being examined.' 但分詞 ἔσχων 之後的賓詞為甚麼是所有格的 μιᾶς γυναικὸς μονῆς（此外，μονῆς = genitive singular of μονή ['room', 約十四 2]！），而不是直接受格的 μίαν γυναῖκα μόνην 呢？(**2**) 有十三世紀的小楷體抄本（編號 460）在一 9 含有這項要求：Μὴ χειροτονεῖν διγάμους μηδὲ διακόνους αὐτοὺς ποιεῖν, μηδὲ γυναικὰς ἔχειν ἐκ διγαμίας = 'Do not appoint those who have married twice or make them deacons, and do not take wives in a second marriage'（*TextC* 584; see also DC 134 n.14; Fee 176）。Collins 320 認為加上底線那部分的意思模棱兩可，最可能的意思是禁止執事與結過婚的婦女結婚（'it enjoins deacons/servants from marrying a woman if her marriage to the deacon were to be her second marriage'）。參一 9 註釋註 41（下面 147）。

獨身漢！[20] 可是，這很不可能是保羅的要求，因這要求使「從未結婚」變成負面的東西，因而與保羅和耶穌的看法不同。保羅明言，上帝給一些人結婚的恩賜，也給另一些人獨身的恩賜（林前七 7b，新普）；他更表示希望人人都像我一樣獨身（林前七 7a，新普），未婚的人和寡婦……最好像我一樣保持獨身（林前七 8，新普）。他不可能一面鼓勵人保持獨身，以致可以不分心地事奉主（林前七 32～35〔35 節〕），同時要求只有已婚者才可以任長老／監督或執事（提前三 2、12）。[21] 耶穌則教導，有人從母腹裏就是不宜結婚的，也有因人為的緣故不宜結婚的，並有為天國的緣故自己不結婚的（太十九 12）。[22] 因此，只作一個婦人的丈夫並不排除未婚者作長老，就如兒女（複數）也是信主的並不表示沒有兒女（或只有一個兒子或女兒）的人不可以作長老。[23]

（二）這話禁止一夫多妻的人擔任監督。[24] 可是，雖然一夫多妻可能出現在一世紀的一些猶太人的貴族當中，但一夫一妻是希羅世

---

20 Pietersen 135 聲稱，作者（不是保羅）以這項要求來 'disqualify . . . the opponents who forbid marriage (1 Tim. 4.3).' Davies II 75 認為，只作一個婦人的丈夫的意思並不清晰，但長老們 'are to be family men whose children are to be believers' 這項要求 'excludes women, unmarried men and slaves from the office of elder. . . . By excluding the unmarried . . . the Pastorals would exclude anyone attracted to asceticism (cf. 1 Tim. 4.3).'

21 Glasscock, 'Requirement' 246.

22 Lock 36.（**1**）Page（'Expectations' 107）指出另一點：一個的對比顯然是「不止一個（more than one）」而不是「一個也沒有（none）」。See also Marshall 155: 'the emphatic position of μιᾶς is strongly against it [the view under discussion].'（**2**）Stott 93 指出，耶穌（太十九 10～11）和保羅的教導（林前七 7）'makes the compulsory celibacy of the Roman Catholic priesthood indefensible.'

23 Knight II 289.

24 Calvin 223 斷言，'The only right exegesis is that of Chrysostom, who takes this to be an express prohibition of polygamy in a bishop at a time when it was almost legal among the Jews.' Cf. Simpson 50: '[it is] a prohibition of polygamy'. 更準確的講法是 'proscribing . . . simultaneous polygyny'（Page, 'Expectations' 107〔這不是佩悉尼本身的立場〕）。Baugh 501*b*-2*b* 則認為保羅的意思是，預期作長老的人不應有（一個或多個）妾侍；納妾在當代的希羅社會相當普遍，沒有被認為是姦淫或重婚。Köstenberger（'Pastoral Epistles' 23）認為 '[Baugh] has made a convincing case for interpreting the phrase as barring men who have one or several concubines.' 參陳 19：「只有一位妻子，沒有立妾。」

界惟一合法的婚姻方式，也肯定是猶太教以外的正常情況，而我們可合理地預期，猶太人會遵照社會的婚姻模式。在此時期，一夫多妻是罕見的，亦無證據顯示一夫多妻在基督徒羣體中是個重要問題。新約聖經從來沒有（因為無此需要）告訴信徒不要娶多過一個妻子，因此很不可能須要對預期的領袖提出這項要求。[25] 此外，若**只作一個婦人的丈夫**是禁止一夫多妻，那麼**只作一個丈夫的妻子**（提前五 9）便得理解為禁止一妻多夫，但這種理解不可能正確，因為在希羅世界中，一妻多夫是聞所未聞的。[26]

（三）這話禁止喪偶之後再婚的人擔任監督。[27] 可是，保羅容

---

25 Page, 'Expectations' 108. Fee 80 指出，一夫多妻在異教社會中十分罕見，以致 'such a prohibition would function as a near irrelevancy.'

26 Page, art. cit. 108: 'polyandry was unknown in Graeco-Roman society'; Collins 81: 'Nothing in the New Testament suggests that either polygamy or polyandry was a matter of concern for first-century Christians.' 'Since the phrases [ἑνὸς ἀνδρὸς γυνή, μιᾶς γυναικὸς ἄνδρα/ἀνήρ] are parallel and since polyandry was clearly not in Paul's mind in 1 Timothy 5:9, it is unlikely that he refers to polygamy in 1 Timothy 3:2 [or Tit 1:6]'（Schreiner, 'Overseeing' 97）。（**1**）Ward 55 斷言，'in New Testament times it would have been unthinkable if not as absurd to forbid polygamy as to forbid a Christian life devoted to murder.'（**2**）Stott 93 同意，一夫多妻 'was unheard of even among pagans.' 不過他繼續說，'Nevertheless, this apostolic ban has proved relevant in contemporary polygamous societies (*e.g.* in Africa), where churches tend to admit polygamists to membership by baptism, but not to leadership by ordination.' Stott 175 指出，92-94 的討論之結論是：**只作一個婦人的丈夫**這話所排除的是「一夫多妻者以及離婚後再婚的人」。參下面註 31 之（1）。

27 A. Oepke, *TDNT* 1.362 n.11; Collins 321. 後者（寇雷蒙）的理解是基於兩點「線索（clue[s]）」（82）：（**i**）有別於他的父親亞伯拉罕和他的兒子雅各，以撒只有一個妻子；斐羅因此稱讚他，說：'his lawful wife is the one who shares his home throughout'（*Preliminary Studies* 34）。（**ii**）**只作一個丈夫的妻子**（提前五 9）似乎暗示，一個**真寡婦**（5 節）是個喪偶後沒有再嫁的婦人。Montague 218 認為，保羅這項要求的神學根據很可能就是，'Christian marriage is an icon of the marriage of Christ and his Church', 而第二次結婚不符合此「象徵」，'for Christ never had any other spouse than his Church'.（**1**）Kelly 75（cf. 231）認為**只作一個婦人的丈夫**的 'plain meaning' 是，不管是喪偶後再婚或離婚後再婚的人，都不符合這項資格。（**2**）Hunter（'Titus 1:6' 334）指出，教父時期最通常的解釋就是，這話禁止 'ordaining "digamists" or twice-married men to the clergy'. 這也是羅馬天主教的釋經傳統的趨勢：'Roman Catholic exegesis tends to take the phrase to mean that . . . anyone who has remarried after the death of his first wife or who has remarried after divorce (in the case of a pagan convert) is automatically excluded [from the office]'（C.

許信徒喪偶後再婚（林前七 39；參：羅七 1～3），儘管他的理想是維持獨身像我一樣（林前七 8）；他也勸年輕的寡婦再嫁，生兒育女，好好持家（提前五 14〔新普〕；[28] 亦參：太二十二 23～33 ‖ 可十二 28～17 ‖ 路二十 27～40）；若認為他對長老定下高過一般信徒的道德標準，這假設是有疑問的。[29] 事實上，新約聖經沒有任何地方明確地禁止再婚，不管是對一般信徒或對教會領袖都沒有。討論中的看法（三）亦與教牧書信「反禁慾」的語調不符：禁止嫁娶和禁戒食物被視為屬於邪靈和鬼魔的教訓（提前四 3、1），生兒育女和維持健康的家庭關係（多二 4～5；提前二 15，五 9～10、14）則受到強調。[30]

（四）被禁止任監督的是離婚後再婚的人。[31] 這看法的困難在

Brown, *DNTT* 2.563）。

28 （**1**）Saucy（'Husband' 230）指出，如果只作一個婦人的丈夫（提前三 2 同）禁止喪妻之後再婚的人擔任監督，那麼只作一個丈夫的妻子（提前五 9）亦使喪夫之後再婚的人失去資格，不能登記為接受救濟的寡婦，這樣，聽從保羅的勸告而再嫁的年輕寡婦，老年的時候便不能接受救濟了。（**2**）Streete（'*Askesis*' 309）則認為，這禁令很可能指基督徒監督不可再婚，這使他們有別於年輕的基督徒寡婦（提前五 14）。

29 Ward 55.（**1**）這假設是有疑問的，因為一般而言，教會領袖的各種資格所指的品質，應同樣彰顯在所有信徒身上（Page, 'Expectations' 113）。例外的可能只有善於教導（提前三 2：διδακτικόν〔參：多一 9〕）和不……是初參加教會的（提前三 6〔現修〕：μὴ νεόφυτον）這兩項（115）。（**2**）Stott 94 認為，新約明確地容許鰥夫和寡婦再婚（羅七 1～3；林前七 39）就是確鑿的證據，表示這話並非禁止喪偶而再婚者擔任牧職。有趣的是，斯托得並不把下面註 31 之（1）那種「雙重標準」（離婚後再婚者不可任監督）應用到喪偶再婚者身上。

30 Page, 'Expectations' 113. Banker 35*b*-36*a* 認為，這一項資格緊隨無可指責，這提示只作一個婦人的丈夫應從「它是否罪」、它會否受到不信者的非議（參二 5b、8b、10c 所表達的關注）的角度來理解；從這個角度看，很難認為一個妻子去世之後再婚的人，或是一個從未結婚的人，並不符合這項資格。

31 Carter－Levine, 'Pastorals' 246: 'most likely it disqualifies a divorced and remarried man, or even a remarried widower'; 侯嘉文 69：「他一定不能是離婚再娶的人」；馮譯 445：「即不得休妻另娶」；Hanson I 41: 'not a *divorcé* who has remarried'. 韓遜提出的理由是：只作一個丈夫的妻子（提前五 9）的意思一定是 'she had not been divorced and therefore changed her husband'; 在當代的墓碑上，常有婦人被稱讚為 'of one husband', 意即她從來沒有被休。（**1**）關於這一種人（離婚後再婚者），斯托得認為，雖然耶穌似乎容許因嚴重的性罪行「無辜受害（the innocent party）」的一方離婚和再婚（太五 31～32，十九 9），而保羅亦似乎容許「初信主，但其配偶仍

於，（1）根據耶穌和保羅的教導，在某些情況下離婚是容許的：妻子**不貞**是離婚的正當理由（太五 32，十九 9）；被不信的妻子離棄（林前七 15～16）也是。在猶太教，離婚附帶再婚的權利；上述情況可能有這樣的含意，即離婚的丈夫可以再婚。[32]（2）教牧書信關於教會領袖的資格的各個清單中（多一 6～9；提前三 1～13），都沒有明確提到「離婚」這事情；事實上，教牧書信完全沒有提到這事。**只作一個婦人的丈夫**這話本身只表明，此人僅與一個婦人有關係；其自然的意思是禁止目前與其他異性有（同樣的）關係，而不是對過去的關係定罪。如果這話的確指向過去的關係，則經文並無任何表示，所指的只是以離婚告終的那些關係；所指的可能亦包括配偶去世後再婚。[33] 關於後一

然不信並且不願維持婚姻關係」的人離婚和再婚，但這些允許不適用於神職人員或期望擔任神職的人。雖然 'this [does] erect a double standard . . . but is it not reasonable and right that a higher standard should be expected of pastors who are called to teach by example as well as by words?'（Stott 93-94）。（**2**）Köstenberger（'Challenges' 11*a-b*）同樣認為，離婚（及再婚）的男人不一定不可作長老、監督或執事（提前三 2、12），若離婚的理由是合乎聖經教導的（16 n.45: 妻子不忠〔太十九 9〕；被不信的妻子離棄〔林前七 15～16〕）就更是這樣；不過，鑑於長老／監督必須**無可指責**（多一 6／提前三 2：ἀνέγκλητος/ἀνεπίλημπτον）這項要求，還是最好不要讓離婚者擔當此職。See also Köstenberger, 'Pastoral Epistles' 23-24.（**3**）但是 Madsen（'Ethics' 231）提出警告說，'We should . . . avoid interpretations that set up two standards of morality (vs. ability) in the Pastoral Epistles, that is, a high one for the overseer and a low one for the layman.'（此評語特別適用於上面〔1〕斯托得的解釋。）不過，作者稍後又說（231-32）：'while the phrase μιᾶς γυναικὸς ἄνδρα [*mias gynaikos andra*] concentrates on marital faithfulness, its narrower focus as such does not permit the church to disregard altogether a candidate's history of divorce, if he has one. Multiple divorces would be a "red flag" surely, as would a divorce that occurred precipitously or on grounds that were not biblical. Local congregations also need to consider whether the overseer, if divorced, would still be "above reproach" in the eyes of his own community. All things considered, the answer to this question might be "yes," especially in North America, but that judgment has to be reached on a case-by-case basis. Divorce is not the unforgivable sin, but it can be a significant handicap in some ministry settings.' 參較（2）的立場。（**4**）Glasscock（'Requirement' 251）則認為，若保羅的意思是要排除離婚後再婚的人，'it would have been more easily and clearly said by μὴ ἀπολελύμενον [*sic*, ἀπολελυμένον*], even as he did write [in v. 7b] μὴ πάροινον, prohibiting the abuse of wine, and μὴ πλήκτην, prohibiting physically violent men.'（*此字在來十三 23 的意思是**已經釋放**〔新譯〕。）

32 Page, 'Expectations' 109-10.

33 Page, art. cit. 110. See also Marshall 156: 'the limitation to remarriage after divorce is by

種情況，上文已討論過（見上段）。

（五）**只作一個婦人的丈夫**最自然的字面意義就是，他只有一個活著的妻子。[34] 這裏的關注似乎僅在於教會的領袖要在婚姻關係上忠於他的妻子。[35] 在教會中負責教導和領導的監督，必須在「性與婚姻」

---

no means obvious from the wording, and such a prohibition is not supported elsewhere in the NT.'

34 Hiebert 430: 'he must be the husband of only one living woman.' Taylor 85 指出，**只作一個婦人的丈夫**這要求 'finds no parallel in other Hellenistic lists of duties.'

35 Fee 173, 81（Fee, 'Reflections' 148/150 則認為：'it also is very likely a frowning upon second marriages of any kind' / 'the text also probably prohibits remarriage of widows/widowers'）；Collins 319: 'faithful to one's wife'; Hendriksen 121: 'he must be an example to others of faithfulness to his one and only marriage-partner' (see also 348: 'faithful in the marriage-relationship'); Houlden 78: 'simply an enjoining of marital fidelity'; Jeon I 39: 'The audience hear the phrase as a reference to marital fidelity'; Jeon II 14: 'he must be a faithful husband'; Keener 626*b*: '"Husband of one wife" probably meant "a faithful husband"'; Knight II 289: 'marital and sexual fidelity are required'; Laansma 236: 'a demonstrated purity and faithfulness in his marriage relationship'; Marshall 154: 'best interpreted as faithfulness in marriage'; Mounce 388: 'the idea of fidelity in marriage is to be preferred'; Oden 146/141/142: 'fidelity to the marital covenant / covenant sexual fidelity / covenant fidelity in marriage'; Scott 154: 'nothing more seems to be intended than that the elders must have been faithful in the marriage relation'; Stern, *Comm.* 654: 'faithful to his wife'; Towner I 232, 233; Towner II 224; Towner III 250-51 / III 682: 'fidelity in/within marriage [is meant]'（唐 353-54／995：「婚姻中的忠誠／在婚姻裡的忠實」）；Wild 894*b*: 'a demand for ordinary marital fidelity'; Witherington 110: 'what the phrase in question is dealing with is behavior *within* marriage, which is to say, being sexually faithful to one's own wife, and so not engaging in any sort of extramarital infidelity'; Zehr 247: 'simply . . . a requirement for marital fidelity'. See also Madsen, 'Ethics' 231: 'the phrase . . . means "faithful husband"'; Wieland, 'Grace' 9*a*: 'do they demonstrate faithfulness in that [marriage] relationship?'; 彭編 33*a*：「強調對婚姻的忠實。」

(1) Köstenberger 認為，這項要求（'being, literally, an "of-one-wife-husband"'）可能模仿 'a *univira* [*sic*] (i.e., a "one-husband"-type of wife)' 這羅馬概念。這詞指婚姻上的忠誠，原先用於在生的婦女與丈夫的關係，其後變成丈夫給予去世的妻子的稱號（無數現存的碑文為此作證）（'Challenges' 10*b*, with 16 n.38）。由此看來，原文片語（μιᾶς γυναικὸς ἀνήρ）很可能是個慣用語，最宜翻譯為 'faithful husband'. 平行經文提前五 9 亦支持這種理解：該處指明，寡婦接受教會資助的條件之一是她**只作一個丈夫的妻子**（ἑνὸς ἀνδρὸς γυνή），意即 '[she] has been / was faithful to her husband'（NIV, TNIV, NIV2011 / NLT）。這片語不能解為禁止一妻多夫，因為婦人的丈夫已經去世；也不可能指這寡婦必須不曾作多過一個丈夫的妻子，因為保羅不會一方面**希望年輕的寡婦嫁人，生養兒女**（五 15），另方面卻認為曾作多過一個丈夫的妻子的寡婦沒有資格接受教會對寡婦的資助（ibid. 11*a*; Page, 'Expectations' 112）。See also Köstenberger, 'Pastoral Epistles' 23. **(2)** 如 Hendriksen 122 所言，保羅一定完全同意希伯來書作者的話，後者說：**人人都應該尊重婚姻，婚床也不要玷污**（來十三 4a，新譯）= **要尊重婚姻，在婚姻中要對配偶保持忠誠**（新普；參《來》

這範疇上具有清白無瑕的名聲。[36] 這一項資格是可以明顯地被證實的素質。[37] 這種解釋（五）可取，理由如下：**第一**，它十分符合文理：（**i**）只作一個婦人的丈夫緊隨無可指責（提前三 2 同）；在提摩太前書三章，執事只作一個婦人的丈夫（12 節）則在執事也必須莊重（8 節）之後提及。[38] 至少在本節和提摩太前書三章 2 節，無可指責在長老／監督的資格中是帶頭的一項，可以視為隨後各項的概要，因而借助於在前者（無可指責）來解釋隨後者（只作一個婦人的丈夫）是合宜的。故此，只作一個婦人的丈夫所描寫的，應該是看得見的行為，且是在基督徒羣體內外都受到敬重的。將這詞理解為指婚姻上的忠誠符合這種預期。[39] 二章 4 至 5 節要年長的婦女指教年輕的婦女愛丈夫，愛兒女，並且克己，貞潔；這和只作一個婦人的丈夫（解釋為指

2.429-31）。

36 Stott 94, 175.（**1**）張 176 合併「指要在性生活上聖潔」和「指必須要〔原文照錄〕維持一夫一妻的婚姻制度」這兩種主張。（**2**）Ward 55 的解釋較為特別。他認為，保羅想到的是候選人的資格，這時當問的問題是：'Is he married? Does the marriage "work"? Does it fulfill the ideal of marriage? If it does, the two are one and in particular the man is *husband of one wife*, to whom he is completely joined.'（參周 203：「這包括一夫一妻制，也包括保持婚姻關係的忠實，特別夫婦之間能夠相敬相愛，達到上帝始初設立婚姻時『二人成為一體』之目的。」）可是，二人成為一體（弗五 31）不是成功婚姻的「理想」，而是婚姻的「事實」；完成的結婚之舉（consummated marriage）本身使夫妻二人成為一體（參《弗》875-76）。

37 Quinn 85: 'what is being proposed is intended to be an <u>obviously verifiable</u> quality.' 與此同時，Laansma 236 的提醒是適切的，他說：'Marital infidelity has become almost a fashion in Western society [only?]. Popular culture (television, movies, advertising, magazines) affords a good many registers of that fact. . . . In this context, lest we define sexual relations legalistically, it is necessary to recall Matthew 5:28* and to admit that this applies in the context of men and women, to television, to the Internet, to magazines, to clothing catalogs, to billboards, to the beach, and to the sidewalk. The elder is to be "faithful to his wife."'（這項要求／提醒其實適用於所有已婚的男性基督徒。）（*我〔耶穌〕告訴你們，看見婦女而生邪念的，在心裏已經跟她犯姦淫了〔現修〕；凡是帶著淫念看女人的，心裏已經犯了通姦罪〔新普〕。）

38 無可指責和莊重這（在原文是）三個形容詞，原文依次為 ἀνέγκλητος（多一 6）、ἀνεπίλημπτος（提前三 2），和 σεμνός（提前三 8）。

39 Page, 'Expectations' 114-15. 佩悉尼將提前三 8 的莊重（σεμνούς）同樣視為概要的描寫（114）。這形容詞在提前三 11 也是女執事* 的資格中帶頭的一項（σεμνάς）。但它在多二 2 則只排第二。（*γυναῖκας 指女執事而不是執事的妻子，理由見〔例如〕《恩賜》137-38；Fee 88; Schreiner, 'Overseeing' 111-12.）

婚姻上的忠貞）十分相似。（**ii**）這解釋為只作一個丈夫的妻子（提前五 9）提供了具吸引力的解釋：寡婦登記只限於被公認為曾忠於她們的丈夫的婦女。[40]（**iii**）新約聖經整體的教導亦支持這解釋。新約聖經將婚姻描寫為一夫一妻一生之久的聯合（可十 6～9），是人人都當尊重（來十三 4）的。保羅教導信徒，為了避免淫亂的事，男人當各有自己的妻子，女人也當各有自己的丈夫（林前七 2），夫妻都各要在性事上向對方盡本分（七 3～5）。在新約聖經裏，婚姻以外的一切性活動，包括通姦、同性戀行為、與妓女苟合，自始至終都受到譴責。[41] 既然如此，教會領袖要忠於自己的妻子是自然不過的要求。[42]

第二，這解釋亦與當時的歷史情況相符。亞古士督曾於公元前 18

---

40 Page, art. cit. 116.

41 參（例如）羅一 27（男的和男的彼此貪戀；參《羅》1.312-15），十三 13（好色淫蕩；參《羅》4.325-26）；林前五 1～5、9～11，六 9（新譯：作孌童的*，親男色的**）、12～18；加五 19（淫亂、污穢、放蕩；參《加》1248-50）；弗五 3（淫亂；參《弗》713-14）；西三 5（淫亂、污穢、邪情；參《西・門》530-33）；帖前四 3～7（參《帖前》293-317，尤其是 296-97、305、316）；提前一 10（犯淫亂和親男色的**）；來十三 4（參《來》2.429-33）；彼前四 3（淫蕩、情慾）；彼後二 9～10（放縱污穢的情慾）；啟九 21／二十一 8，二十二 15（淫亂／淫亂的）。（**1**）* μαλακός = **'pert. to being passive in a same-sex relationship, *effeminate*** esp. of *catamites*, of men and boys who are sodomized by other males in such a relationship, opp. ἀρσενοκοίτης'（BDAG 613*b* [s.v. μαλακός, 2]）；「同性戀關係中被動的男伴角色」（《新希》209*b* [s.v.]）。作男妓的（新普）= 'male prostitutes'（NLT, NRSV, NIV, TNIV）這翻譯的意思太過狹窄。（**2**）** ἀρσενοκοίτης = 'a male who engages in sexual activity w. a pers. of his own sex, *pederast*'（BDAG 135*a*, s.v.）；「與男性發生性行為的男士」（《新希》45*b* [s.v.]）。（**3**）LN §88.280 指出，'It is possible that ἀρσενοκοίτης in certain contexts refers to the <u>active</u> male partner in homosexual intercourse in contrast with μαλακός, the <u>passive</u> male partner (88.281).' 因此，NIV2011 marginal note 正確解釋：'The words *men who have sex with men* translate two Greek words that refer to the <u>passive</u> and <u>active</u> participants in homosexual acts.' 但 RSV/REB 以 'sexual perverts/pervert' 一詞翻譯原文兩個名詞，這做法合理地被評為 'lexically unacceptable'（BDAG 135*a* [s.v. ἀρσενοκοίτης]）。

42 Page, 'Expectations' 117. Ramsay 30 認為，'the regulation in [1 Tim.] 3:2, 12 and 5:9 . . . means only "monogamistic" in the fullest and purest sense. It neither forbids second marriage nor enjoins marriage.' Cf. Saarinen 62: 'the apostle simply says that the bishop should not cause any offense in the conduct of his marriage but that he must hold to the accepted monogamous practice in an exemplary manner'; Wall 341: 'Whatever the particular sense, Paul's larger point is that a stable, monogamous marriage is evidence of a successful household that may carry over to leadership of a Christian congregation.'

年立法，使通姦成為不合法。儘管這法例採雙重標準（妻子通姦，丈夫須與她離婚並提出控告；丈夫通姦，妻子可與他離婚，但不能提出控告），又豁免某些情況（例如，與娼妓苟合並不構成通姦行為），但它確實表示婚姻上的忠誠是被欣賞的。婚姻上的忠誠這概念亦見於古代的婚約和希臘道德哲人的著作。由此可見，希臘化時期的世界認識並且贊同這概念。如果教會的領袖達到這種理想，教會便會獲得教外人的尊敬，反之則會使教會傳福音的工作受阻（參二 5、8、10）。鑑於這種歷史情況，教會領袖的資格中包括「婚姻上的忠誠」這一項是十分合適的。[43]

對於這種解釋，基里認為「婚姻關係中的忠誠」可意譯為「不對妻子以外的婦女動淫念」，然後批評不可能從原文得出這個意思來。[44] 但原文是否不可能表達「在婚姻上忠誠」這個意思呢？[45] 答案是否定的。首先，就證據所及，原文片語最早出現的地方就是教牧書信的有關章節（一 6；提前三 2、12），因此，它的意思要根據其本身的文理來決定。其次，從新約聖經及可與之相比的文獻看來，希臘化時期的希臘文（即通用希臘文）似乎沒有明顯的方法表達「婚姻上的忠誠」這個正面的意思（最接近的可能就是**貞潔**一字〔二 5〕），儘管它不乏表達負面的「不合法的性行為」的詞彙。[46] 作者若要表達這個正面的

---

43 Page, art. cit. 117-18.

44 Kelly 75: '. . . that their object is merely to prescribe fidelity within marriage, a suitable paraphrase being "not lusting after women than his wife"－but this is to squeeze more out of the Greek than it will bear.' 留意基里的批評所針對的是他的意譯，不是 'fidelity within marriage' 這概念本身。

45 Goulder（'Wolves' 245 n.14）就認為，原文不能表達「忠於（一個）妻子」這個意思；'we should need μιᾷ γυναικὶ πιστόν [faithful to one wife], if indeed μιᾷ was required at all.' 但見下文。

46 **（1）** 以 μοιχ- 為字根的
（i） 陰性人物名詞 μοιχαλίς（**淫婦**）：羅七 3；
（ii） 動詞 μοιχάομαι（**犯姦淫**）：太五 32*b*；太十九 9 || 可十 11；可十 12；
（iii） 名詞 μοιχεῖα（**姦淫**）：太十五 19 || 可七 22；約八 3；
（iv） 動詞 μοιχεύω（**姦淫**），例：太五 27；可十 19 || 路十八 20；羅二 22，十三 9；

意思，就得自創一個詞語。

第三，假定原文片語內的**一個婦人的**有形容詞的作用，**一個婦人的丈夫**大可以理解為此人是專一地忠於他的妻子的。[47] 最後，保羅的教導是**男人當各有自己的妻子**（林前七 2），一個遵循這教導的男人可自然地描寫為**一個婦人的丈夫**。[48] 由此可見，基里的反對理由並不堅實；第（**五**）種解釋最符合文理和歷史實況，因此至為可取。

（**#3**）**信主的**原文[49] 另有譯為「忠誠、可靠」。[50]（一）班約翰

雅二 11；

（**v**） 陽性人物名詞 μοιχός（犯姦淫者）：路十八 11；林前六 9；來十三 4。

（**2**） 以 πορν- 為字根的

（**i**） 名詞 πορνεία（**不貞／淫亂／淫行**），例：太五 32，十九 9／可七 21；約八 41；徒十五 20；林前五 1；林後十二 21；加五 19；弗五 3；西三 5；啟九 21／帖前四 3；啟二 21；

（**ii**） 動詞 πορνεύω（**行淫／犯姦淫／犯淫亂**），例：林前六 18；啟十七 2／林前十 8a（參十 8b）／啟二 14、20；

（**iii**） 陰性人物名詞 πόρνη（**娼妓／妓女**），例：太二十一 31、32；路十五 30；林前六 15、16／來十一 31；雅二 25；

（**iv**） 陽性人物名詞 πόρνος（**淫亂的人／行淫亂的／犯淫亂〔的〕／淫亂的**），例：林前五 9／林前五 10／林前五 11；提前一 10／林前六 9；弗五 5。

47 Bailey（'Theology' 361）就認為：'At minimum it [the phrase] called for a husband to be singularly focused on his wife and devoted to her.'（**1**）Spencer 14 指出：'having an elder who is (or was) devoted to his spouse (**a one-woman man**) would be a dramatic contrast to many in the larger society. In Crete, as in the rest of the Roman and Greek society, sexual relations between a married free man and a slave or even the wife of a serf were not fined as "adultery." According to the ancient Cretan Gortyn Code, even rape against a household slave received only a penalty of one to twenty-four obols depending on the circumstances (while against a free person was 1,200 obols).'（**2**）Glasscock（'Requirement' 249）也認為原文片語應翻譯為 'a man of one woman' 或 'a one-woman man': 'This understanding emphasizes the character of the man rather than his marital status. Thus even a single man or a man who has been married only once must demonstrate that he is not a "playboy" or flirtatious, but that he is stable and mature in character towards his wife or other females.' μιᾶς γυναικός 可視為 'a genitive of quality'（250），意即 'he is a one-woman type of man'（251）。Cf. Chapell 295: 'an elder must be "a one-woman man." . . . The literal phrasing seems less concerned with one's marital history and more focused on whether the man being considered for office is perceived as living in honesty, faithfulness, and devotion to his spouse.'

48 本段的論證取自 Page, 'Expectations' 119.

49 R. Bultmann（*TDNT* 6.215）聲稱，'The adj. πιστός simply means "Christian"'.

50 I.e., πιστός = 'loyal and trustworthy' (Lock 128), 'trustworthy, loyal' (Classen, 'Titus' 433 n.15, following Lock 130).（**1**）Bassler 186 認為，這字一定要求兒女是**信主的**，但它同時提示 'a pattern of loyalty that is the opposite of

辯證，這種翻譯（理解為對父母忠誠）可能更符合文理：（**i**）兒女對父母忠誠即是對父母順服（與**不受約束**相對），不是過著**放蕩**的生活。[51]（**ii**）在**兒女也是信主的**的原文片語內，明確的人物是**兒女**和分詞**有**字所隱含的**丈夫**一字；[52] 故此，原文的**信**字所表達的關係很可能是**兒女**和這個**丈夫**（即他們的父親）的關係，因而「忠誠」比**信主**更合適。（**iii**）在提摩太前書三章 2 至 4 節有關監督的資格的平行經文中，並無要求他的兒女必須是信主的，[53] 卻有提到他和兒女的關係：**要好好管理自己的家，使兒女順服，凡事莊重**（4 節）。[54]（二）馬歇

rebellion.'（**2**）但 'having brave children'（Classen, 'Epistle to Titus' 51）這片語是令人費解的。

這形容詞（**πιστός**）在保羅書信另外出現 32 次（新約全部 67 次），主要分為兩種用法：（**甲**）用於主動的意思（**信**：提前四 3、10）上，這字指亞伯拉罕對上帝**有信心**（加三 9）、**信主的**人（提前六 2a、2b〔新譯〕），與**不信的人**（林後六 15〔現修〕）相對；亦可用作名詞，指**信主的婦女**（提前五 16）或**信徒**（提前四 12）。以上共八次。（**乙**）用於被動的意思上，這字指（**i**）**忠心**的管家（林前四 2）和**忠心**的主僕與信徒（**提摩太**：林前四 17；**推基古**：弗六 21 ‖ 西四 7；**以巴弗**：西一 7；**阿尼西謀**：西四 9；其他：弗一 1；西一 2）；**凡事忠心**是女執事必須具備的條件（提前三 11）；（**ii**）**可信**的話（提前一 15，三 1，四 9；提後二 11；多三 8）或**可靠**的道理（多一 9）；（**iii**）**可信靠／可信任**的人（林前七 25；提後二 2／提前一 12）；（**iv**）上帝是**信實**的（林前一 9，十 13；林後一 18；帖前五 24），主（基督）也是**信實**（帖後三 3）／**信實可靠**（提後二 13〔現修〕）的。以上共 **24** 次。（甲）（乙）合共 **32** 次。See BDAG 820*b*-21*b* (s.v.);《新希》268*a*（s.v.）。

51 Banker 36*b*.（他的譯文作 'faithful (to him (their father))' [34, 36*a*].）Cf. Bouwman 41: 'The reference is . . . to . . . whether they have learned to submit to his authority as God's appointed family head.'（**1**）**違背父母**是末日的標誌之一（提後三 2）。（**2**）Kidd（'Titus' 204）則把 'faithful' 解釋為「虔誠」（'faithful (*pistos*, that is, pious)'）。Cf. Trebilco, 'Self-designation' 254 (cf. 257): 'believers [or "faithful [to God]"]'（方括號都是作者的）。

52 第 6b 節 τέκνα ἔχων πιστά 內的 ἔχων 之主詞是 6a 節末 μιᾶς γυναικὸς ἀνήρ 內的 ἀνήρ.

53 White 187*a* 對此的解釋是：一個信主的父親有未信主的兒女表示他是初信的，或是不認真（'very careless'）的基督徒。提前沒有提到**兒女也是信主的**這一項要求，證明當時基督教在以弗所比起在克里特已較穩固地建立起來了。

54 Banker 36*b*. Towner I 233, Towner II 225, Köstenberger 607*a* 和 Knight II 290（followed by Blomberg, 'Titus' 353）均認為，一 6 的 τέχνα ἔχων πιστά 相當於提前三 4 的 τέκνα ἔχοντα ἐν ὑποταγῇ（**使兒女順服**）。若是這樣，'then πιστά here means "faithful" in the sense of "submissive" or "obedient," as a servant or steward is regarded as πιστός when he carries out the requests of his master (Mt. 24:45f.; 25:21, 23;

爾則認為，（**i**）難以明白為甚麼要在目前的文理中特別提到「忠誠／可靠」，而且「忠誠／可靠」並不是與「順服」同義的；（**ii**）過著**放蕩**的生活不僅是**不受約束**的表現，也是不信主的表現；（**iii**）在父權的社會中，兒女接受父親所信奉的宗教，比起在現代的（尤其是西方）社會中可能得多。[55] 兩種看法比較之下，筆者認為班約翰的第一、三兩點更具說服力，因此贊同將原文形容詞理解為「忠誠／可靠」之意。[56]

告字原文的意思是**控告**（呂譯、思高）或**指控**（當代）。[57] **沒有人告他們**（新和加上是字）這種翻譯著眼於**沒有人指控**／**控告他們**（當代／新譯）、他們**沒有被控告為**……（呂譯、思高）[58] 的事實。另一種翻譯則表達「〔他們的行為使他們〕不容易受到指控」之意。[59] **放蕩**（同呂譯、思高、新譯、新和、現修）[60] 原文名詞在新約僅再出

Lk. 12:42f.; 1 Cor. 4:2 . . .)'（Knight II 290）。See also Schreinere, 'Overseeing' 107-8: 'The conceptual link between "insubordination" (Titus 1:6) and "submissive" (1 Tim. 3:4) suggests that both texts require the same behavior in children. What is mandated is that the children are obedience, that they are "faithful" children, not that they are believers.'

55 Marshall 158. Cf. idem, 'Congregation' 112: 'It was assumed . . . that children would accept the Christian faith of their fathers (Titus 1:6).'

56 Knight II 289 認為，這裏的**兒女**是仍然住在父親的家中並在父親的權柄下生活的（followed by Schreiner, 'Overseeing' 108）。See also Towner II 225: 'The instruction . . . restricts the elder's accountability to children who are not yet adults.'

57 **κατηγορία** = 'accusation . . . charge' (BDAG 533*b*, s.v.). Johnson II 223 理解為 'the children are to be believers and <u>not criminals</u>.'（**1**）這名詞在希臘文聖經僅再出現兩次，指對長老的**控告**（提前五 19）和對耶穌的**控告**（約十八 29，呂譯、思高、新譯、現修、新普）。參《新希》182*a*（s.v.）。（**2**）同字根的動詞 κατηγορέω 則在新約出現 23 次，絕大多數在四福音（2、3、4、3 次）和使徒行傳（9 次），例外的只有兩次（羅二 15〔參《羅》1.380-81〕；啟十二 10）。See BDAG 533*a-b* (s.v.);《新希》182*a*（s.v.）。

58 See KJV, NAU, NRSV: 'not accused of . . .'. 在 μὴ ἐν κατηγορίᾳ ἀσωτίας ἢ ἀνυπότακτα 這片語內，（**i**）否定詞 μή（通常用於分詞及不定詞）暗示 μὴ ἐν = μὴ ὄντα ἐν（*Idiom* 155-56; Knight II 290）；（**ii**）ἀσωτίας 可理解為 'genitive of content'（Marshall 158），即「指控」的內容就是「放蕩」（參較 Wallace 92-94 所列出的例子）。

59 See RSV, NIV, TNIV, NIV2011, ESV: 'not open to the charge of . . .'; NJB: 'not liable to be charged with . . .'; Fairbairn 261: 'not . . . in a position that such accusation could be brought'.

60 參以下英譯：'debauchery'（NRSV, ESV; Quinn 25）；'dissipation'（NAU, NKJV; G.

現兩次（弗五 18；彼前四 4）；[61] 另二種（較好的）翻譯是**任性**（新普）[62] 和**行為不檢**（當代）。[63] 保羅不是只提到這負面行為本身，而是特別提到**沒有人告他們**有這種行為，這表示保羅在意別人怎樣看他們、他們的行為怎樣影響別人對基督信仰的觀感，就如第二章更清楚地表明的（見二 5b、10c，參 8b）。[64]

不受約束（同當代、新譯；另見一 10）、**不服約束／不受管教**（呂譯、新和／現修）、**不羈**[65]／**叛逆**[66]（思高／新普）或「不服從」[67] 的反義詞是**順服**（二 5、9，三 1）。[68] 兒女不服從的對象很可能是自

Schneider, *EDNT* 1.176*b* [s.v. ἀσωτία]:)；'being profligate'（RSV）；'riot'（KJV）；'a dissolute, debauched, profligate manner of living'（Trench 55 [§xvi]）；「放蕩的生活」（《輔讀》525）。(**1**) Banker 37*b* 認為最好的翻譯是 'debauchery', 解釋為 'Gross indulgence of one's sensual appetites', 即是放縱一己的肉慾。(**2**) Montague 219 則認為，'**Licentiousness** suggests unrestrained sexual activity, which Roman society, at least among the upper classes, tolerated in youth who had reached puberty'.

61 **ἀσωτία**. 這兩次的意思也是**放蕩**（弗五 18；彼前四 4）。同字根的副詞 ἀσώτως 在希臘文聖經只出現一次（路十五 13），指小兒子**生活放蕩**（新普）。See BDAG 148*a* (s.v.);《新希》49*b*（s.v.）。(**1**) 名詞在 LXX 亦僅出現兩次，分別指一個「如牧者般照料（ποιμαίνει）放蕩（ἀσωτίαν）」的人羞辱他的父親（箴二十八 7），以及「聖殿內充滿了外邦人的放蕩和縱飲」（次經《馬加比二書》6.4，思高）。(**2**) ἀσωτία 是複合名詞（from σῴζω + α-privative [see Vine 3.299]）；'the verb σῴζω refers to preservation, hence ἀσωτία gener. denotes "wastefulness"'（BDAG 148*a* [s.v. ἀσωτία]）。此動詞在本書僅出現一次（三 5），但在保羅書信另外出現 28 次，新約全部 106 次（see BDAG 982*a*-83*a* [s.v.];《新希》322*a*）。

62 See also NLT, NIV, TNIV, NIV2011: 'being wild'; BDAG 148*a* (s.v.): 'wild living'.

63 See also NJB: 'disorderly conduct'; W. Foerster, *TDNT* 1.507: '[here] the word signifies wild and disorderly rather than extravagant or voluptuous living.' Marshall 158 則認為，兩個兒子的比喻（路十五 11～32）中的小兒子，就是**任意放蕩**（13 節）者生動的例子（馬歇爾的意思似乎是，**放蕩**亦牽涉「揮霍無度」之意）。

64 Banker 37*a*. Montague 219 指出，'Children may indeed turn out badly through no fault of their parents, but then their father should not be placed in charge of the Church, lest the disobedience of his children give members of the Church license to disrespect the authority of their leader.'

65 See also KJV: 'unruly'; Quinn 25, 80, 87: 'refractory'（= 'resisting control, discipline, etc.'〔《牛津》962*b*〕）。

66 See also NAU: 'rebellion'; NRSV, LN §36.26, H. Balz, *EDNT* 1.112*a* (s.v. ἀνυπότακτος): 'rebellious'; NLT: 'being . . . rebellious'.

67 NIV, TNIV, NIV2011: 'being . . . disobedient'; RSV: 'being . . . insubordinate'; NJB, NKJV, ESV, Davies II 75: 'insubordination'.

68 原文依次為：**ἀνυπότακτος**, ὑποτάσσομαι（二者同字根）。(**1**) 前者在新約僅再出現

己的父親。[69]

這裏對長老兒女的要求，許多中英譯本都錯誤地表達為只有兩項，就是：（1）他們**是信主的**；（2）**沒有人告他們放蕩，不受約束**——這種翻譯將**不受約束**視為與**放蕩**同等，二者是對他們的指控的兩項罪名。[70] 但是原文的結構清楚表示，形容詞**不受約束**並不是

兩次（提前一9：**叛逆的**；來二8：**不服**）。參《新希》32*a*（s.v.）；BDAG 91*b* (s.v. ἀνυπότακτος): 'pertaining to refusing to submit to authority, *undisciplined*, *disobedient*, *rebellious*'; 在本節用於「寵壞了的孩子（spoiled children）」身上。（**2**）這字是複合形容詞（from ὑποτάσσω + α-privative; the *ν* is 'euphonic' [Vine 4.174], 即是 *an-yp* 比 *a-yp* 讀起來更悅耳）；動詞 ὑποτάσσω 在保羅書信一共出現 23 次（新約全部 38 次），詳見《羅》4.225-27 連註 38；《弗》806-9。See BDAG 1042*a* (s.v.);《新希》342*a*（s.v.）。

69 See G. Delling, *TDNT* 8.47: '"rebellious" against one's father'; Hiebert 430: 'refusing to bow to parental authority'; Banker 37*a*: 'neither do (they) refuse to obey (their father)'; 唐 997：「不順服父親的權柄，已到公然藐視〔flagrant disregard〕的地步」（Towner III 683）。（**1**）Marshall 158 則認為，雖然這裏首先指不服從父母，但與假教師**不受約束**（一 10）的聯繫可能是刻意的，所提示的意思就是，在這層次上的不尊重權柄會有廣泛的影響。（**2**）Johnson I 117 認為，**放蕩**和**不受約束**原文是很強的字，表示 'the elder's children <u>may be</u> the sort who could be arrested for carousing or for criminal activity'（see also 127: 'This is a situation where the bishop's son might be arrested for profligacy or public disorder'）。這話有點奇怪，因為有這種兒女的人不能當長老；因此，撇開作者對兩個形容詞的解釋，'may be' 是否應修正為 'must not be' 呢？

70 參以下中英譯本：

- 呂譯：有兒女〔*a*〕是信徒、而沒有被控告為〔*b*1〕放蕩或〔*b*2〕不服約束的
- 思高：所有的子女都〔*a*〕是信徒，又沒有被控告為〔*b*1〕放蕩〔*b*2〕不羈的
- 當代：兒女全都〔*a*〕信主，也沒有人指控他們〔*b*1〕行為不檢，或〔*b*2〕不受約束
- 新譯：兒女都〔*a*〕信主，也沒有人控告他們〔*b*1〕放蕩或〔*b*2〕不受約束
- 新和：兒女也〔*a*〕是信主的，沒有人告他們是〔*b*1〕放蕩〔*b*2〕不服約束的
- NKJV: 'having [*a*] faithful children not accused of [*b*1] dissipation or [*b*2] insubordination.'
- RSV: 'his children [*a*] are believers and not open to the charge of being [*b*1] profligate or [*b*2] insubordinate.' See also Johnson I 117.
- REB: 'Are their children [*a*] believers, not open to any charge of [*b*1] dissipation or [*b*2] indiscipline?'
- NAU: 'having children [*a*] who believe, not accused of [*b*1] dissipation or [*b*2] rebellion.'
- NIV, TNIV, NIV2011: 'whose children [*a*] believe and are not open to the charge of being [*b*1] wild and [*b*2] disobedient.'
- NJB: 'his children [*a*] must be believers and not liable to be charged with [*b*1] disorderly conduct or [*b*2] insubordination.'
- TEV: 'his children [*a*] must be believers and not have the reputation of being [*b*1] wild or [*b*2] disobedient.'

與放蕩同等的，因而並非從屬於名詞告字；[71] 不受約束其實是獨立於沒有人告他們放蕩的另一項目，因而這裏對兒女的要求其實有三項：（1）他們是信主的；（2）沒有人告他們放蕩；（3）他們並非不受約束的。[72] 在本註釋所參考的接近三十本的中英譯本中，正確地表達這種意思的只有四本英譯本，[73] 這是令人感到奇怪的。無論如何，本節

- BV: 'has [*a*] believing children that are not charged with being [*b*1] incorrigible or [*b*2] unruly.'
- Phillips: 'with children [*a*] brought up as Christians and not likely to be accused of [*b*1] loose living or [*b*2] law-breaking.' See also DC 132*a*: '(and should) have children who [*a*] are believers and cannot be accused of [*b*1] loose living and [*b*2] disobedience.'
- *Paraphrase*: 'with children [*a*] who are themselves believers and not open to the charge of being [*b*1] profligate or [*b*2] insubordinate.' See also H. Bietenhard, *DNTT* 1.83: 'his children are not open to the accusation of being [*b*1] profligate or [*b*2] insubordinate'.
- Stern: 'with [*a*] believing children who do not have a reputation for being [*b*1] wild [*b*2] or rebellious.'

將不受約束看為告的（第二）部分內容的釋經者包括：Laansma 237; Towner III 683（唐 997）; Witherington 106, 111; Johnson, 'Titus' 395*b*; Mounce, 'Titus' 105; Knight II 289（但見下註之〔2〕Knight II 290）。

71 **(1)** 在 μὴ ἐν κατηγορίᾳ ἀσωτίας ἢ ἀνυπότακτα 這詞語內，ἀνυπότακτα 既非名詞，亦非所有格，因此不可能是與所有格名詞 ἀσωτίας 同屬於名詞 κατηγορίᾳ 之下。換一個講法，ἀνυπότακτα 是中性複數形容詞，所形容的是中性複數的 τέκνα（Banker 37*b*）。因此，沒有人告他們的他們「可指長老的兒女，也可指長老本身」（陳 20）這話不確。**(2)** 這詞語的結構其實是這樣的：在 μή 之下有兩個項目，由 ἤ 字隔開。這就是說，這裏的兩項要求是：μὴ ἐν κατηγορίᾳ ἀσωτίας 和 (μὴ) ἀνυπότακτα. 'ἀνυπότακτα stands in tandem with the preceding prepositional phrase and its genitive modifier'（Knight II 290）。See also Fiore II 195: 'who are not liable to a charge of debauchery nor disobedient'; Jeon I 12: 'not in accusation of debauchery or rebellious'; Mounce 384: 'not able to be accused of debauchery or rebellious'. **(3)** Tollefson（'Titus' 150*a*）錯誤地將 'avoid loose living' 和 'not be guilty of insubordination' 這兩項都看為對長老（而不是其兒女）的要求。Similarly, Collins 321: 'The Pastor describes the elder whom Titus should appoint as someone who . . . cannot be accused of being profligate or headstrong.' 有趣的是，寇雷蒙早前曾（正確地）將這兩項看為對兒女的要求：'having faithful children who cannot be accused of being wasteful or stubborn'（320），但同時（不正確地）將兩者都視為他們被控訴的內容（also 322）。

72 So also Barclay 234: 'children who are also believers, who cannot be accused of profligacy, and who are not undisciplined.'

73 **KJV**: 'having [*a*] faithful children not [*b*] accused of riot or [*c*] unruly'; **RV**: 'having children that [*a*] believe, who are not [*b*] accused of riot or [*c*] unruly'; **NEB**: 'children [*a*] who are believers, who [*b*] are under no imputation of loose living, and [*c*] are not out of control'; **NRSV**: 'whose children are [*a*] believers, [*b*] not accused of debauchery

對長老的要求似乎假定了，一個人是否適合作教會領袖，可以從他如何管理自己的家看出來。[74] 提摩太前書三章 5 節以修辭問句從反面指出這種邏輯關係：**人若不管理好自己的家，又怎能照顧好上帝的教會呢？（新普）**。[75] 不過，目前的重點不在於這種邏輯關係，而是在於當長老的必須有無可指責的名聲。[76]

---

and [*c*] not rebellious.' 中譯本方面，《新普及譯本》似乎反映這種「三項」的理解：**他的兒女也必須是信徒，不任性、不叛逆**。但這翻譯忽視了原文相當關鍵性的名詞 κατηγορία（告）。這評語同樣適用於《現代中文譯本修訂版》的翻譯：**他的兒女都應該〔*a*〕是信徒，沒有〔*b*1〕放蕩或〔*b*2〕不受管教的事**。

74 Aageson 68: 'Management of the domestic household is thought to indicate the ability to manage the household of God.' Stott 176 斷言：'the logic is plain. Parents cannot be expected to manage God's family if they have failed to manage their own.' 斯托得繼續說，這原則亦隱含於 7 節：監督是**上帝的管家**，他要管理的是上帝的家。Malherbe（'Paulus Senex' 207）指出，'The notion that successful household management was indispensable in the preparation for public service was commonly held and was part of the conservative social philosophy of persons like Plutarch.'

75 （**1**）Zamfir 63 聲稱，這種看法 'draws from the conviction that roles in the *oikos* [household] and in the *polis* [city] are integrated in a divinely instituted cosmic order.' 詳見同書 70-85。（**2**）然則父母要對兒女的行為負責到何時為止呢？答案似乎是，直到他們不再是「未成年的兒女，仍在父母的權柄之下」。See Stott 176. 亦參弗六 1（《弗》898-99 連註 3）；西三 20（《西・門》661 連註 16）。（**3**）有釋經者認為，**沒有人告他們放蕩**這一項要求提示，這裏的**兒女**很可能是年輕的成年人；so Fiore II 198: 'probably young adults'; Bassler 186: 'adult children, not young ones'.（Spencer 15 指出，'adult "children" often continued to live within the household of the parents. The child was responsible to the *paterfamilias* even in adulthood.'）Quinn 88 也認為，**不受約束**所指的不是 'the willfulness of mere youngsters' 而是 'the rebelliousness of young adults in public opposition to the social and political orders.' 不過，**任性**（新普）和**不受約束**並非成年人的專利，任性和不受約束的青少年符合「未成年的兒女，仍在父母的權柄之下」的描述。參註 56（上面 115）。

76 Marshall 159. Horrell（'Ideologies' 118）認為，'The requirements laid down for church leaders in 1 Tim. 3.1-13 (cf. Tit. 1.5-9) restrict leading functions to those who govern their households well. Non-(male) householders, it seems, would be disqualified from such positions.' 這看法似乎合理；參一 5 註釋註 35（上面 96）。

2.2 監督的資格和職能（一 7～9）

一 7a 監督既然是上帝的管家，必須無可指責、

7b 不自負、不暴躁、不酗酒、不好鬥、不貪財；

原文開首有因為（當代、思高、新譯、新普）一字，[1] 它的功用是引進一句解釋的話。保羅首先指明，作長老的必須無可指責，在他的婚姻和家庭生活兩方面都應如此（6 節）；在保羅繼續列出作長老的其他資格（7b～9 節）之前，他首先插入一句話來解釋，為甚麼作長老的必須無可指責：因為長老作為教會的監督乃是上帝的管家，故此必須無可指責（7a 節）。[2] 這插入句同時改變了隨後那些資格的表達方式：在插入句之前，所用的方式是若有人無可指責（6a 節，思高），隨後的項目在文法上皆為主格；[3] 但在插入句之後，所有的項目都依照必須無可指責這種格式，在文法上皆為直接受格。總言之，「第 6 節

1 γάρ = 'For' (KJV, NKJV, RSV, NRSV, NAU, ESV, NLT). 既然／既（同現修／新和）或 'Since'（NIV, TNIV, NIV2011）應該不是原文小字的翻譯，而是 ὡς θεοῦ οἰκονόμον 這片語中的 ὡς 字的意譯（as God's steward => since he is God's steward）。以下譯本也沒有把 γάρ 譯出來：呂譯、新和、現修、和修；NJB, *Paraphrase* 291.

2 Marshall 149. See also Davies I 95: '*Overseer* . . . briefly indicates the role which the elder should play.' Cf. Fee 173-74: 'v. 7a . . . now gives reasons *why* the **overseer** . . . must be **blameless** in the sense of verse 6 (i.e., as a faithful husband and father), namely, because he will also serve as "God's household manager"'; Towner III 686（唐 1000）：'an elder should be blameless in his household [i.e., marriage/children, v. 6] . . . *for* as an overseer, he must be blameless to serve in God's household . . .'（方括號是原來的）。因此，不必認為 'The word is repeated for emphasis'（Mounce 388），更不宜把兩次的無可指責作不同解釋，如在黃編 197：「六節是重在指其生活表現無可指責，本〔7〕節是重在指其性格無可指責。」

3 εἴ τίς ἐστιν, ἀνέγκλητος, μιᾶς γυναικὸς ἀνήρ, τέκνα ἔχων πιστά κ.τ.λ. 代名詞、形容詞、名詞、分詞皆為主格。

和第 7 至 9 節代表兩張不同的清單，分別列出作長老和作監督的資格」[4] 是一種假象；造成此假象的是第 7a 節的插句，這插句改變了隨後的表達方式。[5] 解釋性的插句過後，保羅就繼續列出他對長老／監督的要求。[6]

---

4 Zehr 237: 'Titus must . . . put elders and an overseer in place'; 245: 'Appointment of Elders, 1:6', 'Appointment of a Bishop, 1:7-9'; Schnelle, 'Pastoral Letters' 345: 'both forms of church order simply stand alongside each other without really being connected.' See also G. Bornkamm, *TDNT* 6.667: 'the change from plur. to sing. and the separate enumeration of qualifications are arguments against an equation of the titles.' 可是，5b 節複數的**長老**變成單數的**監督**，這是不足為奇的，尤其因為 6a 節的主詞已變為單數的人（Marshall 160）；* 至於 'the separate enumeration of qualifications', 這是一種假象，如正文所解釋的。*Cf. Marshall, 'Congregation' 118: 'The shift from the plural "elders" to the singular "overseer" or "bishop" is natural in the detailed discussion of the qualities required. Furthermore, it is paralleled elsewhere－notably in 1 Tim 5:3-16, where the author oscillates between the singular [vv. 4-5, 9] and the plural [vv. 3a, 3b, 11, 16a, 16b] with reference to widows'. 另見（Merkle, *Elder* 143-44）：提前二 8／12（τοὺς ἄνδρας / ἀνδρός）；二 9、10／11、12（γυναῖκας, γυναιξίν / γυνή, γυναικί）；五 17／19（πρεσβύτεροι/πρεσβυτέρου）。**(1)** Karris 110 則認為，6 節和 7～9 節是來自不同傳統的資料，作者（不是保羅）以後者補充前者。Quinn 85 同樣認為，作者（不是保羅）將 'two previously existing lists of qualifications for ecclesial ministers' 合併起來；對作者此刻的目的而言，'they were practically synonymous', 儘管二者源自不同的猶太環境。See also Bassler 185: 'The shift in terminology from elders to bishop . . . may indicate that two earlier lists have been combined here'; Miller 127: 'two previously independent pieces have been brought together here': 長老（複數）的資格（5～6 節）、監督（單數）的資格（7～9 節）。作者甚至認為（127-28），7～9 節本身也是混合物：有關監督的簡短規定（7a 節 + 9a 節）後來被插入一列籠統的惡行／美德（7b～8 節）。此見解並無說服力。見 Marshall 16-18 對 Miller 之命題的批評。**(2)** 另有認為 7～9 節是被人加插進經文裏的（e.g. Richards 81-82）。但古卷的證據完全不支持此說（Kelly 231）。詳細的反駁見 Van Neste 237-38.

5 Marshall 149 (cf. 159). Banker 37*b* 則認為，從文法的角度來看，很可能是第 6b 節關於長老的兒女較為複雜的描述，使保羅覺得要開始新的一句。

6 多一 5～9 所列出作長老／監督的資格，有不少與提前三 2～4 所列舉監督的資格相似或相同，如下表所示：

多一 5～9		**提前三 2～7**
6a 節：無可指責（ἀνέγκλητος）		2 節：無可指責（ἀνεπίλημπτος）〔原文二字大致上同義：見一 6 註釋註 9 之（3）= 上面 102〕

上一段已經解釋，為甚麼第 5 節的**長老**在這裏變成**監督**。**監督**著眼於這位領袖的功能，**長老**則著眼於其地位。[7] 原文二字是同一個

6a 節：只作一個婦人的丈夫（μιᾶς γυναικὸς ἀνήρ）	=	2 節：只作一個婦人的丈夫（μιᾶς γυναικὸς ἄνδρα）〔ἄνδρα = ἀνήρ 的直接受格〕
6b 節：兒女也是信主的，沒有人告他們放蕩，〔並非〕不受約束（τέκνα ἔχων πιστά, μὴ ἐν κατηγορίᾳ ἀσωτίας, [μὴ] ἀνυπότακτα）		4 節：兒女順服，凡事莊重（τέκνα ἔχοντα ἐν ὑποταγῇ, μετα πάσης σεμνότητος）〔ἔχοντα = ἔχων 的直接受格；順服與不受約束同字根；莊重與（不）放蕩相近〕
7b 節：不酗酒（μὴ πάροινον）	=	3 節：不酗酒（μὴ πάροινον）
7b 節：不好鬥（μὴ πλήκτην）	=	3 節：不打人（μὴ πλήκτην）
8 節：樂意接待外人（φιλόξενον）	=	2 節：樂意接待外人（φιλόξενον）
8 節：克己（σώφρονα）	=	2 節：克己（σώφρονα）
9 節：能〔以〕健全的教導勸勉人（δυνατὸς . . . παρακαλεῖν ἐν τῇ διδασκαλίᾳ τῇ ὑγιαινούσῃ）		2 節：善於教導（διδακτικόν）〔這形容詞與左欄的名詞 διδασκαλία（教導）同字根〕

(1) 剛信主的，不可作監督（提前三 6）這項要求，沒有在提多書本段出現。好些釋經者認為這就提示，比起以弗所教會，克里特的眾教會是較新近成立的（e.g., Fee 172; Guthrie I 186; Guthrie II 198; 古特立 34、200；Johnson I 116; Johnson II 223; Mounce 385; Merkle, *Elder* 141, 146; Wieland, 'Grace' 9*b*）。Davies I 96（cf. Davies II 76）說，'this epistle depicts a situation in which all believers would be new converts.' 古特立指出，提前三 6 的要求沒有在本段出現，這事實本身就是 'an indirect confirmation of the veracity of the account, which it is difficult to imagine came from the pen of a Paulinist after the end of the century'（Guthrie, *NTI* 626-27）。唐書禮也認為，'The church setting depicted in the letter to Titus is completely at odds with theories of late authorship'（Towner III 51〔唐 72〕）。**(2)** 羅拔臣指出，提多書本段所提到（但沒有在提前該段提及）的正直、聖潔（8 節），是必須經過一段時間才能培養出來的品德；堅守合乎教義的可靠之道（9 節），亦暗示一段相當長時間的受教，以致能掌握使徒的教訓到一個程度，能〔以〕健全的教導勸勉人，又能駁倒爭辯的人。這就是說，在提多書本節，作長老／監督的同樣不是個剛信主的人（Robertson, 'Pastor' 83-85）。不過，'while there may have been Christians in Crete for some time, it seems doubtful that the church had thrived for very long'（Mounce 386）。Mounce 389 則承認，6 節表示克里特的教會 'cannot have been too young, for there must have been time for fathers and their children to be converted (if πιστά is understood as "believing").' 但 πιστά 的意思較可能是「忠誠／可靠」而不是信主的；參一 6 註釋（**#3**）= 倒數第四段（上面 113-15）。

7 Barrett 129: 'whereas *elder* describes an official, *bishop* describes his function.' 參《腓》

職位不同的稱謂。[8] 有力地支持這看法的另兩點是，(i) 第 6 節提及

71-72；Collins 322; Keegan I 58, Keegan II 92; Laansma 238; Marshall, 'Timothy and Titus' 187*b*; Mounce 390; Stott 90. See also Guthrie, *Theology* 740: 'The combination of "elder" and "bishop" in this context shows clearly that the latter is no more than a function of the former' (cf. 763: 'The *episkopos* was . . . an elder who performed the special function of oversight'); Hendriksen 346: 'as to their age and dignity [they] are called *elders*, and as to their task [they] are called *overseers*'; Hiebert 430; Scott 155: 'No doubt the alternative name is now given him because of its literal meaning of "overseer," which itself indicates the duty of a steward.' 如 Köstenberger（'Challenges' 10*b*）所指出的，一般而言，'*presbyteros* is Jewish in origin, signifying seniority, while *episkopos* is Greek, indicating a person's superintending role.' (1) Johnson I 116 則認為長老和監督是兩個不同的職位：'a board of elders has a revolving office called the overseer, held in turn by one or more of the elders.' 侯嘉文 148 也認為，「『監督』是指一間教會的長老團的主席（後來變成整個教區的領袖）」。(2) Young 110 認為，長老們構成教會的 'governing council, which had the authority to appoint and advise the *episkopos*'（cf. Harding II 63-64）。但卡森－穆爾（〈教牧書信〉552）指出，「這顯然不是提多書第一章 5 至 9 節的解釋，她指稱長老委任監督的說法，亦幾近於空想出來。」

8 See esp. Merkle, 'Ecclesiology' 182-86. See also Fiore II 11: 'the letter seems to be talking about one person with two different titles', 198: 'the office is the same, but has two names'; Stepp 200 n.3: 'interchangeable names for the same office'; L. Coenen, *DNTT* 1.199: 'probabl[y] . . . interchangeable'; J. Rohde, *EDNT* 3.149*b* (s.v. πρεσβύτερος, 3 d): 'the term is interchangeable with ἐπίσκοπος in Titus 1:7'; Achtemeier－Green－Thompson, *INT* 459; Brindle, 'Titus' 252; Chapell 297; Fee, 'Reflections' 147: 'the grammar of Titus 1:5, 7 demands that "elder" and "overseer" are interchangeable terms (as in Acts 20:17, 28)'; Hagner, *New Testament* 633: 'there appears to be no essential difference between elder and bishop'; Herzer, 'Perspective' 561: 'ἐπίσκοπος serves as another term for πρεσβύτερος, and the singular form ἐπίσκοπος refers to each single person of the same group of leading people (πρεσβύτεροι)'; Ladd, *Theology* 352: 'the two terms are used interchangeably'; Long 258: 'two terms for the same office'; Merkle, 'Ecclesiology' 198: 'the terms . . . were used interchangeably to represent the same office'; Murphy-O'Connor, '2 Timothy' 408: '[They are] synonymous titles'; Ridderbos, *Paul* 457: 'we have to do here with one and the same office'; Schreiner, 'Overseeing' 93-94, 106; Wall 340; Wieland 184: 'both terms refer to the one <u>function</u>'; 曾 138：「這裏提到的……是一個職分的兩面。」古特立 30 指出，「提多書一 5～7 確實將這兩個字用來形容同樣的人，這個事實已經在新約學者間廣泛的被接受。」
(1)Dunn 864*b* 同意兩個名詞 'were regarded as near synonyms'. 但他同時認為可以這樣推論：'just as the elder was appointed from among the older men, so also the more specific role of overseer emerged from that of the elders.' 這等於說，長老和監督是不同的職位。Cf. Burkett, *INT* 440: 'The bishop is apparently one of the elders who occupies a place of preeminence'; North, '*Presbuteroi*' 319: '"the bishop" of 1 Timothy and Titus refers . . . to a presiding bishop, a "first amongst equals"'; Oden 139: 'all *episkopoi* (overseers) were *presbuteroi* (elders), though the reverse was not always true'; 140-41: 'The presbyter-overseer appears distinguishable from the ordinary presbyter in that certain duties of oversight are added, as seems indicated by the title'; Saarinen 172: 'The plain sense of 1:7-9 is that much more is required of bishops than of elders.' (2)Quinn 88 指著單數的監督（τὸν ἐπίσκοπον）說：'The awkward expression that could easily have been ironed out indicates that he [the author] did not consider them [πρεσβυτέρους, τὸν ἐπίσκοπον] completely synonymous.' Strecker（'Sound

---

Doctrine' 588）更認為，'since the Pastorals speak of the bishop only in the singular, but of the presbyters only in the plural, at least a step has been taken in the direction of the monarchical episcopacy of the later Catholic Church.' 但這單數的字只是延續了 6a 節單數的 εἴ τις（若有人）（Knight II 291）。如 Fiore II 198 所指出，單數的**監督**（δεῖ γὰρ τὸν ἐπίσκοπον）並不表示只有一位監督，即是單一監督制（monarchical episcopacy）內的 'monarchical bishop'；而是由於這字位於一列資格之前：參提前三 2（δεῖ οὖν τὸν ἐπίσκοπον），五 9（Χήρα καταλεγέσθω）。See also H. W. Beyer, *TDNT* 2.617: 'the reference is to the bishop as a type . . . There is no reference to monarchical episcopate'; L. Coenen, *DNTT* 1.192: '[the singular "bishop"] offers little support for the theory of monarchical episcopacy with a single bishop supervising all other office holders. This system triumphed in the 2nd and 3rd centuries, partly because of individuals with outstanding gifts and partly because of the need for tighter organization.' 單數的 ἐπίσκοπον 'is rather to be understood generically'（J. Rohde, *EDNT* 2.36*a* [s.v. 2]），即它是 generic singular（Davies II 75, 77; Hendriksen 346; Kelly 13, 14, 231; Knight II 291; Towner III 686〔唐 1001：「作為總稱」〕。Fitzmyer ['Ministry' 587] 則稱之為 'generic or collective [singular]'. 但 'collective singular' 通常是指一個集體的單數名詞，例如「人羣／羣眾」：ὄχλος/πλῆθος〔可二 4／三 7〕; see Wallace 400-1）。如 Ward 240 所說：'When we say that "a soldier must be brave" we mean "all soldiers."' 因此，Marshall（'Deception' 797）的見解不可取，他說：'the letter to Titus has "Paul" advocate a community with a single authoritative bishop over the church'. See also Bassler 186: 'it is likely that the bishop was chosen from the ranks of the elders as leader over them and over the church of a particular locale'; Drury 1231*b*: 'perhaps, as in Jewish communities of the diaspora, the *episkopos* was drawn from the ranks of the elders.' Collins 328 也認為，單數的**監督**提示 'that a singular overseer is to be appointed for each community, supervising each house church'; 300: 'the overseer is to be chosen from among the community's elders.'
(3) Kelly 229-30 則這樣區別長老和監督：首先，'there is a board of elders, or presbyters, who . . . form a court of notables with general responsibility for each community.' 然後，'there are executive officers known as overseers . . . who actually performed the ministerial and pastoral duties required.' 他們是從長老中選出來的，因而兩個稱謂幾乎是（但嚴格地說並非）可交換使用的（see also 232）。亦參張 326：「可能是每一所地方教會有數位長老，但卻〔只〕有一位監督，作為長老中的主席。」See also Zehr 248: 'the weight of evidence seems to point in the direction of calling out one person from among the elders who is especially gifted in management and teaching as the bishop of the congregation.' **(4)** Taylor 81 認為，教牧書信將兩種制度融合起來：'The churches of Paul did not have elders, but at least in Philippi they had bishops (Phil. 1:1). In contrast, Palestinian Christianity had adopted leadership patterns from the synagogue, which was governed by elders. In the Pastorals the two systems are fused.' **(5)** Young 則認為安提阿主教伊格那丢（約 35 至約 107）的描述—— 'let all respect the διάκονοι as Jesus Christ, even as the ἐπίσκοπος is the "type" of the Father, and the πρεσβύτεροι God's συνέδριον and as the συνέδριον of the Apostles'（《致他拉勒人書》3）（'On Ἐπίσκοπος' 148）——為監督、長老、執事這三者的關係提供了線索：原先只有監督和執事這兩種「職位（officers）」（144），長老則是後來才出現的「顧問團（an advisory council）」（145）。她的 'admittedly tentative hypothesis' 是這樣的：教會的管理人員（長期的基督徒習慣稱之為監督）開始獲得猶太人**會堂主管**（the ἀρχισυνάγωγος〔例：可五 22；路八 49〕）的功能，執事們則獲得會堂的賑濟員和服務員的功能（還有與基督徒聖餐有關的功能）；教會的「長者（seniors）」構成「管理局（a kind of governing council）」，有權委任監督並向他提供意見（147-48）。**(6)** 關於長老與監督的關係，詳盡的討論可參 Marshall 170-81，尤其是

的作長老的資格，也出現於提摩太前書三章 2 至 4 節作監督的資格中；[9]（**ii**）保羅對以弗所教會的長老（徒二十 17）說，聖靈立你們作全羣的監督（28 節）。[10] 從教牧書信可見，**監督**的功能包括三方面：教導（多一 9；提前三 2〔監督必須善於教導〕)、牧養（提前三 5b〔呂譯、當代／現修：照顧／看顧上帝的教會〕[11])、行政（由管理自己的家〔三 4、5a〕[12] 暗示）；而從教牧書信和使徒行傳可見，**長老**的功能同樣是這三方面：宣揚主道（提前五 17b：講道和教導〔現修、新譯、新普〕)、牧養信徒（徒二十 28：牧養上帝的教會），[13] 和治理教會（提前五 17a：督導／領導／管理／治理〔同呂譯、思高／現修／新和、當代／新譯〕[14])。[15] 在使徒行傳，教會的牧者被稱為監督（徒二十

177-81。就多一 5～7 而論，馬歇爾的結論是：'Tit 1.5-7 is concerned with the appointment of people to be elders and [*sic*] who are to act as overseers and stewards of God's people'（181）。筆者認為，後半部分若改為 'who are to act as God's stewards and overseers of God's people'，意思就更為準確和清晰。

9 見註 6 表格的頭三欄（上面 121-22）。利斐特 25（Liefeld 32）認為，「保羅在腓立比書的問候語中用了 *episkopoi* 和 *diakonoi* 這兩個詞，而不是 *presbyteroi*，顯見他信手拈來就把其中一詞〔*episkopoi*〕用作另一詞〔*presbyteroi*〕的同義詞。」筆者倒認為這論證不是很有說服力，反而有「假定了所要證明的」之嫌。

10 更詳細的辯證見 Merkle, *Elder* 142-48.

11 照管原文動詞是 ἐπιμελέομαι: 'care for, take care of'（BDAG 375*b* [s.v.]）。《新希》127*b*（s.v. I 2）則認為，這動詞在該節的意思是「考慮；關心；留意着好作回應——恰當地考慮一些問題或事情」。

12 管理原文動詞是 προΐστημι: 'manage'（BDAG 870*b* [s.v. 1]）。《新希》283*a*（s.v. I 1）則認為，此動詞在這裏的意思是「引導；指引；帶領——影響別人，使他們跟從所建議的方法行動」。此解釋可以視為指出了有效管理的技巧！

13 牧者和教師（弗四 11）的關係特別密切：教導是牧養的重要方式，也是牧者的重要職能；因而教師藉著教導也是在牧養信徒。參《弗》578，580 之（2）。

14 原文動詞也是 προΐστημι（見上面註 12）。Fiore II 11 認為，提前五 17 可能表示，在當時教會的職位尚未固定的情況下，'some who presided might have chosen to preach, others to teach, and others to do both'（see also 198: 'not all elders teach, as suggested by 1 Tim 5:17b）。不過，原文的結構（ἐν λόγῳ καὶ διδασκαλίᾳ: 兩個名詞從屬於同一個介系詞）似乎提示，與督導教會區別出來的，不是「講道」和「教導」（兩樣東西），而是在講道和教導上勞苦的／特別努力的（新譯／現修；see also RSV, NRSV, ESV / NAU, NJB / *Paraphrase* 307: 'those who labor in / work hard at/in preaching and teaching'），即是講道和教導被視為一樣東西。

15 因此，「『監督』似乎是長老羣中為首的，專責牧養和教導／〔他

28）或長老（二十 17，參十四 23）；在彼得前書，他被稱為長老（彼前五 1～4，見 1 節）；[16] 由此可見，在保羅事奉的後期，長老、監督和牧者（弗四 11）這些名稱都是指同一職分，粗略地等同「教會領袖」。[17]

上帝的管家一詞暗示，教會是上帝的家（提前三 15）。[18] 上帝的管家是由上帝指派的（參：路十二 42；林前九 17）。[19] 因此，作上帝

是〕長老羣中專責牧養教會的為首的『執行長老』／〔他是〕專責牧養教會的長老／首席長老」（周 411／414／415／414）這看法值得商榷。

16 Stott 90 說，'Peter appealed to the "elders" among his readers to serve as "bishops" of God's flock'，作為「新約時期長老和監督是同一職位的不同稱謂」的理據之一。他的話反映他接受彼前五 2 原文有分詞 ἐπισκοποῦντες（照顧他們；cf. NKJV, NIV: 'serving as overseers'; NAU, ESV / NRSV: 'exercising oversight / the oversight'; TNIV, NIV2011: 'watching over them'; NLT/NJB: 'Watch/watch over it'），但這讀文是不確定的（see *TextC* 625）。

17 參《弗》579。LN §53.71 就把 ἐπίσκοπος（監督）翻譯為 'church leader'. Wild 894*b* 同意教牧書信作者（並非保羅）將長老和監督二詞等同；不過他認為，由於古代（富有的）家庭由一個管家管理，這裏提到上帝的管家，可能暗示每一個家庭教會由一個長老／監督負責。參一 5 註釋註 28（上面 94）。

18 這種教會觀合併了教會（*ekklēsia*）和家（*oikos*）兩個觀念（Zamfir 60）。
（1） Tomlinson（'Purpose' 77 [cf. 83]）認為，'Paul apparently views himself as the "chief steward" of the household, having sent Timothy [1 Tim. 1:3] and Titus on temporary assignments as his delegated agents to check on the household churches. . . . Apparently Paul viewed his responsibility for these churches as like that of a chief steward overseeing scattered household estates.'
（2） Herzer 則質疑 'household' 是否提三 15 οἶκος 一字合適的翻譯（'Perspective' 559）。他認為 οἶκος θεοῦ 喚起的概念主要是教會乃上帝的殿（560），而提前的作者（不是保羅）故意選用 'house' 而不用 'temple' 一字，'because it would better fit his purpose to include this Pauline idea into his concern of the οἰκονομία θεοῦ (1 Tim 1:5). In this perspective, the congregation represents the house of God—a new kind of spiritual temple, whose primary function is to be solid and strong, a fortification to protect and keep the truth of the faith'（561）。不過，Marshall 508 較早前已辯證，'the language here primarily reflects the concept of the church as a household, but the thought of the church as temple is secondarily present.' Cf. idem, 'Congregation' 113: 'The dominant metaphor for the nature of the church in the Pastoral Epistles is that of the household.'

19 **（1）** 管家原文（οἰκονόμος）在新約另外出現九次：八次的意思都是管家（路十二 42，十六 1、3、8；林前四 2〔所求於管家的，是要他忠心〕；加四 2），其中兩次（如在本節）按其隱喻性意義使用（林前四 1；彼前四 10），餘下一次指某種官吏（羅十六 23；詳參《羅》4.797-802）。See

的管家的教會監督，像作**上帝的僕人**（1a 節）的保羅一樣，都是向上帝負責的，都要向上帝交賬。比較兩個片語，可見本節的字序使**上帝的**一字受到強調。[20] 有釋經者認為，**必須**[21] 在這裏可能有「因為這是上帝的旨意」的含意；[22]「上帝的旨意和性情就是倫理和敬虔的準則」。[23] 不過，文理提示另一種意思：監督之所以**必須**無可指責，是由於他是**上帝的管家**，他的屬靈品格必須配得上他所代表的上帝，並使上帝獲得稱讚而不是使祂的聲譽受損。[24]

（**#1**）**無可指責**重複自第 6a 節，因為第 7a 節是解釋第 6 節首句的：為甚麼**無可指責的人**才可以立為長老呢？因為長老作為教會的監督乃是**上帝的管家**，故此**監督……必須無可指責**（7a 節）。**無可指責**兩次都是籠統用法，引入長老或監督在家庭生活中（6 節）以及在個人品格上（7～9 節）所必須具備的條件。[25] 第 6 節已提及另兩項條件：見該節註釋之（**#2**）（**#3**）＝ 上面 103-7）。

隨後的五項都冠以否定詞不字：[26]（**#4**）**自負**（同思高）原文的

BDAG (s.v.);《新希》233*a*-33*b*（s.v.）。（**2**）原文是個複合名詞（from οἶκος + νόμος, 'one who rules a house' [Vine 2.169]）。名詞 οἶκος 見一 11 註釋註 11 之（2）＝ 下面 167）；名詞 νόμος 在保羅書信出現 141 次（新約全部 195 次）。

20 See Banker 38*a*. 兩個片語依次為 δοῦλος θεοῦ（正常次序）和 θεοῦ οἰκονόμον.

21 動詞 δεῖ（**必須**）在下文再出現兩次（一 11a、11c），保羅書信另外出現 22 次（包括提前三 2、7／提後二 14；這三節同樣指出**監督**／**主的僕人**必須是怎樣的），新約全部 101 次。見 BDAG 213*b*-14*b* (s.v.);《新希》73*a-b*（s.v.）。

22 W. Grundmann, *TDNT* 2.21 (cf. *TDNTA* 140]).

23 W. Popkes, *EDNT* 1.279*b* (s.v. δεῖ, 2): 'God's will and nature are the norms of ethics and piety'.

24 Marshall 160. Van Neste（'Message' 20*b*）認為，**無可指責**被重複提及，反映了保羅一方面的關注：不信主的世界在觀看，教會的聲譽攸關。但見註 2 及所屬正文（上面 120）。

25 Clark, 'Structure' 106. 其中的三樣見於一世紀中葉的哲學家 Onosander（或 Onasander [Marshall 183]）的作品中：'we must choose a general, not because of . . . but because he is temperate [σώφρονα], self-restrained [ἐγκρατῆ], . . . free from avarice [ἀφιλάργυρον] . . .'（DC 158）。比較一 8 的**克己**（σώφρονα）、**節制**（ἐγκρατῆ），和一 7 的**不貪財**（μὴ αἰσχροκερδῆ）。

26 （**1**）'The anaphoric μη [*sic*, μή] is . . . employed to highlight the five vices in 1:7'

意思包括**任性**（呂譯、新譯、新和）[27]「頑固」，[28] **傲慢**（現修、新普）[29]「自大」。[30] 監督是**上帝的管家**，即他的身分是上帝的僕人，他所照管的家是上帝的而不是他自己的，他當然不能任性自大。[31]

（**#5**）**暴躁**（同呂譯、新和、現修，新普同）原文的意思大抵不是**發怒**（思高），[32] 而是「性急、暴躁、易怒」，[33] 因而**隨便動怒**（新

(Genade 26). On 'anaphora' ('ἀνα-φορά, a reference back': 'Repetition of one or more words in successive statements'), see Harris, *Colossians* 290（引句出處）；BDF §491.（**2**）Quinn 89 認為，以不字開始的這五項解釋了**無可指責**的意思。他更聲稱，路加的比喻中那**不義的管家**（路十六 8）的行為，與多一 7b 的五項惡行相符：'The conduct of the vicious manager in the Lukan parable corresponds to the five vices that are listed in Titus 1:7b.' 筆者認為這聲稱言過其實；參《比喻》47-51。

27 See KJV / NKJV, NAU: 'selfwilled / self-willed'; G. Schneider, *EDNT* 1.178*a* (s.v. αὐθάδης): 'self-willed, arrogant'. *Paraphrase* 291 作 'self-assertive'（倔強）；Spencer 13, 17 作 'self-pleasing'. O. Bauernfeind（*TDNT* 1.509 [*TDNTA* 87]）則認為，'the related adjectives suggest meaning b', i.e. 'arbitrary' (508).

28 參當代：**剛愎自用**。'Stubborn perverseness that will not admit error is in mind' (Barrett 129).

29 See also RSV, NRSV, NJB, ESV, NLT, LN §88.206, DC 132*a*, Mounce cviii, Quinn 25, Witherington 106, 112: 'arrogant'; REB, NIV, TNIV, NIV2011: 'overbearing';《輔讀》525：「高傲的，任性妄為的」。 LN 認為，傲慢是任性和固執導致的（'as the result of self-will and stubbornness'）。

30 See BDAG 150*a* (s.v. **αὐθάδης**): 'self-willed, stubborn, arrogant';《新希》50*a*（s.v.）：「自負的；固執的——因為任性和頑固而自覺了不起的」。（**1**）此字在新約僅再出現一次（彼後二 10：**任性**），在 LXX 出現三次（創四十九 3，箴二十一 24／創四十九 7〔LXE: 'self-willed' / 'willful'〕）。（**2**）αὐθάδης 是複合形容詞（from αὐτός + ἥδομαι, to please; αὐθάδης '= αὐτοάδης, or αὑτῷ ἁδῶν, as Aristotle informs us' [Trench 349 (§xciii)]）：'[it] denotes one who, dominated by self-interest, and inconsiderate of others, arrogantly asserts his own will, "self-willed"'（Vine 3.342）；'self-willed, obstinate in his own opinion, arrogant, refusing to listen to others'（Lock 130）。

31 Fee 174. 不用說，即使在自己的家中，任何人（更遑論教會的監督）都不應任性頑固、傲慢自大。

32 See also LN §175: 'angry'. *Paraphrase* 291 作 'quarrelsome'. 當代作**暴戾急躁**；但「暴戾」的意思是「暴虐」(《國語》347*b*)。

33 See KJV: 'soon angry'; NKJV, RSV, NRSV, NAU, NIV, TNIV, NIV2011, ESV, NLT, LN §88.175, G. Schneider, *EDNT* 2.530*b* (s.v. ὀργίλος): 'quick-tempered'; REB: 'short-tempered'; NJB: 'hot-tempered'; Fairbairn 261, DC 132*a*, Fiore II 195, Witherington 106, 112: 'irascible'; Quinn 25: 'irritable'; BDAG 721*b* (s.v.): 'inclined to anger, quick-tempered';《新希》239*a*（s.v.）：「脾氣暴躁的；易怒的；愛發怒的——有動怒的傾向的」。（**1**）此字（**ὀργίλος**）在新約不再出現；它在 LXX 出現四次（詩十七 49〔十八 48；LXE: 'angry enemies'〕；箴二十一 19，二十二 24，二十九 22〔LXE 三次都譯作 'passionate'，但所譯自的希臘文所翻譯的希伯來字，在和

譯）。[34] 箴言指出，**易怒的人極易惹起紛爭**（箴二十九22，思高）；更警告人說，**脾氣暴躁的人，不要與他來往，免得你效法他的行徑，自己就陷在網羅裡**（二十二24b～25，新譯）。[35] 暴躁的人顯然不適合做**上帝的管家**。

（**#6**）**酗酒**（同當代、現修，新普同）原文若視為名詞，其意思便是「酒徒」（＝常常喝醉的人）；[36] 但若視為形容詞（像前三項一樣），它的意思便是**嗜酒／好酒**（思高／新譯）、「沉迷於酒」。[37] **豪飲**（呂譯）或**喝酒太多**（新普頁邊註）[38] 會導致**因酒滋事**（新和），[39] 但後者並非原文本身的部分涵義。[40]

修依次譯作**易怒的**、**暴怒的**，和**暴怒的**〕）。（**2**）與此字同字根的名詞是 ὀργή. Sewakpo（'Titus' 10-11）認為，希臘文用來指「憤怒」的兩個字之中，θυμός（誤作 θύμος；例：羅二8；弗四31；西三8）指 'the anger that quickly blazes up and quickly subsides', ὀργή（例：羅二8；弗四31；西三8）則指 'the wrath which a man nurses to keep it warm'. 可是，這樣區分二字是有疑問的；其實二字之間並無強烈或實質上的分別（參《羅》1.354-55；《弗》693-94；《西・門》549-50），儘管保羅的傾向是用 θυμός 指人的憤怒，以 ὀργή 指上帝的憤怒（詳見《西・門》549 連註 13）。有趣的是，Sewakpo 一早指出形容詞 ὀργίλος 的字面意義是 'to be [*sic*] prone to anger, irascible or passionate', 其後的解釋又提到 'A choleric* individual that has no proper command over his own temper', 即是直接地和間接地都贊同本註開首對此字的解釋，而不是支持他對名詞 ὀργή 的理解（'this long-lived, purposely maintained anger'）。（* =「易激怒的；常發怒的」〔《牛津》199*a* [s.v. 'choler']〕。）

34 Bailey（'Theology' 361）指出：'In ministry people can try an elder's patience. The root issues of selfishness, insecurity, and feelings of inferiority need to be addressed to slow a quick temper.'

35 Cf. Spencer 17-18.

36 RSV, ESV, LN §88.288, *EDNT* 3.42*b* (s.v. πάροινος): 'a drunkard'. See also NJB, NLT: 'a heavy drinker'.

37 KJV, NKJV / NRSV, NAU: 'given/addicted to wine'; NIV, TNIV, NIV2011: 'given to drunkenness'; BDAG 708*a* (s.v.): 'given to drinking too much wine, *addicted to wine, drunken*.' 若視為「名詞化用語」，這字的意思便是「酗酒者——習慣飲太多酒的人，因此變成酒鬼」（《新希》255*a* [s.v. I 2]）。此字在希臘文聖經僅再出現一次，就是在本節的平行經文提前三3（論監督的資格）。

38 See also NLT margin: 'drink too much wine'.

39 Towner III 688（唐 1003）：'it was common wisdom that excessive drinking [#6] often led to violence [#7]'; Spencer 18: 'sometimes excessive drinking can lessen inhibitions that cover more hidden aggressive [#7] emotions, especially if a person is prone to **anger** anyway (*orgilos*) [#5].'

40 （**1**）Lock 130 認為，πάροινος 在本節不一定具有字面意義，也許其意思只是像喝多了的人那樣「咆哮（blustering）」、「惡言惡語（abusive）」。但提多要勸年長的婦

（**#7**）**好鬥**（同現修）原文是人物名詞。[41] 一個好鬥的人隨時能夠**動武**（當代）或**使用暴力**（新普）[42] **去打人**（呂譯、新譯、新和）。[43] 這人隨時準備好去攻擊對手，[44] 他可能也是個「恃強凌弱的人」。[45]

（**#8**）**貪財**（同當代、現修）[46] 原文形容詞在這裏的意思可能只是「貪婪」，[47] 但較可能包括「貪、財、不誠實」這三個元素在

女**不作酒的奴僕**（二 3：μὴ οἴνῳ πολλῷ δεδουλωμένας），**不好酒**也是對作執事者的要求（提前三 8：μὴ οἴνῳ πολλῷ προσέχοντας），而兩個片語都必須按酒字的字面意義來理解；因而多一 7 對監督的這項要求同樣應理解為具字面意義（Banker 38*b*）。Cf. Marshall 162: 'The context here describes the roughest behaviour, and drunkenness fits best.'（**2**）威瑟靈頓說：'The vices are listed in a way that would lodge them in the hearer's aural memory': '*orgilos* and *paroinos* [## 5, 6] have rhyming endings, as do the next pair *plēktēs* and *aischrokerdēs* [##7, 8]'（Witherington 112 n.77）。其實，這四個字在本節皆為直接受格，因而只有前兩個押韻（*orgilon*, *paroinon*），後兩個則並不（*plēktēn*, *aischrokerdē*）。

41 *EDNT* 3.106*a*（s.v. πλήκτης）譯作 'a *quarrelsome man*'. 參較註 32（上面 128）。

42 See also NLT, NKJV, RSV, NRSV, NIV, TNIV, NIV2011, NJB, ESV, Mounce cviii, Malherbe, 'Medical Imagery' 125: 'violent'. Cf. *Paraphrase* 291: 'subject to a violent temper' =「受制於暴烈的性情」。思高則譯作**暴戾**；參較註 32（上面 128）。

43 See also KJV / Fairbairn 261: 'striker / a striker'. μὴ πλήκτην = 'not hasty to strike an opponent' (Lock 131).《輔讀》525 則解為「脾氣暴躁或粗暴的人」。但這使此字與**暴躁**（#5）的意思部分重疊。

44 Hiebert 431: 'ready to assail an opponent, either with fists or by bellicose behavior'. Barclay 237 認為原文名詞在這裏可能指一個使用語言暴力（來威嚇或使人就範）的人（'one who *browbeats* his fellow-men'）。Sewakpo（'Titus' 11）同樣認為，這字的意思包括 'a violent speech'. Cf. Marshall 162: 'the term may extend [beyond physical violence] also to ideas of anger and violence and verbal abuse'.

45 《新希》269*b*（s.v. πλήκτης）；BDAG 826*a* (s.v.): '[a] pugnacious person, bully'. See also LN§88.137, Quinn 25: 'a bully'; NAU, Spencer 13, 17, 18, 57, Witherington 106, 112: 'pugnacious'; Marshall 162: 'bully, pugnacious person'.（**1**）此字在希臘文聖經僅再出現一次（提前三 3；參上面註 37）。（**2**）Fiore（'Pastoral Epistles' 274-75）認為，**不好鬥**這一項資格可能反映了伊壁鳩魯主義（亦稱享樂主義）者（Epicureans）的一種主張，就是反對體罰奴隸這長期存在的傳統，這個主張可能被納入了教牧書信對如何**管理自己的家**（提前三 4）的理解中。

46 See NKJV: 'greedy for money'; RSV, NRSV, ESV; Mounce cviii / Fairbairn 261: 'greedy for/of gain'. G. Schneider（*EDNT* 1.41*b* [s.v. αἰσχροκερδής]）譯作 'repulsively greedy'.（**1**）Quinn 25 則僅譯為 'money-minded'（以金錢為念）。（**2**）末世時，人會⋯⋯**貪愛錢財**（提後三 2）；原文用的是另一個字（φιλάργυρος）。

47 NJB: 'avaricious'. 但「貪婪」在保羅書信是通用名詞 πλεονεξία（羅一 29；弗五 3；西三 5；帖前二 5）或人物名詞 πλεονέκτης（林前五 10、11，六 10；弗五 5）表達

內，[48] 就如好些中英譯本所反映的：**貪可恥／無義／不義之財**（呂譯／新和／新譯）。[49]（一）白新港認為，**可恥**是指以圖利為進入職事的目的。[50] 但這解釋不合適地限制了原文形容詞的意思。[51]（二）巴列特認為，**貪財**不是指以不誠實的方法獲得利益，而是指從基督教的服務中獲得利益。[52] 不過，保羅在提摩太前書五章 18 節申明，**工人得工資是應當的**，這原則同樣適用於教會的長老（17 節）。因此，（三）**貪財**較可能指想要發財，擁有多過自己生活所需的（參：提前六 5～10）。[53] 無論如何，**不貪財**顯然與克里特假教師的**貪不義之財**（一 11）相對。[54]

的。思高明確地翻譯為**貪污**。

48 BDAG 29*b* (s.v.): '<u>shamelessly</u> greedy for money, *avaricious*, *fond of dishonest gain*'; LN §25.26: 'pertaining to being <u>shamefully</u> greedy for material gain or profit'; DC 132*a* / Banker 38*b*: 'fond of dishonest/shameful gain';《新希》10*b*（s.v.）：「無恥地貪圖財富與利益的。」留意兩個英文副詞的分別：'shamelessly' =「無恥地、厚著面皮地」（指貪財者本身），'shamefully' =「可恥地、不體面地」（指他們的行為）。（**1**）Stott 177 則認為，保羅在此禁止的 'is not so much dishonesty of practice as greed of motive.' 參較下面註 52（Barrett）。（**2**）此字（**αἰσχροκερδής**）在希臘文聖經僅再出現一次（提前三 8，論執事的資格）。但參多一 11c 的 αἰσχροῦ κέρδους χάριν（**貪不義之財**）；見一 11 註釋第四段（下面 169-71）。（**3**）此字是複合形容詞（from αἰσχρός + κέρδος, 這兩個字都在多一 11c 出現）；αἰσχρός 在新約出現的另三次，其意思也是**可恥的**（林前十一 6〔現修〕，十四 35；弗五 12）；κέρδος 在新約出現的另二次，其意思都是**利益**（思高：腓一 21，三 7）。（**4**）同字根的副詞在希臘文聖經只出現一次，指作長老的牧養羣羊，應該不是**因為貪財**（αἰσχροκερδῶς），**而是出於樂意**（彼前五 2）。

49 See also KJV / Vine 2.99: 'given to / greedy of filthy lucre'; NAU: 'fond of sordid gain'; NIV, TNIV, NIV2011: 'pursuing dishonest gain'.（**1**）新普（**欺詐錢財**）只表達二個元素（see also NLT: 'dishonest with money'）。（**2**）張 185 認為原文的意思是「貪於賺取錢財」。但「（以正當工作）賺取」得來的錢財，為甚麼稱為**不義之財**（新譯）呢？

50 White 115*a* ('an object in entering the ministry').

51 See Banker 38*b*-39*a*. Hanson I 110 則將**不貪財**理解為，'he should not take up a trade unsuitable to his position as bishop'. 這假定監督是「帶職事奉」的。但這假設與提前五 17～18 的含意是否相符呢？

52 Barrett 129 (followed by Fee 174): 'It is the sordidness of making profit out of Christian service . . . that is here condemned.' 這使人想起以弗所的假教師：對他們來說，**敬虔的表現只是謀利的途徑**（提前六 5，新普）。

53 Mounce 390.

54 至少在這方面，'the elder is the Cretan antitype*'（Jeon I 42）。*此字在這裏的意思是「相反的類型」，而不是神學意義的、與「預表（type）」相對的「對範（預表之本體）」（《宗教》18*b*）。

一 8 卻要樂意接待外人、好善、克己、正直、聖潔、節制，

本節繼續列舉監督的資格。這裏以連接詞卻（同呂譯、新譯）、但（思高）、相反（新普）[1] 開始，不是因為本節的六項[2] 和上一節的不自負、不暴躁、不酗酒、不好鬥、不貪財那五項相反（因為負負得正，加上了不字的負面項目變成了正面的項目），[3] 而是和減去不字的自負、暴躁、酗酒、好鬥、貪財相反。[4]

（**#9**）樂意接待外人原文形容詞[5] 的意思是好客（思高、當代），[6] 就一世紀的處境而論，可能是特指樂意接待旅客（呂

1 ἀλλά = 'But/but' (KJV / NKJV, RSV, NRSV, NAU, NJB, ESV), 'Rather' (NIV, TNIV, NIV2011, NLT); 'on the contrary' (*Paraphrase* 291). 'The purpose of the antithesis [μή . . . μή . . . μή . . . μή . . . μή . . . ἀλλά] is to emphasize the second, positive member' (Malherbe, 'Paraenesis' 304).

2 克拉遜指出，頭兩項有相同的前綴（φιλ-），後四項在希臘哲學討論的傳統中是緊密相連的（Classen, 'Titus' 343, 'Epistle to Titus' 52-53）。Wild 894*b* 認為，後四項是 '[a] version of the four cardinal virtues of Greco-Roman antiquity.' 這就是說，這裏的第三項（聖潔：ὅσιον）取代了傳統的 ἀνδρεία（courage）一項。但這裏也沒有傳統的 φρόνησις 一項；參二 12 註釋註 2 之（1）（2）= 下面 290。

3 也許就是為了這緣故，**（1）**新和、現修不把 ἀλλά 譯出，使本節的六項和上一節的六項一氣呵成（不過，兩者都在 7 節末使用分號，將 6 節以負面形式表達的五項，和本節以正面形式表達的六項稍微分開）；**（2）**當代更以並且開始本節。**（3）**留意 Jeon II 14 的觀察：'a candidate is not qualified simply because he is *not* a bad fellow; rather, he must also demonstrate positive qualities evident to all who know him.'

4 這似乎就是 Sterling（'Philosophy' 326）可以將 'Titus 1:7 and 1:8' 列入新約中的 'four compound [vice and virtue] lists' 的原因。作者列出的另三個例子是 'Gal. 5:19-21 and 22-23; Eph. 4:31 and 4:32-5:2; Col. 3:5-8 and 12'. 參《加》1243-45；《弗》696-97、698；《西》529。

5 φιλόξενος 是複合形容詞（from φίλος + ξένος [see Vine 2.235]）。**（1）**形容詞 φίλος 在新約出現 29 次，其意思是 'loving, kindly disposed'（BDAG 1059*a* [s.v. 1]），如在徒十九 31（保羅的朋友直譯是 'friendly to him' [NRSV]）；用作名詞，其意思便是朋友（例：耶穌被識為稅吏和罪人的朋友〔太十一 19 ‖ 路七 34〕；約翰自喻為新郎的朋友（約三 29）；亞伯拉罕稱為上帝的朋友（雅二 23）；與世俗為友〔雅四 4〕直譯是「世界的朋友」）。詳見 BDAG 1058*b*-59*a* (s.v.);《新希》347*b*（s.v.）。**（2）**形容詞 ξένος 在保羅書信出現三次（羅十六 23：東道主〔呂譯〕；弗二 19／12：外人／局外人），新約另外十一次。See BDAG 684*a*-*b* (s.v.);《新希》230*a*（s.v.）。

6 φιλόξενος = 'hospitable'（BDAG 1058*b* [s.v.]; *EDNT* 3.427*b* [s.v.]; NKJV, RSV, NRSV, NAU, NIV, TNIV, NIV2011, NJB, ESV, *Paraphrase* 291），'showing hospitality to strangers'（LN §34.85）。**（1）**Banker 39*a* 認為原文的意思是籠統的 'hospitable' 而

譯）。[7] 同字根的抽象名詞[8] 在新約出現兩次：樂意款待旅客的事要力行（羅十二 13，呂譯）；別忘了樂意款待旅客（來十三 2）。三段經文所指的似乎都是接待基督徒客旅，理由如下：（i）在羅馬書十二章，異鄉客，要殷勤款待（13b 節）緊隨聖徒有缺乏，要供給（13a 節），兩句按先後次序似乎是弟兄彼此相愛的原則（10a 節）籠統的和確切的具體應用；（ii）在希伯來書十三章，不可忘記用愛心接待旅客（2a 節）更是緊接著原文的弟兄相愛（1 節）一詞，前者似乎是後者的一種表達方式；（iii）相同的現象見於彼得前書四章，在「要恆常不變地彼此相愛」一句（8a 節）[9] 之後就是要互相款待（9a 節）。[10] 這個三重的事實有力地提示，討論中的外人或旅客不是未信主的人，[11] 而是基督徒客旅。[12]

不僅是對 'strangers' 的接待。新普（熱情好客）加入了「熱情」之意；see also NLT / Mounce, 'Titus' 105: 'enjoy having guests/others in his home';《新希》347*b*（s.v.）：「款待周到的——殷勤招待陌生人的。」（**2**）這形容詞在希臘文聖經僅再出現兩次：提前三 2（監督必須樂意接待外人）；彼前四 9（信徒要互相款待）。

7 （**1**）KJV 的翻譯不可取，因 'a love of hospitality' 容易被誤解為「喜歡接受款待」而不是樂意接待人（現修）。（**2**）要接待客旅（新譯）這翻譯也不可取，因這翻譯表達的是一項命令，但文理是在談及一項資格。

8 φιλοξενία = 'hospitality' (BDAG 1058*b* [s.v.]; LN §34.57).

9 τὴν εἰς ἑαυτοὺς ἀγάπην ἐκτενῆ ἔχοντες. ἐκτενής = 'pert. to being persevering, with implication that one does not waver in one's display of interest or devotion' (BDAG 310*a* [s.v.]); see also LN §68.12: 'love one another without ceasing'. 另一可能是 ἐκτενής = 'eager . . . earnest'（LN §25.71）;「熱切的；熱誠的」(《新希》107*a* [s.v. I 2]）。

10 彼前四 9 用的是與 φιλοξενία 同字根的形容詞 φιλόξενος（參上面註 6 之〔2〕)。

11 S. C. Mott (*DPL* 271*a*) 認為，羅十二 13 的 φιλοξενία 是指款待「非信徒」(《辭典》396*b*）。

12 M. J. Selman（*IBD* 2.665*b*）指出，雖然接待異鄉人的例子在整本聖經都有，但是這方面惟一的明確命令，是關乎基督徒對他的基督徒同道的責任。（**1**）Witherington 116 則認為，'Here in Titus, however, it would appear that Paul also has in mind [besides the help offered to 'traveling missionaries', 115] the hospitality offered to fellow Christians who met in the elder's or congregational patron's house.'（**2**）威瑟靈頓進一步認為，外人包括非基督徒。他聲稱：'Most early Christians, particularly Gentile ones, likely came to Christian faith not by hearing about it in a synagogue, but by hearing the message over or after a meal in a friend's home'（116）。可是，至少從使徒行傳的證據看來，「早期基督教的佈道模式很可能是以會堂為其焦點；基督教開始時被視為一世紀之猶太教的一派（參徒十八 15，二十八 22），基督教最初的宣教士都是猶太

這些基督徒客旅包括：教會的帶信人（參：羅十六 1～2）；因受逼迫而逃難的信徒（參：徒八 1，十一 19）；[13] 巡迴佈道者，**他們為主的名出外，並沒有從教外人接受甚麼**，因而應被所到之地的教會接待（參：約叁 5～8〔引句 7 節，新譯〕），儘管這種接待含有冒險成分（參：徒十七 5～9）。古代的客店是既昂貴又不安全，且是聲名狼藉的場所（客店主人常與邪術有關聯；開客店跟開妓寨被視為不相伯仲之事〔根據猶太傳統，妓女喇合是個客棧的主人〕；旅客可在客店找到「商業性」女伴是普遍的假設），因而尤其不適宜基督徒入住。[14] 早期教會的宣教士如彼得（徒十 6、48；參十八 27）、保羅（門 22；參：羅十五 24；林後一 15～16；徒二十七 3，二十八 14）、提摩太（林前十六 10～11）及馬可（西四 10），和耶穌自己（路十 38），都依靠信徒的接待。[15]

樂意接待外人這一項美德，假定了監督具有為教會接待基督徒客旅的能力；這就是說，他有一所夠大的房子，或許同時在家庭教會內擁有權柄，可以接待或拒絕接待過境的客旅（參：約叁）。[16]

（**#10**）**好善**（同新和）在希羅世界是特別受敬重和負責任的公

人，因此猶太基督徒在會堂中分享他們的信仰是很自然的事（參徒十一 19，十八 19、24～26，十九 8）。即使是向外邦人傳福音的工作，其最佳土壤也是皈依猶太教的外邦人以及『虔敬的人』；保羅在外邦城市傳福音時的一貫做法，是首先在安息日進入會堂，以外邦人及『虔敬的人』為其對象（參：徒十三 5、14，十四 1，十七 1～2、10、17，十八 4）」（《羅》1.65-66）。無論如何，（**3**）'What sometimes passes for hospitality today (the entertainment of friends and church members, often with the expectation of a return invitation) is a rather dim reflection of the New Testament concept. . . . hospitality required sacrificial sharing and stretching. It was a very practical expression of love, not a source of entertainment'（Towner II 227）。

13 Jeon I 43 認為，'The quality has in view hospitality to Christian refugees and . . . .'

14 See Malherbe, *Social Aspects* 67;《來》2.426 連註 11。B. M. Rapske（*DNTB* 1246*b*）指出，現有的文學及考古學方面的資料顯示，古代的客店一般都沒有好好的打理所提供的設備：最小量的傢具和陳設品、生滿臭蟲的牀鋪、劣質的食物和飲料；而且店主不可靠，住客形迹可疑，道德一般低落。

15 以上兩段，參《羅》4.153-54。See also Quinn 90; 昆謝隆認為，（#9）所指的就是 'an ungrudging provision of food and shelter to Christian missionaries'（參三 12～15）。

16 MacDonald, *Pauline Churches* 212.

民的特色；[17] 因此，這字常見於頌揚的銘文上。[18] 原文的意思不僅是喜歡做好事（現修），[19] 而是籠統意義的好良善（呂譯）或喜愛良善（新譯、新普）。[20] 這一項美德與末世（即是現今）之假教師的不愛

17 BDAG 1055*b* (s.v. φιλάγαθος): '***loving what is good*** (in the Gr-Rom. world a characteristic of an esp. respected and responsible citizen'). **(1)** 此字在希臘文聖經僅再出現一次：舊約次經《所羅門智訓》7.22（φιλάγαθον 相當於思高智慧篇 7.22 的「好善的」）。這是智慧的 21 項特色的其中一項（Montague 221）。**(2)** 這字是複合形容詞（from φιλέω + ἀγαθός）。動詞 φιλέω 見三 15a～b 註釋註 16（下面 472）；形容詞 ἀγαθός 見一 16 註釋註 35 之（2）= 下面 213。
(3) 除了本節這兩個字（φιλόξενος〔樂意接待外人〕，另見提前三 2；彼前四 9〔款待〕；φιλάγαθος〔好善〕），**以 φιλ- 開始的複合字**（see C. Brown, *DNTT* 2.549-50）
(i) 在本書還有：φίλανδρος（二 4：愛丈夫）、φιλότεκνος（二 4：愛兒女）、φιλανθρωπία（三 4：慈愛；此字另見徒二十八 2〔友善〕）。
(ii) 在教牧書信還有：φιλαργυρία（提前六 10：貪財）、φιλάργυρος（提後三 2〔另見路十六 14〕：貪愛錢財）、φίλαυτος（提後三 2：專愛自己）、φιλήδονος（提後三 4：愛享樂〔新譯〕）、φιλόθεος（提後三 4：愛上帝）。
(iii) 在其他的保羅書信還有：φιλαδελφία（羅十二 10／帖前四 9：愛弟兄／弟兄間的手足之情；此字另見來十三 1；彼前一 22；彼後一 7a、7b）、φιλόνεικος（林前十一 16：「〔好〕爭辯」〔新普〕）、φιλοξενία（羅十二 13：款待〔另見來十三 2：接待〕）、φιλοσοφία（西二 8：哲學）、φιλόστοργος（羅十二 10：相親相愛〔思高、現修〕= 'loving dearly' [BDAG 1059*b*, s.v.]）、φιλοτιμέομαι（羅十五 20：〔以之為〕抱負〔現修、新普〕；此字另見林後五 9；帖前四 11）。
(iv) 在新約其他的書卷還有：φιλάδελφος（彼前三 8：相愛如弟兄）、φιλανθρώπως（徒二十七 3：以仁慈待〔思高〕）、φιλονεικία（路二十二 24：爭論〔eagerness to contend－＞contention [Vine 1.234]〕）、φιλοπρωτεύω（約叁 9 節：好作領袖）、φιλόσοφος（徒十七 18：哲學家）、φιλοφρόνως（徒二十八 7：友善地〔新普〕）。
(v) 還包括以下兩個地名：Φιλαδέλφεια（啟一 11，三 7：非拉鐵非）、Φίλιπποι（徒十六 12，二十 6；腓一 1；帖前二 2：腓立比）；和五個人名：Φιλήμων（門 9 節：腓利門）、Φίλητος（提後二 17：腓理徒）、Φιλιππήσιος（腓四 15：腓立比人）、Φιλόλογος（羅十六 15：非羅羅古）、Φίλιππος——可指（see D. H. Wheaton, *IBD* 3.1213*a*-15*a*）：（*a*）大希律王與其第三任妻子 Mariamne II 所生的腓力（太十四 3 ‖ 可六 17）；（*b*）大希律王與其第五任妻子 Cleopatra of Jerusalem 所生的分封王腓力（路三 1；凱撒利亞．腓立比〔太十六 13 ‖ 可八 27〕的意思是斐理伯的凱撒勒雅〔思高〕）；（*c*）門徒和十二使徒之一的腓力（例：太十 3 ‖ 可三 18 ‖ 路六 14；徒一 13）；（*d*）耶路撒冷教會選出來辦理供給之事的七人之一（徒六 5），其後從事傳福音的工作（八 5～40），更被稱為傳福音的腓利（二十一 8）。

18 BDAG 157*b* (s.v. ἀφιλάγαθος): 'the affirmative φιλάγαθος is freq. in honorary ins'. See also DC 133*b*: '"Love of what is good" (φιλαγαθία) appears frequently in the honorary inscriptions.'

19 樂善（思高、當代）這翻譯容易使人想到「樂善好施」=「樂於做善事，喜歡施捨」（《成語》360*b*），因而被局限於「樂於行善」之意。參陳 21：「行善已成為其愛好之一。」

20 NAU, *EDNT* 3.424*a*, Mounce cviii, Spencer 13, 17, 18: 'loving what is good'; LN

良善（提後三 3）[21] 剛好相反。[22]

（**#11**）**克己**（同呂譯）即是能夠控制自己。[23] 原文[24] 主要的意思是「心思健全」；[25] 這字在本節的幾種翻譯可謂都與健全的心思有關聯：「有判斷力的、明理的」；[26] **通情達理**（當代），即是「很懂道理，說話、做事合情合理」；[27] **行事有智慧**（新普）。[28] 另二種翻譯是**慎重**（思高），即是「謹慎持重不苟且」，[29] 和**自律**（新譯）。原文形容詞在舊約偽經《馬加比四書》出現八次，英文的《標準修訂版》和《新標準修訂版》翻譯為「有節制的、適度的」有七次，[30] 餘下一次

---

§25.105: 'liking or loving what is good';《新希》346*b*（s.v.）：「喜歡或喜愛美善事物的。」（**1**）多數英譯本的翻譯將形容詞化為人物名詞：'a lover of good/goodness'（ESV / RSV, NRSV, NJB; W. Grundmann, *TDNTA* 4; Jeon I 13; Matera, 'Moral Guides' 240-41）；'a lover of / one who loves what is good'（NKJV* / NIV, TNIV, NIV2011）；'a lover of all that is good'（*Paraphrase* 291）。See also LN §25.105: 'one . . . who loves what is good'.（*修正了 KJV 的 'a lover of good men'.）（**2**）古特立則認為，*philagathos* 一字 'includ[es] / can include things as well as persons'（Guthrie I 186 / Guthrie II 198; 古特立 200）。Barclay 238 就翻譯為 'a lover of all good things and all good people'. See also Mounce 391: 'it probably includes both [loving good people and good things] here'; Lock 131: 'ready to welcome all good men, or probably "goodness wherever he sees it"'.（**3**）Calvin 360 譯作 'devoted to kindness'. 他的理由（筆者認為不具說服力）是，'Paul seems to be connecting this virtue with hospitality and contrasting them both with greed and meanness.'

21 ἀφιλάγαθος（= φιλάγαθος + α-privative）在希臘文聖經僅此一次。

22 Ward 241 則認為，**喜愛良善**可理解為<u>包括</u> 'loving good people' 之意（參上面註 20 之〔2〕），與**專愛自己，貪愛錢財**（提後三 2）相對。

23 See NIV, TNIV, NIV2011, ESV, LN §88.84: 'self-controlled'; RSV: 'master of himself'.

24 σώφρων，在本書再出現兩次（二 2、5），在提前出現一次（三 2，論監督的資格）；新約僅此四次。同字根的抽象名詞 σωφροσύνη 在教牧書信出現兩次（提前二 9、15：**克制**）。參一 14 註釋註 27 之（5）= 下面 195。

25 BDAG 987*b* (s.v. σώφρων): 'prim. "one of sound mind"'. 參下面註 33（Blaiklock）。

26 NAU, NJB, *EDNT* 3.330*a* (s.v.), Quinn 26: 'sensible'（所引中譯見《牛津》1056*a* [s.v. 1]）。See also Fee 185: 'It has especially to do with being "sensible" or "sound-minded"'.

27 《成語》621*a*。

28 NLT: 'live wisely'; Fee 175: 'close to "having his wits about him"'. See also Marshall 186:（同字根的名詞）σωφροσύνη 'has . . . the nuance of acting thoughtfully and wisely.'

29 《國語》267*a*。See Fairbairn 261: 'discreet' =「謹慎的；有智慮的」（《牛津》337*b*）。**莊重**（新和）及**莊敬自重**（現修；《輔讀》525〔第一解釋〕加上「的」字）則含「嚴謹、認真、莊嚴」等意思。See NKJV: 'sober-minded' =「認真的；嚴肅的」（《牛津》1113*b* [s.v. 1]）。

30 所引中譯見《牛津》1213*a*（s.v. 'temperate', 1）。

則翻譯為「自我控制」。[31]「自我控制」這意思將會由第十四項清楚表達（見下文）；目前這第十一項的意思可能比第十四項更為廣闊，[32] 涵蓋數個意思：「審慎的、深思的、自制的」、[33]「適度的、有節制的」。[34]

（**#12**）**正直**（同現修）[35] 的另一些翻譯是**正義**（呂譯）、**公正**（思高、新譯、新普）、[36] **公正嚴明**（當代）、**公平**（新和）。[37] 在希羅傳統裏，一個正直、公正、公平的人，就是一個「維護那些導致秩序井然的文明社會的種種行為習俗和標準（包括尤其是公共服務）」的人。[38] 但是對一個在基督羣體中的監督而言，正義的標準較可能是上帝的要求。[39]（**#13**）**聖潔**（同新譯、新和、現

---

31 《馬加比四書》1.35, 2.16, 2.18, 3.17: ὁ σώφρων νοῦς = 'the temperate mind'; 2.2: ὁ σώφρων Ιωσηφ = 'the temperate Joseph'; 2.23: βασιλεία σώφρων = 'a kingdom that is temperate'; 3.19: σώφρων λογισμός = 'temperate reason'; 15.10: σώφρων = 'self-controlled'.

32 Kidd（'Titus' 204）則認為**克己**（#11）與**節制**（#14）同義（'are synonyms'）。但見註 54 及所屬正文（下面 140）。

33 BDAG 987*b* (s.v. σώφρων): 'pert. to being in control of oneself, *prudent*, *thoughtful*, *self-controlled*'. See also NRSV: 'prudent' =「審慎的；三思而後行的」(《牛津》915*b*)；Blaiklock 81: 'The Greek word speaks of a wise self-control, . . . a strength of mind which knows how to avoid folly as well as vice, which shuns all excess, which keeps all desire, all activity, all thought, in rightful place. It suggests that it is a sane and ordered reason which makes for virtue, not mere emotion.' 留意此解釋對心思和理性的著重（參上面註 25）。

34 LN §88.94: 'moderate' =「適度的；有節制的」(《牛津》738*b* [s.v. 1])；《新希》323*a*（s.v.）：「明智的；有節制的——一個人的行為屬於明智而適度的」；REB, Fairbairn 261: 'temperate'（參上面註 31 及所屬正文）；KJV, *Paraphrase* 291: 'sober' = 'self-controlled; temperate; . . . 自制的；適度的；……'(《牛津》1113*b* [s.v. 1])。See also Marshall 184: 'it communicates . . . the idea of "a suitable restraint in every respect", a self-control which leads to behaviour appropriate to the situation'; 'it depicts a balanced demeanour characterized by self-control, prudence and good judgement.'

35 See also RSV, NRSV, NIV, TNIV, NIV2011, NJB, ESV: 'upright'.

36 See also KJV, NKJV, NAU, NLT, *Paraphrase* 291: 'just'.

37 Cf. Arichea – Hatton 272: '"fair," "impartial," or "unbiased" are all good [translation] models.'

38 BDAG 246*a* (s.v. δίκαιος, 1 a α): 'In Gr-Rom. tradition a δ. pers. is one who upholds the customs and norms of behavior, including esp. public service, that make for a well-ordered, civilized society'.

39 See LN §88.12· δίκαιος = 'pertaining to being in accordance with what God requires'; G. Schrenk, *TDNT* 2.191: 'his life should be in accordance with the divine norm'.（**1**）

修）[40] 另有譯為**虔聖**（呂譯）、**心虔意誠**（當代）、[41] **過敬虔⋯⋯的生活**（新普）。[42] 這兩項分別指對人和對上帝的恰當的行為。[43]

正直和**聖潔**這兩個形容詞在此連著出現，使人想起另二節經文：在帖撒羅尼迦前書二章 10 節，保羅說帖人可以見證，他對待他們**是何等聖潔、正直**（原文所用的是副詞「聖潔地、正直地」)。在以弗所書四章 24 節，保羅指出：照著上帝的形像造的**新我**，是「在真理的**公義和聖潔中**」（原文直譯）被造的。**公義**和**聖潔**若分開來解釋，可依次指對人和對上帝的正當關係和行為，但這種在古典希臘文常見的區別，似乎不能轉移到二字在新約的用法。**公義**和**聖潔**二詞一起可能指有品德的生活整體。[44] 按這種理解，這裏對監督的要求包括他要過一種有品德的生活。不過，本節的**正義**、**虔聖**（呂譯）二字中間並無連詞（不像上述的另二節），而且前後還有另四個項目，也是以無連詞的

Hendriksen 347 則解釋為 'performing one's duty toward man'.《新希》84*b*（s.v. I 3）解釋為「適當的或對的，證明了是完全合理的」。(**2**) 這形容詞（**δίκαιος**）在保羅書信另外出現十六次，新約全部 78 次：參《新希》84*b*(s.v.)；BDAG 246*a*-47*a* (s.v.).

40 See also KJV, NKJV, RSV, NJB, ESV: 'holy'. 思高的**熱心**未知是如何得來的。

41 See also NRSV, REB, NAU, NIV, TNIV, NIV2011, Quinn 26: 'devout'; *Paraphrase* 291: 'pious'; BDAG 728*a* (s.v. ὅσιος, 1): 'pert. to being without fault relative to deity, *devout, pious*, *pleasing to God*, *holy*'; H. Balz, *EDNT* 2.536*b* (s.v. 3): 'godly, pleasing to God'. 此形容詞（**ὅσιος**）在新約另外出現七次：(i) 三次分別指上帝是**神聖**的（啟十五 4），基督是**聖潔**的大祭司（來七 26〔參《來》1.473〕），信徒禱告時舉起的手應是**聖潔**的（提前二 8）；(ii) 另四次用作名詞，分別指上帝是**聖者**（啟十六 5），基督是上帝的**聖者**（徒二 27，十三 35〔引詩十六 10〕），以及所應許予大衞那**神聖⋯⋯的恩典／恩福**（徒十三 34，現修／新譯）。See BDAG 728*a*-*b* (s.v.);《新希》240*b*(s.v.)。

42 NLT: 'live a devout . . . life.' F. Hauck（*TDNT* 5.492）認為，'Echoed here is . . . the general Gk. use for "what is right and good before God and man."'

43 Mounce 391; cf. 393: 'just toward people, and holy in conduct toward God.' 在聖經別處，二字都是形容上帝的：摩西稱上帝為「公義和聖潔的」（LXX 申三十二 4：δίκαιος καὶ ὅσιος）；詩人（詩一四五 17）讚嘆，'the Lord is righteous [δίκαιος] in all his ways, and holy [ὅσιος] in all his works'（LXX 一四四 17 [LXE]）；在啟十六 5，一位天使對上帝這樣說：**昔在、今在的聖者**（ὁ ὅσιος）**啊！你是公正**（δίκαιος）**的**（新普）。另見偽經《所羅門詩篇》10.5：'Our Lord is just and holy [δίκαιος καὶ ὅσιος] in his judgments forever'（LXE）。參較徒三 14：彼得稱耶穌為**那聖潔公義者**（τὸν ἅγιον καὶ δίκαιον）。

44 詳見《弗》657-58，連註 9-11。

形式出現；因此，二字不必視為構成一個單元，而可（或應）分開來處理，如在上一段所建議的。

（**#14**）**節制**、**有節**（思高）、**能節制**（呂譯）[45] 更好的翻譯是**自制**（新譯）、[46] **能管束自己**（現修）、[47] **過……自律的生活**（新普），[48] 所指的就是能夠控制自己的情感、衝動，或慾念。[49] 同字根的名詞[50] 在新約出現四次：保羅對腓力斯講論的，包括**自制**（徒二十四 25，新譯）；**自制**是聖靈的果子之一（加五 23，當代）；[51] **自制**也是彼得要信徒努力追求的品質之一（彼後一 6a、6b，當代）。同字根的動詞[52] 在新約只出現兩次，分別指性慾方面的**自制**（林前七 9）和運動員在各方面都必須**自制**（林前九 25，當代）。[53] 總

---

45 新和作**自持**。當代翻譯為**莊敬自持**，與之前的**通情達理**，**公正嚴明**，**心虔意誠**（##3-5）四字組合一致。KJV 則翻譯為 'temperate'（參註 30、31、34 及所屬正文〔上面 136、137〕）。

46 參《新希》94*a*（s.v. ἐγκρατής）：「自制的——指操練自我控制的。」

47 See also NKJV, RSV, NRSV, REB, NAU, NJB, *Paraphrase* 291, LN §88.84, Quinn 26: 'self-controlled'.

48 NLT: 'live a . . . disciplined life.' See also NIV, TNIV, NIV2011, ESV: 'disciplined'.

49 BDAG 274*b* (s.v. ἐγκρατής): 'pert. to having one's emotions, impulses, or desires under control, *self-controlled, disciplined*'. H. Baltensweiler（*DNTT* 1.496）解釋為 'not a dissolute character'（能自制 = 不放縱自己）。這字在新約出現僅此一次。(**1**) White 188*a* 則這樣區別這字和 σώφρων（#11）：這字指 'bodily appetites', 該字亦指 'the desires of the mind'; 'ἐγκράτ. concerns action, σώφρ. thought.' (**2**) H. Goldstein（*EDNT* 1.378*a* [s.v. ἐγκράτεια, 3]）認為，ἐγκρατ- 這組字在新約出現的七次都首先指 'sexual abstinence, but then is extended to include positive, general self-control and discipline'. (**3**) Witherington 106-7 指出，在一 5～9 這一段裏，除了有三個字在新約不再出現（5b 節：ἐπιδιορθόω; 8 節：φιλάγαθος, ἐγκρατής），還有十五個字不見於教牧書信以外的保羅書信，儘管其中有九個字在教牧書信裏再次出現；威瑟靈頓認為這事實支持他的看法：'The voice is that of Paul, but the hand is that of Luke, who is far more attuned to speaking in a Hellenistic manner'（即提多書及提前是保羅假路加的手筆寫成的〔102〕）。

50 ἐγκράτεια, 'restraint of one's emotions, impulses, or desires, *self-control*' (BDAG 274*a*, s.v.). 參《新希》94*a*（s.v.）：「對自己的慾念和行為實行完全的控制。」

51 詳見《加》1282-84。

52 ἐγκρατεύομαι, 'to keep one's emotions, impulses, or desires under control, *control oneself, abstain*' (BDAG 274*b*, s.v.), 'to exercise complete control over one's desires and actions' (LN §88.83);「完全控制自己的慾念和行為」(《新希》94*a* [s.v.])。

53 Hiebert 431 認為，(##12-14) 這最後三項可視為對人、對神，和對己的要求。參較二 12 註釋註 52 及所屬正文（下面 299）。比較本節的三個形容詞和該節的三個

而言之，**節制**這字的焦點在於「對身體及其慾望的自我控制」，**克己**（#11）則較多關注思想方面的審慎、適度，以及所帶來行為方面的自制。[54]

副詞：

一 8	δίκαιον（對人）	ὅσιον（對上帝）	ἐγκρατῆ（對己）
二 12c	σωφρόνως（對己）	δικαίως（對人）	εὐσεβῶς（對上帝）

54 Marshall 186: 'self-control of the body and its desires . . . is the focus of this word, whereas σωφροσύνη would appear to be more concerned with sobriety in one's thinking and in the resulting behaviour.' Similarly, Towner III 690（唐 1006）。

一 **9a** 堅守合乎教義的可靠之道，

9b 就能將健全的教導勸勉人，

9c 又能駁倒爭辯的人。[1]

本節提出了作監督的最後一項資格（**#15**），其重點不再是監督的個人品格和家庭生活，而是監督在教會中教導的職能。[2] 第 6 至 8 節的各項絕大多數都只是一字形容詞，[3] 或是加上否定詞的一字形容詞或名詞，[4] 或三個字的分詞片語，[5] 只有論監督的兒女的一項較長（九個字）；[6] 但本節這一項卻是由一個分詞片語（9a 節〔七個字〕）加上目的子句（9b～c 節〔十四個字〕）構成。它的長度和較複雜的結構，使它與之前的各項分開，凸出了監督的教導角色。之前的那十四項都是其他的信徒也應該有的品格，但教導和駁斥的能力卻是監督所具「有區別作用的標誌」。[7]

---

1 Clark（'Structure' 106）聲稱：'Chiastically, the command to rebuke [ἐλέγχειν] is enlarged on first in 1.13b-16, and the command to encourage [παρακαλεῖν] second in 2.1-14.' 他又認為，'these two verbs are repeated in reverse sequence in 2.15, the verse which sums up 2.1-14, thus forming a chiastic inclusio.' 其實，在二 15 如在一 9，兩個動詞的次序都是 παρακαλεῖν 在先，ἐλέγχειν 在後。因此，祈勒克的 'chiastic inclusio' 不是指兩個動詞的次序本身，而是「先指兩個動詞的功能 + 後指兩個動詞的次序」：（甲）一 13b～16（駁倒〔ἐλέγχειν〕爭辯的人）；（乙）二 1～14（勸勉〔παρακαλεῖν〕人）；（乙'）二 15a 上（παρακάλει）；（甲'） 二 15a 下（ἔλεγχε）。不過，我們可以這樣說，在勸戒人和責備人這兩方面，監督（一 9）與提多（二 15）有同樣的職能。

2 Jeon II 18 認為，'The sequence of these qualifications may reflect Paul's understanding of the basic principle that a person must win credibility [by being above reproach] before he is able to speak effectively.' 毫無疑問，這原則是正確的；不過，這最後一項資格在經文中的次序，似乎有更好的解釋。見本段下文，及（尤其是）「一章 9 節在本書結構中的獨特功能」（下面 148-52）。

3 第 6a 節和 7a 節的 #1，以及 8 節的 ##9-14。

4 第 7b 節的 ## 4-6、8（形容詞）和 #7（人物名詞）。

5 第 6a 節的 #2。

6 第 6b 節的 #3。

7 本段見 Van Neste, 'Message' 21*a*. 引句英文原作 '*the* distinguishing mark (of the elder)'. (**1**) 馬賀比指出，在提前三章「監督的資格」中，善於教導在接近開首的位置（三 2：διδακτικόν）出現；但在這裏，這項資格居於名單的頂端，並且獲得

（一）動詞**堅守**（同呂譯、新和、現修）的意思不只是**堅信**（新普：**他要堅信自己領受了……的信息**），[8] 也不僅是對這信息有透徹的理解，[9] 而是對這信息**堅守不移**（當代）並且專心致力於這信息。[10] **可靠之道**意即**值得信賴的信息**（新普），[11] 這信息被描寫為**合乎教義**的；[12] 正是由於它是**合乎教義**的，它是**值得**

擴充（Malherbe, 'Soteriology' 338）。這也支持正文的論點。Houlden 144 認為，本節是提前三 2 那個形容詞的 'expanded equivalent'; cf. Ramsay 71: 'That [what is said in Tit. 1:9] was all implied in the single word [in 1 Tim. 3:2] "apt to teach," as Paul used it.'（**2**）Wild 894*a-b* 則認為，6～8 節可能得自一份傳統的長老資格；若是這樣，9 節是作者（並非保羅）加上去的。

8 NLT: 'He must have a strong belief in the trustworthy message'.

9 NRSV/NJB: 'He/he must have a firm grasp of the word / of the . . . message'.

10 See BDAG 87*b* (s.v. ἀντέχω, 1): 'cling to, hold fast to, be devoted to'; H. Balz, *EDNT* 1.108*a* (s.v. ἀντέχομαι) / LN §31.49: 'holding firm/firmly to'; *Paraphrase* 291: 'devoted to the . . . message';《新希》227*b*（s.v. I.2）：「牢固地執着……含有『照着信念而行動』的意思。」See also H. Hanse, *TDNT* 2.828: 'it means "to be concerned" to keep preaching faithful to the received doctrine, i.e., "to hold fast."' Cf. Johnson II 224: 'personal commitment to the right understanding of the gospel "according to the teaching."'（**1**）但前一本辭典又認為，由於教會的監督 'could be expected to do more than hold fast to correct instruction'，這字也許應理解為 'to have strong interest in'（BDAG 87*b* [s.v. 2]）之意。（**2**）Fiore II 199 認為，**堅守**的意思是 'maintaining the true teaching both in content and as applied to life practice.' 若是這樣，保羅對監督的期望就像他對提摩太的囑咐一樣：**要留心你的行為和你的教導……你必須持守真理**（提前四 16，新普）。（**3**）原文動詞在新約僅再出現三次（皆為中間語態），分別指僕人**忠於**所服侍的主人（新譯：太六 24 ‖ 路十六 13），以及信徒應**扶助**軟弱的人（帖前五 14）。

11 See also NIV, TNIV, NIV2011, NLT, *Paraphrase* 291 / G. Barth, *EDNT* 3.98*a* (s.v. πιστός, 2 b): 'the trustworthy message/word'; BDAG 821*a* (s.v. πιστός, 1 b): 'trustworthy, faithful, dependable'.（**1**）Quinn 26, 81 則翻譯為 'the message that is meant to be believed'.（**2**）**道**字（λόγος）拾起一 3 的**他的道**，即是關於基督的福音信息。參一 2b～3a 註釋末段（上面 71）。Cf. Marshall 215 n.192: 'Tit 1.9 refers to the gospel as trustworthy.'（**3**）DC 133*b* 認為 λόγος（**道**）在這裏的意思是「宣道（preaching）」（如在提前五 17；thus also Knight II 293: ' the "preaching" or "proclamation" that the prospective overseer/elder has heard'），9a 節的意思即是：'he should be concerned with [ἀντεχόμενον]* the preaching [τοῦ λόγου] that is reliable [πιστός] with respect to the teaching [κατὰ τὴν διδαχήν]'（132*a*）。（*參上註之 H. Hanse.）不過，9b 節的目的子句表明，ἀντεχόμενον 的目的是要**能夠以健全的教導**勸勉人，並且駁斥（改正）爭辯的人。鑑於這種對純正教義的強調，分詞較可能的意思是 'holding firm' 而不是 'be[ing] concerned with'（cf., correctly, Marshall 166）。

12 κατὰ τὴν διδαχήν = 'in accordance with the teaching' (NRSV, NAU).（**1**）曾 116 聲稱，「ἀντεχόμενον τοῦ κατὰ τὴν διδαχὴν πιστοῦ λόγου 這個短語實際上可以譯

信賴的。[13] **堅守**所教**真實的道理**（新和）這翻譯，似乎將這裏的教義理解為提多的教導，[14] 但**教義**其實是指監督所**領受了**（新普）的[15] 使徒傳統的教訓。[16] **合乎教義**的教導就是忠實地反映那**教義的規範**（羅六 17，新譯）的教導。[17] **合乎教義**和**可靠**這兩個意思這樣連在一起，

成：『按照信實之言所教導的』。所強調的是教導的行動和信息的整全。」「信息的整全」這意思是如何得來的呢？答案是：「『所教導的』和『信實之言』都是單數，強調的……是教導上的統一性。」可是，這解釋完全忽視了開首的兩個字 ἀντεχόμενον τοῦ, 從而錯過了整個分詞片語的要旨。其實，這片語要表達的意思有兩方面：（**i**）監督要**堅守〔那〕可靠之道**（ἀντεχόμενον τοῦ . . . πιστοῦ λόγου）；（**ii**）那可靠之道是**合乎教義的**（τοῦ κατὰ τὴν διδαχὴν πιστοῦ λόγου = τοῦ πιστοῦ λόγου τοῦ κατὰ τὴν διδαχήν）。曾氏的翻譯等於從整個分詞片語中單把 κατὰ τὴν διδαχὴν πιστοῦ λόγου 抽出來，從而得出「按照信實之言所教導的」這意思；這做法並不合理。「長老必須堅守正確的教義」（曾 139）較符合原意。
（**2**）名詞 **διδαχή**（新約共 30 次）在本書只出現這一次；在教牧書信僅再出現一次，指**教導**的活動（提後四 2）；在保羅書信另外出現四次，分別指**教義的規範**（羅六 17，新譯〔參《羅》2.289-90〕）、羅馬信徒**所學的教義**（十六 17，新譯；該節的 παρὰ τὴν διδαχήν 與本節的 κατὰ τὴν διδαχήν 剛好相反〔Quinn 93〕）、**教導**的活動（林前十四 6）和內容（十四 26）。See BAGD 192*a-b*, BDAG 241*b* (s.v.);《新希》82*a*（s.v.）。（**3**）K. Wegenast（*DNTT* 3.770）聲稱，διδαχή 一字在教牧書信的用法有別於羅馬書（六 17，十六 17）和林前（十四 6、26）：在後二書，此字指 'the whole of his [*sic*]* apostolic teaching . . . the scope of the word is left undefined'; 但是在多一 9 和提後四 2，'*didachē* has probably become a given body of doctrine which is to be inculcated as such.' 可是，羅六 17 的**教義的規範**（新譯）和十六 17 的羅馬信徒**所學的教義**（新譯）何嘗不是同樣提示 'a body of doctrine' 呢（參《羅》2.293-98）？（*參《羅》4.768：羅十六 17 所指的顯然不是保羅的使徒教訓之全部，「因保羅從未踏足羅馬，羅馬教會整體而論亦非保羅建立……而是保羅與其他教師共享的、初期教會的基本教義，這教義可認同為讀者所曾『被交付』給的『教義的規範』」。）（**4**）διδαχή 在這裏與下一句的 διδασκαλία（**教導**）同義，都是指 'a normative body of doctrines and precepts'（Marshall 166）。

13 Classen, 'Titus' 434, 'Epistle to Titus' 53. 終極而言，此信息之所以值得信賴，是由於它是來自**那無謊言的上帝**（一 2）的福音信息（Stott 178）。

14 See Fiore II 195: 'holding fast to the trustworthy message in accord with his teaching'.

15 NLT: 'the trustworthy message he was taught'; KJV/NKJV: 'as he hath/has been taught'. 參當代：**對傳給他們的確實可靠的真理……**。

16 RSV / NIV, TNIV, NIV2011: 'as taught / as it has been taught'; ESV: 'the trustworthy word as taught'; NJB: 'the unchanging message of the tradition'; *Paraphrase* 291: 'which accords with the apostolic teaching'. See also Lock 132: 'the teaching of the Apostle himself'; Banker 40*a*: 'the teaching they had received from Paul and Titus'. 在教牧書信，保羅的身分顯著地是**教師**（提前二 7；提後一 11）；他告訴提摩太，**你要持守所學習的和所確信的，因為你知道是跟誰學的**（提後三 14）。

17 Kelly 233. 在羅六 17，原文不是說這**教義的規範**被傳授給你們，而是說讀者曾被交付給這**教義的規範**（新譯）；詳見《羅》2.289-91。羅十六 17 則稱這教義為**你們所**

強調那被認可的使徒教義，就是福音信息之可靠性的惟一標準。[18] 如此，監督職能的第一方面就是：他必須堅守那可靠、符合教義的教訓（現修）。

（二）就能（同新和）或這樣，他就能夠（現修、新普）這種翻譯，將原文連接詞視為引進堅守的結果。[19] 較自然的理解是以連接詞為表達目的，因而翻譯為好使（呂譯、新譯）或好能（思高）。[20] 這目的包括兩方面：[21] 積極方面，監督要能夠用健全的教義勸勉人（呂譯）；消極方面，他要能夠駁倒爭辯的人。（**A**）健全的教導[22] 或健全的教義[23]／道理（呂譯、現修／思高）的另一種翻譯是純正的教訓／

學的教義（新譯），即是你們已領受的教導（新普）。

18 Marshall 167.

19 參當代：這樣，才可以⋯⋯。I.e., ἵνα = (ecbatic) 'then' (NLT; *Paraphrase* 291).

20 I.e., ἵνα = (telic) 'that' (KJV, NKJV), 'so that' (RSV, NRSV, NAU, NIV, TNIV, NIV2012, NJB, ESV). Malherbe（'Paraenesis' 300）認為，此目的子句 'is implicitly imperatival'.

21 ἵνα δυνατὸς ᾖ <u>καὶ</u> παρακαλεῖν . . . <u>καὶ</u> . . . ἐλέγχειν ('both . . . and': KJV, NKJV, NRSV, NAU, NJB). (**1**) LN 給予 δυνατός 兩種可能的翻譯和解釋：'able'（§74.2）或 'specially competent'（§74.4）。筆者認為，並無足夠理由在本節採納後一個意思，儘管它可能適合徒十八 24。(**2**) J. Zmijewski（*EDNT* 1.360*b* [s.v. δυνατός, 3]）則從這字看出「監督之『權力』」的意思來：'The episcopal "power" is to be understood as essentially that of a teaching and disciplinary office.'

22 See also NLT: 'wholesome teaching'.

23 See also KJV, NKJV, RSV, NRSV, NAU, NIV, TNIV, NIV2011, NJB, ESV, *Paraphrase* 291: 'sound doctrine'; C. Brown, *DNTT* 3.61: 'the healthy doctrine'. 後者認為這詞語提示有一種「教導集（a corpus of teaching）」存在。(**1**) 名詞 **διδασκαλία** 在新約一共出現 21 次，除了（**i**）**兩次**之外（太十五 9 ‖ 可七 7：人的規條被當作教義），全部在保羅書信中：在本書再出現三次（二 1、7、10），在教牧書信另十一次，其他的書信四次。(**ii**) 這**四次**分別指教導的活動（羅十二 7）或教導之舉（羅十五 4），以及教導的內容（弗四 14：負面意義的教義〔呂譯、思高、新普〕；西二 22：由人製定的教條〔呂譯〕）。(**iii**) 在教牧書信的**十五次**中，只有一次是指鬼魔的教訓（提前四 1：<u>複數</u>的 διδασκαλίαις），其餘十四次（全部為<u>單數</u>）皆具正面意義：四次在健全的<u>教導</u>／健全〔的〕<u>教義</u>一詞中出現（多一 9，二 1；提後四 3／提前一 10），其餘十次或指教導的活動（四次：多二 7；提前四 13，五 17；提後三 16），或指所教導的內容（六次：多二 10：上帝的教導；提前四 6：好教義／好教訓〔呂譯／思高〕；四 16：提摩太自己的教訓〔新和、新譯〕；六 1：他〔上帝〕的教導／我們〔保羅〕的教導（新普／現修）；六 3：合乎敬虔的教導；提後三 10：保羅的教導）。參較《新希》82*a*（s.v.）；BAGD 191*b*, BDAG 240*b*（s.v.）。(**2**) 這名詞在 LXX 只出現四次；有趣的是，單數的有好的意思（箴二 17；次經《便西拉智訓》24.33, 39.8），複數的則有壞的意思（賽二十九 13），像這字在教牧書信的用法一樣（Quinn 95）。

道理（新和／新譯、新普）。健全原文動詞的字面意義是健康（路五31；約叁 2；參路七 10，十五 27），但它在教牧書信出現的八次都是比喻用法，指正確無誤[24]（＝純正）的教導／教義或信仰。[25] 就本節而論，健全的教導就是上文剛提到的合乎教義的可靠之道。但是將健全的教導勸勉人（參新和：將純正的教訓勸化人）是甚麼意思呢？原文介系詞若視為具地方意義，所得出的意思便是「在健全的教義上指導、勸勉或鼓勵人」。[26] 不過，介系詞較可能具媒介意義，所得出的意思也就更為清晰：以健全的道理勸戒……人（思高），用健全的教義

---

24 BDAG 1023*a* (s.v. ὑγιαίνω, 2): 'to be sound or free from error, *be correct*'; LN §72.15: 'to be correct, to be sound, to be accurate';《新希》336*a*（s.v. I.2）：「觀點正確」；U. Luck, *TDNT* 8.312: 'Sound doctrine is true and correct teaching in contrast to perverted doctrine, to μῦθοι καὶ γενεαλογίαι ἀπέραντοι [myths and endless genealogies], 1 Tm. 1:4.' 這動詞（ὑγιαίνω）衍生自同字根的形容詞 ὑγιής（二 8 的健全）。因此，ἡ διδασκαλία ἡ ὑγιαίνουσα 'means that relatively fixed "orthodoxy" which the churches have received and which it is their duty to preserve against heresy'（K. Wegenast, *DNTT* 3.770）。Cf. Hagner, *New Testament* 629: 'The idea of "sound doctrine" . . . is an obvious way of referring to orthodox teaching'.

25 以四個不同的形式出現：（**i**）<u>ἐν</u> τῇ διδασκαλίᾳ τῇ ὑγιαινούσῃ（多一 9：以健全的教導）；（**ii**）τῇ ὑγιαινούσῃ διδασκαλίᾳ（多二 1：健全的教導；提前一 10：健全〔的〕教義），τῆς ὑγιαινούσης διδασκαλίας（提後四 3：健全的教導）；（**iii**）ὑγιαίνωσιν <u>ἐν</u> τῇ πίστει / ὑγιαίνοντας τῇ πίστει（多一 13：在信仰上健全／二 2：在信心……上健全）；（**iv**）ὑγιαίνουσιν λόγοις / ὑγιαινόντων λόγων（提前六 3：純正的話語／提後一 13：健全的言論）。（**1**）'The[se] expressions . . . represent a major theme of the letters, namely, that orthodox teaching alone issues in a moral life'（Malherbe, 'Medical Imagery' 121）。以健全的形容基督教的教導（與假教師「不健全的*」教導相對〔Stott 186; cf. Marshall 169〕），是教牧書信的獨特用法。（*保羅說：若有人傳別的教義，不符合我們主耶穌基督純正的話語與合乎敬虔的教導〔提前六 3〕，這種人顯然喜歡〔νοσῶν περί = 'has an unhealthy craving for / an unhealthy interest in / an unhealthy desire to' [ESV/NIV/NLT]〕辯論，喜歡在字句上吹毛求疵〔六 4，現修〕。他們的言論好像毒瘤一樣〔提後二 17，新譯〕擴散開去〔新普〕。）（**2**）U. Luck 指出，形容詞 ὑγιής（二 8 的健全）在世俗希臘文可具有 'the gen. sense of "rational," "intelligent," "pertinent"'（*TDNT* 8.308）；他認為本註開首的那些詞語應按其「希臘文－希臘化時期（Greek-Hellenistic）」的背景來理解，故此，'To be avoided is the mistake of thinking that the reference is to the teaching which makes whole, whose goal is health of soul'（312）。正確的理解見上註。提後二 17 是比喻性用法（n.32）。

26 RSV, ESV / NAU / NJB: 'give instruction / exhort / giving encouragement <u>in</u> sound doctrine'. See also *Paraphrase* 291: 'encourage his hearers in sound doctrine'; Knight II 294: 'in the sphere of . . . "sound doctrine"'; Marshall 167: 'in the sphere of doctrine'.

勸勉人（呂譯），[27] **用純正的道理勸勉／勉勵人**（新譯／新普[28]）。[29] 無論如何，沒有人應該在教會中作長老／監督，除非他有能力教導別人。[30] 這一項要求暗示，(**i**) 這樣的人在被委派為長老／監督之前，已經在運用他所擁有的教導的恩賜，因而（**ii**）教導的恩賜並非只限於長老和監督。[31]

闡釋真理的另一面（較不受歡迎的一面[32]）是（**B**）**駁倒爭辯的人**（參新和）。[33] 另外的翻譯包括：（**i**）**使頂撞的人自知有罪**（呂譯）；[34]（**ii**）「責備那些反駁（這健全的教導）的人」；[35]（**iii**）**駁斥抗辯的人**（思高），[36]「駁斥那些反駁（這教導）的人」，[37]「駁斥

---

27 See also KJV, NKJV: '<u>by</u> sound doctrine . . . to exhort'.

28 See also NLT / NIV, TNIV, NIV2011: 'encourage others <u>with</u> wholesome teaching / <u>by</u> sound doctrine'; Johnson I 117: 'exhort (the faithful) with healthy teaching'; Mounce 384, 392: 'exhort with healthy doctrine'.

29 παρακαλέω = 'to urge strongly, *appeal to*, *urge*, *exhort*, *encourage*' (BDAG 765*a*, s.v. 2). NRSV 則翻譯為 'preach'; 現修譯作感化。

30 See Van Neste, 'Message' 28*c*-29*a* n.19 ('there is, by definition, no such thing as a "non-teaching elder"). Witherington 117 強調，'the elder must be <u>rhetorically</u> adept . . . These leaders must be able to argue for and against . . . which requires at least a rudimentary knowledge of rhetoric. . . . The rhetorical strategy of Luke* and Paul here is to train Titus to use enthymemes and comparisons and paradigms – the elementary rhetorical tools for persuasion – and so equip and train the elders to do likewise.' 對筆者而言，這看法並無說服力。(*威瑟靈頓認為路加是保羅的代筆人。)

31 Marshall 176, 166. Cf. idem, 'Congregation' 121: 'there was evidence of their ability to teach before their appointment.' Keener 627*a* 則認為，'Elders had to be trained to refute current false teachings before they were appointed'. 但這意思在經文中並不明顯。

32 Stott [1997] 178: 'The negative aspect of this teaching ministry is particularly unfashionable today.' 這句話到了今天仍然是真的；或者可以說，在客觀真理的存在受到質疑的時代，這句話尤其適切。

33 當代則加入「沒有原因」之意：駁倒<u>無端</u>爭辯的人。

34 See also F. Büchsel, *TDNT* 2.474: 'It means "to show someone his sin and to summon him to repentance."'

35 ESV: 'rebuke those who contradict it'; Knight II 294: '"Rebuke" (or "reprove") would seem . . . to be the likely nuance here also [as in v. 13]'; Smith 334: 'the primary nuance of ἐλέγχω here is "rebuke" rather than "convict".' 因此，'no one translates "rebuke" there [in 1:9c]'（Banker 51*a*）這話不確。Jeon I 46 選擇 'reprove'（thus also Spencer 20）這翻譯，他解釋說：'"Refute" seems to focus on correcting false doctrine, "rebuke" on bad behavior. "Reprove" captures both dimensions'（n.42）。

36 See also NJB: 'refuting those who argue against it'.

37 NAU; BDAG 89*a* (s.v. ἀντιλέγω, 1) / REB: 'refute those who contradict / raise

那些反對（這教導）的人」；[38]（iv）向反對的人指出他們的錯誤（新普），[39] 折服反對的人（新譯），[40] 糾正那些反對的人的錯誤（現修）。[41] 第一個原文動詞在第 13 節再次出現時，它的行動的目的是使他們在信仰上健全；我們很難預期，這目的可以藉著嚴厲〔的〕責備（13b 節）達到，但他們若被說服自己錯了，就有改變的可能。[42]

---

objections'; RSV; Johnson I 117 / NRSV: 'confute/refute those who contradict it'; Trench 13 (§iv): 'ἐλέγχειν is . . . so to rebuke another, with such effectual wielding of the victorious arms of the truth, as to bring him, if not always to a confession, yet at least to a conviction, of his sin (Job v. 17; xix. 25), just as in juristic Greek, ἐλέγχειν is not merely to reply to, but to refute, an opponent.'

38 NIV, TNIV, NIV2011: 'refute those who oppose it'.（Witherington 106 的 'able to . . . oppose opponents' 似是 'refute opponents' 之誤；cf. 112: 'and can refute those who oppose . . . such teaching'.）Richards 81 卻翻譯為 'and the nay-sayers to oppose [ἐλέγχειν]'（方括號是原來的）；如此，不定詞與分詞 ἀντιλέγοντας 變成幾乎同義的。

39 NLT: 'show those who oppose it where they are wrong'. See also NKJV: 'convict those who contradict'; BDAG 315*a* (s.v. ἐλέγχω, 2): 'to bring a pers. to the point of recognizing wrong-doing, *convict*, *convince* someone of someth.'; H.-G. Link, *DNTT* 2.141: 'convicting opponents of their error'; Barrett 130: 'ἐλέγχειν . . . means to expose, and by exposing, convict. Those who contradict the truth must be shown their errors'; DC 132*a*: 'convict the opponents'; Fee 175: 'convict';《輔讀》525（第一解釋）：「指出錯誤」。**(1)** 這動詞（**ἐλέγχω**）在教牧書信另外出現四次（一 13，二 15；提前五 20；提後四 2），保羅書信另三次（林前十四 24；弗五 11、13〔參《弗》749-53，756-57〕），新約另九次。See BDAG 315*a*-15*b* (s.v.);《新希》108*b*-9*a*（s.v.）。**(2)** 反對的人（現修、新譯、新普）原文為 τοὺς ἀντιλέγοντας（冠詞 + 分詞 = 名詞）。動詞 **ἀντιλέγω** 在下文再出現一次（二 9：頂撞），保羅書信僅再一次（羅十 21：頂嘴〔參《羅》3.449-50〕），新約另外八次：路二 34（反對〔思高、新譯、新普〕），二十 27（否認〔思高、現修、新譯〕，假定原來的讀文是 ἀντιλέγοντες 而不是 λέγοντες〔see *TextC* 145-46〕），二十一 15（反駁／駁倒〔新普／新譯〕）；約十九 12（背叛／與……為敵〔同思高、新和／新譯〕）；徒四 14（辯駁〔呂譯、新譯〕），十三 45（反駁〔新譯、新普〕），二十八 19、22（反對）。See BDAG 89*a*-*b* (s.v.);《新希》31*b*（s.v.）。

40 See also KJV: 'convince the gainsayers'; Banker 34, 40*b*: 'to convince those who oppose (what is correct) (that they are wrong)'. Stott 178 解釋為「在辯論中打敗他們（to overthrow them in argument）」。

41 See also Guthrie I 186, Guthrie II 199: 'correcting those who contradict the truth.'（「指證那些敵對真理的」〔古特立 201〕這翻譯並不準確。）在原文，ἐλέγχειν 是一 9 的最後一字。但在十三世紀一份三語的小楷體抄本中（第 460 號，附有拉丁文和阿拉伯文版本），這字之後還有很長的一段話；其開首部分曾引於一 6 註釋註 19 之（2）= 上面 104。詳見 *TextC* 584; Mounce 384 n.d.

42 Banker 51*a*. **(1)** Marshall 204 則認為，'the opponents talk nonsense and will not listen to reason', 因此提多只能 'refute strongly those who hold to the false teaching'（= view

由於第 9c 節和第 13c 節是在談及同一個題目（第 9c 節直接引入第 10 至 16 節這一段），因此動詞在這兩節的意思極可能是相同的。這就是說，在上述的四種翻譯中，後兩種比前兩種較符合文理，而第四種比第三種更為清晰，因而最為可取。這些人所反對的自然是本節上文所提到的**合乎教義…之道**和**健全的教導**。[43] 在原文，**堅守**和**反對**是有同一前綴的複合分詞，它們分別置於本節的開首和末尾，強調了提多所委任的長老和那些反對者之間的對立。[44]

一章 9 節在本書結構中的獨特功能——在列舉教會領袖的資格這數節（6～9 節）中，末後這一節較為特別。在此之前的各項主要是倫理性的，[45] 但本節列出的則聚焦在教義和教導上。[46] 另外，本節的造句法也比之前的數節複雜多了：之前數節主要是把各項資格簡單地

(iii))。但 'refute (someone)' 的意思是 'prove (sb) wrong in his opinions: . . . 證明（某人）看法不對'（《牛津》963*b* [s.v.]），而這顯然牽涉到提出理由。(**2**) Towner III 693（唐 1011）更認為：'With the situation of an opposing inferior teaching particularly in mind, the correctional and disciplinary dimension of the leader's ministry is viewed more narrowly in terms of condemning the false teaching by insisting on what is correct, and "silencing" the opponents by forceful admonition backed up by apostolic authority (1:11; 3:10; 1 Tim 1:20; 2 Tim 2:25).' 不過，作者稍後（696〔唐 1015〕）正確指出：'At this point in the engagement [1:11] . . . there still exists hope that the rebellious teachers <u>can be reasoned with</u>, and it is turning them back, not throwing them out, that Paul hopes to accomplish (1:13).'

43 Genade 26 聲稱，διδαχή（**教義**）和 διδασκαλία（**教導**）在這裏是可互換的。不過，從句子本身的結構（τοῦ κατὰ τὴν διδαχὴν πιστοῦ λόγου . . . ἐν τῇ διδασκαλίᾳ τῇ ὑγιαινούσῃ）看來，和**教導**相對應的並不是**教義**，而是與這教義相符的**道**（λόγος）；提多要堅守這道，並以這道（= **健全的教導**）勸勉人。

44 See Genade 26-27. 原文分詞依次為單數的 ἀντεχόμενον 和複數的 ἀντιλέγοντας（後者加上冠詞合成名詞）。

45 Van Neste（'Structure' 127）指出，8 節的最後四項——**克己**、**正直**、**聖潔**、**節制**（σώφρων, δίκαιος, ὅσιος, ἐγκρατής）——都被 LN 歸入 'Moral and Ethical Qualities and Related Behavior' 這第 88 範疇（domain）內。筆者留意到，被歸入這範疇的還有 6b 節的**放蕩**（ἀσωτία）和 7b 節的**不自負**、**不暴躁**、**不酗酒**、**不好鬥**（αὐθάδης, ὀργίλος, πάροινος, πλήκτης）。以上九項，依次見 LN §88.94, §88.12, §88.24, §88.84, §88.96, §88.206, §88.175, §88.288, §88.137.

46 **合乎<u>教義</u>的可靠之道**（τοῦ κατὰ <u>τὴν διδαχὴν</u> πιστοῦ λόγου）；**健全的<u>教導</u>**（τῇ <u>διδασκαλίᾳ</u> τῇ ὑγιαινούσῃ）；**勸勉**（παρακαλεῖν）；**駁倒**（ἐλέγχειν）。Genade 27 認為，保羅以本節結束本段，這表示作長老／監督最重要的資格就是 'the ability to teach the word'.

逐一列出（只在第 6b 節有關兒女的一項較長），[47] 但本節這個項目的形式則是一個分詞片語，內含直接受詞，這受詞進一步由一個目的子句解釋。[48] 這兩點將本節和前數節區別出來，使本節特別適合用來標示過渡。

范尼斯因此認為，這目的子句本質上是個「雙重的鈎」，它結合了一個「鈎狀鑰字」和一個「遠距離的鈎狀鑰字」，詳細的解釋如下：[49] **首先**，目的子句的第二部分提到監督必須能夠駁倒爭辯的人（9c 節）；這是信上首次提到有反對的人（新普）。緊隨的一段（一 10～16），雖然沒有使用「反對」一詞，但其焦點卻是在於這種人確實存在，並且必須受到責備（13 節）。[50] 如此，駁倒爭辯的人就像「鈎狀鑰字」般使思想過渡到下一段有關反對之人的討論。[51] **其次**，目的子句的第一部分是，就能〔以〕健全

47 τέκνα ἔχων πιστά, 'having children who believe' (NAU) = 兒女也是信主的（但見一 6 註釋〔#3〕= 倒數第四段〔上面 113-15〕）。隨後還有形容兒女的 μὴ ἐν κατηγορίᾳ ἢ ἀνυπότακτα（見一 6 註釋末段〔上面 117-19〕）。

48 Van Neste（'Structure' 127; see also Van Neste 280）稱之為 'a participial phrase with a direct object [which (phrase) is] further explicated by a dual ἵνα-clause.' 原文作：ἀντεχόμενον τοῦ κατὰ τὴν διδαχὴν πιστοῦ λόγου（這是個 'participial phrase', 其中的 τοῦ πιστου λόγου 是分詞 ἀντεχόμενον 的 'direct object'〔ἀντέχομαι 的直接受詞取所有格〕）ἵνα δυνατὸς ᾖ καὶ παρακαλεῖν ἐν τῇ διδ ασκαλίᾳ τῇ ὑγιαινούσῃ καὶ τοὺς ἀντιλέγοντας ἐλέγχειν（這是由連接詞 ἵνα 引入的目的子句；'a dual ἵνα-clause' 的意思不是說 ἵνα 出現兩次，而是指 'the t wo parts of the ἵνα-clause'——'that he may be able to' 之後有兩部分〔καὶ . . . κ αὶ . . .〕，就是將健全的教導勸勉人和駁倒爭辯的人）。參一 9 註釋首段（上面 141）。

49 Van Neste, 'Structure' 127 (see also 132). 引句英文原作 'a "double hook," combining a hooked keyword and a distant hooked keyword.' '[A] hooked keyword' 是從一段轉到另一段的修辭技巧，'in which the words involved in the "hook" figure prominently in one of the units being connected'（126）。「鈎狀鑰字／鑰詞」的另一些例子見：一 16 註釋註 36 及所屬正文，二 9～10 註釋註 48 及所屬正文（下面 213-14，278-79）。

50 駁倒和責備在原文是同一個動詞（ἐλέγχω）：ἐλέγχειν（不定詞），ἔλεγχε（限定動詞）。

51 Van Neste 255. Genade 127 同樣認為，τοὺς ἀντιλέγοντας 'functions as a transitional device that introduces the next section.'

的教導勸勉人（9b 節）。[52] 勸勉是二章 1 至 10 節的兩個主要動詞之一（見原文第 6 節，另一個是第 1 節的講字；勸勉在二 15 的要旨重述中再次出現），而該段的勸勉被形容為合乎那健全的教導（1 節）。事實上，除了一章 9 節，名詞教導在信上僅再出現三次，都是在二章 1 至 10 節之內（1、7、10 節）。由此看來，一章 9 節的就能將健全的教導勸勉人，就像一個「遠距離的鈎狀鑰字」，引介二章 1 至 10 節的勸勉。[53]

回到目的子句的第二部分，監督必須能夠駁倒爭辯的人（9c 節）這話，不但引介緊隨其後的一章 10 至 16 節，亦引介同樣是論到如何對待反對的人的另一段——三章 9 至 11 節，因為這兩段（一 10～16，三 9～11）的關係密切，它們不但討論相同的題目，並且像一對書立般把書信本體的其餘部分（討論「與福音相符的生活」的兩段：二 1～15，三 1～8）夾在中央。[54] 而三章 9 至 11 節亦與一章 9c 節這個「鈎」有語意上的聯繫：分門結黨的人（三 10）與反對健全的教導的人（一 9c）是一丘之貉；警戒之後拒絕交往（三 10，呂譯）是與駁斥（一 9c，思高）同類的行動。如此，一章 9 節的目的子句之第二部分（即 9c 節）的功能，就是引介書信本體（一 5～三 11）其餘兩部分——「如何對待反對的人」（一 10～16，三 9～11），「與福音相符的生活」（二 1～15，三 1～8）——的其中一部分（一 10～16，三 9～11），即大綱之「叁」「陸」。[55]

---

52 名詞教導和動詞勸勉原文依次為 διδασκαλία, παρακαλέω.

53 以上一段的主旨可以用圖表表達如下：

甲 將健全的教導勸勉人（=「遠距離的鈎狀鑰字」，連於甲’）
　　乙 駁倒爭辯的人（=「鈎狀鑰字」，連於乙’）
　　乙’ 一 10～16（要責備反對的人
甲’ 二 1～10（勸勉和教導）

這裏呈現交叉配置模式（范尼斯沒有使用這詞），參較註 1（上面 141）。

54 見大綱之「叁」「肆」「伍」「陸」（上面 31-35）。

55 Van Neste 280.（有趣地，在 ‘The call to “rebuke” (ἐλέγχω, 1.9) and to “warn”

再回到目的子句的第一部分（一 9b），**就能〔以〕健全的教導勸勉人**（9b 節）不但像一個「遠距離的鈎狀鑰字」引介二章 1 至 10 節的勸勉（見再上一段），更可視為引介二章 1 節至三章 8 節這一整段，因為二章 1 節的**你所講的總要合乎那健全的教導**，大可以包括二章 2 節至三章 8 節的內容。三章 1 節並無過渡性陳述，而只是繼續上文的勸勉，因此，二章 1 節至三章 8 節可以看為合一的大段落，細分為平行的兩段（二 1～15 ‖ 三 1～8）。[56] 如此，一章 9 節的目的子句之第一部分的功能，就是引介書信本體其餘兩部分（見上段）的另一部分（二 1～15，三 1～8），即大綱之「肆」「伍」。[57]

總結以上四段，可以看見一章 9 節的目的子句的兩部分，引介了書信本體的其餘部分：**就能〔以〕健全的教導勸勉人**（9b 節）引介二章 1 節至三章 8 節（即大綱之「肆」「伍」），而**又能駁倒爭辯的人**（9c 節）則引介一章 10 至 16 節和三章 9 至 11 節（即大綱之「叁」「陸」）。一章 10 節至三章 11 節這一整段（即是書信本

(νουθεσία, 3.10), followed by shunning, are similar’ 這句子裏面，單數的主詞 ‘call’ 和複數的動詞 ‘are’ 並不協調；重複主詞，問題就解決了：‘The call to “rebuke” . . . and the call to “warn” . . . are similar.’）

56 Cf. Van Neste, ‘Structure’ 129-30. Van Neste 275 詳細指出兩段之間的相似之處：**(一)** 二 **1～10** 和三 **1～2** 這兩段皆以命令式動詞（二 1，**講**；三 1，**提醒**）引進關於倫理生活的勸勉；兩個動詞皆為現在時態主動語態命令式語法單數第二人稱（present active imperative 2nd person singular: λάλει, Ὑπομίμνησκε）；兩段隨後的指示皆以從屬於開首的命令式語法動詞之不定詞來表達；兩段結束時皆用了 πᾶσαν (. . .) ἐνδεικνυμένους（**顯出**）這些字眼（二 10，三 2）；順服權柄是兩段共同的關注（二 5、9，三 1）。**(二)** 上述兩段勸勉的話隨後皆以「因為（γάρ）」一字引入教義性的一段（**二 11～14，三 3～7**）。除了**救主**（二 10、13，三 4、6〔三 5 **救**〕）、**生活／生**（二 12／三 7）和**盼望**（二 13，二 7）這些字詞上的聯繫之外，這兩段在內容上亦有重要的相似之處：兩段都描寫離棄罪惡（二 12，三 3～4）以及救恩的倫理層面；兩段都把有罪的私慾（二 12，三 3）看為與救恩的新生命相違；兩段都提到等候盼望的實現（二 13，三 7）。**(三)** 這教義性的兩段隨後都回到對提多的勸勉（**二 15，三 8**），以現在時態命令式語法動詞（**講明；堅持**）要提多教導信上的內容（**這些事** = Ταῦτα/τούτων）。‘Thus there are two parallel sections calling for proper behavior based on proper doctrine.’

57 Van Neste 280-81.

體減去一 5～9）呈現交叉配置模式。[58] 在這模式裏面，受強調的是中間的兩段（大綱之「肆」「伍」），即是關於「與福音相符的生活」的教導。[59]

58 再看大綱之「叁」「肆」「伍」「陸」（上面 31-35）。

59 Smith（'Structure' 106-7）則認為，一 9b（他的一 9c）引介二 1～三 7 這一整段（標題為 'Teach sound doctrine'），一 9c（他的一 9d）則引介一 10～16（標題為 'Silence false teachers'）。如此，他的交叉配置模式（他稱之為 'Criss-cross chiasmus'）把重點放在這模式的外面兩段，而這是反常的。'Whereas normal chiasmus emphasizes the central elements, this technique gives greatest natural prominence to the peripheral items. Two things signal the natural prominence of the items: (1) in the announcement, the item mentioned first is most emphasised; (2) in the exposition, the item receiving the greater amount of space is most emphasised' (ibid. 107). 參一 5 註釋註 10（上面 90-91）。

叁　如何對付反對的人：之一（一 10～16）

10a　因為也有許多人不受約束，說空話欺哄人，
10b　　　　　　　尤其是那些奉割禮的人。
11a　　　　這些人的口必須堵住，
11b　　　　因為他們……敗壞人的全家。
11c　　　　　　　　貪不義之財，將不該教導的事教導人，
12a　克里特人中有一個本地的先知說：
12b　　　　「克里特人常說謊話，是惡獸，貪吃懶做。」
13a　這個見證是真的。
13b　為這緣故，你要嚴厲地責備他們，
13c　　　　　　　使他們在信仰上健全。
14a　不要聽猶太人無稽的傳說
14b　　　　和背棄真理之人的命令。
15a　在潔淨的人，凡物都潔淨；
15b　在污穢不信的人，甚麼都不潔淨，
15c　　　　　連心地和天良也都污穢了。
16a　他們宣稱認識上帝，
16b　　　卻在行為上否認他；
16c　他們是可憎惡的，是悖逆的，不配做任何好事。

本段把一章 9 節所引入的對立（堅守和反對真教義的雙方）加以擴充。[1] 雖然本段的主角從上一段（一 5～9）的長老／監督轉到敵

1　Genade 29. 參一 9 註釋註 44 及所屬正文（上面 148）。保羅在這裏使用了「比較（*synkrisis*）」的修辭技巧：'A rhetorical comparison . . . most often an example

對者，但是本段如上段一樣關注倫理行為。就如上一段列出教會領袖應具備的倫理品質，本段描寫那些敵對者所展現的、應該避免的倫理品質與行為（下表頭兩行），而這相同的倫理關注由重複一些相同的詞彙更清晰地表明出來（後三行）：[2]

教會領袖	反對的人
正直、聖潔（8 節）	污穢、可憎惡（15c、16c 節）
好善（8 節）	不配做任何好事（16c 節）
不貪不義之財（7b 節，新譯）	貪不義之財（11c 節）[3]
兒女並非不受約束（6b 節）	不受約束（10a 節）[4]
兒女是信主的（6b 節）	不信（15b 節）[5]

本段亦延續了上一段對信仰上的忠誠的關注。（**i**）在上一段，長老／監督不但要在倫理方面無可指責（6a 節），也要堅守合乎教義的可靠之道，因而能夠〔以〕健全的教導勸勉人（9a、b 節）。在本段，敵對者不僅在倫理方面是污穢了（15c 節），也將不該教導的事教導人（11c 節）；他們是背棄真理的人（14b 節）。（**ii**）在上一段，監督必須堅守合乎教義的可靠之道（9a 節）；在本段，提多也要嚴厲

---

of comparison by contrast'（Witherington 117; cf. 127: 'a clear rhetorical *synkrisis*'）。

2 Van Nestle, 'Structure' 123 (see also 131).（筆者省略了 'characterized by an orderly home (v 5)' 與 'upsetting families (v 11)' 之對比。）范尼斯以此辯證兩段之間存有 '[a] significant continuity under the cohesion field of "topic"'（122）。See also Van Neste 253-54.

3 原文依次作：μὴ αἰσχροκερδῆ（7b 節），αἰσχροῦ κέρδους（11c 節）。呂譯依次作：不貪可恥之財，可恥之利。

4 原文依次作：ἀνυπότακτα, ἀνυπότακτοι. 前者為 ἀνυπότακτος 的複數中性直接受格，與 τέκνα 相符；後者為複數陽性主格。

5 原文依次作：πιστά, ἀπίστοις. 前者為 πιστός 的複數中性直接受格，與 τέκνα 相符；後者為 πιστός 之反義詞 ἄπιστος 的複數陽性間接受格。但前者的意思可能是「忠誠、可靠」；見一 6 註釋之（**#3**）＝ 倒數第四段（上面 113-15）。

地責備[6] 敵對者，使他們在信仰上健全（13b～c 節），不聽從（當代）猶太人的傳說和人的命令（14 節）。[7]

6 解釋見一 13b～c 註釋末段（下面 184-86）。
7 兩個動詞在原文是同字根的：ἀντέχω（堅守），προσέχω（聽從）。以上一段參 Van Nestle, 'Structure' 125. 另見 Van Neste 254.

3.1 假教師的描述（一 10～13a）

簡內德認為，保羅在本段使用了修辭學上的「詆毀」策略。[1] 根據希羅修辭學，這是使聽眾疏遠一己之敵對者的主要伎倆，即是盡量負面地描寫（＝抹黑）他們。[2] 但保羅所事奉的是**無謊言**的上帝（一 2b），他強調**真理**（1b、14b 節）和真實（13a 節），反對**欺哄人**和**常說謊話**的人（10a、12b 節）；如果他自己卻「詆毀／誣衊／醜化／抹黑」對手，這無異於「賊喊捉賊」！因此筆者認為，保羅在此並非使用了「詆毀」的修辭策略。[3]

---

1 簡內德以 'Discrediting the Illegitimate Teachers'（「使那些非法教師的名譽受損」）為其專題研究第四章（論提一 10～16）的標題（Genade 29 [see also 114, 116, 121]），並重複申述保羅所用的修辭技巧是 'the vilification of the opposition' / 'the vilification of the illegitimate leaders'（27 [see also 125] / 27, 29）。See also Dunn 865*a*: 'the warning against false teaching . . . draws on the familiar rhetoric of vilification'; 866*b*: 'The final clause [1:16c] reverts to vilification'.

2 參《加》251 連註 13；Genade 29: 'Vilification is a persuasive technique used by an author or speaker to present opposing parties or the parties' viewpoints in a negative light, by magnifying some aspects of character or propositional weakness, with a view to influence [*sic*] audience members to disassociate themselves from the opposition or the viewpoint and endorse the position of the speaker or writer.'

3 Cf. Marshall 43: 'There need be no doubt that this description [the author's description of Paul's opponents in the PE] is based on observation of the opponents'. Johnson（'Titus' 379*a*）說，'the genuine Paul is not immune from the use of slander against rival teachers (cf. 2 Cor. 11:13-15; Gal. 5:12; 6:13; Phil. 3:2).' 可是，'slander' 是指毫無根據的誹謗或詆毀，但是（**i**）在加六 12～13，不見得保羅使用了「詆毀」的修辭技巧（見《加》1394-96）；（**ii**）保羅不會認為他在腓三 2 對假師傅（見《腓》336-39）和他在林後十一 13～15 對假使徒的描述是無根據的詆毀；（iii）在加五 12，保羅更只是以嚴厲的「願望」表達他的憤怒（見《加》1186-88）。

一 **10a** 因為也有許多人不受約束，說空話欺哄人，
10b 尤其是那些奉割禮的人。

因為解釋了為甚麼監督必須具有第 9 節（尤其是 9c 節）所提到的資格。這是由於克里特教會遇到為數不少的（許多[1]）敵對者。[2] 這裏提到他們的三點特色：[3]（**#1**）他們不受約束（同新譯），[4] 尚不服從（思高），[5] 是悖逆的人（新

1 πολλοί. 參較提前一 3 的某些人（τισίν = 'some' [KJV, NKJV], 'certain persons/people' [RSV, ESV / NRSV, NJB]）。Laansma 246 認為，'it is probably more rhetorical (meaning they are a significant presence) than numerically descriptive'.

2 Marshall 191: 'This section [1:10-16] gives the reason why elders apt at teaching are required'; 194: 'The reason for selecting leaders who are properly equipped to teach is given in vv. 10f.'; cf. 21: '1.10-12 is a unit which explains why the specific instruction in 1.9b [= my 9b-c] is given.' Banker 47*a* 稱 9c 節和 10a 節的關係為 'a lower-level relationship', 即 γάρ 字所指向的並非一 10～16 和一 6～9 這兩段之間的 'higher-level relationship'.（**1**）另一些釋經者則認為，因為指出 'why elders are needed'（Schreiner, 'Overseeing' 93），或是指出為甚麼克里特教會需要有 5～9 節所描寫的教會領袖：e.g., Fee 177; Hendriksen 336, 350, 358; Kelly 234; Mounce 395; Van Neste 253; 周 416；張 323。Stegemann（'Prejudices' 282）甚至認為，'the instructions for the extension or establishment of institutional structures [1:5-9] refers precisely to the task of setting the deviants straight.' 但見導論第伍節註 28（Banker 46*b*, 上面 38）。（**2**）Lock 133 認為，γάρ 字主要引進監督必須能夠駁倒爭辯的人（9c 節）的理由，但同時亦引進 5～9 節這一整段的理由。Witherington 119 則把因為子句連於 'Elders must rebuke those who oppose the right teaching': 'Because there are many who rebel against it'.（**3**）Levinsohn（'Constraints' 320）認為，10 節所提供的資料，一方面支持 9 節，同時提供 11 節的理由。

3 ἀνυπότακτοι, ματαιολόγοι καὶ φρεναπάται.（**1**）Genade 30 稱之為 'emphatic clustering' 的修辭技巧。這裏有「和（καί）」字將後面二字連起來，因此不能稱為 asyndetic emphatic clustering（參一 12 註釋註 7〔下面 174〕），但也不能稱為 polysyndetic emphatic clustering（參一 16 註釋註 2〔下面 207〕），因為並無 καί 字也把前面二字連起來。（**2**）在 πολλοί 和 ἀνυπότακτοι 之間是否有 καί（也）字，（**i**）*TextC* 584-85 給予此字的評級是 C 級，意即多數的編委接納它是原來的讀文，但是由於有重要的古卷缺少這字，因此把它放在方括號內，表示並非十分肯定。（**ii**）BDF §442(11) 指出：'Καί after πολύς before a second adjective' 是古典希臘文的做法，但從英語用法的角度看，καί 字是多餘的。（**iii**）Marshall 193 認為，可能有抄寫員認為這字是多餘的而把它刪去。

4 參呂譯、新和：不服約束；KJV: 'unruly'; Johnson II 225, 226: 'unrestrained'. Cf. REB: 'undisciplined'; Dunn 865*a*: 'lacking in personal discipline'.

5 See also NKJV, NJB, ESV, Stott 180: 'insubordinate'; RSV / *Paraphrase* 291: 'insubordinate men/characters'.（**i**）Banker 47*b* 認為，他們不受任何人約束：'they do

普）；[6] 另一些翻譯則更明確地表示，他們叛道（現修），是不受真理約束的叛徒（當代）。[7] 這裏的原文形容詞重拾了一章 6 節的同一個字。[8] （**#2**）他們說空話，好談虛妄事／好空談／好說空談／好講空話（呂譯／思高，新普／當代／新譯）。[9] 也許原文的意思是：他

---

not obey (anyone)'; (**ii**) Wild 894*b* 認為他們 'disobey church authority and tradition';(**iii**)古特立認為，他們公然藐視教會的正式規管（'flouting the official rule of the church' [Guthrie I 187; Guthrie II 199]; 古特立 201 作「藐視教會的規矩」)；(**iv**) Donelson I 179 則認為，在教會的「秩序」(τάξις: 次序〔林前十四 40〕、秩序〔西二 5，思高〕) 內，每個成員都有自己的位置；因此，假教師被指控為不受約束時，(ἀνυπότακτος 與 τάξις 同字根)，'they are not only being condemned for being out of position but for undermining the taxis of the church.' Cf. Stegemann, 'Prejudices' 282: 'a large number of group members . . . refuse to submit . . . to the order structure favoured by the author.' 可是，後三種看法都不大可能，因為 'there was no church structure yet in Crete (1:5)'（Mounce 396）。

6 See also NAU / NRSV, NIV, TNIV, NIV2011, NLT: 'rebellious men/people'.

7 See also (**i**) Hendriksen 351: 'disobedient to the Word of God'; Knight II 296: 'unwilling to be subject to God and his law'; (**ii**) Marshall 194: 'refusal to submit to (apostolic) authority'; Jeon I 48: 'this group does not honor the apostolic authority that God has established through Paul'; 唐 1012：「拒絕順服教會和使徒的權柄」(Towner III 694)；Zehr 255: 'These persons . . . refuse to submit to apostolic authority and the gospel';(**iii**)Mounce 396: '[the term] speaks of a person who rebels against the gospel (v 9) as taught by Paul and Titus'; Griffin 288: 'Their rebelliousness was against the truth of the gospel (cf. v. 14)'; (**iv**) G. Delling, *TDNT* 8.47: 他們不服從 the 'proponents' of 'sound teaching'; (**v**) 張 329：「不服神的律法，或是真理的教導」。

8 ἀνυπότακτος, 參一 6 註釋倒數第二段（上面 116-17）。(**1**) Classen ('Titus' 434, 'Epistle to Titus' 53) 提出這種思想上的聯繫：沒有不受約束的兒女的監督，會懂得如何處理那些不受約束的 'members of the congregation'. See also Van Neste 255 (with reference to Bassler 186-87). (**2**) Genade 31 則聲稱，在這裏從 6 節重複這字的效果，就是 'to evoke strong disapproval from the congregation for childish behavior on the part of the opposition.' Genade 32 認為：'they prove to be outsiders who are predatory and harmful to families.' See also Johnson, 'Titus' 396*a*: 'In Titus, these opponents are outsiders, evidently Jewish rivals.' (**3**) 范尼斯則像克拉遜一樣認為，這些人是 'in the church': 'While elders have not yet been appointed, false teachers have already arisen'（Van Neste, 'Message' 22*b*）。See also Guthrie I 188 / Guthrie II 200-1（古特立 203）：'The apostle is about to urge Titus to take a strong hand [v. 13b] with the unruly element in the Church/church'; Stegemann, 'Prejudices' 280: 'Since . . . it is clear that the group portrayed so negatively here [in 1:10-16] is to be found within the Christian community, I use the term "deviant Christian group."' 一 13b～c 和三 10 都提示，敵對者是教會內的人。

9 They (**i**) 'talk wildly/nonsense' (REB/NJB), (**ii**) 'engage in useless talk' (NLT), (**iii**) are '[*a*] vain / [*b*] empty / [*c*] idle / [*d*] foolish / [*e*] frivolous / [*f*] futile / [*g*] mere talkers' ([*a*] KJV / [*b*] RSV, NAU, ESV; LN §33.378, 31.13; E. Tiedtke, *DNTT* 1.552; Barclay 240; Genade 30 / [*c*] NKJV,

們從事於無用的、無益的閒談！[10] 不過，與說空話同字根的詞彙典型地描寫偶像崇拜和異教的信仰和行為，[11] 因而這裏的說空話同時提示謬誤與真理的對比。[12] 保羅在下文將會囑咐提多，要遠避愚拙的辯論、家譜、紛爭和因律法而起的爭辯，因為這都是虛妄無益的（三 9）；也許說空話欺哄人就是指這些假教師所參與的口頭的辯論和爭辯。[13] 他們是堅守合乎教義的可靠之道（9 節）的監督的相反。**（#3）** 他們欺哄人或欺騙人／別人（思高、新譯／新普），[14] 是欺騙人的人（呂譯）。[15] 文理（尤其是 11 節）提示，

NRSV, Fiore II 203 / [*d*] DC 135*b*; Banker 45*a* / [*e*] Kartzow 8, 194; Richards 82 / [*f*] Kelly 233, 234 / [*g*] NIV），（**iv**）'full of meaningless talk' (TNIV, NIV2011),（**v**）'spouting nonsense' (Quinn 26, 97, 98, 105) =「喋喋不休地說無意義的話」。

10 BDAG 621*a* (s.v. ματαιολόγος): '***talking idly***, subst. ὁ μ. *an idle talker*, *windbag*'; H. Balz, *EDNT* 2.396*a*: 'talking idly, empty talker'; LN §33.378: 'one who engages in empty and idle talk'; Marshall 194: 'empty prattler'; Mounce cv: 'senseless babbler';《新希》211*a*（s.v.）：「講話空洞無聊的人」。《輔讀》525 則理解為「說荒唐無稽的話的人」。（**1**）原文為複合形容詞（from μάταιος + λέγω [Vine 4.109]）；形容詞 μάταιος 見三 9 註釋倒數第二段之（乙）= 下面 440；動詞 λέγω（say）在保羅書信出現 115 次，新約全部 2,258 次！（**2**）這複合形容詞在希臘文聖經出現僅此一次；同字根的抽象名詞 ματαιολογία 亦只出現一次（提前一 6：空談）；同字根的動詞 ματαιολογέω（'to engage in idle talk' [LN]）一次也沒有出現。

11 （**i**）形容詞 μάταιος——這些虛妄的事（徒十四 15：τὰ μάταια）= 這些虛無之物／無用的東西（思高／新普），即是虛幻的偶像（現修）；虛妄的行為（彼前一 18：ματαία ἀναστροφή）；（**ii**）動詞 ματαιόω——在思想上成為虛妄（羅一 21〔思高〕：ἐματαιώθησαν），即是思想無價值的事物；（**iii**）名詞 ματαιότης——存著虛妄的意念（弗四 17〔新譯〕：ἐν ματαιότητι τοῦ νοὸς αὐτῶν），即是他們的思想虛妄（現修）=「無用、無效、（因而）沒有價值」（《弗》627）。

12 See Towner III 695（唐 1012-13）。Cf. Jeon I 48; Spencer 21: 'Paul describes those people whose words have no value most likely because their content is not in accordance with truth.' See also Calvin 362: 'Ματαιολογία is the opposite of useful and solid teaching'.

13 Karris, 'Polemic' 553. 本節的 ματαιολόγος 是與三 9 的 μάταιος 同字根的複合形容詞。Cf. Spencer 67: 'The circumcision party wastes its time in such words.'

14 See also NLT: 'who . . . deceive others'; Banker 47*b*: 'they deceive others'; *EDNT* 3.438*a*: '*those who deceive* the Church.'（**1**）BDF §119(2) 則把 φρεναπάτης 解釋為 'one who deceives his own mind, i.e. conceited'. 當代加上「自欺」之意：他們自欺欺人。但「自欺」應有代名詞，如在加六 3：φρεναπατᾷ ἑαυτόν.（**2**）這字（**φρεναπάτης**）是複合名詞（from φρήν + ἀπατάω, 'a mind-deceiver' [Vine 1.280]），其中的 'second element "governs" the first'（BDF §119）。名詞 φρήν 在新約只出現兩次（林前十四 20：在心志上不要作小孩子……在心志上總要作大人）；動詞 ἀπατάω 亦只出現三次（弗五 6；雅一 26／提前二 14：欺騙／受騙）。

15 See also KJV, NKJV, RSV, NRSV, NAU, NIV, ESV, LN §31.13: 'deceivers'; TNIV,

這是指他們散播假教義，使別人（教會中無戒備之心的信徒）受到欺騙。[16] 他們是**無謊言的上帝**（2 節）的相反。

一些譯本將（#2）（#3）看為有某種邏輯關係，從而得出以下的意思：他們**說虛空話欺哄人**（新和），[17] **用荒唐無稽的話欺騙別人**（現修），「他們試圖使別人相信他們所說的廢話」。[18]

保羅說許多人都有上述的三點特色，**尤其是那些奉割禮的人**。**尤其是**表示，**那些奉割禮的人**是擁有許多人的「反對陣營」[19] 中的猶太派，[20] 這反對健全教義的運動基本上是由這些人帶領

NIV2011: 'full of . . . deception'; Quinn 26, 97, 98, 105: 'seducing minds'; BDAG 1065*a* (s.v. φρεναπάτης): 'deceiver, misleader';《輔讀》525：「騙子」;《新希》227*b*（s.v.）：「騙子——在真理上誤導別人的人」。這字在希臘文聖經不再出現；同字根的動詞 φρεναπατάω 也只出現一次（加六 3，見上註之〔1〕）。

16 Marshall 195; Towner III 695（唐 1013）。Cf. REB: '[who] lead others astray.'

17 See *Paraphrase* 291: 'who deceive people's minds with their empty arguments'.

18 NJB: 'who talk nonsense and try to make others believe it'. 溫特指出，說空話、欺哄人，和貪婪（11c 節）這三點批評，也是一世紀的雄辯者（'the *virtuoso* orators who had come to dominate first-century teachers in education, especially those at the tertiary level'）從哲學家及其他人（包括斐羅）所受到的（Winter, *Roman Wives* 146; 詳見 146-48）。

19 Sumney（*Opponents* 291）認為，**許多人**可能是 'polemical exaggeration to increase alarm about their presence.' 但見下面註 22：該處的講法不必牽涉誇大其詞。

20 Genade 31; Wieland 183-84: 'the adverb μάλιστα seems to specify οἱ ἐκ τῆς περιτομῆς as a particular group among the many ἀνυπότακτοι . . . who threaten the church.'（**1**）Quinn 98 則認為，'*Malista* may here specify who the *many* are, as would the English, "I mean namely"'. 意即**許多人**就是**那些奉割禮的人**，「不服約束的人**正是**這一羣 "奉割禮的" 人」（利斐特 332〔Liefeld 315〕）。See also Fee 178: 'The word **especially** . . . in this instance probably means something like "in other words"'. 這種見解是基於 Skeat 的文章（'Parchments'）。Marshall 195 也認為，鑑於克里特異端的猶太色彩（一 14，三 9），μάλιστα 在這裏的意思可能是 Skeat 所提議的 'namely'; thus also Towner III 695 n.75（唐 1013 註 6）。（**2**）Skeat 認為，如果保羅的意思是 'especially among Jewish converts'（NEB, REB [see also NJB: 'particularly among those of the circumcision']），'he would have needed to write ἐν τοῖς ἐκ περιτομῆς'，因此，原文的英譯是 'in other words, the Jewish converts'（art. cit. 174）。可是，原文片語（οἱ ἐκ τῆς περιτομῆς）不必像 NEB 那樣翻譯，其意思大可以是 'especially those of the circumcision'（NRSV, NKJV, NAU）或 'especially those of the circumcision party/group'（ESV / NIV, TNIV, NIV2011）。（**3**）Poythress（'Meaning' 524）指出，Skeat 的文章並無說服力，因有以下三個問題：

> '1. Skeat's article fails to consider that the expression τοῦτ' ἔστιν is already available to represent the meaning "that is", making less plausible a claim that

的，[21] 而他們的跟隨者為數不少。[22] 這裏所用的原文片語[23]（或稍微不同的形式）在使徒行傳和保羅書信另外出現四次，[24] 全部五次的意思都是「那些從割禮之舉取得他們的身分的人」。[25] 但是一個詞的意

---

this meaning belongs to μάλιστα.

2. All cited instances in Skeat's article are ambiguous at best, and can easily be interpreted in another way.
3. In the absence of unambiguous evidence, meanings are not to be multiplied.'

詳見 524-25, 525-31, 531.

(4) Kim（'Interpretation' 361-65）審視了 Skeat 文章的論據，認為它們並無說服力（見 365-68 的總結）。關於費歌頓（Fee 183）特別倚重的、Skeat 在聖經以外找到的例子（Skeat, 'Parchments' 175-77），金氏則認為無須討論，他的理由是（365）：'The conclusive documents for our discussion are the Pastorals. If it were used with that connotation in all the other verses in the Pastorals [I Tim. 4:10; 5:8; II Tim. 4:13; Tit. 1:10], we could be convinced that its usage in I Tim. 5:17 must be in the same thread. However, such an attempt to find examples of such a unique usage in other writings, sometimes even from ambiguous or academically invalid sentences, would not prove or strongly support the hypothesis that the word is employed with the unfamiliar usage in the biblical verse. Therefore, it is unnecessary to discuss the rest of Skeat's examples here.' Poythress（'Meaning' 526-31）早已把金氏沒有討論的例子詳細審視，他的結論是：'All in all, every example that Skeat offers [including 2 Tim 4:13; Tit 1:10; 1 Tim 4:10] is either spurious or inconclusive. There is no firm evidence here for a new meaning of μάλιστα'（531）。**(5)** 這副詞（**μάλιστα**）在保羅書信另外出現七次，新約另四次，其意思都或是*更是*／*更*（提前四 10；門 16 節；彼後二 10／徒二十六 3；加六 10）、*特別是*／*特別*（提後四 13／腓四 22）、*尤其是*／*尤其*（提前五 8、17／徒二十五 26），或是最（徒二十 38），沒有一次是「即、就是，換句話說」之意。See BDAG 613 (s.v.);《新希》209*b* (s.v.). 誠如 Köstenberger 548 所說，'the NT pattern of usage speaks decisively in favor of the meaning "especially" here [in Tit 1:10] and elsewhere in the PE . . . in the sense that a larger group is first named from which a subsegment is separated out and brought into focus'. **(6)** Kim（'Interpretation' 368 n.27）指出，'no support can be found for Skeat's hypothesis in BAGD [488*b*-89*a*, s.v.] or LSJ*.'（**A Greek-English Lexicon*, by H. G. Liddell and R. Scott, 9th edition revised by Henry Stuart Jones [Oxford: Clarendon, 1976; with Revised Supplement 1996].）

21 Banker 48*a*. **(1)** DC 135*b* 認為本段可能表示，教牧書信所見的整個異端運動都與猶太主義／猶太教有關（'had something to do with Judaism'）。**(2)** Blaiklock 76 則認為，克里特的異端部分源於猶太教（*那些奉割禮的人*），部分源於異教（*說空話欺哄人*）。See also Zamfir 176: 'The adverb seems to invite the audience to look beyond those of the circumcision to others who do not share this affiliation.'

22 Sumney, *Opponents* 295: 'they have garnered a significant following.'

23 οἱ ἐκ <u>τῆς</u> περιτομῆς.

24 不包括徒十 45 *那些奉割禮的信徒*（οἱ <u>ἐκ περιτομῆς</u> πιστοί）。比較上註，可見這裏的介詞片語不是直接連於冠詞，並與冠詞一起構成名詞，而是形容名詞 οἱ πιστοί 的；整個片語相當於 οἱ πιστοὶ οἱ ἐκ περιτομῆς.

25 參《羅》1.603 註 8。

思是一回事，該詞指甚麼是另一回事。[26] 在本節以外的另四次中，三次僅指「受了割禮的人」（即是猶太人：羅四 12；加二 12；西四 11），[27] 其餘一次則指耶路撒冷教會的割禮派（徒十一 2），他們認為外邦信徒若不照摩西的規例受割禮，就不能得救（徒十五 1〔新譯〕，參 5 節）。[28] 就提多書本節而論，那些奉割禮的人推銷猶太人無稽的傳說和背棄真理之人的命令（14 節），這些命令關乎潔淨與不潔淨的區別（15 節）；而且他們從事「關於家譜（或由家譜引起）的辯論」和「關於律法（或因律法而起）的爭辯」（三 9）。[29] 有認為（一）那些奉割禮的人所指的，就是那些主張行割禮的猶太人（當代），[30] 更明確地說，就是那些主張受割禮的猶太基督徒（現修），[31] 即那些堅持受割禮才能

---

26 此即 meaning 和 referent 的區別。

27 τοῖς . . . ἐκ περιτομῆς（羅四 12；參《羅》1.603），τοὺς ἐκ περιτομῆς（加二 12；詳參《加》481-85）；οἱ ὄντες τῆς περιτομῆς（西四 11；參《西・門》743-45）。

28 加拉太的煽動者（猶太派的基督徒）很可能和耶路撒冷教會的割禮派有關連（參《加》117-20）。

29 參三 9 註釋第六段之（三）= 下面 438-40。

30 （1）See also RSV, *Paraphrase* 291 / Fiore II 203, 204: 'the circumcision party/faction'; NIV, TNIV, NIV2011 / ESV: 'those of the circumcision group/party'; Fiore II 206: 'the circumcisionists'; 222: 13～16 節所批評的是 '[t]he circumcisionist position and religious regulations . . . , particularly regarding purity'. （2）張永信認為，他們「高抬割禮的地位」（張 45），「這些猶太裔的信徒極力標榜割禮，以反映出沒有受過割禮的提多，在屬靈的地位上是遜色的」（330）。馬唐納 559*a-b* 認為，他們「是那些自稱是基督徒，並且堅持基督徒必須要受割禮和遵守禮儀律法的猶太人教師。」（3）昆謝隆認為，克里特的教會主要是猶太基督徒構成的（'predominantly Jewish-Christian' [Quinn 20]），故此，他們受到反保羅的奉割禮教師的誘惑，其後又產生關於「摩西律法在基督徒生命中的功用」之爭論，都是可理解的（16）。其實，克里特的小教會只是被教牧書信的作者（並非保羅）想像為相對地新成立的猶太基督徒的教會，因而「提多」所傳遞的教導，代表了保羅對於這種教會之組成所能作出的貢獻。按這理論，保羅、提多、克理特的教會都被賦予 'a typical or representative function'（21; see also 16）！（4）古特立 40 有這樣的講法：「在提多書一 10 很特別的提到，有人說虛空的話，<u>在奉割禮的事上</u>，欺哄人。」其實，這翻譯偏離了原文的意思：'In Titus 1:10 / Tit. i. 10 a significant reference to empty talkers <u>of the circumcision party</u> clearly shows . . .'（Guthrie II 42 / Guthrie I 35）。

31 See also Oden 62: 'converts from Judaism who insisted that to be a Christian one had to submit to Jewish ceremonial ordinances (cf. Acts 15:1-29; Gal. 5).' Keegan II

得救的人（新普）。[32] 不過，由於信上完全沒有提到他們堅持外邦人必須受割禮，[33] 因此另一種理解較為可取：（二）那些奉割禮的人或那些守割禮的人（新譯）僅指那些受過割禮／割損的人（呂譯／思高），[34] 即他們是猶太

94（Keegan I 59）也認為，「克里特教會中有眾多的猶太基督徒，可能面對的問題與保祿要處理的問題相似：外邦人皈依後，要遵守猶太律法的規定，諸如割損及食物規條」。See also Johnson I 119: 'We have here a situation remarkably close to that which Paul faced in the Galatian churches'; Fiore II 204: 'Here Titus faces similar opponents [as those in Gal 2:3-5]'; Stern, *Comm.* 654: 'it denotes, as in Galatia, a group . . . whose distinctive was that they favored circumcising Gentile believers.' Keener 625 更明確地說，'Paul's old opponents, those of the circumcision group he encountered in Galatia, apparently continue to follow on his heels to "correct" his converts (1:10, 14).' Fairbairn 264-65 則質疑這種見解。

32 NLT: 'those who insist on circumcision for salvation'. See also LN §11.51: 'οἱ ἐκ περιτομῆς: (a set phrase . . .) those who insisted on circumcising Gentiles if they were to be regarded as true believers in Jesus Christ'; Dunn 865*a*: 'It presumably . . . denotes Jews who . . . had believed in Jesus as Messiah and continued to think as Jews－that is, they continued to assume that the way for Gentiles to share in Israel's covenant blessings (the Messiah!) was for them to be circumcised and become proselytes'; Wall 333 (cf. 344): '[They] believe that converts to Christianity should be purified by Torah observance and circumcision before their initiation into the community of "elect ones"'; 《新希》264*a*（s.v.）：「設定短語……堅持外邦人若要被當作耶穌基督的真正信徒，就要行割禮的人」；彭編 97*a*：「那些主張外邦人須受割禮才能成為基督徒的猶太基督徒」（底線是原來的）。

33 Cf. Marshall 44: 'there is no specific attack on circumcision in the letter and no indication that there was a dependence upon "works of the law" for salvation.'

34 參《輔讀》525：「受過割禮的人」；H. C. Hahn, *DNTT* 1.309: 'the Jews'; Ngewa 346: 'simply ethnic Jews'; Zehr 254: 'the Hellenistic Jews'. **(1)** 不少釋經者都認為他們是「猶太基督徒」（侯嘉文 150）= 'Jewish-Christian believers'（Ehrman, 'Pastoral Epistles' 452*a*），'believers of Jewish origin'（Murphy-O'Connor, '2 Timothy' 415），'Hellenistic Jewish converts'（Fee 11），'Jewish Christians'（Arichea－Hatton 275; Knight II 297; Witherington 87, 124 n.108; deSilva, *INT* 735*b*; Fatum, 'Christ' 184; Goulder, 'Wolves' 243: 'it sounds as if the opposition is Jewish-Christian'; Hanson III 175; 韓遜進一步聲稱：'We do not find Jews, as distinguished from Jewish Christians, referred to in the Pastorals' [182]）。**(2)** S. Martin 211 認為這片語只是一種（對猶太人的）「種族誹謗（ethnic slur）」，指 'a cultural/religious/national heritage'. 但見 Montague 226: 'it is possible that the statement could be heard today . . . as an ethnic slur . . . The danger of this misinterpretation is probably the reason why this text is never read in the liturgy.' **(3)** Johnson II 213 則認為，那些假教師也許並非猶太人，而是（像加拉太的煽動者一樣）受到猶太教師的影響的外邦人；他們想遵守猶太律法（227-28）。Stegemann（'Prejudices' 287-88）同樣辯證：假教師不是猶太人，也不是所謂的「猶太基督徒」；他們是基督徒，又是克里特人。教牧書信的作者 '*deliberately* moves the protagonists of the deviant group into the proximity of Judaism, which he clearly sees in a negative light.' 他顯然要 'charge the Christian deviants with prejudices about

人；[35] 他們自稱為基督徒，但他們的信仰卻是不健全的（參一13）。[36]

Judaism and to discredit them because of their proximity to Jewish traditions.' 作者對他們的辱罵有可能暗指加拉太書，為要將他們置於保羅在該書與之爭辯的那些「敵對者」的鄰近；**那些奉割禮的人**（οἱ ἐκ τῆς περιτομῆς，參：加二 12，τοὺς ἐκ περιτομῆς）、**背棄真理之人**（參：加二 14，**與福音的真理不合**；五 7，**不順從真理**）和**欺哄人**（參：加六 3，**自欺**；亦參加三 1 及下）等詞語，可能支持這見解。

35 Calvin 362: 'the Jews'. Wieland 184-85 指出，'Roman Crete had a significant Jewish population, with links to the Jewish community in Alexandria.'

36 See Marshall 195: 'Since activity in the church is implied, the reference must be to Jewish Christians'; BDAG 807*b* (s.v. περιτομή, 2 a): 'Judean (Jewish) Christians'; Fiore II 193, Kelly 234, Quinn 11, 26, Streete, '*Askesis*' 302, Wild 894*b*: 'Jewish Christians'; Ward 243: 'Jews . . . professing the Christian faith'; White 188*b*: 'Christian Jews'; 周 416：「奉基督教的猶太人」。H. Balz（*EDNT* 1.239*a* [s.v. γαστήρ]）也談到 'the Jewish-Christian false teachers who were appearing on Crete.' 另見上面註 34 之（1）。**（1）**Hendriksen 351 進一步解釋為 'Jewish church-members of the Pharisaic type tinged with incipient Gnosticism'（cf. Robertson, *Pictures* 4.600）。Hiebert 432 認為他們是 'gnosticizing Judaists who as professed Christians sought to infiltrate the churches with their misguided teaching.'**（2）**Aune（'Pastoral Letters' 551）指出，'Even though the identification of "Jewish Christian Gnostics" as a broad designation for the heresy reflected in the Pastorals is widely held, that rubric is the result of synthesizing the various, sometimes contradictory, characteristics of the opponents and is therefore virtually useless historically. The problem of identifying the heresy or heresies addressed in the Pastorals therefore remains unsolved.'**（3）**Towner III 40（唐 57）則認為，他們是 'Christian teachers (Jewish: "especially those of the circumcision") who refuse to break free from the value system corrupting Crete and so in the churches become opponents of the apostle and his mission.' '[They] are apparently rebellious Jewish-Christian teachers unwilling (or unable) to evaluate cultural assumptions critically'（Towner III 76〔唐 106 把 'cultural assumptions' 翻譯為「文化的自負」，但 'assumptions' 在這裏的意思較可能是「假設」而不是「傲慢」〕）。這些悖逆的教師拒絕保羅的權柄，'and continue to ply the communities with a lowest-common-denominator Christian faith that makes plenty of room for Cretan vices'（Towner III 47〔唐 67：「他們不斷灌輸給基督徒群體的教導，所包含的基督徒信仰因素微乎其微，並且給革哩底* 的罪惡留下很多空間」〕）。（*和合；新和、和修：克里特。）亦參一 5 註釋註 20 之（2）＝ 上面 92。

一 **11a** 這些人的口必須堵住，

11b 因為他們……敗壞人的全家。

11c 貪不義之財，將不該教導的事教導人，

這些人的口必須堵住[1] 原文直譯作「必須使他們沉默無聲」。[2] 一些中譯本把它視為對提多的命令，[3] 因而意譯為你務要堵住他們的嘴（新譯），你一定要使他們住口（新普），你應該勒住他們的口（呂譯），你必須禁止這些人說話（現修）。[4] 班約翰指出，經文並無明言誰要負責堵住他們的口；這些人原文是關係代名詞，第 11a 節是關於這些假教師的一長列描述中的一個子句，這描述一直延伸至第 12 節

---

1 參新和（這些人的口總要堵住）；思高（應杜塞這些人的口）。BDAG 382*a*（s.v. ἐπιστομίζω）指出，原文動詞的字面意義是 'to put someth. on the mouth'; 因此，'[it] can apply either to a bridle or a muzzle'（Scott 158）。See also Blaiklock 76 / Quinn 26, 97, 98, 105: 'Such people should / these people must be muzzled'; Fiore II 203, 204: 'It is necessary to gag these'; Collins 333: 'These troublemakers must be "reined in" [as in the reining in of horses]'. 這動詞在希臘文聖經出現僅此一次。

2 οὓς δεῖ ἐπιστομίζειν, 'whom it is necessary to silence' = 'who/They/they must be silenced' (NAU, BDAG 382*a* [s.v. ἐπιστομίζω] / NIV, TNIV, NIV2011, NJB, ESV, NLT, *Paraphrase* 291 / RSV, NRSV), 'it is necessary to silence them' (LN §33.124).

3 Cf. Laansma 246: 'Paul ordered Titus to shut their mouths'. Hendriksen 351 認為，文理（一 5～9）提示堵住這些人的口是提多和長老們的工作。Knight II 297 稱這要求為 'the essential demand placed on Titus and the leaders.' Collins 333 同樣認為，抑制他們是提多的責任，可能是透過監督們來執行。Cf. Jeon I 49: 'it is primarily the exhortation and reproof of the elders that will "gag" these mouths'; Schreiner, 'Overseeing' 93: 'surely this is one of the responsibilities of the elders.'

4 參《輔讀》525：「禁止說話」；《新希》129*a*（s.v.）：「使人停止講話。」See also BDAG 382*a* (s.v. ἐπιστομίζω): 'The mng. *bridle*, *hinder*, *prevent* . . . is also prob.'（**1**）Hanson III 175 認為，可能指革除他們的會籍。（**2**）Van Neste（'Message' 23*a*）解釋為「不要再給他們機會散播他們的謬誤」。Thus already Blaiklock 76: 'A sure method of dealing with a corrupting minority in a church is by all means to deny them opportunity to talk.'（**3**）古特立則認為，使假教師閉口的方法，大抵就是巧妙地陳述 9 節提到的真教義（Guthrie I 187, Guthrie II 200: 'presumably by the skilful presentation of the true doctrine mentioned in verse 9'；「這或許是因為第 9 節裡所提到，能把爭辯的人駁倒了」〔古特立 202〕這翻譯，跟原文相去頗遠）。Similarly Mounce 392: 'they are to be muzzled through the proper teaching of the gospel'; 396: 'the muzzling is to be done by instruction (so v 9 . . .)'; Oden 63: 'not physically or coercively but by proper argument'; Towner II 233: 'by publicly correcting their false doctrines with the approved teaching of the apostle.' 亦參陳 25：「要用真理確切地指出其錯誤與動機，使他們不能再有什麼機會用錯誤的教訓敗壞人。」

末，然後第 13a 節以這個見證是真的來結束「假教師的描述」這一小段。因此，這些人的口必須堵住不宜看為一句勸勉的話；真正的勸勉是在第 13b 節（你要嚴厲地責備他們），第 13c 節表達這勸勉的目的（使他們在信仰上健全），而第 14 節則表達在信仰上健全的一種表現（不聽假教師的教導）。隨後兩節再回到對他們的描述。這種交叉配置模式[5] 提示，本段只有一句勸勉的話，而那並不是第 11a 節。[6] 與此同時，很難認為第 11a 節完全沒有勸勉的意味：這些人的口必須堵住這直接描述，同時是間接的勸勉；本段開首所引的意譯（新譯、新普、呂譯、現修），就是將這含意表達了出來。[7]

第 11b 節的他們原文是關係代名詞，在這裏可能具有「他們是這樣的一種人」之意。[8] 他們的「特色」就是：他們……敗壞人的全家（11b 節，同新和、新譯）。[9] 原文動詞在新約聖經僅再出現兩次：一次指耶穌推翻在聖殿外院兌換銀錢的人的桌子（約二 15）；另一次的用法與本節相同（提後二 18：他們……敗壞了好些人的信心）。《呂振中譯本》在後兩節都把動詞翻譯為傾覆，[10] 另有在本節翻譯為「分

---

5 描述（10～13a 節），勸勉（13b～14 節），描述（15～16 節）。參導論第伍節之「乙叁」（上面 31-32）。

6 Banker 45*b*.

7 班約翰自己早前（44）就這樣翻譯：'They . . . should be prevented from teaching (the things they teach) (by you and the leaders you appoint')'（also 48*a*）。留意第二次括號內的話和上註所屬正文所引的看法似乎產生衝突。班約翰的解釋是（45*b*-46*a*）：有可能保羅的用意是說，使他們（假教師）住口的方法就是說服他們的跟隨者，他們（假教師）是錯的（13b～c 節）。See also Simpson 99: ἐπιστομίζειν 的意思是 'silencing by force of reason'; Ward 244: 'A man can sometimes *be silenced* by a demonstration of the falsity of his views and even of their silliness (1 Tim. 4:7).' 如此，11a 節肯定具勸勉的意味，是間接的勸勉。

8 參呂譯：這種人；NJB: 'people of this kind . . .'; BAGD 587*a*, BDAG 729*b* (s.v. ὅστις, 2 b): '[used here] to emphasize a characteristic quality, by which a preceding statement is to be confirmed'; Knight II 297（endorsing BDAG）。

9 在原文，全家被放在動詞敗壞之前，表示賓詞受到強調。正常的字序是動詞先於賓詞的（see BDF §472(1)）。參較一 12 註釋註 4 之（1）= 下面 172。

10 參本節的以下英譯：'who subvert whole houses/households' (KJV/NKJV), 'they are upsetting whole families' (RSV, NRSV, NAU, ESV; LN §59.29), 'people of this kind

裂」。[11] 不過，動詞在本節的意思較可能是「破壞」：**他們……破壞人的整個家庭**（思高），[12] 即是使這些家庭不再相信正確的教導。[13] 這種效果是如何達到的呢？是**用不該傳講的學說**（現修）達成的：他們**將不該教導的事教導人**（同新和）。[14] 這就為**破壞**提供了進一步的解

---

upset whole families' (NJB). Wall 343 則譯作 'they are shaking up entire households'.

11 TNIV, NIV2011: 'they are disrupting whole households'（在提後二 18 則譯作 'destroy'）。See also Scott 158: 他們影響一兩個家庭成員，使全家陷入分裂與痛苦（'dissension and misery'）之中。

12 See also BDAG 74*b* (s.v. ἀνατρέπω, 2): 'they ruin whole families'; O. Michel, *TDNT* 5.130: 'Tt. 1:11 complains of false teachers leading whole houses astray and ruining them'; Marshall 197: 'almost certainly the defection of entire families to the false teachers'. 亦參現修：**他們破壞了許多家庭**。但原文動詞是現在時態的（ἀνατρέπουσιν）：'they are ruining whole families' (NIV). 亦參上註。(**1**) Genade 32 認為，這裏的 'οἶκοι'(*sic*, 其後改正為 οἶκοι) 可指家庭或家庭教會。Thielman（'Old Convictions' 307 n.58）也認為，'These "househoulds" (*oikoi*) were probably not merely individual families but the churches that met in their houses as well.' Wild 894*b* 認為這裏的家很可能就是指家庭教會。Cf. Long 261/262: 'whole families' = 'entire/whole house churches'; Mounce lxxiv-v (cf. liii): 'The opponents have upset entire house churches'; Ellis, 'Pastoral Letters' 661*b*: 'Some house churches were ravaged and near collapse'（《辭典》957*b* 作「有些家庭教會不堪一擊，接近崩潰」，但英文的意思應該是「受到嚴重破壞，瀕臨崩潰」）。另有認為，複數的家字「指全教會的各家」（陳 25；周 417〔無「的」字〕）。(**2**) 名詞 **οἶκος** 在保羅書信另外出現十四次（新約全部 114 次〔包括約七 53〕; see BDAG 698*b*-99*b* [s.v.];《新希》233*b*），多次是在**上帝的家**（提前三 15）、「某人的家」（林前一 16；提後一 16，四 19）、「某人家裏的教會」（羅十六 5；林前十六 19；西四 15；門 2 節）等詞語中；另見林前十一 34，十四 35；提前三 4、5、12，五 4（皆指字面意義的家）。以上的資料提示，多一 11 本節的 οἶκοι 應該是指家庭而不是指家庭教會，因後者通常是用「冠詞＋介詞片語＋名詞」這種形式表達的：τὴν κατ' οἶκον αὐτῶν/αὐτῆς ἐκκλησίαν（羅十六 5／西四 15），τῇ κατ' οἶκον αὐτῶν / οἶκόν σου ἐκκλησίᾳ（林前十六 19／門 2 節）。(**3**) 唐 1015-16 指出：「家庭……是哲學性背誦〔philosophical recitations〕和修辭操練〔rhetorical performance〕的典型場合」（Towner III 697）。此事實亦支持假教師以「家庭」為其活動場所的看法。

13 Banker 44, 48*b*: 'They cause whole families to stop believing in the correct teachings'. 參《新希》25*b*（s.v. ἀνατρέπω, II）：「推翻信念——打垮原有的信念，或根本否定既有信念。」Stegemann（'Prejudices' 282）則認為，亦有可能 'the deviants' activities have caused social conflicts within Christian families.' Keener 627*a* 認為，也許 'they are undermining the authority structures current in the culture (Tit 2:4-5, 9-10)'. Fatum（'Christ' 185）明確認為，**敗壞人的全家的**是**禁止嫁娶**（提前四 3）的教導。

14 參呂譯：**教授所不該教授的**；思高：**教導那不應教導的**；新譯：**教訓一些不應該教導的事**。分詞 διδάσκοντες = participle of means（Wallace 630: 'who upset whole houses **by teaching** things that they should not'; similarly, NEB, REB; Barclay 240; Kelly 233）。*Pace* Ngewa 459 n.74: 'The participle *didaskontes* may be taken as a participle of manner,* stating how the ruining is achieved, or as a causal participle'; 350:

釋：他們用錯誤的教導使許多人全家偏離真理（新普），[15] 破壞……許多基督徒全家人純正的信仰（當代）。[16] 提摩太後書二章 18 節（見上文）支持這種理解。他們……敗壞人的全家這種講法提示，這些假教師不是在教會的全會眾面前宣揚他們不該傳講的學說（現修），而是向不同的家庭灌輸他們錯誤的教導（新普）。[17] 這裏浮現的圖畫是，教導信徒的工作在許多不同的家庭中進行。[18]

將不該教導的事教導人（11c 節）有解釋為「他們無權教導，卻仍然教導」。[19] 但原文清楚的意思是：他們教導一些不應該教導的事

'The teachers cause disruption by what they do and because of what they do.' (*On the participle of manner, see Wallace 627-28.)
（1）Quinn 15 認為，也許他們特別透過富有的女贊助者達到他們的目的（見提後三 6～7），這些婦女分享了他們對無稽的傳說和冗長的家譜（提前一 4；參：多一 14，三 9）的濃厚興趣，以及他們對婚姻的排斥（提前四 3），這種排斥完全是「非猶太」的（'quite un-Jewish'）。See also Hanson I 110: 'Probably to be taken in the same sense as 2 Tim. 3: 6.' 但是 Marshall 196-97 指出，這一點並不明顯（'not clear'）。（2）原文動詞（διδάσκω）在本書出現僅此一次（用於假教師身上）；在教牧書信另外出現四次（提前二 12，四 11，六 2；提後二 2），都具正面意義；在保羅書信另外出現 11 次，新約全部 97 次（參《帖後》269-70；BAGD 192*a*, BDAG 241*a-b* [s.v.];《新希》82*a* [s.v.]）。

15 See also NLT: 'they are turning whole families away from the truth'; Köstenberger 609*b*: 'plunging their devotees into spiritual turmoil by overturning their previous convictions through persuasive argument.'（1）Bassler 189 則認為，敗壞人的全家的方法也可能是 'through the quarrels and divisions the opponents fomented (3:9; 1 Tim. 6:4-5), [or] through moral corruption (3:11)'.（2）Bouwman 40 的看法（若筆者沒有誤解）是奇怪的，他認為：'As their children saw through their hypocrisy [see 1:16], "whole families" were upset'——被破壞的是假教師自己的家庭！

16 筆者省略了字（見上面註 12）。See also LN §31.72: 'who upset the faith of entire households'. Fiore II 7 認為，教牧書信的一個特色，就是把信仰視為認識真理（'their view of faith as knowledge of the truth'）；作者聲稱，在這方面，教牧書信與希羅的觀念相似，即知識有拯救的效能並帶來行動。

17 Ward 244. 參：提後三 6：有人潛入別人家裏，操縱無知的婦女。Marshall 42 認為，教牧書信中保羅的對手 'are engaged in teaching, both in the church meetings and in private conversations in people's homes.' 不過，單就提多書而論，華德的見解似較可取。

18 Fee 178. 參：徒二十 20，保羅對以弗所的長老說：或在公眾面前，或在每一個人的家裏，我都教導你們。

19 Genade 30: 'teaching without the right to teach'. See also RSV: 'teaching . . . what they have no right to teach'; 但留意 'what' 字，參下註。

（新譯），[20] 那些事情是不該傳講的學說（現修），[21] 是錯誤的教導（新普）[22]——不指明其確切內容表示貶抑[23]——與保羅所教導的合乎敬虔的真理（一 1b）和保羅要提多用來勸勉人的健全的教導（一 9b）相對。[24] 這些錯誤的教導在第 14 節被解釋為猶太人無稽的傳說和背棄真理之人的命令。在教牧書信裏，只有這裏提到反對者的教導；這表示教導——真正的和錯謬的——是本書特別關注的題目。[25]

貪不義之財原文有「因／為了」一字：這是他們將不該教導的事

20 Zamfir 186: 'the opponents teach what they should not'. διδάσκοντες ἃ μὴ δεῖ = 'teaching things they ought not to teach / that they ought not to [teach] / which they ought not [to teach] / teaching . . . what they ought not to teach' (NIV, TNIV, NIV2011 / NJB / KJV, NKJV / ESV), 'teaching things they should not *teach*' (NAU); 'teaching . . . what it is not right to teach' (NRSV). 參思高／呂譯：教導那不應教導的事／教授所不該教授的。參較提前五 13：一些年輕的寡婦好管閒事，說些不該說的話（λαλοῦσαι τὰ μὴ δέοντα）。

21 （**1**）Genade 33 將 ἃ μὴ δεῖ 翻譯為 'things not necessary'（also 42, cf. 54, 64; see also Jeon I 55, 65, 114, 124, 126: 'teaching what is not necessary' [thus also Spencer 20]），又聲稱關係代名詞 ἅ 字凸出了他們的教導之無足輕重：'The illegitimate teachers simply teach things.' 筆者認為作者將太多的貨品放在 ἅ 這小艇上，這是由於（或導致）他從 διδάσκοντες ἃ μὴ δεῖ 這分詞片語把 ἃ μὴ δεῖ 抽出來，然後給予後者不正確的翻譯（參較上註）。（**2**）Griffin 289 根據 'things which are not necessary' 這種不合宜的翻譯而認為，這表示克里特的假教導 'is the attempt to add "works" in some form as a requirement for Christian salvation'. 作者稍後採納 'teaching things they ought not to teach' 這正確的翻譯（290；參上註及本註下文）。（**3**）BDF §428(4) 指出，'Relative clauses with the indicative have οὐ* except in two instances'（多一 11；彼後一 9）；此辭典認為，'ἃ μὴ δεῖ is probably merely a mixture of τὰ μὴ δέοντα [1 T 5: 13] and ἃ οὐ δεῖ [Job 19:4]'（endorsed by BDAG 214*a* [s.v. δεῖ, 2 a]; 方括號內的兩段經文依次由 BDF 及 BDAG 提供）。*See Zerwick §440: 'for the NT οὐ is used with the indicative and μή with the other moods, including the infinitive and the participle'.

22 See also *Paraphrase* 291: 'they subvert whole households with their false teaching'.

23 Marshall 197.

24 Hanson I 110 則認為，不該教導的事可能像不該說的話（提前五 13〔見上面註 20 末〕）一樣，指 'magical practices'. 由於提前五 13 好管閒事的原文形容詞（περίεργοι）在徒十九 19 加了冠詞（τὰ περίεργα）的意思是邪術或法術（新普），韓遜就認為提前五 13 的不該說的話可能指 'charms and magical formulae'（Hanson I 60; see also Hinson 283: 'They may also have engaged in some kind of magical rites'）。對筆者而言，這論證並無說服力。如馬歇爾所指出：'Surrounding references to the apostolic teaching [1:9, 14] . . . suggest the general meaning of false teaching'（Marshall 197）。

25 Faber, 'Titus' 143. 作者說 'a concern particular to this letter'（= 此信獨有的關注）；筆者略加修改如上。

教導人的原因（因貪不義之財〔新和〕）或目的（為了可恥之利／為了貪圖錢財〔呂譯／現修[26]〕）。原文形容詞有各種不同的意思，從外表的「醜的、難看的」到道德意義上「卑鄙的、卑劣的」都包括在內。在以「榮譽－恥辱」為導向的社會中，這詞特別重要；它一般指未能達到社會所預期的道德或文化標準，因而是「社會上或道德上不可接受」之意。[27] 討論中的片語在中英譯本的多種翻譯中，[28] 為了可恥之利（呂譯）即是可恥的利潤／利益（思高／新譯），[29] 解釋為「為了

---

26 參新普：他們這樣做只是貪圖錢財（NLT: 'only for money'）。當代則理解為為了騙取錢財。（1）提前六 5 所譴責的假教師以敬虔為得利的門路。（2）「貪財」是希臘哲學家對「詭辯派」（《宗教》282*b*）的標準批評（Karris, 'Polemic' 552: 'a stock criticism of the sophist'*）。*Sophists 的另一翻譯是「智者」；他們是「公元前 5 世紀在希臘周遊各地講授詭辯術、治國之道和哲學的教師」（《聖神》486*b*）。參三 9 註釋註 6 第二段（下面 434）。

27 BDAG 29*b* (s.v. αἰσχρός): 'pert. to being socially or morally unacceptable, *shameful*, *base*'. See also G. Schneider, *EDNT* 1.41*b* (s.v.): 'repulsive, shameful'. 這字（**αἰσχρός**）在新約僅再出現三次（林前十一 6〔羞愧〕，十四 35〔可恥的〕；弗五 12〔可恥的〕）；參《新希》10*b*（s.v.）。同字根的抽象名詞 αἰσχρότης 在希臘文聖經只出現一次（弗五 4：猥褻〔思高〕，參《弗》718-19），同字根的另一名詞 αἰσχρολογία 也只出現一次（西三 8：「辱罵性的言語」〔參《西・門》553〕）。

28 尚未提及的包括：（**i**）'for filthy lucre's sake' (KJV)——這翻譯被評為 'unfortunate in suggesting that "lucre" is of itself FILTHY' (Leaney 116); 'it wrongly suggests to modern ears that it was the money itself that was wrong whereas it was their motives' (Mounce 397); 'It is only money gained by bad or false teaching that is disgraceful; and the passage might be rendered, "who make a gain that is dishonorable by teaching what they ought not"' (Ramsay 33); cf. Kümmel, *INT* 378: 'The opponents . . . take money for their instructional lectures (Tit 1:11, I Tim 6:5);（**ii**）'for sordid gain / for the sake of sordid gain/profit' (NRSV / NAU, NJB / Kelly 233, 234);（**iii**）'for base gain' (RSV; H.-G. Link, *DNTT* 3.564), 'all for sordid gain / base love of material gain' (NEB, REB / *Paraphrase* 291), 'for the sake of base/disgraceful gain' (Witherington 119);（**iv**）「為了令人不齒的好處」（彭編 97*a*）。Van Neste（'Message' 19*a*）引希臘史家 Polybius（Πολύβιος, 公元前三至二世紀）對克里特人的描寫：'So much in fact do sordid love of gain [αἰσχροκέρδεια] and lust for wealth prevail among them, that the Cretans are the only people in the world in whose eyes no gain is disgraceful（*Histories* 6.46; see also DC 135*b*-36*a*; Knight II 299; Köstenberger 610*a*; Marshall 198 n.126; Witherington 123; Kidd, 'Titus' 191; Tollefson, 'Titus' 151*b*）。這描寫證實保羅對他們貪不義之財的指控。Cf. Lock 122: 克里特的居民 'had a bad name . . . for love of money'; Quinn 106: 'The greed of Cretans was almost as proverbial as their mendacity', 意即他們的貪婪幾乎像他們的說謊成性一樣眾所周知。

29 See also ESV / G. Schneider, *EDNT* 284*a* (s.v. κέρδος); Banker 45*a*, 49*a*; Fiore II 203, 204 / LN §57.192 / Johnson II 225: 'for shameful gain / for the sake of shameful gain /

不誠實地獲得利益」，[30] 最為可取。[31]

貪不義之財重拾了第 7 節的**貪財**；[32] 如果教會的監督必須**不貪財**，這些假教師卻是**因為……貪不義之財**而作教師，[33] 那麼，這些假教師是絕對不可能合法地在上帝的家中服侍的。如此，**他們貪不義之財**這項控訴，同時暗示警告，彷彿保羅說：「小心，他們企圖要利用你們！」這種警告的得益者是信徒，因而保羅寫信的主要對象其實是克里特教會的信徒。[34] 或者應該這樣說，這封信確是寫給提多的，但是信上提出的種種教導，都是為了信徒的益處。

---

for the shameful purpose of gain / for a shameful profit'. Cf. R. Bultmann, *TDNTA* 30: '*aischrós* means "what is disgraceful"'. Hendriksen 351 解釋說，他們所獲利益之所以為**可恥**，是因他們為了自肥而使別人衰敗；班約翰則認為，'shameful' 是指他們圖利的目的（Banker 49*a*）。

30 NIV, TNIV, NIV2011, NKJV, DC 135*b*: 'for the sake of dishonest gain'. See also BDAG 29*b* (s.v. αἰσχρός): 'dishonest gain'. (**1**) Wall 344 認為，'This may mean that their financial support comes from misled members of the congregation.' 但之前一句已將 'dishonest profit' 解釋為 'both spiritual and material (see 1 Tim 6:3-10).' (**2**) Banker 49*a* 也認為，「利益」不必只限於金錢，亦可包括其他形式的物質好處。See also Blaiklock 77: 'the gain can be measured in position, influence and standing as well as in cash.'

31 在上文提及的三語古卷 460 中（見一 9 註釋註 41〔上面 147〕），在一 11 最後一字（χάριν）之後加上一句，英譯作：'The children who abuse or strike their parents you must check and reprove and admonish as a father his children'（*TextC* 585; see also DC 134 n.14; Fee 183; Mounce 394 n.c）。

32 原文依次為：αἰσχροῦ κέρδους, αἰσχροκερδῆ 參一 7 註釋末段，尤其是註 48 之（2）= 上面 131。Simpson 99 指出：'αἰσχρὸν κέρδος is written as two words because the literal meaning has stress laid upon it', 即是要強調這**財**是**不義**的。

33 Sumney（*Opponents* 292）則聲稱，'this is another stock polemical charge that yields no good evidence about these teachers.'

34 Genade 33. 在 'The next two words, αἰσχροί [*sic*] κέρδοι, are further examples of paronomasia'（ibid.）這話裏面，αἰσχροί κέρδοι 二字（複數陽性主格）是奇怪的。因為保羅的用詞是 αἰσχροῦ κέρδους（二字皆為單數所有格），其主格形式應為 αἰσχρὸν κέρδος（見上面註 32； κέρδος 是中性名詞，其形容詞也應是中性的 αἰσχρόν 而不是陽性的 αἰσχρός），而後者的複數應為 αἰσχρὰ κέρδη 不是陽性的 αἰσχροὶ κέρδοι（這錯誤的形式似乎是由於簡內德把原來的 κέρδους〔中性〕誤認為陽性而導致的）。

一 **12a** 克里特人中有一個本地的先知說：

12b 「克里特人常說謊話，是惡獸，貪吃懶做。」

克里特人中的一個本地先知（新和）原文直譯是：「他們當中的一個人、他們自己的先知」。[1] 從文法的角度而言，「他們」的前述詞是第 11a 節的這些人，即是第 10 節提到的那些人；但是文理表示(引句表示本節是一種自我描述)，「他們」指隨後的克里特人。[2] 如果那些敗壞人的全家的人（11b 節）是克里特的猶太人，兩者的差異就解決了。[3] 這樣重複「他們」一詞，暗示「他們」和「我們」的對立；更為重要的，重複這詞的作用，是證實（使用引句而作出的）對那些假教師的指控——這是有關他們的根本品格的可靠消息！[4] 學者一般認為，這位克里特的先知（新普）是公元前六／五世紀的先知和詩人

---

1 τις ἐξ αὐτῶν ἴδιος αὐτῶν προφήτης = 'One of them, a prophet of their own / their very own prophet'（NKJV / NRSV），'One of themselves, a prophet of their own'（RSV, NAU）。但 'one of Crete's/their own prophets' (NIV, TNIV, NIV2011 / NJB) 這種翻譯暗示克里特出了一些先知，但原文並無此意（Hiebert 432）。（**1**）在這種 'Orienter-Head relationships, in which the first proposition introduces the second', 並無連詞將二者連起來（'asyndeton': Levinsohn, 'Constraints' 331-32）。參較二 1～2 的 'Head-Specific' relationship; 見二 2 註釋註 1（下面 221）。（**2**）ἴδιος αὐτῶν, 'their own' 意即 'not another nationality'（MHT 3.191）；因此，本地的是正確的意譯。

2 See Towner III 699-700（唐 1019）; Van Neste 240. Knight II 298 就認為：'Both occurrences of αὐτῶν refer to the Cretans.'

3 See Houlden 144: 'the Cretans specially in mind in v. 12 are Cretan Jews, converted but now gone astray'; Oden 63: 'it was probably Jewish Cretans against whom Paul was mainly contending rather than ethnic Cretans'; Drury 1231*b*: 'They are native Cretans, converted to Christianity from Judaism and now apparently reverting in some way to their old faith'; Winter, *Roman Wives* 148: 'Christian teachers of Jewish origins had absorbed the values of secular orators or followed their conventions.'

4 Genade 33 ('here we have information about the false teachers from the proverbial horse's mouth').（**1**）張 331 註 102 聲稱，「『說』（*eipen*）是處強調的位置」。這話不確，因為以動詞開始一句，是希臘文的正常字序（see BDF §472(1);《弗》248 註 9；《西‧門》214 註 8 第二段）。（**2**）說字原文動詞（**λέγω**）在下文再出現一次（二 8）；它在教牧書信另外出現六次，全部具有深思熟慮的正式宣告的含意（Quinn 126）：假教師的（提前一 7；提後二 18）、保羅的（提前二 7；提後二 7），和聖靈的（提前四 1）或聖經的（提前五 18）。

伊皮麥尼德；[5] 保羅在雅典的亞略巴古證道時，可能亦曾引述他的一

---

5 Epimenides（Ἐπιμενίδης），中譯見《宗教》97*a*（'Epimemes' 這名字〔C. Martin 433*a*〕似是 'Epimenides' 之誤。）另有譯為「伊壁曼尼德」（彭編 97*a*）。See, e.g., MHT 2.8-9 n.3, 2.137; MHT 3.96; C. H. Preisker, *DNTT* 3.81 ('from whose *Theogony** a proverbial saying is quoted'); Gray, 'Titus' 303 n.3.（*Theogony = 'an account of the origin and genealogy of the gods' =「神譜」。）'Its attribution to Epimenides is found in Christian writers, Clement of Alexandria and Jerome'（Marshall 200）。**（1）** Aune 475*b*（also F. Hauck, *TDNT* 5.856 n.26; Hanson I 110）認為所指的是公元前三世紀的希臘詩人「迦立馬庫」（《宗教》50*b*）：'Callimachus, *Hymn to Zeus* 8: "Cretans are confirmed liars"'.（彭編 97*a*、97*b* 的 'Collimachus', 譯作「<u>克里馬古</u>」〔底線是原來的〕，似為 'Callimachus' 之誤。）'But Callimachus was not from Crete but from Cyrene and does not have the entire statement quoted by Paul' (Knight II 298).（Mounce 399 的 'Callimachus, a <u>Cretan</u> poet of the third century B.C.' 是否 'Cyrenian' 之誤？）**（2）** Kidd（'Titus' 193-94）指出：'Titus 1:12 marks the first appearance of the saying in its entirety in any extant source. Prior to this, the first member of the saying appears for the first time (and that in this precise wording, "Cretans are always liars") in Callimachus'; 這位詩人隨即解釋他為何稱克里特人為常說謊者：'For a tomb, O Lord, Cretans build for you; but you did not die, for you are forever'（*Hymn to Zeus* 8-9 [see DC 136*b*; Mounce 399]）。Barrett 131 認為，'part of the hexameter line [by Epimenides] was taken over by Callimachus'; cf. Mounce 398: 'Callimachus appears to be quoting a known saying.'**（3）** Lee（'Epimenides'）則認為 G. L. Huxley（*Greek Epic Poetry from Eumelos to Panyassis* [London: Faber and Faber, 1969] 81-82）的臆測頗為可能：多一 12 的引句是德爾斐／特耳菲（《聖神》160*a*／《宗教》79*b*：Delphi）的阿波羅神殿之女祭司（'the Pythoness'）和 'the insolent Cretan seer' 互相辱罵時，前者對後者的回應（Köstenberger 612 認為 '[this] is possible'）；這句話自然地被包括在伊皮麥尼德的語錄（'a collection of Epimenides' sayings'）中。Lee 認為若是這樣，保羅（或提多書這部分的作者，不管他是誰）就不只是引用了一句名言，而是在一神喻集的原處見過這句話（'had seen it *in situ* in a collection of oracles'），而可以想像，這神喻集是深奧難解的。可是，'the biblical text attributes the saying to a Cretan, not someone from Delphi'（Mounce 398）。**（4）** 馬賀比指出：'this statement . . . had become proverbial by the first century AD and is insufficient evidence of a firsthand knowledge of the works of Epimenides'（Malherbe, *Social Aspect* 43）；在 MacDonald（*Pauline Churches* 191）的引用下，'by the first century' 變成了 'by the <u>end of</u> the first-century'; 這假定了提多書並非出自保羅的手筆。**（5）** Marshall 200-1 經討論後這樣下結論：'We are left with some uncertainty regarding both the origin of the material cited and the source from which the saying of Tit 1.12 derives. But the probability is that the author thought that he was citing Epimenides' (201). **（6）** Koskenniemi（'Liar' 69）的研究則達到不同的結論：'Apparently the quotation is proverbial and the writer – well aware of the logical problem – considers the content of the verse to be excellent though deeper conclusions are hazardous. To connect it with the historical Epimenides requires a lot of credulity, and we have no reason to believe that the writer ever saw the alleged work Χρησμοί* of Epimenides.'（*Nestle-Aland [margin ad. loc.] 指向 'Epimenides, de oraculis / περὶ χρησμῶν [On oracles]'; E. M. Yamauchi [*DPL* 386*b*] 也認為，在本節 'Epimenedes' [*sic*] *De Oraculis* is cited'〔《辭典》571*a*：「《神諭》」〕。）

句話：我們生活、行動、存在都在於他（徒十七 28）。[6]

這位本地先知對克里特人有三重的描寫，[7] 保羅似乎認為這描寫適用於克里特的假教師。[8]（**#1**）常說謊話（同新和）[9] 另一種翻譯是

6 See Bruce, *Acts* 338; *Book of Acts* 338-39 with n. 75; Munck, *Acts* 171; but cf. Haenchen, *Acts* 524 n.3 ('[This]is not the case'); Williams, *Acts* 205.（**1**）Simpson 100 指出，伊皮麥尼德在希臘文獻一直被稱為先知，柏拉圖也為這稱號背書（cf. Marshall 199: 'Epimenides . . . (like some other Greek poet-philosophers) was regarded as a prophet by Plato, Aristotle, Cicero and others'）。辛普遜認為，當保羅寫到「他們自己的先知」時，他的眼睛是閃亮的，因為他的引述使克里特人進退維谷：如果他們贊同這位先知的話，等於承認自己道德墮落；但若否定這先知的話，則使克里特的守護神變成說謊者（endorsed by Hanson III 177; see also Hiebert 433）。（**2**）就事實而論，伊皮麥尼德這句話已被充分證實了：（**i**）就如得自 Κόρινθος（哥林多）的動詞 κορινθιάζω（'to act like a Corinthian'）的意思是「通姦（to commit fornication）」（see Fee, *First Corinthians* 2），得自 Κρήτης（克里特人）的動詞 κρητίζω（'to act like a Cretan' = 'to lie'）特指克里特人說謊成性的品格（see F. Hauck, *TDNT* 5.856 n.26; Fiore II 204-5; Winter, *Roman Wives* 149-50），同字根的名詞 'κρητισμός denotes *falsehood*'（Simpson 100; see also Hendriksen 353: 'Cretism' 指 'Cretan behavior', 即是 'lying'〕）。（**ii**）πρὸς Κρῆτα κρητίζειν, 'to Cretize against a Cretan', 意即「對說謊者說謊（to lie to a liar）」（Blaiklock 77），'to match lies with lies'（Barclay 243）或 'to meet craft with craft'（Simpson 100）！由此可見，作者複述克里特人常說謊話這一句時，他完全正確地反映了古代對克里特及其居民的看法（Wieland, 'Crete' 346）。

7 並無「和（καί）」字將三者連起來，故此簡內德稱之為 'asyndetic . . . clustering' 的例子（Genade 128）。另一例子是二 2 的 νηφαλίους . . . , σεμνούς, σώφρονας, ὑγιαίνοντας 和隨後的 τῇ πίστει, τῇ ἀγάπῃ, τῇ ὑπομονῇ. 參該節註釋註 38 之（1）= 下面 227。（**1**）一 12b 原文是 'a hexameter'（A. Strobel, *EDNT* 2.149*a* [s.v. θήριον, 3 a];「六音步的詩或詩行」〔《牛津》547*a*〕）。Blaiklock 77 認為把它翻譯為 'The Cretans are liars all, wild beasts, just indolent bellies' 可保存其原貌；Quinn 107 則翻譯為：'Liars ever, men of Crete, / Nasty brutes that live to eat'（endorsed by Mounce 398）。See also DC 135*b* (cf. 136 n.7): 'Cretans are mostly liars / brutes and loitering gluttons'. 不過，原文並無動詞（see Wallace 55 n.59），但以上英譯皆無法避免使用動詞。（**2**）Kidd（'Titus' 189）的描述（'Cretans are prevaricators, predators, and profligates'）呈頭韻現象，但「恣意揮霍／放蕩」跟貪吃懶做在意思上相去頗遠。

8 H. Balz, *EDNT* 3.499*b* (s.v. ψεύστης): 'The Cretans' proverbial falseness is used against false teachers on Crete'; Griffin 289: 'Paul evidently applied this quotation to the Cretan false teachers, not to Cretans in general.'（**1**）Faber（'Titus' 137）正確強調，保羅引用全句，是由於其中的每一部分都跟緊接的和整體的文理所發展的論證有關。（**2**）馬特羅卻認為，冒名的作者選擇克里特作為提多書虛構的目的地，就是因為只有這樣他才可以引用這句諺語來描寫他的對手（Martin, 'Titus' 13）。

9 參思高：常是些說謊者；新譯：是常常說謊的。（**1**）名詞 **ψεύστης** 在本書出現僅此一次，在保羅書信僅再出現兩次（羅三 4；提前一 10）；它在新約另外出現七次，

總是撒謊（現修）、永遠是撒謊者（呂譯），[10] 二者分別代表了原文副詞兩個可能的意思。[11] **撒謊者和無謊言的上帝**（2b 節）構成不明言的對比，兩者的品格是完全相對的。[12] 伊皮麥尼德稱克里特人為說謊者，是由於他們聲稱，在他們的島上有宙斯的墓！[13] 這等於把宙斯的地位貶為由人變成的英雄人物。從傳統希臘宗教的角度（超凡的神明和地上的人是不同類的）而言，這是克里特人的異端信仰（以為許多的希臘神明都是在克里特出生的）！[14] 因此，在迦立馬庫的詩中，[15] **克里特人常說謊話**這一句是用來譴責他們的異端信仰的。保羅寬鬆地拿提多的對手（他們**說空話欺哄人**〔10 節〕）和克里特人作比較，暗示假教師的神學信念是與基督教的真理對立的。[16]

（**#2**）**惡獸**（同呂譯、當代、新和、現修、新譯；新普同）的意

都是在約翰文獻裏：除了魔鬼（約八 44），被歸類為「說謊者」的人包括不認識上帝的猶太人（八 55）、口裏說「**我認識他**」，**卻不遵守他的命令**的（約壹一 10）、說「**我愛上帝**」，**卻恨他的弟兄**的（四 20），以及**那不認耶穌為基督**的（二 22）。另見一 10／五 10（**我們若說自己沒有犯過罪／不信上帝的，就是把上帝當作說謊的**）。（**2**）這名詞在 LXX 出現四次：詩人驚奇地說，**人都是說謊的**（詩一一六 11〔LXX 一一五 2，參：羅三 4〕）；**做窮乏人比做撒謊人好**（箴十九 22，呂譯）；「說謊的人不會思念〔智慧〕」（次經《便西拉智訓》〔思高《德訓篇》〕15.8）；智者所恨惡的三種人包括「富有的說謊者」（25.2〔思高《德訓篇》25.4 作「詭詐的富人」〕）。

10 英譯本多採納這種意思：'always' (KJV, NKJV, RSV, NRSV, NAU, NIV, TNIV, NIV2011, ESV, *Paraphrase* 291); see also NJB: 'never anything but liars'. （**1**）NLT 的翻譯（'The people of Crete are all liars' =「克里特人都是說謊者」〔新普〕）沒有準確譯出原文副詞的意思。Fiore II 204, 205 意譯為「積習成癖、根深蒂固（inveterate）」。Mounce（'Titus' 105-6）作 'pathological liars'！（**2**）原文副詞（**ἀεί**）在新約另外出現六次（徒七 51；林後四 11，六 10；來三 10；彼前三 15；彼後一 12）。

11 即 ἀεί 指 'duration of time as continuous, *always*' 或 'duration of time as episodic, of a freq. recurring action or situation *continually*, *constantly*'（BDAG 22*b*, s.v. 1, 2）；「一段時間，可以是連續不斷的或無止境地偶然發生」（《新希》8*a* [s.v.]）。LN（vol. 2, p. 4*b*）只提出一個意思：'always'; Marshall 201 則認為 'ἀεί . . . means here "from time immemorial"'（followed by Jeon I 52）。

12 Genade 34: 'an instance of *implicit contrasting*' (see also 126, 130).

13 Lock 134; DC 137*a*; Fee 179. 這聲稱被「譽」為「近代最駭人的異端（the most outrageous heresy of recent times）」（Blaiklock 77）。

14 See Towner III 701（唐 1021）。

15 參註 5 之（2）= 上面 173。

16 Faber, 'Titus' 138.

思不僅是<u>可惡</u>的野獸（思高），[17] 而是「邪惡的、殘忍的、有害的、危險的野獸」，[18] 指捕食的野獸。[19] 其實，克里特享有境內並無捕食生物的野獸之稱譽，因而克里特的惡獸就是島上的人民！[20] 這是延伸了獸字的字面意義的比喻用法，指具獸性的邪惡的人。[21] 有認為保羅引用這詞來指向提多的對手的強暴行為，[22] 但更符合文理的解釋是，「有害的[23] 野獸」指向假教師所造成的破壞[24]（參 11b 節：敗壞人的全家）。

（**#3**）貪吃懶做、好吃懶做／懶作（現修／新譯）、又饞又懶（當代、新和、新普）這些翻譯，[25] 其實都只是原文的意譯；原文直譯作

---

17 參《新希》170*b*（s.v. κακός, I.2）：「價值上本質是惡劣和不易取悅人的。」

18 κακὰ θηρία = 'evil/pernicious beasts' (KJV, NKJV, RSV, NAU, ESV, Genade 30 / Kelly 233, 235, 236), 'Nasty/evil/vicious/wicked brutes' (Quinn 26 / NIV, TNIV, NIV2011 / NRSV, REB / Fiore II 204, 205); 'cruel animals' (NLT); 'dangerous animals/beasts' (NJB / *Paraphrase* 291); 'vicious beasts' (Kidd, 'Titus' 190). 形容詞 **κακός** 在本書出現僅此一次，保羅書信另 25 次（參《帖前》435-36〔435 誤作：24 次〕），新約全部 50 次；詳見 BDAG 501*a*-1*b* (s.v.);《新希》170*b*-71*a*（s.v.）。

19 W. Foerster, *TDNT* 3.134: 'the adj. κακός gives the clear sense of "beasts of prey"'.

20 參彭編 97*b*：「本句為反諷的修辭，指出『<u>克里特</u>島無須有野獸，因為有<u>克里特</u>人就夠了』。」（底線是原來的。）'Behind this aspect of the Cretan reputation was a history of inter-city wars, piracy and selfishness' (Marshall 202). Cf. Towner III 701（唐 1022）：在克里特人……是惡獸這批評的背後，是克里特出名的野蠻行為，這與島上無數的城市之間的戰爭傳統、海盜猖獗，以及宗教儀式中的同性戀行為有關。

21 BDAG 456*a* (s.v. θηρίον, 2): 'wicked person, someone w. a "bestial" nature, *beast, monster*'; cf. LN §88.119: 'a bad person, in the sense of being both harmful and dangerous'. 名詞 **θηρίον** 在新約另外出現 45 次，或是指真正的野獸，或是指「好像野獸」的超然活物；詳見 BDAG 455*b*-56*a*（s.v. 1）；《新希》155*b*（s.v. I, II.2）。

22 Faber, 'Titus' 139. See also Kidd, 'Titus' 190; Wieland, 'Crete' 347. Cf. Griffin 290: 'their rebellious, out-of-control nature [1:10a] proved them to be "evil brutes"'.

23 See BDAG 501*b* (s.v. κακός, 2): 'pert. to being harmful or injurious, *evil*, *injurious, dangerous*, *pernicious*'.

24 Jeon I 52: 'The term "beasts" . . . taken with the adjective . . . "harmful" . . . highlights the destructive impact of the opponents.' See also Spencer 25-26: 'Probably he [Paul] would understand "evil beasts" in its Old Testament context, comparing these false teachers to destructive animals who destroy people by attacking them and destroying their healthy faith.'

25 思高作貪口福的懶漢。（**1**）「口福」意即「飲食」（《國語》107*a*），因此思高的翻譯屬於此處。Similarly NKJV, RSV, NRSV, REB, NAU, NIV, TNIV, NIV2011, ESV, NLT, BDAG 128*b* (s.v. ἀργός 2), LN §23.19, Fiore II 204, 205, Genade 30: 'lazy gluttons'. See also DC 135*b*: 'loitering gluttons'. （**2**）《串釋（增簡）》1754*b* 聲稱，引句「證明

懶惰的大腹者（呂譯）。[26] 不過，他們之所以是**大腹者**，大抵是由於他們**貪吃**造成的，因而「腹」的比喻用法就是指貪吃的人。[27] **懶惰**是指他們不願意工作、慣性地拒絕工作。[28] 再一次，保羅寬鬆地拿提多的對手和克里特人作比較：伊皮麥尼德將克里特人描寫為貪吃的人，保羅以**貪吃懶做**來暗指對手以不誠實的方法來取利。[29]

貪心與說謊（參 11 節）是該地人民的通病。」但**貪吃**不等於「貪心」。

26 γαστέρες ἀργαί = 'idle bellies' (*Paraphrase* 291; Fairbairn 266; Banker 49*b*; Kidd, 'Titus' 191), 'idle/lazy stomachs' (Genade 34 / Witherington 124). (**1**) KJV 譯作 'slow bellies'; cf. Hendriksen 350, 352, 359: 'bellies inactive'. NJB 的翻譯（'all greed and laziness'）似乎將「貪吃」化為籠統的「貪婪」之意（參上註末句），理由不詳。《輔讀》526 則作「貪吃暴食」；但「暴食」並非「貪吃」的必然伙伴。（**2**）Riesner（'Once More' 248）稱 γαστέρες ἀργαί 為 'the language of illness'，理由不詳。（**3**）ἀργαί（野獸）與 ψεῦσται（肚腹）押韻。BDF §487 認為，除了這裏、徒十七 28 和林前十五 33 的引句外，'[t]he search for verses and fragments of verses . . . i.e, for rhyme, is a needless waste of time and those that are found are of such quality that they are better left unmentioned'! E. M. Yamauchi（*DPL* 386*b*）認為，新約中「只有〔這〕三處確定是引用古典希臘文學」（《辭典》571*a*）。

27 BDAG 190*a* (s.v. γαστήρ, 1 b): 'metaph., or pers. defined by primary interest *glutton*'). See also LN §8.68: 'literally "lazy bellies [so also Kelly 233; Quinn 99]," but meaning "gluttons"'.（**1**）Winter（*Roman Wives* 150）引蒲魯他克所描述克里特的公共食堂（'the "public mess" (ἀνδρεῖα)'）的情景，來說明克里特人在飲宴時的自我放縱。飲酒過量和不道德行為是互相伴隨的；而蒲魯他克所用的字 ἀνδρεῖα 'denoted "courage" or "manliness" which was also a euphemism for the male sexual organ.'（**2**）這字（**γαστήρ**）在新約另外出現八次，都是指字面意義的「腹」，且都是在 ἐν γαστρί (ἔχειν) / (συλλημφθῆναι*) ἐν γαστρί =「懷孕」這片語中（太一 18、23，二十四 19；可十三 17；路二十一 23；帖前五 3；啟十二 2／路一 31）。（*= aorist passive infinitive of συλλαμβάνω, 見路二 21。）

28 BDAG 128*b* (s.v. ἀργός 2): 'pert. to being unwilling to work, *idle*, *lazy*'; LN §88.248: 'pertaining to habitually refusing to work'；《新希》43*b*（s.v. I.2）：「指習慣性地拒絕工作；有比較『無所事事的』（ἄτακτος*）更令人討厭的含意。」（*帖前五 14：**不守規距**。）（**1**）這形容詞（**ἀργός**）在保羅書信僅再出現兩次（提前五 13a、13b：**懶惰**），新約另外五次，分別指**閒話**（太十二 36）、**閒站**的人（太二十 3、6）、**沒有用的**信心（雅二 20），和**懶散**（彼後一 8）。See BDAG 128*a-b* (s.v.);《新希》43*b*（s.v.）。（**2**）彭編 97*b* 則解釋如下：「此處『饞』用來描繪克里特人追逐利益時的貪得無厭，而『懶』應為反諷修辭，指出克里特人汲汲營營於爭鬥、利益，並性方面的不道德，卻懶於德行的建立」（底線是原來的）。（**3**）Kidd（'Titus' 191）將 #3 和 #2 這樣連起來：'unbridled appetites make for bestial behavior.' Similarly, Towner III 702（唐 1023-24）：'. . . complete lack of control somehow fueling the beastly behavior.'

29 Marshall 201: 提多書的作者以**貪吃懶做**來指對手欲藉著欺騙他們的學生（'by duping their pupils'）來取利。Cf. Arichea－Hatton 277: '**lazy gluttons** refers back to the preoccupation of the false teachers in "making money"'; Griffin 290: 'their desire for "dishonest gain" proved them to be "lazy gluttons."' Faber（'Titus' 139）則認為，保羅

大致上說，在保羅的引用之下，**常說謊話**提示真教義與假教義的對比，**惡獸**和**貪吃懶做**則提示正當與不正當行為之對比。[30] 由此可見，保羅引用伊皮麥尼德的詩句，不是作為種族主義的辱罵、[31] 攻擊性的謾罵，或哲學性的難題；[32] 他的目的是要表明，教義上的謬誤是由道德腐敗伴隨著的。[33] 假教師的教導（一 11、13b～14，三 9）和他們的行為（一 15～16，三 10～11）都是保羅所譴責的。[34]

暗示假教師（像詩句中的克里特人）同樣誤解了人的食慾的角色；他們的**污穢**（一 15）源自他們錯誤的教導（一 14：**人的命令**），這錯誤的教導反映於他們不正確的飲食習慣。

30 Faber, 'Titus' 139: 'the first half of the hexameter concerns true and false teaching, the second half proper and improper conduct.' 作者認為，保羅使教義和行為的關係變得明確，'when he completes his argument in v. 16 with a reference to the quotation'（140）：**不配做任何好事**（ἔργον）回望 12b 節的**懶惰的大腹者**（呂譯；γαστέρες ἀργαί），因為形容詞 ἀργαί 'is derived from α-εργαι ("non-working"; cf. Jas 2:20), [and this] may be the source for the play upon words in the phrase πρὸς πᾶν ἔργον ἀγαθὸν ἀδόκιμοι'（139）。（Cf. Vine 1.98: 'ἀργός . . . denote[s] idle, barren, yielding no return, because of inactivity'; BDAG 128*a* (s.v.): 'ἀργός . . . contr[acted] fr. ἄεργος "without performance"'.）筆者倒認為，不能確定保羅是在玩文字遊戲，讀者會否認出他是在玩文字遊戲也是有疑問的。

31 Aune, 'Pastoral Letters' 559: 'Titus 1:12 contains a quotation of an ethnic slur'.

32 Hanson I 111: 作者（不是保羅）使用這普及的看法，為要使假教師左右為難（'to impale [them] on the horns of a dilemma'）：若接受引句的話為真確，就定自己的罪；若否定引句，就定自己的先知的罪。

33 Faber, 'Titus' 145: 'The citation . . . is not intended as a racist slur, polemic invective, or philosophical dilemma; rather, its purpose is to show that doctrinal error is accompanied by moral corruption.'

34 Towner III 702（唐 1024）。

一　**13a**　這個見證是真的。[1]

這個見證是指那個克里特先知所說的話（12b 節），[2] 即是那先知對克里特人的品格與行為所作的見證。[3] 由於說克里特人常說謊話這句話的，是個克里特人，那麼按照邏輯推論，那句話本身就可能不是真的。[4] 祈勒克認為也許這個見證是真的語帶幽默，其意思是：「無

1　Clark（'Structure' 105）認為，12～13a 節屬插句性質，'probably adding a touch of wry humour.' 第 12 節開首呈現「無連詞（asyndetic）」現象。'In such [a case] the function of the independent clause is implied from the literary context'（Wallace 658）。

2　參新普：這話是真的（NLT: 'This is true'）；思高：這話說得很對；當代：這話一點也不錯；現修：他這話沒有講錯；NJB: 'that is a true statement.' 即 αὕτη 是 'anaphoric' 用法（Clark, 'Structure' 106）；參較一 5 的 τούτου（上面 87-88 註 1）。'Paul's testimony is also true (1:13)'（Spencer 7）這話是奇怪的。

3　BDAG 619*a* (s.v. μαρτυρία, 3): 'attestation of character or behavior'. 這字（μαρτυρία）在保羅書信僅再出現一次，指監督必須在教外有好名聲（提前三 7），即「基於對一個人品行的評價而講的話」（《新希》210*b* [s.v. I.3]）。在新約另外出現 35 次，除了 5 次（馬可福音 3 次、路加福音與使徒行傳各 1 次），其餘都是在約翰文獻中（約翰福音 14 次，約翰書信 7 次，啟示錄 9 次）。See BDAG 618*b*-19*a* (s.v.);《新希》210*b*（s.v.）。

4　Fiore II 205 談到 'its inherent paradox'; cf. Gray, 'Titus' 302: 'one of the most (in)famous antinomies of the ancient world.' Genade 34 甚至稱之為 'a logical impossibility'. Ward 245 則認為，'Paul would not have the patience to consider the fallacy involved, even if he had thought of it. . . . Paul's point is sufficiently clear.'（**1**）Thiselton（'Logical Role' [1994] 208）認為，這個見證是真的這話 'becomes self-contradictory because it may function to endorse *either the truth or the falsity* of the liar's assertion, and thus endorses *neither*.' 因此，一 13a 這話應視為 'an ironic comment on logical regress *ad infinitum*'（212）。提多書作者使用一 12 的 'liar paradox quite specifically to demonstrate the self-defeating ineffectiveness of making truth-claims which are given the lie by conduct which fails to match them'（214）；作者將克里特人常說謊話這句話放在一個克里特人的口中，其目的是要 'demonstrate that, *anchored to an inappropriate behaviour context, first-person* utterances can become *self-defeating*'（219）。Cf., earlier, A. C. Thiselton, *DNTT* 3[1978].887: 'The logical puzzle is the status of the assertion that "all Cretans are liars", if this is spoken by a Cretan. If the statement is true then it is falsified by a Cretan's speaking it truly; whilst if it is false, to assert it would be untrue. Its conclusion in the Pastorals with the added statement "this testimony is true" suggests not that the author has misunderstood the philosophical point, but that the Cretan antinomy constitutes a valid example of the kind of profitless controversy described above, which makes truth a merely theoretical matter. By contrast, "the truth" in the Pastorals, especially in the sense of Christian revelation, is wholesome and health-giving'.（**2**）Koskenniemi（'Liar' 67）認為 Thiselton 'has convincingly shown that the writer recognized the logical problem: To say the maxim in the first person means a different thing than to say it in the third. To be true, the verse

論如何，這個見證倒是真的！」[5] 亨捷晨的看法是，保羅的意思不外於「當這個克里特先知說『一般而論，克里特人經常說謊』時，他說的是真話」。[6] 另有認為，提多書的作者故意使自己落在這三段論的陷阱中，為要凸出某種論述的反效果性質，作者告訴提多要阻止克里特的信徒參與這類活動。[7] 也許較可取的解釋是，保羅無意控訴所有的克里特人（畢竟，提多要設立的長老就是克里特人，他們要教導真理），[8] 他只是提醒讀者，就克里特的假教師而論，克里特人自己

---

itself contains no paradox, but it does, when the writer attributes it to a Cretan "prophet".' Saarinen 174 也認為，'there may be some point in the claim [Thiselton's] that Paul is here showing that the futile nature of idle talk leads only to self-refuting contradictions, whereas a true virtue is not verified by words but in action (cf. 1:16).'（**3**）馬歇爾則認為，'the use of the material here [in 1:12] gives no evidence of any awareness of a logical problem. There does not appear to be any ancient evidence that the saying was regarded as paradoxical, or as intending a paradox'（Marshall 203）；因此，'the <u>complicated</u> interpretation* by Thiselton [1994] . . . would appear to be unnecessary'（n.153）。唐 1023 同樣認為，「沒有證據顯示使用這材料時有意識到這邏輯上的矛盾」（Towner III 702）。（*筆者對此複雜的解釋只能說「似懂非懂」，因而只能滿足於引述另一些釋經者對它的評估。）（**3**）到此為止，「真理」與「謊言（或說謊者）」的出現呈現交叉配置模式（Genade 34-35）：（**A**）ἀληθείας（真理〔一 1b〕）（**B**）ἀψευδής（無謊言〔2b 節〕）（**B'**）ψεῦσται（說謊話的〔12b 節〕）（**A'**）ἀληθής（真的〔13a 節〕）。在所涉及的四個字（ἀλήθεια, ἀψευδής, ψευστής, ἀληθής）當中，只有第一個在本書再出現一次（14b 節）。

5 Clark, 'Structure' 106: 'This testimony at any rate is true!' Köstenberger 610*a* 認為，保羅說這話時是 'tongue firmly in cheek', 即是開玩笑的。Cf. Long 263: 'the Pastor . . . is attempting to make a joke.'

6 Hendriksen 354: 'This particular Cretan, namely Epimenedes [*sic*], spoke the truth when he described Cretans as, generally speaking, constant liars.'

7 Gray, 'Titus' 309: 'the author springs this syllogistic trap – on himself! – in order to highlight the counterproductive nature of the types of discourse Titus is told to discourage among his Cretan co-religionists.' 參上面註 4 之（1）。Gray（ibid.）又認為，由於隱含的收信人與隱含作者的關係密切，後者可合理地預期前者會領會他的笑話。

8 Stott 181-82. 斯托得認為，有一些克里特人在五旬節那天在耶路撒冷領受了改變生命的聖靈（參：徒二 11、41）。See also Marshall 202: 'it is surely taken for granted that the converted members of the church would be regarded as delivered from the sins of their race, and that the attack is on those who were never converted or have fallen away'; Mounce 398: 'Sweeping generalizations by nature do not always claim to be true in every situation; they are generally true. Paul is just trying to make a point.' Calvin 364 則認為，'these vices [are not] charged against a few individuals, but the whole nation is condemned.'

的先知對克里特人的見證是真的。[9] 保羅認同這見證，有認為是基於他自己對克里特人的認識，[10] 但更可能是由於他對克里特假教師的認識。[11] 保羅引用這先知的話的結果，是一種強有力的反諷：一個非基督徒「先知」對一些想要做基督徒領袖的人的描述是真的，後者因其假教義和不當的行為是「真・克里特人」，他們全是說謊者。[12]

9 Fee 179. Cf. Marshall 203: 'Presumably "always" was not taken *au pied de la lettre* [literally]'; Montague 226: 'The context shows that Paul is applying this not to every Cretan but to the false teachers (1:13)'; Stern, *Comm.* 655: '[Paul applies this] entirely and only to the false teachers'; Spencer 24: 'Paul is simply saying that his [Epimenides'] testimony about the general nature of Cretans (in ancient times) was true and applicable in this case'; Towner II 22: 'Paul applies the quote specifically to a group of agitators in the church'; Brauch, 'Titus' 676*a*: 'What Paul intends to communicate forcefully is clear; namely, in the case of these teachers who peddle false teaching, Epimenides' dictum is in fact shown to be true.' 故此，不必像 Wild 894*b* 那樣認為，提多書作者的 'emphatic agreement with this sentiment' 相當清楚地表示，這並不是一封真正寫給克里特基督徒的信。如果有人問，為甚麼這封信要引用一位異教徒的話呢？屈梭多模的答案是：上帝用人們可以明白的話來對他們說話（see Twomey 195）。

10 Banker 50*a*: 'based on his own experience with the Cretans.' So also Hiebert 433. Kelly 236 甚至認為，句子的語調提示，保羅 'has had bitter personal experience on the island.' 周 419 也說，「這句話顯示保羅在革哩底〔和合；新和、和修：克里特〕島上曾經親歷過受騙的沉痛經驗」。

11 (**1**) Fee（*Presence* 777）指出，這是保羅書信中惟一的一次，先知一字不是指舊約或新約的先知；他認為保羅稱伊皮麥尼德為先知，只是反映了此人在一般人心中的名聲，而此人所說關於克里特人的話在假教師的身上被證實了，這使保羅可以接受此人被稱為先知；但這並不表示保羅認為伊皮麥尼德是受聖靈的感動而說話的先知。See also DC 136*a*: 'Epimenides . . . is probably considered a prophet by the author of the Pastorals . . . because of the correctness of his testimony.'(**2**)Hodge(*Romans* 389 1st n.）則認為，'As poets were supposed to speak under a certain kind of inspiration, they too were called prophets. Paul used the word in this sense.' Cf. Calvin 363: 'poets are sometimes called prophets in Greek . . . Thus Adimatus in the second book of Plato's *Republic*, having called poets "sons of the gods", adds that they were also their prophets'; Köstenberger 612: 'Poets, like prophets, were considered inspired in Greco-Roman culture and thus were occasionally called "prophets" . . . .' Similarly, Montague 223-24.

12 Fee, *Presence* 777.

3.2 對他們的回應（一 13b～14）

一 **13b** 為這緣故，你要嚴厲地責備他們，

13c 使他們在信仰上健全。

為這緣故[1] 回望上文（10～13a 節）。[2] 責備（同新和、現修、新譯）或指責／譴責（呂譯／新普）[3] 的原文是信上首次出現的命令式語法動詞。[4] 另有翻譯為規勸（思高、當代）、「駁

1 δι' ἣν αἰτίαν 是個 'causal conjunction'（BDF §456(4)），在新約另外出現五次：路八 47〔緣故〕；徒二十二 24〔甚麼緣故〕；提後一 6、12，來二 11〔為這緣故〕）。

2 See Banker 50*a*.（**1**）第 12 節開首並無連詞，這可能提示 10～11 節和 12～13a 節是兩個平行的單元，二者一起為 13b～14 節的結論提供理據（Levinsohn, *Discourse Features* 120-21）。（**2**）另一可能是，12～13a 節提供了 10～11 節（尤其是 10 節）的理據；有一古卷在 12 節開首有 γάρ（for）字，反映了這種理解（ibid. 25, 121）。按這種理解，13b 節的為這緣故仍是回望 10～13a 節；12 節開首並無連詞，正是由於 12～13a 節和 10～11 節的關係是密切的（see ibid. 118: 'Asyndeton is found . . . when there is a *close* connection between the information concerned (i.e., the information belongs together in the same unit'); 但反之亦然：'Asyndeton is found . . . when there is *no* direct connection between the information concerned (i.e., the information belongs to different units'!)）。筆者認為，（2）較（1）可取。（**3**）Marshall 204 則認為，為這緣故（僅）指 12～13a 節：'because of the character of the Cretans, which we know to be a fact.'

3 參以下英譯：（i）'rebuke'（KJV, NKJV, RSV, NRSV, NIV, TNIV, NIV2011, ESV; Hanson III 177）；（ii）'reprove'（NAU; Fairbairn 53, 267）；（iii）'reprimand'（NLT）。動詞 ἐλέγχω 已在一 9 出現過；參該節註釋之（二）（B）＝ 第四段（上面 146-48）。

4 ἔλεγχε, 現在時態。命令式語法動詞在本書再出現十三次（除了特別註明的三次，其餘皆為現在時態）：λάλει（二 1），παρακάλει（二 6），λάλει, παρακάλει, ἔλεγχε（二 15a），περιφρονείτω （二 15b），ὑπομίμνησκε（三 1），περιΐστασο（三 9a），παραιτοῦ（三 10），σπούδασον（三 12b，過去不定時時態），πρόπεμψον（三 13a，過不定），μανθανέτωσαν（三 14a），ἄσπασαι（三 15b，過不定）。參 Himes（'Use' 81）之圖表；該圖表同時顯示，命令式語法動詞在提前出現 44 次，只有三次是過去不定時時態（五 1，六 12、20）；在提後出現 34 次，其中 18 次為過去不定時時態。關於這些命令式動詞在教牧書信的用法，作者的結論是（74）：'it is safest to view the aorist imperative as the default, generic imperative and prohibition and that, in contrast to the present imperative and prohibition, no significance should be drawn from the tense *in of itself* [*sic*, in and of itself], either for *aktionsart* or verbal aspect. In other

斥」，[5]「糾正」，[6] 或「使（他們）知罪」。[7] 原文動詞已在第 9 節出現過，在該節行使這職能的是監督；加上本節，可以看見駁斥／責備假教師及其跟從者的責任由提多和長老們分擔；合理的假設是，提多會告訴長老們，這也是他們的工作。[8]

責備的賓詞是**他們**；**他們**指何人有三種答案：（一）僅指那些敵對者。[9] 這看法的主要根據是，到目前為止，本段在談論的一直都是那些**說空話欺哄人**（10 節）的人，這些人為了可恥之利**將不該教導的事教導人，敗壞人的全家**（11 節）。這些人極可能就是保羅透過克里特的先知的話描寫為**撒謊者**（12b 節，呂譯）的那些人，尤其因為從文法的角度而言，「他們當中的一個人、他們自己的先知」（12a 節）的「他們」自然地指第 11a 節的**這些人**，即是第 10 節提到的那些人。[10] 同樣地，第 13b 節的**他們**自然地指第 12b 節的撒謊者，亦即是第 10 至 11 節所談及的**說空話欺哄人**的人。[11]

---

words, the aorist imperative is significant only in its insignificance. In contrast, the present does seem to possess a durative or habitual force. The propensity of the present imperative in the PE, then, can be attributed to an emphasis on a habitual, consistent lifestyle.' 較籠統（不限於教牧書信）的討論見 Wallace 719-21（aorist imperative），721-722（present imperative），723-25（prohibitions），499-504（aspect）。

5 *Paraphrase* 291, Quinn 26: 'refute'. Cf. Saarinen 175: 'A cognitive therapy is to be offered that . . . shows that sound doctrine is to be preferred. . . . At least since Aristotle, *elenchus* means the refutation of the opponent's position'.

6 See NJB: 'be severe in correcting them'; Fiore II 204, 205: 'correct them rigorously'.

7 BDAG 315*a* (s.v. ἐλέγχω, 2): 'to bring a pers. to the point of recognizing wrong-doing, *convict*, *convince* someone of someth.'; Hiebert 433: '"convict," effectively showing the error of the teaching that is being opposed.'

8 Marshall 191. Genade 35 甚至認為，提多要向長老們示範如何執行他們的工作。Similarly, Griffin 290: 'Titus's dealings with the false teachers would serve as an excellent example for the Cretan elders to follow.'

9 E.g., Quinn 109 ('Jewish Christians who oppose Paul'); Arichea－Hatton 277 ('the false teachers'); Chapell 316 ('the Cretan opponents').

10 文理則表示（引句表示本節是一種自我描述），「他們」指隨後的**克里特人**。如果那些敗壞人的全家的人（11b 節）是猶太派的克里特人，兩者的差異就解決了。見一 12 註釋註 3 及所屬正文（上面 172）。

11 See Banker 50*a* (not his own view). See also Mounce 400. 張 333 引用提後二 25～26 來支持這立場：該兩節表示，「即使是泥足深陷的假教師，保羅亦相信他們是能夠回轉的，可見此處亦是針對假教師而說的」。

（二）他們僅指被那些領袖欺騙的人。[12] 第 13b 至 14 節的勸勉聽起來不像是對欺騙者本身、而是對被欺騙的人而發的。這裏對提多的勸勉不是「不要讓他們教導」或「要他們住口」，而是要嚴厲地責備他們，使他們在信仰上健全（13b 節）；前者適用於欺騙者，後者較適用於被欺騙者。第 14 節清楚顯示，本段其實談及兩班人：（甲）有一些人正在聽從無稽的傳說和背棄真理之人的命令，或處於這種危險之中；他們就是提多要嚴厲地責備……使他們在信仰上健全（13b 節）的那些人。（乙）另一些人事實上背棄了真理，傳播猶太人無稽的傳說和背棄真理之人的命令，並以他們的教導欺騙人。他們就是那些欺哄人（10a 節）、破壞……許多基督徒全家人純正的信仰（11b 節，當代）、將不該教導的事教導人（11c 節）的人。[13]

（三）他們同時指領袖和跟隨者，因為不宜將領袖和跟隨者嚴格地分開。[14] 可能開始時保羅的焦點確是在假教師身上（10～11 節），但是到了引句（12 節），也許是由於假教師和跟隨者都是克里特人，兩班人的分別開始變得模糊。在第 13b 節，他們可能指所有仍可教化的那些人，他們可以透過嚴厲的改正恢復健全的信仰。[15] 但他們亦可包括假教師本身，因為三章 10 節對於分門結黨即是製造分裂的人經

12 E.g., Knight II 300: 'them, the Cretans'; G. Stählin, *TDNT* 4.788: 'ἔλεγχε αὐτοὺς (sc. the Cretan Christians)'; 曾 117：「那群被圍困的會眾」。Cf. Johnson, 'Titus' 396*a*: 'those being seduced by the Jewish opponents [outside the church]'.

13 See Banker 50*b* (not exactly his own view). Knight II 300 認為，'the decisive argument is that those who are to be rebuked (v. 13) are, in fact, distinguished from those "who turn away from the truth" (v. 14).' Hiebert 433 認為他們主要指受到危害的教會成員。

14 So, e.g., Hendriksen 355 ('The errorists and those who listen to them'); Laansma 251; Smith 335 ('chiefly . . . the proponents of the deceptions, and secondly . . . those who had been seduced by their message'); Van Neste 254 n.12. Fee 180 則認為，文理要求，他們首先指那些假教師；但使他們在信仰上健全這個目的，以及 14 節的內容，可能指向所有的信徒（'all the believers'）。

15 Banker 50*b*-51*a*. 不過，班約翰的譯文似乎較接近第（二）看法：'those Cretan believers who follow false teachings'（45*b*, 50*a*, 51*a*）。

警告後回轉，仍然抱持盼望（參：提後二 25～26）；[16] 而第 14 節的描寫（減去**不要**）同樣適用於假教師和他們的跟隨者（參：提前四 1；提後四 4）。[17] 顯然地，作者首要的關注是要制止假教義繼續傳播，並且對付帶頭的那些假教師，但是克里特教會的問題是整個異端運動，包括它的領袖和跟從者。[18] 可以肯定的是，保羅假定教會內有些人已主動地或被動地牽涉於偏離正道的信仰和行為之中。[19] 但經文並沒有將假教師和跟隨者，也沒有將克里特眾教會內的猶太基督徒和克里特基督徒，清楚地區別出來。[20] 這第三種看法可取。

上文已經辯證，**責備**原文動詞在第 9c 節和 13b 節的意思相同，最符合文理的意思是「使他們認識自己的錯誤」：[21] 認識自己的錯誤才有改變的可能，**嚴厲地責備**不大可能會達到**好使他們在信仰上健全**（新譯）[22] 這目的。班約翰認為，副詞**嚴厲地**（同呂譯、思高、現修、新譯，新普同）[23] 可理解為「毫不妥協地」，即是「毫不含糊

16 見該節註釋首二段（下面 442-44）。

17 更準確地說，**聽猶太人無稽的傳說**同時適用於假教師和跟隨者，**聽……背棄真理之人的命令**則特別適用於跟隨者。

18 Marshall 204-5. Cf. Jeon I 58 n.2: 'the reproof is primarily for the false teachers, but applies secondarily to their followers'.

19 Johnson I 118: 'Paul assumes that some members of the community are actively or passively involved in the deviance.'

20 Marshall 205.

21 參一 9 註釋第四段（上面 146-48）；黃編 200，《輔讀》526（第一解釋）：「指出錯誤」。亦參註 7（'convict', 上面 183）。

22 *ἵνα ὑγιαίνωσιν ἐν τῇ πίστει* = 'that they may be sound in the faith' (KJV, NKJV, RSV, NAU, NIV, ESV). See also NRSV: 'so that they may <u>become</u> sound in the faith'; *Paraphrase* 291 / NJB: '<u>teach them to be</u> / <u>make them</u> sound in the faith'. 四種翻譯的含意都是，他們的信仰在目前並不健全。這原文子句合併了上文出現過的動詞 ὑγιαίνω（9b 節）和名詞 πίστις（1b、4a 節）。

23 當代作**嚴正地**。**(1)** 英譯多作 'sharply'（KJV, NKJV, RSV, NRSV, ESV, *Paraphrase* 291; G. Schneider, *EDNT* 1.147*a* [s.v. ἀποτόμως]; Kelly 233），'severely'（NAU, NIV, TNIV, NIV2011 [see also NJB: 'be severe']），'sternly'（NLT）。參《新希》42*a*（s.v.）：「苛刻地；嚴厲地——嚴格猛烈、不寬容」；張 333：「尖刻地」。**(2)** 這副詞（**ἀποτόμως**）在新約僅再出現一次（林後十三 10：**嚴厲地**），在 LXX 只出現一次（次經《所羅門智訓》5.22：江河必〔無情地〕〔RSV, NRSV / NJB: 'relentlessly / without pity'〕淹沒愚頑人）。同字根的名詞 ἀποτομία 在希臘文聖經僅出現兩次，指上帝的**嚴厲**（羅十一 22a、22b）。同字根的形容詞 ἀπότομος 不見於新約，但在 LXX 出

地」[24] 使他們知道自己的錯誤。不過，副詞更合乎文理的翻譯是「嚴緊地、縝密地」，[25] 所得出的意思就是，提多要以嚴緊縝密的方式訴之以理，使那些假教師知道自己的錯誤。**健全**的原文動詞已在第 9 節出現過；在這裏的意思也是「正確無誤」，[26] 因而**在信仰／真道上健全無疵／純全無疵**（呂譯／新和）這些翻譯中的「瑕疵」是指信仰上的錯誤，[27] 而**好使他們有健全的信仰**（現修）意即「好使他們在信仰上康復過來」、[28] **好使他們持守純正的信仰**（當代）。[29] **好使他們有健全的信仰**與**聽猶太人無稽的傳說和背棄真理之人的命令**（14 節）的對比提示，提多要呼召他的對手（重新）經歷像歸主般的改變。[30]

現五次，分別指上主的「盛怒（ἀπότομον ὀργήν）」（次經《便西拉智訓》5.20〔思高《智慧篇》5.21〕）、「嚴厲的審判（κρίσις ἀπότομος）」（6.5〔6.6〕）、「嚴厲〔的〕君王（ἀπότομος βασιλεύς）」（11.10〔11.11〕）、「嚴厲的言語（λόγῳ ἀποτόμῳ）」（12.9）、「無情的戰士（ἀπότομος πολεμιστής）」（18.15）。

24 Banker 51*a*: 'uncompromisingly', i.e., 'in no uncertain terms'. See also Hendriksen 355: 'decisively'; Simpson 100: 'incisively', 即是「清楚直接地」。亦參黃編 200：「毫無保留地」。

25 I.e., ἀποτόμως = 'rigorously'（BDAG 124*b* [s.v.]; Classen, 'Epistle to Titus' 54; Fiore II 204, 205; Spencer 28）。

26 見一 9 註釋註 24-25 及所屬正文（上面 145）。'The message is clear: sound doctrine begets sound faith'（Jeon I 59）；**健全的信仰**（現修）來自**健全的教導**（一 9）。

27 （**1**）Genade 35 認為 τῇ πίστει 和一 1b 的 '*the* truth' 是同義詞。（一 1b 無冠詞的 ἀληθείας 其實相當於有冠詞的 τῆς ἀληθείας. 此點見一 1～2a 註釋註 47 之〔1〕= 上面 58。）唐 1026 將 'the faith' 理解為「組成基督徒道路的正統教義、信仰、和傳統的模型」（Towner III 704: 'the matrix of orthodox doctrines, beliefs, and traditions that make up the Christian way'）。（**2**）思高（**在信德上健全無瑕**）則似乎將 πίστις 理解為「信心」。See also Marshall 215: 'for the writer faith is the key characteristic of the Christian (cf. . . . Tit 1.13; 3.15).' 不過，馬歇爾隨即補充一句，說：'The objective . . . and subjective aspects are hard to disentangle'.

28 Quinn 26: 'so that they may recover their health in the faith'. （**1**）Wild 894*b* 指出，教牧書信將謬誤看為疾病，只有真理能治好它。（**2**）連接詞 ἵνα（'that / so that (they may) . . .' [KJV, NKJV, RSV / NRSV, NAU）在此表達目的；另有認為它表達「結果」（張 333 註 114；see also NIV, TNIV, NIV2011: 'so that (they will) . . .'）。

29 See also LN §72.15: 'that they might be correct in their faith'. 按這種理解，**好堅定他們的信仰**（新普；cf. NLT: 'to make them strong in the faith'）這種翻譯就不夠準確。

30 Collins 335 ('. . . Titus is to call his opponents to a kind of conversion').

一 **14a** 不要聽猶太人無稽的傳說

14b 和背棄真理之人的命令。

就原文的結構而論，本節是從屬於上一節的目的子句好使他們有健全的信仰（13c 節，現修）的分詞片語。它表達了持守純正的信仰（當代）的負面含意；這就是說，有健全的信仰必然牽涉這裏的不……聽。[1] 聽字在這裏的意思是「密切留意」、聽信（思高）、聽從（當代）。[2] 原文動詞與第 9a 節的堅守同字根：監督必須堅守合乎教義的可靠之道；在信仰上健全（13c 節）牽涉到不……再聽信猶太人無稽的傳說（新普）。[3]

形容詞猶太人的（呂譯）在新約僅見此處。原文更準確的翻譯是「猶太的」，即是「屬猶太民族的」。[4] 無稽的傳說（同思高，新普

---

1 Thus also Jeon I 59: 'Being sound in the faith entails "not paying attention to Jewish myths . . ."'.

2 BDAG 880*a* (s.v. προσέχω, 2): 'to pay close attention to someth., *pay attention to*, *give heed to*, *follow*'; *EDNT* 3.170*a* (s.v.): 'pay attention to, follow, listen to'. 參以下英譯：（**i**）'giving heed to'（KJV, NKJV, RSV; cf. *Paraphrase* 291: 'pay no heed to'）;（**ii**）'paying attention to'（NRSV, NAU; cf. NIV, TNIV, NIV2011: 'pay no attention to'）;（**iii**）'listening to'（NLT）。（**1**）按這種理解，原文的意思就不僅為 'taking notice of'（NJB）。（**2**）動詞 **προσέχω** 在保羅書信另外出現四次：提前一 4（不要聽從無稽的傳說），三 8（執事必須不好酒），四 1（末後的時期必有人聽信那誘惑人的邪靈），四 13（提摩太要以宣讀聖經，勸勉，教導為念）；只有最後一次具正面的意思。在新約另外十九次（即新約全部 24 次）；詳見 BDAG 879*b*-80*a* (s.v.);《新希》286*a*（s.v.）。

3 兩個動詞依次為 ἀντέχομαι, προσέχω. See Genade 35; Jeon I 59.

4 依次見《輔讀》526，《新希》163*a*（s.v. Ἰουδαϊκός）。See also BDAG 478*a* (s.v.): 'Judean (Jewish)'; LN §93.171: 'pertaining to the Jewish nation – "Jewish"'. (**1**) W. Gutbrod（*TDNT* 3.382）認為，'what is meant is not so much the nature of the fables as their derivation and connection. These μῦθοι circulate among Jews and are spread by them . . . ; they are not Jewish by nature.' Thus also G. Schneider, *EDNT* 2.193*a* (s.v.): ''Ιουδαϊκός probably refers to their derivation and associations'; Marshall 206: 無稽的傳說被形容為猶太人的，表示那些傳說在猶太人當中流傳，但並不表示它們的性質必然是猶太人的。(**2**) Stern（*Comm.* 655）認為，'Ιουδαϊκός = 'Jewish' 這通常的翻譯 'is misleading and, in the ambience of the present world, anti-Semitic, insofar as it causes people to think less of normative non-Messianic Judaism.' 因此他建議將這字翻譯為 '"Judaistic," that is, imitative of Judaism without actually emanating from

同）[5] 原文只是一個字；[6] 這字在保羅書信僅再出現三次，也是在教牧書信裏（提前一 4，四 7；提後四 4），意思與本節相同。[7] 在提摩太後書四章 4 節，**掩耳不聽真理**和**偏向無稽的傳說**是一體的兩面，**無稽的傳說**與**真理**相對；由此看來，**無稽的傳說**的涵義包括三個元素：「虛假的故事作為教義的基礎」。[8] 在這裏，**不……聽猶太人無稽的傳說是在信仰上健全**（13c 節）的部分涵義；在三章 9 節，提多要**遠避愚拙的辯論、家譜**。在提摩太前書一章 4 節，提摩太要囑咐某些人**不要聽從無稽的傳說和冗長的家譜**；該節一口氣提到在提多書分開來提及的那兩個項目（**無稽的傳說**和**家譜**），這表示後兩個項目只是克里特假教義的不同部分，而一章 10 至 16 節和三章 9 至 11 節所談及的假教師是同一班人。[9] 至於**無稽的傳說**究竟指甚麼，保羅沒有給我們

---

normative Judaism.'（**3**）F. Büchsel（*TDNT* 4.788）的判斷較可取，他說：'here the Jewish nature and origin of the μῦθοι is most evident (cf. not only the attribute 'Ιουδαϊκός but also the link with ἐντολαί).'（**4**）此字（**'Ιουδαϊκός**）在 LXX 也只出現一次（次經《馬加比二書》13.21）：ἐκ τῆς Ιουδαϊκῆς τάξεως = 'from the ranks of the Jews' (RSV, NRSV), 'of the Jewish army' (NJB). 同字根的副詞 'Ιουδαϊκῶς 在希臘文聖經也只出現一次（加二 14：**按照猶太人的樣子生活**〔參《加》496-99〕）。

5　參現修（**荒唐的傳說**〔呂譯缺「的」字〕）、當代（**荒誕的……傳說**）；新譯（**無稽之談**）；《輔讀》526：「無稽之談，荒唐傳說」。

6　μῦθοι, 英譯本多翻譯為 'myths'（RSV, NRSV, NAU, NIV, TNIV, 2011, NJB, NLT, *Paraphrase* 291）或 'fables'（KJV, NKJV）。

7　此字（**μῦθος**）在新約僅再出現一次（彼後一 16：**無稽傳說**）；它在 LXX 也只出現一次（次經《便西拉智訓》20.19：「故事」〔思高《德訓篇》20.21〕；μύθος ἄκαιρος = 'a story told at the wrong time' [RSV], hence 'an inappropriate story' [NRSV]）。See also BDAG 660*b* (s.v.): 'tale, story, legend, myth'; Classen, 'Epistle to Titus' 54: 'tales';《新希》222*b*（s.v.）：「傳奇故事或描述，通常涉及超自然的生物、事情或民族英雄；在新約裏往往〔總是〕表示不好的內涵。」

8　Banker 52*a*.

9　See Banker 42*a-b*. 關於這兩段的連貫性，另見三 9～11 註釋引言第二段（下面 431-32）。（**1**）Witherington 128 則聲稱，除了一 10～16 本段，'our author does not deal with the false teachers again in this document'. 他認為三 9～11 所處理的是 'those not willing to believe'（92）。（**2**）Hendriksen 350 指出一 10～14 與提前一 3～10 的相似之處，亨捷晨認為這些相似之處表示兩段所談論的是同一班人：

足夠的線索，我們也就無從知道[10]（至少不能確定）。

多一		提前一	
10a 節	不受約束（ἀνυπότακτοι）	叛逆的（ἀνυποτάκτοις）	9 節
10a 節	說空話（ματαιολόγοι）	轉向空談（ἐξετράπησαν εἰς ματαιολογίαν）	6 節
11c 節	將不該教導的事教導人（διδάσκοντες ἃ μὴ δεῖ）	囑咐某些人不可傳別的教義（μὴ ἑτεροδιδασκαλεῖν）	3 節
12b 節	常說謊話（ἀεὶ ψεῦσται）	說謊話的（ψεύσταις）	10 節
13c 節	使他們在信仰上健全（ὑγιαίνωσιν ἐν τῇ πίστει）	違背健全教義（τῇ ὑγιαινούσῃ διδασκαλίᾳ ἀντίκειται）	10 節
14a 節	不要聽猶太人無稽的傳說（μὴ προσέχοντες Ἰουδαϊκοῖς μύθοις）	不要聽從無稽的傳說和冗長的家譜（μηδὲ προσέχειν μύθοις καὶ γενεαλογίαις ἀπεράντοις）	4 節

Spencer 22 的圖表（‘Heterodoxy Compared’）更全面地比較提多書和提前的假教師與假教導。但見註 27 之（3）（4）= 下面 194-95。正文上文借用提前一 4 相同的詞彙（無稽的傳說和……家譜）把多一 14 的猶太人無稽的傳說和三 9 的家譜連起來，這做法似乎合理，可視為有別於該註所反對的做法。

10 Fee 42: ‘It must finally be admitted that we simply do not know, because Paul does not give us enough clues’; Griffin 291: ‘The actual content of these Jewish myths remains unknown.’（**1**）Fee（‘Reflections’ 142）認為，無稽的傳說和冗長的家譜（提前一 4）是指「有關舊約的臆測（speculations about the OT）」。Carter－Levine（‘Pastorals’ 243）認為，‘the myths may comprise interpretations of Israel’s Scriptures.’ Mounce 402 也認為，猶太人……的傳說和人的命令是指 ‘Pharisaic oral tradition as it reinterpreted the Hebrew Scriptures.’ Cf. Long 266: ‘“Jewish myths” . . . is almost surely the same sort of speculative and over-spiritualized exegesis of the Old Testament that was in play in Ephesus’.（**2**）Marshall 207 認為，幾乎可以肯定，無稽的傳說的內容與舊約聖經有關。Davies I 97 認為它們大抵（‘presumably’）是關於亞伯拉罕的傳說。Knight II 300 認為，它們很可能（‘likely’）是 ‘concocted stories related to the “genealogies” spun out from those given in the OT.’ Wall 345 說，‘“legends” is Paul’s term for speculative midrash about OT characters used to authorize beliefs and practices that opposed and even subverted Paul’s witness.’ Towner II 24 認為猶太人無稽的傳說和家譜（三 9）可能都是 ‘descriptions of a speculative use of the Old Testament creation material and stories about famous personages, from which proof texts and spiritual lessons (or bizarre doctrines) were drawn’.（**3**）布魯斯認為，這些無稽的傳說（提前一 4 同）也許是 ‘a mixture of Jewish and incipient Gnostic speculation’; 老婦的無稽傳說（提前四 7）很可能是同一類的東西（F. F. Bruce, *DNTT* 2.645）。Lightfoot（‘Heresy’ 413）早就認為，教牧書信所抗衡的異端是 ‘an early phase of *Jewish Gnosticism*, very similar in character to, but more advanced and definite than, that which appears in the Epistles to the Colossians and Ephesians.’ See also Bassler 189: ‘speculations, perhaps, of a Gnostic character rooted in the scriptures of Judaism’; Köstenberger 611*a*: ‘The . . . “Jewish myths” were apparently ascetic, an amalgam of Jewish food laws . . . and a dualistic (proto-gnostic) rejection of the material’; Ellis, ‘Authorship’ 52: ‘the error seems to

背棄真理之人就是第 10 至 11 節所描寫的那些人，亦即是第 9 節末那些反對健全的教導的人；他們反對並拒絕接受真理。[11] 背棄（同

reflect a Gnosticizing Judaism'（cf. Kelly 12: 'a Gnosticizing form of Jewish Christianity'）; Ellis, 'Pastoral Letters' 661*b*: 'a judaizing-gnostic countermission'（《辭典》957*a*：「猶太教 / 諾斯底派」），663*a*: 'gnosticizing judaizers'（《辭典》959*b*：「鼓吹諾斯底主義的猶太派基督徒」〔但筆者加上底線一詞似乎過度解釋了 'gnosticizing' 一字，後者的意思可能只是「有諾斯底色彩／傾向的」〕）; Hagner, 'Titus' 548: 'an early form of Jewish gnosticism'; C. Brown, *DNTT* 3.1119: 'it would seem to be some form of gnosticizing Judaism.'（**4**）Dunn 783（= Dunn, 'Titus' 278*b*）特別反對稱教牧書信所見的假教義為 'Judaizing Gnosticism', 因他認為 '"Judaizing" means "living as a Jew," and no gnostic system that we know of taught the need to Judaize.' 參《加》83 註 19。（**5**）Hanson III 178 認為，猶太人無稽的傳說是指 'Gnostic theogonies* propagated by Christian Jews, or by Gentile Christians influenced by a Jewish form of Gnosticism.'（*Theogony = 'an account of the origin and genealogy of the gods' =「神譜」。參一 12 註釋註 5〔上面 173〕。）但是 Marshall 207 斷言：'There is nothing in this description to suggest Gnostic doctrines'. Cf. idem, 'Timothy and Titus' 194*a*: 'there is no clear reflection of typically Gnostic beliefs in the [Pastoral] letters'; Marshall 90: 'The heresy . . . shows little relationship to second-century Gnosticism'; 49-50: 'what we have is rather the presence of "Pre-Gnosticism", i.e. of elements that later went to make up the Gnostic package but which are not yet themselves compounded together in the characteristically Gnostic fashion.' See also Guthrie I 37, Guthrie II 44: 'the evidence is far from conclusive that the writer is, in fact, combating developed gnosticism'（「所有的證據都不足以證明，教牧書信的作者是直接與發展中的諾斯底主義對抗」〔古特立 42〕這翻譯，將 'developed' 誤讀為 'developing'）。（**6**）H. Balz（*EDNT* 2.445*a* [s.v. μῦθος]）認為，這字在新約出現的五次 'perhaps all point to cosmological, genealogical, and angelological speculations of a Hellenistic-Jewish Gnosticism, which is somewhat comparable to the so-called Colossian heresy (cf. Col 2:8-23) and which was found to be an increasing threat to the Church esp. in the postapostolic era.' 但所謂的歌羅西異端是甚麼東西，同樣沒有確定的答案（詳參《西．門》39-83，尤其是 81-83）。Cf. Fee 8: 'As with Colossians . . . the *nature* of the false teaching [in 1 Tim] is difficult to define with precision.'（**7**）古特立認為，這裏明言這些無稽的傳說是猶太人的，提前一 4 的描述則較為籠統，因此可以假定，克里特的異端者比以弗所的假教師更傾向於贊同猶太教（'more Judaistically inclined than their Ephesian counterparts' [Guthrie I 189; Guthrie II 201]；「克里特的異端比較傾向於是猶太人的問題，尤有甚於以弗所人」〔古特立 203-4〕這翻譯，似乎沒有掌握英文原句的意思）。

11 Banker 44*b*-45*a*. See also Fee 180: 'the false teachers with their "commandments of men."' 亨捷晨則認為，有別於 10 節那些奉割禮的人，背棄真理之人並非教會成員，而是不信主的猶太人，他們影響著克里特的假教師：'These false teachers . . . were under the influence of men who stood entirely outside the church, namely, Jews, Pharisaic propagandists, who completely rejected Christ'（Hendriksen 355）。參一 16 註釋註 38（下面 214）。

思高、現修）原文在這裏的意思不僅是**轉離／偏離**（呂譯／新譯），[12] 而是**離棄／背離**（新和／新普），即是「拒絕，從而離棄」。[13] 原文分詞的現在時態表示，這些人不斷地拒絕真理，拒絕真理是他們的特色。[14] 在原文，**真理**是本節的末後二字，與上半節的末後一字**無稽的傳說**平行和相對。[15] 這裏再次隱含了假教師與保羅（因而與提多、

---

12 See also KJV, NKJV: 'turn from'.

13 BDAG 123*a* (s.v. ἀποστρέφω, 3): 'turn away from by rejecting, *reject*, *repudiate*'; LN §31.62: 'to turn away from, to reject'.（ἀποστρεφομένων 是中間語態現在時態分詞。）See also NAU, NJB: 'turn away from'; RSV, NRSV, NIV, TNIV, NIV2011: 'reject'（thus also G. Schneider, *EDNT* 1.146*a* (s.v.); Banker 44）。當代意譯為**真理叛徒**。(**1**) Witherington 125 指出，'The reference to these false teachers "abandoning the truth" indicates that they had once embraced it'. (**2**) *Paraphrase* 291 的意譯（'Jewish myths and human regulations which subvert the truth'）將分詞 ἀποστρεφομένων 連於「猶太人的傳說和人的規條」，但分詞只與「人的（ἀνθρώπων）」同格（都是複數所有格），因而**背棄**是那些人的行動。(**3**) G. Stählin（*TDNT* 4.789 n.153）認為有此可能：'ἀποστρέφομαι alludes directly to allegorical falsification [of haggadic and halachic . . . pieces].' 但這純屬臆測。(**4**) **ἀποστρέφω** 在新約另外出現八次：(**i**) 兩次為中間語態（如在本節），分別指**拒絕**想借貸的人（太五 42，思高、新譯、新普）和**拒絕**從天上說話的上帝（來十二 25，現修、新普）；(**ii**) 另一次為第二過去不定時時態被動語態，指在亞細亞省的人都**離棄了**保羅（提後一 15）；(**iii**) 其餘五次都是及物的，分別指把劍**放回**原處（太二十六 52，思高），**煽惑／煽動**百姓（路二十三 14，同思高、新譯／現修），**使**〔人〕**離開**罪惡的道路（徒三 26，新普），**使**〔不虔〕**轉離**雅各（羅十一 26，呂譯），**使**〔耳朵〕**轉離**真理（提後四 4，呂譯）。See BDAG 122*b*-23*a* (s.v. ἀποστρέφω);《新希》41*b*-42*a*（s.v.）;《來》2.413 註 14。

14 因此，NLT 的翻譯（'who have turned away from the truth'）值得商榷。Lock 135 則理解為 'who are now turning away from . . . the truth'; 但不見得「他們此刻正在背離真理」是經文的焦點（so Banker 52*a*）。

15 與此同時，本節的上下兩半呈現交叉配置模式，如下：

μὴ προσέχοντες [A] Ἰουδαϊκοῖς [B] μύθοις
καὶ [B'] ἐντολαῖς [A'] ἀνθρώπων ἀποστρεφομένων τὴν ἀλήθειαν.

Quinn 109 聲稱：(**i**) AB 和 B'A' 依次指猶太文獻的〈哈加達〉(*Haggadah*) 和〈哈拉卡〉(*Halakah*)*（cf. Collins 335: '[the Pastor] is undoubtedly referring to Jewish haggadah and halakah'; G. Schrenk, *TDNT* 2.549 n.12: 'Tt. 1:14 speaks of ἐντολαὶ ἀνθρώπων (Halacha) and Ἰουδαϊκοὶ μῦθοι (Haggada)'; G. Stählin, *TDNT* 4.788-89; *TDNTA* 613: 'probably the allegorical development of haggadic and halakic pieces'; Keener 627*b*: 'Jewish "myths" would especially be *haggadoth*'; Marshall, 'Timothy and Titus' 187*b*-88*a*: 'this [form of Jewish teaching] appears to have been a speculative, allegorical interpretation of Jewish stories and genealogies from which probably some strange rules of conduct were drawn'）；前者是經過修飾的、載於摩西五經猶太人出埃及的「敍事」，後者是解釋如何遵行摩西律法的口傳傳統（參《聖

長老／監督）的對比：這些人[16] 背離**真理**，但保羅的整個事奉，都是**為了使上帝的選民信從與認識合乎敬虔的真理**（1 節）。[17] 如在該節，**真理**指構成福音的客觀真理，[18] 即是基督教的信仰（參提前二 4：**上帝願意人得救，並得以認識真理**）。[19]

背棄真理之人的命令表明這些命令來自背棄真理的人；它們不僅是人的教導（參西二 8：**人間的傳統**），[20] 更是背棄真理的人[21] 的教

神》239*b*、240*b*）。（**ii**）克里特的猶太基督徒反對陣營試圖用這種哈加達式和哈拉卡式的註釋來縮短以色列的聖經和使徒的信仰（**真理**）之間的差距。（**iii**）雖然教牧書信的作者（不是保羅）鄙視這些試圖，但其實 'Haggadic development appears in 1 Tim 2:13-15 and 2 Tim 3:8; halakic commentary, in 1 Tim 5:17-19; both are implied in 2 Tim 3:14-17.' *有趣的是，Quinn 110 同時承認：'The materials from the rabbinic *haggadah* and *halakah* that are adduced as illustrating the "Jewish tales" are . . . sparse and unsatisfying (cf. D-C, pp. 16-17).'

16 名詞 **ἄνθρωπος** 在本書再出現四次（二 11，三 2、8、10），在保羅書信另外 121 次（新約全部 550 次），較特別的組合包括：**照著人的看法／觀點說**（羅三 5／加三 15：κατὰ ἄνθρωπον λέγω）；**照著世人的樣子／照一般人的看法／從人的觀點看來／按照人的意思**（林前三 3／林前九 8／林前十五 32／加一 11：κατὰ ἄνθρωπον）；**屬上帝的人**（提前六 11；提後三 17）。See MGM 71*b*-73*a*; 詳參 BDAG 81*a*-82*b* (s.v.);《新希》28*a*-29*a*（s.v.）。

17 Genade 36. 'It is especially against error that ἀλήθεια is "true teaching"' (R. Bultmann, *TDNT* 1.244).

18 參一 1～2a 註 47 所屬正文（上面 58）。

19 Fiore II 205.（**1**）Mounce 401 則認為，在目前的文理中，保羅主要想到的是 'the ascetic practices of the opponents and the declaration of the gospel that all food is ritually clean'.（**2**）Stegemann（'Prejudices' 283）卻指控提多書的作者（不是保羅）對猶太教存有種族偏見：'this connection with Judaism is reason enough for him to reproach the opposing group with falling away from the truth (1:4 [*sic*, 1:14]). There is an early indication, then, that a heterophobic* attitude on the part of the author towards Judaism has either given rise to, or reinforced, the ostracism of the deviant Christian group.' Cf. 284: 'the rejected group is connected with *implicit* prejudices [on the part of the author] about Judaism'.（*Heterophobia = 對異性戀者非理性的恐懼、厭惡或歧視。但是在作者筆下，這字有另一個意思：'A. Memmi introduced the term "heterophobia" in his book about racism [*Rassismus* (Frankfurt, 1987), esp. 97-124; reprinted in D. Claussen, *Was heist Rassismus?* (Darmstadt, 1994) 203-222]. By this he wants to render the concept of "those phobic and aggressive constellations which are directed against others and are justified with various – psychological, cultural, social or metaphysical – arguments' [quotation from Memmi (in Clausen) 220-21].）

20 Scott 158 正確指出：'the Colossian heresy is itself obscure,* and it would be hazardous to assume that the one denounced here was identical with it.' *參註 10 之（5）末（上面 190）。

21 （**1**）張 334 把「人的誡命」理解為「出於人意的誡命」；如此，ἀνθρώπων 便是 'genitive

導，貶抑之意再清楚不過。**命令**（新普同）[22] 或**誡命**（呂譯、新和）[23] 也許可以理解為那些假師傅聲稱他們帶有上帝所賦予的權柄，因而他們的教導就是（上帝的）命令。[24] 不過，很難想像保羅對此聲稱不加修飾，而沿用他們的「命令」一字；因此，原文名詞在這裏的意思較可能只是**規定／規例／規條**（思高／現修／新譯），[25] 因它所指的是並無上帝認可的、僅屬教派性質的指示。[26] 下文顯示，這些指示是有關外表潔淨的規條（15 節）。[27]

---

of source'（註 121）。但這字較可能是主詞所有格（所有格名詞的語意功能，就是作為帶頭那個名詞所隱含之動詞的主詞）：'commandments/commands of men'（KJV, NKJV, NAU / RSV）或 'the commands of people/those who . . .'（ESV, NLT / NIV）可化為 'what men / people who . . . / those who . . . command'. 這符合 Wallace 113 所提供的 subjective genitive 的 'Key to Identification'. **(2)**「（不要順從）轉離真理的，人的誡命」（張 334）這句子裏的逗號，錯誤地使「轉離真理的」變成形容「誡命」或「人的誡命」而不是形容「人」。

22 See also RSV, NIV, TNIV, NIV2011, NLT: 'commands'; NJB: 'orders'.

23 See also KJV, NKJV, NRSV, NAU: 'commandments'. **教唆**（當代）是過度鬆散的意譯。

24 See Classen, 'Titus' 435, 'Epistle to Titus' 54: 'the μῦθοι [myths] are put forward with a claim to authority'.

25 See *Paraphrase* 291; Jeon I 59, 60 / Kelly 233, 236: 'regulations/rules'. 亦參《串釋（增簡）》1754*b*：**誡命**（新和）「指這些異端分子所制定的、有關食物與外表潔淨的規條」。Mounce（'Titus' 106）則意譯為 'demands'.

26 BDAG 340*a* (s.v. ἐντολή, 2 a): 'instruction of a sectarian nature and without divine sanction'. Sumney（*Opponents* 293）認為，'Such a description of their teaching shows only that the author of Titus rejects it and intends for the readers to do the same because it is not teaching from God, while Paul's and Titus's is (1.1-3).' **(1)** 耶穌引以賽亞的預言（LXX 賽二十九 13）指責法利賽人，**把人的規條**（ἐντάλματα, 複數）**當作教義教導人**（可七 7）；又指控他們為了人的**傳統**（παραδόσεις, 複數）而離棄／廢棄上帝的誡命（ἐντολή, 單數）（七 8／9）。多一 14 的**命令**（ἐντολαῖς, 複數）相當於耶穌談及的**規條和傳統**。留意人的規條／傳統（複數）和上帝的命令（單數）的對比，前者與後者相違（see Quinn 112）。**(2)** 這字（**ἐντολή**）在教牧書信僅再出現一次（提前六 14：**要守這命令**），在保羅書信另十二次（計為：羅七 8～13 的**誡命**〔六次〕；羅十三 9 複數的**誡命**；林前七 19 複數的**神的誡命**，十四 37 單數的**主的命令**；弗二 15 複數的、構成律法的「誡命」〔參《弗》347-48〕，六 2 單數的**誡命**；西四 10 複數的**指示**），新約另外 53 次（全部 67 次）。See BDAG 340*a*-40*b* (s.v.);《新希》116*a*（s.v.）。

27 **(1)** Banker 52*b* 認為，15 節的話很難明白，除非我們假定 14 節的**命令**有一些是關乎食物（可能還有其他）的禮儀潔淨的。See also Perkins 1443*b*: 'The reference to purity in v. 15 suggests that the commandments in question concerned purity or kosher regulations.' **(2)** White 190*a* 認為，這些**命令**的性質與西二 22 的**命令**相同，都是 'arbitrary ascetic prohibitions'. See also Marshall 206: 'The application [of the phrase

"the commandments of men"] to ascetic teachings in Col 2.22 is perhaps nearest to this passage's intent.' 不過，西二 22 的**人的命令**（ἐντάλματα）的禁慾性質是明顯的，因它們是「**不可拿、不可嘗、不可摸**」**等類的規條**（21 節〔參《西‧門》482-84〕）；這裏的**背棄真理之人的命令**（ἐντολαί）則並無明顯的禁慾含意，文理（15 節）只提示它們與禮儀潔淨有關。

(**3**) Scott 161 認為，這些**命令**的性質可從提前四 3～6 得知：'prohibitions imposed on marriage and on certain meats and drinks.' 參周 419：「禁止嫁娶以及禁戒某些食物。」Similarly, Kelly 236. 但是唐書禮正確認為，'it is not wise to assume that the situations overlap that completely'（Towner III 706 n.128〔唐 1029 註 59〕）；'It is not warranted to import elements from the Cretan description to fill out the Ephesian profile, <u>and vice versa</u>'（Towner III 44〔唐 63〕）。馬歇爾指出，雖然這裏用了與提前相同的詞彙來描寫克里特的假教師——**無稽的傳說**（μῦθοι: 一 14a；提前一 4，四 7；提後四 4）；**家譜**（γενεαλογίαι: 三 9a；提前一 4）——又表明他們的教導的猶太性質（<u>**猶太人**</u>**無稽的傳說**；參：提前一 4：**想要作**<u>**律法**</u>**教師**）和禁慾的趨勢（一 15；參：提前四 3〔但見上面（2）末〕），但並無提到**他們禁止嫁娶**（提前四 3），亦見不到**復活之事已過去**（提後二 18）這種實現末世論的謬誤正在影響著克里特的教會；由此看來，儘管克里特的異端和以弗所的異端十分類似，兩者可能仍是分開來發展的（Marshall 192）。Cf. Kelly 10: '[the false teaching] took somewhat different forms in Ephesus and Crete'. See also Sumney, *Opponents* 302: 'we have found a separate group of opponents in each of these letters [the Pastorals]. While two of the groups [those in 1 Tim. and Titus] are similar, we have no evidence that they are identical or are both part of a larger movement—and some evidence to the contrary.' Cf. Johnson, 'Titus' 379*a*: 'The composite sketch [of the nature of the opponents or heresy they attack, 378*b*] . . . ignores the real differences between the letters themselves, each of which is internally consistent and need not be read in light of the others'; Johnson II 13: 'The composite sketch . . . ignores the fact that each of the letters deals with a different set of "opponents," whether they are real or simply literary foils.' Murphy-O'Connor（'2 Timothy' 414）斷言，'Nowhere has the assumption of the unity of the Pastorals been more pernicious than in treatments of the errors they oppose.'

(**4**) Sumney（*Opponents* 298）更認為，'Th[e] use of another letter [1 Tim.] to identify the opponents of the primary text [Titus] is <u>methodologically unsound</u>. Unless we can be certain that the very same opponents are in view in both letters and that they have not modified their view, such borrowing cannot be permitted. . . . Thus, we cannot use 1 Timothy to expand our understanding of the opponents of Titus. So we are left with only the knowledge that the opponents are concerned about purity laws that are based on the Mosaic Code. It is possible that food laws were among their concerns. . . . But purity laws encompass a much broader spectrum of life than food prohibitions and sex regulations [cf. 1 Tim. 4:3]. Verse 15 gives us no basis to narrow the concerns of these teachers to these or any other matters or to explicitly include them among their concerns. This verse suggests only that they regard matters about purity as important, without specifying any particular areas on which they concentrate their attention.' 按上述的原則，以下的看法便有部分值得商榷：Faber（'Titus' 138）認為：'The traditional view, that the teachers form a group of Jewish Christians who promoted <u>abstinence</u>, ritual purity, and the Mosaic law on foods (cf. 1 Tim. 4:3), remains the most plausible one.' Similarly, Mounce 395: 'This passage [1:10-16] clearly shows that the teaching was primarily Jewish and taught <u>asceticism</u> and guidelines for ritual purity and defilement.' Cf. Mounce lxxi: 'The heresy taught <u>asceticism</u> (cf. Titus 1:15)'; Marshall 44:

'permanent abstinence from certain foods on principle [1 Tim 4.3] . . . appears to be connected with ritual requirements regarding purity (Tit 1.15)'; Murphy-O'Connor, '2 Timothy' 415: 'They taught abstinence from food explicitly (1 Tim 4:3) and implicitly (Titus 1:14-15) – and the obvious reference point is the one recommended by the context, Jewish dietary laws.' 因為 'abstinence' 和 'asceticism' 這些意思其實是從提前四 3 得來的。因此，唐書禮的看法較為可取；他認為 'The absence of explicit reference to the sort of asceticism linked to the movement in Ephesus may place these teachers into another category'（Towner III 47〔唐 67〕）。

（5） Streete 辯證，教牧書信的作者將假教師視為「假的禁慾主義者」，因他們欠缺或假裝具有苦行的標誌，即是「克制（σωφροσύνη）」（參一 8 註釋註 24〔上面 136〕），他們所推行的只是「假冒的苦行主義（bogus asceticism）」（'*Askesis*' 300）；教牧書信的作者則聲稱自己擁有「真確的（authentic）」保羅教導，並在這基礎上建構 'an ascetic subjectivity that undermines and opposes the power of the asceticism of his opponents'（303）。這就是說，教牧書信的教導才是「真確的禁慾／苦行主義」。如此，對文章的作者而言，'ascetic' 與 'disciplined' 同義（312: 'Although the sexuality advocated by the Pastoral Epistles appears not to be an ascetic sexuality understood as celibacy, for example, in 1 Corinthians 7, it is similarly "ascetic" in that it is disciplined within the bonds of marriage'）。鑑於保羅對苦待己身的負面評估（西二 22；參《西・門》494-99），筆者十分懷疑保羅會將基督徒克己自制的生活視為「真確的禁慾／苦行生活」。

3.3 假教師的定罪（一 15～16）

一 **15a** 在潔淨的人，凡物都潔淨；

15b 在污穢不信的人，甚麼都不潔淨，[1]

---

1 在原文，這兩個子句呈現反義平行及交叉配置模式（Witherington 125: 'the use of antithetical parallelism . . . and chiasm'）：

πάντα καθαρὰ (A) τοῖς καθαροῖς (B),
τοῖς δὲ μεμιαμμένοις καὶ ἀπίστοις (B') οὐδὲν καθαρόν (A').

中譯本的翻譯將這模式變成 ABA'B'. 但原文的次序是有原因的：15～16 節所關注的，主要不是**潔淨的人**，而是**污穢不信的人**，因此 15a 節就不以 τοῖς καθαροῖς（to the pure）開始；但 15b 節開首的 δέ（but）字引入與**潔淨的人**相反的另一班人，因而 15b 節就以 τοῖς . . . μεμιαμμένοις καὶ ἀπίστοις（to the defiled and unbelieving）開始（Levinsohn, *Discourse Features* 25）。

（1）Genade 36-37 (see also 127) 則認為，這兩個子句所呈現的模式是 AABA*。其理由是，保羅拿潔淨的和不潔淨的作對比，而第一、二、四這三項都用了正面的 καθαρός 一字，只有第三項是用負面的 μιαίνω 和 ἄτιστος 二字。（作者的 'the verb <u>με</u>μί<u>α</u>νω' 含有至少兩點錯誤：the acute accent [´] 不可能放在長音的 ω 之前的第二位置；更嚴重的，開首的 με 其實只是完成時態分詞 <u>με</u>μιαμμένοις 或限定動詞 <u>με</u>μίανται〔15c 節〕的前綴〔reduplication of μ〕，不是動詞本身〔μι<u>αί</u>νω〕一部分。）可是，第四項的 οὐδέν 一字使 οὐδὲν καθαρόν 成為負面意義的（nothing is clean = everything is unclean!）。因此，即使以潔淨或不潔淨作為區分的標準，作者的 AABA* 模式亦宜修正為 AABB* 模式。事實上，這兩種模式都遠不及上述的交叉配置模式那麼自然：在後者，首末兩項（all things are clean; nothing is clean）和中間兩項（**潔淨的人；污穢不信的人**）都十分工整地相對應。有趣的是，作者在前一頁認同這裏呈現<u>交叉配置模式</u>的看法：'He continues his vilification campaign by elaborating on the description of the teachings he introduced in verse 14. He accomplishes this through a technique described as . . . antithetic <u>chiasmus</u>'（36, with reference to Quinn 101 ['antithetical chiasmus']）。但筆者剛解釋過，作者的 AABA* 其實是 AABB* 模式，而兩者都不是 'antithetic chiasmus'.

（2）Köstenberger 611*a* 認為本節的交叉配置模式是這樣的：

'All things are pure to the pure.
But to those who are corrupted
and do not believe,
nothing is pure.'

可是，與末行相對應的只是首行的前半部分（'All things are pure'），而首行的後半部分（'to the pure'）則顯然與第二、三行（視為一個單元）相對應。因此，首行應分拆為<u>兩個</u>單元，第二、三兩行則應視為<u>一個</u>單元。換句話說，本註開首指出的那

15c 連心地和天良也都污穢了。

本節和下一節進一步描寫那些假教師，為第 13b 至 14 節的勸勉提供進一步的理由。[2] 祈勒克認為，本節頭兩行是那些**背棄真理之人**所說的話。[3] 不過，筆者同意亨捷晨的理解，即那些假教師主要是**奉割禮的人**（10 節），他們高度評價猶太人的〈哈拉卡〉；[4] 因此，他

個交叉配置模式才是經文所呈現的。

（3）Classen（'Titus' 436, 'Epistle to Titus' 55）聲稱：'No one can fail to be impressed by the polyptoton καθαρά－τοῖς καθαροῖς－καθαρόν'. 不過，這裏的情形並不符合 Rowe ('Style' 132) 對此字的解釋：'Polyptoton is the repetition of a noun or pronoun in different cases at the beginnings of successive clauses'; 因為首末二字都是所有格，並且第二、三兩個字都是在所屬子句的末後而非開首。參較《加》213 註 6。

（4）Jeon I 60 則聲稱，聽眾會從 15～16 節聽出 'a mini-chiasm' 來：（甲）凡物（πάντα, 15a 節），（乙）污穢（μεμιαμμένοις, 15b 節），（乙'）污穢（μεμίανται, 15c 節），（甲'）任何（πᾶν, 16 節）。可是，這樣將形容詞 πᾶν 字抽出來使之與名詞 πάντα 相對應，等於忽視 16 節其餘部分重要得多的內容——最明顯的是 16a 節與 16b 節的雙重對比：宣稱認識上帝，卻在行為上否認他；作者本身就稱 16a～b 節為 'a final and devastating assessment of the opponents'（62），又稱 16c 節為 'a devastating condemnation'（63）。

2 Banker 52*b*.

3 Clark, 'Structure' 107: 其譯文在 15 節開首加上 '[saying]' 一字（方括號是作者的；see also 108: 'They say'）。祈勒克指出，（i）在林前六 12 和十 23，一共四個引句之後，都一貫地各以但字（ἀλλά）引進保羅的反駁。（ii）以希臘文為母語、並且身為聯合聖經公會希臘文聖經第四版的編委之一的 John Karavidopoulos 教授也堅信，如果這裏包含引句，它一定是延伸到 15b 節末。祈勒克又認為（107-8）他的看法有兩個優點：第一，可以免去試圖理解使徒保羅為甚麼會說出這樣的話的困難，因為這樣的話很容易被誤用（'a clause readily capable of ethical misuse'）。第二，有上述林前兩段經文支持：該處的 πάντα (μοι) ἔξεστιν（凡事〔我〕都可行）被廣泛地承認為引自保羅的敵對者。按這種理解，一 15c 是保羅的反駁：「相反地（ἀλλά），污穢了的（μεμίανται）是他們的* 心地和良心（αὐτῶν* καὶ ὁ νοῦς καὶ ἡ συνείδησις）。」（*但見註 46 之〔3〕= 下面 205。）（1）White 190*a* 早就認為 15a、15b 節是 'a maxim of the Judaic Gnostics', 15c 節是保羅的反駁。See also Martin, 'Titus' 16-17 n.40: 15a、15b 節表達對手的觀點，15c 節才是提多書作者（他並非保羅）的觀點；F. Hauck, *TDNT* 4.646: 'the inner defilement . . . results from adopting Gnostic libertinism.'（2）Lock 132 只將 15a 節放在引號內。Cf. Richards 83: 'the apparent proverb of 1.15[a]'.

4 「猶太文獻用語，可拼寫為 *Halakah* 或 *Halachah*，是指自聖經記事年代以來所逐漸形成的猶太宗教禮儀、日常生活和行事為人的律法和典章。〈哈拉卡〉有別於五經的律法，是專為保存口傳傳統」（《聖神》240*b*）。

們的道德倫理守則應是嚴謹[5] 而非寬鬆的（**凡物都潔淨**）。[6]

凡物都潔淨與羅馬書十四章 20 節的**一切都是潔淨的**相似，[7] 後一句話很可能是羅馬教會中的「強者」的口號，他們聲稱**一切食物都可以吃**（現修）；保羅在引述（和暗示同意[8]）之餘，也隨即提出修正。[9] 在本節，**凡物都潔淨**則是保羅自己的意見。[10] 本節（尤其是第一行）使人想起耶穌講過的話；針對法利賽人的禮儀主義，耶穌曾說：**從外面進去的不能玷污人，惟有從裏面出來的才玷污人**（可七 15；參太十五 11）。[11] 耶穌同樣將禮儀上的潔淨和道德上的潔淨放在對立面。[12] 禮儀上的潔淨可能正是假教師的教導中一個主要的

---

5 L. Goppelt（*TDNT* 6.146 n.7）認為，'[a] similar demand [to Col. 2:21] is raised by the related error combated in the Past. (1 Tm. 4:3; Tt. 1:14 f.)'.

6 Hendriksen 356, n.192 (continued). 正文的辯證並不要求 14 節的**背棄真理之人的命令**就是指猶太人的〈哈拉卡〉(見該節註釋註 15〔上面 191-92〕)，儘管亨捷晨將二者連起來（'these errorists were for the most part . . . people who esteemed very highly the Jewish *Halacha* (verse 14 . . .)）。

7 原文依次為 πάντα καθαρὰ τοῖς καθαροί, πάντα μὲν καθαρά.

8 參：羅十四 14：**我憑著主耶穌確知深信，凡物本來沒有不潔淨的**。

9 參《羅》4.458-59。**(1)** 費柯利認為，本節是羅十四 14 的變體（Fiore II 205），這裏所指的是飲食方面的限制（207: 'Dietary restrictions' 構成**不信**的一項明證；see also 215: 'Jewish dietary regulations are superseded'）。Goulder（'Wolves' 243）也認為，15a 節 'should be understood to be a refusal to have Jewish *kashrut* regulations imposed on Gentile Christians.' **(2)** 祁勒克則認為，本節的文理並無任何提示，這裏談論的是類似的題目（Clark, 'Structure' 107）。Fee 183 斷言：'Except for the language used, there is scarcely any other point of contact with Romans 14.'

10 亨捷晨將**凡物**理解為上帝所造的每一樣食物(提前四 4)。See Hendriksen 356('I Tim. 5:5' 是 'I Tim. 4:4' 之誤)。

11 Wendland（'Discourse' 347）則認為，一 15 使用了 'a religious maxim/commonplace'（例如：太十七 17～19，十五 11、17～20）來支持 14 節暗示的指示（= 13 節的**要……責備他們**）。

12 Banker 53*a* 有這樣的陳述：'Note that, in the second occurrence of "unclean" here in Mark, Jesus is using "unclean" in its moral sense, <u>but that his starting point is the use of "unclean" in its moral sense,</u> but that his starting point is the use of "unclean" in its ritual sense, something very similar to what Paul is doing in Titus 1:14-15.' 筆者加上底線的部分與文理發生衝突，似乎是應被刪去卻沒有被刪去；把它刪去，全句的意思才清晰和合理。按這種理解，班約翰似乎認為可七 15 的首個**玷污**是指禮儀上的污穢，第二個則指道德上的不潔。筆者倒認為，第一次的**玷污**也是指道德上的污穢；see Lane, *Mark* 254: 'Jesus sets in radical opposition material purity and moral purity. . . . a man is not <u>defiled</u> by what he eats, even when his hands are not properly <u>washed</u>.'

特色。[13]

潔淨的人與污穢不信的人相對，[14] 這就提示第一個（原文次序為第二個）潔淨是指道德方面的潔淨。[15] 第二（原文次序為第一）和第三個潔淨則指禮儀上的潔淨。[16] 所得出的意思就是：對（道德上或靈性上）潔淨的人來說，[17] 一切都是（禮儀上）潔

---

13 Genade 37.（**1**）耶柔米也認為，一 15 'is entirely directed against the Jewish distinction of clean and unclean, which was maintained on a mistaken view of abolished laws'（Gorday 293*a*）。See also Blaiklock 77: 'The words must be set in the context of regulation-ridden Judaism, with its overwhelming list of "unclean" things'; Sumney, *Opponents* 297: 'The most probable implication of these comments about purity [in v. 15] is that they are related to their interpretation of the Law and so involve purity laws of Judaism'; 300-1: 'they are a group of teachers who are largely or at least originally Jewish Christians who advocate interpretations and observances of the Law that the author of Titus rejects. They probably give particular attention to some purity regulations from Judaism, but we cannot isolate any particular laws within the purity code on which they place special emphasis. . . . Their disputing about the Law may well include more than matters about purity, but we cannot determine what other matters of interpretation or observance they raise.'（**2**）Knight II 11 則認為，15、16 兩節提示，假教師有不道德行為的傾向（'a tendency toward . . . immorality'）。這見解似乎是基於經文提到他們的心地和天良也都污穢了。

14 （**1**）Levinsohn（*Discourse Features* 115-16）指出，15b 節開首的 δέ 字引進了真正的對比：在 15a 節和 15b 節這兩個子句之間，（i）有一共同的要素：潔淨（καθαρά, καθαρόν），（ii）同時有兩對相反的詞：一切與沒有一樣（思高、新譯）相對（πάντα vs. οὐδέν），在潔淨的人與在污穢不信的人相對（τοῖς καθαροῖς vs. τοῖς . . . μεμιαμμένοις καὶ ἀπίστοις）。（**2**）BDF §447(2) 解釋，雖然以 μέν 和 δέ 提出對比是古典希臘文的基本特色，但在新約裏 μέν 字常被省略（如在這裏：τοῖς ⌊μὲν⌋ καθαροῖς· τοῖς δὲ μεμιαμμένοις）。

15 See BDAG 489*b* (s.v. καθαρός, 3): 'pert. to being free from moral guilt, *pure*, *free* fr. sin'; DC 138*a*: 'The second "pure" (καθαρός) refers to ethical purity';《新希》167*b*（s.v. I.4）：「道德上沒有過失的人；無罪的人。」Chapell 315 則認為，'Paul contends that for those whose <u>motives</u> are pure in Christ, virtually nothing makes them impure.' 但作者並無提出理由支持其說。

16 See BDAG 489*b* (s.v. καθαρός, 2): 'pert. to being cultically/ceremonially pure, *ritually pure*';《新希》167*b*（s.v. I.2）：「在禮儀上是未污染的」。原文的交叉配置模式（見註 1 開首〔上面 196〕）支持這種理解。除了本節的三次，這形容詞（**καθαρός**）在保羅書信另外出現五次（新約全部 27 次），除了一次指一切〔食物〕都是潔淨的（羅十四 20），其餘四次皆指清潔／純潔的心（提前一 5／提後二 22）或清白／純潔的良心（提前三 9／提後一 3）；在新約另外十九次（全部 27 次）。See BDAG 489*b* (s.v.);《新希》167*a*-67*b*（s.v.）。

17 Marshall 209 認為，καθαροῖς 'indicates either that all things are clean in the opinion of pure people or that all things are clean for their use'. 這就是說，這字或是 'ethical dative'（see Wallace 146-47），意即 'as far as they are concerned', 或是 'dative of

淨的；[18] 但對那些污穢和不信的人來說，沒有一件東西是（禮儀上）潔淨的（現修）。[19] 又由於污穢與不信相連（15b 節），污穢就不是指禮儀上的不潔（如在約十八 28：恐怕染了污穢），而是指德性上的污染。[20] 如此，潔淨的人就是被耶穌基督潔淨（二 14）了、被上帝……藉着聖靈所施〔1〕重生和更新的〔2〕洗……拯救了（三 5，現修）[21] 的人，即是藉著……上帝的靈，已經洗淨，成聖，稱義了（林前六 11，新和）的人，亦即是那〔些〕信而明白真理的人（提前四 3）。污穢不

---

advantage'（see Wallace 142-44）。筆者認為前者較後者可取。

18 Mounce 401: 'all things are [ritually] clean to the [morally] clean'（方括號是原來的）。孟威廉由此推論，保羅的敵對者則這樣教導人：道德上潔淨的人仍然會因吃了不潔的食物或觸摸了不潔之物而變成不潔（參：該二 10～14）（ibid.）。M. Reasoner（*DPL* 776*b*）則認為，'The perception of things as pure to the pure in Titus 1:15 seems related to Jesus' logion now preserved in Matthew 6:22-23'（留意引句的後半部分在《辭典》1119*a-b* 變成〔修正為？〕「這似乎與路加福音十一章 40～41 節耶穌的話有關」）。

19 Mounce 401: 'To the (morally) impure, all things are (ritually) impure.' Banker 44, 53*b* 則認為第三個潔淨的是指 'pure (ritually or spiritually)'. 他的理由是（53*b*）：'when Paul amplifies *ouden katharon* in 1:15c and says even their minds and consciences have been defiled, he is talking about moral purity. It may be, then, that is [*sic*, in] *ouden katharon* "nothing (is) pure", Paul is not making a distinction as to ritual or moral purity, since he seems to be relating it to ritual purity on one side [15a] and moral purity on the other [15c].' 筆者倒認為，15c 節並不是 15b 節末甚麼都不潔淨的擴充，而是 15b 節開首污穢……的人（τοῖς . . . μεμιαμμένοις）進一步的描寫；如此，甚麼都不潔淨不必牽涉道德上的不潔。事實上，連心地和天良也都污穢了（15c 節）的人，不會關心道德上的不潔。

20 See Banker 44: 'people who are defiled (spiritually)'; LN §88.260: '[the verb means] to cause someone to be morally tainted or defiled'; BDAG 650*a* (s.v. μιαίνω, 2): 'to cause the purity of someth. to be violated by immoral behavior, *defile*'. 此辭典指出，'The primary sense "to stain" . . . prepares the way for the transf. sense of causing defilement through socially or cultically unacceptable behavior.'（**1**）Fee 181 指出，15b 節表達了一個猶太人的常見主題，那就是，任何東西被不潔淨的人觸摸過，也就變成不潔淨的（參：該二 10～14；斐羅，《律法釋義》3.208-9）。參下面註 25 及所屬正文。（**2**）Wallace 437 將本節列於 'the suppression of the agent for rhetorical effect' 的例子當中，可惜他沒有指明他想到的是分詞 μεμιαμμένοις（15b 節）、動詞 μεμίανται（15c 節），還是兩者；更沒有解釋不提出「誰人使他們污穢了」如何達到修辭效果（他的意思是否說，不提出「誰人」使重點落在他們「是污穢的」的狀況上？）。（**3**）分詞和動詞的完成時態表示，二字的著眼點都是在於「已污穢了，因而是污穢的」的狀況。從文法的角度而言，二者都是 intensive/consummative perfects（see Wallace 574-76）。

21 詳見該節註釋第四至九段（下面 386-91）。Cf. Ridderbos, *Paul* 302: 'to him who lives by faith in Christ no gift or food is wrong in itself.'

信的人就是不信靠基督，未曾經歷上帝的潔淨和拯救的非信徒，[22] 在文理中特指那些奉割禮的假教師（10 節）。他們所不信的就是他們所拒絕的真理，即是保羅受託傳揚（一 3）的關於大衛的後裔、耶穌基督的福音（提後二 8）。他們企圖以遵守人的命令（14 節）即是人所訂立的規條，來使自己及別人成為或保持潔淨，這樣做不但徒勞無功（因為外表的、禮儀上的潔淨不等於內在的、道德上的潔淨），更表明了他們是污穢的（因為道德上潔淨的人不須要任何的潔淨規條來使自己在禮儀上潔淨），不屬於上帝子民的信心羣體，而是不信的人，[23] 他們的不信使他們的罪污（罪的污染）沒有獲得潔淨。[24] 由於他們仍然受到罪的污染，對他們而言，就甚麼都不潔淨；保羅似乎將哈該書二章 13 至 14 節的原則應用到他們身上。[25]

末句（15c 節）證實，本節的污穢是內在而非外在的：連心地和天良也都污穢了。[26] 心地（新和、現修）原文作心思／理性（呂譯、

---

22 Cf. Calvin 367: 'Since in God's sight there is no purity apart from faith, it follows that unbelievers are all unclean.'

23 Cf. Fee 181. See also Banker 53*b*: 'people who . . . do not trust (in Christ Jesus)'; Fiore II 206: 'Their opposition has placed them outside the community of the faithful.'（1）新普作不信上帝（NLT 只作 'unbelieving'）。但補充上帝作為不信的賓詞，這做法很不可能是正確的，因為文理顯示，那些假教師是奉割禮的人（10 節），即是猶太人（他們信奉獨一的上帝），而且他們宣稱認識上帝（16 節）。（2）ἄπιστος 在保羅書信另外出現十五次（新約全部 23 次），四次指不信的妻子／丈夫（林前七 12、14a／13、14b），其餘十一次（林前六 6，七 15，十 27，十四 22a、22b、23、24；林後四 4，六 14、15；提前五 8）皆為「名詞化用語」，指「不信的人；不相信耶穌基督福音的人；非基督徒；並不屬於基督徒羣體的人」（《新希》36*a* [s.v. I.3-4]）。Cf. BDAG 103*b*-4*a* (s.v.).

24 Knight II 302. Montague 225 將 μεμιαμμένοις καὶ ἀπίστοις 視為「重言法（hendiadys）」，所得出的意思就是 'defiled by disbelief',「被不信所玷污」。

25 So Knight II 303. 該二 13～14 的信息是：「凡帶有罪愆的人，不單污染他們手下的各樣工作，亦玷污他們在壇上所獻的祭物」（盧玉音，《小先知書》301）。參上面註 20 之（1）。

26 原文動詞（μιαίνω）在新約僅再出現三次，分別指控告耶穌的猶太人不進總督府，恐怕染了污穢（約十八 28）；一個背道者可以令教會所有其他成員被染污（來十二 15〔呂譯〕，參《來》2.385）；以及做夢者污穢身體（猶 8 節）。See BDAG 650*a* (s.v.);《新希》219*b*（s.v.）。

當代、新普／思高）；[27] 天良（同當代、新和）即是良知／良心（呂譯、現修、新普／思高、新譯）。對保羅而言，良心並不是一種內在的道德標準，更非與上帝的聲音等同，它也並不對人的行為提供指引；良心乃是一種中性的下判斷的「機件」，它根據既定的道德標準對人的行為作出客觀的判斷（或是負面的批評，或是正面的肯定），使人知道自己的行為是否（或到甚麼程度）符合那些準則，而人與良心的關係就是人要對良心負責。[28] 費阿利認為，「心思」（亦見提前六 5；提後三 8）和「良知」（亦見提前一 5、19，三 9，四 2；提後一 3）[29] 表達了教牧書信中基督徒生命的兩方面——理性的一面和實際的一面：[30] 心思是認識和認可真理（即是福音或上帝的啟示）的器官，[31] 良知[32] 則

27 F. Hauck（*TDNT* 3.424）則理解為 'inner being'. 名詞 **νοῦς** 在保羅書信另外出現二十次（包括三次在主／基督的心思一語中〔呂譯：羅十一 34；林前二 16a／16b〕），新約另外僅三次（路二十四 45；啟十三 18，十三 9）；詳參《帖後》146-47；BDAG 680 (s.v.);《新希》228*a*（s.v.）。

28 See Marshall 218; 參《羅》1.378-79。

29 在這五次，「良知」四次是正面的（見下面註 32 之〔iv〕）；餘下一次（提前四 2）是負面的（見同註之〔v〕）。

30 Fiore II 206.

31 Towner III 708-9（唐 1032）：'The "mind" . . . within Paul's anthropology is the organ that perceives and approves "the truth" (i.e., the gospel or God's revelation).' Cf. G Harder, *DNTT* 3.127: νοῦς 在這裏指 'a religious understanding, a religious faculty of judgment'.

32 名詞 **συνείδησις** 在新約一共出現 30 次（三份之二在保羅書信中）：除了兩次特指罪的意識／罪疚感（來十 2，呂譯、現修／新普）和領會……上帝的旨意（彼前二 19，現修），其餘 28 次皆指人的道德意識或良知：
（**i**）良心與己分開而對己作證（羅二 15〔參《羅》2.377-78〕，九 1；林後一 12）；
（**ii**）良心有判斷的功能（林後四 2，五 11）；
（**iii**）良心（包括自己的／別人的）是行事的動機（羅十三 5；林前十 25、27／28、29a、29b）；（**iv**）良心有多種：（負面的）軟弱的（林前八 7、10／12：ἀσθενής/ἀσθενοῦσα [ἀσθενέω]）、邪僻的（來十 22〔思高〕：πονηρά）＝ 充滿罪咎的（當代）；（正面的）無虧的（徒二十四 16：ἀπρόσκοπος）、清白／純潔的（提前三 9／提後一 3：καθαρά）、清白的／無愧的／無虧的（ἀγαθή: 徒二十三 1／提前一 5*、19／來十三 18；彼前三 16、21）；（*Cf. Marshall 226: 'the idea of being in good working order, operating on true norms [and making good judgement, 225], is essential to the concept of a good conscience. On the other hand, the believer's aim is that this good conscience will also be "clean" in that it does not condemn for an inconsistency between faith and action. Both motifs are present, but the emphasis may well shift to and

根據人對上帝及其旨意的認識而對人的行為作出判斷。[33] 既然假教師的心思已被污染，他們對上帝及其旨意的認識就是錯的；他們的良心根據這種錯誤的認識而對自己的行為作出的道德判斷，也就是錯的，故此，他們的良心也被描寫為**污穢了**。[34] 在另兩卷教牧書信，**心思敗壞與喪失真理**（提前六 5，思高）和**反對真理**（提後三 8，現修、新普）皆密切相關；[35] 但前者和後二者的關係則有點模棱兩可。[36] 照樣在提多書本段，馬歇爾認為污穢的心思（和良心）導致**背棄真理**（14 節），以及因背棄真理而生的禁慾規條（15a 節）；[37] 唐書禮則認為，幾乎可以確定，假教師的**心思和良知都敗壞了**（新普）乃是他們**不信**（＝**背棄真理**）的結果。[38] 但若心思和良知的關係就如上述（「見註 33、

---

fro between them.' C. Maurer [*TDNT* 7.918] 認為，**無愧的良心**指向 'the renewal of man by the new creation in faith, which embraces the whole life of the Christian'. 'We should . . . trace the origin of the renewed conscience to that renewal by the Holy Spirit of which Tit 3.5 speaks so eloquently' [Marshall 226].）

（**v**）良心可以**受污染**（林前八 7：μολύνεται [μολύνω]），可以成為**染污了**（多一 15〔呂譯〕：μεμίανται [μιαίνω]）的，甚至變成**像是給熱鐵烙死了**（提前四 2〔現修〕：κεκαυστηριασμένη [καυστηριάζω]**）；cf. Marshall 219: '[in the Pastoral Epistles] the qualification of the term in each occurrence (good, clean, defiled, seared) and its relation to acceptance or rejection of the faith, shows that it is viewed from a theological perspective and that the interest is in its condition, which is the result of belief or unbelief.'（**給熱鐵烙死了的良心 'has ceased to operate at all' [Marshall 225].）

（**vi**）舊約底下的供物**不能使敬拜的人在良心上得以完全**（來九 9〔參《來》2.70〕），只有基督的血**能洗淨我們的良心**（來九 14）。See BAGD 786*b*-87*a*, BDAG 967*b*-68*b* (s.v.);《新希》317*a*（s.v.）。

33 Marshall 223 (with reference to Towner I 158).

34 Cf. Marshall 225: 'The conscience is useless if it has been defiled, so that it gives wrong judgements'.

35 兩次的**心思敗壞**在原文用了略為不同（但是同字根且意義相近）的動詞：διεφθαρμένων [from διαφθείρω] . . . τὸν νοῦν（提前六 5）；κατεφθαρμένοι [from καταφθείρω] τὸν νοῦν（提後三 8）。

36 （**1**）Marshall 211 認為，兩段所提示的情況似乎是，心思敗壞使人不能理解真理，或導致人反對真理（'its [νοῦς] corrupt condition prevents apprehension or leads to rejection of "the truth"）。（**2**）唐書禮則認為：提前六 5 提示，'the corrupted mind of the false teacher either stems from rejection of the truth or frustrates correct perception of it'（Towner III 397〔唐 564〕）；在提後三 8，保羅將對手描寫為 'people with malfunctioning minds, as revealed (and also probably caused) by their rejection of the gospel (= "the truth")'（565〔唐 819〕）。但見下面註 38。

37 Marshall 211.

38 Towner III 707-8（唐 1031；cf. Towner I 156: 'the force of the perfect tense (*memiantai*)

34 所屬正文」)，筆者認為合理的推論是這樣：背棄真理（甲）是因，心思和良知敗壞（乙）是果，而後者進一步強化前者，即是使不信更為堅固（甲'）。[39] 無論如何，保羅對假教師作出本節的指控，大抵是由於他們以為違反某些有關禮儀潔淨的規例會使人成為不潔，更因為他們想要將這種**人的規條**（14 節，新譯）加在**上帝的選民**（1 節）——就是**已信上帝**（三 8）和**救主耶穌基督**（二 13，三 6）的人——身上。[40]

---

is probably to indicate a state arising out of a past act or decision, which in all likelihood is alluded to at the end of v. 14: *apostrephomenōn tēn alētheian*'; Collins, 'Theology' 61: 'Denial of the truth leads to the corruption of mind, conscience, and action'）。但是作者稍後又這樣說(709〔唐 1032〕)：'In their defiled condition, the opponents typically not only fail to apprehend the truth but actively "reject" or resist the truth (1:14; 1 Tim 6:5; 2 Tim 3:8).' 這等於說，他們**背棄真理**是由於他們的心思和良心**也都污穢了**。不過，作者進一步的闡述也許可以解釋這種表面的衝突；見下註。

39 見唐 1033（Towner III 709）：「這段經文後面的假設是，基督徒行為始於接受使徒的信仰〔the apostolic faith〕（以不同的方式指稱〔referred to in various ways〕），心地理解、贊同、並將這些資料組織成為認知的倫理架構來過聖潔的生活〔The mind apprehends, endorses, and organizes these data into the cognitive-ethical framework for holy living〕；而天良則藉著作正確的道德決定來實踐倫理生活。藉濫用〔perverting = 扭曲〕或棄絕〔jettisoning〕傳統的福音來拒絕『真理』，會打斷導致敬虔生活的這個程序。取而代之的是另一程序：被不信欺哄的心地贊同錯誤的教義，使失常的天良將之塑造為劣質的倫理〔the mind, deluded in unbelief, approves false doctrines that the equally dysfunctional conscience shapes into inferior ethics〕。在保羅的架構中，不信(或不全然脫離異教的道路〔pagan ways = 異教徒的生活方式〕)或拒絕福音似乎是根本的錯誤。但當保羅察覺並面對〔observes and engages〕已成為敵對思想體系和生活方式的不信時，這程序已成為自我延續〔self-perpetuating〕了：不信混淆了理性的認知和判斷，這又造成另一些行為和思想模式，來堅固不信〔unbelief confuses rational perception and judgment, which produces patterns of behavior and thought that reinforce unbelief〕。」上註「作者……又這樣說……」那句話是否可以理解為 'reinforce[d] unbelief'（強化了的不信）的表現呢？

40 See again Sumney, *Opponents* 298: 'we are left with only the knowledge that the opponents are concerned about purity laws that are based on the Mosaic Code. It is possible that food laws were among their concerns. . . . But purity laws encompass a much broader spectrum of life than food prohibitions and sex regulations [cf. 1 Tim. 4:3]. Verse 15 gives us no basis to narrow the concerns of these teachers to these or any other matters or to explicitly include them among their concerns. This verse suggests only that they regard matters about purity as important, without specifying any particular areas on which they concentrate their attention.'（參一 14 註釋註 27 之〔4〕= 上面 194-95。）Cf. Marshall 207-8: 'it is . . . likely that some kind of Jewish teaching is being foisted on Gentile believers here.' 由此看來，假教師不大可能是（如巴刻的理解）「不信主的

末句（15c 節）在原文以強烈的反語詞開始，[41] 這詞很難翻譯為「因為」，如在《現代中文譯本修訂版》：**對那些污穢和不信的人來說，沒有一件東西是潔淨的，因為他們的心地和良心都污穢不堪**，[42] 儘管就事實而論，這種翻譯所表達的意思可能是保羅思想的一部分。[43] 另一方面，在《呂振中譯本》的翻譯裏——**在染污的和不信的人、甚麼都不潔淨，反而連他們的心思和良知也都染污了**（呂譯）——亦難看出在**反而**之前和之後的兩個思想是如何彼此對立的。因此，《新國際譯本》的「事實上」可能是取佳選擇，[44] 所得出的整個意思就是：「對那些受了污染和不信[45] 的人來說，沒有一樣是潔淨的；事實上，他們的[46] 心思和良心都是受了污染的」。[47] 如此，第 15c 節其實是對那些

放縱者」：巴刻認為動詞 μιαίνω 在這裏 'is used . . . of the moral defilement of mind, conscience . . . which results from becoming a faithless libertine'（J. I. Packer, *DNTT* 1.448）。

41 ἀλλά = 'but' (KJV, NKJV, NAU).

42 參新普：因為他們的心思和良知都敗壞了；NLT: 'because their minds and consciences are corrupted'.

43 See Fairbairn 269: 'In saying this, he no doubt indicates the reason why nothing external is pure to them: but he does not give it formally as a reason . . .'（下接註 48）。See also Marshall 201: 'ἀλλά is not "but even", but "but nothing is clean because . . ."'.

44 NIV, TNIV, NIV2011: 'In fact'（also Banker 44, 54*a*）; Towner III 708: 'In fact [what I mean is]' =「實際上〔我的意思是〕」（唐 1032；方括號和六角括號都是原來的）。NJB 以破折號取代 ἀλλά（'. . . nothing can be pure－the corruption is both in their minds and in their consciences'），具有類似的果效。NRSV/RSV 也不把 ἀλλά 譯出，而是將 15c 節視為獨立句子／子句：'. . . nothing is pure. Their very minds . . . / nothing is pure; their very minds . . .'.

45 （**1**）R. Bultmann（*TDNT* 6.215 with n.313）認為 ἄπιστος 的意思是 'non-Christian'. Scott 161 則認為幾乎可以肯定，原文形容詞在本節必須理解為廣義的 'irreligious' 之意，即是 'devoid of any feeling for God.'（**2**）形容詞 **ἄπιστος** 在保羅書信另外出現 15 次（林前六 6，七 12、13、14a、14b、15，十 27，十四 22a、22b、23、24；林後四 4，六 14、15；提前五 8），新約全部 23 次；除了一次（徒二十六 8：不可信），其餘皆為「不信」之意。See BDAG 103*b*-4*a* (s.v.);《新希》36*a*（s.v.）。

46 αὐτῶν（他們的）放在 ὁ νοῦς καὶ ἡ συνείδησις（心思和良心）之前，（**1**）Knight II 303 及 Marshall 210 n.177 皆認為這表示此字受到強調。（**2**）Levinsohn（*Discourse Features* 64）這樣解釋：'pronominal genitives may sometimes be preposed when the referent of the pronoun is *thematically salient* (i.e., the center of attention).'（**3**）MHT 3.190 則認為，αὐτῶν 放在兩個名詞之前只是為免重複（'to save repetition'），並無強調之意。此解釋似最可取。

47 兩次的「受了污染」原文皆為完成時態（依次為分詞 μεμιαμμένοις 和動詞

污穢不信的人進一步的形容。[48] 而這（內在的污染）就是他們的問題的根源（參：可七 14～23）：他們內在的道德污穢使他們所觸摸之物和所作之事都受到污染。[49]

μεμίανται），描述 'a state of being, / a state of corruption resulting from past actions or/and decisions'（Towner III 707/708〔唐 1031/1032〕）。A. Sands（*EDNT* 2.479*b* [s.v. νοῦς, 4]）則從 15c 節得出這樣的意思來：'the *understanding* of the unbeliever is characterized as without conscience.' 其中的邏輯是否這樣：不信之人的良心是染污了（因而失效）的，因此他（同樣是染污了）的心思是「沒有良心的」？

48 See Fairbairn 269:（接上面註 43）'. . . he rather advances it as an additional disclosure of their defilement'; Banker 54*b*: '1:15c is probably best analyzed relationally as amplification'; Knight II 303: 'a further enlargement of the contrast already begun with δέ'. Classen（'Titus' 436, 'Epistle to Titus' 55）則認為 15c 節開首的 ἀλλὰ μεμίανται 修正了 15b 節末尾的 οὐδὲν καθαρόν: 'No one can fail to be impressed . . . by the *correctio* οὐδὲν καθαρόν, ἀλλὰ μεμίανται'.

49 Cf. Towner III 708（唐 1032）。參註 20 之（1），註 25 及所屬正文（上面 200，201）。

一　**16a**　他們宣稱認識上帝，[1]

16b　　　卻在行為上否認他；

16c　他們是可憎惡的，是悖逆的，不配做任何好事。[2]

認識上帝是猶太人特別誇耀的事情；[3] 而在舊約及猶太人眼中，不認識上帝（加四 8；帖前四 5；帖後一 8）是外邦人的特色：他們不認識獨一真神，即以色列的上帝。[4] 在聖經裏，認識上帝意即宣認上帝是真神，並且按照祂的命令來生活，即是過正義的生活（參：耶二十二 15～16：你〔約雅敬〕的父親……施行公平和公義……認識我不是在此嗎？）。[5] 宣稱（同現修）原文在這裏的意思不是宣認（如在羅十 9、10；提前六 12〔現修〕），[6] 而是聲稱（新譯、新普）[7] 或自稱

1　MHT 3.146 以 θεὸν ὁμολογοῦσιν εἰδέναι 為 'Subject of infin. not expressed' 的例子；作者提到 'the class. rule that the subject of a dependent infin. is not expressed again if it is the same as the subject of the independent verb.' 但在這裏 'the subject of the independent verb [ὁμολογοῦσιν]' 也沒有表達出來啊！

2　βδελυκτοὶ (ὄντες) καὶ ἀπειθεῖς καὶ (πρὸς πᾶν ἔργον ἀγαθὸν) ἀδόκιμοι 這三個形容詞由兩個 καί 字串連起來。Genade 37 稱之為 'polysyndetic *emphatic clustering*' 的修辭技巧（see also 128）；參二 12 註釋註 37 之（1），二 15 註釋註 2 之（1）（下面 297，341）。

3　Guthrie I 190, Guthrie II 202（古特立 204）：'Judaistic pride in monotheism is here in mind.' 馮譯作口稱認得上帝；未知認得是甚麼意思。羅二 17～18 描述了猶太人的自我意識中的六點特色，其中的三點是：（**i**）自稱為猶太人，即是聲稱自己是獨一真神的宣認者；（**ii**）以上帝誇口，所提示的意思是：猶太人（自認為）真的認識上帝，真的敬拜那揀選以色列的神；（**iii**）已經受法律的薰陶，知道上帝的旨意（18 節，現修）（依次參《羅》1.389，390-91，391）。

4　參《加》967-68 連註 2；《帖前》306-7；《帖後》91。

5　Montague 225-26.

6　O. Michel（*TDNT* 5.210）則認為，在本節（如在羅十 9、10）'ὁμολογεῖν = "to make solemn statements of faith," "to confess something in faith"（209）。

7　See also KJV, NKJV, RSV, NRSV, NAU, ESV, *Paraphrase* 291: 'profess'; NIV, TNIV, NIV2011, NJB, NLT, BDAG 708*b* (s.v. ὁμολογέω, 4 a): 'claim'; O. Hofius, *EDNT* 2.514*b* (s.v. 3 a): 'assert'.（**1**）Cf. Johnson II 227: 'they claim special knowledge of God'; Jeon II 38: 'they claim to have a deeply personal relationship with God'.（**2**）Hiebert 434 則認為「聲稱」可指猶太人自誇為認識上帝，或諾斯底主義者自稱對上帝有祕傳的（'esoteric'）知識，很可能兩者兼備；這是由於作者將那些奉割禮的人（一 10）理解為 'gnosticizing Judaists'（432）。Cf. Barrett 133: 'it seems to be a Jewish kind of gnosticism with which we are dealing.' 亦參一 10 註釋註 36 之（1），一 14 註釋

（思高）。[8] **自稱為認識上帝**（呂譯）的含義就是，他們也聲稱能夠引導人歸向上帝。[9] **聲稱認識**（新譯、新普）與**在行為上否認**構成反義平行，[10] 兩者的賓詞都是**上帝**。[11] 有認為**在行為上否認他**的意思是，他們以其禁慾行為否認上帝的創造之美善。[12] 較可能的意思是，這裏

註 10 之（3）（5）（6），一 15 註釋註 3 之（1）＝ 上面 164，189-90，197。

8　**（1）**動詞 **ὁμολογέω** 在保羅書信出現僅此四次，在新約另外 22 次。See BDAG 708*a*-9*a* (s.v.);《新希》236*a*（s.v.）。**（2）**同字根的名詞 ὁμολογία 在新約出現六次，保羅書信和希伯來書各半：林後九 13（宣認……福音〔現修〕）；提前六 12（「宣認了那美好的宣認」：ὡμολόγησας τὴν καλὴν ὁμολογίαν）、13（美好的宣認〔現修〕）；來三 1（我們所宣認為使者、為大祭司的耶穌），四 14（我們應該持守我們所宣認的信仰〔現修；信仰是正確的補充〕），十 23（讓我們堅定不移地持守我們所宣認的盼望〔現修〕）。

9　Fee 182. Similarly, Marshall 44: 'it may reflect a claim that the only, or the true, way to know God was through acceptance of the teaching and practices of the opponents.' 參：羅二 19～20：（猶太人）深信自己是給盲人領路的，是在黑暗中人的光，是無知的人的師傅，是小孩子的老師。這四重描述「全都指向以色列作為外邦人的教師和嚮導所扮演的角色」（《羅》1394）。

10　16a 節:　**θεὸν** ὁμολογοῦσιν [A]　　εἰδέναι [B],
16b 節:　　　　τοῖς δὲ ἔργοις [A']　ἀρνοῦνται [B'].
（1）動詞 **ἀρνέομαι** 在保羅書信另外出現六次，以人為賓詞（如在本節）和以物為賓詞的各半：**（i）**我們若不認〔基督〕，他也必不認我們（提後二 12b）；他不能否認自己（二 13）；**（ii）**信徒若不照顧親屬，尤其是自己家裏的人，就是背棄信仰（提前五 8）；一些人有敬虔的外貌，卻背棄了敬虔的實質（提後三 5）；上帝的恩典教導信徒，要棄絕不敬虔的行為和屬世的私慾（多二 12，現修）。**（2）**此動詞在新約另外出現 26 次：12 次以人為賓詞（太十 33a、33b；路九 23，十二 9；約十三 38；徒三 13、14，七 35；彼後二 1；約壹二 22b、23；猶 4 節），兩次以物為賓詞（啟二 13，三 8），另 12 次以一項陳述為賓詞（太二十六 70、72 ‖ 可十四 68、70 ‖ 路二十二 57 ‖ 約十八 25、27；路八 45；約一 20；徒四 16；來十一 24；約壹二 22a）。

11　這是「省略（ellipsis）」的例子：'The verb *arnountai*, "deny," lacks a direct object; "God" (*theon*) must be supplied'（Collins 336 n.29; cf. Knight II 303; Towner III 710 n.147〔唐 1035 註 78 之延續〕）。**（1）**Barclay 244 認為他們在行為上所否認的是 'their profession [that they know God]'. Similarly, Ngewa 351. **（2）**Mounce 403 則認為，否認的賓詞是基督，因為這動詞在別處是指否認基督；參：提後二 12；太十 33a ‖ 路十二 9；約十三 38；徒三 13～14；彼後二 1；約壹二 22b、23；猶 4 節。但見上註之（2）其他的用法：以物或以一項陳述為賓詞。

12　Kelly 238. See also Young 50: 'their actions [=] presumably their hindering of marriage and their abstention from foods as indicated in 1 Tim. 4.3ff.'; Mounce 403: 'the works that prove the opponents do not know God are their insistence on asceticism and possibly their lifestyle in general'; Marshall 211-12: 'These people deny God by rejecting his good creation (Dibelius-Conzelmann, 104), i.e. by asceticism (Knight, 303).'（馬歇爾稍後又說，'their corrupt behaviour is a tacit denial of God' [212]. 這似乎表示，他把他們的禁慾行為等同為腐敗的行為。）張 336 同樣認為，行事（新

假定正義的行為是認識上帝的證據，[13] 但是他們的行為（見 10～12 節的描繪，及 16b 節）並不是認識上帝的人應有的表現，他們「在道德行為上不符〔上帝〕的要求」。[14]

下一句再次（參 15c 節）描寫假教師本身的狀況（16c 節）。**（1）可憎惡的／可憎的／可恶的**（同思高、新和／呂譯、新譯、新普／現修）[15] 原文形容詞在箴言十七章 15 節用來指被上帝**憎惡**的兩種人：

和）「是指其強烈要求別人要守潔淨禁戒之誡命的言行……他們如此堅持潔淨之誡命，反而證明了他們是否定了神在基督稣裏的應許，便是凡物只要感謝着接受，都是好的，都成了聖潔（提前四 4～5）。」但見一 15 註釋註 40 = 上面 204。

13 Marshall 211: 'It is assumed that "knowing God" is evidenced by righteous behaviour.'

14 彭編 99*a*。See also Towner III 710（唐 1034-35）：'their "deeds" . . . are a rejection of God. . . . there is no reason to limit the scope of the reference just to asceticism'; Jeon II 21: '[they] invalidate their confession of faith by their evil deeds'; Mounce lxxvii: 'their deeds (praxis) prove they do not [know God]'. Oden 9 甚至斷言，假教師否定上帝的方法是 'by their licentious actions'.（**1**）Banker 54*b*-55*a* 不必要地把 16b 節分拆為兩個意思：我們知道他們並不認識上帝，因他們的行為邪惡。班約翰稍後的陳述較為可取：'They deny God by their actions [see also 60] . . . they show that they do not know God by the bad things they do'（56*b*）。（**2**）Ward 247-48 認為，保羅在本節已離開了 13 節那些仍有機會把他們挽回的假教師，轉到那些行為與言語相左的「極端分子（extremists）」。（**3**）卡羅拔則認為（**i**）多一 16（和提前三 5）那些對手言行不一，只說不做（'the opponents do not practice what they preach; they are all words, but no action'），並認為（**ii**）'This objection is also paralleled in the polemic against the sophists' *（Karris, 'Polemic' 552-53）。（*參一 11 註釋註 26 之〔2〕= 上面 170。）可是文理提示，'what they preach' 是**欺哄人的空話**（10 節），是**不該教導的事**（11 節），是**無稽的傳說和背棄真理之人的命令**（14 節）。因此，卡羅拔所認為的第一點是有疑問的，因而其第二點亦同樣成疑。

15 βδελυκτός = 'pert. to a pers. or thing that stirs up feelings of repugnance, *abhorrent, detestable*' (BDAG 172*a* [s.v.]), 'detested, detestable, abominable, abhorrent' (LN §25.188); 'horrid, abominable' (H. Balz, *EDNT* 1.210*a* [s.v.]);「屬於那該當被厭惡或視為可憎惡的人或事」(《新希》58*b* [s.v.])。參以下英譯：'abominable' (KJV, NKJV; DC 135*b*; Johnson II 225, 226), 'detestable' (RSV, NRSV, NAU, NIV, TNIV, NIV2011, ESV, NLT, *Paraphrase* 291; Banker 45*a*; Fiore II 204; Ward 228), 'repugnant' (Banker 44, 55*a*).(**1**)NJB 則把這字(βδελυκτοί)緊連於隨後一字(ἀπειθεῖς)而得出 'outrageously rebellious' 這翻譯，即是將這字理解為「駭人的、無恥的、無法接受的」之意。但見註 24 之（1）= 下面 211。(**2**) Stegemann（'Prejudices' 284）將這字的意思減弱為 'abnormal, and thus fall[ing] out of the basic categories of order in human society.'(**3**)Ngewa 352 於解釋此字時說，'Proverbs 6:16-19 lists seven things that are detestable to the Lord'. 不過，LXX 該段完全沒有使用本節的形容詞 βδελυκτός 或同字根的名詞（'The noun form of this adjective'）βδέλυγμα 或 βδελυγμός. 事實上，LXX 箴六 16（有別於 MT 及中英譯本）是這樣說的：ὅτι χαίρει πᾶσιν οἷς μισεῖ ὁ κύριος συντρίβεται δὲ δι' ἀκαθαρσίαν ψυχῆς = 'For

定惡人為義的和**定義人為有罪的**；[16] 同字根的名詞在七十士譯本常用來指偶像和不潔的可憎之物。[17] 如此，這裏將舊約用來指道德上及禮儀上的不潔的詞彙，諷刺地用於這些力圖維護他們禮儀上的潔淨的假教師身上。[18] 在本節，上文在談論的是這些人與上帝的關係（16a～b節），因此**可憎惡的**也是指「對上帝來說」他們是可憎惡的；[19] 同理，**（2）悖逆的**是指他們對上帝悖逆。[20] **悖逆的**（同呂譯、思高、新和、新譯；新普同）[21] 原文的意思是「不服從」；[22] 他們服從**人的命令**（14

---

he rejoices in all things which God hates, and he is ruined by reason of impurity of soul'（LXE）。**（4）**同字根的動詞 βδελύσσω 在 LXX 詩十三 1（中英譯本十四 1）指心裏說**沒有上帝**的愚頑人 'have corrupted *themselves*, and become abominable (ἐβδελύχθησαν) in their devices'（LXE）。Towner IV 913*a* 認為，該節 'expresses the same sentiment of denying the existence of God by acts of abominable behavior [as Tit 1:16]'. 筆者倒認為較自然的理解是，心裏說**沒有上帝**是根，敗壞和變成可憎是果。

16 這字在希臘文聖經僅再出現一次，用於禱文中祈求上帝「眷顧那些被人……憎惡的（τοὺς . . . βδελυκτούς）」（次經《馬加比二書》1.27，思高〔《瑪加伯下》〕）。**（1）**同字根的名詞 βδέλυγμα 在新約出現六次，其中兩次指**施行毀滅的褻瀆者**（太二十四 15 ‖ 可十三 14），原文直譯「帶來荒廢的厭惡性事物」（《新希》58*b* [s.v. II]）；另四次指**可憎惡的**東西（路十六 15）、**可憎之物**（啟十七 4、5）和**可憎……之事**（啟二十一 27）。See BDAG 172*a* (s.v.);《新希》58*b*（s.v.）。

17 βδέλυγμα, 參（例如）：（偶像）申七 25、26；（不潔之物）利十一 10、11、12、13、20、23、41、42。

18 See Marshall 212-13.

19 Calvin 367 認為，'he [Paul] seems to be alluding to the pretended sanctity to which they gave their whole attention.' Stott 183 則解釋為，他們的信條使上帝的子民生厭（'their tenets provoke a certain disgust in the people of God'）。

20 Arichea－Hatton 280; Banker 55*b*; O. Becker, *DNTT* 1.593: 'the context suggests disobedience to God'. **（1）** Griffin 293 則認為，'They were "disobedient" both to the truth of the gospel and to the apostolic authority'. Young 49 解釋為「不忠」於他們先前所掌握的真理：'having been unfaithful to the truth they once grasped'. **（2）**張 336 聲稱，「以上兩種形容，可能本來是假教師用來形容那些不聽從他們教導的人，即不守各種禁忌之人」。筆者認為，此說不大可能，尤其因為**可憎惡的**是那麼罕見的字（見上面註 16）。

21 參現修：**是叛徒**；NJB: 'outrageously rebellious'（見上面註 15 之〔1〕）。

22 ἀπειθής = 'disobedient' (BDAG 99*b* [s.v.]; KJV, NKJV, RSV, NRSV, NAU, NIV, TNIV, NIV2011, ESV, NLT, *Paraphrase* 291);「繼續不服從的」（《新希》34*b* [s.v.]）。Witherington 119 譯作 'intractable'（難駕馭的、難對付的）。**（1）**這形容詞（ἀπειθής）在新約再出現五次，其中三次也是在惡行目錄中（多三 3；提後三 2；羅一 30；另見路一 17；徒二十六 19）；另在 LXX 出現七次（民二十 10；申二十一 18〔翻譯了希伯來文的**頑梗**〕；賽三十 9；耶五 23〔**忤逆**〕；亞七 12〔翻譯了希伯來文的堅

節），對上帝本身卻「不服從」。[23] 這字和本段開首的不受約束（10 節）前後呼應。[24]

（3）不配做任何好事另有翻譯為在各樣善事上是可廢棄的（新和）。但原文形容詞本身的意思並不是可廢棄的，[25] 而是經不起考驗（如在林後十三 5、6、7；提後三 8），[26] 由此而得「不合格」、[27]「被取消資格」（林後九 27）、[28]「卑劣」、「無用」等意

硬〕；次經《便西拉智訓》16.6 / 47.21: 'a disobedient nation' [RSV, NRSV] / 'a rebel kingdom' [NRSV, NJB]）。（2）**ἀπειθής** 是複合形容詞（from πείθω + α-privative; [Vine 1.319]）。Genade 38 聲稱，ἀπειθής 是比 'ἀπίστος'（*sic*, ἄπιστος〔15b 節的不信〕）更強的字：'they are beyond persuasion'（see also Stegemann, 'Prejudices' 278: 'cannot be persuaded'; Vine 1.319: 'unwilling to be persuaded . . . disobedient'）。這樣解釋 ἀπειθής 可視為「『詞源研究』在釋經上的誤用」的（另）一個例子，因為聖經語言應該從語意而不是從詞源的角度來解釋（見黃錫木：〈語言學〉90-91〔引句出自 90〕；參《羅》4.705 註 2；參較《羅》1.488 註 6 及所屬正文）。（3）提多書有三個「惡行目錄」（catalogue of vices or vice lists），其中兩段是描寫敵對者（一 10～16，三 9～11），另一段則描繪信徒歸主之前的景況（三 3）。所牽涉的詞彙，詳見 Van Neste 265-67.

23 Fee 182. Zehr 258 則解釋為 'they do not yield to the gospel as taught by the apostles'; 參一 10 註釋註 7 之（ii）= 上面 158。

24 （1）Quinn 26, 97, 104, 114 將 βδελυκτοί 和 ἀπειθεῖς 連起來而得 'disobedient abominations' 這翻譯；參註 15 之（1）= 上面 209。但是，將二字分開更能收辭令之效，就如 Quinn 115 自己所指出的：'The crescendo of repudiation reaches its peak in the triple characterization of the opposition as abominable, contumacious, incompetent (*bdelyktoi, apeitheis, adokimoi*)'; 'The indictment reaches its climax in the expansive third member'.（2）P. Bläser（*EDNT* 1.119*a* [s.v. ἀπειθέω, 3]）認為 '*disobedient* is explicated by "unfit for any good deed."' 但不配做任何好事如何解釋是悖逆的呢？反而他們是悖逆的可以解釋為甚麼他們不配做任何好事。

25 See also KJV: 'reprobate'. 也不是 NJB 的 'quite untrustworthy'.

26 ἀδόκιμος 是複合形容詞（δόκιμος + α-privative [Vine 3.283]）；而其反義詞 δόκιμος 的意思之一就是經得起考驗（林前十一 19；林後十三 7；提後二 15）；亦參羅十六 10，雅一 12：經過考驗。Cf. H. Haarbeck, *DNTT* 3.808: 'meaning that which has not stood the test, that which has been shown to be a sham, and has therefore been rejected'.

27 See RSV / NRSV, ESV: 'unfit for any good deed/work'; NIV, TNIV, NIV2011: 'unfit for doing anything good'. B. Reicke 將 πρός 理解為表達目的（*TDNT* 6.724: 'Final : a. of the aim of a given action "with a view to"'）；較自然的解釋是：'After adjectives [as here and 3:1] and participles *for*'（BDAG 874*b* [s.v. πρός, 3 c β]）。

28 See NKJV: 'disqualified for every good work'; *Paraphrase* 291: '[they] have disqualified themselves for any good work.' 這是由於他們 'fail to stand the test of Christian character'（Zehr 258）。按這種翻譯，16c 節的英譯便構成頭韻：'being detestable, disobedient, and disqualified for any good action'（Kelly 233, see also 238; Zehr 258）；'they are detestable and disobedient, disqualified for any good work'（REB;

思。[29] 在本節，最後這個意思最可取：他們在各樣的善事上，是毫無用處的（新譯），[30] 實質意義等於說，他們做不出甚麼好事來／甚麼好事也做不出來（現修／新普）！好事是有價值的事。[31] 好事以各種形式出現，包括幫助有迫切需要的人（三 14），養育兒女，收留外人，謙卑地服侍別的信徒（提前五 10），以及分享一己的財富（提前六 18）。[32] 預備行各樣善事是人歸信基督之後應有的表現（三 1）。由此

---

cf. Wall 343）。

29 BDAG 21*b* (s.v. ἀδόκιμος): '"not standing the test", then ***unqualified, worthless, base*** of pers'; G. Schneider, *EDNT* 1.33*b* (s.v.): 'not standing the test, useless'; Leaney 119: 'useless (tested and found unfit)'.（**1**）'Paul describes the false teachers as ἀδόκιμος (abominable or detestable)'（Genade 37）這話含有兩點錯誤：ἀδόκιμος（單數）應為 ἀδόκιμοι（複數，與複數的 'teachers' 相符）；作者誤把 βδελυκτός 的意思歸給 ἀδόκιμος. 簡內德稍後對這字解釋如下（38）：'The last word in the trilogy, ἀδόκιμος, means unapproved, unworthy, spurious, or worthless.' 他似乎沒有意識到早前的錯誤。（**2**）除了正文提到的五次和本節，這字（**ἀδόκιμος**）在新約僅再出現兩次，分別指敗壞的心（羅一 28〔現修、新譯〕，參《羅》1.317-18）和被廢棄的田地（來六 8，參《來》1.372-73）。參《新希》7*b*（s.v.）。它在 LXX 只出現兩次，分別形容「有渣滓」的銀子（箴二十五 4）和銀子變成「無用的」（賽一 22）。

30 參呂譯／思高：在各樣善行上都不中用／在一切善事上是無用的；NAU / NLT: 'worthless for any good deed / doing anything good'.（**1**）C. Brown（*DNTT* 3.197）認為，πᾶς 的意思是 'not all, in an absolute and inclusive sense, but all kinds of'. 若是這樣，呂譯、新譯的各樣才是正確的翻譯。（**2**）在 πρὸς πᾶν ἔργον ἀγαθὸν 這介詞片語內，πρός 的意思是 'with reference to'（Marshall 213 n.190），即是「關於、有關」（關於善事，他們毫無用處），英譯多作 'for'（NKJV, RSV, NRSV, NAU, NIV, TNIV, NIV2011, NJB, ESV, NLT）。See also BDAG 874*b* (s.v. 3 c β): 'After adjectives and participles *for*'.（**3**）這介詞片語亦見於三 1（見下段開首）及提後三 17：上帝默示的聖經有各種功用，其目的是要叫屬上帝的人得以完全，預備行各樣的善事。參林後九 8 的能多做各樣善事（εἰς πᾶν ἔργον ἀγαθόν）。

31 Marshall 213: 'what is approved and commended by God as being morally good and acceptable'; BADG 3*a*（s.v., 1 b β）：有內在價值（尤其是道德價值）的事；參《新希》1*b*（s.v. I.1）：「具有最基本正面的素質。」（**1**）BDAG 4*a*（s.v. ἀγαθός, 2 a β）則認為是指 'things characterized esp. in terms of social significance and worth'. But see Marshall 229: 'here [in the PE] and elsewhere the stress is more on the fact that certain things are good because they are ordained or approved by God'.（**2**）Collins 336 稱 πᾶν ἔργον ἀγαθόν（'every good work'）為「正確行為的密碼（a cipher for correct behavior）」（參三 1，提前五 10，提後二 21，三 17〔πᾶν ἔργον ἀγαθόν〕；提前二 10〔ἔργα ἀγαθά〕）。但不見得這片語在寇雷蒙所引各節皆指正確的行為。參較二 7～8a 註釋註 8（Collins 344,下面 259）。

32 Marshall 229. Young 31 則認為，'probably they [good works] also embrace all the qualities and moral standards approved in these letters.' Cf. Banker 56*b*: 好事不僅指為

看來，這些假教師或是回到了他們從前的景況，或是從來沒有歸信基督。[33] 他們是很好的反面教材，讓人看見真正的宗教的三點特色：其來源是上帝，不是**背棄真理之人**（14 節）；其本質是屬靈的，不是著重外表的禮儀（15 節）；其效果是結出道德的果子，不是沒有任何的好行為（16 節）。[34]

好事在三章 1 節再次出現：提多**要提醒眾人……預備行各樣善事**。複數的「善行」在第二、三兩章出現四次（二 7、14，三 8、14）。[35] 這樣看來，本節的**各樣善事**（新和）是作者將本段（一 10～

了別人而作的事，亦包括籠統的好行為。

33 Marshall 213. Cf. Towner III 711（唐 1036）：'their "faith" produces no legitimate fruit; they are outside the faith.'

34 Stott 183: 'True religion is divine in its origin, spiritual in its essence and moral in its effect.'

35 原文為 **(甲)** καλὰ ἔργα（good works; 另見〔單數 καλὸν ἔργον〕提前三 1；〔複數 ἔργα καλά〕提前五 10a、25，六 18）。一 16 和三 1 的**好事**則為 **(乙)** ἔργον ἀγαθόν（另見羅二 7；林後九 8；腓一 6；西一 10；提前五 10b；提後二 21，三 17；參帖後二 17；〔複數 ἔργα ἀγαθά〕弗二 10；提前二 10；ἀγαθὸν ἔργον 見羅十三 3a）。很難看出（甲）（乙）兩種詞語在意思上有甚麼分別（so, correctly, Clark, 'structure' 111）；參《羅》1.351-52 註 4；《加》1359-60 註 5；Murphy-O'Connor, '2 Timothy' 414: '1 Tim 5:10 [ἐν ἔργοις καλοῖς . . . ἐν παντὶ ἔργῳ ἀγαθῷ] makes it impossible to postulate any substantive difference between the two expressions'; Marshall 227: 'Paul uses καλός in the same sense as ἀγαθός.' 但見二 7～8a 註 6 之（1）末尾（下面 259 ）。

(1) 名詞 **ἔργον** 在本書出現八次（本節兩次，正文提及的五次，另見三 5），在提前後十二次，保羅書信另 48 次（即保羅書信共 68 次）；參《帖前》63-64 註 27。常見的或較特別的組合包括 **(i)** 律法的<u>行為</u>（〔複數〕羅三 20、28；加二 16〔三次〕，三 2、5、10；參〔單數〕羅二 15〔現修：法律的<u>要求</u>〕）；**(ii)** 黑暗的<u>行為</u>／黑暗之……<u>行為</u>（羅十三 12〔思高、新普〕／弗五 11〔呂譯〕）；肉體之<u>行為</u>（加五 19，呂譯）；**(iii)** 上帝的<u>工作</u>（羅十四 20）；主〔的〕<u>工</u>〔作〕／主的<u>工作</u>（林前十五 58／十六 10）；基督的<u>工作</u>（腓二 30）；**(iv)** 以言語，以<u>行動</u>（羅十五 18，思高）；在言語上……在<u>行事</u>上（林後十 11，思高）；在言語上或在<u>行為</u>上（西三 17，思高）；在……善<u>行</u>善言上（帖後二 17）；**(v)** 邪惡的<u>行為</u>（西一 21〔呂譯、思高、現修〕）；兇惡／邪惡的<u>事</u>（提後四 18，思高／新譯）。新約另外 101 次（全部 169 次）。詳見 BDAG 390*a*-91*b* (s.v.);《新希》132*a*-32*b*（s.v.）。

(2) 形容詞 **ἀγαθός** 在保羅書信一共出現 47 次，常見的組合是 ἔργον ἀγαθόν（見本註首段之〔乙〕）和單數的 τὸ ἀγαθόν（羅二 10，五 7，七 13a、b，十二 9、21，十三 3c、4，十四 16，十五 2，十六 19；加六 10；弗四 28；帖前五 15；門 14 節）及複數的 τὰ ἀγαθά（羅三 8，十 15）；參《帖前》242-43。新約另外 55 次（全部 102 次）。詳見 BDAG 3*a*-4*a* (s.v.);《新希》1*b*-2*a*（s.v.）。

16）和下文多段（二 1～10，二 11～14，三 1～8，三 12～14）串連起來的一個「鈎狀綸詞」，[36] 善事或「善工」是貫徹全書的一個主要關注。[37] 不過，保羅此刻的要點是，不能期望這種善事或「善工」會出自那些假教師和他們的跟隨者：[38] 他們根本做不出甚麼好事來（當代）！

36 此詞參一 9 註釋註 49 及所屬正文（上面 149），二 9～10 註釋註 48 及所屬正文（下面 278-79）。Lock 137 說：'The whole of 2[1-13] is a contrast to this phrase [πρὸς πᾶν ἔργον ἀγ. ἀδόκιμοι].'

37 Fee 12: 'The dominant theme in Titus . . . is *good works* . . . that is, exemplary Christian behaviour and that *for the sake of outsiders* (2:5, 7, 8, 10, 11 [*sic*]; 3:1, 8)'; 215: 'This [doing what is good] is the recurring theme of the entire letter'. See also Stott 207.

38 Genade 38.（**1**）Hendriksen 357 則認為他們指 14 節那些背棄真理之人，即是不信主的猶太人，他們影響著克里特的假教師：'[Paul here refers] to *the Jews* (particularly, the Pharisaic leaders who, though outsiders, are exerting a sinister influence upon the false leaders within the churches of Crete)'. 參一 14 註釋註 11（上面 190）。（**2**）但是 Knight II 304 認為，'the error spoken of here is not what was typical of Jews. These false teachers . . . do not insist on circumcision and OT ceremonial rites. . . . Being "of the circumcision" they do have some views that come from the Jewish community ("myths and endless genealogies"), but their views go beyond Judaism. It is unnecessary, therefore, to say Paul has shifted from the false teachers within the Christian community to those outside.'

肆 與福音相符的生活：之一（二 1～15）

4.1 健全的行為（二 1～10）

1 至於你，你所講的總要合乎那健全的教導。
2 勸老年人要有節制、端正、克己，在信心、愛心、耐心上都要健全。
3 又要勸年長的婦女在操守上恭正，不說讒言，不作酒的奴隸，用善
道教導人，
4a 好指教年輕的婦女
4b 愛丈夫，愛兒女，
5a 克己，貞潔，理家，善良，順服自己的丈夫，
5b 免得上帝的道被毀謗。
6 同樣，要勸年輕人凡事克己。
7a 你要顯出自己是好行為的榜樣，
7b 在教導上要正直、莊重，
8a 言語健全，無可指責，
8b 使那反對的人，……自覺羞愧。
8c 因說不出我們有甚麼不好而
9 要勸僕人順服自己的主人，凡事討他的喜悅，不可頂撞他，
10a 不可私竊財物；
10b 要凡事顯出完美的忠誠，
10c 好事事都能榮耀我們救主上帝的教導。

一章 5 節已經讓我們看見，提多在克里特的任務至少包括兩方

面：明確地，他要按照保羅的指示**在各城設立長老**；較籠統地，他要改正教會的一些缺陷。[1] 本段<u>開始提出</u>保羅要提多給予克里特教會的教導。[2] 由此看來，教會的「缺陷」跟教會的教導有關；似乎克里特的信徒當中有一種趨勢，就是容忍那些傳講不是**健全的教導**（二 1）的假教師，[3] 必須有人用純正的教義改正他們，而保羅自己因某些原因必須離開克里特，故此這改正缺陷的任務就交給了提多。

這一段的主要關注是信徒（在家庭和教會中）的倫理行為，[4] 因而繼續了一章 5 至 16 節的倫理關注。[5] 再一次，詞彙上的關聯提示，保羅刻意拿克里特的敵對者作對比：提多要**顯出自己是<u>好行為</u>的榜樣**（7 節），不像他們**不配做任何<u>好事</u>**（一 16c）；描寫他們的第一個形容詞是**不受約束**（一 10a），但年輕的婦女要**順服**自己的丈夫（二 5a），僕人也要**順服**自己的主人（二 9）；[6] 一章 9 節初次提到敵對者

---

1 參一 5 註釋第二段之（**甲**）= 上面 91-93。

2 Stegemann（'Prejudices' 282）的看法頗為奇怪：他認為本段的教導是 'instructions for relations <u>between</u> the Christian communities (Tit. 2:1ff.)'.

3 See Genade 43: 'the tendency . . . to tolerate unhealthy teachers.'

4 See Van Neste, 'Message' 24*a*: 'Paul explains what Christian behavior looks like . . . within the family and church (2:1-10).'（**1**）鄧雅各指出，'no word of counsel is given to the primary male member of the household: the husband, father and master (cf. Col 3:19, 21; 4:1).' 他認為其含意可能是，在上帝的家庭（教會）裏，這角色是提多的（Dunn 869*a*）。可是，鄧雅各看出來的含意可能並不存在，因為本段的架構（根據年紀和性別分為：年老的男人、年長的婦女、年輕的婦女、年輕的男子 + 提多、奴僕）根本有別於歌羅西書（及以弗所書）的家庭規範（妻子與丈夫、兒女和父親、奴僕與主人）。'We clearly have no household table here, no direct address to the members of the household spoken to as paired opposites'（Witherington 131）。因此，本段並非家庭規範（Quinn 50: 'A domestic code'）的另一例子，而是 'the station code schema'（MacDonald, *Pauline Churches* 208; see also Harding II 52-53）的例子。Cf. Marshall 22: 'in 2.1-8 we have not so much a *Haustafel* as a *Gemeindetafel*; it deals with different relationships within the church rather than within the family'; 15 n.27.（**2**）關於 'household codes'（以「家庭之內的相互關係」為結構的規範）和 'station codes'（以「家庭內外的社會階層」為結構的規範）二者的區別，詳見《西・門》640 註 10。馬賀比稱二 1～10 的教導為 'Gemeindeparänese'（Malherbe, 'Paraenesis' 305, 306, 309, 316, 317），意即給基督徒羣體的勸勉。

5 參一 10～16 註釋引言首段（上面 153-54）。

6 有關的原文依次為同一字根的 ἀνυπότακτοι（from ἀνυπότακτος），ὑποτασσομένας（from ὑποτάσσω），和 ὑποτάσσεσθαι（ὑποτάσσω 的中間語態）。

的時候，稱他們為爭辯的人，但僕人不可頂撞主人（二 9）。[7]

除了繼續第一章的倫理關注，本段亦同樣延續了上文對教義的關注。[8] 本段所提倡的倫理行為，被稱為合乎那健全的教導（1 節）；提多要宣揚能反映純正道理的生活方式（新普）。這種倫理行為或生活方式會防止上帝的道被毀謗（5b 節），會榮耀我們救主上帝的教導（10c 節）。本段的教導與假教師的行徑也是用教義的詞彙來作出對比：提多要教導老年人在信心上要健全（2 節），但敵對者顯然並不是在信仰上健全的，因為提多要責備他們，使他們在信仰上健全（一 13）。[9] 年長的婦女應該教導人美善的事（二 3，新普），提多在教導上要正直（7 節），但敵對者將不該教導的事教導人（一 11）。[10]

7 有關的原文依次為 τοὺς ἀντιλέγοντας, μὴ ἀντιλέγοντας（from ἀντιλέγω）。以上一段參 Van Neste, 'Structure' 124 (see also 131). Van Neste 256 又認為，本段三次提到的克己（二 2、5a、6 節）所要求的節制，跟敵對者是惡獸，貪吃懶做（一 12）這描寫構成對比。但見一 12 註釋第三、四兩段所提供更好的解釋（上面 175-77）。

8 參一 10～16 註釋引言第二段（上面 154-55）。

9 原文結構略為不同：ὑγιαίνειν ἐν τῇ πίστει（一 13），ὑγιαίνειν τῇ πίστει（二 2）。

10 以上一段參 Van Neste, 'Structure' 125.

4.1.1 籠統的序言（二 1）

二 1 至於你，你所講的總要合乎那健全的教導。

至於你[1] 將提多和上一段（一 10～16）所談及的那些假教師（一 10～12）作對比（參：提前六 11；提後三 10、14，四 5）。[2] 你所講的總要合乎……與他們將不該教導的事教導人（11c 節）形成對比。[3] 講字原文是信上第二次使用命令式語法的動詞（參新普：你要宣揚），第一次是一章 13 節的責備，兩次都與健全的教導或信仰有關聯：提多要以嚴緊縝密的方式訴之以理，使那些將不該教導的事教導人的人，知道自己的錯誤（一 13b），[4] 好使他們在信仰上健全（一 13c，新譯）；他必須講即是教導[5] 合

---

1 Σὺ δέ [*Sy de*], 'But as for you' (NKJV, RSV, NRSV, NAU, ESV).

2 除了以上的五次，σὺ δέ 在新約另外出現十二次；這十七次幾乎全部都有這種強調對比的意義：太六 6、17；路九 60，十六 7、25；羅十一 17、20，十四 10（參《羅》4.397）；來一 11、12；雅四 12。另見路一 76。

3 λάλει ἃ πρέπει τῇ ὑγιαινούσῃ διδασκαλίᾳ 對 διδάσκοντες ἃ μὴ δεῖ（see Classen, 'Titus' 436, 'Epistle to Titus' 55）。**（1）** Genade 41 更認為，由於二者（加上底線的部分）的節奏相似，而且二者都以母音 α 開始、以雙元音 ει 結束，聽者會立即留意到二者的讀音相似，並領會保羅欲表達的、這裏「對提多說的話」和早前「論及那些假教師時所說的話」二者之間的分別。**（2）** 與此同時，從段落的層次來看，二 1～15 和一 10～16 這兩段的主題並不是相對的，因為兩段分別是提多要「如何處理假教師和假教義以及鼓勵信徒追隨健全的教導」這問題的兩個步驟（see Banker 41*b*）。

4 見一 13b～c 註釋末段（上面 185-86）。

5 λάλει = 'speak' (KJV, NKJV, NAU), 'you . . . must speak' (*Paraphrase* 291); 'teach' (RSV, NRSV), 'You must / You . . . must teach' (NIV /TNIV, NIV2011). 'Titus is urged to "speak" in the sense of "teach"' (Knight II 305; see also Arichea－Hatton 281).（'But you are speaking' [Spencer 33] 這翻譯是奇怪的。）**（1）** Genade 40-41 問道：為甚麼保羅不使用動詞教導（一 11）而用講字呢？簡內德提出三個可能的答案：（i）保羅要在提多和假教師（他們將不該教導的事教導人〔一 11〕）之間製造一點空間或距離。（ii）保羅不用動詞「教導」，免得這動詞影響了本節末的名詞教導（διδασκαλία）的獨特或專門意思。（iii）不用動詞「教導」，為要避免重複（簡內德說 'to avoid redundancy', 但 'redundant' 的意思是「多餘、不需要」，而這意思並不合適，因此

乎[6] **那健全的教導**的事（二 1）。由於二章 1 至 10 節所關注的主要是信徒的倫理行為，本句應理解為「你要宣揚與健全的教導相符的行為」。[7] 本段餘下的部分（2～10 節），就是與**健全的教導**相符之行為的具體說明。[8]

健全的教導一詞重複自一章 9 節，指權威性的使徒教義。[9] 在

筆者修改如上）。這答案似最可取。（**2**）Simpson 103 指出，希臘化時期的希臘文（即通用希臘文）已將 'λαλεῖν, *to chatter*' 和 'λέγειν, *to speak*' 這古典希臘文的區別幾乎完全消除，儘管 λαλεῖν 仍指 'vocal utterance'（有聲的說話），λέγειν 則指 'regular discourse (cf. Latin *sermo**)'（*= discussion, speech）。（**3**）從以上兩點看來，Hendrikson 362 的解釋（λαλεῖν 指提多的 'informal daily *conversation*'）是有疑問的。

6 原文動詞 **πρέπω**（呂譯：適合）在新約另外出現六次，其中兩次用來表達某種行動的原因（πρέπον ἐστίν = 'it is fitting, proper, right' [BDAG 861*b* [s.v.]）：實行上帝的要求是**應該的**（太三 15，新普）；某些事情即使談論也不可，**如此纔合乎聖徒的身分**（弗五 3，思高）。另外四次分別指：保羅要哥林多人自己判斷，女人不蒙著頭禱告是否**合宜**（林前十一 13）；以善行打扮自己，**才與自稱為敬畏上帝的女人相稱**（提前二 10）；上帝以「使他們救恩的創始者及領導者藉著受苦成為完全」的方法來達到**領許多兒子進入榮耀**的目的，這是**合宜的**（來二 10；詳參《來》1.146-55）；來七 26b～27 所描寫的**這樣的一位大祭司，對我們本是合適的**（26a 節〔新譯〕；參《來》1.471-72）。See BDAG (s.v.);《新希》280*a*-80*b*（s.v.）。

7 See（**i**）NJB: 'It is for you, then, to preach the behaviour which goes with healthy doctrine'; Van Neste, 'Message' 24*a*: '"*things* which are fitting for sound doctrine" . . . must refer to behaviors or lifestyles';（**ii**）NLT: 'promote the kind of living that reflects wholesome teaching'; Laansma 260: 'The overarching charge of verses 1-10 is simply this: "Promote the kind of living that reflects wholesome teaching"'; 新普：**你要宣揚能反映純正道理的生活方式**；（**iii**）Mounce, 'Titus' 106: 'you, Titus, are to teach a way of living that is based on solid Christian doctrine.'

8 （**1**）'The basic relationship between 2:1 and 2:2-10 is that of generic-specifics' (Banker 63*a*); 'Titus 2:1 is the topic sentence or the idea which is fleshed out in 2:2-10'（Schreiner, *Interpreting* 123〔施賴納：《詮釋》138〕）。留意 NKJV 在 1 節末用冒號：'speak the things that are proper for sound doctrine: that . . .'. See also Genade 43: 'it sets out to answer the question, what does sound doctrine *look* like?'; Marshall 238: 'Ethical conduct that befits orthodox teaching is the theme.'（**2**）Wieland 197-98 則認為，'the theological passage [2:11-14] may supply something of the content of that teaching. The ὑγιαινούσῃ διδασκαλίᾳ that Titus is to teach (2:1) is specifically ἡ διδασκαλία ἡ τοῦ σωτῆρος ἡμῶν θεοῦ (2:10). This corresponds to the theme of God's soterial goals and activity expounded in 2:11-14.' 可是，作者似乎忽視了一點：提多所要教導的（1 節）並不是**那健全的教導**本身，而是合乎**那健全的教導**之事，而緊接的文理提示，這些事是關乎信徒的行為的。此評語同樣適用於馬賀比這句話：'The social responsibilities in which that community is instructed are tantamount to the sound teaching'（Malherbe, 'Medical Imagery' 126）。

9 Towner III 719: 'the authoritative apostolic doctrine'（唐 1048：「權威性的使徒教訓」）。原文依次為 τῇ διδασκαλίᾳ τῇ ὑγιαινούσῃ（一 9）和

該節，要用健全的教義勸勉人（呂譯）的是教會的監督；在這裏，提多要講合乎那健全的教導的事；重複的健全的教導一詞把提多和監督連起來。如此，保羅將提多和長老／監督描寫為盟友或夥伴，把那些將不該教導的事教導人（11 節）的假教師描寫成異族。[10] 在上一段（一 10～16），假教師宣稱認識上帝，卻在行為上否認他（16 節）；在本段，提多「要宣揚與健全的教導相符的行為」；由此可見，健全的教導和與之相符的行為不可分割，而這就是本段的修辭目的的中心。[11] 不但如此，本節和一章 16 節的強烈對比顯示，本段所教導的行為或生活方式，才是認識上帝的證據（不像假教師以其行為否認上帝）；不按這裏的教導來生活，則使一己的得救成疑，因為上帝的拯救恩典就是教導這樣的生活方式的（二 11～14）。[12]

τῇ ὑγιαινούσῃ διδασκαλίᾳ（二 1），兩者不同的字序構成 'a low profile chiasmus'（Clark, 'Structure' 110）。後者是 'dat. of respect'（see Wallace 144-46）：'it indicates that in respect of which Titus's teaching is to be "appropriate"'（Marshall 238）。

10 Genade 45, 41.「異族」英文原作 'aliens'.

11 Genade 43.

12 Cf. Van Neste, 'Message' 24*a-b*. See also Van Neste 256: 'The primary thematic contrast is seen between 1.16 and 2.1.'

4.1.2 年老的男人（二 2）

二 2 勸老年人要有節制、端正、克己，在信心、愛心、耐心上都要健全。[1]

本節原文開首並無動詞；[2] 勸（同呂譯、當代、新和、現修、新譯）或教訓／教導（思高／新普）都是中譯本按文理補充進來的。[3] **老年人**原文跟一章 5 節的**長老**同字根；前者在新約僅再出現二次：施洗約翰的父親撒迦利亞和保羅都自稱為**已經老了**（路一 18）或**上了年紀**（門 9 節）。[4] 在保羅當代，**老年人**或「年長的男人」似乎是個五十至

---

1 本節（和 3、6、9 節）開首並無連詞（asyndeton）。在這種 'Head-Specific relationships, in which the second proposition [v. 2] gives a specific instance of the more generic proposition that precedes it [v. 1]', 並無連詞將二者連起來（Levinsohn, 'Constraints' 332; cf. idem, *Discourse Features* 118-19, 稱為 '*GENERIC-specific*' 關係）。參較一 12 的 'Orienter-Head' relationship; 見一 12 註釋註 1 之（1）= 上面 172。

2 See KJV/NKJV: 'That the aged men be / that the older men be . . .'.

3 **(1)** 英譯本多補充 'Bid'（RSV）、'Tell'（NRSV）、'Teach'（NIV, TNIV, NIV2011, NLT, *Paraphrase* 291）或化為命令式語法的句子：'Older men are to be / should be . . .'（NAU, ESV / NJB）。不過，本節的 εἶναι 不必視為「命令式不定詞（imperatival Infinitive）」（MHT 1.179; cf. DM 216; Knight II 305: 'εἶναι and the other infinitives in vv. 2-10 may well function as imperatives'. Wallace 608 認為 imperatival infinitive 在新約只有三個例子：羅十二 15〔χαίρειν . . . κλαίειν〕；腓三 16〔στοιχεῖν〕，而最後這個 'more resembles a hortatory subjunctive than an imperative'）。*Idiom* 126 認為 'νηφαλίους εἶναι is perhaps a quite normal Accusative and Infinitive after λάλει'. 更明確地，Towner III 720 n.16（唐 1050 註 9）認為 'λάλει in v. 1 should be understood to control the thought of vv. 2-5', 就如 'παρακάλει [in v. 6] governs 2:6-10'. **(2)** 張 344 則根據提前五 1（**不可嚴責老年人，要勸他如同父親**）在這裏補充「勸」字。但作者稍後又說，不定詞 εἶναι「在此處有如命令語之用法」（345 註 10）。兩種看法並不一致：如果 εἶναι 相當於命令式語法，Πρεσβύτας νηφαλίους εἶναι 的意思便是 'Older men are to be sober minded/temperate / Older men should be reserved'（ESV/NAU / NJB），而這有別於**勸老年人要有節制**（新和）。換句話說，如果 εἶναι 相當於命令式語法，便無須補充「勸」字。**(3)** DC 140*b* 說：'all the regulations for the members of the congregation are disguised this way in the Pastorals: as regulations which are handed over to the apostle's assistant!'「喬裝」一詞含貶意；作者們認為教牧書信並非保羅寫的。

4 原文皆為 πρεσβύτης（與一 5 的 πρεσβύτερος 和二 3 的 πρεσβῦτις 同字根）；

五十六歲的人。[5] 但是五十六歲以上的男性，亦會包括在提多要勸的老年人當中；這樣，這第一組別是五十歲或以上的男性。[6]

有節制（**#1**，同呂譯、新和、新譯）、[7] **應／必須節制**（思高／

'*presbytēs* and *presbytis* [v. 3] . . . refer simply to length, or greater length, of life and mean old man and woman respectively'（L. Coenen, *DNTT* 1.197）。（**1**）在門 9 節，思高的**年老的**現修作**大使**，後一種翻譯有兩種可能的解釋：或是假定了 πρεσβευτής（大使）才是原來的讀文，或是認為 πρεσβύτης （老人）只是 πρεσβευτής（大使）的另一拼法；詳細的討論可參《西・門》881-91。（**2**）Spencer 33-34 聲稱，二 2 的 πρεσβύτας 和二 3 的 πρεσβύτιδας 亦可指 'church leadership positions (male and female "elders")'. 她認為：πρεσβύτης 在以下四節 'clearly refer[s] to ambassadors or envoys': LXX 代下三十二 31；次經《馬加比一書》14.22; 15.17;《馬加比二書》11.34。伯二十九 7～8 和哀五 14 提到在城門判案的長老；一些譯本在門 9 節翻譯為「大使」。可是，在這七節經文中，（**i**）三節所用的字是 πρεσβευτής（代下三十二 31；次經《馬加比一書》14.22; 15.17〔如在 13.21; 14.21; 14.40〕），不是多二 2 的 πρεσβύτης.（**ii**）在門 9 節，**年老的**（思高）而非**大使**（現修）才是正確的翻譯；詳見《西・門》881-91。（**iii**）在餘下的三節，《馬加比二書》11.34 清楚指「羅馬人的使者（πρεσβῦται）」（思高瑪加伯下）。伯二十九 8 說：'The young men [νεανίσκοι] saw me [Job], and hid themselves; and all the old men [πρεσβῦται] stood up'（LXE）；後者可能是指「長老」（Carol A. Newsom, in *NIB* 4.538*a*）。在哀五 14（LXE），'the elders'（πρεσβῦται）與 'the chosen men'（ἐκλεκτοι）相對（在中譯本是**老年人**與**年輕人**的對比）；前者可能指「長老」：「老年人不受尊敬和喪失了他們處理社會事務的權利」（Gordon McConville, 於《證主 21 世紀聖經新釋 2》〔香港：福音證主協會，1999〕758*b*）。由此看來，在 Spencer 所引用的七節中，πρεσβύτης 可能指「長老」的只有兩節。因此筆者認為，她用以支持「多二 2 的 πρεσβύτας 是指長老」的論據相當薄弱。決定性的反對理由見二 3 註釋註 2（下面 230）。

5 （**1**）斐羅根據《託希坡克拉底名書》（*Pseudo-Hippocrates*）* 將人生分為七個階段：'παιδίον [little boy] (0-7); παῖς [boy] (8-14); μειράκιον [lad] (15-21); νεανίσκος [young man] (22-28); ἀνήρ [man] (29-49); πρεσβύτης [elderly man] (50-56); γέρων [old man] (57-)'（Marshall 239）。（* Hippocrates, 公元前約 460-377，被譽為古希臘之「醫學始祖／之父」〔《宗教》145*a*／《聖神》257*b*〕。）參較《西・門》884 連註 13。（**2**）Quinn 129 引 Aulus Gellius 指出，在羅馬世界，男性按年齡分為三組：十七歲以下是 'boys', 17-46 歲是 'younger men', 46 歲以上是 'elders'. 但 Quinn 139 將**年輕人**解釋為 'men up to fifty'.（**3**）Towner III 720（唐 1050）則認為：'Depending on which ancient classification of age groups we follow, old men are at least somewhere upward of forty years old, possibly into their fifties or sixties.'

6 Marshall 239. Mounce 408 提出另一可能：'Paul appears to be addressing all the adult members in the Cretan church, so old and young are relative in reference to each other rather than to a time of life.' 參二 4a 註釋註 13 之（2）＝ 下面 240。

7 See also RSV, NRSV, NAU, NIV, TNIV, NIV2011, Banker 60, 63*a*, Quinn 26, 116, 118: 'temperate'; P. J. Budd, *DNTT* 1.515: 'abstemious'（節制的）。（**1**）在 'we have now . . . a series of accusations with the infinitive'（Fairbairn 271）這句話裏面，'accusati<u>ons</u>' 是 'accusati<u>ves</u>' 之誤。（**2**）本節四個直接受格的形容詞（νηφαλίους, σεμνούς, σώφρονας）

當代）或**操練自律**（新普）[8] 的另兩個翻譯是**嚴肅**（現修）[9] 和「沉默寡言」。[10] 下一節清楚提到，提多要勸年長的婦女**不作酒的奴隸**，這就有力地提示，**有節制**同樣是針對傳統希臘文化中老年人醉酒的問題。[11] 新約聖經另有好幾處提到醉酒的問題：哥林多教會守主的聖餐時，竟然**有人飢餓，有人酒醉**（林前十一 21）；[12] 有稱為弟兄的人卻仍**醉酒**（五 11，參六 10）；非信徒向基督徒施壓，要他們回復從前的生活方式，包括**醉酒**（彼前四 3）；教會的監督必須**不酗酒**（多一 7；提前三 3），執事也必須**不好酒**（提前三 8）。[13] 提摩太則示範了不同的生活方式，保羅要這樣勸他：**為了你的胃，又常患病，不要只喝水，要稍微喝點酒**（提前五 23）。聖經傳統整體亦強烈地貶抑醉酒的行為。[14] 在上述的事實底下，**有節制**的原文形容詞可能特指在飲用含酒

和分詞（ὑγιαίνοντας）都是 predicate accusatives. 如 Wallace 190 所解釋：'The accusative substantive (or adjective [as here]) stands in predicate relation to another accusative substantive [here πρεσβύτας]. The two will be joined by an equative verb, either an infinitive [here εἶναι] or participle. Neither type is especially frequent outside of Luke or Paul.'

8 NLT: 'exercise self-control'.

9 See also Fairbairn 271, REB: 'sober'; O. Bauernfeind, *TDNT* 4.941: 'sober . . . The reference is to the clarity and self-control necessary for sacred ministry in God's work'; ESV: 'sober-minded' =「認真的；嚴肅的」(《牛津》1113*b* [s.v. 1])。

10 NJB: 'reserved'. 形容詞 νηφάλιος 在希臘文聖經僅再出現兩次：監督和女執事都必須**有節制**（提前三 2、11）。See BDAG 672*b* (s.v.);《新希》226*a*（s.v.）。

11 Marshall 186, endorsing Quinn 130-31. See also Jeon I 66: 'νηφαλίους . . . refers to moderation in alcohol consumption'; Calvin 369: 'excessive drinking is a fault all too common in old age.' Ward 250 指出，**不作酒的奴僕**這項勸告仍然十分適切：'When older men are converted they have more sins in their experience than younger men, and the pressure of their past is all the stronger'（參：約八 7～9；留意 9 節的**從老的開始**〔'They had more sins on their conscience as they had lived longer'〕）。

12 本節含有許多釋經問題，詳見（例如）Fee, *First Corinthians* 540-43. 從下一節可見，保羅<u>在這裏</u>的關注不是有人酒醉，而是有人飢餓（543）。

13 以上七節，原文使用了五種不同的詞彙來指醉酒：動詞 μεθύω 的主動語態（林前十一 21）；人物名詞 μέθυσος（林前五 11，六 10）；抽象名詞 οἰνοφλυγία（彼前四 3）；形容詞 πάροινος（提前三 3；多一 7）；分詞片語 οἴνῳ πολλῷ προσέχων（提前三 8）。亦參下註。

14 參：箴二十 1，二十三 20a（**不可與好飲酒的人**〔οἰνοπότης〕**在一起**）、21a（**因為⋯⋯好酒的**〔μέθυσος〕**必致貧窮**）、29～35（30a 節，**流連飲酒**〔οἱ ἐν χρονίζοντες ἐν οἴνοις〕）；次經《傳道經》19.1-2（思高德訓篇 1a 節：「好醉酒的工人〔μέθυσος〕不會致富」），31.25-31（參較德訓篇 31.30-40）；次經《多比傳》4.15b（思高多俾

精飲料時有節制；[15] 若翻譯為「清醒」，[16] 亦宜理解為不僅是比喻意義的頭腦冷靜，而是指字面意義的、與醉醺醺相對的、因為不飲酒（至少是飲酒有節制）而保持的清醒。[17]

端正（#2）、**端莊**（思高、新和）或**莊重**（呂譯、當代、新譯）[18] 另有翻譯為**有好品格**（現修）、**配受尊敬**（新普）、[19]「感覺或表現尊敬的；虔敬的」。[20] 原文在新約另外出現三次：兩次指執事和女執事的一項資格（提前三 8、11：**莊重**）；另一次指信徒應當思念的事包括**凡是可敬的**（腓四 8）。它在七十士譯本出現九次：兩次分別指安息日為那「至聖」的日子，及上帝的「聖」名；[21] 一次指出自智慧口中的

亞傳：「喝酒不要喝醉〔εἰς μέθην〕；醉酒〔μέθη〕不可在你的路上與你同行」）；馬加比一書 16.15-16；羅十三 13，加五 21（**醉酒** = μέθη）；弗五 18（**醉酒** = μεθύσκεσθαι οἴνῳ）。另見上註。

15 BDAG 672*b* (s.v. *νηφάλιος*, 1): 'pert. to being very moderate in the drinking of an alcoholic beverage, *temperate*, *sober*'; Thayer 425*b* (s.v. *νηφάλεος* [*sic*]): 'abstaining from . . . its immoderate use'; *Paraphrase* 291: 'temperate in the use of wine'. 俄利根說：'Sobriety is the mother of virtues, drunkenness the mother of vices'（Gorday 295*b*）。

16 KJV, NKJV: 'sober'; Knight II 305, Köstenberger 614*a*: 'clear-headed'; BAGD 538*b* (s.v. *νηφάλιος*): 'sober, clear-headed, self-controlled'; Laansma 261: 'restrained, level-headed, sensible, controlled'; Mounce 409/cvii: 'clear-minded, sober in judgment, self-controlled / clearminded'; Ngewa 360: 'having a clear mind'; LN §88.87: 'pertaining to behavior in a sober, restrained manner – "sober, restrained."' 參彭編 33*a*：「宜作『審慎』、『頭腦清醒』」。Hiebert 436 認為這字的意思是 '"clear-headed," manifesting self-possession under all circumstances'.

17 Marshall 187. 班約翰則認為，形容詞 *νηφάλιος* 在這裏的比喻意思（Banker 63*b*: 'well-balanced, self-controlled'）間接地包括 'temperance in the use of wine' 之意（64*a*）。

18 See also KJV, Fairbairn 271: 'grave' =「嚴肅的」（《牛津》513*a* [s.v.]）；RSV, NRSV, Quinn 26, 116, 118: 'serious' =「嚴肅的；莊重的」（《牛津》1058*b* [s.v. 1]）；W. Foerster, *TDNT* 7.195: 'serious and worthy'.「莊重」意即「端莊鄭重」（《國語》700*d*〔但此辭典並無「端莊」這一條；《新雅》也沒有〕）。

19 NLT, NIV, TNIV, NIV2011, Knight II 305, Köstenberger 614*a*, Marshall 240, Towner III 720: 'worthy of respect'（唐 1051：「配得尊敬」）；Quinn 131: 'respectable';《新希》300*a*（s.v. σεμνός）：「可尊敬的；值得敬重的」。See also REB, NAU, NJB, ESV, Fiore II 208, Mounce 405, 409: 'dignified' =「可敬的；高貴的」（《牛津》331*a* [s.v. 'dignify']）。

20 NKJV, *Paraphrase* 293: 'reverent'. 所引中譯見《牛津》988*a*（s.v.）。

21 次經《馬加比二書》6.11（ἡ σεμνοτάτη ἡμέρα: 'that most holy day' [RSV, NRSV]），8.15（τὸ σεμνὸς . . . ὄνομα αὐτοῦ: 'his holy . . . name' [RSV, NRSV]）。

「嚴肅的」真理，[22] 另五次則有「可敬／尊敬」等意思。[23] 同字根的抽象名詞在新約出現三次：提多在教導上要**莊重**（多二7）；信徒要為在位者禱告，好讓自己能夠**莊重地**過活（提前二2，新譯〔參呂譯〕）；監督的資格包括能夠使兒女順服，凡事**莊重**（提前三4）。[24] 它在七十士譯本只出現一次，指聖殿的「神聖、尊嚴」（次經《馬加比二書》3.12）。[25] 同字根的副詞在希臘文聖經只出現一次，指透過律法上的教育「虔誠地」學習屬上帝的事（偽經《馬加比四書》1.17）。[26] 由此看來，作為一項倫理品質，這組字彙所表達的，基本上是一種**配受尊敬**（新普）的**好品格**（現修），意味著一種對生命「嚴肅」的態度，[27] 以及**莊重**的生活行為。[28] 班約翰正確地強調，贏得別人的尊敬的是品德方面的特質。[29]（對於現今「窮得只剩下錢」＝道德淪亡、依附權貴、

---

22 箴八6 LXE: 'I will speak solemn *truths* [σεμνά]'. 箴六8的 σεμνός 意思不明（Marshall 188: 'the force in 6.8 is uncertain'）。

23 箴十五26 LXE: 'the sayings of the pure are held in honour [σεμναί]'; 次經《馬加比二書》（思高瑪加伯下）6.28：「可敬的法律」（οἱ σεμνοὶ . . . νόμοι: 'the venerable . . . laws' [NJB]）；偽經《馬加比四書》5.36（μου τὸ σεμνὸν γήρως στόμα: 'the honorable mouth of my old age' [RSV, NRSV]）；7.15（σεμνὴ πολιά: 'venerable grey hair' [RSV, NRSV]）；17.5: 七子之母「令人敬畏」（σεμνή: 'august' [RSV, NRSV]）。

24 如果本節末的 μετὰ πάσης σεμνότητος 是形容動詞，所得出的意思就是**端端莊莊地使兒女順服**（新和貝邊註）；see Marshall 189.

25 See RSV, NRSV: 'the sanctity . . . of the temple'; NJB: 'the . . . majesty of a Temple'; 思高《瑪加伯下》：「聖殿〔的〕神聖⋯⋯的尊嚴」。

26 RSV, NRSV: '. . . education in the law, by which we learn divine matters reverently [σεμνῶς]'.

27 See Guthrie I 191, Guthrie II 204: 'A seriousness of purpose particularly suits the dignity of seniors'（「嚴肅的用意特別符合那些資深之士」〔古特立 206〕這翻譯，沒有譯出「長者的尊嚴」這個意思）；Marshall 189: 'A Christian's behaviour should be such as to win respect from other people because they [*sic*] take life seriously and devoutly and do not trifle.'

28 See BDAG 919*a* (s.v. σεμνός, a α): 'pert. to evoking special respect . . . *worthy of respect/honor*, *noble*, *dignified*, *serious*'; Banker 60, 63*a*, 64*b*: '(that they should) behave in such a manner that all people will respect them'; Marshall 189: 'In the PE the word-group signifies serious, dignified behaviour that is worthy of respect'; LN §88.47: 'honorable, worthy of respect, of good character'; 《輔讀》527（第一解釋）：「莊敬自重的」；張 184：「形容人的嚴肅和配受尊重」；《腓》446。

29 Banker 64*a-b*: '*Semnos* designates a person who has those moral qualities that are respected by others. He is respected because of the moral quality of his life, not because of the position he holds or any seemingly pleasant outward deportment that is not based

一切向金錢、權力和利益看的社會／國家，這種強調尤其重要。）

克己（**#3**）一詞已在一章 8 節出現過，[30] 在本段再出現一次（5 節）。**克己**是作監督的一項資格（一 8；提前三 2），也是年老的男人（本節）、年輕的婦女（5 節）、年輕的男子（6 節）都要具備的美德。[31] 上一項（#2 **端正**）也是做執事和女執事（提前三 8、11：**莊重**）必備的條件；同樣，再上一項（#1 **有節制**）也是作監督（提前三 2）和女執事（提前三 11）的資格之一。由此看來，教會領袖要示範正常基督徒生命應有的品質。[32]

以上三項基本上取自希羅倫理的手冊，隨後一項則明確地是基督徒的美德。[33] **(i) 在信心……上健全**（**#4**，[34] 呂譯）的原文已在一章

---

on inner moral quality.' Cf. Dunn 784 (= Dunn, 'Titus' 279*b*): 'Notable here is . . . the concern for a proper respectability, or better, respect-worthiness as a measure of Christian conduct.'

30 原文為形容詞 σώφρων（參一 8 註釋之〔#11〕= 第六段〔上面 136-37〕）。另有翻譯為「理智的（sensible）」：LN §88.94; Marshall 240; Quinn 26, 116, 118; Towner III 720（唐 1051：「明智的」）。二 4 的動詞**指教**（σωφρονίζω）和二 12 的副詞**克己**（σωφρόνως）皆與此形容詞（σώφρων）同字根。（Genade 45 的 'νηφαλίοι σεμνοίσώφρονοι' 是 'νηφάλιοι σεμνοί σώφρονες' 之誤；'the adjective σώφρονος' 是 'the adjective σώφρων' 之誤，前者是所有格，後者才是主格。）

31 (**1**) Barclay（'Age' 237）認為，那些已經把**年輕人的私慾**（νεωτερικαὶ ἐπιθυμίαι, 提後二 22）放下的人，可被預期有上述三項（##1-3）美德。(**2**) Keegan II 97（Keegan I 61）認為，上述三項是「精英公民的優良社會品質（social qualities found in leading citizens）」，最後一項則指「特殊的基督徒德性（specific Christian virtues）」。

32 Marshall 238: 'church leaders . . . are to exemplify the qualities which typify the normal Christian life.'

33 Cf. Witherington 134: 'the first three basically are drawn from the Greco-Roman manual, while the last three are more specifically Christian'（'the last three' 指**信心、愛心、耐心**；但保羅的重點是**在信心、愛心、耐心上都要健全**）。Collins 339 聲稱，作者為這些五十來歲的**老年人**所勾勒的道德面貌含有六項美德，'arranged as a pair of triads', 即是把**在信心、愛心、耐心上都要健全**這一項，分拆為「在信心上健全，在愛心上健全，在耐心上健全」這三項。Genade 45 認為，這裏的三個正面品質似乎平衡了一 12 的引句中那三個負面品質。可是，這三個名詞都是從屬於帶頭的分詞 ὑγιαίνοντες，全部一起只構成一項美德（簡內德自己也說：'The participle ὑγιαίνοντες is the fourth quality in this list and is modified by three nouns'）。因此，不宜將三個名詞從所屬的分詞片語中抽出來，作為一 12 那三個品質的平衡物。

34 Blaiklock 82 認為第四項（**在信心、愛心、耐心上都要健全**）解釋了第三項：'This is exactly "sophron [*sic*]," the word so difficult to render.' Towner II 236（followed by

13 節（**在信仰上健全**）出現過。在該節，提多要以嚴緊縝密的方式訴之以理，使那些假教師知道自己的錯誤，[35] 為要使他們成為**在信仰上健全**；在這裏，年老的信徒要**在信心**[36]**……上健全**，這是提多所講的**合乎那健全的教導**之事（二 1）的一小部分。在信心（信的主觀意義）上健全必定包括**有堅定的信心**（新普）和正確的信仰（信的客觀意義）。[37] 除了**信心**，保羅還加上**愛心**和**耐心**。[38] **(ii)**「在愛心上健全」意即「真誠地愛」，[39] 甚或**充滿愛心**（新普），這愛是捨己為人的服事。[40] **(iii)** **耐心**（同現修，新普同）原文不是提摩太後書三

Chapell 327-28）認為，第四項可能表達了 'the cause or means of the behavior described above [in the first part of v. 2]'. 筆者對這兩種見解都不敢苟同。

35 見一 13b～c 註釋末段（上面 185-86）。

36 由於隨後的**愛心**和**耐心**都是信徒的主觀品質，τῇ πίστει 應理解為**信心**（thus also Kelly 240; Knight II 306; Towner III 721 n.21〔唐 1052 註 14〕; White 191*a*; Witherington 136; cf. Mounce cxxxi, 409: 'trust'）而不是「信仰」（e.g., Mounce cxxx-xxxi: 'in a creedal, objective sense'）；和本節類似的美德目錄（提前四 12，六 11；提後二 22，三 10）亦支持這種理解（Marshall 240）。**(1)** 由此可見，'the presence of the article does not automatically demand an objective meaning [of πίστις]'; 參：提後三 10：**我的……信心**（τῇ πίστει）、**寬容**、**愛心**、**忍耐**（Marshall 214）。*Pace*, e.g., Aageson 51: 'steadfast in the faith'. **(2)** Quinn 27, 116, 118 則翻譯為 'robust in faithfulness'.

37 See Banker 65*a*; 他意譯為 '(And tell them that they should) firmly believe in the correct teachings'（also 60）。Cf. Laansma 261: 'calling it [faith] "sound" unavoidably suggests its contents at the same time.' See also D. Müller, *DNTT* 2.171: 'to be "sound in faith" . . . means to hold the received apostolic doctrine as normative and binding.' Jeon I 66 則認為，'to be "sound in faith" includes both holding fast to sound doctrine and living according to godliness.'

38 **(1)** τῇ πίστει, τῇ ἀγάπῃ, τῇ ὑπομονῇ 'is another instance of asyndetic *emphatic clustering*' (Genade 45 [cf. 128]). 前一個例子在一 12；參該節註釋註 7（上面 174）。參較一 10a 的 'emphatic clustering'（但非 'asyndetic'; 見一 10 註釋註 3 之〔1〕= 上面 157），一 16c 的 'polysyndetic *emphatic clustering*'（見一 16 註釋註 2〔上面 207〕）。**(2)** 三個名詞皆為 dative of reference/respect（see Wallace 144-46）。**(3)** 三個名詞都有冠詞，強調了每一項美德都是重要的（Quinn 132）。三個名詞之前的冠詞可理解為特指「他們的」信心、愛心和耐心（Fairbairn 271; Hendriksen 363; Hiebert 436）。留意這裏 πίστις 有冠詞並不表示所指的是「所信的內容」，就如三 15 無冠詞的 πίστις 並不表示所指的是「信心」（參三 15a～b 註釋註 21 及所屬正文〔下面 473〕）。Quinn 273 解釋如下：'The appearance (or absence) of the article has far more to do with the grammatical and rhetorical patterns of Hellenistic Greek than with systematic theological distinctions.'

39 Banker 65*a*: 'to sincerely love'.

40 Towner III 721: 'sacrificial service done for another'（唐 1052：「為他人作的犧牲」）。

章 10 節的**寬容**一字，而是隨後的**忍耐**一字。[41] 若二字可加以區別的話，本節**耐心**的意思就可能不是（對不易相處的人的）**忍耐**（思高、當代、新和、新譯），而是（對困難的環境的）**堅忍**（呂譯）。[42] **在……堅忍上健全**（呂譯）意即「常常堅忍、一直堅忍下去」。[43] 這裏的三組合不是「信、望、愛」（林前十三 13）或「信、愛、望」（帖前五 8），而是「信、愛、堅忍」。[44] 三者合成基督徒生命首要的美德。[45] 保羅同樣勉勵提摩太要追求「信心、愛心、**堅忍**〔呂譯〕」（提前六 11），又表示提摩太**已經了解**（新譯）他（保羅）的「**信心、……愛心、堅忍**」（提後三 10〔呂譯 10～11〕）。在教牧書信這三節，「堅忍」取代了「信、望、愛」這組合中的第二項或「信、愛、望」這組合中的第三項，<u>彷彿</u>「堅忍」和「盼望」是同義的。[46] 帖撒羅尼迦前書一章 3

41 這就是說，多二 2 所用的字<u>不是</u> μακροθυμία（保羅書信另外八次，包括提前一 16；提後四 2；參《加》1275-76），<u>而是</u> ὑπομονή.（**1**）除了提後三 10，二字在保羅書信中一起出現只有另一次（西一 11）。（**2**）名詞 **ὑπομονή** = 'fortitude/steadfastness'（REB / Quinn 27, 116, 118, 133; Fiore II 208）在保羅書信另外出現十四次，包括提前六 11（參《帖前》67-68），新約全部 32 次。See BDAG 1039*b*-40*a* (s.v.);《新希》341*b*（s.v.）。

42 詳見《西・門》164。（**1**）Lock 137 意譯為 'sound . . . in their power of enduring persecution'; cf. 139: 'their power of endurance must be able to hold out against the provocations and persecutions of the world around them'.（**2**）Banker 65*b* 則認為，**堅忍**在這裏主要是指 'unwavering loyalty to the received faith'.（**3**）Quinn 133 認為，原文名詞 'has an active nuance that suggests heroic steadfastness against evil', 這在希臘化時期的世界（'the Hellenistic world'）會被理解為 'an aspect of what that society knew and admired as courage or fortitude (*andreia** . . .).'（*參二 12 註釋註 2 之〔1〕= 下面 290）。（**4**）Bouwman 63 則解釋為 'not anemic in their determination to fulfill their God-given role in life, but robust－even in old age－in exercising their (remaining) gifts and opportunities to God's glory and the neighbor's benefit.'

43 See Banker 65*b-a*: '"being truly steadfast," "completely steadfast," or "always steadfast."'

44 如在伊格那丢《致坡旅甲書》6.2（DC 139*b*）。因此，Clarke（*Problems* 159）稱堅忍為 'a variant for hope'.

45 Verner 171: 'They stand together as primary virtues of the Christian life.'

46 因此，Witherington 137 的解釋未能使人感到滿意，他說：我們若問為甚麼這裏（二 2）似乎以堅忍（'constancy'）取代盼望，it is perhaps because this is <u>addressed to older men</u> who need to be encouraged to persevere and remain constant to the end of their lives.' 另外兩節（至少提前六 11）相同的現象不能這樣解釋。

節提供了解釋這現象的線索：在該節，保羅將堅忍與盼望緊密相連：他不住地記念收信人因信心所做的工作，因愛心所受的勞苦，因盼望我們主耶穌基督所存的堅忍。也許保羅從他豐富的經驗發現，在信徒的生命中，盼望是以堅忍的形式發生功效的。[47] 由此看來，在……堅忍上健全（呂譯）可能是指堅毅地等候永生的盼望（一 2，三 7）的實現。[48]

本節所要求於年長的男人的美德，幾乎全部都包括在提摩太前書所列出的監督或執事的資格中：有節制（提前三 2〔監督〕）；端正＝莊重（提前三 8〔執事〕）；克己（提前三 2；多一 8〔監督〕）；「在信心上健全」（參：提前三 9〔執事〕，固守信仰的奧祕）。這種重疊現象證實，最可能找到教會領袖的地方，就是在年長（較有經驗和智慧）的男人當中。[49]

---

47 參《帖前》67-68。(**1**) Scott 163 認為，教牧書信的作者（不是保羅）以「堅忍」代替「盼望」，也許是由於他尤其想到老年人，他們現階段對生命的態度就是「無奈的接受（resignation）」。參馬唐納 561*b*：「年老就有輭弱和殘疾，很多時很難忍受。」Cf. Griffin 298: 'The latter years of life, especially for men, can be filled with regrets, a sense of uselessness or worthlessness, feelings of despair, self-absorption, or even a tendency to relax moral standards because of old age.' (**2**) Marshall 241 則認為，鑑於正統信仰受到反對，作者有需要強調 'the ingredient of patient perseverance'. Similarly Laansma 263: 'the concern here may be specifically with the present opposition'; Jeon I 66-67: 'In the immediate context, the presence and influence of false teachers and apostates indicate a setting charged with conflict. To maintain "faith" and "love" will require tremendous fortitude and steadfastness.' Cf. Towner III 721-22（唐 1053）：'This element of perseverance could envision the conflict setting or more generally the struggle to live as believers in rough Cretan social conditions'. (**3**) Mounce ('Titus' 106) 僅理解為 'They must . . . carry through on whatever falls to them to do.'

48 參彭編 53*b*：「對主再臨的盼望，其體現便是用忍耐面對今生各樣的困難（帖前 1:3）。」(**1**) Bassler 193 則認為，本節的堅忍可能指等候永生盼望之實現，或是指 'steadfastness in doing good works (2:14; 3:1, 8, 14; cf. Rom 2:7) or in adhering to the truth (1:1; cf. 1:14).' (**2**) 無論如何，'The particular witness that the aged can give is their lifelong fidelity. Such witness . . . adds luster even to the witness of Jesus, who, dying young, was not able to show in his own body what kingdom living in advanced age would look like. This is the privilege of the elderly faithful' (Montague 231)。另一方面，'faith, love, and endurance . . . may become more difficult with age, since the experience of shattered dreams and broken promises can make the aged skeptical and advancing weakness can make them impatient. That is why serenity, love, and joy in the aged are all the more powerful a [*sic*] witness to the presence and power of the Holy Spirit'（同上）。

49 Dunn 869*a-b*.

4.1.3 年長的婦女（二 3～4a）

二 3 又要勸年長的婦女在操守上恭正，[1] 不說讒言，不作酒的奴隸，用善道教導人，

年長的婦女[2] 大抵是和上一節的**老年人**＝「年長的男人」年紀相若的婦女。[3] **又**字似乎是原文**照樣**（新譯、新普）的意譯；**照樣**（＝ 6 節的**同樣**）意即「像你要**勸老年人**一樣」（參 2 節）。[4] 這裏的四個

---

1 原文在 Πρεσβύτιδας ὡσαύτως 之後，假定了從 2 節補充 εἶναι（to be）一字（Clark, 'Structure' 110）。

2 原文名詞（πρεσβῦτις）在希臘文聖經僅再出現一次（偽經《馬加比四書》16.14）；作者這樣稱呼七子之母：'Mother, soldier of God in piety's cause, elder [πρεσβῦτι] and woman withal'（H. Anderson, in *Pseudepigrapha* 2.561）。Spencer 34 n.9 認為，'even the term *presbytera* has been used for women elders in 1 Tim 5:2'（*presbytera* = 一 5 的 *presbyteros*〔長老〕的陰性）。部分基於這兩點，Spencer 35-36 聲稱多二 3 的 πρεσβύτιδας 是指居領導地位的婦女（女長老）。可是，在提前五 1～2，保羅顯然是根據性別和年齡來區別四種人：

<u>πρεσβυτέρῳ</u> . . . παρακάλει ὡς πατέρα, <u>νεωτέρους</u> ὡς ἀδελφούς
老年〔男〕人 要勸 如同父親 年輕人 如同弟兄
<u>πρεσβυτέρας</u> ὡς μητέρας, <u>νεωτέρας</u> ὡς ἀδελφάς
老年婦女 如同母親 年輕婦女 如同姊妹

同樣，多二 2、3、4、6 也是根據性別和年齡來區別四種人：老年〔男〕人（πρεσβύτας）、年長的婦女（πρεσβύτιδας）、年輕的婦女（νέας）、年輕〔男〕人（νεωτέρους）。因此，文理絕對不利於 Spencer 的聲稱。參二 2 註釋註 4 之（2）＝ 上面 222。

3 見二 2 註釋註 5 及所屬正文（上面 222）。Cf. Collins 340: 'presumably women in their early fifties.'

4 BDAG 1106*b* (s.v. ὡσαύτως): '*(in) the same (way), similarly, likewise* . . . The verb is to be supplied fr. the context'; cf. Griffin 299: 'The term "likewise" . . . indicates that the verb forms, which are lacking in the exhortations to the older women, are to be supplied from the exhortations to the "older men" given previously.'（**1**）Towner II 237 則認為，'Paul's instructions to the older women have the same goal (*likewise*) of Christian respectability.' Cf. Jeon I 67: 'The adverb "similarly" . . . indicates to the audience that the same standard of godliness is expected of both genders despite their distinct roles'; Witherington 137-38: 'the elderly women are basically to practice the same virtues as the elderly men'; Schreiner, *Interpreting* 123: 'the women are to live their lives in

項目在形式上（不是事實上）呈現交叉配置模式：正負負正。**在操守上恭正**（**#1**）原文片語[5] 在希臘文聖經出現僅此一次。**操守**的另一翻譯是**行為**（現修）；[6] 原文包括表裏兩方面的意思（有諸內形諸外）。[7] **恭正**原文的另一些翻譯是**謹慎**（當代、現修）、**恭敬**（新和）、**聖善**（思高）、[8]「端

---

accordance with sound teaching "in the same way" (ὡσαύτως) as the older men'（施賴納：《詮釋》138）。黃編 208 也認為，**照樣**的「意思是說，第二節對老年人的勸導，也同樣適用於老年婦人。」（**2**）比較本節和 2 節，可以看見 'topic changes that nevertheless involve a degree of parallelism may be characterized by asyndeton'（Levinsohn, 'Constraints' 331 with n.73）。參提前三 8。

5 ἐν καταστήματι ἱεροπρεπεῖς = '<u>reverent</u> in behavior / their behavior / their demeanour / in the way they live' (NKJV, RSV, NRSV; *EDNT* 3.150*a* [s.v. πρεσβῦτις] / NAU / REB / NIV, TNIV, NIV2011). (**1**) 名詞 **κατάστημα** 在希臘文聖經不再出現。(**2**) 形容詞 **ἱεροπρεπής** 在新約僅此一次，但在偽經《馬加比四書》出現兩次，用來形容一位「道德崇高（saintly [RSV, NRSV]）」的年輕人（9.25, 11.20）。這字是複合形容詞（from ἱερός + the adjectival form of πρέπω [Vine 1.106]）；ἱερός 在新約僅出現一次，指<u>聖</u>經（提後三 15）；πρέπω 則出現七次，詳見二 1 註釋註 6（上面 219）。

6 《輔讀》527（第一解釋）同。κατάστημα = 'behavior, demeanor' (BDAG 527*b* [s.v.]), 'demeanour' (*Paraphrase* 293);「涉及個人道德標準的行為表現」(《新希》179*b* [s.v.])。See also KJV / NKJV, RSV, NRSV, NAU, ESV / Mounce cxii: 'behaviour/behavior'; DC 139*b*, H. Balz, *EDNT* 2.269*a* (s.v.): 'conduct'. 亦參當代：言行。(**1**) 其他的翻譯還有：(**i**) **舉止**（思高）;「舉止」=「人的行動」(《國語》684*d*)；(**ii**) **行動舉止**／**舉止行動**（呂譯／新和）；(**iii**) 'in the way they live' (NIV, TNIV, NIV2011)，**生活**（新普〔NLT: 'live'〕)，「生活方式」(《輔讀》527〔第二解釋〕)。(**2**) Calvin 369 認為這裏的意思是，她們要 'show by their very dress that they are holy and godly.' Verner 171 認為，'κατάστημα probably refers both to dress and more broadly to deportment.' Cf. Montague 231: 'it suggests that women consecrated by baptism should manifest that consecration in how they dress, speak, and act'. (**3**) Collins 340/341 則翻譯為 'station/state in life'; 341 解釋如下：'Classical writers used "state in life" (*katastēmati* [*sic*, *katastēma*]) to refer to a person's state, condition, or demeanor; Hellenistic Jewish authors used this term to refer to behavior or disposition.'

7 Johnson II 231 認為此字可指 'an internal disposition', 亦可指 'external bearing'; 'the translation "demeanor" seeks to capture the combination.' Marshall 243 也認為，這字同時表達 'general demeanour' 以及 'a corresponding inward dimension that yields outward calm and poise' 這兩方面的意思。See also Towner III 722（唐 1054）：'conduct understood as the interplay of inward and outward realities'; n.30（註 23）：'Combining the inward and outward, the term arrives at a notion of an inward condition that yields an observable result'.

8 See also LN §9.37: 'lead a <u>holy</u> life'; G. Schneider, *EDNT* 2.176*a* (s.v. ἱεροπρεπής [1st meaning]): 'holy'; NJB / Fiore II 208: 'behave <u>as befits / as is appropriate for religious people</u>'.

莊」、[9]「配受尊敬」。[10] 不過，原文的意思最可能是**敬虔**（新譯）。[11] 馬歇爾認為，**恭正**跟上一節的**端正**（#2）差不多。[12] 不過，二字的區別可能是這樣：第 2 節的**端正**是指令人尊敬，本節的**敬**

---

9 *Paraphrase* 293: 'dignified'.

10 Davies I 99, Marshall 244, Classen, 'Epistle to Titus' 56: 'worthy of reverence'. See also Marshall 243: 'the word properly means "befitting a holy person, thing", hence "holy, worthy of reverence".' Cf. H. Balz, *EDNT* 2.269*a* (s.v. κατάστημα): 'honorable'（值得尊敬）。Bouwman 69 則認為，**在操守上恭正**原文直譯是 'in behavior befitting a temple', 即是將 ἱεροπρεπής 這字內的 ἱερο- 視為代表 ἱερόν = 'temple'.

11 See also Mounce cxii, G. Schneider, *EDNT* 2.176*a* (s.v. ἱεροπρεπής): 'reverent' (2nd meaning). 亦參上面註 5 所引的英譯本。(**1**) Genade 46 說，ἱεροπρεπής 的意思是 'to act like a sacred person'; see also DC 139*b*, 140*a*: 'priestly'; Hanson I 113: 'literally "priestlike"'; Dunn 869*b*: 'as befits a priest'; Knight II 306: 'befitting a holy person'; Johnson II 230, 231: 'befitting a priestess', 234: 'They are . . . to have the bearing of priestesses'; Fee 186: 'acting like a priestess'; Lock 140: 'like people engaged in sacred duties'; Quinn 27, 116, 134: 'to be as reverent . . . as priests'; Kelly 240 / Hiebert 436: 'the adjective suggests the behaviour / the adjective . . . conveys the image of a good priestess carrying out the duties of her office'; Witherington 131: 'exhorted . . . to the sort of reverent and godly behavior characteristic of priestesses and other holy persons'; 134: 'older women should behave like priestesses'; 137: 'each one of them is to "behave like a priestess"'; Zehr 264: 'in the manner of a priestess in the temple'; 呂譯：**有聖役上的恭敬**；彭編 100*a*：「虔敬」 = 「合乎獻祭要求的態度」。Hanson III 180 贊同 'carry themselves as befits a holy calling' 這翻譯。(**2**) Wieland（'Crete' 344）指出，在 Gortyn（克里特最大的考古遺址〔彭編 97 有「戈突納（Gortyn）主後六世紀聖提多教會遺址」的圖片；「戈突納為克里特主後一世紀時的首府」〕）出土的雅典娜神廟的還願供物中，包括一些少女的像，她們被禁制於某種建築物內（'young females in the confinement of some kind of structure'）；這種禁制可能指那些少女曾在廟裏侍奉，那可能是她們的教育的一部分（with reference to M. Prent, *Cretan Sanctuaries and Cults* [Leiden/Boston: Brill, 2005] 636）。Wieland 問道：'Is Titus 2.3-4 hinting at an analogy to service performed by women in the temples, indicating that the behaviour of Christian women in their households could have the character of service offered to God?' 筆者認為，作者的辯證相當迂迴，且臆測成分頗高，故此問題的答案應是「值得懷疑」。

(**3**) BDAG 470*a-b* (s.v.) 正確地認為：'The more specialized mng. *priestlike* (so Dibelius) . . . is less prob. here'; 這裏的意思是 'reverent, venerable'. See also LN §53.6 / §41.8 : 'devout/pious';《新希》160*b*（s.v.）：「虔誠的；篤信宗教的；虔敬的」。(**4**) G. Schrenk（*TDNT* 3.254; followed by Best, 'Sacrifice' 290）認為，ἱεροπρεπής 最好的解釋是提前二 10：**這才與自稱為敬畏上帝的女人相稱**（ὃ πρέπει γυναιξὶν ἐπαγγελλομέναις θεοσέβειαν）；前一個字是後一句描述的縮寫（thus also Mounce 410）。這個字的要旨在於提醒那些年長的婦女，'since they belong to God by faith in Jesus Christ, they should live and act accordingly, i.e., with the consonant reverence'（G. Schrenk, *TDNTA* 354），意即她們的生活行動應表現出與她們屬於上帝這事實一致的敬虔。

12 Marshall 189: 'with much the same significance'.

虔則指對上帝的恭敬虔誠。[13]

不說讒言（**#2**，同呂譯、新和、新譯）原文是否定詞 + 形容詞，這形容詞與名詞「魔鬼」相同。[14] 說讒言的意思不僅是說長道短（當代）或搬弄是非（現修）。[15] 讒字的意思是「說別人壞話」、[16]「說假話毀謗好人」，[17] 因此不說讒言意即不毀謗人（思高）；[18] 提多要教導老年婦女，她們不可毀謗別人（新普）。[19]

不作酒的奴隸（**#3**，同現修）較貼近原文的翻譯是不被酒奴役（新譯）。[20] 被酒奴役或做〔了〕酒奴（呂譯）的表現，就是好酒貪杯（當

---

13 See Banker 66*a*: '(tell them that they should) behave in a holy, reverent manner.' 陳 32 合併兩方面的意思：「對神敬虔，對人端莊之態度」。

14 （**1**）Schreiner（*Interpreting* 123）／施賴納（《詮譯》136）的翻譯在這一項之前補充 '*That is*'／「即是」二字；因他認為第二至四項「較詳細解釋〔第一項〕敬虔生活的本質」（《詮譯》138〔*Interpreting* 125〕）。筆者倒認為，這裏的四項較可能是同等的，像上一節的四項一樣。（**2**）**διάβολος** 在保羅書信出現八次：五次是名詞，指魔鬼（弗四 27，六 11；提前三 6、7；提後二 26），其餘三次是形容詞，分別形容女執事（提前三 11：讒謗〔思高〕）、末世的人（提後三 3：惡言中傷〔新譯〕），和年長的婦女（多二 3 本節）。新約另外 29 次，也都是指魔鬼（除了約六 70 可能是指 'a devil' [KJV, NKJV, RSV, NRSV, NAU, NIV, TNIV, NIV2011, NJB, ESV, NLT] 而不是 'the devil'）。See BDAG (s.v.);《新希》77*a*（s.v.）。

15 這兩種翻譯相當於英文的 'gossip'. See also NAU: 'not malicious gossips'; *CGEDNT* 42*a* (s.v. διάβολος): 'given to malicious gossip'.（在前一種翻譯，'gossips' 是人物名詞：「愛說三道四的人」；在後一種翻譯，'gossip' 是「流言蜚語」之意。）留意兩種英文翻譯都加上「惡意的（malicious）」一字。Quinn 27, 116, 119 的意譯 'devils at gossip' 似乎企圖帶出此字與「魔鬼」的聯繫（見上註）。See also NJB / REB, *Paraphrase* 293; Davies I 99: 'scandal-mongering / scandalmongers'（散播醜聞／散播醜聞的人）。

16 《國語》773*d*。See BDAG 226*b* (s.v. διάβολος): 'pert. to engagement in slander, *slanderous*'.

17 《新雅》690*a*。See also KJV: 'false accusers'.

18 See also NKJV, ESV: 'not slanderers'; RSV, NRSV, NIV, TNIV, TNIV, Fiore II 208: 'not . . . slanderers'.

19 NLT: 'They must not slander others'.

20 μὴ οἴνῳ πολλῷ δεδουλωμένας = 'not . . . enslaved to much wine / heavy wine drinking' (NAU / Fiore II 208). See also REB: 'not . . . slaves to excessive drinking'; Quinn 27, 116, 119, 134: 'not slaves to drink'.（**1**）黃編 208 認為，「被酒奴役〔的〕程度比『好酒』（參提前三 8）更惡劣。」不過，該處原文作 μὴ οἴνῳ πολλῷ προσέχοντας, 而 'addicted to / indulging in much wine'（RSV, NAU, ESV / NRSV, NIV, TNIV, NIV2011）其實與本節的 'addicted / enslaved / slaves to much wine'（NIV, TNIV, NIV2011 / NAU / ESV）無異。（**2**）δεδουλωμένας 是 **δουλόω** 的完成時態被動語態分詞。這動詞（**i**）在保羅書信再出現五次：四次為被動語態，分別指信徒作了義的／上帝的

代、新普)、**沉湎於酒**(思高)。[21] 如彼得後書二章 19 節所說,**人被甚麼東西所支配,就是甚麼東西的奴隸**(新普)。在這裏,這東西就是「酗酒」;年老的婦女不可**作酗酒的奴隸**(新普頁邊註)。[22] 在希羅社會中,婦女過度飲酒是個普遍的現象。[23] 諷刺的是,她們以愛酒開始,結果卻成為酒的奴隸。[24]

奴僕(羅六 18/22);信徒在成為上帝的兒子之前**被世上粗淺的學說所奴役**(加四 3〔參《加》924-27、976-91〕);以及在婚姻關係中,若不信的一方堅持要離開信主的伴侶,信主的一方就**不再受約束**(林前七 15,當代),即是**不必受奴轄**(呂譯)去維持這段婚姻(see Fee, *First Corinthians* 302-3)。餘下的一次為主動語態,指保羅**使自己成了眾人的奴僕**,為要多得一些人(林前九 19,思高)。(**ii**)在新約僅再出現二次,一次為主動語態(徒七 6),另一次為被動語態(彼後二 19)。See BDAG 260*b* (s.v.);《新希》89*a*(s.v.)。

21 See also KJV, NKJV / NIV, TNIV, NIV2011: 'given/addicted to much wine'; NJB: '(no) addiction to wine'; NLT: 'be[ing] heavy drinkers'.(**1**)*Paraphrase* 293 作 'over-addicted to wine'. 為甚麼是 'over-addicted' 而不僅是 'addicted' 呢?因原文有 πολύς 一字:布魯斯將 'addicted to <u>much</u> wine' 化為 '<u>over</u>-addicted to wine'.(**2**)回到思高的翻譯,**沉湎於酒**其實含有贅述,因湎字本身已經是「沉/沈迷於酒」(《新雅》381*b*/《國語》444*d*)之意。

22 NLT margin: '(They must not) be enslaved to much wine'; see also RSV, NRSV / ESV: 'slaves to drink / to much wine'.

23 Fiore II 209. See also Johnson I 125: 'the repetition here [see 1:7] suggests that drinking as an enslaving vice is a problem for this population.' 亦參:彼前四 3:**你們從前……生活在……醉酒**(ἐν . . . οἰνοφλυγίαις)**……中**。(**1**)Scott 164 指出**被酒奴役**(新譯)和**說讒言**的關係:'In ancient times, when wine was the only beverage, it was at their little wine-parties that old women would tear their neighbours' characters to pieces.' See also Marshall 245: 'drunkenness and talkativeness or slanderous talk were common elements in the typical description of old women in Hellenistic culture.' Cf. Towner III 723(唐 1055):'"Addiction to much wine" was probably . . . the cause of the slanderous talk'.(**2**)Towner III 723-24 認為,酗酒和毀謗是「解放了的羅馬婦女(liberated Roman women)」在宴會上的典型行為,而這些行為同時與缺乏克己(σωφροσύνη〔參 5 節開首的 σώφρων〕)——這是確保女性在性方面貞忠的主要美德——和性濫交有關連。這些含意是社會交流('social discourse')夠強的一部分(唐 1056「這些含意就是<u>非常強烈的社會講論</u>的一部分」英文原作 'These implications were <u>a strong enough</u> part of the social discourse'),以致保羅不必提及就已暗示出來。'His intentional echoing of this stereotype is meant to ensure that Cretan Christian older women rid themselves of this "typical" reputation.' 參註 29 之(3)= 下面 236。(**3**)White 191*b* 說:'It is proved by experience that the reclamation of a woman drunkard is almost impossible.'「戒酒無名會(Alcoholics Anonymous)」的成立(1935 年於美國)和努力不懈,應使這句話在今天不再適用。

24 'Tt. 2:3 . . . refers to women who from lovers of wine have become its slaves'(K. H. Rengstorf, *TDNT* 2.279 n.1)。

用善道教導人（#4）原文是形容詞（在希臘文聖經僅此一次）。它的意思其實不是用善道教導／教訓人（同新譯／當代、新和），[25] 因它並不包含道字；不是作好榜樣（現修）或用好榜樣教導人（呂譯），[26] 也不（僅）是教人行善（思高），而是十分籠統的教導人美善的事（新普）。[27] 與此同時，較年長的婦女所教導的對象，可能不是籠統的「人們」（原文並無指明賓詞），而是較年輕的婦女，因為

25 參《輔讀》527（第一解釋）：「教好的道理的」。

26 See also Barrett 134, White 191*b*: 'by example'; Scott 164: 'as patterns of a good life'; Blaiklock 83: '"Teachers of virtue." Primarily by example'; Hanson III 180: 'their method of teaching is by their lives and behaviour'; Marshall 242: 'largely through example and informal instruction'; Towner II 237: 'The adjective *teaching what is good* denotes informal teaching by lifestyle'; Faber, 'Titus' 143: 'καλο- functions as internal accusative and means informal teaching by word and example';《輔讀》527（第二解釋）：「作好榜樣的」;《串釋（增簡）》1754*b*：「在家庭裏（參提前 2:12）以身作則教導後輩」（黃編 208 同）。REB 譯作 'they must set a high standard'（這隱含了以身作則之意）。反對的理由見二 4a 註釋首段（下面 237-38）。

27 See also NAU; BDAG 504*a* (s.v. καλοδιδάσκαλος); K. Wegenast, *DNTT* 3.768; H. Balz, *EDNT* 2.244 (s.v.) / Classen, 'Epistle to Titus' 56: 'teaching what is good / good things'; ESV / RSV, NRSV: 'They/they are to teach what is good' (cf. NIV, TNIV, NIV2011: 'but to teach what is good'); NLT: 'they should teach others what is good.' See also K. H. Rengstorf, *TDNT* 2.159: 'The older women are to keep the younger to their duties, i.e., to every καλὸν ἔργον.'（**1**）化為人物名詞就變成 'teacher of what is good, teacher of what is right'（LN §33.249），'teachers of good things / all that is good / all good things'（KJV, NKJV / *Paraphrase* 293 / DC 139*b*），'teachers of what is good and beautiful'（Collins 338, 341），'teachers of virtue'（Wall 346, 349, 350）。《新希》171*b*（s.v.）明確解釋為「教正確道理的教師」。（**2**）原文是複合形容詞（from καλός + διδάσκω）；形容詞 καλός 見二 7～8a 註釋註 6 之（2）－ 下面 259；動詞 διδάσκω 見一 11 註釋註 14 之（2）= 上面 168。（**3**）Hanson I 113 認為原文 'means literally "one who is a good teacher"'; Johnson II 230/234 也翻譯為 'effective/good teachers'. 參較下面之（4）。但是 Marshall 246 指出，雖然 'teaching what is good' 和 'good at teaching' 都是此字可能的意思，但有兩個與此類似的字——κακοδιδασκαλέω（teach what is bad）和 κακοδιδασκαλία（evil teaching）（see K. H. Rengstorf, *TDNT* 2.160）——顯示，前者才是正確的意思。Smith 72 也指出，提前一 7 的 νομοδιδάσκαλος（律法教師）和一 3，六 3 的 ἑτεροδιδασκαλέω（傳別的教義）提示，多二 3 這字是指 'the content of the teaching.'（**4**）Towner III 724（唐 1056）認為，由於文理聚焦於年長婦女的品格，因此 'good teachers'（thus also Witherington 128, 137; Winter, *Roman Wives* 155; cf. Jeon I 68, 72: 'commendable teachers'）是較好的翻譯。MHT 2.278 指出，'Καλοδιδάσκαλος . . . being a ἁ.λ. [hapax legomenon], might be taken as *noble teacher*; but this would probably be καλλιδιδάσκαλος'.（最後此字也是複合形容詞，得自 κάλλος + διδάσκαλος, 就如羅十一 24 的 καλλιέλαιος〔好橄欖〕得自 κάλλος, beauty + ἐλαία, olive tree [Vine 3.136]）。

隨後的子句（4～5 節）開首就說，**好指教年輕的婦女**（4 節）。[28] 這子句同時顯示，年長的婦女所教導的內容，主要是年輕的婦女在家庭裏的正確行為。[29]

---

28 Banker 66*b*. Ward 252 也認為，**教導**是指以言語和行為影響年輕的婦女。Quinn 27, 116, 134 則把 καλοδιδασκάλους 連於 ἵνα σωφρονίζωσιν τὰς νεάς（4a 節），從而得出 'They are the right teachers for spurring on younger women' 之意。

29 See NJB: 'they must be the teachers of right behaviour'; Mounce 410: 'Context shows that this refers . . . to informal, one-to-one encouragement (σωφρονίζωσιν [v 4])（方括號是原來的）。**（1）**古特立認為，**教導人美善的事**（新普）一定是指 'ministry <u>in the home</u>'（Guthrie I 193; Guthrie II 205; 古特立 207）。See also Fee 191: 'Formal teaching is hardly in view; rather, it is that "everyday" kind of instruction that takes place <u>in the home</u> by word and example'. 但是 Witherington 131 提出，'We may wish to ask which younger women the older women are to instruct . . . Why should we simply assume that it is women within their own home rather than younger Christian women in general? I see no good reason for such a limitation.' 因此，**（2）**較可取的講法是，教導的內容（4～5 節）'has to do with being a model, godly wife'（Fee 186）。See also A. Oepke, *TDNT* 1.788: 'the elder women have the duty of exhorting the younger to family life as Christians'; G. Stählin, *TDNT* 9.457: '. . . to lead younger women to proper marriage and family life'; Kartzow 148: 'older women are to <u>teach</u> the younger ones <u>what is good</u> [καλοδιδασκάλους], that is to love their husbands and children'; 136: 'they shall <u>teach others to do well</u> [καλοδιδασκάλους]; that means to direct the young women to manage their households, love their husbands and children . . . (Tit 2:3-5).'（方括號是原來的。）如此，'The Christian tradition of domestic virtue is transmitted through the female line'（Houlden 148）。**（3）**Towner III 77 認為：'At this juncture it is possible to see the mark of the "new woman" trend, which challenged women to let go of dress codes and pursue promiscuity, spreading throughout the empire.'（「在這裡，可能可以看到『新女性』趨勢的迹象，這種趨勢挑戰婦女放棄服飾規範，並追求<u>在帝國境內蔓延的</u>性雜交」〔唐 108〕這翻譯，錯誤地將分詞片語 'spreading throughout the empire' 視為形容 'promiscuity'; 其實，這分詞片語是形容 'trend' 字的，英文的原意是：「……可以看到『新女性』趨勢的迹象<u>在帝國境內蔓延</u>，這種趨勢挑戰婦女放棄服飾規範並追求性雜交。」）參註 23 之（2）= 上面 234，二 4b～5a 註釋註 19 之（4）= 下面 245。

二 4a 好指教年輕的婦女……[1]

連接詞好字似乎引入了第 4 至 5a 節頗長的目的子句。（一）理論上，這目的子句可視為連於第 3 節的四個項目（**在操守上恭正、不說讒言、不作酒的奴隸、教導人美善的事**〔新普〕），[2] 所得出的意思

---

1 τὰς νέας 是冠詞用作 'substantiver' 的例子，即是冠詞 + 形容詞 = 名詞（Wallace 231）。(**1**) Classen（'Titus' 437, 'Epistle to Titus' 56）力辯，論年輕婦女的 4～5 節（從**年輕的婦女**開始）應視為與 3 節分開的一段，'even though τὰς νέας has to be taken as the object of σωφρονίζωσιν'. 他認為作者在 4 節似乎是從一種結構（σωφρονίζωσιν τὰς νέας）轉入另一種結構（τὰς νέας φιλάνδρους εἶναι），後者與早前的 νηφαλίους εἶναι（2 節開首）平行，且仍是從屬於 1 節的動詞 λάλει 的。可是，將原來一氣呵成的 σωφρονίζωσιν τὰς νέας φιλάνδρους εἶναι 一分為二（且牽涉到將 τὰς νέας 一物二用），這做法殊不自然（儘管克拉遜聲稱，'an infinitive construction following [σωφρονίζειν]' 並無他例可援）。(**2**) 雖然如此，筆者在這裏仍然將 3～4a 節（給**年長的婦女**的教導）和 4b～5 節（給**年輕的婦女**的教導）分開（as in Classen, 'Titus' 444, 'Epistle to Titus' 66），不是由於克拉遜的上述理由，而是（i）由於年長婦女要教導年輕婦女的，顯然可以視為提多對後者的教導，而且（ii）給予 4b～5 節本身的標題，才可以在大綱裏反映內容上的平行（AA'BB'）以及交叉配置模式（XYY'X'）：

4.1.2	年老的（A）	男人（X）	（二 2）
4.1.3	年長的（A'）	婦女（Y）	（二 3～4a）
4.1.4	年輕的（B）	婦女（Y'）	（二 4b～5）
4.1.5	年輕的（B'）	男子（X'）	（二 6）

(**3**) Ward 254 認為值得留意，保羅將對年輕婦女的要求包括在年長的婦女應該給予的訓練之內；**年長的婦女**看來很像**女執事**（提前三 11）。(**4**) Quinn 10 認為，二 4～5 含有 'a citation from a marriage charge'. 筆者認為以上二說均流於臆測。(**5**) Griffin 302 認為，'That Paul has given more attention to the young women and has been more specific in his exhortations suggests that the behavior of this group was creating more problems for the Cretan church than perhaps the behavior of other groups designated in 2:2-10.' 但是，對奴僕的指示佔了更多的篇幅（9～10 節〔原文為 27 字，開首的**僕人**不算在內；相對於 4b～5 節的 18 字〕），這是否表示奴僕比年輕的婦女引起更多的問題？

2 即連接詞 ἵνα 是從屬於（depends on） 3 節開首、在副詞 ὡσαύτως 之後所隱含的不定詞 εἶναι（重複自 2 節）一字。參陳 32：好字表示，「老年婦人自己先有了三節的各種品德，這樣才可以指教家中少年的婦女……」; Schreiner, *Interpreting* 125: 'I take it to be a purpose clause since in the pastoral [*sic*] Epistles both behavior and words are necessary for healthy teaching.* Thus, the older women teach the younger women not only with words but by the way they live.'（*「教牧書信同樣需要就人的行為和言語作出健全的教導」〔施賴納：《詮釋》138〕這翻譯沒有掌握英文原意。）

就是，年長的婦女要藉著上述的行為以身作則地影響年輕的婦女。但若這是第 3 至 5 節的主要思想，保羅大可以用類似**要顯出自己是好行為的榜樣**（7a 節）這樣的話來表明此點；但是他沒有這樣做。而且，上述的四個項目與下文（4b～5 節）所要求的行為（七個項目）並沒有緊密的關連；如果**指教**是指藉著榜樣來教導，那麼在「年長的婦女應當怎樣」和「年輕的婦女應當怎樣」二者之間應有更緊密的聯繫。[3] 較可取的看法是，（二）這目的子句在思想上是連於上一節末的形容詞**教導人美善的事**〔新普〕所隱含的動詞**教導**；[4] 這動詞和本節的**指教**都肯定提示藉著言語來教導之意。雖然保羅一定同意年長的婦女應**以身作則**（馮譯），但是他此刻的焦點是在於她們口頭上的教導。[5] 另一方面，很難理解**指教年輕的婦女**如何是**教導人美善的事**的目的；因此，也許（三）討論中的子句應視為表達命令，[6] 它只是延續了上一節的四個項目，就如一些譯本所表明的：……**她們應該教導人美善的事，訓導年輕婦女愛丈夫**……（新普）。[7]

---

3 Banker 67*a*.（**1**）這評語同樣適用於另一種看法，就是將 ἵνα 子句視為表達結果：'Then they can train/urge the younger women . . .'（NIV / TNIV, NIV2011）；'and so train the younger women to love their husbands . . .'（RSV, ESV）；'Then in their turn they will encourage the younger women . . .'（*Paraphrase* 293）；**她們這樣才能教導年輕的婦女**……（當代）。（**2**）D'Angelo（'Family Values' 160）則認為，'there is no indication that they teach other than by example (2:3-6).'

4 見二 3 註釋註 27 之（2）= 上面 235。

5 Banker 66*b*, 67*a*.

6 See BDAG 476*b* (s.v. ἵνα, 2 g): 'ἵνα w. subjunctive as a periphrasis for the impv.' 不過，多二 4 並不在這辭典所例舉的例子之中。Mounce 411（with 406 n.c）則認為，indicative σωφρονίζουσιν（不是 subjunctive σωφρονίζωσιν）才是原來的讀文。

7 NLT: 'These older women must train the younger women to love their husbands . . .'. Witherington 139（引 Collins 341 的意見）指出，在古代，貧窮的婦女一般不會飲酒，較富有的婦女才會飲酒；對後者而言，飲酒表示她們較富裕的地位。因此，威瑟靈頓認為，保羅在這裏假定（i）部分的聽眾至少頗為富有，並且擁有自己的家庭；（ii）即使她們較為年長，也許沒有很多可自由支配的收入（'perhaps would have less discretionary income'），她們仍然負擔得起飲酒的花費；（iii）又有時間教導會眾中（而不僅是自己家中）的其他成員。這提示保羅在這裏想到的是 'some elite women who are capable of being good teachers.'

指教（同新和）、**教育**（馮譯）或**教導**[8]／**訓導**（思高、當代／新普[9]）原文動詞在希臘文聖經不再出現；同字根的名詞也只出現一次（提後一 7：**自制的心**）。[10] 另一譯本合併了「指導」和「訓練」[11] 兩個意思：**要……善導年輕婦女，訓練她們……**（現

---

8 See also KJV: 'teach'; LN §25.37, §33.229: 'to teach'. Cf. NJB: 'show'.

9 See also NKJV, DC 140*b*: 'admonish'. Zamfir 108 翻譯為 'reason . . . with'.

10 二字依次為：σωφρονίζω, σωφρονισμός. **(1)** 前者是使役（factitive）動詞，意思是 'bring one to one's senses'（*EDNT* 3.329*b* [s.v.]）。以下英譯似乎企圖表達這種使役意思：'bringing *the younger women* to the sensible practice of loving *their husbands and children*'（Ward 252）；'to give younger women the good sense to be . . .'（Fiore II 208）；'make sensible'（Jeon I 14, 68）；'make [them] soberminded'（Calvin 370）；'"make them modest" (*sōphron-izōsin*). "Modesty" was the epitome of feminine virtue in the Hellenistic world'（Collins 342; cf. Witherington 136: 'the older women are to make the younger women modest. Heliodorus stressed that "modesty is the distinctive virtue of women" . . . , especially younger women (Demosthenes . . .)'）。**(2)** 溫特力證這字的意思是 'good teachers bringing their charges back to their senses'（Winter, *Roman Wives* 159; see 155-59; followed by Smith 339, 340）。唐 1058 也認為，保羅選用這字，就是由於它能夠表達「隱喻性、使人清醒的『給人一巴掌』之意（即『讓人清醒過來』）」（Towner III 725: 'the idea of a figurative, sobering "slap in the face"' [followed by Jeon I 68]）。亦參彭編 100*b*：「**指教**……宜作『使……謹守』、『使……節制』、『使……合宜』，在此有『回歸正途』之意」。**(3)** 不過，此使役動詞在這裏可能已減弱為勸告之意；cf. D. Zeller, *EDNT* 3.330*b* (s.v. σωφροσύνη, 4): 'the factitive vb. σωφρονίζω here is weakened to *admonish*'; Marshall 247: 'σωφρονίζω is "to make somebody sober, bring them to their senses, make of sound mind", hence "to encourage, advise, urge"'; Dunn 869*b*: 'it may have the weaker sense of "encourage," "advise," "urge"'; Mounce 405, 407, 410, Krause II 609: 'encourage'; Johnson II 230: 'advise'. **(4)** Witherington 128 翻譯為 'train in self-control'，大抵是由於他認為動詞 σωφρονίζω 包含了同字根的形容詞 σώφρων* 的意思。（*在二 2 翻譯為**克己**。）**(5)** Genade 47 認為，這裏用**指教**而不用一 11 的**教導**（διδάσκω），為要使合法的教師和不合法的教師保持距離；參二 1 註釋註 5 之（1）（i）= 上面 218。**(6)** Fairbairn 273 則認為，由於受教者是年輕的婦女，這裏的**指教**屬於 'the more severe and urgent kind'. 他引用以下例子支持他的看法：'δεῖ τοὺς μὲν λόγοις νουθετεῖν, τοὺς δὲ ἀπειλαῖς σωφρονίζειν', 意即「必須對一些人用話語來勸戒、教導，對另一些人則用**威嚇**〔弗六 9〕來 σωφρονίζειν」。不過，是否有此可能：這裏的對比不在於兩個動詞，而在於兩個名詞（兩個名詞都放在不定詞之前，表示受到強調）；換一個講法，'more severe and urgent' 的意思不是來自不定詞 σωφρονίζειν, 而是來自名詞 ἀπειλαῖς（dative of means）？

11 See RSV, NIV, ESV, NLT, Banker 60, 66*a*: 'train'; Marshall 184: 'training'. NRSV 修訂為 'encourage'（thus also NAU, *Paraphrase* 293），TNIV 和 NIV2011 則修訂為 'urge'（see also BAGD 802*a* [endorsed by Knight II 307], BDAG 986*b*-87*a* [s.v. σωφρονίζω]: 'encourage, advise, urge'）。但後兩個意思（'encourage, urge'）保羅通常用 παρακαλέω 來表達（參一 9 註釋註 29〔上面 146〕）。此評語亦適用於 Quinn 27,

修）。[12] 年長的婦女教導的對象只是**年輕的婦女**，[13] 因而保羅在這裏的指示跟提摩太前書二章 12 節（**我不許女人教導**）並無衝突。[14] 從下文的幾個項目（尤其是 #1、2、5）看來，**年輕的婦女**可能特指已婚的年輕婦女。[15] 值得留意的是，提多本身要教導老年人和年長的婦女（2、3 節）以及年輕的男人（6 節），

116, 134, 135 的意譯：'spurring on'. **提醒**（新譯）恐怕也不是原文的意思；三 1 的**提醒**原文動詞是 ὑπομιμνῄσκω.

12 參《新希》323*b*（s.v.）：「教導；訓練」。呂譯作**好修練年輕婦人**。Wall 346, 350, 383 譯作 'mentor'（動詞）。Carter－Levine（'Pastorals' 246）卻認為，這些婦女 'are given the role of controlling other women'.

13 **年輕的婦女**原文只是 τὰς νέας, 'the young'（陰性）。Collins 342 認為她們是 'in their twenties'（cf. Wall 349: 'those "twenty-somethings"'）。利斐特 345（Liefeld 328）則認為，「"少年婦人" 不只是指年輕的成人，而是包括了任何不算年老的婦人。」**(1)** 形容詞 **νέος** 在保羅書信另外出現七次（新約全部 24 次），分別指（**i**）基督信徒應該像**沒有酵母的新麵／麪團**（林前五 7，現修／新普），他們已**穿上了新人**（西三 10）；（**ii**）（比較級用作原級）**年輕人**（男性；多二 6；提前五 1）、**年輕婦女**（五 2）、**年輕的寡婦**（五 11、14〔從 11 節補充**寡婦**一字〕）。See BDAG 669*a*-69*b* (s.v.);《新希》225*a*（s.v.）。**(2)** Barclay（'Age' 226 n.3）則認為，本節的 νέαι 形式上是原級，但其實具有比較級的意思，因它與 6 節比較級的 νεώτεροι（'younger men' [NJB, cf. RSV, NRSV, ESV]）並排。巴約翰進一步認為，'the terms "young" and "younger" are in most contexts synonymous (as are "old men" and "older men"); in other words, even the non-comparative forms generally carry an implicit comparative sense, since such age labels are almost always defined *by comparison with* each other.' 參二 2 註釋註 6（上面 222）。

14 Fiore II 209. Cf. Zamfir 258: 'There is nothing in the context to suggest that such teaching should be carried out in public, although an all-female community may be envisaged. More significantly, the content of this instruction does not encompass doctrinal matters, but addresses exclusively . . . the attitude required from women in the *oikos* [household]' 參二 3 註釋註 29 之（2）＝ 上面 236。

15 Towner III 725 n.44（唐 1057 註 37）：'younger wives who are still occupied with raising children and keeping house.' Cf. Towner II 237: '*younger women* means younger married women, for in that day most would have been married.'（**1**）Keener 628*b* 也直言，'"Young women" were almost always wives, because Jewish and Greco-Roman society generally frowned up women's singleness and men seemed to have outnumbered women.'（**2**）White 192*a* 認為，也許保羅只想到 'recently married women'（see also Hiebert 436: 'the newly married'）。問題在於她們的**兒女**有多大；在習慣早婚* 的文化中，一個婦女的兒女可能已踏入青少年期，但本身仍屬**年輕的婦女**，卻不能稱為 'recently/newly married'.（*Winter, *Roman Wives* 163-64: 'While it is known that soon after reaching puberty young women married, usually between the ages of fourteen and seventeen, the age at which young men took the *toga virilis*** was around eighteen.'）（** = 'toga of manhood',「表示成年的托加袍」，參《加》882 註 6。）

但是教導年輕婦女的責任則落在年長的婦女身上；斯托得認為，如果長老／監督是未婚的，這宗旨是特別有意義的，但即使他已經結婚，這可能仍是明智的做法。[16]

16 Stott 188. See also Montague 232: 這做法是 'a measure of prudence, avoiding even the possible appearance of any sexual irregularity if their formation were confided to men'; Chapell 329: 'Paul . . . apparently desires to establish a pattern of instruction in the church that does not lead to sexual temptation.' Gannett（'Titus 2' 86-87）從如何實踐多二 1～5 的角度指出，「年長」和「年輕」可以是比較性的觀念，她認為用「生命的階段（stage of life）」（比起用年齡）來定義「年長的婦女」可能更有幫助：'Each stage brings different challenges: emotional, physical, relational, and spiritual. An "older" woman may be defined by a bride as a woman who has gone through the adjustment of the first few years of marriage. To a mother of teenagers, an "older" woman may be a mother whose children have left home and entered the working world. The "older" woman to the recent widow may be a chronologically younger woman who has already been through the stages of grief after the premature death of her husband.'

4.1.4 年輕的婦女（二 4b～5）

二 **4b** 愛丈夫，愛兒女，

5a 克己，貞潔，理家，善良，順服自己的丈夫，

愛丈夫（**#1**）原文[1] 在希臘文聖經出現僅此一次。在古代「盲婚啞嫁」的情況下，希羅倫理所盼望或要求於妻子的，至多也只是尊敬和順服丈夫，不是愛；因此，愛丈夫的妻子會被視為特別好的妻子。[2] 愛在這裏所指的不是愛的感覺或激情，不是羅曼蒂克的愛，更不是性愛，[3] 而是自我犧牲、服事對方。[4] 作丈夫的……要愛自己／你們的妻子（弗五 25／西三 19），所指的也是這種在意志及行動上尋求對方的最高福祉的愛。[5]

---

1 φίλανδρος. See LN §25.37: 'having love . . . having affection for one's husband'. (**1**) 原文為複合形容詞（from φιλέω + ἀνήρ）；動詞 φιλέω 見三 15a～b 註釋註 16（下面 472）；名詞 ἀνήρ 見一 6 註釋註 15 之（2）= 上面 104。(**2**) Calvin 370 認為保羅在這裏 'is continuing with his list of the duties of women which apply to the older women as well. . . . in reminding older women of their duties, he at the same time offers to the younger an example they should follow, and so teaches both at once.' 其意思大抵是，這裏的七個項目仍是指著年長的婦女說的，她們要立下榜樣給年輕的婦女跟隨。

2 So Witherington 133.「盲婚啞嫁」英文原作 'arranged marriages'.

3 Oden 116 則似乎認為這裏所指的是性愛：'women would counsel women on how to treat their husbands with affection. . . . Paul thought that it was not to be left merely to natural impulse. Here lie deep Jewish-Christian roots of what we today call sex education.'

4 Stott 188: 'love is . . . not so much the love of emotion and romance, still less of eroticism, but rather of sacrifice and service.' Arichea－Hatton 284 指出，'In a society of arranged marriages, where women did not have a say at all on the choice of their husbands, this quality is very important and needs to be emphasized.' See also Spencer 40: 'Cretan marriage was a public, state-controlled ceremony, involving those who belonged to the same age-grade and same social class. However, the wives usually did not join the husbands' homes until later when the young women had learned how to manage household affairs. Most marriages were arranged. . . . Thus, love for one's husband had to be learned.'

5 參《弗》850 連註 9，852 註 20；《西・門》653，連註 3-5。

愛兒女（**#2**）原文在新約不再出現。[6] **愛兒女**不是母親的天性嗎？古特立認為，鑑於假教師所用的「破壞家庭」的策略（一 11），這一項要求具特殊意義。即使在現代，信主的基督徒婦女若把自己的事業置於兒女的福祉之上，就是展現了「缺乏母愛」（即是母親不愛自己的兒女）的重要症狀。[7]

克己（**#3**）原文形容詞已在上文出現兩次，分別用於監督（一 8）和老年人（二 2）身上。[8] 同字根的抽象名詞在提摩太前書二章 9 節，指女人要以**克己**／**莊重**／**自律**／**克制**（呂譯／思高／新譯／和修）為裝飾。[9] 克己（抽象名詞，相當於「貞潔」）就是古代婦女的主要美德，

---

6 〔**1**〕此字（φιλότεκνος）在偽經《馬加比四書》出現三次：一次形容「愛兒女」的父母（15.4）；另二次為比較級（φιλοτεκνότερος），分別指母親比父親更「熱愛她們的兒女（devoted to their children [RSV, NRSV]）」（15.5），以及七子之母比任何其他的母親更「愛她的兒女」（15.6）。（**2**）這字是複合形容詞（from φιλέω + τέκνον [Vine 1.188]）。動詞 φιλέω 見上面 註 1 之（1）；名詞 τέκνον 見一 4a 註釋註 2 之（3）= 上面 76 。（**3**）這裏的 φίλανδρος 和 φιλότεκνος 二字與一 8 的 φιλόξενος 和 φιλάγαθος 遙遙呼應。Genade 128 稱之為 'Anaphora' 的例子。筆者認為這稱謂並不合適，因這字所指的應為 'the identity of the initial <u>words</u> in each member [of a parallelism]'（BDF §489），但上述四字只是其前綴（φιλ-）相同。新約聖經裏 anaphora 最長的例子是來十一 3～31 的 Πίστει 一字（共 18 次：3～5、7～9、11、17、20～24、27～31 節）（BDF §491）。

7 Guthrie I 193; Guthrie II 205（古特立 208）。（**1**）Ward 253 指出，'love does not always flow out of a person, even a wife and mother, as from a mountain spring. Love in the family requires thoughtfulness and the mother has to work at it.'（**2**）Johnson I 131 甚至認為：'The evidence surrounds us in frightening fashion that our [American] culture is one which hates children. . . . Ours is a kingdom which increasingly has no place for children: not simply the retarded and the crippled and the ugly but all children. . . . We have to give ourselves to them without much recognition or payment. So we rationalize turning over their care to others – "it is good for them," we say, perhaps meaning, "it is good for us."'（**3**）Barclay 251 斷言，'It is infinitely more important that a mother should be at home to put her children to bed and hear them say their prayers than that she should attend all the public and Church meetings in the world.' 參註 25 Chapell（下面 246）。

8 σώφρων, 參一 8 註釋之（**#11**）= 上面 136-37；二 2 註釋之（**#3**）= 上面 226。

9 μετὰ . . . σωφροσύνης: 'with . . . sobriety/moderation/propriety/self-control' (KJV, RV / NKJV / NIV, TNIV, NIV2011 / ESV), 'sensibly / decently / soberly / discreetly / modestly' (RSV / NRSV / NEB / NAU / NJB). 這名詞（σωφροσύνη）在新約僅再出現兩次，分別指保羅所說<u>清醒</u>的話（徒二十六25）和女人的**克制**／**克己**／**自律**（提前二15，和修／呂譯／新譯）或**莊重**／**端莊**（思高／新普）。

此美德使婦女能夠愛丈夫和保護他的名譽。[10] 本節的形容詞用於婦女身上也是指在性方面的忠誠，[11] 在這裏特指對丈夫的忠誠。[12] **貞潔**（**#4**）有翻譯為「誠懇地」。[13] 但**貞潔**（同呂譯、新和、現修、新譯，新普同）[14]（尤指性方面的清潔）無疑更符合文理，所指的是在性方面對丈夫忠誠。[15] 如此，**克己**和**貞潔**皆指妻子在性方面對配偶忠誠，[16] 重複提及表示強調；不過，二字並非完全同義：**貞潔**的重點在於「清潔、沒有玷污」的性質，[17] **克己**的重點則在於克制慾望與衝動。[18]

---

10 Winter, *Roman Wives* 102: 'It was the cardinal virtue for women in the ancient world'; Towner III 207（唐 294）：'In reference to women . . . "self-control" (= chastity) takes in behavior and dress that signifies the restrained and modest wife, able by it to protect the honor of her husband.'

11 Winter, *Roman Wives* 145: 'This term . . . in relation to women refers to sexual fidelity.' Cf. D. Zeller, *EDNT* 3.330*b* (s.v. σωφροσύνη, 4): 'Applied to women here, σώφρων . . . is used to mean *modest*, *chaste*'; S. Wibbing, *DNTT* 1.502: 'chaste, pure'; Banker 64*b*: 'self-control in one's sex life'; Laansma 264: 'here it applies to purity within marriage'.

12 彭編 100*b*-1*a*：「在此的重點為節制慾望，用於女性，往往指在性方面對自己的配偶忠誠。」Fee 187 則認為，這字是當代作者最常用來描寫好妻子的字詞之一，而它最常有的意思是指「有品德」的婦女。

13 DC 139*b*, 140*b*: '[to live] in sincerity'. See also F. Hauck, *TDNT* 1.122: 'It signifies "moral purity and sincerity"'; Saarinen 180: '"chaste" (*agnē* [*sic*]) refers to blameless and sincere character in a broad sense'. Arichea－Hatton 284 則解釋為 'free from any moral defect in thought, word, and deed.'

14 See also KJV, NKJV, RSV, NRSV, REB, NJB, H. Baltensweiler, *DNTT* 3.101: 'chaste'.

15 Marshall 248: 'Sexual fidelity to the husband is meant.'

16 Bassler 196: 'a wife's sexual fidelity to her spouse'. See also BDAG 987*b* (s.v. σώφρων): 'Esp. of women <u>*chaste*</u>, *decent*, *modest*'; 13*b* (s.v. ἁγνός, b): 'Esp. of women <u>*chaste*</u>, *pure*'; 即是這兩項被視為意思相近。

17 H. Balz, *EDNT* 1.22*b* (s.v. ἁγνός): 'pure, undefiled'.（**1**）原文形容詞 **ἁγνός** 在保羅書信另外出現四次，新約另三次，分別指提摩太要保守自己<u>純潔</u>（提前五 22），哥林多人表明了自己是<u>無可指責的</u>（林後七 11），保羅要把他們如同<u>貞潔的</u>童女獻給基督（林後十一 2），信徒當思念的事包括凡是<u>純潔的</u>（腓四 8，思高〔參《腓》447-48〕）；那從天上來的智慧首先是<u>純潔的</u>（雅三 17，新普），妻子<u>純潔的</u>品行（彼前三 2）能感化不信的丈夫，每一個盼望基督顯現的人都會保持自己的純潔（ἁγνίζει），正像基督是<u>純潔的</u>（ἁγνός）一樣（約壹三 3，現修）。See BDAG 13*b* (s.v.);《新希》5*a*（s.v.）。（**2**）同字根的名詞 ἁγνεία 在新約僅出現兩次（提前四 12，五 2：純潔〔新譯、現修、新普〕），在 LXX 亦僅出現四次（民六 2、21；代下三十 19；次經《馬加比一書》14.36）。（**3**）另一個同字根的名詞 ἁγνότης 在希臘文聖經僅出現兩次（林後六 6，十一 3），指「道德上純全的素質」（《新希》5*a* [s.v.]）。

18 See Towner III 727: 'it was to manifest itself above all <u>in dignified conduct characterized</u>

理家（**#5**）與提摩太前書五章 13 節那些年輕寡婦的**挨家閒逛**構成鮮明的對比。原文在希臘文聖經不再出現。[19] 但提摩太前書五章 14 節對年輕的寡婦表達了類似的願望：（**在嫁人、生養兒女之後**）**治理家務**。[20] 有英譯本和釋經者將**理家**和**善良**（**#6**）連起來成為一項；[21] 這

---

by restraint of the passions and urges that might jeopardize fidelity to her husband.'（唐 1060「其高尚舉止特別顯明在克制那些會危及對丈夫貞節的情慾與衝動上」這翻譯，可能節約了英文的原意。英文的原意是，**克己**這美德尤其要由「高尚舉止」顯明出來，這「高尚舉止」的特徵就是「克制……的情慾與衝動」。）

19 οἰκουργός 是複合形容詞（from οἶκος + a root of ἔργον [Vine 2.228]）；名詞 οἶκος 見一 11 註釋註 12 之（2）= 上面 167；名詞 ἔργον 見一 16 註釋註 35 之（1）= 上面 213。（**1**）RSV 翻譯為 'domestic'（also G. Schneider, *EDNT* 2.505*a* [s.v. οἰκουργός]; Classen, 'Epistle to Titus' 56; cf. KJV: 'keepers at home'）。這反映異文 οἰκουρούς, 'staying at home, domestic'（BDAG 700*a* [s.v. οἰκουρός]; see also MHT 2.273: 'house-guardian'）。但 οἰκουργούς 才是原來的讀文（see *TextC* 585）。馬歇爾認為，οἰκουργός 'is a Hellenistic variant of οἰκουρός / a variant of the Cl. οἰκουρός'（Marshall 243/248）。（**2**）Twomey 204 則認為，'keepers at home'（KJV）這翻譯可能更為準確，因為 '*oikourgous* does not imply active participation in decisions concerning the household economy but rather the simple fact that one works in the house (Bassler 1996: 196; Knight 1992: 308).'（**3**）Quinn 27, 116, 120, 135, 136, 137 的翻譯 'tending the hearth' 以部分（the hearth）代替全部（the home），即是使用了 synecdoche 的修辭技巧。（**4**）Winter（*Roman Wives* 160 [also cited by Laansma 265]）提到，斯特拉波（Strabo, 約公元前 63－公元 24；斯多亞派的希臘地理及歷史學者〔《聖神》490*a*〕）記載了克里特島獨有的一種結婚習俗：丈夫們 'did not take their girls whom they married to their own homes immediately, but as soon as the girls were qualified to manage the affairs of the house'（Strabo, *Geography* 10.4.20）。溫特認為：'This fits well with Titus 2:5. Young wives who had not been instructed in the management of their households are called to undertake that for which they were deemed qualified before they ventured into the marriage home.' 溫特聲稱：'This further suggests that in Crete there was now an option of an alternative lifestyle for young married women – that which was promoted by the "new" Roman women.' 筆者認為，這聲稱從**理家**一詞看出太多的意思來。參二 5b 註釋註 3 之（3）（4）= 下面 250-51。

20 原文動詞為 οἰκοδεσποτέω: 'manage the house / their households / their homes'（NKJV / NRSV, ESV / NIV, TNIV, NIV2011）。這動詞同樣在希臘文聖經不再出現，但同字根的人物名詞 οἰκοδεσπότης 則出現十二次，分別指**一家／一個家的主人**（太十 25，二十 1；太二十四 43 ‖ 路十二 39／太十三 52，二十一 33）= **一家之主**（路十三 25）、**那家的主人**（太二十 11；可十四 14 ‖ 路二十二 11）、田地的**主人**（太十三 27）、僕人的**主人**（路十四 21）。

21 TEV: 'to be good housewives'; LN §46.3; Collins 338; Fiore II 208 / Towner I 193: 'good/efficient homemakers'; Banker 60, 67*a*, Hanson III 180: 'good workers at home'; Chapell 331: '*useful* home-workers'; Donelson II 176: 'good household managers'; Stern: 'to take good care of their homes'. See also Fiore II 209: 'good homemaking' is among 'the domestic virtues the letter promotes'.

樣，有關年輕婦女的六項便可分成三對：**愛丈夫，愛兒女；克己，貞潔；**好的家庭勞動者，**順服自己的丈夫**。[22] 不過，第五項原文本身的意思已經是**勤理／勤於家務**（思高／現修），[23] 這意思和「好的家庭勞動者」相當近似，若翻譯成**善理家務／善於持家**（當代／新普）[24] 就更是這樣。因此，**理家**和**善良**較可能是分開的兩項，[25] **順服自己的丈夫**則為第七項。[26]

---

22 Banker 67*b*.

23 οἰκουργός = 'busy at home' (NEB, REB, NIV, TNIV, NIV2011), 'busy at home, carrying out household duties' (BDAG 700*a* [s.v.]), 'working at home' (Mounce cvii, 405, 411). See also *Paraphrase* 293: 'do their housework'; Bouwman 86: 'That is "homeworking," where all her activity is directed to what benefits her family';《新希》227*b*（s.v.）：「照顧家庭的；打理家務的」;《輔讀》527：「專務家事的」。MHT 2.274 翻譯為 'home-worker'（cf. Knight II 308: 'women should be diligent homeworkers'; Blomberg, 'Titus' 354: 'wives . . . should become diligent "homeworkers"'）；這翻譯使筆者（聯）想到，香港不少的中小學學生，尤其是在 TSA* 的壓力下，都不幸地變成名副其實的 'homework-ers'（課外作業者）!（*TSA = The Territory-wide System Assessment, 這是香港考試及評核局「受教育局委託，在小三、小六……及中三級舉行的全港性系統評估，所有接受政府資助的學校在指定的時段均須參與評估」〔www.hkeaa.edu.hk/tc/sa_tsa/tsa/, 2016.04.06 瀏覽〕。後記：「小三 TSA 」已演變為教育局準備推廣至全港小學的「2017 小三基本能力評估研究計劃 [BCA = Basic Competency Assessment]」〔www.bca.hkeaa.edu.hk/web/TSA/zh/2009_priNews.html#, 2017.07.07 瀏覽〕。）

24 See also NRSV, Davies I 100, Davies II 82, Saarinen 180: 'good managers of the household'; BV, Hanson I 113, Johnson I 126, Johnson II 230, 231, Witherington 137: 'good housekeepers'（cf. Witherington 128: 'a good housekeeper'; 但 139 則似乎一物二用：'encouraged to . . . be good housekeepers . . . being self-controlled and kind'）。Collins 342 用了三種翻譯：'good housekeepers', 'good householders', 'good homemakers'. Wall 346, 350 用第三種。

25 關於**理家**一項，Mounce 411（followed by Blomberg, 'Titus' 354 n.41）指出：'It does not require a woman to work only at home (cf. Prov 31), but it does state that she does have duties at home.' Chapell 330-31 直言，'Any woman who makes career status or financial advantage a higher priority in her life than the welfare of her marriage, children, or home transgresses Scripture as well as the signals of a heart sensitive to God's Spirit.' 參註 7 之（3）= 上面 243。

26 （**1**）Quinn 122 反對 'good housekeepers' 這翻譯的理由就是，'this sense alters the formal structure of the list, which is adjectival to *neai* and septuple.' 即是這個意思改變了本列的結構——**年輕的婦女**有七重的形容（see also 129: 'The younger women are to cultivate a septet of virtues'; 135: 'the content of the exhortation for the younger women is spelled out in the seven qualities that follow'）。（**2**）這反對理由同樣適用於 *Paraphrase* 293 的做法——把第六、七兩項連起來而得 'be good and obedient to their husbands' 之意。（**3**）另一個反對理由是，頭四項都並無修飾語，將 #6 看為 #5

善良（**#6**）或良善（思高）[27] 的意思是「仁慈的」。[28] 司各脫解釋為，勤於家務的婦女必須避免把全部精神都花在家務上，卻要保持高度的同情心。[29] 這籠統的意思可包括待人有恩（新和）和慈善／好慈善／多行善事（現修／呂譯／新普[30]）等意思在內。[31] 不過，文理支持較明確的意思，就是仁慈地對待在履行家庭職責中所接觸到的所有人，包括家中的奴僕。[32] 到此為止的六項可分為三對，分別描寫作妻子／母親的在其家庭關係中的主要關注（愛丈夫，愛兒女），她個人的虔誠（克己，貞潔），以及她的活動範圍和她對身邊的人的態度和行動（理家，善良）。[33]

的修飾語跟上述模式不符（Hendriksen 365 n.197; Knight II 308）。（**4**）Quinn 134 認為：就教牧書信而言，很難想像年長的婦女不必實踐她們教導年輕的婦女要做的事；3 節沒有提到前者要順服自己的丈夫，乃是由於她們與丈夫年紀相若，因而與他們分享在家中的領導地位。但見二 6 註釋註 24 所屬正文（下面 257）。

27 See also KJV, NKJV: ‘good’; Blaiklock 83: ‘good housewives, good women’.

28 I.e., ἀγαθάς = ‘kind’ (RV, RSV, NEB, NAU, NIV, TNIV, NIV2011, ESV; Guthrie I 194; Guthrie II 206*), ‘kind-hearted’ (Phillips).（*古特立 208 只是沿用新和的待人有恩。）

29 Scott 164: ‘They must be careful to preserve the larger sympathies which the too active housewife is so apt to lose.’

30 NLT: ‘to do good’.

31 另有翻譯為和藹（當代）、‘gentle’（NJB），‘good-natured’（BV）。Stott 189 則理解為 ‘[being] hospitable’.

32 Marshall 249: ‘the wife is to exhibit kindness towards all those with whom she comes in contact as she applies herself to her domestic duties’ (followed by Jeon I 70); Mounce 412: ‘[this refers] to the young woman’s kind treatment of those in her household’; Towner III 727（唐 1061）：‘she is to show consideration to those with whom she has contact in carrying out her household duties’; Zehr 265: ‘kind to all the persons she meets in her domestic duties’; Winter, *Roman Wives* 161: ‘This would encompass others beyond the confines of her family and include any of her household servants.’ Cf. Lock 137: ‘kindly to their servants’; 141: ‘“kindly,” *i.e.* mainly, “to their servants”’; Quinn 121: ‘considerate and kindly in dealing with her domestic help’, 137: ‘her considerate supervision of others who work for her’; see also White 192*b*. (**1**) Ward 253 認為，‘To be kind is the natural expression of love for husband and children.’ Hiebert 437 認為，善良的對象是「別人，尤其是家人」。See also Bailey, ‘Theology’ 358: ‘they are to demonstrate kindness . . . to their husbands’. (**2**) Hendriksen 365 則認為，除了丈夫和妻子，善良的對象亦包括奴僕：‘*kind* . . . not only to husbands and children but also to slaves.’ See also Kelly 241: ‘she should not forget the kindly sympathy she owes to her family and her domestic helps.’ 但是關於家人，上文已有明確的指示：愛丈夫，愛兒女；下文再提到順服自己的丈夫。此點不利於以上二說。

33 Knight II 308; Marshall 246.

這裏的七個項目以**愛丈夫**開始（先於**愛兒女**），又以**順服自己的丈夫**（#7）[34] 結束，昆謝隆認為這反映了對婚姻生活之心理學的睿見。[35] 的確，配偶的位置被兒女取代的婚姻關係是不理想的。**順服**提示妻子選擇自願順從丈夫之意，[36] **愛丈夫**則提示，妻子對丈夫的順

---

34 Cf. NEB/REB: 'respecting the authority of their own / their husbands'; Young 91: 'respectful of their husbands' authority'; Mounce, 'Titus' 106: 'It's important that they allow their husbands to lead'.「妻子應順服丈夫是由於〔上帝〕在家庭中設立了領導和權柄的角色，而順服就是謙卑地承認〔上帝〕所設定的次序」(《弗》830)；詳細的討論見同書 829-38。(**1**) Padgett ('Submission' 50-51) 則認為，雖然保羅相信在基督裏男女是平等的，但是為使教會可以繼續生存，繼續傳揚福音，並且免受更大的非議和逼迫，他就在兩害之間取其輕，要求妻子順服丈夫：'Paul's concern is for the advancement of the church in the face of first century opposition. . . . It was therefore necessary to yield the right of women Christians to equality with men, so that the gospel could go forth. Although Paul knew women to be equal in Christ to men, he soon discovered that they had to submit to their pagan husbands, if the church was to survive, and to avoid greater slander and persecution.' 作者聲稱，'The Pastorals make a choice between two evils: the destruction of the church as a whole, including women and slaves; or the suffering of women and slaves for the sake of the church and her good news' (51-52). (**2**) Köstenberger 616 批評 Padgett 'unduly presupposes that Paul held an "egalitarian" view of gender roles.' 另見 Knight II 316-18 和 Mounce 417-19 對 Padgett 一文的批評和反駁。

35 Quinn 136: 'A shrewd insight into the psychology of married life puts the husband first (ahead of children) as well as last in the list.'

36 See Quinn 138: 'This freely chosen subordination . . .'; Marshall 247: 'the middle voice implies willing subjection and makes it the responsibility of the wife to give it rather than for the husband . . . to take it'; Padgett, 'Submission' 41: 'the word *hypotassesthai* . . . means a voluntary submission to a recognized authority'; Towner III 728: 'the wife is to show submission to the husband of her own free will' =「妻子當自願順服丈夫」(唐 1062)；《弗》830-33。(**1**) G. Delling (*TDNT* 8.43) 認為，'in the commonly required subjection of wife to husband according to the biblical understanding . . . the issue is keeping a divinely willed order'. 筆者同意；參《弗》830。(**2**) Fee 188 認為，保羅在「妻子順服丈夫」這一點上，只是假定了 'the cultural norm of what a good wife was expected to be like'. 但是 Knight II 309-10 指出，保羅認為在某些基本的事上，非基督徒的倫理意識也是正確的（例：提前五 8；林前五 1），因為**律法的功用刻在他們心裏**（羅二 15）〔詳參《羅》1.374-77〕)。本段關於**老年人**、**年長的婦女**、**年輕人**的教導，都反映 'Christian norms rather than merely contemporary cultural norms'，因而以類似的格式與這些教導並列的對**年輕的婦女**的教導，也是如此。本段提到**美善的事**（3 節，新普）和**好行為**（7a 節），其中的**美善**和**好**都是指 'that which is good from God's point of view, not of that which society happens to regard as good.' 這就是說，沒有理由把妻子要**順服自己的丈夫**這一項視為例外；這一項（像所列出的其他的美德）並非 'merely cultural', 而是 'a transcultural standard'. 筆者同意。(**3**) Arichea－Hatton 284 根據弗五 21（**要……彼此順服**）而認為，'the husband also is commanded to submit to the wife.' 但見《弗》806-13 的討論；特別留意 813 註 21

服應該不是勉強的或敷衍了事，而是帶著愛心的。[37] 洛窩特認為，不管丈夫是否基督徒，妻子都應順服（參：提前六 1、2）。[38] 二章 9、10 兩節的指示，可能是對所有奴僕發出的，不管他們的**主人**是信主或不信主的；[39] 這一點支持洛窩特的看法，因為在一個家庭之內，丈夫、父親（本書沒有提及）和主人是同一人。[40] 值得強調的是，新約聖經從來沒有「丈夫要使妻子順服自己」這種講法。[41] 婦女要**順服自己的丈夫**與奴僕要**順服自己的主人**（二 9）前後呼應；兩者的要旨皆在於把順服的命令局限於家庭內的特定關係，而不是把它應用於整個羣體：妻子要順服的是自己的丈夫，[42] 不是一般的男人；奴僕要順服他們自己的主人，不是羣體內所有的自由的人。[43]

之（1）。**（4）**動詞 ὑποτάσσω 在保羅書信另外出現 22 次，新約另 15 次（合共 38 次）。詳見《弗》807-9。

37 Köstenberger 615*b*: 'Their submission is not to be grudging or perfunctory but loving'.

38 Lock 141. Cf. Tollefson, 'Titus' 153*b*: 'Paul urged voluntary submission on the part of women to their unbelieving husbands', **免得上帝的道被毀謗**。

39 參二 9～10 註釋第二段（下面 270-71）。

40 亦參《西・門》657 註 20 之（1）。

41 Correctly, Quinn 137. See also Mounce 412: 'In both the husband/wife and master/slave relationship, Paul does not allow the former to demand submission but instructs the latter to give it. This is a significant distinction'; Ngewa 367-68: 'Husbands should not regard themselves as entitled to demand submission. It must be a gift offered by the wife, not a right demanded by the husband.' 亦參《西・門》657 註 20 之（1）：「夫妻各有自己的命令，任何一方都不能把使徒對另一方的命令變成自己對配偶的命令。」

42 **（1）** Johnson II 234 就著**順服自己的丈夫**問道：'Can we detect a hint of the influence of other male teachers making inroads into the structure of domestic authority (see 1:11)?' Winter（*Roman Wives* 162）認為，**順服自己的丈夫**這最後指示 'sought at the very least to counter a prevalent view of marriage in which a wife might pursue a life of pleasure as some of the Roman wives did.' 它也可能針對姦淫的問題，若如是，'then the use of "own" (ἰδίοις) contrasted with any sexual rendering of themselves to another man.' **（2）** 筆者認為這些看法並不穩妥；留意 REB 已將 NEB 的 'their own husbands' 修正為 'their husbands'（見上面註 34），表示 REB 的譯者認為 ἰδίοις 並無強調之意。

43 Marshall 250.

二 5b **免得上帝的道被毀謗。**

這目的子句是回溯上文哪些人的呢？祈勒克認為，它所回溯的範圍不僅是**年輕的婦女**（4 節），也包括**年長的婦女**（3 節），可能還有第 2 節的**老年人**。[1] 不過，下文第 8 節的目的子句（**使那反對的人**）和第 10 節的目的子句（**好事事都能榮耀**）都分別只是回溯所屬的組別（提多、僕人）；這就提示，目前的子句只是年輕的婦女所受教導之行為（4b～5a 節）的目的。[2] 她們所受的教導都聚焦在夫妻和親子關係上，因為這方面的壞見證會危害基督教信息的可信性。[3]

---

1 Clark, 'Structure' 111. 他認為 'the structure of the whole sentence' 支持這看法（「整個句子」大抵指二 1～5）。持這看法（目的子句表達 2～5a 節的目的）的還有 Schreiner, *Interpreting* 125（施賴納：《詮釋》138-39）。

2 持此立場的釋經者包括 Arichea－Hatton 285; Banker 68*a*; Hendriksen 365; Hiebert 437; Knight II 309; Marshall 250; Mounce 412. See also Gannett, 'Titus 2' 84.

3 Genade 48.（**1**）Witherington 130 指出，這目的子句是「省略三段論法（enthymeme*）」的第三部分，如下：（*70: 'Enthymemes are miniature syllogisms in which usually one of the elements or argumentative premises is omitted.'）

> '1. Younger women should submit themselves to their own husbands,
> 2. [For outsiders will judge our faith based on their behavior,]
> 3. So the Word of God will not be discredited by observers.'

（第二行的方括號是原來的，表示該行是被省略的部分〔'a suppressed premise'〕。）不過，筆者認為第一行不應限於**順服自己的丈夫**這一點，而應包括 4b～5a 節的全部內容（見上註所屬正文）。參二 8b～c 註釋註 1 之（2），二 9～10 註釋註 41（下面 266，277）。

（**2**）古特立認為，5b 節提示，一些被福音解放了的婦女在濫用她們新近獲得的自由，其方式不被當代社會所認可（Guthrie I 194, Guthrie II 206: 'Contravention of these Christian qualities . . . would be an affront to the Christian message, suggesting that some women, emancipated by the gospel, were abusing their new-found liberty in ways which were not approved in contemporary society.'）。（「那些在福音裏被釋放的婦女，若濫用了這自由，行不被當時社會所容許的事，將是對這信息的公然污辱」〔古特立 208〕這翻譯，沒有掌握作者的原意。）（**3**）Winter（*Roman Wives* 166-67）更明確地列出在甚麼情況下基督教信仰的名譽會受損：'if young wives (i) did not return to their role of loving their husbands and children; (ii) did not exercise self-control but indulged in debauchery; (iii) were not pure, or committed to managing their own households; (iv) were not kind or submissive to husbands in the intimacy of marriage but engaged in casual sexual liaisons.' 溫特認為（168），克里特的年輕已婚婦女 'had been influenced by some of their secular married sisters. Terminology used in Titus to counter

上帝的道[4] 就是來自上帝的信息，[5] 也就是上帝的福

---

the situation in Crete fits well with what is known of the "new" Roman women's conduct with their lack of interest in the welfare of the household which Cretan women had to demonstrate their ability to run before marrying. The neglect of her husband as well as her children presumably in favour of a social life that might involve casual extramarital affairs is also commented on. The call, therefore, was for the young Christian wives to come to their senses and no longer follow the secular trend.' 她們採納了羅馬的「新女性」的前衛行為方式（'the *avant-garde* ground rules of the "new women"）；這些行為方式可能使她們在另一範疇獲得更大的自由——'inappropriate liaisons with those not their husbands with the resulting neglect of their own spouses and children'（168）。參二 4b～5a 註釋註 19 之（4）= 上面 245。**(4)** 不過，溫特的專題研究受到頗多的批評和質疑：（**i**）Suzanne Dixson (*JTS* n.s. 56.2 [2005] 560)：'I remain unconvinced of his central thesis about the existence of a "new woman" and of the impact of such a concept on the whole Mediterranean Roman empire.'（**ii**）James R. Wicker (*SWJT* 47.2 [2005] 252): 'Although his research is interesting and enlightening, he ultimately fails to prove his point. The evidence is sometimes questionable (such as using poets, who tend to exaggerate or excessively titillate, 24-30), scanty (proof of the new woman in the eastern Roman empire is sparse, 32-37), and overstated (202-3). The alleged new woman *Sitz im Leben* [life-setting] seems to be an excuse to wrongly relegate all of the "problematic" NT passages about women as culture bound and irrelevant for today.'（**iii**）Edgar Krentz (*CurTM* 34.3 [2007] 217*b*): 'The appendix on the "new woman" is based largely on Roman love poetry and satirical poetry. But are Catullus, Ovid, Juvenal, and Martial representative of the bulk of Roman society－and of society in the Greek east? Certainly the views of Musonius Rufus and Plutarch, along with much epigraphic evidence, would give a different picture.'（**iv**）Kenneth D. Litwak (*The Covenant Quarterly* 63.1 [2005] 45): 'in a culture that lacked modern media, and in which a large proportion of the population were slaves or poor, one must ask how much of what can be learned about the new Roman woman is of general relevance for all or even the majority of women in the eastern empire in Paul's day.'（**v**）Shelley Matthews (*CBQ* 67.1 [2005] 162): 'The major problem with W.'s argument comes into focus in his suggestion that the New Woman lurks behind all the biblical passages he exegetes in part 2 [1 Cor. 11:2-16; 1 Tim. 2:9-15; 1 Tim. 5:11-15; Tit. 2:3-5]. To explain and defend these restrictions on women, W. repeatedly resorts to the specter of this sexually aggressive, inappropriately dominant, and otherwise immoral figure.'（**vi**）Mary Rose D'Angelo (*JR* 85.3 [2005] 481): 'Most classicists seem rather chary of claiming that adultery remained (or ever was) a social sport in any significant sector of the Roman aristocracy.' 正面的評估包括（但不限於）：Kathleen E. Corley (*Interpretation* 58.3 [2004] 318*b*): 'The overall thesis of Winter's book is certainly sound, and his exegetical discussions based on his evidence are well worth reading.'

4 ὁ λόγος τοῦ θεοῦ（主格）在保羅書信另外出現三次（羅九 6；林前十四 36；提後二 8）；τὸν λόγον τοῦ θεοῦ（直接受格）出現三次（林後二 17，四 2；西一 25），無冠詞的 λόγον θεοῦ 一次（帖前二 13）；無冠詞的 λόγου θεοῦ（所有格）一次（提前四 5）。

5 TEV: 'the message from God'. See also Quinn 122: 'The genitival "of God" emphasizes the divine origin of the message'. I.e., τοῦ θεοῦ = genitive of author/origin, but not 'subjective genitive' (*pace* Marshall 250 n.54), 因為 λόγος 並不是 verbal noun. Banker 68*a* 則理解為 'that message which is both from God and about God'.

音，[6] 亦即是基督的福音[7]＝關於基督的福音（羅十五 19，現修）。[8] 被毀謗（同新和）[9] 或受毀謗／謗讟（新譯、現修／呂譯[10]）的另一些翻譯是「受到懷疑」、[11] 蒙受恥辱（新普）。[12]

但見下文。

6 εὐαγγέλιον τοῦ θεοῦ / τὸ εὐαγγέλιον τοῦ θεοῦ / τὸ τοῦ θεοῦ εὐαγγέλιον（直接受格：羅一 1／羅十五 16；帖前二 2、8、9／林後十一 7）。

7 τὸ εὐαγγέλιον τοῦ Χριστοῦ（直接受格：羅十五 19；林後二 12，九 13〔思高、新譯、新普〕；加一 7）；τοῦ εὐαγγελίου τοῦ Χριστοῦ（所有格：腓一 27）；τῷ εὐαγγελίῳ τοῦ Χριστοῦ（間接受格：林前九 12）。

8 Hanson III 181 則認為，'this must mean simply the Christian religion.'

9 See also Quinn 27, 135-36, 138: 'so that the message of God not be defamed.' Cf. NIV, TNIV, NIV2011: 'so that no one will malign the word of God'.

10 See also KJV, NKJV: 'be blasphemed.' ESV 作 'be reviled'.

11 RSV, NRSV: 'that the word of God may not be discredited'; REB: 'will not be brought into disrepute'; O. Hofius, *EDNT* 1.220*b* (s.v. βλασφημία, 2 b): 'be *slandered* or *brought into ill repute*'.

12 See also NAU: 'be dishonored'; NJB: 'disgraced'; NLT: 'Then they will not bring shame on the word of God.'（**1**）動詞 **βλασφημέω** 在下文再出現一次（三 2：不要毀謗），保羅書信另外六次（新約全部 34 次），分別指有人毀謗保羅（羅三 8），保羅把許米乃和亞歷山大交給撒但，讓他們學會不再褻瀆（提前一 20）；保羅勸喻羅馬教會的「強者」，不可讓你們的善被人毀謗（羅十四 16〔參《羅》4.431-36〕），一個人不應因著所感恩的食物〔而〕被人毀謗（林前十 30），上帝的名在外邦人中受了褻瀆（羅二 24〔參《羅》1.401-3〕），作奴隸的要尊敬自己的主人，免得上帝的名和教導被人褻瀆（提前六 1）。最後這一節的意境與多二 5 本句相似。See BDAG 178*a* (s.v.);《新希》60*a*-60*b*（s.v.）。（**2**）同字根的名詞 βλασφημία 在保羅書信僅出現三次（毀謗：弗四 31；西三 8；提前六 4），新約另十五次；詳見《西‧門》533 連註 27；《新希》60*b*（s.v.）；BDAG 178*a*-78*b* (s.v.).

4.1.5 年輕的男子（二 6）

二 6 同樣，要勸年輕人凡事克己。

同樣即是第 3 節的照樣（新譯、新普），意即「像你要勸老年人，又要勸年長的婦女一樣」（參 2、3 節）。[1] 這裏的動詞從第 1 節的講字變為勸字。[2] 祈勒克認為這改變的理由可能是，保羅認為勸字不適用於較年輕的提多對較年長的人說的話，但是用於與提多同齡的組別說的話是合適的。[3] 可是，祈勒克自己指出，勸字在提摩太前書五章 1 節的對象正是老年人；勸字的意思比講字更明確，但它在這裏只是重複了第 1 節在功能上同義的講字，同時重拾了已在一章 9 節出現過的同一個字（勸勉）。[4] 其實，二章 1 節不用勸字而用講字的理由可

---

1 參二 3 註釋註 4（上面 230）。See also Mounce 412: 'ὡσαύτως . . . joins this discussion to the previous one in usual fashion for the PE (cf. v 3).'（**1**）Stott 189 則認為，同樣指年輕的男人像年輕的婦女一樣要克己。See also Marshall 253: 'in the present context it may stress the repetition of the concept of σωφροσύνη which is required of each of the groups to be addressed'; Jeon I 15 (cf. 71): 'Exhort . . . the younger men to be similarly sensible about all things'; Padgett, 'Submission' 49; Winter, *Roman Wives* 151.（**2**）黃編 210 卻認為，「這裏的意思是說，<u>第四、五節對少年婦人的勸導，同樣適用於少年人</u>」。但作者立即加上：「但『愛丈夫』（參 4 節）和『順服自己的丈夫』（參 5 節），宜作『愛妻子』和『愛自己的妻子』（參弗五 24～25）。」必須如此改寫經文正好表示，作者對「也要照樣地」的解釋是錯的。

2 παρακάλει. 這是信上第三次使用命令式語法的動詞；參二 1 註釋首段（上面 218）。這裏重新使用命令式語法動詞，似乎偏離了 2 節和 3 節所用的結構（該二節使用倚賴 1 節的講字的不定式語法）；但是由於對年輕的婦女的指示（4b～5 節）是間接地由 ἵνα 子句引入而不是直屬於 1 節的講字，因此，在這裏改用明確的命令式語法是明智的（Van Neste 242）。Cf. Marshall 253: 'The repetition of a verb instructing Titus what to say is necessary after the lengthy previous instruction (contrast 2.3)'; Towner III 730（唐 1064）。

3 Clark, 'Structure' 109. See also Montague 233-34: 'notice the <u>slightly stronger</u> verb here, delicately nuancing the method of instruction appropriate to the difference of age'; Guthrie I 194 / Guthrie II 206): '*exhort* / *encourage* [is] a <u>much stronger</u> directive than "speak" / that found in verse 1'; Mounce 412: 'παρακάλει . . . is <u>stronger</u> than its parallel λάλει . . . in v 1'.

4 Clark, 'Structure' 110. See KJV, NKJV / RSV, NRSV, NAU, NJB, ESV / NIV, TNIV, NIV2011, NLT: 'exhort / urge / encourage'. 思高則補充教訓（參一 11）一詞。

能十分簡單：第 1 節動詞的賓詞不是一些人，而是一些事，[5] 因而在該節沒有理由用**勸**字，**講**字才是合適的。

年輕人原文是比較級形容詞用作名詞，因此直譯可作「較年輕的男人」。[6] 如果**老年人**或「年長的男人」是個四十九／五十至五十六歲的人，[7] 那麼「較年輕的男人」就是四十九或五十歲以下的人。[8] 不過，比較級的形容詞有時用作原級的形容詞（例：徒五 6〔**年輕人**把亞拿尼亞抬出去埋葬〕；彼前五 5〔**你們年輕的，要順服年長的**〕）；本節可能是另一例子，[9] 因而**年輕人**（現修同）、**年青人／青年人**（新普／思高）、**年輕的男子**（新譯〔呂譯無「的」字）是正確的翻譯。[10]

---

5 λάλει ἃ πρέπει τῇ ὑγιαινούσῃ διδασκαλίᾳ, 'speak <u>the things which</u> are fitting/proper for sound doctrine' (NAU/NKJV). 參呂譯：你總要講健全教義上所適合講<u>的事</u>。

6 I.e., τοὺς νεωτέρους = 'younger men / the younger men' (NJB / RSV, NRSV).

7 見二 2 註釋註 5 及所屬正文（上面 221-22）。

8 參較 Hendriksen 366 n.198.

9 BDAG 669*a-b* (s.v. νεός, 3 b β): 'comp. . . . with little comp. force'. I.e., Τοὺς νεωτέρους = 'Young men / the young men' (KJV / NKJV, NAU, NIV, TNIV, NIV2011, NLT; G. Schneider, *EDNT* 2.463*a* [s.v. 2 b]), 'the young men as a class in the community' (J. Behm, *TDNT* 4.898). Behm（897 [followed by Köstenberger 617*a*]）認為年輕人是 20 至 30 歲的人。See also Towner III 730（唐 1065）：'younger men might be from twenty to thirty years of age, with some flexibility at the upward end.'

10 （**1**）Collins 343 指出，'A "young man" (*neaniskos*) is someone between twenty-one and twenty-eight years of age', 儘管本節所用的字不是 νεανισκός（例：徒二 17，五 10，二十三 18、22）而是 νεώτερος.（**2**）Wieland（'Crete' 342-43）指出，（**i**）克里特文化的特色包括 'the practices of male communal dining in ἀνδρεία (men's halls) and the separation of children into age groups for education and eventual initiation into adult society';（**ii**）克里特的文化又將男性分為三組：'Among males παῖδες (children), νεώτεροι (young men) and πρεσβύτεροι (older men) are distinguished.' 後兩組在本段出現：**年輕人**（6 節：νεώτεροι），**老年人**（2 節：πρεσβῦται）。後一個名詞（單數 = πρεσβύτης）與用作名詞的形容詞 πρεσβύτεροι（單數 πρεσβύτερος）意思相近：πρεσβύτης 指 '[an] old man, aged man'（BDAG 863*a* [s.v.]），「年老的男人」（《新希》280*b* [s.v.]）；πρεσβύτερος 亦可指「年老的男人」（《新希》280*b* [s.v. I 2 a]），cf. BDAG 862*a* (s.v. 1): 'pert[aining] to being relatively advanced in age, *older, old*'.（**3**）Bouwman 94 指出，'There is . . . a subgroup today known as "kidults";* these are the twenty-somethings who shy away from responsibility and so keep living at home, and have Mom make their lunch and do their laundry while they float from job to job.'（*'Kidult' 是由 'kid' 和 'adult' 二字得來的複合字，其通常的意思〔用作名詞〕是「童心未泯的成年人」或〔用作形容詞〕「同時適合兒童和

凡事意即「在一切事上」或「在各方面」。[11] 凡事二字在原文是第 7 節的開首，這反映於多數譯本該節的翻譯，例如：你凡事要顯出你自己是好行為的榜樣（呂譯），無論在甚麼事上都要有好行為（現修），各方面都做一個善功的模範（馮譯）。[12] 少數譯本則把原文片語連於上文，從而得出要勸年輕人凡事克己或在一切事上要慎重（思高）的意思。[13] 祈勒克觀察到，老年人、年長的婦女，和僕人（2、3、9 節）在所屬子句中都是首個項目（原文次序），這提示有關提多的教導也是以你自己（新和、現修、新普）一字開始，因而之前的凡事二字是連於上文的，就如第 9 和 10 節的凡事都是連於上文一樣。[14] 這種理

成年人口味的〔電視節目等〕」。）

11 περὶ πάντα = 'In/in all things' (KJV / NKJV, NAU), 'in all respects' (RSV, NRSV, ESV; MHT 3.270), 'in all aspects of life' (Towner I 194).

12 另見新和、新普；KJV, NKJV, RSV, NRSV, NAU, NIV, TNIV, NIV2011, ESV, NLT.（新普和 NLT 的翻譯在意思上略有出入：而你自己，要在各樣的善行上為他們作榜樣，不完全等於 'you yourself must be an example to them by doing good works of every kind.'）See also L. Goppelt, *TDNT* 8.250: 'In all things shewing thyself a pattern (in the doing) of good works'; Guthrie I 195 / Guthrie II 207（古特立 209）：'to show an example *in all things* / *in everything*'; Arichea－Hatton 286; Johnson II 230; Lock 142; Smith 71: 'In all things, Titus was to present himself as a model of good works'（但見下註）; Witherington 128, 140; Malherbe, 'Paraenesis' 301. 馬歇爾指出，'the phrase is not altogether appropriate with the following words'（Marshall 253）。

13 See also REB: 'Urge the younger men . . . to be temperate in all things'; NJB: 'urge younger men to be moderate in everything that they do'. Similarly, Bassler 197; DC 139*b*, 141*a*; Fee 188; Fiore II 208; Griffin 304; Houlden 149; Köstenberger 617*a*; Marshall 253; Mounce 405; Quinn 123; Smith 285: '. . . urge and teach . . . them to show self-control in all things'（但見上註）; Towner II 240; Towner III 730 with n.67（唐 1065 連註 60）。

14 Clark, 'Structure' 110. See also Banker 68*b*-69*a*. 另一理由是：'σωφρονεῖν . . . is such an important, all-encompassing term in the PE that περὶ πάντα . . . reads naturally with it'（Mounce 412）。因此，並無理由接受周 428 的臆測：「也許保羅故意把這兩個字擺在中間，好叫人明白，不僅少年人要凡事謹慎，提多本人也要在凡事上作信徒的好榜樣。」**(1)** περὶ πάντα 這介詞片語在希臘文聖經出現僅此一次。**(2)** 類似的 περὶ πάντων 在保羅書信出現四次（但只是所屬片語的一部分：〔περὶ πάντων ὑμῶν〕羅一 8；帖前一 8；〔περὶ πάντων τῶν ἁγίων〕弗六 18；〔περὶ πάντων τούτων〕帖前四 6），沒有一次用來開始一個題目。**(3)** 保羅書信確有八次以「περὶ δέ + 所有格」這種結構來引進新的題目（林前七 1、25，八 1，十二 1，十六 1、12；帖前四 9，五 1），但本節的 περὶ πάντα 既無 δέ 字，πάντα 亦非所有格（而是直接受格）。See Banker 69*a*.

解使第 7 節開首**你要顯出自己是好行為的榜樣**一句中的〔你〕**自己**一詞獲得它應有的著重。[15]

（一）**克己**（同呂譯）、**自律**（新譯）或**管束自己**（現修）[16] 原文不定詞[17] 的（二）另一些翻譯是**謹守**（新和）、**慎重**（思高）、[18] **在生活上謹慎**（新普）、[19] **檢點言行**（當代）、「心智清醒」、[20]「明智的」。[21] 這些意思可以並存不悖，但重點可能是在第一種意思。[22] 斯托得認為，保羅想到的一定是年輕的基督徒男子必須控制自己的脾氣和舌頭、野心和貪念，尤其是身體的慾望，包括性衝動，以致他們可以持守「婚前貞潔、婚後忠誠」這不能改變的基督徒標準。[23]

---

15 Kelly 242; Mounce 412. 原文為 <u>σεαυτὸν</u> παρεχόμενος τύπον καλῶν ἔργων. Hiebert 437 卻認為，'a connection [of περὶ πάντα] with v.7 gives proper emphasis to "yourself."'

16《輔讀》527(第三解釋)同。See also RSV / NRSV, NIV, TNIV, NIV2011, ESV: 'to control themselves / to be self-controlled'; D. Zeller, *EDNT* 3.330*a* (s.v. σωφροσύνη, 4): 'the young should . . . control themselves'; Blaiklock 83: 'Self-mastery is a magnificent achievement for youth.'

17 σωφρονεῖν, here 'an infinitive in indirect discourse'(see Wallace 603)。動詞 **σωφρονέω** 在新約僅再出現五次，分別指曾被鬼附的人**神智清醒**（可五 15 ‖ 路八 35），使徒的**清醒**（林後五 13，與**癲狂**相對）；信徒要將自己**看得適中**（羅十二 3〔新譯〕，參《羅》4.76-77），並因萬物的結局近了而要**謹慎自守**（彼前四 7）。See BDAG 986*b* (s.v.);《新希》323*a*-23*b*（s.v.）。此字沒有在 LXX 出現。

18 See also U. Luck, *TDNT* 7.1103: 'young men should be summoned to . . . a measured and orderly life.' NJB 則翻譯為 'to be moderate' =「適中的」。

19 NLT: 'live wisely'.

20 KJV/NKJV: 'sober minded / sober-minded'; *Paraphrase* 293: 'sober'.

21 NAU: 'sensible'. See also LN §32.34: 'to be wise and sensible'; Quinn 27, 116, 138, 139: 'to use common sense'.

22 See BDAG 986*b* (s.v. 2): 'to be prudent, <u>with focus on self-control</u>, *be reasonable*, *sensible*, *serious*, *keep one's head*'; Marshall 253: 'The basic idea appears to be that of self-control'. Kartzow 136 解釋如下：'This term means that they shall exercise self-control and have all aspects of their lives under control, a typical virtue for a male citizen in the ancient world.' Banker 68*b*（正確地）將原文動詞和同字根的形容詞 σώφρων（一 8，二 2、5）看為表達同一種品質；參一 8 註釋之（**#11**）（上面 136-37）。

23 Stott 189. Cf. Verner 172: 'In the case of younger men as in that of the younger women [v. 5a] there is probably a sexual connotation [in the word σώφρονας/σωφρονεῖν].' 參二 4b～5a 註釋第三段（上面 243-44）。

有別於對年輕婦女的教導，本節沒有提到年輕男子的責任，這「可能與當時女性的適婚年齡為 14-15 歲，而男性適婚年齡相對晚許多（可到 30 歲）有關。」[24]

24 彭編 101*a*。

4.1.6 提多的教導（二 7～8）

二 **7a** 你要顯出自己是好行為的榜樣，

7b 在教導上要正直、莊重，

8a 言語健全，無可指責，

顯出（同呂譯、新和、新譯）或**顯示**（思高）[1] 原文是個分詞，[2] 附屬於第 6 節**要勸年輕人凡事克己**的限定動詞**勸**字。[3] 但這並不表示，這兩節是屬於「對年輕人的勸勉」的一部分；相反，這兩節是和第 6 節分開、特別針對提多的另一單元，其重點落在提多本身的教導上。[4]

---

1 「導致，使……得到，給」（《輔讀》527）這些意思並不符合文理。參較下面註 10 之（1）。

2 παρεχόμενος, 中間語態；古典希臘文會用主動語態的 παρέχων. See BDF §316(3): 'Παρεχόμενον σεαυτὸν τύπον T 2:7 = παρέχων is contrary to classical usage.' Robertson（*Pictures* 4.603）稱之為 '(redundant middle) participle of *parechō* with the reflexive pronoun *seauton* as if the active voice *parechōn*.'（**2**）Quinn 124 認為，中間語態強調提多要 'keep doing certain things *himself* over and above exhorting others.' 但是 *Idiom* 24 早就指出，主動語態和中間語態的區別 'has become blurred by the N. T. period'.

3 因此，不必將分詞看為 'an independent imperatival participle'（Ngewa 460 n.102; cf. RSV, NRSV, NAU, NIV, TNIV, NIV2011, NJB, NLT）。（**1**）*EDNT* 3.39*b* (s.v. παρέχω) 翻譯為 'by *showing yourself to be* an example', 即是將原文分詞視為 participle of means（cf. Wallace 625: 'often [the present participle] follows a present imperative as a participle of *means*'），所得出的意思就是，提多要以**顯出自己是好行為的榜樣**作為**勸年輕人凡事克己**的方法；如此，使**年輕人凡事克己**就是**顯出自己是好行為的榜樣**的目的。但是二 8b～c 顯示，**顯出自己是好行為的榜樣**的目的，並不是要使**年輕人凡事克己**。（**2**）παρεχόμενον 可視為 adverbial participle of accompanying circumstance, 所得出的意思就是：**要勸年輕人凡事克己**（6 節），'<u>while showing</u> yourself to be an example of good works'; 在提多勸年輕人凡事克己的同時，他也要**顯出自己是好行為的榜樣**。

4 詳細的討論見導論第伍節註 8，尤其是該註之（2）= 上面 32-33。Cf. Mounce 413: 'Mention of the younger men reminds Paul to address some personal concerns directly to Titus, who himself was probably young*' (cf. 407).（*但見下面註 9 中文部分。）

（**#1**）好行為一詞在信上首次在此出現，下文會再出現三次（二 14，三 8、14）。[5] 這詞暗示提多與假教師的對比：他們根本做不出甚麼好事來（一 16，當代），但提多要在各樣的善行上為他們作榜樣（新普）。[6] 原文並無「為他們」，這表示所要求於提多的，不是僅對年輕的男子作榜樣，[7] 而是對所有信徒作好行為（即是真正的、名副其實的基督徒行為[8]）

5 四次原文皆為複數所有格的 καλῶν ἔργων. 複數另見提前五 10，六 18（不同次序的間接受格：[ἐν] ἔργοις καλοῖς），五 25（不同形式和次序的直接受格：τὰ ἔργα τὰ καλά）。單數的 καλὸν ἔργον 在提前三 1 形容監督的職分。保羅書信僅此八次；參一 16 註釋註 35 之（甲）= 上面 213。亦參一 16 和三 1 單數的各樣善事（πᾶν ἔργον ἀγαθόν）。

6 由此可見，這裏的 καλὸν ἔργον 和一 16 的 ἔργον ἀγαθόν 是同義詞（Genade 127）。（**1**）Quinn 13-14 則認為，ἔργα καλά（見上註開首）的意思不僅是 'good deeds (*agatha*; 1 Tim 2:10)'，而是 'visibly and attractively good actions (Titus 2:7, 14; 3:8, 14; etc.).' See also 139: 'works that are both good and visibly attractive'; 175: 'what is aesthetically pleasing to Greek eyes, the visibly good'; 227: 'for the PE good deeds are not enough; they must be visibly good and attractive (*kala* as distinct from *agatha*).' Cf. Murphy-O'Connor, '2 Timothy' 411: '"Show yourself an example of beautiful works"'; Marshall 228: 'καλός may . . . carry the nuance of "beautiful" in that the good deeds done by believers are seen as "attractive".'（**2**）形容詞 **καλός** 在保羅書信另外出現 40 次（參《帖前》451-52）；新約全部 101 次。See BDAG 504*b*-5*a* (s.v.);《新希》171*b*-72*a* (s.v.)。此字數次在 ποιεῖν τὸ καλὸν / τὸ καλὸν ποιεῖν 這片語內出現（行善：羅七 21／林後十三 7〔呂譯、思高〕；加六 9；雅四 17〔無冠詞〕），又多次與惡字（κακός: 羅七 21，十二 17；林後十三 7；來五 14）或壞字（πονηρός: 太七 17b、18a，十三 38／σαπρός: 太七 17b、18b ‖ 路六 43；太十二 33，十三 48）相對。

7 REB: 'set them an example of good conduct yourself'; Towner III 731（唐 1066）：'Titus . . . is set into this context as a model for the young men'; Collins 337: 'Titus is to give an example to younger men'; 300: 'Titus is to act in such a way that he can serve as a role model for younger men'; Davies II 73: 'He is . . . to show himself a model of good deeds for younger men'; Spencer 44: 'Titus is a . . . **model** for the younger men'; Richards 98: 'Titus is a model for the younger men'; Witherington 74: 'Titus . . . is called upon to be an example "to the younger men"', 134: '. . . with Titus especially providing an example to younger men'; Schreiner, *Interpreting* 125: 'Timothy should set an example for the younger men by his own life'（施賴納：《詮釋》139）。See also Drury1232*a*: 'Titus is urged to be a model for younger men in his behaviour and teaching'. 但 'and teaching' 並不適用於其他的年輕男子；*pace* Long 270: 'Younger men . . . should train themselves to be sound teachers.'

8 Fee 200: 'genuinely Christian behavior'. Cf. Collins 344: καλὰ ἔργα = 'a cipher for the Christian life'. 參較一 16 註釋註 31 之（2）= 上面 212。（**1**）Montague 234 則認為，'Paul probably considers the ministry of teaching to be the primary good work that Titus should be doing, as the next phrase indicates.'（**2**）Schreiner（*Interpreting* 123）／施賴納（《詮譯》136）的翻譯在 'in your teaching'／「在教導上」之

的榜樣。[9] 在提摩太前書四章 12 節，保羅更明確地勸勉他的年輕副手要在言語、行為、愛心、信心、清潔上，都作信徒的榜樣。[10]

前補充 '*That is*'／「即是」二字；因他認為保羅在 7b～8a 節「說明他心目中的好行為是怎樣的」(《詮譯》139〔*Interpreting* 126〕)。此解釋值得商榷，因它與上文發生衝突。先引述作者的翻譯（*Interpreting* 123／《詮譯》136〔斜體、方括號和黑體都是原來的〕）：

7a *in that* you show yourself as an example of good works in all things,
7a **[因為]** 無論在甚麼事上你都要顯出好行為的榜樣
7b-8a *that is*, in your teaching show integrity, dignity, and healthy speech which is beyond reproach.
7b-8a **[即是]** 在教導上要純全、要莊重，言語要純正，無可指摘

按施賴納的理解，7a 節說，「你要在一切事上都顯出你自己是好行為的榜樣」，但 7b～8a 節卻把好行為解釋為（**[即是]**）「在你的教導上要顯出正直、莊重，和無可指摘的健全的言詞」。如此，7a～8a 節的整個意思豈不是變成「你要在一切事上都顯出好行為的榜樣——即是在教導上要顯出正直、莊重，和無可指摘的健全的言詞」=「你要在一切事上都在教導上顯出正直、莊重，和無可指摘的健全的言詞」？

9 Hiebert 437. Cf. Johnson II 212: 'Titus is to show himself to the community as a model of good deeds (2:7-8)'; Smith 370: 'all Christians, not just the young men, would benefit educationally from Titus' example'; Bassler 197: 'certainly for the young men but probably for the rest of the church as well'; Mounce lxxxi: 'Both Timothy (1 Tim 4:7, 15) and Titus (Titus 2:7) are models to their churches.' 在古代，作榜樣的角色是交給較年長的人和領袖扮演的，因此，雖然提多在這裏出現，我們不應假定提多必然是年輕的（Marshall 254）；至於提摩太，唐書禮認為他雖然年輕卻有資格作榜樣，是由於他具有領袖及保羅同工的地位（Towner III 731 n.70〔唐 1066 註 63〕）。

10 提前四 12 的講法是 τύπον γίνου τῶν πιστῶν（作信徒的榜樣），多二 7 的用詞是 παρεχόμενος τύπον καλῶν ἔργων（作好行為的榜樣）。**(1)** 動詞 **παρέχω** 在保羅書信另外出現四次（新約全部十六次），三次是主動語態，分別指上帝厚賜百物給我們享受（提前六 17），某些事只會引起爭論（提前一 4），加拉太的煽動者「給（保羅）引起／製造麻煩」（加六 17；參《加》1430-31）；餘下一次是中間語態（如在多二 7），指作主人的要公平地對待僕人（西四 1，新譯）。See BDAG 776*b*-77*a* (s.v.);《新希》254*a*（s.v.）。**(2)** 名詞 **τύπος** 在保羅書信另外出現六次（新約另外七次），分別指亞當是基督的預表（羅五 14〔當代、現修、新譯〕，參《羅》2.129-30）；道理的規範（六 17〔新譯〕，參《羅》2.289-91）；以色列人留給新約信徒的鑑戒（林前十 6），即是負面的「榜樣」；以及（如在本節）正面的榜樣（腓三 17；帖後三 9）甚或模範（帖前一 7〔思高、當代、現修〕，參《帖前》89-90）。See BDAG 1019*b*-20*b* (s.v.);《新希》334*a*-34*b*（s.v.）。同字根的副詞 τυπικῶς 在希臘文聖經僅出現一次，指舊約發生的某些事是要對新約信徒作為鑒戒（林前十 11）。同字根的複合名詞 ὑποτύπωσις 在希臘文聖經僅出現兩次，分別指基督使保羅成為信他得永生的人的榜樣（提前一 16），保羅要提摩太持守從我這裏學到的純正道理作為典範（提後一 13，新普）。**(3)** Quinn 141 認為，τύπος 在多二 7 除了具有倫理榜樣（see BDAG

在教導上這介詞片語和下文的關係有幾種不同的理解：[11]（一）這片語只是連於緊隨其後的那個名詞，所得出的意思就是：**在教導上不腐化**（呂譯）或**在教訓上要純全**（當代）。[12]（二）這片語是連於隨後的兩個名詞，意即：（A）**在教導上應表示純正莊重**（思高），**在教導上要純全，要莊重**（新譯）；[13]（B）**在教訓／教導上要正直、端莊／莊重**（新和／和修〔留意頓號〕）；或（C）**教導人要誠懇、嚴肅**（現修），〔**要**〕**反映出你的教導是又誠實又認真的**（新普）。[14]（三）**在教導上**有三個修飾語：「在你的教導上要顯出誠實／正直、[15] 莊重，和無可指摘的言詞。」[16] 這種

1020*a* [s.v. 6 b]: 'example, pattern'）的意思外，還有另一重意思：提多肯定是保羅的**真兒子**（一 4），而兒女是父母的 *typoi*（= 'copy, image' [BDAG 1020*a*, s.v. 2]）；如此，提多是以保羅的生命和教導為**典範**（提前一 16）塑造出來的活模型（'a living *typos* stamped out of the life and teaching of the Pauline model, *hypotyposis* [*sic*]'），因而 'the *typos* . . . look[s] <u>simultaneously</u> to the past and to the future'. 筆者認為，這種論證過分巧妙（over-subtle）。就 τύπον καλῶν ἔργων 這片語本身的語意而論，τύπον 的意思只是**榜樣**，儘管就事實而論，我們可以如此<u>推論</u>：提多之所以能作好行為的榜樣，是由於他是「以保羅的生命和教導為**典範**（提前一 16）塑造出來的活模型」。

11 Calvin 371 則把**在教導上**連於<u>上文</u>（7a 節末）的**好行為**，所得出的意思就是，提多要在自己的生命中顯出他所教導的好行為：'having enjoined Titus to inculcate zeal for good works in his teaching [καλῶν ἔργων ἐν τῇ διδασκαλίᾳ] he wants the good works that correspond to this teaching to be seen in his own life [τύπον, *typon*].' 但若這是保羅的意思，他需要表達得清晰一點。

12 I.e., ἐν τῇ διδασκαλίᾳ ἀφθορίαν = '(let them see in you) purity of doctrine' (*Paraphrase* 293). See also NAU: '*with* purity in doctrine'; Quinn 27, 117: 'wholesome in preaching'; Fiore II 208: 'exhibiting integrity in teaching', 214: 'teaching impeccability . . . impeccable teaching'; Van Neste 256: 'Titus is to be "incorrupt in doctrine"'.

13 See also Hendriksen 361, 366: 'in your teaching (showing) incorruptibility, dignity'; Mounce 405, 413 / 417: 'pure [and] dignified in your teaching / pure and dignified in how he teaches'（方括號是原來的）; DC 139*b*: 'pure and dignified as a teacher'. 後一種翻譯將 ἀφθορία 理解為 'innocence' 之意（141*a*）。

14 See also NLT: '(Let everything you do) reflect the integrity and seriousness of your teaching'; NJB: '(set an example) by sincerity and earnestness [ἀφθορίαν, σεμνότητα], when you are teaching [ἐν τῇ διδασκαλίᾳ]'; P. Fiedler, *EDNT* 3.238*b* (s.v. σεμνότης, 4): 'teach in such a way as to show integrity and dignity'.

15 參下面註 19。

16 NIV, TNIV, NIV2011: 'In your teaching show integrity, seriousness and soundness of speech that cannot be condemned'; REB: 'In your teaching you must show integrity and seriousness, and offer sound instruction to which none can take exception';

理解可取。[17]

（**#2**）**正直**（同新和）、[18] **誠實**（新普）[19] 或**誠懇**（現修）[20] 原文的另一種翻譯是**不腐化**（呂譯）、[21] **純正**（思高）[22] 或**純全**（當代、新譯）。[23]

RSV, NRSV / ESV: 'in your teaching show integrity, gravity/dignity, and sound speech that cannot be censured/condemned'. See also Banker 60, 70*a*; Barclay 252; Collins 338; Fairnbairn 55; Johnson I 124; Kelly 242; Köstenberger 617*b*; Lock 137, 142; Marshall 254; Malherbe, 'Paraenesis' 309; Padgett, 'Submission' 49; Zehr 267; Stott 190（三者依次指提多的教導之動機、方式和內容），191（'Titus [in his teaching] was to combine purity of motive, soundness of matter and seriousness of manner'）。(**1**)按正文的理解，διδασκαλία 指教導的活動（K. Wegenast, *DNTT* 3.771: 'The word denotes an activity [here]'），如在提前四 13，五 17；提後三 16；羅十二 7，十五 4（H.-F. Weiss, *EDNT* 1.317*a* [s.v. 2]: 'in the active sense of *the action of teaching* or *instruction*'）。ἐν τῇ διδασκαλίᾳ = 'In/in your teaching' (NIV, TNIV, NIV2011 / RSV, NRSV). H.-F. Weiss（loc. cit. [s.v. 3 a]）認為這片語可翻譯為 'as a teacher'.(**2**)按 NKJV 的翻譯，提多在教義上要顯出四樣東西：'in doctrine *showing* integrity, reverence, incorruptibility, sound speech that cannot be condemned'. 第三樣反映（從提後一 10 得來的）異文 ἀφθαρσίαν. 這裏的異文還有 ἀδιαφθορίαν（'sincerity'）、ἀδιαφορίαν（'indifference'）和 ἀφθονίαν（'freedom from envy'）；see *TextC* 585.

17 Knight II 312-13 則認為他所列出的 'all the various alternatives are possible', 因而無法確定哪一種理解才是正確的。Hagner（'Titus' 554）卻將 7b～8a 節視為對年輕人說的：'younger men are told "in your teaching . . . show integrity, gravity and sound speech . . . ."'

18 《輔讀》527（第一解釋）同。

19 See also NKJV, RSV, NRSV, NIV, TNIV, NIV2011, ESV, NLT: 'integrity'. 這個英文字同時有「正直」和「誠實」之意：'integrity' = '[the] quality of being honest and upright in character'（《牛津》603*a-b*）。Quinn 27, 125 / 117, 139, 142 則翻譯為 'openhanded with the / with instruction'（不吝賜教？）。

20 《輔讀》527（第二解釋）同；張 350：「在教訓上有誠懇的態度」。See also NJB: 'sincerity'. 這種翻譯是否反映異文 ἀδιαφθορίαν（見上面註 16 之〔2〕末部分）呢？不一定，因為雖然原來的讀文是 ἀφθορίαν, 但 Banker 70*a* 根據這讀文而翻譯為 '(Teach) sincerely'; see also Blaiklock 83: 'utterly sincere';《新希》227*b*（s.v.）：「誠懇；真摯」。(**1**) 這字（**ἀφθορία**）在希臘文聖經只出現這一次；同字根的形容詞 ἄφθορος 也只出現一次（斯二 2，指 'chaste . . . young virgins' [LXE]）。(**2**) 前一個字是複合名詞（from φθείρω + α-privative, 'uncorruptedness, free from (moral) taint' [Vine 1.244]）；動詞 φθείρω（'to destroy by means of corrupting' [Vine 1.242]）在保羅書信出現六次，新約另三次；詳見《弗》651 註 21。

21 See also KJV: 'uncorruptedness'; *TextC* 585, Quinn 142: 'incorruption'; Genade 50: 'incorruptible'; Collins 344: 'literally . . . "without decay" (*a-phthoria*)'; Marshall 254-55: 'ἀφθορία must mean "incorruption, soundness", i.e. freedom from guilt.'

22 See also NAU: 'purity in doctrine'; *Paraphrase* 293: 'purity of doctrine'; BDAG 156*a* (s.v.): '***soundness***, lit. incorruption . . . of pure doctrine'; H. Balz, *EDNT* 1.181*a* (s.v.): 'soundness [in teaching]'; Hanson III 181: 'preserving orthodoxy pure'.

23 LN §88.43 認為原文的意思是 'integrity in teaching' = 'teaching the whole truth'.

前一種翻譯將原文名詞理解為提多教導的動機或方式，[24] 後一種翻譯則理解為提多的教導之內容。前者較為可取，因為（i）上文剛提到提多要顯出自己是好行為的榜樣；（ii）隨後的抽象名詞莊重顯然是指方式而非內容，在它之前的這另一個抽象名詞較可能也是指方式或動機而非內容。[25]

（**#3**）莊重（同呂譯、思高、當代、新譯）或端莊（新和）[26] 另有譯本作嚴肅（現修）[27] 或認真（新普）。[28] 原文名詞與二章 2 節的形容詞端正同字根。[29] 在教導上……莊重指教導者的態度和教導的方式。[30]

（**#4**）言語健全所指的可能不僅是「恰當的」言語，[31] 而是「健

---

24 Barclay 252: 'purity of motive'; Fee 189: 'pure motive'; Kelly 242: 'By **integrity** Paul means purity of motive, the absence of any desire for gain'; Towner II 240: '"with *integrity*" probably focuses on motive of teaching'. Cf. G. Harder, *TDNT* 9.103: 'It is used with σεμνότης to describe the moral attitude of Titus'; 黃編 211：「『正直』重在指動機的純潔真摯，沒有絲毫貪念」。

25 Banker 70*a*. See also Scott 165: 'sincerity . . . of motive, in contrast to the self-seeking of the false teachers'（11c 節：貪不義之財）；周 428：「要有正直無私的動機」；White 193*a*: 'These [ἀφθορίαν, σεμνότητα] refer respectively to the principles and the manner of the teacher, while λόγον, κ.τ.λ., describes the matter of his teaching'; Smith 71: 'Titus was to . . . show himself to have both integrity and seriousness in his *manner* of teaching . . . and soundness in the *content* of his teaching'. Lock 137 認為正直是指動機（'your motives [are to be] sincere'）；其後則解釋為 'purity of motive . . . and purity of doctrine'（142）。

26 參《輔讀》527（第二解釋）：「行為端莊合宜」。

27 《輔讀》527（第一解釋）同。

28 See also Lock 137: 'your manner [is to be] such as to inspire respect'; Guthrie II 207 (cf. Guthrie I 195): 'If the words of the Christian teacher are to earn respect he must teach in a serious manner'（古特立 209 作「以莊重的態度來教導人」）；Zamfir 107: 'Respectability (σεμνότης) is demanded from Titus'.

29 依次為 σεμνότης（名詞）、σεμνός（形容詞）。後者參二 2 註釋第三段（上面 224-26）。名詞 **σεμνότης** 在新約僅再出現兩次：提前二 2（端正地生活），三 4（兒女凡事莊重）；在 LXX 僅出現一次（次經《馬加比二書》3.12，指聖殿的「神聖」[RSV, NRSV: 'sanctity']）。Quinn 27, 117, 125, 139 在本節意譯為 'a reverent man'; Simpson 105 則認為 'high-mindedness' 最貼近原文的意思。

30 Kelly 242: '**gravity** denotes a high moral tone and serious manner'; Fee 189: 'respectful demeanor'; Mounce cvi: 'godly dignity'; Marshall 255: 'seriousness in teaching'; Towner II 241: 'the dignified bearing that bespeaks the importance of the Christian task.' See also W. Foerster, *TDNT* 7.195: 'σεμνότης relates to [the way he teaches] . . . σεμνότης is the σχῆμα [outward form] which corresponds to the content of the doctrine, namely, "gravity," "dignity"'; 黃編 211：「『端莊』重在指態度的誠懇莊重，沒有輕佻隨便。」

31 《簡明》175*b*（s.v. ὑγιής）。Cf. *EDNT* 3.380*a* (s.v.): '*healthy/sound* speech'; 曾 117：

全的教導或宣講」。[32] **健全**的原文形容詞在保羅書信出現僅此一次，[33] 但（i）同字根的動詞在教牧書信出現的八次，都是指正確無誤的教導／教義或信仰；[34] 加上（ii）這動詞與名詞**言語**的原文在提摩太前書六章 3 節和提摩太後書一章 13 節（如在本節）連著出現，分別指**耶穌基督純正的話語**和提摩太**從我〔保羅〕聽到那健全的言論**，兩者都肯定是指教導或教義的內容；這就有力地提示，本節的**言語健全**同樣是指「健全的教導或宣講」。[35]

有釋經者認為，鑑於隨後的目的子句（8b～c 節），**無可指責**[36] 應視為與**言語健全**分開，所指的是提多作為傳道者的生活。[37] 不過，**無**

「日常對話」（124 則理解為指「教導的修辭」）。

32 BDAG 1023*a* (s.v. ὑγιής, 2): '*sound teaching* or *preaching*'. See also LN §72.14: ὑγιής = 'pertaining to being accurate, as well as useful and beneficial－"right, accurate, sound"'. LN §72 n.4 認為，在本節，此字的 'focal element appears to be "that which is right"'. Lock 142 則解為 'the message in true proportion, well-balanced'.

33 **ὑγιής** 在新約另外出現十次（約五 4 不算在內），全部為字面意義，分別指**痊癒**的人（太十五 31；可五 34；約五 6、9、11、14、15，七 23；徒四 10；）和**康健**的手（太十二 13〔呂譯〕）。See BDAG 1203*a* (s.v.);《新希》336*a*（s.v.）。

34 見一 9 註釋註 24、25 及所屬正文（上面 145）。

35 Banker 70*a-b*. 參《輔讀》527（第一解釋）：「健全正確的（教訓）」。**(1)** Griffin 304 將**言語健全**理解為 'a healthy, persuasive, well-thought-out, and attractively delivered presentation of the Christian gospel'. **(2)** 張 350 則認為提多的**言語**包括「其所講的道〔及〕平日說的話」；參黃編 211：「所講的道，以及平日所說的話」。Cf. Hiebert 438: 'his personal word spoken while teaching or in ordinary conversation'. **(3)** Quinn 27, 117, 125, 139, 142 翻譯為 'wholesome in preaching'; 即是將形容詞 ὑγιῆ 視為形容提多本身，λόγον 則為 accusative of respect. 'Such a further change in construction is unlikely'（Marshall 256; see also Towner III 732 n.79〔唐 1068 註 72〕）。

36 **(1)** 形容詞 **ἀκατάγνωστος** 在新約出現僅此一次，在 LXX 亦只出現一次（次經《馬加比二書》4.47），指一些被判死刑的人其實應被判「無罪」（思高；RSV, NRSV: 'uncondemned'）而獲釋。在這裏的意思是 'above criticism'（LN §33.415），'beyond reproach'（BDAG 35*a* [s.v.]）=「沒有值得被批評的地方」（《新希》12*b* [s.v.]）。**(2)** 這複合形容詞得自 α-privative + καταγινώσκω. 後者本身是複合動詞（κατά + γινώσκω = 'to know something against . . . hence, to think ill of, to condemn' [Vine 1.221-22]），其意思是「定罪」（加二 11〔參《加》472〕；約壹三 20、21；see BDAG 515*b* [s.v.]: 'condemn'）。

37 See Quinn 143; also Fee 189; 張 350（「指提多的整個人之表現」）。Calvin 371 則把 ἀκατάγνωστον 視為形容之前的三個項目，所得出的意思就是，'that you may prove yourself unblamable in gravity, integrity and sound speech.' 亦參下面註 40 之（2）。

可指責[38] 較可能應與言語健全連起來成為一個單元，作為提多在教導上要顯出的第三個特色，[39] 所得出的意思就是「無可指責的、健全的宣講」。[40] 這就是說，提多所宣講的信息必須是正確和健全的，以致無人可以合理地批評它。[41]

38 G Schneider（*EDNT* I.48*b* [s.v.]）則翻譯為 'incontestable'.

39 參註 16 及所屬正文（上面 261-62）。

40 Collins 344: 'a sound and irreproachable message'; Fiore II 208: 'sound preaching beyond reproach'; Johnson I 124: 'His teaching . . . is to be . . . "a healthy word without reproach"'; Kelly 242: 'sound speech to which no exception can be taken'; Lock 137: 'your message [is to be] sound and not open to criticism'; Mounce 414: 'his presentation of the apostolic gospel must be beyond reproach'; 407: '[Paul asks Titus] to keep the healthy word above reproach'; Towner I 194: 'preaching that is sound in doctrine and which therefore cannot be reproached.'（1）按這種理解，兩個形容詞 'are linked together and form a mixed metaphor': 健全屬於健康的範疇，無可指責（其字面意思是 'nothing known against'〔見上面註 36 之（2）〕）是法庭用語（Collins 344; Zehr 267）。（2）唐書禮則把 λόγον ὑγιῆ ἀκατάγνωστον 理解為 accusative of respect（首二字）+ 形容詞（後一字）：'"Sound teaching" is that in respect of which Titus is to be "irreproachable"'（Towner III 732 n.76〔唐 1068 註 69〕）。Cf. Mounce 405, 413, 418: 'beyond reproach [in your] healthy instruction'（方括號是原來的）。亦參上面註 37。

41 Banker 60, 70*b*: 'teach what is correct which no one can (justly) criticize.' See also Towner II 241: 'This true gospel cannot be condemned by those outside the church as giving rise to disorder and unseemly behavior.'（1）Mounce 414 則認為：'Context shows that the issue was Titus's behavior more than the content of his instruction. . . . Paul is emphasizing that believers should behave in such a way that no charges can justifiably be brought against the message of the gospel.' 但 417 仍解釋為 'beyond reproach in what he teaches'.（2）Montague 234 將 ἀκατάγνωστον 翻譯為 'free from censure', 所指的責備來自基督：'the Christian message itself must not be corrupted by infidelity to the apostolic Tradition and thus incur the censure ultimately of Christ as judge.'

二 **8b** 使那反對的人，……自覺羞愧。
8c 因說不出我們有甚麼不好而

使這字引入了提多要按照上述指示(7～8a 節)而行的目的。[1] 那反對的人意即敵人或對手。[2] 這敵人或對手可能是「教外的異教徒」，[3] 或是傳異端的假教師；[4] 最可能是主要指一章 10 至 13 節那些反對健全的信仰的人，但不排除教外人士。[5] 說不出我們有甚麼

---

1 I.e., ἵνα = 'so that' (RSV, NAU, NIV, TNIV, NIV2011, NJB, ESV). (**1**) 這連接詞將目的子句連於 7a 節的分詞 παρεχόμενος（顯出）; see also Banker 71*a*; Towner II 241. 另有中英譯本將連接詞 ἵνα 視為表達結果：'Then/then'（NLT, *Paraphrase* 293 / NRSV），這樣（現修）。參二 9～10 註釋註 37（下面 276）。(**2**) Witherington 130 指出，這目的子句是「省略三段論法（enthymeme）」的第三部分，如下：

> '1. Titus must set a good moral example and offer teaching with integrity,
> 2. [For opponents are looking for inconsistencies in our leaders,]
> 3. So that the opponents can find nothing to criticize.'

（第二行的方括號是原來的，表示該行是被省略的部分〔'a suppressed premise'〕。）參二 5b 註釋註 3 之（1）= 上面 250；二 9～10 註釋註 41（下面 277）。

2 ὁ ἐξ ἐναντίας [sc. χώρας], 'someone on the opposite side' (Fiore II 208) = 'the opponent' (G. Schneider, *EDNT* 1.449*b* [s.v. ἐναντίος]; Bassler 197-98; Knight II 313; Marshall 256; Mounce 405, 414) or '[the] enemy' (Newman 60*a* [s.v.]). (**1**) 原文的單數是 'an individualizing mode of representing a class'（Fairbairn 276）或 'a generic reference'（Smith 99），意即 '*any*/any opponent'（Banker 71*a*/*b*）。亦有把它翻譯為複數的：LN §39.6: 'those who are hostile (to you)'; 馮譯：那些作對的。Jeon I 73 則認為，'the audience hear the phrase "the opponent" . . . as a reference to a specific individual, although an entire group is in view by association.' (**2**) 這形容詞（**ἐναντίος**）在保羅書信僅再出現一次（帖前二 15，指猶太人與眾人為敵），在新約另外出現六次，分別指逆風（太十四 24 ‖ 可六 48；徒二十七 4，思高、現修），百夫長在耶穌的對面站著（可十五 39），保羅從前認為必須竭力反對耶穌的名（徒二十六 9），以及保羅沒有做任何反對他的同胞或祖先的規例的事（二十八 17，思高、新譯）。See BDAG 330*b*-31*a* (s.v.);《新希》113*a*（s.v.）。

3 張 351。See also Lock 142: 'the main thought is of pagan criticism' (followed by Padgett, 'Submission' 50); Towner I 194: 'almost certainly the outsider, who would put evidence of antisocial behavior in the church to use in slandering the "new religion".'

4 Hanson III 181. Quinn 143 認為那反對的人 'is Jewish, probably Jewish-Christian'.

5 See Hendriksen 367: 'The reference is especially to any one of the Cretan errorists described in Titus 1:10-16'; Kelly 243: 'its primary reference is to ill-disposed individuals in the community itself'; Fee 189: 'The primary reference is almost certainly to the opponents within, although in the full context of verses 1-10 it may also include

不好這話[6] 裏面的形容詞**不好**，在新約另外出現五次，一貫用於行為而不是言語；[7] 由此推論，保羅想到的可能是**我們**[8] 不要行惡，免得敵人有機會批評他們。不過，**不好**這字在七十士譯本亦用來指人的言語，[9] 而且在本目的子句之前剛提到提多（i）**要顯出自己是好行為的榜樣**（7a 節），（ii）又**在教導上**「要顯出誠實／正直、莊重，和無可指摘的言詞」（7b～8a 節）；保羅要提多在行為和教導兩方面有上述的表現，其目的就是使反對者因**說不出我們有甚麼不好**而自覺羞愧。[10] 因此文理提示，敵人所批評的較可能是保羅及其宣教同工（包括提多）的行為及教導。[11] **自覺羞愧／慚愧**（同呂譯、當代、新和，

---

the pagan critic'; Smith 100: 'both are on [*sic*] view'; Mounce 414; Marshall 256: 'the primary reference' is to 'heretical teachers'. 亦參彭編 101*a-b*：「泛指教會內外所有反對基督教健全教導的人」。

6 說字原文（λέγω）見一 12 註釋註 4 之（2）= 上面 172。

7 **凡作惡的人都恨光**（約三 20）；**各人要按著本身所行的，或善或惡受報**（林後五 10）；**行善的，復活得生命；作惡的，復活被定罪**（約五 29）；雙胞胎雅各和以掃的**善惡還沒有行出來**（羅九 11），上帝就作出祂的揀選（12 節）；**哪裏有嫉妒和私心，哪裏就有混亂和種種惡行**（雅三 16，新普）。See BDAG 1050*b*-51*a* (s.v. φαῦλος);《新希》345*a*（s.v.）。

8 昆謝隆認為，由於這兩節（7～8 節）是特別針對提多的勸勉，這裏突然重現的複數第一人稱**我們**（參一 3、4）最自然的理解是指保羅和他的助手（Quinn 143, see also 144）。另有認為**我們**是指「全教會」（張 351）= 'the Christian community as a whole / the Christian community'（Knight II 313 / Smith 71）。Mounce 414 則認為，**我們**暗示 'corporate responsibility: Titus must behave properly so that the opponent has nothing bad to say about ἡμῶν, "us," the plural including Paul, the Cretan Christians, and probably all Christendom.' Cf. Smith 99: 'The identity of "us" . . . was primarily Titus and Paul, but also the Cretan Christians, and probably Christians generally.'

9 這形容詞（**φαῦλος**）在 LXX 出現十次（除非另外註明，以下英譯皆取自 LXE）：（**i**）三次指人的言語：'my words are vain'（伯六 3）；'the words of a true man are vain'（六 25）；'Those who eat [the fool's] bread are evil-tongued'（次經《傳道經＝便西拉智訓》20.17〔NRSV 20.16〕）；（**ii**）五次指人：'a worthless woman'（箴五 3〔LXE 5:2〕），'a worthless man'（二十九 9）；'sin makes worthless the ungodly'（十三 6）；'the worthless die'（伯九 23）；'*Men* call the wise and understanding evil'（箴十六 21）；（**iii**）兩次指邪惡：'He that sows wickedness shall reap troubles'（箴二十二 8）；一些人 'incline constantly to evil'（偽經《馬加比三書》3.22）。

10 馬泰拉卻把 8c 節（只）連於 8a 節，從而得出這樣的意思：'opponents will have nothing evil to say [v. 8c] if Titus's speech is sound (2:8[a])' / 'his speech is to be sound so that it cannot be censured'（Matera, 'Moral Guides' 242/245）。

11 Towner III 734 n.86（唐 1071 註 79）：'[likely] a general reference to the behavior and

新普同／新譯）原文動詞在這裏的意思不是主觀的**感到羞愧**（思高）或**覺得慚愧**（現修），[12] 而較可能是「蒙羞」（原文為被動語態）。[13] 這不是說，當敵人發現自己的指控無法成立時，他會顯得很愚蠢；[14] 而是說，當敵人對保羅的宣教同工的指控證實為毫無根據時，他們便會失去別人的尊重，他們的聲譽和信息便會受到懷疑。[15]

---

teaching of the Pauline mission team'. Marshall 256 則以 φαῦλον = 'worthless'，所得出的意思就是：'[the opponent has] no report of our worthlessness.' Witherington 140 的講法（'so that they will have nothing worthless to say concerning Titus or Paul'; similarly Laansma 257: 'having nothing worthless to say about us'）則有點古怪（「關於提多或保羅，他們沒有不值得講的話」？）。

12 See also KJV, NKJV, NIV, TNIV, NIV2011 / NLT: 'may/will be ashamed'; G. Schneider, *EDNT* 1.461*a* (s.v. ἐντρέπω): 'be ashamed'. 原文動詞（**ἐντρέπω**）在新約另外出現八次，其中一次（帖後三 14）和本節相同（ἐντραπῇ, 被動語態）；其餘七次分為兩種用法：一次為主動語態，意思是**使（你們）覺得慚愧**（林前四 14，現修），六次為被動語態（但有中間語態的主動意思），意思是**尊敬**（太二十一 37 ‖ 可十二 6 ‖ 路二十 13）、**尊重**（路十八 2、4）、**敬重**（來十二 9）。See BAGD 269*b*, BDAG 341*a* (s.v.);《新希》116*a*-16*b*（s.v.）。

13 RSV, NRSV, NAU, ESV, Mounce 405, 414, Towner III 734: 'be put to shame'.

14 White 193*a*: 'An antagonist who finds that he has no case "looks foolish," as we say'; Hiebert 438: 'made to look foolish because he is shown to have no case.'（**1**）類似的意思是 'feeling foolish'（Oden 119），「感到尷尬（may/will be embarrassed）」（Ward 256 / Quinn 27, 117, 125, 126, 139）和「不知所措」= 'will be at a loss'（REB, NJB）。（**2**）DC 139*b* 則翻譯為 'may be converted'. Cf. Saarinen 180: 'The expression "will be put to shame" (*entrepō*) contains the wish that the opponents will be converted to orthodoxy.'

15 Towner III 734（唐 1071：「他們的聲譽就會被敗壞」）。Cf. Griffin 305: 'hostile critics will ultimately be "ashamed" . . . in the sense of publicly suffering loss of respect as it becomes apparent that their criticisms are groundless.'

4.1.7 家裏的奴僕（二 9～10）

二 9 要勸僕人順服自己的主人，[1] 凡事討他的喜悅，不可頂撞他，
10a 不可私竊財物；
10b 要凡事顯出完美的忠誠，
10c 好事事都能榮耀我們救主上帝的教導。

第 9 節原文並無勸字，但僕人是直接受格（賓詞），表示這裏假定了第 6 節的動詞勸字。[2] 僕人原文是奴隸（思高），即是作奴僕的（現修、新譯、新普）。在羅馬時代，有多種原因可以使人成為奴僕：他們是戰俘；他們是被判有罪的人；他們欠債；他們是被綁架的；他們被父母賣作奴僕；他們生下來就是奴僕。[3] 主人原文是複數，[4] 因此隨後兩個動詞的賓詞（儘管原文並無表達）亦應是複數的他們（新普：討他們喜悅；現修：不可頂撞他們）。凡事原文居於順服和討他的喜悅之間，若把它連於後者，所得出的意思就是凡事討他的喜悅（亦

---

1 ἰδίοις δεσπόταις（自己的主人）並無冠詞（τοῖς）；BDF §286(2) 稱之為 'a kind of assimilation to anarthrous δούλους', 意即可以這樣說：在無冠詞的 δούλους 之影響下，δεσπόταις 也變成無冠詞的。

2 Marshall 259; Mounce 415; Hiebert 438; Clark, 'Structure' 110. BDF §389 提到 'the accusatives with inf. in T 2:2-10 with a single occurrence of παρακάλει in *v.* 6.'（**1**）與此同時，有別於 3 節／6 節，本節並無使用照樣（新譯、新普）／同樣（ὡσαύτως）一字；有認為這表示，作者 'does not discern significant parallelism between the instructions to slaves and those to earlier groups'（Levinsohn, 'Constraints' 331 n.73）。但 Wendland（'Discourse' 346）在此補充 '[likewise]'.（**2**）Malherbe（'Paraenesis' 300 n.12）則認為，'Probably ὑποτάσσεσθαι and εἶναι in 2:9 are imperatival and not dependent on παρακάλει in 2:6.' 但見二 2 註釋註 3 之（1）= 上面 221。

3 Hendriksen 191. 為甚麼保羅（及其他新約作者都）沒有對奴隸制度提出譴責並要求把它廢除呢？哈里斯指出，這是基於歷史、社會，以及宗教的三重因素；詳見《西・門》694-95，亦參 811-13。Cf. G. Delling, *TDNT* 8.44: 'Slavery is accepted as a social reality which primitive Christianity was not in a position to abolish externally.'

4 '[The plural] is surely distributive'（Marshall 259），即是指奴僕（一個或多個）所屬的（一個）主人。和修譯作單數的他字也許就是要表達這個意思。

參呂譯、當代、新和、現修），[5] 但若把它連於前者，所得出的意思就是要凡事順服／要事事順服／在一切事上要服從自己的主人（新譯／新普／思高）。[6] 這種理解可取，因為：（**i**）下一節末（原文次序）的事事（原文與本節的凡事相同）只能夠是連於上文的；（**ii**）同一個介詞片語在教牧書信另外出現三次（提前三 11；提後二 7，四 5），頭兩次只能夠是連於上文，後一次很可能也是連於上文；（**iii**）若把凡事連於下文（凡事討他的喜悅），此片語便居於顯著地位，而在這樣籠統的勸勉中，似乎沒有理由要特別強調凡事之意。[7]（**iv**）凡事順服自己的主人（新譯）與第 10c 節的凡事尊榮……上帝的道（新和）構成更好的平衡。[8]（**v**）平行經文歌羅西書三章 22 節（要凡事聽從你們肉身的主人）也支持這種理解。[9] 凡事意即「在一切事上」、「在每事上」、「在每一方面」。[10]

有認為（一）這裏可能假定奴僕的主人是信主的（提前六 2），因為基督徒奴僕有時為了良心的緣故而不能順服信奉異教的主人；[11] 由於信主的奴僕可能會因自己與信主的主人是主內弟兄而輕看他們

---

5 亦參以下英譯：'to please them well / to be well-pleasing in all things'（KJV/NKJV），'to give them satisfaction all around'（Moffatt, cited in Guthrie I 196）。

6 See also NAU / NIV: 'to be subject to their own masters / their masters in everything'; ESV: 'to be submissive to their own masters in everything'; NJB: 'be obedient to their masters in everything'; REB: 'to respect their masters' authority in everything'; Davies I 100; Lock 142; Marshall 259; Mounce 405; Quinn 27, 117, 126, 144; Collins 345: 'to be subject to their masters in all things and in every way'; Towner III 736 n.95（唐 1074 註 88）。

7 以上三點理由見 Banker72*a*.

8 Kelly 243.

9 Hiebert 438. 亦參：弗五 24：妻子也要……凡事順服丈夫。

10 I.e., ἐν πᾶσιν = 'in all *things*/respects' (KJV, NKJV / Kelly 238, 243), 'in everything' (NAU, NIV, TNIV, NIV2011, NJB, ESV), 'in every respect' (RSV, NRSV; Hendriksen 361).

11 Guthrie I 196; Guthrie II 208（古特立 210）。See also Fee 190; Kelly 243: 'Presumably he has Christian households in view, and is not prescribing blind obedience to orders of doubtful morality'; Quinn 146: 'these slaves can be directed "to be subject . . . in all matters," with the presumption that the Christian master or mistress would not command unchristian acts.'

（提前六 2），保羅就提醒他們當盡的責任。[12] 不過，（二）第 10c 節所提出的理由（**好事事都能榮耀我們救主上帝的教導**）表示，保羅的關注是基督徒奴僕的行為會影響教會的聲譽（參 5b、8b～c 節）。[13] 因此，這裏的指示可能是對所有奴僕發出的，不管他們的主人是信主或不信主的；[14] 而背後則隱含著「奴僕對主人的順服不是絕對的，乃要符合基督徒的原則」這種限制。[15] **自己的**在此並無與「別人的」有任何對比的含意，因而在翻譯上可以省略而無損作者要表達的意思：**要他們服從主人**（現修，參當代）。[16] **順服**原文在第 5 節曾用來指妻子

---

12 See Scott 166.

13 Barrett 136 指出，'Christian *slaves* constituted a special danger to the good repute of the Church. Their Christian freedom could if wrongly expressed lead to the opinion that they and their brethren were social revolutionaries. Accordingly they must be careful to *respect their masters' authority in everything*.'（斜體字代表所引用的 NEB 的譯文。）Portefaix（'Women's Position' 151）也認為，'Presumably the "one-in-Christ" formula (Gal. 3.28), concealing social and political implications, had tended to place master and slave on an equal footing outside the community and had attracted the attention of non-Christians.'

14 Laansma 267: 'Since nothing in this passage indicates whether the masters are believers or unbelievers . . . , it is probably best to assume that the teaching is meant to apply to either situation.' Marshall 260 也認為，'the duty of slaves in any situation is in mind.'（**1**）Hanson III 182 則認為，10c 節提示奴僕可藉著他們的行為將福音推薦給他們信奉異教的主人，故此作者可能是對在異教家庭中的奴僕說話（本段並無給予主人的勸告，可能因他們不是信主的）。Bailey（'Theology' 358）同樣假定他們的主人是未信主的，他說：'Slaves were to earn the trust of their bosses with the goal of attracting <u>them</u> to the Savior'.（**2**）Richards 98 認為，在克里特島上，'While slaves are members of these communities, slave-owners significantly are not.' Cf. 86: '. . . the omission of an address to "masters" would seem to suggest that Christians in the Titus-community do not themselves own slaves.'（**3**）Ho（'Mission' 245）也認為，'This admonition evidently was given with the non-Christian masters in mind since "masters" are not mentioned in the *Haustafeln* in Titus'.（不過，二 1～10 並不是「家庭規範」的例子，而是 station code 的例子；見本段（二 1～10）註釋引言註 4〔上面 216〕。）

15 Mounce 415. See also Calvin 371: 'this desire to please must be limited to things that are right'. Knight II 314 將**凡事**解釋為 'in all aspects of their service that a Christian slave can render without sinning.' Davies II 89 則認為，'Slaves are . . . to show "complete and true fidelity" [2:10b] to their masters, irrespective of their masters' demands, and <u>whether their demands might conflict with God's demands</u>'（參註 25〔下面 273〕）。

16 （**1**）以下英譯本將 ἰδίοις δεσπόταις 翻譯為 'their masters' 而不是 'their own masters': RSV, NRSV, NIV, TNIV, NIV2011, NLT.（**2**）名詞 δεσπότης 在保羅書信僅再出現三次，分別指奴僕的**主人**（提前六 1、2）和器皿的**主人**（提後二 21，思高、新普）；在新約另外六次，分別指**主**／**主宰**－上帝（路二 29／徒四 24；啟六 10）、

要**順服**丈夫；昆謝隆認為這裏的重點（如在該節）在於人際關係中應有的秩序，而不在於一方居於另一方之下。[17] 不過，本節的**順服**可同樣理解為自願順服之意：就如妻子要自願地順服丈夫，奴僕也要自願地順服主人；如此，他們必須**服從**主人是不能改變的事實，但他們可以選擇在心態上自願地（而不是不情願地）**順服**主人。[18]

在（**#1**）**要凡事順服自己的主人**（新譯）這籠統的要求之後，是四項明確的說明，這四項分為兩對，每一對以正負的形式出現，一起構成交叉配置模式，如下：**討他的喜悅**（正），**不可頂撞他**（負），**不可私竊財物**（負），**要……顯出完美的忠誠**（正）。[19] 這樣，**要事事順**

主人／**主宰**－基督（彼後二 1／猶 4 節），和奴僕的**主人**（彼前二 18）。See BDAG 220*a* (s.v.); 《新希》75*b*（s.v.）。(**3**) Knight II 314（followed by Blomberg, 'Titus' 354 n.43）認為，保羅在此選用 δεσπότης, 可能是因它更精準地描寫不信主的主人。(**4**) Quinn 146 認為，δεσπότης 'suggests unqualified ownership and the right to dispose of a particular property without answering to anyone', κύριος 則指 'one who has the governance and use of property but not necessarily an absolute title to it.' Trench 96 (§28) 也認為，κύριος 意指這位「主」的權力是受到限制的（也許只是道德上的限制），並且暗示使用權力者會顧及受這權力管轄者的好處，δεσπότης 則運用 'a more unrestricted power and absolute domination'. 不過作者隨即指出，就保羅的用法而論，他時而稱奴僕的主人為 κύριοι（弗六 9；西四 1），時而稱他們為 δεσπόται（提前六 1、2；提後二 21），似乎二字在意思上並無分別（97）。另一方面，用在上帝（或基督）身上，δεσπότης 比 κύριος 更能表達上帝（或基督）絕對的權力／能力，而祂的能力 'is never disconnected from wisdom and from love'（97-98〔引句出自 97〕）。

17 Quinn 147: 'As in that passage, the emphasis here is on the order (*tassein*, *taxis*) that ought to prevail in human relationships, not on a *sub*mission, *sub*jection, or *sub*ordination designated by the prefixed *hypo*-'. 可是，中間語態的 ὑποτάσσεσθαι 的意思正是「把自己置於（*tassesthai*）別人之下（*hypo*）」。古特立認為，這裏的**順服**（ὑποτάσσω = 'to be in subjection' [*sic*]）是比弗六 5 和西三 22 的**聽從**（ὑπακούω = 'to obey'）更強（'stronger'）的字；這也許提示，克里特的基督徒奴僕有更大的傾向濫用他們新近獲得在基督裏的解放（Guthrie I 196; Guthrie II 208〔古特立 210〕）。不過，這樣區別二字更好：'to be submissive'（RSV, NRSV, ESV）的意思比 'to be obedient'（KJV, NKJV）較廣，所指的不僅是服從明確的命令（參《西．門》649 註 8）。

18 Cf. Oden 111: 'Paul called bond servants to exercise their freedom very intentionally in a paradoxical way: in voluntary submission to conditions that could not under the circumstances be changed by their volition'; Witherington 141: 'Paul is calling them to be proactive rather than reactive to their bondage'.

19 Banker 72*a*; Knight II 315. 這樣分析 9～10 節勝於 Quinn 147 的分析：基督徒奴

服自己的主人（新普）實際上等於「依從他們的要求而不頂嘴；不私竊財物，而是表現出自己是完全誠實可靠的」。[20]

（#2）討他的喜悅即是討主人的喜歡（現修）、令主人滿意（當代）。[21]

（#3）頂撞（同呂譯、新和、現修）另有翻譯為抗辯（思高）[22]和「倔強」。[23] 但在目前的文理中，[24] 頂撞、頂嘴（新譯、新普）[25] 或「反駁」[26] 是原文較明顯的意思，即是用言語表達違反主人意願的自

僕的美德有五項，'two positive [vv. 9a, 9b], then two negative [vv. 9c, 10a], and a concluding characteristic [v. 10b] that expands with a *hina* clause [v. 10c]'.

20 NEB: 'to comply with their demands without answering back; not to pilfer, but to show themselves strictly honest and trustworthy', endorsed by Barrett 136 (followed by Banker 72*a*).

21 I.e., εὐαρέστους εἶναι = 'give / to give satisfaction' (BDAG 403*b* [s.v. εὐάρεστος] / RSV, NRSV; Banker 72*a*, 73*a*; Barclay 254; Fiore II 208, 210). See also REB; Kelly 238 / *Paraphrase* 293: 'to give them satisfaction / to . . . give them satisfactory service'; 馮譯：處處讓他滿意；黃編 212：「意指所有的表現令主人相當滿意。」（1）**εὐάρεστος** 是複合形容詞（= εὐ + ἀρεστός, 'well-pleasing' [Vine 1.20]）。在新約另外出現八次，其對象（是誰所喜悅的）都是上帝（羅十二 1，十四 18；腓四 18；參羅十二 2〔參《羅》4.69〕；來十三 21〔參《來》2.483〕）或主（= 基督：林後五 9；弗五 10；西三 20〔參《西‧門》662〕）。See BDAG 403*b* (s.v.);《新希》137*a*（s.v.）。此字在 LXX 僅出現兩次（次經《所羅門智訓＝智慧篇》4.10, 9:10），其對象也是上帝。（2）Mounce 415 認為，鑑於這字在新約一致的用法，不能排除這裏的對象也是上帝（參：弗六 6～7；西三 22）。不過，順服和頂撞的對象都是奴僕的主人，因此討他的喜悅的「他」較可能也是指主人。（3）H. Balz（*EDNT* 2.74*b* [s.v.]）認為，這字 'is a comprehensive fundamental term in parenetic language involving the believer's task of examining the will of God in one's particular situation.'「審視上帝的旨意」這意思在本節並不明顯，儘管下一節的目的子句（10c 節：好事事都能榮耀我們救主上帝的教導）提示，不能將這意思完全排除。

22 See also NAU, ESV: 'argumentative'; NJB: 'do what is wanted without argument'.

23 RSV: 'be refractory'. See also Johnson I 127: 'They are not to be "refractory"'; Fiore II 208, 210: 'being obstinate'. 古特立則認為 'answering again / talk back'（KJV/NIV）應理解為較廣義的 'opposition' 之意（Guthrie I 196-97; Guthrie II 208-9〔古特立 211「對立」〕）。

24 原文動詞（ἀντιλέγω）已在一 9 出現過；參該節註釋註 39 之（2）= 上面 147。

25 See also NKJV / REB / NRSV, NIV, TNIV, NIV2011, NLT: 'answering back / answer back / talk back'; Davies I 100: 'They are *not to answer back*, <u>even in response to a master's immoral demands</u>'（參註 15〔上面 271〕）。

26 *Paraphrase* 293, DC 139*b*, Saarinen 181: 'contradict'. 黃編 212 則認為，「『頂撞』不單指言語的頂嘴，也指態度的不遜。」

己的意願，意譯可作「拒絕聽命」。[27]《當代聖經》的**以言詞冒犯**可理解為：拒絕遵從主人的要求或命令是冒犯主人的行為。

（**#4**）**私竊財物、私取財物**（新譯）或**私拿東西**（呂譯、新和）[28] 原文只是**竊取／偷竊**（思高／現修、新普），[29] 所指的也許是「小量的、一點一點的偷竊」。[30]

（**#5**）第 10b 節開首原文有**卻**字（呂譯），[31] 表達強烈的對比**不可／不要……卻要**（現修／新譯）。**要凡事顯出完美的忠誠**原文片語[32] 中的「信」字，理論上可理解為奴僕對主人的信任，但第 10b 節

---

27 Banker 73*a*: 'refuse (to obey them (their masters))'. 按這種理解，#3 和 #4 是一對：'"well-pleasing" and "not rebellious" in disposition'（Hendriksen 369）。Baugh 505*b* 舉例說明，'to the ancients the insolent slave was a typical item of conversation portrayed in their literature and plays.'

28 在**不可私拿別人的東西**（當代）這翻譯裏，**別人的**宜改譯為「主人的」（see NIV, TNIV, NIV2011: 'not to steal from them'－'them' 的前述詞是 9 節的 'their masters'）。Quinn 149 指出：'The slave stealing from his master was proverbial in the ancient world, whether Jewish . . . Greek . . . or Roman'.

29 See also KJV: 'purloining'; NIV, TNIV, NIV2011, NLT: 'steal'.

30 NKJV, NAU, NJB, ESV; Fiore II 208, 210 / RSV, NRSV, REB; DC 139*b*, Banker 60: 'pilfering/pilfer'. See also G. Schneider, *EDNT* 2.478*a* (s.v. νοσφίζομαι): 'set aside for oneself, embezzle'. 馮譯作**勿尅扣**，指「替主人管賬或收租時」（夾註）。(**1**) 原文動詞（**νοσφίζω**）在新約聖經僅再出現兩次（都是中間語態），指亞拿尼亞把變賣田產所得的錢留下一部分（徒五 2、3）。See BDAG 679*a* (s.v.);《新希》227*b*（s.v.）。MHT 2.408 指出，'Νοσφίζω . . . has in the two [*sic*] NT occurrences (Ac $5^{2.3}$, Tit 2^{10}) a special middle force, *to purloin*, supported by the papyri (see *Vocab. s.v.* [MM 430*b*]).' (**2**) 此字在 LXX 也只出現兩次，一次指以色列人（亞干）偷取了部分的當滅之物（書七 1），另一次指「默乃勞……由聖殿中偷去一些金器」（次經《馬加比二書》4.32，思高）。

31 ἀλλά = 'but' (KJV, NKJV, RSV, NRSV, NAU, NIV, TNIV, NIV2011, ESV).

32 πᾶσαν πίστιν ἐνδεικνυμένους ἀγαθήν（各種異文見 Wallace 188 n.44），直譯作 'all faith showing good' = 'showing all good faith/faithfulness'（NAU, ESV / Knight II 315）。(**1**) Wallace 188-89（also 312-13）指出，按這種理解，形容詞 ἀγαθήν 與它所形容的無冠詞的名詞 πίστιν 被分詞 ἐνδεικνυμένους 隔開，而這是不尋常的。因此他認為應把 ἀγαθήν 看為述語，所得出的意思就是 'demonstrating that all [genuine] faith is productive'（方括號是作者的；cf. Jeon I 74: 'those who demonstrate that all faith is good'; 75: '"All faith" . . . refers to "faith" that is complete – "faith" that is genuine because it demonstrates a "recognition of truth according to godliness" [1:1b]）。(**2**) 可是，(**i**) 將 πᾶσαν 理解為 'genuine' 十分牽強。沃雷司提出的理據是（Wallace 189 n.49 = 313 n.52）：'"Genuine" may either be implied from the flow of argument or may be considered a part of the field of meaning for πᾶς when it is used

是第 10a 節的反面，因而「信」字所指的是奴僕對主人的忠誠可靠，與偷竊主人的東西相對。[33] 故此，這裏的要求是，奴僕對主人要表現出自己是絕對可靠……的（新普），[34] 要事事表現忠厚可靠／表示自

---

with abstract nouns (cf. BAGD, s.v. πᾶς, 1.a.δ).' 然而，BAGD 的解釋（'to denote the highest degree *full, greatest, all*' [similarly BDAG 783*b*, s.v. 3.a]）並不支持沃雷司的理解，而是支持通常的理解。（**ii**）πίστις 在本節的意思肯定不是 'faith'（信心），而是 'trustworthiness/faithfulness'（忠誠，可靠）；cf. Towner III 738 n.105（唐 1076-77 註 98）。

（**3**）動詞 ἐνδείκνυμι 'means not merely "to prove" but "to demonstrate" powerfully and visibly'（Marshall 260）。（**4**）這動詞（**ἐνδείκνυμι**）在新約另外出現十次（八次在保羅書信裏）：一次指一事表明另一件事（羅二 15，新譯〔參《羅》1.374-76〕），另一次的意思是向人做一些事（提後四 14，現修、新普）；四次指神彰顯祂的大能（羅九 17），和顯明祂的忿怒（羅九 22）、恩典（弗二 7）、忍耐（提前一 16）；其餘四次指人顯明愛心的憑據（林後八 24），以及表現溫柔／愛心（新譯：多三 2／來六 10），和熱心（來六 11，思高）。See BDAG 331*b*-32*a* (s.v.);《新希》113*a*（s.v.）。（**5**）同字根的動詞 ἐπιδείκνυμι 在新約出現七次，分別指法利賽人請耶穌顯個……神蹟給他們看（太十六 1）；耶穌叫門徒拿一個……錢給我看（二十二 19），又叫祂治好的痲瘋病人把身體給祭司檢查（路十七 14）；門徒把聖殿的建築指給〔耶穌〕看（太二十四 1），約帕的眾寡婦拿多加……所做的內衣外衣給〔彼得〕看（徒九 39）；亞波羅引聖經證明耶穌是基督（十八 28）；上帝為要更有力地顯明他的旨意不可更改，就以起誓作保證（來六 17）。See BDAG (s.v.);《新希》125*b*（s.v.）。

33 Banker 73*b*. 參新譯：要顯示絕對的誠實；Lock 123: 'thoroughly loyal to their masters.' Marshall 214 則以這裏的 πίστιν 為 'a continual activity or process [of faith]'.

34 筆者省略了「、善良」。因為在原文（見註 32 開首），最後一個形容詞並不是分詞顯出的第二個賓詞（第一個是 πᾶσαν πίστιν），而是像首個形容詞 πᾶσαν 一樣形容名詞 πίστιν 的，整個片語 πᾶσαν πίστιν ἀγαθήν 意即 'all good fidelity'（KJV, NKJV），'entire and true / complete and perfect fidelity'（RSV/NRSV）。See also REB: 'to show themselves absolutely trustworthy'; NIV, TNIV, NIV2011: 'to show that they can be fully trusted'; White 193*b* / Hendriksen 361, 368, 369 n.200 (continued): 'displaying/evincing the utmost trustworthiness.'（**1**）Kelly 238-39 則翻譯為 'displaying all-round honest trustworthiness'; 張 352 翻譯為「全然〔、〕美好之忠誠」，（按兩個形容詞的相反次序）解釋為「其忠誠應有良好的表現，並且涉及生活的各層面。」（**2**）Quinn 149 則認為，放在末尾因而受到強調的 ἀγαθήν 一字表示，一個基督徒奴僕對基督徒主人的忠誠是有限制的：'If the latter commands his slave to do something evil, the performance of it is not "good evidence of complete reliability," literally "all good loyalty."' 但這解釋與作者早前的假設不符——基督徒主人不會命令奴僕作 'unchristian' 的事（參註 11 末部分〔上面 270〕）。（**3**）Towner III 738 作：'but showing complete faithfulness in [with respect to] what is good'（方括號是原來的，但在唐 1077 被省略了）。但陰性的 ἀγαθήν 較自然地是形容 πίστιν（也是陰性）的，卻很難視為 accusative of respect（'what is good' 要求中性單數的 ἀγαθόν 或複數的 ἀγαθά）。

己實在忠信（現修／思高），[35] 總要用行動表現自己是個完全可靠的人（當代）。[36]

第 10c 節的好或好使（思高、現修、新譯）一字表達目的。[37] 這目的並非只是要事事表現忠厚可靠（10b 節，現修）的目的，而是奴僕應按照上述指示（9～10b 節）而行的目的，[38] 理由有二：（1）第 10c 節的事事或在一切事上（呂譯、思高）[39] 的意思是在所做的一切事上（現修），[40] 其範圍超越了第 10b 節的要事事表現忠厚可靠，亦包括之前提到的凡事順服主人，討他的喜悅，不違反他的意願，不偷竊（9～10a 節）。（2）第 5b 節的目的子句（免得上帝的道被毀謗）表達了年輕的婦女所受教導之行為（4b～5a 節）的目的，第 8b 節的目的子句（使那反對的人……自覺羞愧）表達了提多要按照上述指示

35 **（1）**事事和總（當代）翻譯了 πᾶσαν 的意思：‘consistently’（*Paraphrase* 293），‘at all times’（NJB; Banker 73*b*）。Marshall 260 認為 πᾶς = ‘in all respects, on all occasions’. **（2）**實在翻譯了 ἀγαθήν 的意思：這形容詞 ‘denotes the genuineness of the fidelity’（Banker 73*b*）; see also Marshall 261: ‘true, genuine’; RSV: ‘true fidelity’.

36 唐書禮認為，以上五項要求所暗示的、奴僕對主人不敬的行為，有可能就是假教師敗壞人的全家（一 11b）的部分結果（Towner II 241）。

37 I.e., ἵνα = ‘so that’ (RSV, NRSV, NAU, NIV, TNIV, NIV2011, ESV, NJB). 另有中英譯本將 ἵνα 視為表達結果：‘Then/thus’（NLT / *Paraphrase* 293），這樣（當代、新普）、以致（新和；張 352）。參二 8b～c 註釋註 1 之（1）= 上面 266。

38 Hendriksen 336, 360, 382 認為好使表達各類的家庭成員要按二 2～10b 的教導來生活的目的。但 Hendriksen 369 在二 10c 的註釋中正確地將本句解釋為只是二 9～10b 對奴僕之要求的目的。Cf. Chapell 287-88: ‘Only one class of believers [namely, slaves] is directly instructed in this epistle to order their actions so as to make the faith credible to those outside the Christian community.’

39 ἐν πᾶσιν = ‘in everything’ (RSV, NRSV, ESV), ‘in all things’ (KJV, NKJV). See also NIV, TNIV, NIV2011, NJB: ‘in every way’. 此片語位於目的子句的末尾，Hiebert 438 認為它是受到強調的。

40 See Banker 74*b*: ἐν πᾶσιν = ‘in all that they do’.**（1）**克拉遜則認為，ἐν πᾶσιν（10c 節）的意思是「在一切的人當中（包括奴僕）」：‘. . . this message should be made attractive amongst all people without restriction, including slaves’（Classen, ‘Titus’ 438, ‘Epistle to Titus’ 57-58）。克拉遜認為，隨後一段幾乎要求這種翻譯，尤其是緊接著的 11 節，該節重拾本節的數個字：比較 τοῦ σωτῆρος ἡμῶν θεοῦ . . . ἐν πᾶσιν（10c 節）和 ἡ χάρις τοῦ θεοῦ σωτήριος πᾶσιν ἀνθρώποις（11 節）。See also W. Foerster, *TDNT* 7.1017: ‘“all men” occurs in Tt. 2:11, and it is also in view in the preceding verse . . . ἐν πᾶσιν.’ **（2）**新普的翻譯（在各方面都能吸引人 = ‘attractive in every way’ [NLT]）將 ἐν πᾶσιν 實質上變成上帝的教導的形容詞。

（7～8a 節）而行的目的；這就有力地提示，第 10c 節的目的子句同樣是表達奴僕要按照上述指示（9～10b 節）而行的目的。[41]

動詞榮耀或尊榮（新和）的另一種翻譯是給〔它〕增光彩（呂譯）。[42] 多本英譯本翻譯為「裝飾」[43] 或「為〔它〕作飾物」。[44] 不過，裝飾（馮譯）是比喻用法，其真正的意思可能是使〔它〕能吸引人（新普），[45] 或更可能是使〔之〕獲得光榮／使……得著尊榮（思

---

41 See Banker 74*a-b*. Witherington 130 認為，這目的子句是「省略三段論法（enthymeme）」的第三部分，如下：

> '1. Slaves must subject themselves and give evidence of complete reliability,
> 2. [So that they will even be a good witness to their own masters,]
> 3. For by doing so they will add honor and luster to the teachings of our Savior.'

（第二行的方括號是原來的，表示該行是被省略的部分〔'a suppressed premise'〕。）不過，沒有理由將 10c 節開首的 ἵνα = 'So that' 放在被省略的部分，並以 'For' 取代它的位置。因此筆者認為，第二、三兩行可改寫如下：

> 2. [For by doing so they will be a good witness to their own masters,]
> 3. So that they will add honor and luster to the teachings of our Savior.

如此，這省略三段論法便與之前的兩個例子的模式一致：參二 5b 註釋註 3 之（1），二 8b～c 註 1 之（2）= 上面 250，266。

42 See also Quinn 27, 117, 127, 144: 'add luster . . . to'; NEB, REB; Marshall 257; idem, 'Timothy and Titus' 188*a* / Perkins 1444*b*; Marshall, 'Congregation' 111: 'add lustre/luster to'.

43 KJV, NKJV, RSV, NAU, ESV, H. Sasse, *TDNT* 3.867, K. Wegenast, *DNTT* 3.771, Marshall 261, Johnson II 230, Young 52: 'adorn'; J. Schneider, C. Brown, *DNTT* 3.220: 'adorns'; J. Guhrt, *DNTT* 1.524: 'decorate, adorn'; Liefeld 34: 'adorn, decorate'（利斐特 28：「增加美觀、裝飾」；參較下面註 45）; Kelly 239, 243: 'embellish'. 參《輔讀》528（第一解釋）：「裝飾」；黃編 213：「僕人的好行為能成為我們救主神之教訓的榮美裝飾」。

44 NRSV: 'be an adornment to'; *Paraphrase* 293: 'be ornaments to'.

45 NIV, TNIV, NIV2011, NLT: 'make . . . attractive' (also Fiore II 210; Hiebert 439; Witherington 115; Mounce, 'Titus' 106). See also Guthrie I 197, Guthrie II 209: 'to make it appear beautiful in the eyes of all onlookers'（「旁觀者」在古特立 211 變成「外人」）; Lock 137: 'make the teaching about God our Saviour more attractive'; 138-39: 'to add fresh luster to the doctrine and make it attractive to the heathen'; Montague 236: 'make the gospel shine before the pagan world, increasing its attractiveness'; Mounce 416: 'to make the gospel as attractive as possible for those around them'; White 194*a*: 'it must . . . be rendered attractive to them that are without'; Zehr 269-70: '. . . increase the attractiveness of the gospel in the hearts of the pagans'; Liefeld 329: 'make the teaching about God . . . attractive'（利斐特 346-47：「使"神的教義更具吸引力"」；參較上面註 43）；彭編 102*a*：「使……吸引人」；曾 139-40：「令神我們的救主的教導顯

高／新譯），即是「使〔它〕獲得稱讚和尊敬」。[46]

我們〔的〕救主上帝（10c 節）一詞已在一章 3 節出現過；**我們的**意即「我們所有基督信徒的」。[47] 它在本段的末尾再次出現，具有特別的作用：下一段（二 11～14）一開始就提到上帝拯救……的恩典（二 11，現修）；第 13 節繼而提到我們偉大的〔上帝〕，救主耶穌基督（新譯）。如此，第 10 節的**我們〔的〕救主上帝**一詞具有「鈎狀鑰詞」的功能，它引介下一段，並且將它所屬的本段（二 1～10）與下一段（二 11～14）連接起來。[48]

得吸引。」**(1)** '[T]o make the Christian teaching all the more decorous'（Fiore II 224）這種講法值得商榷，因為「彬彬有禮（decorous）」通常指人的行為舉止，不適宜用於「教導」。**(2)** 周 429 則合併「有吸引力，受人尊重」兩個意思（後者見下文）。

46 See also NJB: 'are . . . a credit to'; BDAG 560*b* (s.v. κοσμέω, 2 b β): 'do credit to' (thus also Marshall 261; Young 78; Classen, 'Epistle to Titus' 57, 64); H. Balz, *EDNT* 2.309*b* (s.v.): '*give honor* to it'; Collins 347: 'bring honor to' (cf. 346: 'by the first century C.E. its meaning was often "to honor"'); Arichea－Hatton 290 ('everyone will show great respect for the teaching about God our [inclusive] Savior . . .'（方括號是原來的）。亦參現修：讓〔它〕更受尊重；《串釋（增簡）》1755*a*：「叫福音真道在人眼中倍覺榮美和尊貴。」**(1)** Jeon II 5（cf. 26）把動詞榮耀的主詞視為奴僕的主人：'so that their masters, who (presumably) were unbelievers, "might adorn the doctrine of God our Savior"'. 張 353 同樣認為「他們尊榮」（κοσμῶσιν）的「他們」是指「僕人的主人」，繼而聲稱：「由此可見，此處的主人，大概都是未信主的人士，他們能因着信主之僕人的好行為，尊敬僕人所信的基督教信仰」。可是，上文的每一個不定詞（順服、討他的喜悅一詞開首的 εἶναι）和分詞（頂撞、私竊財物、顯出）的主事者都是僕人，這裏的限定動詞「他們尊榮」的主事者不可能（在沒有任何預示之下）突然變成僕人的主人。**(2)** 動詞 **κοσμέω** 在保羅書信僅再出現一次，指婦女應以端正、克制……打扮自己（提前二 9）。新約另外八次，分別指從前那些仰望上帝的聖潔婦女……以服從丈夫來妝飾自己（彼前三 5，現修〔三 3 的妝飾原文為同字根名詞 κόσμος〕）；污靈發現從前的住處打掃得乾淨整齊（新普：太十二 44 ‖ 路十一 25），文士和法利賽人裝飾義人的墓（太二十三 29，思高），比喻中的童女整理她們的燈（太二十五 7，新譯）；聖殿是用美石和供物裝飾的（路二十一 5）；聖城新耶路撒冷好像新娘打扮整齊（啟二十一 2），城牆的基石用各種寶石裝飾（啟二十一 19，現修）。See BDAG 560*a*-60*b* (s.v.);《新希》190*b*（s.v.）。

47 參一 3b 註釋註 3 之（2）及註 4 所屬正文（上面 73）。W. Foerster（*TDNT* 7.1017）則認為，我們〔的〕救主上帝意即上帝是 'the Saviour of all men; the σωτήρ [*sic*, ἡμῶν?] means that God is the Saviour whom we know and in whom we believe.'

48 Van Nestle, 'Structure' 126 (see also 132). 引句英文原作 'a hooked keyword'. 這是一位作者從一段轉到另一段的修辭技巧，'in which the words involved in the "hook" [here "God our Savior"] figure prominently in one of the units being connected [here 2:11-14].' See also Van Neste 258. Cf. Banker 74*b*: '"the teaching of our Savior God" is

我們救主上帝的教導可能意即「屬於或源自」我們救主上帝的教導。[49] 不過，這片語較可能的意思是**有關我們救主上帝的教義**（現修）。[50] 在二章 5 節，年長婦女指教年輕婦女應有的行為表現，其目的是負面的**免得上帝的道被毀謗**；但是在這裏，提多要給予僕人的指導，其目的卻是正面的**榮耀我們救主上帝的教導**。保羅將這種至高榮譽的可能，給予在社會上的低下階層！[51] 他所用的修辭技巧，就是以崇高的目標來鼓勵他們，而不僅是告訴他們<u>不可</u>怎樣作。[52] 無論如何，信徒行為的最後依據是**上帝的教導**。

本段的三個目的子句（二 5b、8b～c、10c）突出了一件重要的事實：信徒的行為，會左右人們對上帝和祂的福音的評價。[53] **不合乎那**

---

a tail-head link with 2:11-14.' 亦參一 9 註釋註 49 及所屬正文，一 16 註釋註 36 及所屬正文（上面 149，214）。

49 Barrett 136 ('teaching which proceeds from him'); Genade 52 ('belonging to or originating from God'). 原文為 τὴν διδασκαλίαν <u>τὴν</u> τοῦ σωτῆρος ἡμῶν θεοῦ.（1）第二個冠詞的功用相當於關係代名詞：'the teaching which [is] of our Saviour God'（see Wallace 213-14）。MHT 4.104 認為，這裏重複冠詞是 'in Semitic fashion'.（2）原文的另二種表達法是（i）τὴν <u>τοῦ σωτῆρος</u> <u>ἡμῶν θεοῦ</u> διδασκαλίαν 和（ii）τὴν διδασκαλίαν（不重複冠詞）τοῦ σωτῆρος ἡμῶν θεοῦ（See MHT 3.217）。MHT 4.96 指出：'In Biblical Greek and increasingly in the papyri as time went on . . . the attributive genitive followed its governing noun without repetition of the article' =（ii）。

50 See also NIV, TNIV, NIV2011, NLT: 'the teaching about God our Savior'; similarly, Arichea－Hatton 290; Banker 74*b*; Collins 347; Johnson II 232; Knight II 315; Marshall 261; Towner III 739（唐 1078）。（1）Banker 74*b* 認為，原文的次序（**我們的救主**被放在**上帝**之前）表示前者受到強調，這提示**有關我們救主上帝的教義**（現修）特指關於救恩的教義（二 11～14）。See also Classen, 'Titus' 438: 原文片語的意思是「關於<u>上帝是救主</u>的教導」。（2）Towner III 739 則認為，「有關我們的救主上帝的**教導**」並不表示這教導的內容是「侷限於救恩的信息」（唐 1078）。二 10 的**教導**和二 1 的**教導**（原文皆為 διδασκαλία）前後呼應，「將其間的所有內容都歸入這『教導』的範疇〔category〕內」（Towner III 738-39〔唐 1077，引句出處〕）。

51 Ward 257 稱 '*in everything* to *adorn the doctrine*' 為 'the apex of Paul's vision for the slave'. 足以和前者匹敵的是門 16 節：**不再是奴隸，而是高過奴隸，是親愛的弟兄**（參《西‧門》926-29）。

52 See Genade 52-53. Malherbe（'Soteriology' 340）則認為，雖然 'to adorn the teaching of God their Saviour <u>among all people</u>*' 這話只是用在奴僕身上，但是按照教牧書信的情操（'sentiment'），這話適用於所有基督徒。Cf. Towner III 738（唐 1077）：'Logically, any of the *hina* clauses [vv. 5b, 8b, 10c] could apply to all of the instructions.'（*參註 40 之〔1〕＝ 上面 276。）

53 Jeon II 23: 'there is a missiological purpose for Christian conduct.' Cf. Malherbe,

健全的教導（1 節）的行為，會使上帝的道蒙受恥辱（5b 節，新普）；合乎那健全的教導的行為，則至少會（8b～c 節）使那些敵對的人，因為找不到我們的錯處（現修）而自覺羞愧，不再說我們的壞話（新普），甚至會讓有關我們救主上帝的教義更受尊重（10c 節，現修）。[54] 在這三個目的子句當中，第三個是正面的，不像第一個是負面的，也比第二個籠統，因而最適合在本段的結尾這最具策略性的位置上出現。[55]

'Paulus Senex' 205: 'the reaction of outsiders serve[s] as motivation for the conduct of the community (Titus 2:5, 8, 10)'.

54 See Van Neste, 'Message' 24*b*-25*a*. 范尼斯引兩位舊約人物的事迹以資說明：消極方面，大衞與拔示巴行淫的事，叫耶和華的仇敵大得褻瀆的機會（撒下十二 14，註）；積極方面，但以理的政敵找不到他任何的把柄和過失，只能從他上帝的律法中下手（但六 4～5），這導致但以理受迫害（6～17 節），但至終使上帝受到異教君王的稱讚（25～27 節）。See also Wendland, 'Discourse' 342 with n.17.

55 Banker 59*a*. 在這三個目的子句當中，第一、三兩個分別是關乎年輕的婦女（4a 節）和僕人（9 節）的行為的。（**1**）Witherington 148-49 從當代的社會背景解釋如下：'Going all the way back to the remarks of Augustus himself and the various *leges Juliae* [Julian laws], there had been grave concern in the first century that Romans and others were not practicing the traditional family virtues of marrying, having civil and loyal children, raising them properly, cultivating various domestic virtues, and the like. There was particular concern about <u>women</u> who got involved in foreign cults and neglected their family duties, and there was also a serious and ongoing fear of <u>slave</u> revolts (e.g., like the Spartacus revolt). Since there were a considerable number of <u>women and slaves</u> involved in the Christian movement, it is not a surprise that churches gave special attention to their behavior to make sure that the Christian witness would not suffer because of their actions.'（**2**）P. H. Towner（*DPL* 419*a*）指出，保羅的目的是要 'promote a manner of social behavior that was respectable in the eyes of those outside the church'（尤其見多二 5、8、10；提前三 7，六 1）；「這似乎是保羅的一貫特色，就是認可社會上公認的家庭規範所帶來〔<u>encouraged in</u> the household codes〕循規蹈矩的生活方式，認為這有助於信徒在敵對的世界中〔a <u>potentially</u> hostile world〕傳福音的使命」（《辭典》618*b*）。See also M. B. Thompson, *DPL* 922*b*（《辭典》1322*a*）。

4.2 教義性基礎（二 11～14）

11 因為，上帝救眾人的恩典已經顯明出來，
12a 訓練我們
12b 除去不敬虔的心和世俗的情慾，
12c 在今世過克己、正直、敬虔的生活，
13a 等候福樂的盼望，
13b 並等候至大的上帝和我們的救主耶穌基督的榮耀顯現。
14a 他為我們的緣故捨己，
14b 為了要贖我們脫離一切罪惡，
14c 又潔淨我們作他自己的子民，熱心為善。

二章 13b 節所提到的至大的上帝和我們的救主耶穌基督，與上一段末的我們〔的〕救主上帝（二 10c）前後呼應；後者就是將它所屬的一段（二 1～10）與本段（二 11～14）連接起來的「鈎狀鑰詞」。[1] 上一段的首尾分別提到那健全的教導（二 1）和我們救主上帝的教導（二 10c），該段的內容就是健全的教導的具體說明；本段則引進上一段的健全的教導（二 1～10）之教義性基礎（留意二 11 的因為）：我們救主上帝的教導（二 10c）是基於上帝的恩典已經顯明，而這恩典對我們有所要求（二 11～14）。[2] 與此同時，本段對救恩的

1 這一點見二 9～10 註釋註 48 及所屬正文（上面 278-79）。
2 'γάρ introduces the theological basis for 2.1-10 as a whole' (Marshall 266; see also Lau 154-55). (1) Fee 193 認為，二 11～14 提供了一 10～二 10 這一整段（'the

闡釋，亦可視為有關我們救主上帝的教義（二 10c，現修）的一種解釋。[3]

本段（在原文只是一長句）[4] 的主題從上一段的倫理行為轉到上帝的救恩，因此，本段滿是那些屬於救恩的語意範疇的詞彙：救、恩典（11 節），福樂的盼望、救主（13 節），他為我們的緣故捨己、贖、潔淨（14 節）。[5] 與此同時，保羅是用倫理的詞彙來討論這救恩的。首先，上帝拯救的恩典訓練信徒要過克己……的生活（12c 節），而克己正是老年人和年輕的男女在上一段被勸勉要作的事（2、5a、6 節）。[6] 其次，基督自我犧牲的目的是要救贖人脫離罪惡（14b 節，新譯作不法的事），並且潔淨他們，使他們熱心為善（14c 節）；如此，基督的工作使信徒生出善工（新譯），而提多正是要作好行為的榜樣（7 節）。[7] 第三，上帝拯救的恩典也訓練信徒要棄絕不敬虔的行為和屬世的私慾（12b 節，現修），後者（棄絕……）一定可以包

"imperative"')的神學基礎('the "indicative"')。Fee 194 則說：'An explanatory **for** . . . closely ties verses 11-14 to 2-10'. 筆者認為，後一種講法較為正確，因為二 11～14 與一 10～16 並無明顯的 indicative-imperative 關係；二 15 才與一 10～16 有明顯的關聯（見二 15 註釋註 6 所屬正文〔下面 341-4 2〕）。(**2**) Chapell 334 則認為，'In context the words [v. 11] encourage slaves to remember that even societal superiors who have been corrupted by their worldly privileges are objects of the grace of God and thus should not be denied the message of salvation by slaves who already possess the higher privileges of eternity.')

3 以上一段參 Van Neste 272.

4 (**1**) Genade 120 誤稱二 11～15 在原文是一句。其實，15 節在句法上是和 11～14 節分開的另一句。Genade 128（'2:11-14'）修正了早前的錯誤。(**2**) 昆謝隆認為，二 11～14 是「洗禮的認信（baptismal confession）」(Quinn 10, 64, 166)。(**3**) 艾利斯將二 11～14 放在 'admonitions'（'preformed traditions' 的一種）之列（Ellis, 'Traditions' 238 with n.9），但隨即又以這幾節為一首詩歌（238 with 239 n.12; 244: 'a confessional hymn'）。

5 Banker 75*a*.

6 有關的原文依次為：σωφρόνως（形容詞 σώφρων 的副詞）. . . ζήσωμεν（12c 節），σώφρονας（形容詞 σώφρων 的複數陰性直接受格，2、5a 節）和 σωφρονεῖν（動詞 σωφρονέω 的不定詞，6 節）。加上底線的二字是同字根的；4 節的 σωφρονίζωσιν（指教，from σωφρονίζω）也是。

7 善工和好行為在原文是同一個片語：καλῶν ἔργων（所有格；主格為 καλὰ ἔργα. 一 16c 的好事是這片語的單數直接受格：ἔργον ἀγαθόν）。

括不說讒言、不作酒的奴隸（3 節）和不……私竊財物（10 節）。這樣的棄絕亦與敵對者以他們的行為否認上帝（一 16a）構成對比。[8] 如此，本段保留了很強的倫理元素，延續了上一段（二 1～10）的倫理關注。[9]

8 棄絕（ἀρνησάμενοι）和否認（ἀρνοῦνται）是同一個動詞（ἀρνέομαι）所具有的意思。

9 以上一段參 Van Neste, 'Structure' 124-25. See also Van Neste 258.

4.2.1 上帝恩典的顯明（二 11～13）

班約翰認為：（1）這一小段呈現「夾心式」的排列法：位於兩端的**顯明**（11 節）和**顯現**（13b 節）——二字原文是同字根的動詞和名詞——將所希望見到的行為夾在中央（12 節）。（2）若把第 12 節分拆為正負兩面，這一小段便呈現交叉配置模式：（甲）上帝的恩典顯明（11 節），（乙）信徒要除去的行為（12a～b 節），（乙'）信徒應該過的生活（12c 節），（甲'）耶穌基督的顯現（13 節）。[1] 可是，關於（1），「所希望見到的行為」其實包括第 13 節的內容；關於（2），第 13 節的內容其實是信徒應該過的生活的一部分，即（甲'）其實應納入（乙'）之內。因此，將這一小段的結構看為「夾心式」或「交叉配置模式」皆有其弱點，都不可取。

1 Banker 82*a*. See also Simpson 107.

二 11 因為，上帝救眾人的恩典已經顯明出來，

因為這詞表示，保羅現在為上一段關於健全行為的教導（二 1～10）提出教義性的基礎。[1]（甲）另一種翻譯將**眾人**連於句子開首的動詞**顯明**，[2] 所得出的意思就是：「帶來救恩的、上帝的恩典，已經向眾人顯明。」[3]（乙）**上帝救眾人的恩典**（新和同）這種翻譯，[4] 則把句末的**眾人**二字連於形容詞[5] **帶來拯救**（新

---

1 參二 11～14 註釋引言註 2 及所屬正文（上面 281）。Lock 143 認為，**因為**表示，二 11～14 解釋了為甚麼信徒能夠按二 1～10 的勸勉而行：'do this for you *can*, God's grace was given for this very purpose.' 筆者倒認為，本段較可能是解釋為甚麼信徒應該按上一段的勸勉而行：'It proceeds to explain why God's people should live as exhorted in 2-10'（Fee 194）。

2 **顯明**原文動詞（ἐπεφάνη [from ἐπιφαίνω]）在下文再出現一次（三 4，也是被動語態）；**ἐπιφαίνω** 在新約僅再出現二次，都是主動語態（路一 79：照亮；徒二十七 20：**顯露**〔新和〕）。See BDAG 385*b* (s.v.);《新希》130*b*（s.v.）。

3 Ἐπεφάνη γὰρ ἡ χάρις τοῦ θεοῦ σωτήριος πᾶσιν ἀνθρώποις = 'For the grace of God that bringeth/brings salvation hath/has appeared to all men' (KJV / NKJV, NIV [endorsed by Arichea－Hatton 291]). See also Zehr 280 / Collins 349: 'the saving grace / For the saving beneficence of God has appeared to all people'; Fiore II 208: 'The salvific favor of God . . . has appeared to all people'.（Fiore II 210 更聲稱，全世界都得救〔'Universal salvation'〕在教牧書信的教義中佔有顯著的地位〔參提前二 4〕。）**(1)** 按這種理解，(**i**) 祈勒克聲稱原文呈現交叉配置模式：[A] ἐπεφάνη γὰρ [B] ἡ χάρις [C] τοῦ θεοῦ [B'] σωτήριος [A'] πᾶσιν ἀνθρώποις（Clark, 'Structure' 112），但 [A] 和 [A'] 的「對應」是牽強的；(**ii**) Collins 349-50 認為 [A']（'to all people'）可能是針對猶太人的排外主義而發（參：提前二 4～5，四 10），不管他們是會堂的猶太人（聲稱上帝的救恩只屬猶太人所有），抑是類似羅馬書、加拉太書及徒十五章所處理的猶太派基督派（堅持外邦信徒必須受割禮方能得救）。**(2)** Spencer 49 將這句翻譯為 'For God's grace illuminated with saving power all humans'. 但 πᾶσιν ἀνθρώποις 是間接受格，不是直接受格，因而不可能是 ἐπεφάνη 的賓詞；因此，後者也可能不是及物動詞（'illuminated'），而是不及物動詞（'appeared'）。

4 另見呂譯：**上帝的恩、給全人類施拯救的**；思高：**天主救眾人的恩寵**；當代：**上帝救世人的恩典**；新譯／現修：**神／上帝拯救萬人／全人類的恩典**；新普：**上帝的恩典……為所有人帶來拯救**。彭編 103*a* 認為，「從 2:13 來看，〔上帝〕應指耶穌基督。」可是，到此為止，θεός 在上文已出現九次，全都是指**父上帝**（一 4；另見一 1a、1b、2、3、7、16，二 5、10），因此不大可能在這裏（在毫無預警之下）突然變為指基督。

5 形容詞 **σωτήριος** 在新約聖經另外出現四次，都是「名詞化用語」（《新希》323*a* [s.v.]），指上帝的**救恩**（路二 30，三 6；徒二十八 28；弗六 17）。See also BDAG 986*b* (s.v.). 它在 LXX 出現五次，呈現兩種意思：(i)「有益健康的（wholesome [RSV, NRSV]; see also NJB: 'have health in them'）」，與「致命的毒素（fatal poison [NJB]）」

普）。[6] 支持這立場的理由包括：在原文，**眾人緊隨著帶來拯救**；[7] 動詞**顯明**本身的意思已是完整的，不必由「向眾人」補充；[8] 形容詞**帶來拯救**並無冠詞，這表示它不是定語的，而是謂語的，[9] 它引進「上

相對（次經《便西拉智訓》＝ 思高《德訓篇》1.14）；（ii）「與獲救有關的」（偽經《馬加比三書》6.31; 7.18;《馬加比四書》12.6; 15.26）。

6 Ἐπεφάνη γὰρ ἡ χάρις τοῦ θεοῦ σωτήριος πᾶσιν ἀνθρώποις = 'For the grace of God has appeared, bringing salvation to all / to all men / for all people' (NRSV / NAU; J. Schneider, C. Brown, *DNTT* 3.221 ['for] / ESV; Mounce 420, 421). See also NLT: 'For the grace of God has been revealed, bringing salvation to all people'; NJB: 'God's grace has been revealed to save the whole human race'; NEB, REB: 'For the grace of God has dawned upon the world with healing for all mankind'（有底線的三個字是譯者加上的）；馮譯：**上帝的恩典已彰明，要拯救萬民**。（**1**）持此立場的釋經者包括 BDAG 986*b* (s.v. σωτήριος, a); Arichea－Hatton 291; Barclay 256; DC 142*a*, 144*a*; Fairnbairn 55, 277; Fee 194; Hendriksen 370; Johnson II 238; Marshall 268; White 194*b*; Witherington 128-29; Edwards, 'Christology' 144; 侯嘉文 156。Wallace 174-75 以本節的 πᾶσιν ἀνθρώποις 為 'dative after certain adjectives' 的例子。（**2**）LN §21.28 在兩種立場之間不作選擇。（**3**）'For the grace of God has been manifested for the salvation of all men'（Kelly 244）這翻譯只能視為意譯，因為（i）σωτήριος 是主格形容詞（所形容的是**上帝……的恩典**），在基里的譯文卻變成相當於間接受格的 'for the salvation'（所形容的是動詞**已經顯明出來**）；（ii）πᾶσιν ἀνθρώποις 是間接受格，在基里的譯文卻變成相當於所有格的 'of all men'.（**4**）Mott（'Ethics' 33）認為 'the predicate σωτήριος is explained by παιδεύουσα', 意即上帝的恩典是藉著**訓練我們**而帶來徹底的道德改變（παιδεία 在希臘倫理傳統中具有解救的功能〔'delivering role'〕）。筆者倒認為，**帶來拯救**（新普）較自然的解釋是在下文所述**救主**（σωτήρ, 13b 節）**為我們**所作的一切（14 節），12 節所提及的道德改變只是其中一部分。See e.g. Harris, 'Deity' 263.

7 See Quinn 27, 150, 162: 'Revealed was the grace of God for the rescue of all human beings.' Simpson 107 指出，'σωτήριος followed by a dative case . . . is a classical idiom . . . for *bringing deliverance to*'（endorsed by Guthrie I 198; Guthrie II 210〔'the noun *sōtērios*'（古特立 212「這裏的名詞 *sōtērios*」）是 'the adjective *sōtērios*' 之誤〕）。Wieland 201 將這形容詞化為副詞：'Grace appeared "soterially."'

8 Fairnbairn 277. 這動詞（ἐπεφάνη）在三 4 就是單獨使用，並無修飾語（White 194*b*）。Marshall 268 甚至認為，將「向眾人」連於這動詞 'would . . . produce a false statement'.

9 「定語的」= attributive;「謂語的」= predicative. See BDF §269(3): 'An adjective (participle) following a gen. must have the article (ὁ υἱός μου ὁ ἀγαπητός Mt 3: 17), otherwise it is predicate: T 2: 11 ἐπεφάνη ἡ χάρις τοῦ θεοῦ (ἡ add. C[c] al.) σωτήριος πᾶσιν ἀνθρώποις.' Similarly MHT 3.186-87; Mounce 422: 'σωτήριος is a predicate nominative functioning adverbially, describing the effects of the appearing.' See also Towner III 745 n.7: 'the grace of God appeared with saving power' =「神的恩典帶著拯救的能力顯現」（唐 1086 註 7）。TNIV, NIV2011 的翻譯——'For the grace of God has appeared that offers salvation to all people'（endorsed by Towner III 746 n.10〔唐 1087 註 10〕）——則把 σωτήριος πᾶσιν ἀνθρώποις 視為形容詞。但見

帝的恩典是帶來拯救的」這個意思。眾人並不是明確地指全人類（呂譯、現修）[10] 而是籠統地、不加選擇地指所有人（新普）。[11] 本節這句話的要旨在於，上帝的救恩是為所有人的（參：徒十七 30；提前二 4～6）；[12] 這暗示沒有人可以在別處得到救恩（參：徒四 12）。[13]

本註開首（BDF）。

10 另見上面註 6 之 NJB. **(1)** 眾人一詞的原文在保羅書信另外出現十四次，其中多次是在教義性的文理中：（**i**）複數間接受格（如在本節：πᾶσιν ἀνθρώποις）兩次——要讓眾人知道你們謙讓的心（腓四 5）；不信主的猶太人與眾人為敵（帖前二 15〔參《帖前》189、193〕）；（**ii**）複數直接受格（πάντας ἀνθρώπους）六次——死……從罪而來，於是死就臨到所有的人（羅五 12）；因一次的過犯，所有的人都被定罪；照樣，因一次的義行，所有的人也就被稱義而得生命了（羅五 18〔參《羅》2.156-59〕）；上帝願意所有的人都得救（提前二 4，思高）；信徒對眾人總要顯出溫柔（多三 2）；在婚姻一事上，保羅說我願眾人像我一樣（林前七 7）；（**iii**）複數所有格（πάντων ἀνθρώθων）六次——眾人以為美的事要留心去做（羅十二 17〔參《羅》4.176-78〕）；若是可行，總要盡力與眾人和睦（羅十二 18）；我們若靠基督只在今生有指望，就比所有的人更可憐了（林前十五 19）；對保羅而言，哥林多人就是他的推薦信，被眾人所知道（林後三 2）；教會要為所有的人……祈求、禱告、代求、感恩（提前二 1，現修）；永生的上帝……是萬人的救主，更是信他的人的救主（提前四 10，現修）。**(2)** 這詞的單數在保羅書信出現四次：間接受格（παντὶ ἀνθρώπῳ）一次——保羅對每一個受割禮的人（加五 3，呂譯）——即想憑著受割禮討上帝喜歡（新普）的人——指出，他有義務遵行全部的律法；直接受格（πάντα ἄνθρωπον）三次——保羅及其同工用〔思高以〕諸般的智慧，勸戒各人，教導各人，要把各人完完全全地獻上（西一 28），即把各人獻上，做在基督裏長大成熟的人（呂譯）。

11 見上面註 6 之英譯本（除了 NJB）。See Fairnbairn 278: 'without respect of persons . . . indiscriminately'. **(1)** K. H. Schelkle（*EDNT* 3.326*b* [s.v. σωτήρ, 3]）認為，這裏強調所有人（新普），也許是 'a reaction against Gnostic thought that divides people into the chosen and the rejected'. Oden 9 也認為，眾人或人人（提前二 4，四 10）在教牧書信是個重要的字，因為以弗所和克里特的假教師認為，救恩和屬靈的知識是少數精英的專利品。See also Saarinen 182: 'False teachers may have wanted to limit salvation to specified groups'. **(2)** 另有解為「每一種族、每一類別的人」：'salvation for every race and class of men [= people]'（Lock 137），'to all classes of men, even slaves'（143 [endorsed by Knight II 319]; also Calvin 373: 'all classes of men'）。但是唐書禮認為，這種意思 'seems foreign to the text'（Towner III 746 n.11〔唐 1087 註 11〕）。

12 'This speaks of a universal provision, not universalism' (Akin, 'Mystery' 143); 'the universal applicability of the Christian gospel is declared' (Wieland 202). See also Harris, 'Savior' 174: 'God's grace had appeared with a view to achieving the salvation of all people'. J. M. Gundry-Volf（*DPL* 960*a*）正確指出，二 11 及提前二 4，四 10 這些經文可視為表達「神絕對的心意〔God's antecedent or absolute will〕是要所有的人都得救恩」，這有別於上帝的「附帶條件的旨意〔God's consequent or conditioned will〕」——'only those who believe are saved'（《辭典》1373*b*）。

13 Marshall 268.

已經顯明出來（新普同）這翻譯，正確地表達了原文動詞[14] 的過去不定時時態的意思，即顯明的行動已經完成。[15] 同字根的名詞**顯現**稍後在第 13 節出現：**耶穌基督的榮耀顯現**指基督再臨之日，**會帶著榮光顯現**（新普）。這就提示，**上帝救眾人的恩典已經顯明出來**是指這恩典藉著基督的首次降臨（不僅指祂的道成肉身，[16] 也包括祂在地上的生命與受死〔參 14 節〕和復活[17]）**已經顯明出來了**（當代、現修、新譯）。這種理解由提摩太後書一章 9 至 10 節證實了：第 9 節談到上帝**萬古之先在基督耶穌裏賜給我們的恩典**，第 10 節隨即解釋，**這恩典藉著我們的救主基督耶穌的顯現已經表明出來；他把死廢去，藉著福音，將不朽的生命彰顯出來**。由此可見，**上帝救眾人的恩典已經顯明出來**是指這恩典已經在基督的首次來臨顯明出來，就如三章 4 節**我們的救主上帝已經顯出他的慈悲和仁愛**（現修）同樣是指基督的首次來臨。[18] 但是信徒經歷這已顯明的恩典，則是在他們**聽信福**

---

14 ἐπεφάνη（被動語態）。這字在下文再出現一次（三 4），指**我們的救主上帝已經顯出他的慈悲和仁愛**（現修）。這動詞（**ἐπιφαίνω**）在新約僅再出現二次，都是主動語態：一次指（比喻意義的）清晨的日光（指彌賽亞耶穌基督）**要照亮坐在黑暗中死蔭裏的人**（路一 79），另一次指（字面意義的）**太陽和星辰多日不顯露**（徒二十七 20，新和）。這字在 LXX 多次用來指上帝的顯現，例：創三十五 7；申三十三 2；耶三十六〔二十九〕14；結三十九 28；番二 11；次經《馬加比二書》3.30，12.22，14.15。

15 因此，Wieland 200 的解釋不可取。他認為 'the reference is to the making known of God's gracious saving in the proclaiming of the gospel. . . . Χάρις would then stand here for the message of grace.' 這種持續的行動（'missionary proclamation'）與動詞時態的含意不符。

16 Bailey, 'Theology' 344: 'the term was used for the incarnation of Christ'.

17 Kelly 244; Hiebert 439. Cf. Lau 156: 'The term [ἐπεφάνη] denotes the historical fact that the revelation of God's grace was embodied in the whole earthly appearance of Christ, thus embracing his birth, life, death, and resurrection' (cf. 252, 264); Marshall 266: 'χάρις . . . refers to the whole of God's saving act in Christ'; Mounce 422: 'Here it refers to the totality of Christ's life: from the incarnation through the resurrection and redemption'.

18 Knight I 89.（**1**）DC 145*a* 聲稱，χάρις（**恩典**）'in Tit 2:11 means divine power, whereas in 3:7 it is used in a Pauline sense.' 但**上帝……的恩典**（二 11）與**上帝的恩慈和慈愛**（三 4）顯然是幾乎同義的。（**2**）**顯現**在這兩次都 'refer[s] primarily to Christ as the vehicle, and not the content, of the epiphany'（Bassler, 'Epiphanies' 313）；兩次所顯明

音（加三 2）[19] 而歸向基督的時候，亦即是他們經歷**聖靈所施重生和更新的洗**（多三 5，現修）[20] 之時。[21]

的內容都是 'God's fundamental salvific purpose and saving grace'（318）。**（3）**馬歇爾認為，動詞**顯現**所表達的思想不僅是基督的顯現，而是 'the whole of the saving event including the actual salvation of individuals who experience new birth and justification [3:5c, 7a]'（Marshall 294-95）。這「拯救事件」含有三個元素：'the redemptive death of Jesus [2:14], the proclamation of the gospel [1:3], and the personal acceptance of salvation by faith [3:7, 8c]'（Marshall 296）。但是唐書禮指出，這種看法可能 'confuse the past event of Christ's coming with its ongoing effects on people (right into the present and future) through proclamation of that event'（Towner III 417〔唐 594〕, with reference to Towner I 70-71）。**（4）**唐書禮又指出（Towner III 745），**顯明**的詞彙在希臘化時期（尤其是關於羅馬皇帝）的宗教及政治論述中——關於神明、英雄人物，尤其是羅馬皇帝——有重要的位置，又在七十士譯本用來指耶和華的作為。「這些關聯使保羅得以取用並組合〔access and combine〕一些觀念，即先存性、神顯現以行拯救、和君王蒞臨。這一切使得基督事件有了不能見的神大舉進入〔massive incursion〕可見的人類歷史的特性」（唐 1087）。See also Belleville, 'Piety' 228-29. **（5）**留意 Johnson II 31 的觀察：'For fellow workers of Greek education [Titus was of Greek background, Gal. 2:3; Timothy had a Greek father, Acts 16:1], we might well expect . . . a Christology in which the appearance of a savior figured prominently'. 參一 1～2a 註釋註 42 之（3）末尾（上面 57）。

19 原文的介詞片語 ἐξ ἀκοῆς πίστεως 最可能的意思是 'by hearing with faith'（RSV, NAU），即是「由於他們聽見了**耶穌基督釘十字架**（1 節）的宣講並對此宣講起了信心的回應」；詳見《加》628-36 的討論。

20 這翻譯勝於**重生的洗和聖靈的更新**，詳見三 5 註釋第四至九段（下面 386-91）。

21 參三 4 註釋註 7 所屬正文（下面 378-79）。

二 **12a** 訓練我們

12b 除去不敬虔的心和世俗的情慾，[1]

12c 在今世過克己、正直、敬虔的生活，[2]

保羅把上帝的恩典擬人化，將它視為具有教育（訓練）的功

---

1 二 12a～b 呈現由重複 α 這母音而造成的準押韻（assonance）現象：παιδεύουσα ἡμᾶς, ἵνα ἀρνησάμενοι τὴν ἀσέβειαν καὶ τὰς κοσμικὰς ἐπιθυμίας（Genade 58）。簡內德聲稱，這現象強調了恩典所成就之事的重要性；筆者認為這聲稱值得商榷（參註 52 之〔2〕= 下面 299）。

2 （1）DC 142*a* 聲稱，在希臘倫理的四個主要美德（justice [δικαιοσύνη], wisdom / prudence [φρόνησις], fortitude/courage [ἀνδρεία], temperance / moderation / self-control [σωφροσύνη]; cf. Collins 324: 'prudence, justice, temperance, and fortitude'; Sterling, 'Philosophy' 326: prudence, moderation, justice, courage）之中，這裏只少了「勇氣（ἀνδρεία）*」一項（so also Donelson 173 n.152）。See also P. Fiedler, *EDNT* 2.85*a* (s.v. εὐσέβεια, 3): 'the life of the Christian is determined (with understandable sacrifice of ἀνδρείως*) by the cardinal virtues'.（*參二 2 註釋註 42 之〔3〕= 上面 228。Davies II 21 認為，'since that virtue [courage] was associated with valour in war, it was emphasized less during periods of empire.'）但是 Classen（'Titus' 439 n.36, 'Epistle to Titus' 59 n.42）指出，這裏還缺少 φρόνησις（prudence）一項，因而只有該四個主要美德中的兩項（**克己**〔σωφρόνως→σωφροσύνη〕、**正直**〔δικαίως→δικαιοσύνη〕）。**（2）** Quinn 167 認為，'with regard to form alone, the triad in Titus obviously does not correspond to the tetrads of secular Greek authors; furthermore, the fluid order and the terminology within the tetrads never precisely coincide with the order and terms in Titus.' 不過，希臘倫理的主要美德其實有不止一個版本，例如（Malherbe, 'Soteriology' 341, 342, 343）：（**i**）斐羅認為人的靈魂有雙重性格，'the senior character honouring the cardinal virtues of wisdom, temperance, justice, courage, and virtue ([a] φρόνησις, [b] σωφροσύνη, [c] δικαιοσύνη, [d] ἀνδρεία, [e] ἀρετη), and the junior honouring such things as wealth, reputation, office and good birth.'（**ii**）狄奧屈梭多模（Dio Chrysostom）以 'temperance, manliness and justice ([b] σωφροσύνη, [d] ἀνδρεία, [c] δικαιοσύνη)' 為主要的美德。（**iii**）斐羅 'adds [f] εὐσέβεια to the standard Stoic virtues. Lucian, too, adds [f] εὐσέβεια to [b] σωφροσύνη and [c] δικαιοσύνη, to which he then appends other nobles qualities, all of which he describes as adornments with which the soul is adorned'. **（3）**G. Schrenk（*TDNT* 2.188）指出：'In Tt. 2:12 . . . the mode of expression corresponds to Greek ethics, yet this characteristic of the Past. does not imply material agreement with the Greek view of virtue.' 如 Towner I 251 指著教牧書信整體所解釋的，'many of the terms used by the author were current in pagan ethical thought where they served to define respectable conduct. Thus the author's description of the observable dimension of the Christian life reflects an awareness of the outsider's standards and expectations. But by anchoring this side of the new existence firmly in faith and in the Christ-event (esp. Titus 2.11-12), the author distinguishes Christian ethics from that which the pagan ethicists enunciated.'

能。[3] 值得留意的是，上帝救眾人的恩典藉著基督的首次降臨已經顯明出來（11 節），但是這恩典對信徒的訓練是在繼續進行中。[4] 訓練（同現修、新譯）[5] 原文的另一種翻譯是「引導」[6] 或「導致」。[7] 第三種翻譯是教督（呂譯）、教訓（新和）、教導（思高）。[8] 這種翻譯最

---

3 Mott, 'Ethics' 37: 'One who educates is a person; an abstract quality is presented as acting as a person . . . it is a personification.' 莫特辯證，上帝的恩典（二 12）、恩慈和慈愛（三 4）——這些都是「恩人的美德（the virtues of a benefactor）」（43-46）——被擬人化，類似斐羅常把上帝的品性或美德擬人化（36-39）。但是 Marshall 267 的解釋可能更為正確：上帝的恩典被擬人化，乃是由於顯明（ἐπεφάνη：二 11，三 4）的主要元素（'the essential element in the epiphany'）就是耶穌基督「作為上帝給予人類的恩慈禮物（as God's gracious gift to humanity）」向人顯現。

4 Banker 79*a*. 分詞 παιδεύουσα 的現在時態 'indicates an on-going training'（Wieland 204）。（**1**）動詞 **παιδεύω**（**i**）在保羅書信另外出現四次，分別指（被動語態）信徒被（主）管教（林前十一 32），保羅似乎受懲罰／刑罰（林後六 9，同思高／現修），背道者受教訓，不再褻瀆上帝（提前一 20，新普），（主動語態）主的僕人要溫柔地教導／矯正反對的人（提後二 25，新普／呂譯）。（**ii**）在新約另外八次，分別指彼拉多提議以鞭打（現修、新普）的方式責打耶穌（路二十三 16、22），上帝／基督施行管教（來十二 6〔10b 原文並無此字〕／啟三 19），父親管教兒子（來十二 7、10a）；（被動語態）摩西受了訓練（徒七 22，呂譯），受過……教育（二十二 3，思高）。See Thayer 473*a* (s.v.); BDAG 749*a-b* (s.v.);《新希》246*a*-46*b*（s.v.）。（**2**）同字根的名詞 παιδεία 在保羅書信出現兩次（弗六 4：主的教導；提後三 16：教導人學義〔和修〕），新約另四次（來十二 5、7、8、11：管教〔詳參《來》2.356-57〕）。（**3**）同字根的人物名詞 παιδευτής 在新約出現兩次，分別指猶太人自視為無知的人〔即外邦人〕的師傅（羅二 20〔參《羅》1.393〕），以及「我們曾有我們肉身的父親作管教者」（來十二 9，原文直譯）。（**4**）同字根的形容詞 ἀπαίδευτος 在新約僅出現一次，指無知的辯論（提後二 23，現修、新普同）。

5 《輔讀》528（第三解釋）同。See also RSV, NRSV, ESV: 'training us'; Banker 40: 'God graciously trains us'. Quinn 27, 150, 152 / W. Foerster, *TDNT* 7.182 則翻譯為 'It/grace disciplines us'; cf. Mounce 423: 'to teach by discipline'; Zehr 281: 'it means discipline through education'; NEB, REB: 'by it we are disciplined to . . .' 亦參彭編 103*a*：「管教訓誨……希臘文字根與『孩童』有關，在此有管教啟蒙之意。」Towner I 110 正確指出，'the ideas of the chastisement and suffering of God's people are foreign to this context.'

6 *Paraphrase* 293: 'this grace leads us to . . .'. Cf. G. Schneider, *EDNT* 3.4*a* (s.v. παιδεύω, 3): '[used] in the sense of (spiritual) correction and guidance'.

7 BDAG 749*a* (s.v. 2 a): 'lead to'. 幫助（當聖）是不準確的意譯。

8 《輔讀》528（第一解釋）同。參以下英譯：（**i**）'T/teaching us' (KJV / NKJV; Collins 349; Mounce 420); 'It teaches us / it has taught us' (NIV, TNIV, NIV2011 / NJB);（**ii**）'instructing us' (NAU; Fiore II 208, 211); 'we are instructed' (NLT);（**iii**）'It/it educates us' (Johnson II 236 / DC 142*a*); 'grace is now "educating us"' (Genade 58 [quoting Classen, 'Epistle to Titus' 58]; see also Guthrie I 198, Guthrie II 210: 'educating us in

符合文理：本章 1 節提到**那健全的教導**，隨後一段（2～10 節）具體說明了符合**健全的教導**的行為，其中重複使用**教導**和**指教**等詞彙不下四次之多：年長的婦女要**教導人美善的事**（3 節，新普），也要**指教**（＝教導）年輕的婦女（4 節）；提多**在教導上要正直**（7 節）；作奴僕的可以藉著好行為**榮耀我們救主上帝的教導**（10 節）。[9] 這種種的教導是與上帝恩典的教導同一陣線的。[10] 上帝的恩典**教導我們**（思高）——**我們**指基督徒羣體——所用的方法，就是透過上文提到的**那健全的教導**（1 節，參一 9b），[11] 即是那**合乎教義**（＝使徒傳統的教訓）**的可靠之道**（一 9a）。[12] 上帝的恩典所教導的內容分為消極的（12b 節）和積極的（12c～13 節）兩方面。[13]

---

the art of living'; 古特立 212：「教育我們如何生活」). (**1**) Johnson I 128 強調同字根的名詞 παιδεία（參上面註 4 之〔2〕）在希臘文化的意思：'*Paideia* meant an education in culture and in civilized behavior; it meant how to be a human being in the social world. In effect, Paul is saying that God's grace itself *educates* people in humanity'; see also Johnson II 241: 'Paul's point, then, is that in this instance grace itself educates in humanity'; Johnson, 'Titus' 397*b*: 'the grace of God itself has an educative function: it trains people toward the goal of becoming human social creatures.' (**2**) 馬賀比認為，'the notion that God's saving grace educates believers to live moral and healthy lives' 是提多書作者的 'personal contribution'（Malherbe, 'Paraenesis' 317）。(**3**) Wall 352 的翻譯作 'For the grace of God has appeared, educating us about salvation for all people'. 這翻譯不可取，因它不合理地將 'the grace of God . . . bringing salvation to all people'（σωτήριος πᾶσιν ἀνθρώποις）改為 'educating . . . about salvation for all people'.

9 原文所用的是人物名詞 καλοδιδάσκαλος（3 節），動詞 σωφρονίζω（4 節），抽象名詞 διδασκαλία（7b、10c 節）。

10 Van Neste（'Message' 26*b*）說得好：'One cannot claim to be a recipient of saving grace if he is not a pupil of educating grace.'

11 G. Bertram, *TDNT* 5.623: 'the means used in this . . . is undoubtedly the ὑγιαίνουσα διδασκαλία, the Word of God, which does its educative work by admonition, warning, correction and instruction.' (**1**) Bassler（'Christology' 210）認為平行的神學性段落（三 3～7）提示，這種訓練是 'through the action of the Holy Spirit' 而發生的。但她隨即補充說，'The divine training is, however, certainly complemented, if not effected, by the exhortations in this letter, which have the same goal of instilling moral virtue.' (**2**) Goodwin 1757*a* 則認為，這裏所指的是道成肉身的基督以自己正義生活的榜樣來「訓練」=「教導」（'"training" in the sense of education'）信徒。

12 參一 9 註釋第二段（上面 142-44）。

13 這種理解假定，12b 節開首的 ἵνα 引進 12a 節分詞 παιδεύουσα 的內容（i.e., 'the ἵνα clause is a content clause' [Mounce 423]）：'instructing us to / It teaches us to'

消極方面：除去（同新和、新譯）或除掉（當代）原文的另一種翻譯是擯棄（馮譯）、棄絕（呂譯、思高、現修、新普）。[14] 這動詞直譯可作「否認」，[15] 即是「對之說『不』」；[16] 如此，這動詞突出了兩班人之間的完全相對：接受上帝的恩典教導的人，對不敬虔的行為和屬世的私慾（現修）說「不」，但是假教師卻在行為上否認他（一16）。[17] 班約翰指出，除去原文分詞的過去不定時時態表示，除去的行動是先於限定動詞過……生活（12c 節）所表達的行動，這表示除去不敬虔的心和世俗的情慾是過克己、正直、敬虔的生活的先決條件。[18] 不過在實質上，除去和過生活之間的時間上的間隔可以看為短

（NAU / NIV, TNIV, NIV2011），'it has taught us that'（NJB）。（**1**）White 194*b* 則認為，即使這樣將二字連起來（παιδεύουσα ἵνα），ἵνα 所引進的並不是所教導的內容（KJV/NKJV: 'Teaching/teaching us that'），而是教導的目的（RV: 'Instructing us, to the intent that'）。See also G. Bertram, *TDNT* 5.623: 'The goal [of the instruction] is twofold'; Lock 138: 'It was the divine purpose in the Incarnation that man should live a moral and religious life (ἵνα . . . ζήσωμεν)'. Mott（'Ethics' 32）也認為，本節將 παιδεύειν 和克己、正直、敬虔這三項美德連起來，乃是由於源流久遠的希臘倫理傳統，這傳統反映了 παιδεία 與 ἀρετή 的基本關係，如下：'The work of παιδεία is <u>to produce</u> virtue, and virtue requires proper παιδεία.'（**2**）白新港本身的看法是，παιδεύουσα ἡμᾶς 之後應有逗號（如在 Nestle-Aland），而 ἵνα 是連於 11 節開首的動詞 ἐπεφάνη 的，所得出的意思即是 ἐπεφάνη . . . ἵνα . . . ζήσωμεν: 上帝救眾人的恩典已經<u>顯明</u>出來，<u>為了</u>使我們可以<u>過</u>克己、正直、敬虔的<u>生活</u>（White 194*b*）。不過，這種理解使 παιδεύουσα ἡμᾶς（訓練我們）二字沒有任何解釋，難怪不獲中英譯本或釋經者的支持採納。（**3**）Malherbe（'Soteriology' 341）說，'Here [in v.12] we are knee-deep in philosophical formulations.' 詳見 341-43 的解說。馬賀比繼而指出，'[although the] similarities are numerous . . . the differences are vast'（347）；詳見 347-48。亦參本註之（1）末部分（Mott），及註 2（上面 290）。

14 See also RSV, NRSV: 'renounce'; H. Schlier, *TDNT* 1.469: '"to refuse" or "to reject"'; Banker 75, 80*b*: 'stop doing'; Quinn 27, 150, 152, 163: 'disown' =「聲明與之斷絕關係」。

15 KJV, NKJV / NAU: 'denying / deny'.

16 NIV, TNIV, NIV2011: 'say "No" to'.

17 Genade 58.

18 Banker 80*a*; Towner III 748 n.18（唐 1090 註 18）。即是以 ἀρνησάμενοι 為 aorist of antecedent action. See also White 194*b*-95*a*: 'ἀρνησάμενοι . . . ζήσωμεν represent [two] successive stages in the Christian life'; Johnson II 236: 'once having rejected . . . we might live . . .'; Knight II 319: 'we must be denying (or have already denied) "godlessness and worldly desires" as a condition for the positive goal to which we are called'; Spencer 49: 'Negative behavior needs to end before positive behavior begins'; Bockmuehl, 'Meditation' 3*a*-*b*: 'The negation of evil . . . takes precedence in time . . .

得幾乎不存在，因而兩者其實是同時發生的，是一體的兩面。[19] 本註釋所參考的中英譯本，沒有一本將分詞翻譯為「既已除去」；[20] 很少

---

because nobody among us is like a blank sheet of paper when we encounter the Gospel. Some things will have to be erased.'（1）原文動詞 ἀρνέομαι 已在一 16 出現過（參該節註釋註 10〔上面 208〕)。(2) 張 354 註 87 聲稱：「此處是現在分詞，作 substantival use」（註 91 再說「現在分詞」），兩點都不確。其實，ἀρνησάμενοι 是過去不定時時態分詞，是 adverbial use, 形容隨後的限定動詞過……生活（ζήσωμεν）。這分詞可更準確地視為 adverbial participle of attendant circumstance（see Wallace 640-645）。留意本節與沃雷司所引的其中一個例子（644）很相似：

來十二 1　　ὄγκον **ἀποθέμενοι** πάντα . . . τρέχωμεν
　　　　　　就當卸下各樣重擔……　　　　奔
多二 12　　**ἀρνησάμενοι** τὴν ἀσέβειαν . . . ζήσωμεν
　　　　　　除去不敬虔……　　　　　　過……生活

本節符合沃雷司描寫 participle of attendant circumstance 所具有的五點特色（642）的其中三點：（i）'The tense of the participle is usually *aorist*.'（ii）'The tense of the main verb is usually *aorist*.'（iii）'The participle will *precede the main verb* – both in word order and time of event (though usually there is a very close proximity)*.'（*見正文下文。）另外兩點是：（iv）'Attendant circumstance participles occur frequently in narrative literature, infrequently elsewhere.' 本節不屬敘事文體。(v) 'The mood of the main verb is usually *imperative* or *indicative*.' 但 ζήσωμεν 是 subjunctive mood. 不過，'the subjunctive does sometimes occur, especially the hortatory subjunctive'（642 n.70）。無論如何，'the primary criterion for determining whether a particular participle is attendant circumstance is sense, not structure. And the sense fits well here'（644〔'here' 原指來十二 1〕）：由於分詞和動詞分別表達了訓練我們（思高）的內容的正反兩面（見註 13 及所屬正文〔上面 292-93〕)，ζήσωμεν 在語意上可說相當於（'*semantically* equivalent to' [644]）an imperative（即我們要這樣生活）。

19 Quinn 166 就認為，'The moment that marked the abjuration [ἀρνησάμενοι] of "godlessness and worldly lusts" was also the beginning of a life [ζήσωμεν].' 如此，ἀρνησάμενοι 可視為 'ingressive aorist'（ibid.），而 ζήσωμεν 亦可同樣理解為 'ingressive aorist'（Mounce 421, cf. 424; 此詞見 Wallace 558-59）。但見下面註 22 之（3）。(2) Witherington 143 則認為，'[the] aorist participle . . . refer[s] to a decisive turning point in the work of grace in the individual's life.' 周 432 聲稱，分詞除去原文的時態表示「『一次過』的行動。極可能是指領受洗禮時把過去不敬虔的心……以及世俗的情慾……全然拋棄。」黃編 214 也認為分詞除去「意指乃『一次過』的行動」；Kelly 245 也認為分詞指向洗禮。'But there is nothing in the verb itself that necessitates a reference to baptism' (Mounce 424).

20 But see Mounce 420, 422: 'having denied the ungodliness . . .'; 421: 'having made the decision to deny'.

數的英譯本把分詞翻譯為現在時態，[21] 絕大多數的譯本將兩者視為同等，是訓練我們（思高）的內容的正反兩面。[22]

不敬虔（原文並無「心」字）[23] 與敬虔（一 1）相對。[24] 就如該節的敬虔是指敬虔的生活（新普），本節的不敬虔是指不虔敬的生活（思高）或不敬虔的行為（現修）——與隨後的敬虔的生活（12c 節）相對——而不僅是不虔誠／不虔／不敬虔的心（當代／呂譯／同新和、新譯）。不虔敬的生活（思高）就是目中無神……的生活（新普），[25] 完

---

21 See KJV, NKJV, RV: 'denying'. Chapell 339 聲稱，'the nuance is to renounce on an ongoing basis'.

22 See RSV, ESV / NAU: 'training/instructing us to renounce/deny . . . <u>and</u> to live . . .'
NRSV: 'training us to renounce . . . <u>and</u> . . . to live . . . '
BV: 'it has trained us to deny . . . <u>and</u> to live . . .'
NEB, REB: 'we are disciplined to renounce . . . <u>and</u> to live . . .'
NIV, TNIV, NIV2011: 'It teaches us to say "No" . . . <u>and</u> to live . . .'
TEV: 'That grace instructs us to give up . . . <u>and</u> to live . . .'
Phillips: 'it teaches us to have no more to do with . . . **<u>but</u>** to live . . .'
Paraphrase 293: 'this grace leads us to renounce . . . <u>and</u> live . . .'
Stern: 'It teaches us to renounce . . . <u>and</u> to live . . .'

類似的做法是將 12b 節翻譯為新的一句（cf. Marshall 269: '[to be] taken as indirect command'）：NJB: 'it has taught us that we should give up . . . ; we must be self-restrained . . .'; NLT: 'we are instructed to turn from . . . sinful pleasures. We should live . . .'（**1**）唐書禮則認為：'If it were simply a parallel command, i.e., a parallel object of *hina*, we would expect ἀρνήθωμεν. Instead the sentence seems to predicate pursuit of the new life (v. 12c) on renunciation of the old life (v. 12b).'（**2**）Wall 352 的翻譯使正反兩面的關係變成目的與方法：'in order that <u>by</u> rejecting godlessness and worldly desires <u>we may</u> live modest, upright, and godly lives'.（**3**）按正文的理解，分詞 ἀρνησάμενοι 和動詞 ζήσωμεν 均可視為 constative aorist. Wallace 557 這樣描寫這種用法：'It describes the action in summary fashion, without focusing on the beginning or end of the action specifically. . . . It places the stress on the fact of the occurrence, not its nature [whether the action is iterative, durative, or momentary].' Cf. Fairbairn 280: 'the aorist ζήσωμεν sums it up in one ideal whole'.

23 《輔讀》528（第二解釋）同。See also KJV, NKJV, NAU, NIV, TNIV, NIV2011, ESV: 'ungodliness'; NRSV, *Paraphrase* 293: 'impiety'.（**1**）RSV（also Kelly 244, 245）翻譯為 'irreligion'（'irreligious'=「反宗教的；對宗教無興趣的」〔《牛津》513*a* [s.v.]〕）；see also NJB: 'everything contrary to true religion'.（**2**）原文名詞（**ἀσέβεια**）在新約另外出現五次：羅一 18（人的不虔〔參《羅》1.283-84〕），十一 26（雅各家的不虔不敬〔參《羅》1.283-84〕）；提後二 16（人的不敬虔）；猶 15 節（不敬虔的人所行的不敬虔的事）、18 節（不敬虔的私慾）。

24 Collins 351: 'Impiety (*a-sebeian*) is the total opposite of godliness or piety (*eu-sebeia*).'

25 NLT: 'godless living'.

全不以上帝的意見和命令為依歸，自把自為地過活。[26] 這種生活其實是受制於**世俗的情慾**，即是與世界的系統或標準有關的私慾，[27] 它們反映著今世（其心態與思維皆與上帝為敵）的價值觀；[28] 這些**屬世的私慾**（現修）包括**肉體的邪情私慾**（加五 24）、**肉體的私慾／情慾**（弗二 3a／加五 16；約壹二 16；彼前二 11；彼後二 18）、[29] **眼目的情慾**

---

26 Bockmuehl, 'Meditation' 3*b*: 'We must remove our ungodliness – to be understood exactly in the sense of godlessness – that we lead and decide our lives without seeking God's counsel and command, because we seem to know it all best ourselves.' Marshall 270 認為 ἀσέβεια 尤其是指 'idolatry and the associated behaviour'.

27 LN §41.39: κοσμικός = '(derivative of κόσμος[c] "world system," 41.38) pertaining to the system or standards of the world'. κοσμικός 和二 10 的 κοσμέω（**榮耀**）構成 paronomasia, 'the name given to the recurrence of the same word or word stem in close proximity'（BDF §488(1)）。

28 Fee 195: 'desires that reflect the values of the present age with its antigodly mind-set.' κοσμικός（**世俗的**）有別於提前二 9 的 κόσμιος（**端正……的**），後者指 'what society would respect', 前者則指 'what partook too much of the world in its opposition to God'（Dunn 871*b*）。

29 原文分別為：

單數（無冠詞）的 ἐπιθυμία σαρκός（加五 16）=「在墮落狀況中的人的意圖」，包括他的人生目標和生命取向（參《加》1225-27）

單數（有冠詞）的 ἡ σάρξ . . . σὺν τοῖς παθήμασιν καὶ ταῖς ἐπιθυμίαις（加五 24）=「人在其墮落的狀況中的種種情（感）與慾（望）」（參《加》1297-98）

單數（有冠詞）的 ἡ ἐπιθυμία τῆς σαρκός（約壹二 16）（H. Sasse [*TDNT* 3.897] 將多二 12 的**世俗的情慾**等同於約壹二 16 的**肉體的情慾、眼目的情慾和今生的驕傲**。）

複數（有冠詞）的 αἱ ἐπιθυμίαι τῆς σαρκός（弗二 3a；參《弗》278-80）

複數（有冠詞）的 αἱ σαρκικαὶ ἐπιθυμίαι（彼前二 11）

複數（無冠詞）的 ἐπιθυμίαι σαρκός（彼後二 18）

筆者認為，肉體的慾望的幾個主要範圍是（**i**）金錢（參：太六 24 ‖ 路十六 13）、（**ii**）權力（參：傳四 1）、（**iii**）性（參：羅十三 13〔**好色**是「性交」的雅語〕；帖前四 3〔**淫行**指一切在婚姻以外的性行為，因而包括婚前或婚後的不合法性行為〕），和（**iv**）聲譽（參：結十六 15）。參申十七 14～17 有關以色列人立王的指示：以色列的君王**不可為自己加添馬匹**（16 節），**不可為自己多立妃嬪**（17a 節），**也不可為自己多積金銀**（17b 節）。**馬匹**在當時代表軍力（驕傲的象徵），可否借喻為代表今天的權力？擁有許多妃嬪也是地位的象徵，但肯定亦牽涉到性。參《弗》280 註 18。

（約壹二 16）、[30]「肉體的意念」（羅八 6、7），[31] 和肉體和心中的意念（弗二 3b）。[32] 名詞「慾望」的意思（一如其同字根的動詞）[33] 是中性的，即它本身並無肯定是好或是壞的涵義；它事實上所表達的意思是好或是壞，端視文理而定。[34] 這裏明確地以世俗的形容「慾望」，其含意就是，這些私慾（呂譯、現修）是與上帝為敵或在道德意義上是應受指責的。[35] 信徒在歸主之前作各樣私慾……的奴隸（三 3），但如今在上帝之拯救恩典的教導下，應該對從前奴役他們的私慾說「不」。[36]

積極方面：原文以三個副詞描寫信徒在今世應當過怎樣的生活。這三個副詞放在動詞過……生活之前，表示前者居於顯著的位置，即這裏的重點是在信徒應當怎樣生活。[37]（**1**）克己（同呂

---

30 ἡ ἐπιθυμία τῶν ὀφθαλμῶν =「因眼所見而引起的貪慕之心」（《串釋（增簡）》1807*b*）。

31 τὸ φρόνημα τῆς σαρκός =「在墮落狀況中的人的目標、慾望和生命取向」（《羅》2.578）。

32 τὰ θελήματα τῆς σαρκὸς καὶ τῶν διανοιῶν =「肉體（單數）——和我們的心意（複數）——所想做的事（複數）」（參《弗》280-81）。

33 原文二字依次為（名詞）**ἐπιθυμία**,（動詞）ἐπιθυμέω. 前者在保羅書信共出現 19 次（是新約全部的半數），見下註；後者 5 次（新約共 16 次），壞的意思有四次（羅七 7，十三 9；林前十 6；加五 17），好的只有一次（提前三 1）。

34 在保羅書信的 19 次中，壞的意思有 17 次（多二 12 本節，三 3；羅一 24，六 12，七 7、8，十三 14；加五 16、24；弗二 3，四 22；西三 5；帖前四 5；提前六 9；提後二 22，三 6，四 3），好的只有兩次（腓一 23；帖前二 17）。參《腓》153-54；《加》1229 連註 10；《西》533 註 55。

35 BDAG 561*a* (s.v.): '**pert. to interests prevailing on earth**, *worldly*, w. the implication of that which is at enmity w. God or morally reprehensible'. 這字（**κοσμικός**）在希臘文聖經僅再出現一次（來九 1），在該處並無這種含意，而僅指舊約的會幕是屬世界的聖所（新譯），是地上敬拜的地方（新普）；與此同時，屬世界既指屬於這被造的世界，這字便含有貶抑之意，表示舊約的會幕（及其敬拜的規例）是暫時的和不完全的（參《來》2.49）。參《新希》190*b*-91*a*（s.v.）。

36 奧古斯丁稱之為 'a great and general fasting . . . a Lent of abstinence . . . from iniquities and illicit pleasures'（Gorday 299*a*）。Chapell 342 建議，為要逼使我們回答是否實在願意在今世向世界說「不」向上帝說「是」，'we need to consider specific areas of our lives where the world commonly challenges Christian faithfulness. Determining what God requires in a specific area such as <u>the entertainments we enjoy</u> will provide guidance for godliness in other areas of life.' 詳見 342-48。

37 （**1**）σωφρόνως καὶ δικαίως καὶ εὐσεβῶς 是 polysyndetic emphatic clustering 的另一例子（Genade 128, See 59）。參一 16 註釋註 2（上面 207），二 15 註釋註 2 之

譯）、[38] **自守／自制／自律**（新和／現修／當代、新譯）或**有節地**（思高）[39] 的另一些翻譯是**謹慎**（新普）和「明智地」。[40] 這副詞是第 12c 節的第一個字，與第 12b 節的最後一字**私慾**（現修）相對，但與第 12b 節開首的分詞**除去**一致；換句話說，過克己的生活牽涉到除去世俗的私慾。同字根的形容詞已在上文出現三次，分別指作監督的必須**克己**（一8），[41] 老年人和年輕的婦女也要**克己**（二 2、5）。（**2**）**正直**（同現修）[42] 另有翻譯為**誠實**（當代）、[43] **正義／公義**（呂譯／新和、新普）、[44] **公正**（新譯）或**公正地**（思高）；[45] 但**正直**是最好的翻譯。[46] **正**

（1）=（下面 341）。（**2**）Collins 352 認為，這個「三組合（triad）」可能是作者（並非保羅）仿效帖前二 10 的三組合（ὁσίως καὶ δικαίως καὶ ἀμέμπτως）而得的。不過，「三組合（triad）」已在一 6b（見一 6 註釋註 72 所屬正文該段上半〔上面 117-18〕）和二 2（**信心、愛心、耐心**）出現過；其他形式的三組合另見提前一 5（**清潔的心、無愧的良心和無偽的信心**）、13（**褻瀆、迫害、侮慢上帝**）、17（**不朽壞、看不見、獨一的上帝**），三 8（**不一口兩舌，不好酒，不貪不義之財**）；提後一 7（**剛強、仁愛、自制的心**）；提後二 21（**成為聖潔，合乎主用，預備行各樣的善事**）。Cf. Quinn 168.

38 See BDAG 987*a* (s.v. σωφρόνως): ‘**pert. to being prudent**, *soberly, moderately, showing self-control*’; Banker 79*b*, 81*a*, Mounce cvi: ‘in a self-controlled manner’; NRSV, NIV, TNIV, NIV2011, ESV: ‘self-controlled’; Fiore II 208: ‘a life of self-control’.

39 See also NJB: ‘self-restrained’; KJV, NKJV, Fairnbairn 55, 280: ‘soberly’; RSV, *Paraphrase* 293: ‘sober’.

40 《輔讀》528（第一解釋）。See also NAU: ‘sensibly’ (also LN §53.6, §88.94; Genade 61); Quinn 14, 27, 150, 153, 163, 166, 168: ‘in a sensible . . . way’;《新希》323*b*（s.v.）：「在行為上表現得明智而適度。」See also NLT: ‘with wisdom’; Spencer 49: ‘wisely’; D. Zeller, *EDNT* 3.330*b* (s.v. σωφροσύνη, 4): ‘Titus 2:12 mentions a *reasonable* life (adv. σωφρόνως)’; Fatum, ‘Christ’ 183: ‘live . . . a life of reason’. 這副詞（**σωφρόνως**）在希臘文聖經僅再出現一次（次經《所羅門智訓》9.11），指智慧能引導人「行事明智」（思高《德訓篇》）。

41 参該節註釋之（#11）= 第六段（上面 136-37）。

42 See also RSV, NRSV, NIV, TNIV, NIV2011, NJB, ESV: ‘upright’.

43 See also REB: ‘live a life of . . . honesty’; Quinn 14, 27, 150, 153, 163, 166, 168: ‘in a[n] . . . honest . . . way’.

44 See also KJV, NKJV, NAU: ‘righteously’; NLT: ‘with . . . righteousness’; *Paraphrase* 293: ‘live . . . righteous . . . lives’.

45 《輔讀》528（第一解釋）同。

46 See BDAG 250*a* (s.v. δικαίως, 2): ‘**pert. to quality of character, thought, or behavior,** *correctly, justly, uprightly*’;《輔讀》528（第二解釋）：「正直地」。（**1**）古特立認為這副詞的意思是 ‘[to live] in conformity to/with God’s requirements’（Guthrie I 199 / Guthrie II 211〔古特立 213 意譯為「活在遵行神的旨意中」〕）；Banker 81*a* 認為是 ‘[living] in accordance with the laws of God and man.’（**2**）這副詞（**δικαίως**）在新約

直是監督的必備條件（一 8），如今也是所有接受上帝恩典教導的人的生活素質。[47]（**3**）**敬虔**（同呂譯、新和、現修、新譯）或**敬虔地**（思高）[48] 與開首的**除去不敬虔**前後呼應。保羅被委派去使上帝的選民認識真理，這真理（就是福音）能使他們**過敬虔的生活**（一 1，新普）；而福音所宣告的、上帝的拯救恩典同樣教導信徒要**過……敬虔的生活**。上帝的目的和計劃是一致的。[49] **敬虔**有意譯為**敬畏上帝**（當代）[50] 或**委身於上帝**（新普）。[51] 也許這裏的三副詞組合表達了基督徒對自己、對別人和對上帝的理想行為，[52] 但這一點

僅再出現四次，一次指保羅及同工與帖人關係上的**正直**（帖前二 10〔新普〕，參《帖前》163）；兩次為法庭審判意義的**按公義**受刑罰（路二十三 41，呂譯）和**按公義**審判／**照正義**行審判（彼前二 23，呂譯、新和／思高）；餘下一次的意思是**當**／**應當**／**理當**（林前十五 34，思高／呂譯／新譯）。See BDAG 250*a* (s.v.);《新希》85*a*（s.v.）。

47 在一 8，監督的資格包括**克己**、**正直**（這次序與本節的**克己**、**正直**相同），而該節隨後的**聖潔**與本節隨後的**敬虔**在語意上十分相近，因此 Quinn 166 猜測，這裏所引用的「洗禮認信」（〔參二 11～14 註釋引言註 4 之（2）＝上面 282〕）也許就是一 8 那幾項資格的來源。

48 《輔讀》528 同。參《新希》140*a*（s.v. εὐσεβῶς）：「虔誠地……虔敬地」。這副詞在新約僅再出現一次（提後三 12：敬虔度日）。

49 See Genade 60.

50 See also KJV, NKJV, NAU: 'godly' (adverb); Fairnbairn 55, 280: 'godlily' (now obsolete); BDAG 413*a* (s.v. εὐσεβῶς): 'in a godly manner' (also Banker 79*b*, 81*a*; Mounce cvi); Quinn 14, 27, 150, 153, 163, 166, 168: 'in a . . . godly way'; RSV, NRSV, NIV, TNIV, NIV2011, ESV, *Paraphrase* 293: 'godly' (adjective); Fiore II 208, 210: 'lead a life of . . . piety'. Cf. Bassler 200: 'It implies a reverence for God and moral behavior appropriate to that reverence, including respect for the divinely ordained orders of life such as traditional family structure.' NJB 則翻譯為 'religious'.

51 NLT: 'with . . . devotion to God'.

52 W. Foerster, *TDNT* 7.182: 'Here the adverbs refer in true Greek fashion to the relation of man to self, other men, and God.' Similarly, Chapell 340; Fairnbairn 280; Guthrie I 199; Guthrie II 211（古特立 213）; Hendriksen 372; Hiebert 440; Kelly 245; Knight II 320; Lock 137, 144; Marshall 271 ('Whether by chance or intent'); Montague 239; Quinn 167; Scott 168; Smith 318; Zehr 282; Bailey, 'Theology' 352; 周 432；張 355；黃編 214。參較一 8 註釋註 53（上面 139-40）。See also Smedes, 'Priority' 9: 'the triangle of human life is here set forth. "Soberly" refers to yourself as an isolated human being. "Uprightly" refers to your relationships with your neighbors. And "godly," of course, refers to your living relationship to God.'（**1**）原文的三個副詞（σωφρόνως καὶ δικαίως καὶ εὐσεβῶς）呈現由重複 ω 這母音而造成的準押韻（assonance: -νως, -καίως, -βῶς）和三個 ως 的押韻現象（Quinn 168; Genade 59, 128）。（**2**）Quinn 168 更聲稱，目前這三組合形式（三個副詞、兩個 καί 字、準押韻，和押韻）是 'a cipher that stands

是不確定的。[53]

上述的這種生活，是信徒**在今世**（同思高、新和）要過的。[54] 今

for that fullness of the virtuous life which "the grace of God" generates in his family'. 參註 1（上面 290）。

（3） Kidd（'Titus' 186 [cf. 193, 206]）認為，這裏的三重描述與一 12 對克里特人的三重描寫前後呼應，並且呈現交叉配置模式，如下：

甲 常說謊話（一 12）
　乙 是惡獸（一 12）
　　丙 貪吃懶做（一 12）
　　丙' 過……克己的生活（二 12）= 'not as bellies'
　乙' 過……正直……的生活（二 12）= 'not as beasts'
甲' 過……敬虔的生活（二 12）= 'not as liars'

丙' 和丙可算彼此對應（**克己**就不會**貪吃**），二者皆指對己的行為；乙' 和乙也可算彼此對應（待人**正直**就不會像**惡獸**般傷害人），二者皆指對人的行為；但甲' 和甲則並非彼此對應，因**敬虔**是指對上帝的理想行為，**常說謊話**卻是對別人的行為，* 而且**敬虔**生活的內涵遠超過不說謊，就如**正直**遠超過不傷害人，**克己**遠超過不貪吃。因此筆者認為，作者看出來的交叉配置模式其實並不存在。三組合是教牧書信常見的現象（參註 37 之〔2〕＝ 上面 297-98）。Wieland（'Titus' 348-49）也認為，'the point by point correspondence he [Kidd] proposes may be difficult to sustain'.（*作者把 'impiety' 解釋為 'a dissembling approach to deity', 這等於把與**過……敬虔的生活**相對的**常說謊話**作同樣解釋。）**（4）** Kidd（'Titus' 206）又從二 12 的三重描述看出以下的邏輯關係：'a God-taught right relationship to self [σωφρόνως] enables right relationships with others [δικαίως]; these in turn promote a right relationship with God [εὐσεβῶς] among onlookers.' 可是，前兩個副詞都是指信徒本身的生活，因而第三個副詞很不可能是指「旁觀者」與上帝的關係。

53 Towner III 749（唐 1092）就認為，'the grouping here may be determined more by the traditional presentation of the cardinal virtues in lists than by a desire to intentionally touch on these areas.' Cf. Griffin 311: 'It remains uncertain whether these three adverbs . . . are intentionally employed to refer specifically to the Christian's relationship to himself . . . to others . . . and to God'.

54 **在今世**原文為 *ἐν τῷ νῦν αἰῶνι*（新約僅再出現一次：提前六 17）。名詞 **αἰών** 在保羅書信出現 37 次（新約全部 122 次），常出現在以下的詞語中：

（i） εἰς τὸν <u>αἰῶνα</u>：永遠／到永遠（林前八 13／林後九 9）；
εἰς τοὺς <u>αἰῶνας</u>：永遠／直到永遠（羅十六 27；林後十一 31／羅一 25，九 5，十一 36）；
εἰς τοὺς <u>αἰῶνας</u> τῶν <u>αἰώνων</u>：直到永永遠遠（加一 5；腓四 20；提前一 17b；提後四 18）；
εἰς πάσας τὰς γενεὰς τοῦ αἰῶνος τῶν αἰώνων：直到世世代代，永永遠遠（弗三 21）；
（ii） ὁ <u>αἰὼν</u> οὗτος：這個世界／這世界／這世上／今世（羅十二 2／林後四 4／林前一 20／林前二 6a、6b、8，三 18；弗一 21）；
ὁ νῦν <u>αἰών</u>：今世／現今的世界（提前六 17；多二 12／提後四 10）；
ὁ <u>αἰὼν</u> ὁ ἐνεστῶς：現今的世代（加一 4）；

世原文所指的是「現今的時代」（時間觀念）[55] 過於「現今的世界」（空間觀念）。[56] 在提摩太前書六章，今世與將來相對：提摩太要（現修：）吩咐那些今世福足的人（17 節）行善，多做好事，慷慨施捨，隨時濟助（18 節）。這樣，他們就是在為自己積存財寶，為將來建立堅固的根基（19 節）。[57] 在提多書目前的數節，時間的觀念則從上帝的拯救恩典在過去顯明（11a 節）通過信徒在今世過克己、正直、敬虔的生活（12c 節）進到基督的榮

（**iii**）πρὸ τῶν αἰώνων：在萬世以前（林前二 7）；
ἀπὸ τῶν αἰώνων：歷代以來／歷世（弗三 9／西一 26）。

另見： τὰ τέλη τῶν αἰώνων：末世（林前十 11）；
ὁ αἰὼν τοῦ κόσμου τούτου：「這世界的時代」（弗二 2）；
οἱ αἰῶνες οἱ ἐπερχόμενοι：後來的世代（弗二 7）；
πρόθεσις τῶν αἰώνων：永恆的計劃（弗三 11）；
ὁ βασιλεὺς τῶν αἰώνων：永世的君王（提前一 17a）。

55 See NKJV, NRSV, NEB, NAU, ESV / NIV, TNIV, NIV2011, *Paraphrase* 293: 'in the/this present age'; Stern: 'in this age'. H. Sasse（*TDNT* 1.205）認為，「現今的時代」還有現今這罪惡的世代（加一 4：ὁ αἰὼν ὁ ἐνεστὼς πονηρός）這另外的意思。Cf. G. Stählin, *TDNT* 4.1114: 'the present state of the world'.

56 As in KJV, RV, NJB, BV: 'in this present world'; RSV, TEV: 'in this world'; NLT: 'in this evil world'.（**1**）因此，Bockmuehl（'Meditation' 5*a*）的解釋似乎把重點誤放於後者（空間觀念），他說：'The Christian life . . . is to be lived **in the world**, not by withdrawal from the world, not in the desert, nor in the monastery, or in some homestead in the distant outback.'（**2**）不過，分別代表時間觀念的「時代（αἰών）」和代表空間觀念的「世界（κόσμος）」這兩個名詞，在林前一 20 是可以交換來用的：這世代的（τοῦ αἰῶνος τούτου）詭辯者又在哪裏？〔上帝〕豈不是使這世上的（τοῦ κόσμου）智慧變成了愚妄嗎？（思高）。參：林前三 18a、19a：你們中間若有人自以為在今世（ἐν τῷ αἰῶνι τούτῳ）有智慧的……這世界的（τοῦ κόσμου τούτου）智慧在上帝看來是愚拙的。

57 原文的對比在於 ἐν τῷ νῦν αἰῶνι（= 多二 12c 的在今世）和 εἰς τὸ μέλλον.（**1**）新譯將 εἰς τὸ μέλλον 翻譯為在來世；NIV, TNIV, NIV2011 翻譯為 'for the coming age'. 可是，τὸ μέλλον 是中性，不是陽性的 τὸν μέλλοντα；後者可視為 τὸν μέλλοντα [αἰῶνα] = the coming [age] 的省略寫法，但中性的 τὸ μέλλον 不能這樣理解。τὸ μέλλον 的意思是 'that which is coming'; 因此，εἰς τὸ μέλλον 的意思是 'for the future'（RSV, NRSV, REB, NJB, NAU, ESV, NLT）。NIV, TNIV, NIV2011 的翻譯大抵是將 'the future' 理解為指 'the coming age' 的結果。（**2**）參較：可十 30 在今世……在來世（νῦν ἐν τῷ καιρῷ τούτῳ . . . ἐν τῷ αἰῶνι τῷ ἐρχομένῳ）的對比，和弗一 21 今世……來世（ἐν τῷ αἰῶνι τούτῳ . . . ἐν τῷ μέλλοντι [αἰῶνι]）的對比（參《弗》244-45 連註 18、19）。

耀在將來顯現（13b 節）；**在今世**亦使人想起上帝曾**在萬古之先**應許給人永生（一 2b）。如此，上帝藉著祂在基督裏顯明祂的拯救恩典，兌現了祂在萬古之先的、賜永生的應許；這拯救恩典及其教導，就是信徒在等候基督的榮耀顯現的期間應當過**克己、正直、敬虔的生活**的基礎及原因；而基督的榮耀之顯現，是信徒應當如此生活進一步的動機。

二 **13a** 等候福樂的盼望，

13b 並等候至大的上帝和我們的救主耶穌基督的榮耀顯現。[1]

前兩節先後提到過去（11 節：恩典已經顯明）和現在（12 節：過……生活），本節則突顯出未來。等候原文在保羅書信出現的另二次，其意思都只是接待（羅十六 2；腓二 29）；[2] 但是在這裏，它的意思不單是等候（同當代、新和、新譯）或等待（現修），[3] 更是期待（呂譯、思高、新普），即是殷切地等待之意。[4] 好些英譯本將原文分詞（現在時態）的功用視為回答「何時」的問題，所得出的意思就是：**在今世過克己、正直、敬虔的生活**（12c 節）是「我們<u>在期待</u>福樂的盼望<u>的期間</u>」所應作的事。[5] 較自然的看法是，原文分詞引進了**在今世**

---

1 **（1）** Van Neste（'Message' 26*b*）聲稱，在二 11～14，基督的再來被提出來作為罪的解毒素（'th[e] focus on the return of Christ . . . is presented as <u>the</u> antidote for sin'）。筆者認為這聲稱言過其實，因為更明顯的「解毒素」是上帝的恩典之教導（12 節）以及基督捨己之目的（14 節）。而且 13 節並無<u>明確地</u>以基督的再臨作為信徒潔淨自己的動機，像約壹三 2～3 所作的。**（2）** 范尼斯的聲稱是基於他對 13 節開首的分詞 προσδεχόμενοι 的理解，他認為這分詞 'expresses not merely attendant circumstance ("live godly . . . while awaiting") but also <u>the means by which believers can find the strength</u> to oppose sin and pursue godliness'（29*c* n.35），即是分詞回答了 'how (means)' 的問題。但見下面註 6 之（1）及所屬正文。

2 在這個意義上，此二節所用的複合動詞 προσδέχομαι 與簡單的 δέχομαι 意思相同（W. Grundmann, *TDNT* 2.57）。參《腓》322 註 95。

3 **προσδέχομαι** 在新約另外出現十一次，同樣呈現這兩方面的意思：**（甲）**主動的接納（路十五 2）或接受（來十一 35：拒絕被釋放原文作不願／不肯接受釋放〔思高／新譯〕），或被動的忍受（來十 34〔參《來》2.214〕）。**（乙）**等候（主人〔路十二 36〕；神〔的〕國度‖神的國〔新譯：可十五 43‖路二十三 51〕；千夫長的應允〔徒二十三 21，思高〕）或期待（義人和不義的人都要復活〔徒二十四 15，新譯〕；以色列的安慰者／耶路撒冷蒙救贖〔新譯：路二 25／38〕；耶穌基督的憐憫〔猶 21 節，新普〕）。

4 See *Paraphrase* 293: 'as we wait expectantly'; Van Neste, 'Message' 27*a*: 'eagerly anticipating'; NLT: 'we look forward . . . to'. 以下英譯皆不足以表達這種殷切期待之意：'Looking/looking for' (KJV / NKJV, NAU), 'awaiting' (RSV; A. Palzkill, *EDNT* 3.163*a* [s.v. 4]), 'waiting for / waiting . . . for' (ESV/NJB), 以及下註所引英譯（減去 NLT）。

5 NRSV, NIV, TNIV, NIV2011: '<u>while</u> we wait for the blessed hope'; TEV: '<u>as</u> we wait for the blessed Day we hope for'; *Paraphrase* 293: '<u>as</u> we wait expectantly for our joyful hope'; NLT: 'We should live . . . with wisdom, righteousness, and devotion to God,

過……生活的另一特徵，即是除了克己、正直、敬虔外，還要期待着帶福樂的盼望之實現（呂譯）。[6] 與此同時，文理提示，除了上帝的救贖恩典（11 節），「期待福樂的盼望」是信徒要如此生活的另一動機。[7] 期待這動詞表示，它的賓詞（即名詞盼望）所指的不是主觀的盼望的態度，而是客觀的所盼望之事，即是盼望的實現。[8]

在原文，分詞等候只出現一次；這就是說，下半節並無等候一字。（一）按上引的翻譯，並字（同新和；參思高／當代：和／以及）[9] 將所等候的事分為兩部分：一是福樂的盼望，二是榮耀〔的〕顯現。[10]（二）《新耶路撒冷聖經》將所盼望的福樂視為在基督耶穌的榮耀顯現時來臨。[11]《現代中文譯本修訂版》和《新普及譯本》則把耶穌基督的榮

---

while we look forward with hope to that wonderful day . . . .'

6 See Phillips: 'And while we live this life we hope and wait for the glorious dénouement of the great God . . .'; 新普：並懷着盼望，期待那奇妙的日子來臨。**（1）**這種翻譯將分詞的功用視為回答 'how (manner)' 而不是 'how (means)' 的問題；後者見上面註 1 之（2）。**（2）** Jeon I 14-17 將等候福樂的盼望這分詞片語，視為他從一 13*b*～三 3 這一大段看出來的交叉配置模式的中心；按作者的解釋，'The pivot, i.e., the center of the chiasm, should function as the turning point in the literary structure'（10）。可是，等候福樂的盼望只是信徒在今世過……生活的另一特徵，很難看出它具有作者賦予它的核心地位和功用。

7 參二 12 註釋末段末句（上面 301-2）。Banker 75, 81*b*, 82*a* 甚至根據文理而將分詞視為表達原因：'since . . . we . . . are waiting expectantly for that which . . .'，即是將分詞的功用視為回答 'why' 的問題。回答上述的三個問題（when, how, why）都屬於 'adverbial or circumstantial participle' 的功用：'The adverbial or circumstantial participle is grammatically subordinated to its controlling verb (usually the main verb of the clause [here ζήσωμεν]). Like an ordinary adverb, the participle modifies the verb, answering the question, *When?* (temporal), *How?* (means, manner), *Why?* (purpose, cause), etc.'（Wallace 622）。

8 I.e., ἐλπίδα = 'the realization of the hope' (Banker 82*a*), 'the fulfillment of our expectation' (BDAG 877*a* [s.v. προσδέχομαι, 2 b]), 'used here by metonymy for the content of the hope, its fulfilment' (Marshall 273). Cf. REB: 'looking forward to the happy fulfillment of our hope'. 在提前一 1，我們的盼望就是基督耶穌。Cf. E. Hoffmann, *DNTT* 2.241.

9 I.e., καί = 'and' (KJV, NKJV, NRSV, NAU). 按這種理解，Bassler（'Christology' 210）認為有福的盼望是 'a reference back to the hope of eternal life first mentioned in 1.2'.

10 See also Witherington 144: 'the hope of blessedness/blessed hope *and* the manifestation are spoken of.' 但 129 的譯文作 'awaiting the blessed hope, the manifestation of the glory . . .' = 下文的立場（三）。

11 NJB: 'waiting in hope for the blessing which will come with the appearing of the glory

耀之顯現，看為發生在所盼望的福樂來臨之時。[12] 不過，（三）原文的小字可能有解釋的功用，所得出的意思就是：**等候那有福的盼望，就是……救主耶穌基督榮耀的顯現**（新譯）。[13] 這盼望稱為**有福的盼望**[14] 或**所盼望的真福**／**所希望的幸福**（當代／思高），是由於基督的

---

of our great God and Saviour Christ Jesus.' See also Quinn 27, 150: 'as we wait for the blessed hope revealed in the glory of Jesus Christ'; 170: 'Reading hope and revelation (*epiphaneia*) in hendiadys amounts to saying "hope revealed"'; BDF §442(16): 'The co-ordination of two ideas, one of which is dependent on the other (hendiadys), serves in the NT to avoid a series of dependent genitives'（所列出的例子包括多二 13〔但沒有註明該節的哪一部分；不過，由於 §276(3) 已明確地論及第二個 καί 字（見註 33 = 下面 312），因此可以假定，§442(16) 所暗指的是由第一個 καί 字引進來的 13b 節〕）。本註開首所引 NJB 的翻譯跟這種理解相符。

12 現修：等待我們所盼望那蒙恩的日子來臨；那時候，至尊的上帝和我們的救主耶穌基督的榮耀要顯現；新普：懷著盼望，期待那奇妙的日子來臨；到那日，我們偉大的上帝和救主耶穌基督就會帶著榮光顯現。

13 亦見呂譯：期待着帶福樂的盼望之實現，就是我們的至大上帝……的榮耀之顯現。καί 字的這種用法，見 BAGD 393*a* (s.v. I 3), BDAG 495*b* (s.v. 1 c): 'often explicative; i.e., a word or clause is connected by means of καί w. another word or clause, for the purpose of explaining what goes before it *and so, that is, namely*'; BDF §276(3): 'The article is (naturally) omitted with the second of two phrases in apposition connected by καί'.（**1**）持此立場的**英譯本**包括：（**i**）ESV/RSV: 'waiting for / awaiting our blessed hope, the appearing . . .'（以逗號表示，前者就是後者）；（**ii**）NIV, TNIV, NIV2011: 'we wait for the blessed hope – the glorious appearing . . .'（以破折號表示，後者解釋前者）；（**iii**）*Paraphrase* 293: 'And what is our hope? It is the appearance of the glory . . . .'（**2**）採納這種解釋的**釋經者**包括 Banker 82*b*; Collins 312, 349, 352; Fee 195; Griffin 312; Kelly 246; Knight II 321-22; Simpson 108; Towner III 751 n.35（唐 1095 註 35）; Lamp, 'Titus' 99; Smith – Song, 'Implications' 285. 不過，Smith – Song 一方面說（甲）'The καί . . . is epexegetical'（expressing identity），另一方面又（乙）把 τὴν μακαρίαν ἐλπίδα καὶ ἐπιφάνειαν（the blessed hope and appearing）視為重言法（hendiadys; here 'implying complete identity'），在語意上相當於 τὴν μακαρίαν ἐλπίδα τῆς ἐπιφανείας（the blessed hope of the appearing〔τῆς ἐπιφανείας = epexegetical genitive〕）。亦參奧斯邦：《釋經學》166（Osborne, *Hermeneutical Spiral* 106）：「重名法（hendiadys）是用相接的兩三個名詞來表達同一件事，例如……『有福的盼望和榮耀的顯現』」。可是，按哈理斯的解釋，'the καί used in hendiadys points to a relation, not to an identity'（Harris, *Colossians* 300〔詳參一 4b 註釋註 2 之（2）= 上面 80〕）。因此，（甲）比（乙）可取。（**3**）在 σωτῆρος ἡμῶν Ἰησοῦ Χριστοῦ 這片語內，Ἰησοῦ Χριστοῦ is in simple apposition to σωτῆρος ἡμῶν（'our Saviour, Jesus Christ'）而不是 a genitive of apposition（'our Saviour of Jesus Christ', as in 'the city of Hong Kong'）; see Wallace 98-99.

14 **有福的盼望**（τὴν μακαρίαν ἐλπίδα）拾起卷首的**永生的盼望**（一 2a，新譯）一詞。不過，**盼望**在這裏指「所盼望之事（what is hoped for）」（R. Bultmann, *TDNT* 2.530 n.100; 參上面註 8），在一 2 則指主觀的期望（參一 1～2a 註釋註 66 所屬正文〔上

顯現指基督的再來，[15] 而對信徒而言，基督的再來就是帶福樂的盼望[16] 之實現（呂譯），就是他們所盼望那蒙恩的日子〔的〕來臨（現修）。[17]

面 61〕）。

15 （1）顯現原文名詞（ἐπιφάνεια）在新約再出現五次：一次指基督的首次來臨（提後一 10，現修），其餘四次皆指基督的再來（新普：提前六 14；提後四 1、8），其中一次特指祂再來（παρουσίας）時的榮光（ἐπιφάνεια, 帖後二 8，新普），即是祂的再來所顯現的光輝（新譯〔參《帖後》217-18〕）。（2）由於基督的首次來臨也稱為祂的顯現（提後一 10），因此 Quinn 170 有這樣的講法：'there is a single revelation of Christ that began with his birth and continues to the final Day of the Lord, when it will reach its glorious climax.' 不過，就如我們的主耶穌同他的眾聖者來臨時（帖前三 13，思高〔眾聖者可能指天使，參《帖前》271-75〕）在新約聖經一貫被視為與祂的首次降臨分開的來臨（太二十四 3、27、37、39；帖前四 15，五 23；帖後二 1、8；約壹二 28），指祂的再來（林前十五 23〔現修、新普〕；帖前二 19；雅五 7〔現修、新普〕、8〔新譯、現修、新普〕；彼後一 16〔新普〕；彼後三 4〔現修、新普〕）；照樣，基督再來時的顯現（提前六 14；提後四 1、8）亦應與祂的首次顯現（提後一 10）分開。這就是說，'a single revelation of Christ' 這種講法值得商榷。

16 Towner II 246: '*The blessed hope* means "the hope that brings blessing"'; Smith－Song, 'Implications' 285: 'the blessed hope refers to "the hope that brings blessing" (Fee 1988: 195 . . .).' Wall 355 則認為，有福的盼望是指 'a final justification, when the full effect of the Christ event is to be realized in a new creation freed from all sin and death.'

17 如 Kelly 246 所言，'For the writer this expectation is still vivid and real, and this confirms the early date of the letter.' 形容詞 μακάριος（有福的）（甲）在保羅書信另外出現六次：兩次指可稱頌的上帝／權能者（提前一 11／六 15），三次指某兩種人有福了（羅四 7、8／十四 22〔參《羅》4.467-69〕），餘下一次指寡婦若能守節就比再嫁更有福氣（林前七 40〔原文為 μακάριος 的比較級 μακαριώτερος〕）。（乙）在新約另外出現 43 次，最常見的用法出自福音書的耶穌口中，指（1）某一些人或某人（複數）或（2）某一種人或某人（單數）或（3）某一件事是有福的：

（1）（i）複數第三人稱（不是指形容詞本身，而是指所形容的人）——μακάριοι οἱ . . .（太五 3～10〔八次〕，十三 16〔眼睛〕；路六 20、21a、21b，十 23〔眼睛〕，十一 28，十二 37；約二十 29）；μακάριαι αἱ . . .（路二十三 29）；μακάριοί εἰσιν . . .（路十二 38）；

（ii）複數第二人稱——μακάριοί ἐστε ὅταν/ἐὰν . . .（太五 11；路六 22／約十三 17）；

（2）（i）單數第三人稱——μακάριος ὁ . . .（太二十四 46 ‖ 路十二 43）；μακάριός ἐστιν ὃς . . .（太十一 6 ‖ 路七 23）；

（ii）單數第二人稱——μακάριος εἶ . . .（太十六 17）；μακάριος ἔσῃ . . .（路十四 14）；

（3）μακάριός ἐστιν μᾶλλον . . .（徒二十 35〔這一次是在福音書以外〕）。

另見：**（1）（i）**複數第三人稱——μακάριοι οἱ . . .（啟十四 13，十九 9，二十二 14）；

（ii）複數第二人稱——εἰ . . . μακάριοι（彼前三 14，四 14）；

（2）（i）單數第三人稱——μακαρία ἡ . . .（路一 45，十一 27）；μακάριος ὁ . . .（啟十六 15，二十 6，二十二 7）；μακάριος ὅστις . . .（路十四 15）；μακάριος ἀνὴρ ὃς . . .（雅一 12）；οὗτος μακάριος（雅一 25）；

榮耀顯現（同當代、新和）這種翻譯將所有格的原文名詞榮耀視為相當於形容詞；[18] 信徒所等待的是救主耶穌基督榮耀的顯現（新譯）。[19] 但較好的翻譯保持榮耀的名詞

（ii）單數及複數第三人稱——μακάριος ὁ . . . καὶ [μακάριοι] οἱ ἀκούοντες . . .（啟一 3）；

（iii）保羅自稱——ἥγημαι ἐμαυτὸν μακάριον（徒二十六 2）。

18 See also KJV, NKJV, NIV, TNIV, NIV2011: 'glorious appearing'; DM 115: 'τῆς δόξης means *glorious*'. Bowman（'Jesus Christ' 735-41）為 'glorious manifestation' 這個意思力辯。他認為，'In two-thirds of the occurrences of τῆς δόξης in Paul's writings (12 out of 18, counting Titus 2:13), this same usage of τῆς δόξης is at least possible', 'and of these, several are commonly so understood. All other things being equal, the evidence tips the scale in favor of the attributive use and the translation "glorious manifestation"'（736, 738）。他稍後更聲稱（741），'Paul frequently uses τῆς δόξης attributively in his writings (as much as two thirds of all occurrences).' 但見下註，及註 20 之（1）。

19 從文法的角度而言，這種翻譯是可能的：在 τὴν μακαρίαν ἐλπίδα καὶ ἐπιφάνειαν τῆς δόξης 這組合內，ἐλπίδα 和 ἐπιφάνειαν 同屬一個冠詞之下，因此可以這樣辯證：τῆς δόξης 與 μακαρίαν 對應，因而前者具形容詞的意思（即「榮耀的顯現」與有福的盼望對應）（Harris, 'Deity' 272 n.13 = 'Savior' 175 n.9）。雖然如此，（1）哈里斯指出這種翻譯的兩個問題（'Deity' 264 = 'Savior' 175-76）：（i）這種翻譯破壞了 11 節和 13 節之間字詞上的平行：基督的首次降臨是上帝……的恩典之顯明（11 節：ἐπεφάνη . . . ἡ χάρις τοῦ θεοῦ），基督的二次降臨將會是上帝……的榮耀之顯現（13 節：[ἡ] ἐπιφάνεια τῆς δόξης τοῦ μεγάλου θεοῦ）；後者顯然是與前者對應的，因而榮耀像恩典一樣是名詞，不應視為形容詞。（ii）這種翻譯削弱了榮耀一詞的意義。「上帝或基督的顯現是榮耀的或是由榮耀陪同著的」是一回事；但「上帝或基督本身的榮耀要顯明出來」是另一回事。Fee（*Christology* 443）也指出，這翻譯 'puts the present emphasis in the wrong place: on a description of the *nature* of Christ's coming rather than on the fact that God's own glory is what is going to be revealed at the second "manifestation."' 但見下一段之（4）。（2）Marshall 275 指出另一疑點：'The difficulty is whether there is any precedent for the combination of a Hebraic gen. [τῆς δόξης = 'glorious'] with an ordinary gen. [τοῦ μεγάλου θεοῦ].'
（3）關於上一段之（1）（i），Bowman（'Jesus Christ' 739-40）認為，在教牧書信裏，保羅似乎把名詞 ἐπιφάνεια 留作形容耶穌基督本身的顯現（提前六 14；提後一 10，四 1、8）之用，但以動詞 ἐπιφαίνω 指上帝的恩典（多二 11）及恩慈和慈愛（三 4）的顯明；這種區別支持二 13 的名詞是指「我們偉大的上帝和救主耶穌基督」的「榮耀的顯現」（τῆς δόξης = 'glorious'）。可是，名詞 ἐπιφάνεια 在提前、提後的用法不能決定它在多二 13 的用法（如果提多書是寫於提前、提後之先，就更是這樣），而且動詞 ἐπιφαίνω 沒有在提前、提後出現（提前三 16 的顯現和提後一 10 的表明，原文是 φανερόω, 不是 ἐπιφαίνω），這削弱了上述區別的確定性。此外，褒文自己說（743）：'we would normally understand "the manifestation of the glory of God" as a way of referring to God manifesting himself . . . It is in fact quite *unnatural* to understand "the manifestation of the glory of God" to refer to anything other than God manifesting himself in his own glory.' 既然「上帝的榮耀之顯現」相當於「上帝在其榮耀中顯現」，則 ἐπιφάνεια 在本節仍是用於上帝的顯現（如在提前、提後）。因

性質，[20] 意即所顯現的就是我們偉大的上帝和救主耶穌基督（新普）的榮耀。[21]「『祂的榮耀』之顯現」暗示祂如今是在榮耀中：祂已被

此筆者認為，褒文的異議不足以推翻（1）(i）的論證。**(4)** 關於上一段之（1）(ii)，Bowman（'Jesus Christ' 740-41）認為這異議假定了必須證明之點，即保羅是在論及「上帝的榮耀」之顯現。褒文認為有另一點支持 τῆς δόξης 是用作形容詞。二 13 的兩部分呈現平行情況，如下：

τὴν μακάριαν ἐλπίδα καὶ ἐπιφάνειαν <u>τῆς δόξης</u>
τοῦ μεγάλου θεοῦ καὶ σωτῆρος <u>ἡμῶν</u>

兩部分的結構都是：冠詞 + 形容詞 + 名詞 + καί + 無冠詞的名詞 + 所有格。兩個所有格的功用是相同的：就如我們的形容救主，照樣，「榮耀的」形容顯現。不過，這論證的說服力不大，因為 ἡμῶν by its very nature 只可能是個 'adjectival modifier of the previous noun'（741 n.29），但 τῆς δόξης 卻並非如此。

20 **(1)** 所有格的 δόξης（有或沒有冠詞）緊隨另一名詞之後（如在本節），在保羅書信一共二十次：**(i)** 大部分（十四次）是「非形容詞」用法，即 δόξης 保留其本身作為名詞所具有的榮耀之意——盼望上帝的榮耀（羅五 2），即盼望得享神／分享上帝的榮耀（新譯／新普）；「『上帝兒女之榮耀』的自由」（八 21），即與上帝兒女之榮耀連在一起的自由（參《羅》2.671-72）；他榮耀之豐富（九 23，呂譯），即「『上帝的榮耀』之豐富」（參《羅》3.211）；基督榮耀的福音（林後四 4），即這福音是關於基督的榮耀（現修）的；認識上帝的榮耀（四 6，現修、新普）；極重……的榮耀（四 17）；他〔上帝〕恩典的榮耀／他的榮耀得著頌讚（新譯：弗一 6／12、14）；他榮耀之豐富（三 16，呂譯、馮譯），即「『他的榮耀』之豐富」（參《弗》473-74）；榮耀的盼望（西一 27b，新譯），即得榮耀的盼望（同呂譯）；分享……基督的榮耀（帖後二 14，現修、新普）；上帝之榮耀的福音（提前一 11，呂譯），即「『顯明上帝的榮耀』的福音」（see Marshall 382-83）；耶穌基督榮耀的顯現（多二 13 本節，新譯），即耶穌基督的榮耀要顯現（現修）。**(ii)** 另三次亦可能是「非形容詞」用法——榮耀的主（林前二 8〔see Fee, *First Corinthians* 106-7〕）；榮耀的父（弗一 17〔參《弗》218〕）；基督榮耀的身體（腓三 21：'the body of his glory', 與 'the body of our humiliation' [NRSV] 相對〔參《腓》411-12〕）。**(iii)** 餘下三次則較可能是「形容詞」用法*——他榮耀的權能（西一 11），即「他的『榮耀的能力』」（參《西・門》162 註 10）；榮耀的豐盛（一 27，新譯〔參《西・門》306 註 10 之（1）〕）；榮耀的產業（弗一 18，新普頁邊註〔參《弗》229〕）。*哈里斯則認為，這種用法可能有七次：羅八 21；林後四 4；弗一 17，三 16；腓三 21；西一 11；提前一 11（'Deity' 272 n.12 = 'Savior' 175 n.8）。
(2) 名詞 δόξα 在保羅書信另外出現 57 次（即保羅書信合共 77 次〔新約全部 166 次〕），其中多次用來指（i）「上帝的榮耀」（羅一 23，三 23；林前十一 7；）；(ii)「歸榮耀給上帝」（εἰς δόξαν θεοῦ / τοῦ θεοῦ / τὴν δόξαν τοῦ θεοῦ: 林前十 31；腓一 11，二 11／羅十五 7／林後四 15）；(iii)「主的／基督的榮耀」（林後三 18；帖後二 14／林後四 4，八 19、23）。See BDAG 256*b*-58*a* (s.v.);《新希》87*b*-88*a*（s.v.）。

21 彼前四 13（在他〔的〕榮耀顯現的時候：ἐν τῇ ἀποκαλύψει τῆς δόξης αὐτοῦ），五 1（將來所要顯現的榮耀：τῆς μελλούσης ἀποκαλύπτεσθαι δόξης）有力地支持這種理解（Marshall 275）。**(1)** τῆς δόξης = 主詞所有格（Smith－Song, 'Implications' 286

接在榮耀裏（提前三 16；參：約十七 5）；這如今不被世人認識的榮耀，將要在祂再臨之日完全顯明。[22] 如此，至尊的上帝和我們的救主耶穌基督的榮耀要顯現（現修）與上帝救眾人的恩典已經顯明出來（11 節，參三 4～5）構成對比。[23]

下半節的主要釋經問題是：上帝和救主是同一人，抑是兩個不同的人物？[24]原文末尾的耶穌基督二字與之前的「我們偉大的上帝和救主的榮耀」的關係是怎樣的？這些問題同時牽涉到「耶穌基督是否被稱為上帝」的問題。三者彼此交織，互相連鎖，以下一起討論。（一 A）至大的／至尊的上帝和我們的救主耶穌基督（和修／現修）[25] 這種翻譯，似乎將上帝和基督區別（留意我們的位置）。（一 B）有少數譯本明確地將二者區分；[26] 按這種理解，耶穌基督的末日顯現與上帝的榮

---

n.1）。二 11（上帝救眾人的恩典已經顯明出來）和三 4（上帝的恩慈和慈愛顯明）支持這種理解。See also Lamp, 'Titus' 99 n.19: 'a subjective genitive, in which the noun in the genitive case is viewed as performing the action implicit in the noun that it modifies'; RSV, NAU, NJB, ESV / NRSV: 'the appearing/manifestation of the glory'. 參下面註 27 之 Stern。（2）Fee 195-96 則認為它是受詞所有格，表達 'the "what" of the manifestation'.

22 Hiebert 441.（1）ἐπιφάνεια 在此（指基督的再來）相當於 παρουσία（Marshall 294）；參：帖後二 8：主耶穌要以自己來臨的顯現（思高：τῇ ἐπιφανείᾳ τῆς παρουσίας αὐτοῦ），即是以自己再來所顯現的光輝（新譯）消滅那不法的人（參《帖後》217-18）。（2）耶穌在路九 26 提到，人子〔要〕在自己的榮耀裏，和天父與聖天使的榮耀裏來臨。按正文的理解，多二 13 所指的主要是基督自己的榮耀。

23 Fairnbairn 282. 唐書禮認為，「榮耀（名詞）之顯現」這種講法使名詞顯現的用法有別於這詞在教牧書信另四次（及帖後二 8）的用法：在該五次，顯現一貫指一位人物的顯現（提前六 14〔主耶穌基督〕；提後一 10〔救主基督耶穌〕，四 1〔基督耶穌〕、8〔他〕；帖後二 8〔主耶穌〕），這裏則用於 'the rather impersonal sense of an appearance of "glory"'（Towner III 753〔唐 1097〕）。不過，「上帝的『榮耀』之顯現」相當於「上帝在其榮耀中顯現」，因而實質上 ἐπιφάνεια 在本節仍是用於一位人物的顯現（參上面註 19 之〔3〕）。

24 As in, e.g., Fairnbairn 282-85; Davies I 103; Young 52, 53, 57.（1）MHT 1.84 說，'we must, as grammarians, leave the matter open'. 但見下文。（2）周 434 認為，「兩種讀法都可接納」；「兩種讀法」是指在上帝和我們的救主之間「有沒有和這個字。……假如有和字，則把上帝與耶穌基督分開……假如沒有和字，則是把上帝與耶穌基督聯在一起，即稱耶穌基督為上帝」（433）。其實，原文肯定有和（καί）字；問題只是如何解釋這個字。

25 See also KJV: 'the great God and our Saviour Jesus Christ'.

26 Phillips: 'we hope and wait for the glorious dénouement of the great God and of Christ

耀之彰顯同時發生。[27] 支持「二人」立場的理由包括：（**1**）教牧書信有關「顯現」的經文（三 4～6；提前六 13～16；提後一 9～10，四 1〔參四 8〕），都一致地保留了「基督次於上帝」的講法。雖然基督也被稱為**我們的救主**（如在一 4，三 6；提後一 10），像上帝被稱為**我們的救主**（一 3，二 10，三 4；提前一 1，二 3），這卻不等於「上帝」的稱號也被歸於基督；上帝的救贖功能被轉移到基督身上，卻仍然維持清楚的等級從屬。[28]（**2**）不論在教牧書信或其他書信，保羅都沒有明確地將基督描寫為神（羅九 5 可能是例外）；（**3**）雖然他經常地同時提及上帝和基督（例：一 4，三 4～6），卻總是將兩者區別為不同的人物；（**4**）教牧書信強調上帝的獨特性（例：提前六 16），這一點也不利於「一人」的看法。[29] 但是，這些理由並不是決定性的。[30]

Jesus our Saviour'; Fiore II 208 / DC 142*a*: 'the blessed hope and appearance / the appearance of the glory of the great God and of our savior Jesus Christ / Christ Jesus'.

27 Fiore II 211: 'Jesus' end-time appearance thus coincides with the manifestation of the glory of God'; Stern: '. . . which is the appearing of the *Sh'khinah* of our great God and the appearing of our Deliverer, Yeshua the Messiah.' 但是哈里斯指出：（**i**）任何新約作者都不大可能會將非位格的或只是准位格的主體（**榮耀**）和明確地有位格的主體（**救主**）連起來，讓二者在一種雙重的顯現中一起出現（Harris, 'Deity' 263 = 'Savior' 174: 'it would be strange for any NT writer to conjoin an impersonal or quasi-personal subject (δόξα) and a distinctly personal subject (σωτήρ) in a double epiphany'; cf. Marshall 275: 'the parallelism of the personal Saviour and the impersonal glory is strange'; Knight II 325: 'This construction would be strange for a NT writer in that it joins the impersonal (δόξα) and the personal (σωτῆρος ἡμῶν 'Ιησοῦ Χριστοῦ) on the same footing'）。（**ii**）σωτήρ 是無冠詞的，但若這裏談及的是雙重的顯現，則 σωτήρ 理應有冠詞（καὶ τοῦ σωτῆρος ἡμῶν 'Ιησοῦ Χριστοῦ 與 τῆς δόξης τοῦ μεγάλου θεοῦ 彼此平衡），尤其因為在新約裏 σωτὴρ ἡμῶν 一詞總是有冠詞的（一 3、4，二 10，三 4、6；提前二 3；提後一 10），除非它是跟在無冠詞的 θεός 之後（提前一 1；猶 25 節）（Harris, 'Deity' 263, with 272 n.7 = 'Savior' 175）。

28 DC 143*b*. 作者們認為，在這方面，教牧書信與路加的著作相似。

29 （2）-（4）三點見 Kelly 247. 另見 Marshall 277-78 的討論。

30 （**1**）Marshall 282 這樣評估（1）（4）和另一些異議：'These counter-arguments are far from convincing. It can equally be affirmed that the [Pastoral] Epistles demonstrate a strong functional equality, if not identity, between God [the Father] and Christ which makes the transfer of the title fully possible. It is difficult to see why the One in whom God is fully manifest should not thereby be entitled to the title of God.'（第二個方括號是原來的。）（**2**）關於正文第（2）點理由，哈里斯指出：（**i**）新約較少用 θεός 一字來指耶穌，一個原因可能是由於早期教會認識到，如果稱耶穌為 θεός 與稱上帝

（二 A）另一種翻譯則似乎將上帝和耶穌基督二者等同：**我們偉大的上帝和救主耶穌基督**（當代、新普）。[31]（二 B）許多譯本（尤其是英譯本）都明確地將二者等同：**我們的至大上帝、救主基督耶穌**（呂譯）；**我們偉大的神，救主耶穌基督**（新譯）；**我們的至大上帝與救主，即耶穌基督**（馮譯）。[32] 支持「一人」立場的理由包括：（**1**）在原文，**至大的上帝**和**我們的救主耶穌基督**同屬一個冠詞之下，[33] 表示二者是

為 θεός 的頻密度相若，便會有這樣的危險：猶太人會視基督教為 'incurably deuterotheological'（以基督為第二個神），外邦人則很可能會把它看為多神教（'polytheistic'）（Harris, 'Deity' 265-66 = 'Savior' 177〔除了將 'incurably deuterotheological' 修正為 'ditheistic'〕）。（**ii**）與此有關並饒有意義的事實是：在 (ὁ) θεός 肯定或很可能是指耶穌的那些地方，其緊接的文理通常會有另一項陳述明確地區別上帝的兒子和父上帝。例如：在**道就是上帝**（θεὸς ἦν ὁ λόγος）之前有**道與上帝同在**（ὁ λόγος ἦν πρὸς τὸν θεόν）這一句（約一 1）（'Savior' 177）。雖然羅九 5（**基督是上帝，是統管萬有的那一位**〔新普〕）沒有作出這種區別，但 ὁ Χριστός 隨後有 τὸ κατὰ σάρκα 為其修飾語（**基督按血統說，也是從他們來的**〔思高〕），那是不能用於父上帝的（'Deity' 273 n.20 = 'Savior' 177 n.13）。

31 亦參現修頁邊註 *c*：「我們的至尊上帝和救主耶穌基督」。

32 See also RV, NEB, NJB / NKJV, RSV, TEV, ESV, BV: 'our great God and Saviour/Savior Jesus Christ' (Ward 261: 'There can be little doubt that this is the correct translation'); NRSV, NAU, NIV, TNIV, NIV2011, NLT: 'our great God and Saviour/Savior, Jesus Christ'; REB: 'our great God and Saviour Christ Jesus'.（**1**）愛華斯力證，這種將「我們偉大的上帝和救主」與「耶穌基督」等同的傳統翻譯 'is not valid'（Edwards, 'Christology' 141, 147）。他認為同一位作者在多二 11～14 和提前二 1～7 這兩段 '[1] makes the same claims for universal salvation, [2] gives the same exhortation for godly living, [3] draws on the same influence from Isaiah 42:6-7; 49:6-8, [4] uses the same tradition that is similar to Mark 10:45, [and 5] precedes that tradition with the same vocabulary of θεός plus 'Ιησοῦς Χριστός or Χριστὸς 'Ιησοῦς'（147, 詳見 144-147）。愛華斯首先聲明（144），最重要的是第四、五兩點，頭三點是輔助性的；因此，即使（例如）有人不同意第三點（筆者就是不同意；見二 14 註釋註 22 之〔3〕-〔5〕=〔下面 335-36〕），整體的論證也不受影響（144）。第四、五兩點的要旨在於，提前二 5 顯然區別 θεός 和 Χριστὸς 'Ιησοῦς, 因此多二 13 的 θεός 和 'Ιησοῦς Χριστός 也應視為分指上帝和耶穌基督，否則我們便要這樣下結論：同一位作者在多二 11～14 和提前二 1～7 這兩段 'has a fundamentally different Christology [*sic*]'（142, 147〔引句出處〕）。（**2**）但是 Harris（'Response' 149）指出，討論中的兩節有一重要分別：提前二 5 的關注在於上帝是一位（'the oneness of the Godhead': εἷς . . . θεός）、在上帝與人之間**只有一位中保**（εἷς . . . μεσίτης），以及這一位中保的人性（**成為人的**〔ἄνθρωπος〕**耶穌基督**）。多二 13 則並無這些重點；這裏所強調的可能是與耶穌基督的人性相輔相成（'complementary'）的基督的神性（這絕對不是「基本有別的基督論」），以及祂的榮耀之顯現作為基督徒**福樂的盼望**。

33 τοῦ μεγάλου θεοῦ καὶ σωτῆρος, '<u>the</u> great God and Saviour'. See BDF §276(3): 'The article is (naturally) omitted with the second of two phrases in apposition connected by

同一人。[34] 不錯，二者同屬一個冠詞之下，只能提示基督是神，卻不能證明基督是神，因為只要作者認為二者之間有任何關聯，都可以把它們放在一個冠詞之下。[35] 不過，原文結構完全符合「沙普規則」的要求，表示由**和**字連起來的兩個名詞是同一人。[36]（**2**）公元前二世紀

καί: T 2: 13 (τὴν) ἐπιφάνειαν τῆς δόξης τοῦ μεγάλου θεοῦ καὶ σωτῆρος ἡμῶν ’Ι. Χρ.’（**1**）ὁ μέγας θεός（the great God）一詞在新約不再出現，但在 LXX 出現一次（偽經《馬加比三書》7.2）；ὁ μέγιστος [= superlative of μέγας] θεός 一詞（RSV, NRSV 一貫譯為 ‘the supreme God’）則在 LXX 出現七次：所有格五次（次經《馬加比二書》3.36；偽經《馬加比三書》1.16; 3.11; 5.25; 7.22），直接受格（4.16）和間接受格（1.9）各一次。（**2**）陰性的 ἡ μεγάλη θεά 在新約出現一次，指大女神亞底米（徒十九 27）。

34 DC 143*a* 承認：‘The formulation of the expression itself speaks for the former alternative’, 即立場（二）。See also Scott 169: ‘From a strictly linguistic point of view this is the more natural rendering’; 但是他持立場（一）。（**1**）Clark（‘Structure’ 112）認為，本節的上半部分含有重言法（hendiadys）：τὴν μακαρίαν ἐλπίδα καὶ ἐπιφάνειαν τῆς δόξης（那有福的盼望和榮耀的顯現）; see also RSV: ‘awaiting our blessed hope, the appearing of the glory . . .’; NIV / TNIV, NIV2011: ‘we wait for the blessed hope – the glorious appearing of . . . / the appearing of the glory of’（那有福的盼望就是……之榮耀的顯現）。將 θεοῦ καὶ σωτῆρος 視為另一次重言法使二者成為 ‘rhetorically balanced’.（**2**）但是按哈理斯的解釋，‘the καί used in hendiadys points to a relation, not to an identity’, 意即在「重言法」裏，由「和」字連起來的兩個意思不是相同的，而是主從關係，或是先主後從（例如西二 5 的 χαίρων καὶ βλέπων = ‘rejoicing to see’），或是先從後主（同上，翻譯為 ‘viewing with joy’）（Harris, *Colossians* 300）。另一個例子是弗三 12 的坦然無懼……進到（τὴν παρρησίαν καὶ προσαγωγήν）（參《弗》454）。「上帝和救主」（θεοῦ καὶ σωτῆρος）卻不能這樣解釋，因而不是「重言法」。參一 4b 註釋註 2 之（2）= 上面 80。（**3**）Quinn 171 也認為 ‘God and savior’ 是另一次重言法，也許相當於 ‘divine savior or saving God’, 與 ‘blessed hope and revelation’ 平行（參註 11〔上面 305〕）。可是，這片語之前已有形容詞至大的（μεγάλου），因此，將 θεοῦ 或是將 σωτῆρος 化為形容詞是不自然和多餘的做法。

35 So BDF §185. See also MHT 3.181: ‘In Hell., and indeed for practical purposes in class. Greek the repetition of the art. was not strictly necessary to ensure that the items be considered separately.’（但作者似乎傾向接受立場〔二〕，見註 40〔下面 314〕。）Wallace 270 更清晰地表達如下：‘In Greek, when two nouns are connected by καί and the article precedes only the first noun, there is a close connection between the two. That connection always indicates at least some sort of *unity*. At a higher level, it may connote *equality*. At the highest level it may indicate *identity*. When the construction meets three specific demands,* then the two nouns *always* refer to the same person. When the construction does not meet these requirements, the nouns may or may not refer to the same person(s) / object(s).’（*見下註。）

36 （**1**）「沙普規則」即 ‘Granville Sharp’s Rule’: ‘in the TSKS construction,* the second noun refers to the *same* person mentioned with the first noun when: (1) neither is

的一份文獻，將與**我們偉大的上帝和救主**十分相似的「偉大的上帝、恩人和救主」[37] 這稱號，歸於多利買王朝的君主；而公元二世紀的蒲草紙文獻顯示，「我們偉大的上帝和救主」是說希臘語的基督徒的用詞；兩種稱號所指的都只是一人。[38]（**3**）**救主**一詞在本書另外出現五

---

*im*personal; (2) neither is *plural*; (3) neither is a *proper* name.** Therefore, according to Sharp, the rule applied absolutely *only* with personal, singular, and non-proper nouns'（Wallace 271-72 [see also 735]）。See also DM 147; Fee, *Christology* 443-44. *'The TSKS construction' 指「冠詞 + 名詞 + καί + 名詞」這種結構；'noun' 指 'substantival adjective, substantival participle, or noun'（Wallace 271 n.41）。**θεός 並不是專有名詞（276）。σωτήρ 也不是（see Harris, 'Deity' 268）。（**2**）洛窩特認為，14 節開首的關係代名詞是單數的**他**字，這表示其前述詞只是一人；因此，如果**至大的上帝和我們的救主**是兩個人的話，則最接近**他**字的前述詞**救主**一字應有冠詞（Lock 145 (i) (*a*); see also Hiebert 441 (3)）。不過，加一 3～4 提供了類似的情況。比較兩段：

（多）δόξης <u>τοῦ</u> μεγάλου θεου <u>και</u> σωτῆρος ἡμῶν 'Ιησοῦ Χριστοῦ, <u>ὃς ἔδωκεν</u> ἑαυτόν κτλ.
（加）εἰρήνη <u>ἀπὸ</u> θεοῦ πατρὸς ἡμῶν <u>καὶ</u> κυρίου 'Ιησοῦ Χριστοῦ, <u>τοῦ δόντος</u> ἑαυτὸν κτλ.

在後一段，一個<u>介系詞</u>之下有兩個名詞，隨後的單數冠詞和分詞僅指後一個名詞；同理，在前一段，一個<u>冠詞</u>之下有兩個名詞，隨後的單數關係代名詞可以僅指後一個名詞。因此，哈里斯正確認為，洛窩特的論證 'is of dubious validity'（Harris, 'Deity' 270 = 'Savior' 184; see also Marshall 280 n.144）。

37 τοῦ μεγάλου θεοῦ <u>εὐεργέτου</u> καὶ σωτῆρος（多二 13 並無加上底線一字）。Harris（'Deity' 273 n.26）指出，θεός 和 σωτήρ 是同一位神明不同的稱號。因此，中間的 καί 字 'is not epexegetical'；若是，多二 13 的意思便會變成 '. . . the appearing of the glory of the great God, [namely] our Saviour Jesus Christ'.

38 MHT 1.84; see also Simpson 108-9; Marshall 279 n.140; Towner III 756, point (1)（唐 1102）。（**1**）Witherington 104-5 同意寇雷蒙的看法：'By calling Jesus Christ "God our Savior," the Pastor has appropriated a well-known Hellenistic expression (see 3 Macc 6:29)* to explain the significance of Jesus Christ to his readers'（Collins 313）。（*偽經《馬加比三書》6.29：'the Jews, immediately released, praised their holy God and Savior [τὸν ἅγιον σωτῆρα θεὸν αὐτῶν]' [RSV, NRSV].）（**2**）哈里斯指出，（**i**）'in contemporary usage the θεὸς καὶ σωτήρ formula never referred to two persons or deities'（Harris, Deity' 268 = 'Savior' 180）。（**ii**）如果在 τοῦ μεγάλου θεοῦ καὶ σωτῆρος ἡμῶν 之後並無 'Ιησοῦ Χριστοῦ 二字，前者一定會被理解為僅指一人；'yet 'Ιησοῦς Χριστός is simply added in epexegesis'（'Deity' 266 = 'Savior' 179）；這就是說，加上**耶穌基督**只是解釋了誰是「我們至大的上帝和救主」，並不使整個片語變為指兩個人物。（**3**）班約翰指出（Banker 83*b*-84<u>a</u>），以下的事實加強了正文的第（**2**）點：在**救主**一字在本書另外出現的五次（見下註），τοῦ σωτῆρος ἡμῶν（**我們的救主**）一詞是固定的，這詞有三次指**上帝**，有兩次指**基督耶穌**或**耶穌基督**；而**上帝**和**基督耶穌**或**耶穌基督**是彼此排斥的，意思是說，當**我們的救主**是指**上帝**時，前者就

次，全部有冠詞：三次指上帝，兩次指耶穌基督；[39] 如果本節的**上帝**和**救主**是指兩個不同的人物，那麼在**救主**之前使用冠詞，便會使意思十分清晰；[40] 可是**救主**在這裏是無冠詞的，另外五次則有冠詞，這是奇怪的。[41]（**4**）保羅在本書的每一章，都在很短的篇幅之內先後稱上帝和基督為**我們〔的〕救主**（一 3b、4b，二 10b、13c，三 4、6）；**救主**的稱號這樣可交換地用於上帝和基督身上，提示保羅有意在這裏也將**至大的上帝**這稱號歸於**我們的救主**基督。[42]

不是指**基督耶穌**或**耶穌基督**；反之亦然。按這五次所顯示的「公式」，我們預期**我們的救主**這主題第六次（即是在本節）出現時，它應該以 Χριστοῦ Ἰησοῦ / Ἰησοῦ Χριστοῦ <u>τοῦ σωτῆρος ἡμῶν</u>（一 4／三 6：基督耶穌／耶穌基督我們的救主）這形式出現，但它在這裏的形式卻是 σωτῆρος ἡμῶν Ἰησοῦ Χριστοῦ, 即是（i）σωτῆρος（**救主**）一字並無冠詞，（ii）**耶穌基督**被放在**我們的救主**後面。第（**ii**）點很容易解釋，因為**耶穌基督**可以放在**我們的救主**之前（如在三 6），但亦可以放在**我們的救主**之後（本節），就如**上帝**是放在**我們的救主**之後（一 3，二 10，三 4）。至於第（**i**）點，最好的解釋是：如果**救主**一字有冠詞（**上帝**一字已有冠詞），τοῦ μεγάλου θεοῦ καὶ <u>τοῦ</u> σωτῆρος ἡμῶν Ἰησοῦ Χριστοῦ 便是指**我們的救主**<u>有別於</u>**至大的上帝**；但原文只用了一個冠詞，放在**至大的上帝**之前，表示這冠詞是同時指**至大的上帝**和**我們的救主**，二者是同一人。

39 多一 3，二 10，三 4（<u>τοῦ σωτῆρος ἡμῶν</u> θεοῦ）；一 4／三 6（Χριστοῦ Ἰησοῦ / Ἰησοῦ Χριστοῦ <u>τοῦ σωτῆρος ἡμῶν</u>）。全部（包括二 13，見註 33〔上面 312〕）都是所有格。

40 See MHT 3.181: 'the art. could have been repeated to avoid misunderstanding if separate individuals <u>had been</u> intended.' 這表示作者傾向接受立場（二）。Harris（'Deity' 269）較詳細地指出，如果保羅想毫不含糊地談及兩個人物，他有兩種寫法：

τοῦ μεγάλου θεοῦ καὶ Ἰησοῦ Χριστοῦ <u>τοῦ σωτῆρος</u> ἡμῶν
τοῦ μεγάλου θεοῦ ἡμῶν καὶ <u>τοῦ σωτῆρος</u> Ἰησοῦ Χριστοῦ

他實在的寫法卻是：

τοῦ μεγάλου θεου καὶ <u>σωτῆρος</u> ἡμῶν Ἰησοῦ Χριστοῦ

這種寫法會自然地被理解為，耶穌基督是「我們至大的上帝和救主」；如果保羅相信耶穌絕不是神（'was in no sense θεός'），他不大可能會同意這種寫法。

41 Banker 83*b*. Harris（'Deity' 268 = 'Savior' 181）提及並反駁以下這種說法：σωτήρ 之所以是無冠詞，乃由於作者<u>假定</u> ὁ μέγας θεός 和 σωτὴρ ἡμῶν Ἰησοῦς Χριστός 是不同的人物，因而無須區別兩個不同的主詞。這說法不能解釋為何這裏的做法偏離了教牧書信一貫的做法。哈里斯還提及並反駁了對無冠詞的 σωτήρ 的另三種解釋（'Deity' 268-69: (c) (d) (e) = 'Savior' 182: c. d. e.）。

42 Simpson 109.

（**5**）名詞**顯現**在新約出現的另五次，沒有一次指上帝的顯現，卻總是指基督的來臨。[43]（**6**）新約別處完全沒有將父上帝形容為**至大的**，[44] 儘管有兩個同字根的名詞多次用於上帝身上。[45] 不過，**至大的**原文形容詞相對地較常在《七十士譯本》出現，用來指有別於異教神明的耶和華；[46] 而既然猶太人常用這字來描寫耶和華，因此，如果**至大的**在本節是形容**上帝**的，那也不能說是多餘的，尤其因為**至大的上帝**恰當地總結了提摩太前書六章 15、16 節對上帝的描述。[47] 雖然如

---

43 見註 15 之（1）= 上面 306。同字根的動詞 ἐπιφαίνω 在新約出現四次，也沒有一次是指上帝的顯現；見二 11 註釋註 2（上面 285）。（**1**）哈里斯認為，正文的論證忽視了一點：'it is not the Father himself who will be visibly manifested but the *glory* that belongs to the great God'（Harris, 'Deity' 270）。筆者倒認為，既然名詞 ἐπιφάνεια（或動詞 ἐπιφαίνω）從來不是指上帝的顯現，則以此字來表達的「榮耀」之顯現，大抵也就不是「上帝的榮耀」之顯現。Marshall 281 認為，Abbot 所提出的異議（與哈里斯所提出的相同）沒有掌握到正文論證的要旨，即是：'there is no epiphany of God's glory and grace apart from that in Christ. The NT does not know a future hope of the epiphany of God (the Father). God brings about the epiphany of the Son rather than himself appearing <u>along with</u> him.' *Pace* Wall 352 (cf. 354): 'we wait for the blessed hope and the appearing of the glory of the great God <u>along with</u> our Saviour Jesus Christ'. Wall 379 甚至談到 'two epiphanies of the Creator God' 和 'These co-epiphanies of God and Jesus Christ as co-saviors'.（**2**）哈里斯同意，在猶太天啟文學中，耶和華和彌賽亞從不會一起顯現。See Lock 145 (i) (*d*): 'In Jewish Apocalyptic there is sometimes an anticipation of a manifestation of Jehovah, sometimes of that of a Messiah, but not of both'; Harris, 'Deity' 270 = 'Savior' 184: 'in Jewish apocalyptic . . . never are both said to appear together.' 也沒有任何新約作者談到 'a dual epiphany of Father and Son'（ibid.）; see also Hanson III 184-85: 很難相信 'the author expected God the Father as well as Christ to appear at the parousia'.

44 以弗所的亞底米則被稱為**偉大女神**（徒十九 27〔思高〕：ἡ μεγάλη θεά）。

45 μεγαλειότης: **上帝的<u>大能</u>**（路九 43）; μεγαλωσύνη: **高天<u>至大</u>者的右邊**（來一 3），**天上<u>至大</u>者寶座的右邊**（八 1），**一切榮耀、<u>威嚴</u>、能力和權柄全都屬於他**（猶 25 節〔新普*〕）。*筆者省略了此句開首的願字；留意 NLT 的翻譯（'All glory, majesty, power, and authority <u>are</u> his'）。

46 ὁ θεὸς ὁ μέγας（例：申十 17；尼八 6〔直接受格〕；賽二十六 4；耶三十九〔MT 三十二〕18、19；但二 45，四 37，九 4）；亦參尼一 5，九 32；詩八十五（MT 八十六）10：ὁ θεὸς . . . ὁ μέγας.

47 Harris, 'Deity' 269 = 'Savior' 183 (with reference to E. Abbott).（**1**）White 195*b* 則認為，這裏以 μεγάλου 形容上帝並不是多餘的，**至大的上帝與為我們的緣故捨己**（14a 節）的基督平行。（**2**）Scott 170 的解釋是，'the meaning is that the full effulgence of Divine glory [= the great glory of God] will surround Christ at His coming. The idea of greatness belongs to the glory, although it is transferred to God, from whom the glory emanates.' 筆者認為，兩種解釋都欠缺說服力。

此，若**上帝**一字在這裏是指基督而非上帝，則更容易解釋為何形容詞**至大的**和名詞**上帝**在這裏例外地連著出現：如果作者是借用了「上帝和救主」這公式（見上面之〔**2**〕）並把它應用到基督一人的身上，[48] 那

形容詞 **μέγας**（see BDAG 623*b*-24*b* [s.v.];《新希》212*a*-12*b* [s.v.]）**（甲）**在保羅書信另外出現十二次，（**i**）八次為原級，分別指：保羅為同胞的不信**大大**憂愁（羅九 2，新譯）；有寬大的傳道之門為保羅打開了（林前十六 9）；保羅既然把屬靈的種子撒在〔哥林多信徒〕中間，若從〔他們〕收取養生之物，這還算為**大事**嗎（九 11）；倘若〔撒但〕的僕役也冒充正義的僕役，並不算是**大事**（林後十一 15，思高）；基督和教會的關係是**偉大**的奧祕（弗五 32〔思高〕，參《弗》880-88，尤其是 886-88）；敬虔的奧祕是公認為**偉大的**（提前三 16）；敬虔加上知足就是**大**利（六 6）；**大**戶人家有各種器皿（提後二 20）；（**ii**）四次為比較級，分別指：上帝對利百加說，**年長的**〔以掃〕要服事年幼的〔雅各〕（羅九 12，思高）；信徒要追求那**更大的**恩賜（林前十二 31）；如今常存的有信，有望，有愛這三樣，其中**最大的**是愛（十三 13〔比較級用作最高級〕）；說預言比說方言**更偉大**，除非有人……翻譯（十四 5，新普）。**（乙）**這形容詞在新約另外出現 230 次，最常出現在以下的「大聲」片語中（共 39 次）：

（單數間接受格）φωνῇ μεγάλῃ（20 次：太二十七 46 ‖ 可十五 34；太二十七 50；可一 26 ‖ 路四 33；可五 7 ‖ 路八 28；路十九 37，二十三 46；約十一 43；徒七 57、60，八 7；啟五 12，六 10，七 2、10，八 13，十 3，十四 18）／μεγάλῃ φωνῇ（徒十四 10，十六 28）／μεγάλῃ τῇ φωνῇ（徒二十六 24）
（複數間接受格）φωναῖς μεγάλαις（路二十三 23）
（複數主格）φωναὶ μεγάλαι（啟十一 15）
（單數主格）φωνὴ μεγάλη（啟十六 17）
（單數直接受格）φωνὴν μεγάλην（可十五 37；啟一 10，十二 10，十九 1）
（單數所有格）φωνῆς μεγάλης（啟十一 12，二十一 3）／μεγάλης φωνῆς（十六 1）
（單數介詞片語）μετὰ φωνῆς μεγάλης（路十七 15）／ἐν φωνῇ μεγάλῃ（啟五 2，十四 7、9、15，十九 17）。

（丙）（**i**）同字根的抽象名詞 μεγαλωσύνη 在新約僅出現三次，皆指天上的**至大者**（來一 3，八 1）或其**威嚴**（猶 25 節）。（**ii**）另一個同字根的抽象名詞 μεγαλειότης 也是在新約僅出現三次，分別指上帝的**偉大**／**威榮**／**大能**（路九 43：思高／呂譯／和修、現修、新普），基督的**偉大**／**威榮**（彼後一 16：現修／呂譯、思高、和修、新普），以及亞底米女神的**威榮**／**尊榮**／**尊威**／**威望**／**大威望**（徒十九 27：呂譯、新和、新譯／現修／思高／和修／新普）。（**iii**）其同字根的形容詞 μεγαλεῖος 在新約僅出現一次，為「名詞化用語」（《新希》211*b*（s.v. I.2）），指上帝的**大作為**／**偉大作為**／**偉大的作為**（徒二 11：呂譯、新譯、和修／新普／現修）。

48 Harris（'Deity' 275 n.54）又指出，只有按 Hort 的解釋，θεοῦ 和 σωτῆρος 二字才可以同時指上帝（見註 55 第二段〔下面 319〕）。

麼他同時加上至大的（和我們的），為要抗衡異教對這公式的應用，[49] 那是不足為奇的，所表達的意思就是：「我們偉大的神和救主，耶穌基督。」[50]（**7**）彼得後書一章 11 節我們主－救主耶穌基督（的國度）

49 （**1**）哈里斯指出，有兩點支持「保羅從當前的異教神化詞彙（the current terminology of pagan apotheosis）借用了一個公式，把它應用到基督身上」這看法：（**i**）在緊接的文理中，保羅用了數個與君王的顯現有關的半專門詞語：顯明（11 節），顯現（13b 節），恩典（11 節），σωτήριος（11 節：'bringing aid'），ἐλπίς（13a 節：'high expectation'）。（**ii**）保羅曾在以弗所由底米丟發動的騷亂中聽到羣眾的呼喊，說：以弗所人偉大的（μεγάλη）亞底米女神啊！（徒十九 28、34〔新普〕）。他試圖進到羣眾當中，但被信徒和官方攔阻（30～31 節）；他是否想要向他們談論「我們至大的（μεγάλου）上帝和救主－耶穌基督」呢？無論如何，多二 13 背後的一股動力想必是 'the desire to combat the extravagant titular endowment that had been accorded to human rulers such as Antiochus Epiphanes (θεὸς ἐπιφανής), Ptolemy I (σωτὴρ καὶ θεός), or Julius Caesar (θεὸς καὶ σωτήρ), or to claim exclusively for the Christians' Lord the divine honours/honors freely granted to goddesses such as Aphrodite and Artemis or to gods such as Asclepius and Zeus'，意即一方面抗衡被賦予人間統治者的那些過分的稱號，另一方面宣稱，那些被賦予異教神明的尊榮，其實只屬於基督徒的主。因此，如果 θεὸς καὶ σωτήρ 一詞背後有這種爭論性目的，其中的兩個名詞就不應分開來理解，以前者指父上帝，後者則指耶穌基督（Harris, 'Deity' 267 / 'Savior' 179）。Cf. Leaney 123: 'Probably the present passage owes . . . to a deliberate protest against the use of titles such as "saviour" and "god" applied to kings, including the Roman emperor.' Hanson III 187 同樣認為，作者試圖抗衡羅馬的君主崇拜：'the author of Pastorals [*sic*] was consciously attempting to present Christ as the true saviour of the human race over against the false saviour Caesar.' See also Lock 145 (i) (*c*); Witherington, *Christologies* 120: 'The entire verse seems to be an anti-emperor-cult polemic, now predicating of Jesus what elsewhere was predicated of the emperor.'（**2**）Harris（'Deity' 270 = 'Savior' 183）留意到，二 13 的兩部分呈現平行情況，如下：

τὴν μακάριαν ἐλπίδα καὶ ἐπιφάνειαν τῆς δόξης
τοῦ μεγάλου θεοῦ καὶ σωτῆρος ἡμῶν

兩部分的結構都是：冠詞 + 形容詞 + 名詞 + καί + 無冠詞的名詞 + 所有格。哈里斯認為，如果這種平行是刻意安排的，則至大的上帝就是救主，就如福樂的盼望就是那榮耀的顯現。Marshall 280 直言：'This is hardly compelling!' 其實，這種理解並不符合哈里斯所已接受的「上帝和救主」是個公式的看法。參較註 19 之（4）= 上面 308。

50 Harris, 'Deity' 269 = 'Savior' 183. 哈里斯（'Deity' 269-70 = 'Savior' 183）還提出另一點：14 節描述基督的救贖工作，解釋了耶穌基督作為「我們偉大的上帝和救主」（當代、新普）正是在這救贖工作上展示了祂的偉大：祂不但將會在祂再來時以救主的身分使基督徒所盼望〔的〕上帝的榮耀（羅五 2）得以實現，就是將他們這軟弱必朽的身體，變成榮耀的身體，像他的一樣（腓三 21，新普）；祂更是已經藉著自我犧牲救贖了他們並使他們成為聖潔（二 14），證明了祂是偉大的救主，是上帝救眾人的恩典（二 11）獨一的承載者。針對這一點，Marshall 280 說：'More

的原文結構，大致上跟本節至大的上帝和我們的救主耶穌基督（的榮耀）相同，[51] 而該節的我們〔的〕主和救主一般被認為是同一人。[52]（**8**）「一人」的看法與新約另一些經文完全協調：[53] 多馬稱復活的基督為我的主！我的上帝！（約二十 28）；希伯來書作者引用詩篇的話來稱上帝的兒子為上帝（來一 8）。[54]

現在我們要討論「二人」立場的**另一版本**（一 C），就是將耶穌基督視為與榮耀一字同位，所得出的意思就是，「等候那福樂的盼望，就是『我們至大的上帝和救主』的榮耀，耶穌基督」；簡言之，基督就是上帝的榮耀。[55] 費歌頓提出六點理由支持他這個立場：（**1**）如果

---

convincing is Houlden's suggestion (151) that the writer is contrasting "our deity" with the pagan divinities of surrounding peoples.' 這正是哈里斯的第一點（本註所屬正文）。

51 比較：βασιλείαν τοῦ **κυρίου** ἡμῶν καὶ σωτῆρος 'Ιησοῦ Χριστοῦ（彼後一 11）
τῆς δόξης τοῦ μεγάλου **θεοῦ** καὶ σωτῆρος ἡμῶν 'Ιησοῦ Χριστοῦ（多二 13）

亦參彼後一 1：ἐν δικαιοσύνῃ τοῦ **θεοῦ** ἡμῶν καὶ **σωτῆρος** 'Ιησοῦ Χηριστοῦ. 該節同樣稱基督為我們的上帝和救主（see Wallace 276-77）。（**1**）關於後兩節（多二 13；彼後一 1），沃雷司這樣下結論：'a proper understanding of the rule [Granville Sharp's Rule] shows it to have the highest degree of validity within the NT. Consequently, these two passages are as secure as any in the canon when it comes to identifying Christ as θεός'（Wallace 290; see also 735: 'Validity of the Rule Within the New Testament: always valid'）。（**2**）White 196*a* 則認為，即使這樣理解彼後一 11 是正確的，也不等於要同樣解釋多二 13。可是，借助前者來理解後者是合理的做法。

52 以上三點（〔5〕至〔7〕）參 Banker 84*b*.

53 Hiebert 441 (6): 約二十 28；羅九 5（見下一段）；來一 8；彼後一 1（見上註）。

54 參《來》1.83-84。洛窩特辯證，基督捨己的目的是要贖我們脫離一切罪惡（二 14），而這在舊約是耶和華的工作（詩一三〇8：他必救贖以色列脫離一切的罪孽）；因此，提多書本節將我們的救主耶穌基督等同（'identified with'）至大的上帝，這做法是合理的（Lock 145 (i) (*b*); cf. Marshall 281）。但是 Harris（'Deity' 271 = 'Savior' 184）指出，'similarity of function does not prove interchangeability of titles any more than [it proves] identity of person.'

55 Fee 196: 'Ιησοῦ Χριστοῦ is 'in apposition to "the glory of God." What will finally be manifested is God's glory, namely, Jesus Christ'; Dunn, 'Deutero-Pauline letters' 141: 'Christ is now understood as "the glory of our great God and Saviour"'. Similarly, Towner III 61, 64, 65, 743, 744, 752, 753（唐 87、* 91、92、1083、1085、1096、1098）；758: 'the epiphany of our great God and Savior's glory, Jesus Christ' =「我們至大的神和救主的榮耀——耶穌基督——的顯現」〔唐 1106〕。Towner III 753（唐 1097）指出，名詞 ἐπιφάνεια 在新約出現的其餘五次，全部都是指一個人物的顯現（見註 15 之〔1〕= 上面 306）。（*唐 87：「神的恩典最終將在未來基督顯現時顯明出來（=

保羅只將原文最基本的意思表達出來，那就是「等候上帝的榮耀，耶穌基督的顯現」；若是這樣，沒有人會認為「耶穌基督」是和「上帝」同格的。[56] 可是，救主一詞在信上顯然是受到強調的（另見二 10，一 3、4，三 4、6），因此，我們亦可以假設原文「最基本的意思」較可能是「等候我們的救主耶穌基督的榮耀之顯現」；若是這樣，沒有人會認為「耶穌基督」是和「榮耀」同格的。[57] 事實乃是，保羅所寫的原文是比費氏所假設的「最基本的意思」多，因此不應按後者來理解前者。

提多書二章 13 節的『神的榮耀』)。這翻譯未能準確地反映英文原句所表達的意思——「基督」就是「神的榮耀」：'it will be revealed finally and ultimately in the future epiphany of Christ (= “the glory of God” in Titus 2:13).')
費歌頓表示同意 Hort 的解釋：'The position espoused in the present commentary was first suggested by F. J. A. Hort, *The Epistle of St. James* (London: Macmillan, 1909), pp. 47, 103-4'（Fee 199）。**(1)** *Idiom* 109 稱 Hort 的解釋為 'highly improbable'（endorsed by Marshall 279）。但是 Edwards（'Christology' 143 with n.7, 147 n.17）贊同 Hort 的立場。**(2)** Harris（'Deity' 266 = 'Savior' 178）認為 Hort 的解釋有三個問題；以下三點異議重複於哈里斯對 Edwards 一文的回應（Harris, 'Response' 150）。(**i**)按此解釋，'Ιησοῦ Χριστοῦ 是解釋('in epexegetic apposition [to]')τῆς δόξης 的(上帝的榮耀就是耶穌基督)；若是這樣，在耶穌基督之前加上「就是(ἥτις ἐστίν)」二字（例：太二十七 62）便可除去在 δόξης 和 'Ιησοῦ Χηριστοῦ 之間的那些所有格字詞（τῆς δόξης τοῦ μεγάλου θεοῦ καὶ σωτῆρος ἡμῶν 'Ιησοῦ Χριστοῦ）所引起的模棱兩可（但作者沒有這樣做）。雖然 Edwards（'Christology' 143 n.7）認為 'the apposition . . . is between 'Ιησοῦς Χριστός and the whole phrase: “the glory of our great God and saviour”', 即耶穌基督不是只解釋距離甚遠的榮耀一字，而是解釋「我們至大的上帝和救主的榮耀」這整個詞語（thus also Towner III 754, 755〔唐 1099-100、1101〕; Dunn, 'Anti-Semitism' 164）；但是哈里斯直指，'[this is] a usage that would be difficult to justify'（Harris, 'Response' 150）。(**ii**) 尾隨耶穌基督之後的關係子句（14 節：他為我們的緣故捨己……）將耶穌基督的工作描寫為救贖的工作，因此，將救主（至大的上帝和我們的救主視為一個單元）和耶穌基督分開，是不自然的做法。(**iii**) 教牧書信數次稱耶穌為救主（一 4，三 6；提後一 10），但新約作者從沒有明確地稱耶穌為「上帝的榮耀（δόξα θεοῦ）」。不過，唐書禮指出，林後四 4 稱基督為上帝的像，四 6 更以耶穌基督的臉為上帝的榮耀存放及彰顯之處。這些思想(尤其是後者)很接近 'a precise identification of Jesus Christ *as* “the glory of God”'（Towner III 753〔唐 1098〕)。

56 Fee, *Christology* 444: 'had the present clause been given in its barest essentials, “awaiting the manifestation of the glory of God, Jesus Christ,” no one would have imagined that “Jesus Christ” stood in apposition to God.'

57 Bowman, 'Jesus Christ' 742: 'we are awaiting “the manifestation of the glory of our Savior, Jesus Christ”'. 參：提後一 10：藉著我們的救主基督耶穌的顯現。

（**2**）歌羅西書二章 2 節用了與本節相同的結構：在**好深知上帝的奧祕，就是基督**這話裏面，**基督**不是與**上帝**同位，而是與**奧祕**同位。[58] 這論點由唐書禮解釋得更為清晰：就如在歌羅西書二章 2c 節**基督**是與**上帝的**奧祕同位，照樣在提多書二章 13b 節，**耶穌基督**是與「我們偉大的上帝和救主的榮耀」同位；只不過在前一節，與**基督**同位的是較簡單的**上帝的**奧祕，在後一節，與**耶穌基督**同位的是較長的「我們偉大的上帝和救主的榮耀」；但後者的基本意思其實是「（我們偉大的）上帝（和救主）的榮耀」，如此，「上帝的榮耀，就是耶穌基督」和**上帝的奧祕，就是基督**兩者的結構是完全相同的。而既然**基督**可以與**上帝的**奧祕同位（西二 2c），**耶穌基督**也就可以與「我們偉大的上帝和救主的榮耀」同位。[59] 可是，歌羅西書該節的**基督**是與**上帝的奧祕**同位，這一點是幾乎可以肯定的，[60] 但是提多書本節的**耶穌基督**是與「我們偉大的上帝和救主的榮耀」同位，抑或僅與「我們偉大的上帝和救主」同位，卻仍是爭議所在。換句話說，歌羅西書該節使唐書禮和費歌頓的解釋成為可能，但並不使它成為惟一的可能。不但如此，歌羅西書該節和提多書本節之間有一重要分別：「認識上帝的奧祕」通常不會被理解為只是「認識上帝」的另一種表達方式，因為*「『奧祕』並不指向上帝本體的任何一方面」；但是「上帝的榮耀之顯現」通常會被理解為上帝顯現祂自己，因為**「『榮耀』常指上帝本體的一方面」。事實上，「上帝的榮耀之顯現」惟一自然的理解

---

58 Fee, *Christology* 444.

59 Towner III 754（唐 1099-100）。唐書禮認為，西二 2 提供了 ‘a parallel example of apposition created in this manner’:

西二 2c：**好深知上帝的奧祕，就是基督。**
εἰς ἐπίγνωσιν τοῦ μυστηρίου τοῦ θεοῦ, Χριστοῦ
多二 13b：ἐπιφάνειαν τῆς δόξης τοῦ μεγάλου θεοῦ καὶ σωτῆρος ἡμῶν Ἰησοῦ Χριστοῦ
the epiphany of the glory of our great God and Saviour, Jesus Christ

60 參《西・門》328 註 33。See also Bowman, ‘Jesus Christ’ 744 n.36.

就是指上帝在其榮耀中顯現祂自己；但是，「認識上帝的奧祕」自然的理解就是，這「奧祕」是有別於上帝的。[61] 因此，不論在概念上或從造句法的角度來看，費歌頓和唐書禮的論據，其實都是有困難的。[62]

（3）費歌頓認為，歷代釋經者將**耶穌基督**視為與**我們的救主**或與「我們偉大的上帝和救主」同位，而不是與（上帝的）**榮耀**同位，惟一的理由就是**耶穌基督**和**榮耀**之間的距離：位於末尾的**耶穌基督**，和開首的**榮耀**，被中間的「我們偉大的上帝和救主」隔開。費氏承認這「距離因素」對他的解釋顯然是個困難，但他強調這是惟一的困難，而且這困難不像「保羅或冒名者稱基督為『我們至大的上帝和救主』」（這與保羅或教牧書信的用法都不相符）這極大的困難那麼大！[63] 褒文對此提出反駁：**（i）**一直以來，幾乎所有的釋經者都認為**耶穌基督**是與**我們的救主**或與「我們偉大的上帝和救主」同位的，直到最近一百年才有數個學者倡議將**耶穌基督**視為與**榮耀**同位。[64] 費氏所承認的「困難」對他的解釋委實是不利的。**（ii）**從語意的角度而言，「上帝的榮耀之顯現」這種講法自然地使人預期，所顯現的就是上帝本身（見上段）；如果說所顯現的並不是上帝本身，這是古怪或出乎意料的。[65]**（iii）**一個讀者要為一個個人名字找出它的「同位」者時，如果其他情況都相同，「他（或她）的傾向是以一個公認的個人名稱為答案的」；這就是說，他較可能以「我們至大的上帝和救主」而不是以**榮耀**作為**耶穌基督**與之同位的那個名詞。由此可見，「距離因素」並不是費氏立場的

61 Bowman, 'Jesus Christ' 743. 二引句英文原作 *'"mystery" rarely (if ever) refers to any aspect of God's own being'; ** '"glory" often refers to an aspect of God's own being.'

62 Bowman, art. cit. 751, point (6): 'God's manifesting "glory" is naturally understood as an aspect of God himself (unlike God's "mystery" in Col 2:2), so that construing "the glory" as a designation for Jesus Christ as someone distinguished from God in this context is conceptually as well as syntactically awkward.'

63 Fee, *Christology* 444 with n.87.

64 Harris（*Jesus* 178 n.14）列出六位釋經者，包括 Hort, Fee 196, 199（見上面註 55）和 Dunn, *Romans* 529（參較註 85 之〔1〕〔ii〕= 下面 326）。

65 以上兩點見 Bowman, 'Jesus Christ' 743-44.

惟一困難；本段上述的三點一起指向與耶穌基督同位的是「我們至大的上帝和救主」。[66]

(4) 費歌頓聲稱，以耶穌基督為上帝的榮耀是十分「保羅式的概念」。在哥林多後書三章 7 節至四章 6 節，「榮耀」一字出現不下十三次；雖然保羅沒有明確地稱基督為「上帝的榮耀」，但是他表明基督確是上帝的榮耀之顯現，因基督是上帝真正的像／形像（四 4／三 18）。[67] 可是，這種講法偏離了費氏原先的釋經立場，那就是：在提多書二章 13 節，與耶穌基督同位的是榮耀，不是顯現。[68] 費氏的意譯不止一次表明，他把顯現視為與耶穌基督同位。[69] 但是從文法的角度而言，這立場是不能成立的（顯現原文為直接受格，耶穌基督則為所有格）；而且後者與前者相隔八個字（包括三個所有格的名詞），使這立場變得更為不大可能。[70]

---

66 同上 744. 首引句英文原作 'the reader will tend to "land" on a recognized personal designation.'（Cf. 751, point (5): 'The verbal distance between δόξης and Ἰησοῦ Χριστοῦ, along with the preference for a personal designation (like θεοῦ καὶ σωτῆρος) to serve in apposition to a name, makes Fee's view that Ἰησοῦ Χριστοῦ is in apposition to δόξης syntactically awkward.'）西二 2 是個例外：與基督同位的不是上帝而是奧祕，因為（744 n.36）(**i**) 保羅表達他的關注是要讀者認識上帝的奧祕，這使我們預期保羅會告訴我們這奧祕是甚麼，而隨後的基督；在他裏面蘊藏著一切智慧和知識（二 2b～3）滿足了這預期；(**ii**) 保羅在上文剛明確地將這奧祕等同為基督在你們心裏（一 27）。文理提供的這兩點線索，凌駕於正文的 (iii) 那個原則；但多二 13 的文理並無此等線索。

67 Fee, *Christology* 445; 'he makes it clear that Christ is indeed *the manifestation of God's glory*'. 像／形像在原文皆為 εἰκών. 不過，Bowman（'Jesus Christ' 745）指出，四 4 說不信的人看不見福音的光；這福音是關於基督的榮耀，而基督是上帝的真像（現修）；因此，基督是（或彰顯）上帝的榮耀這觀念不是得自該節，而是得自四 6，這一節提到上帝是用光照亮我們內心的上帝；他使我們認識上帝的榮耀，照耀在耶穌基督臉上（現修）。

68 見註 55（上面 318～319）。

69 Bowman, 'Jesus Christ' 745. See Fee, *Christology* 445: 'Christ is the coming manifestation of God's glory'; 444 n.87: 'Christ is no more "the Glory of God" than he is "the Grace of God," as though titles were in view in either case. The passage has to do with the *manifestation* of God's glory.'

70 Bowman, 'Jesus Christ' 745（cf. 751, point (4): 'It is practically impossible to construe ἐπιφάνεια[ν] as in apposition to Ἰησοῦ Χριστοῦ (which, though technically not Fee's view, is implied by some of his statements about the text'）。費氏又認為很難解釋，為

(5) 費歌頓認為，就保羅的用法而論，稱基督為「上帝」是「反常的現象」。費氏提出兩點理由支持他的看法。**第一**，在哥林多前書八章 6 節，保羅明確地稱父上帝為那一位上帝，又稱子基督為那一位主；保羅一貫地這樣區別父上帝（祂是上帝）和基督（祂是主）。[71] 但是褒文指出，雖然這區別大致上行得通，卻很可能不是絕對的。在哥林多後書六章 17 至 18 節，保羅在兩次使用舊約引句（賽五十二 11；撒下七 14）之後，分別加上主說和全能的主說這些短句，來表示那些引句是上帝所說的話；這一點是費氏自己承認的。[72] 保羅在這兩節原本可以同樣輕易地用「上帝說」和「全能的上帝說」（就如他在第 16 節以就如上帝曾說來引入另一舊約引句），可見他在這裏是刻意地選擇用主這稱號來指上帝。既然保羅可以稱父上帝為主（儘管這並不常見），也許我們就不應太輕易地假定，他不可能稱子基督為「上帝」。[73] 費歌頓自己觀察到，在保羅信集中，提多書是惟一的書信，在其中「主」這稱號完全沒有出現。[74] 這顯然偏離了保羅稱基督為「主」的常規；因此，如果他同時稱耶穌基督為「上帝」，我們也就不應太過驚訝。事實上，保羅在提多書以「上帝」和「救主」這兩個稱號來稱呼耶穌，這在其他的保羅書信是罕見的（前者只見於羅九 5；後者只見於腓三 20 及提後一 10）。[75] 費氏的**第二**點理由是：如果保羅不但稱基督為「上帝」，更稱祂為「偉大的」上帝，這就構成雙重的困難。他聲稱這形容詞所屬的詞組在新約只是用來指上帝的（在舊約則常用

何保羅（或冒名作者）要在這裏提到基督的再來是基督的榮耀的彰顯（Fee, *Christology* 445）。褒文（art. cit. 746）則認為，在目前的文理中提到基督的榮耀並無不當。

71 Fee, *Christology* 445.「反常的現象」英文原作 'anomaly'.

72 See Fee, op. cit. 266, 636-37.

73 Bowman, 'Jesus Christ' 746-47. 哈里斯早就指出，'there is an ever-present danger in literary research in making a writer's "habitual usage" so normative that he is disallowed the privilege of creating the exception that proves the rule"（Harris, 'Deity' 265 = 'Savior' 176-77）。

74 Fee, *Christology* 437.

75 Bowman, 'Jesus Christ' 747.

來指上帝)。[76] 但是褒文指出，這聲稱並不正確，因為這詞組出現時，絕大多數不是指上帝（也不是指基督）。[77] 當這組字用來指神性人物時，所指的也不是限於父上帝。[78]

(6) 最後，費歌頓認為二章 10 節和三章 4 節（兩節都提到我們救主上帝）像一對書立將二章 13 節夾住，而且基督的兩次顯現所顯明的是上帝……的恩典（二 11）和上帝……的榮耀（二 13），因此文理提示，保羅在本節只是再次提出第 10 節所提到的我們救主上帝，為要強調基督再來所顯明的是誰的榮耀。[79] 這就是說，費氏要我們按以下的模式來理解本節：

我們救主上帝	我們偉大的上帝和救主	我們救主上帝
（二 10）	（二 13）	（三 4）

如此，本節的救主就是指父上帝而不是指基督。可是，褒文指出這模式是虛假的，因它不是基於全部事實。事實乃是，救主在本書共出現六次，每章兩次，而且總是在稱上帝為我們救主上帝（一 3，二 10，三 4）之後，稍後就提到我們的救主基督耶穌／我們的救主耶穌基

76 Fee, *Christology* 445 with n.90. 註 90：'Against this is the use of this word group in the NT to refer exclusively to God ("greatness/majesty" [see Luke 9:43; Heb 1:3; 8:1; Jude 25]), and especially its multiplied occurrences in the OT to refer to God.'（方括號是原來的。）

77 形容詞 μέγας 參註 47 第二、三兩段，同字根的另三字見該註第四段（上面 316）。

78 Bowman, 'Jesus Christ' 748.（「神性人物」英文原作 'divine persons'.）見路一 32（他〔耶穌〕將要為大〔οὗτος ἔσται μέγας〕）；我們有一位偉大〔μέγαν〕……的大祭司，就是耶穌（來四 14；十 21：偉大〔μέγαν〕祭司）；羣羊的大〔μέγαν〕牧人——我們主耶穌（來十三 20）；腓一 20（讓基督……照常顯大〔μεγαλυνθήσεται〕）；彼後一 16（主耶穌基督……的威榮〔μεγαλειότητος〕）。褒文繼而認為（748-49），費氏認為是不利於「耶穌基督在本節被稱為上帝」這立場的一個因素（偉大的形容上帝在新約僅此一次），其實是對它有利的。此點參註 44-50 所屬正文之 **(6)** = 上面 315-17。

79 Fee, *Christology* 446.

督／耶穌基督我們的救主（一 4／二 13／三 6）。在這三段（亦只有這三段）裏，保羅都用了名詞盼望（一 2，二 13，三 7）和動詞顯明（一 3，二 11，三 4），[80] 這使以下的模式更為鞏固：

我們的救主上帝（一 3）	我們救主上帝（二 10）	我們救主上帝（三 4）
我們的救主基督耶穌（一 4）	我們的救主耶穌基督（二 13）	耶穌基督我們的救主（三 6）

根據這個模式來看，將本節夾在中央的就不是二章 10 節和三章 4 節，而是一章 4 節和三章 6 節，其含意就是，本節的救主是指耶穌基督。[81] 另一些細節加強這個結論：（i）我們（的）救主上帝（上述三次）正是原文的字序，即是上帝一字緊隨我們（的）救主之後，上帝與我們（的）救主同位，在本節，耶穌基督也是緊隨我們的救主之後，這些句法上的相似提示，耶穌基督是與「我們至大的上帝和救主」同位的。（ii）在三章 4 至 5 節，保羅說：

到了我們救主上帝的恩慈和慈愛顯明的時候，他救了我們，

然後在第 6 節提到我們的救主耶穌基督；照樣，在二章 10 至 11 節，保羅說：

我們救主上帝……上帝救眾人的恩典已經顯明出來，

然後在第 13 節提到我們的救主耶穌基督，只不過這一次，保羅用了一個擴充的稱號「我們至大的上帝和救主耶穌基督」。[82]

費歌頓所提出的六點理由，都逐一被駁倒了。因此，他認為保羅要表達的意思是「『我們至大的上帝和救主』的榮耀，〔就是〕耶穌基

80 在前一節，原文動詞是 ἐφανέρωσεν (from φανερόω)，在後二節是 ἐπεφάνη (from ἐπιφαίνω).

81 Bowman, 'Jesus Christ' 749-50. See also 752, point (9).

82 Bowman, art. cit. 750.

督」，這看法不可取。[83]

總結以上很長的討論，筆者同意第（二）種理解才是正確的，即「這裏明確地把"神"一詞應用在耶穌基督身上」。雖然羅馬書九章 5 節早已稱基督為**在萬有之上，永遠受／可稱頌的神／上帝**（新譯／新和，和修頁邊註），[84] 但提多書這句話是初期信徒對於「在上帝複合的身分中，耶穌基督是與父並排的」這種漸次強烈之認識的高潮。[85] 退

83 Bowman（art. cit. 751）指出，費氏反對「提二 13 稱耶穌基督為上帝」這解釋的主要理由，其實就是他假定了保羅絕不會稱基督為上帝（參註 71 所屬正文：這會是「反常的現象」〔上面 323〕）。褒文提出以下的假設性句子：如果本節這樣說——我們等候

[τὴν] ἐπιφάνειαν τῆς δόξης τοῦ μεγάλου **κυρίου** καὶ σωτῆρος ἡμῶν Ἰησοῦ Χριστοῦ
我們 至大的 **主** 和救主耶穌基督的榮耀之顯現，

沒有人會認為「耶穌基督」是與「榮耀」（或與「顯現」）同位的。而這假設的句子和經文之間的惟一分別，就是前者說「主」而不是「上帝」。由此可見，這些新穎的解釋的真正理由就是「保羅不可能稱耶穌基督為上帝」這個假設。'This assumption simply overwhelms the exegetical evidence'，而這樣做是不對的。

84 詳參《羅》3.71-85 的討論。

85 Marshall, 'Book of Titus' 808*b*, 'Titus' 178. 首引句出自 Marshall:〈提多書〉764*a*; 第二引句英文原作 'the climax in the growing recognition that Jesus Christ is alongside the Father in the complex identity of God.'（**1**）支持「一人」立場的釋經者還包括：（**i**）E. Stauffer, *TDNT* 3.106; W. Grundmann, *TDNT* 4.540, 9.565 n.464; B. Gärtner, *DNTT* 3.319; P.-G. Müller, *EDNT* 2.44*b* (s.v. ἐπιφάνεια, 1);（**ii**）Theodore of Cyr, 屈梭多模（see Gorday 300*a*）; Arichea－Hatton 293; Barclay 256; Barrett 138; Bassler 200-1; Baugh 505*b*-6*b*; Bouwman 132, 168; Chapell 341, 361; Collins 313-14, 352, 353, 365; Collins, 'Theology' 71, 72; Dunn 872*a*（他同時認為 Fee 196 的見解 'is also possible'; 見註 55 〔上面 318〕; Goodwin 1757*a*; Griffin 312-14; Guthrie I 200; Guthrie II 212（古特立 214）; Guthrie, *Theology* 340; Hendriksen 374-75; Houlden 150-51; Keener 629*b*; Knight II 322-24; Köstenberger 619*a-b*; Laansma 270, 274-75; Lau 159, 243-44, 250, 278; Leaney 123; Lock 137 ('Him who is at once the High God in heaven and our Saviour upon earth, Jesus Christ'); C. Martin 433*b*; Montague 239（但 241 仍用 'the "appearance of the glory of the great God and of our savior Jesus Christ"' 這種講法）; Mounce 426-31; Ngewa 386; Oden 54; Perkins 1444*b*; Quinn 27, 150, 155, 168; Spencer 8, 51 with n.72; Stott 194; Taylor 67; Towner I 52, 67; Towner II 247; Towner, 'Pastoral Epistles' 332*b*: 'The deity of Christ . . . is affirmed unequivocally in Titus 2:13'; Twomey 206-7, 211; Wieland 209 (cf. 206-7); Wild 895*a-b*; Witherington 129, 144, 146, 147; Zehr 284;（**iii**）Akin, 'Mystery' 144; Bailey, 'Theology' 344; Belleville, 'Piety' 226, 241; Blomberg, 'Titus' 355; Brindle, 'Titus' 252; Hagner, 'Titus' 550, 552, *New Testament* 611, 637; Kee, 'Pastoral Letters' 273; Kidd, 'Titus' 201, 209; Köstenberger－Kellum－Quarles, 'Titus' 282; Ladd, *Theology* 421, 556; Lamp, 'Titus' 99-100;

一步而言，即使按第（一）種理解，雖然基督沒有明確地被宣告為神，祂與上帝同等的事實仍是十分清楚的。[86]

儘管本節的確宣告基督的神性，這卻不是本節的要旨。本節的要旨是在於表明，當耶穌基督再來的時候，祂的榮耀便要顯明。祂首次降臨時，顯明了自己是世人的救主，但祂的榮耀大致上是隱藏的，並且繼續隱藏直至祂再來的時候。但是當祂再來時，祂的榮耀就要完全彰顯，祂要顯明自己是我們至大的神和救主。「基督的榮耀之完全顯現」就是基督徒**福樂的盼望**，這盼望推動我們**在今世過克己、正直、敬虔的生活，熱心為善**（二 12、14）。[87]

MacDonald, *Pauline Churches* 169-70; Malherbe, 'Soteriology' 348; Marshall, 'Christology' 172, 'Titus' 178; Martin, 'Titus' 14; Matera, 'Moral Guides' 244, 'Pastoral Epistles' 169, 171; Mounce, 'Titus' 106; Richardson, 'Christ-Language' 334; Robertson, *Pictures* 4.604; Smith－Song, 'Implications' 290-91; Thurston, 'Titus' 180; Walters, Review of Collins [2002] 248; 卡森－穆爾：〈教牧書信〉553、568。(**iv**) 侯嘉文 157-58；* 張 357-58；彭編 103*a*；曾 77-80；黃編 214。(**2**) * Hultgren（'Pastoral Epistles' 145）一面承認，在多二 13 'the exalted Christ is even called "God"', 但隨後的解釋是這樣的：'for the writer of the Pastorals, God and Christ are intimately related, so much so that at his parousia Christ will bear the divine glory to complete the saving work of God, and in that sense he will be "God and Saviour"'（cf. 146: 'he will appear at the end of time bearing the divine glory'）。此解釋接近正文所討論及排拒的「二人」立場的**另一版本**（一 C）：基督是「我們至大的上帝和救主」的榮耀（見上面 318-26）。

(**3**)哈里斯說，多二 13 稱耶穌基督為「我們偉大的神和救主」這看法，'[is] a verdict shared, with varying degrees of assurance, by almost all grammarians and lexicographers, many commentators, and most writers on NT Christology,* although there are some dissenting voices'（'Deity' 271）（詳見 275-76 nn. 69-73 [cf. 'Savior' 185 nn. 50-54]; see also Harris, 'Response' 150）。* Harris（'Savior' 185）將 'most writers on NT Christology' 修正為 'many writers on NT theology or Christology'. (**4**) 哈里斯的結論值得接納（'Deity' 272）：'The use of θεός in reference to Jesus confirms what may be established on other grounds and makes explicit what is implied in other Christological titles such as κύριος and υἱὸς θεοῦ, viz. the deity of Jesus Christ.'

86 Marshall 277. Howell（'Interchange'）詳細審視了 'the vast language of interchange* where the apostle Paul describes the person and work of the Son in much the same terms as he does the person and work of the Father'（468）。作者認為他所陳列的證據充分顯示，'There is an ontological element here where Christ's divine nature is given clear expression, not just in a few isolated texts but across the expansive horizon of Pauline thought. . . . such language unquestionably points to the essential oneness in activity and nature of Jesus Christ with God'（479）。

87 Smith－Song, 'Implications' 284, 292.

我們的救主耶穌基督這字序，有別於一章 4 節／三章 6 節的「基督耶穌／耶穌基督，我們的救主」（原文直譯）。[88] 也許這裏將**耶穌基督**放在**我們的救主**之後有它的好處，就是使下一節開首的關係代名詞**他**字緊隨**耶穌基督**之後，儘管**他**字的前述詞是**我們的救主耶穌基督**這整個片語。[89]

---

88 比較：二 13：　(A) σωτῆρος ἡμῶν (B) Ἰησοῦ Χριστοῦ
　　一 4／三 6：　(B) Χριστοῦ Ἰησοῦ / Ἰησοῦ Χριστοῦ (A) τοῦ σωτῆρος ἡμῶν

89 Clark, 'Structure' 112. 筆者留意到，(**i**) 腓三 20～21 呈現相同的情況，即是關係代名詞 ὅς（**他**）緊隨**耶穌基督**（[A] σωτῆρα . . . [B] κύριον Ἰησοῦν Χριστόν）之後；這一點支持祈勒克的解釋。亦參提後一 10：διὰ τῆς ἐπιφανείας [A] τοῦ σωτῆρος ἡμῶν [B] Χριστοῦ Ἰησοῦ, καταργήσαντος. 雖然緊隨**基督耶穌**之後並非關係代名詞**他**（ὅς）字，而是分詞**廢去**，但**廢去**的主詞仍是它所緊隨的**基督耶穌**。(**ii**)彼後則一致地使用**救主耶穌基督**這字序：[A] σωτῆρος [B] Ἰησοῦ Χριστοῦ（一 1、11，二 20，三 18）。

4.2.2 基督救贖之目的（二 14）

二 **14a** 他為我們的緣故捨己，

14b 為了要贖我們脫離一切罪惡，

14c 又潔淨我們作他自己的子民，熱心為善。

本節的內容大致上與第 11、12 節平行：上帝救眾人的恩典在這裏更明確地解釋為〔基督〕為我們的緣故捨己，而後者的目的包括使我們脫離罪惡，熱心為善，這相當於上帝的恩典所教導的除去不敬虔，過敬虔的生活。[1] 為我們（呂譯、思高、新和、現修、新譯、新普）

---

1 Cf. Banker 84*b*-85*a*: 14 節是 11～13 節的「擴充（amplification）」。See also Bassler, 'Christology' 211: 'the purpose of Jesus' self-giving (redemption and ethical zeal) and the result of the appearance of grace (salvation and moral training) are shown to be identical.'（1）Van Neste 244 以圖表表達 11～12 節和 14 節的平行狀況，如下：

'A Past work of Christ – appearing of saving grace
B Goal – Negative – deny sin, etc.
Positive – live soberly, etc.
C Parousia – the blessed hope
A' Past work of Christ – he gave himself for us
B' Goal – Negative – redeem us from lawlessness
Positive – cleanse, good deeds.'

筆者惟一的疑問是關於 B 行的 'Goal' 字：12b 節開首的 ἵνα 並不表達目標（in order that），而是表達內容（'that' [KJV, NKJV]）；參二 12 註釋註 13（上面 292）。（2）Wieland 211-12（cf. 262）認為，作者可能刻意地將一些原始的基督教表述（14 節）化為希臘化時期的聽眾能夠明白的思想方式（11～13 節），兩者之間有某程度的平行。他的圖表如下（筆者以中譯取代了希臘原文）：

Concept familiar to Hellenistic popular philosophy	**Essential religious idea**	**Primitive Christian formulation, derived from OT ideas**
因為，上帝救眾人的恩典已經顯明出來	Entry of divine gift	耶穌基督……他為我們的緣故捨己
訓練我們棄絕不敬虔的行為和屬世的私慾（現修）	Release from immoral state	為了要贖我們脫離一切罪惡

這介詞片語本身的意思不是**替我們**（當代），而是**為我們的緣故**。[2] 不過，**捨己**[3] 指向基督的死亡，而死是罪的**工價**（羅六 23），因此，基督**為我們的緣故捨己**或**為我們死**（羅五 8）——犯罪的是我們，受死的是基督——這話，可能同時有**替我們**死的含意。[4] 原文的介詞片語在保羅書信另外出現十二次，三分之二也是和我們的救贖有關。[5] 我

在今世過克己、正直、敬虔的生活	New, ethically attractive way of life	熱心為善*
等候那有福的盼望，就是我們偉大的神，救主耶穌基督〔之〕榮耀的顯現（新譯）	Self-awareness as a group oriented towards God	又潔淨我們作他自己的子民

* 'Being "zealous for the good" is not unprecedented in Jewish literature (ἐζήλωσα τὸ ἀγαθὸν [*sic*], Sir 51:18)' (210). 參次經《便西拉智訓》51.18：「因為我已決定，要實行智慧的事，熱心行善，我決不會蒙羞」（思高德訓篇 51.24）。

2 Fairnbairn 285: 'ὑπὲρ ἡμῶν, not exactly in our room or stead (which ἀντὶ ἡμῶν would have expressed), but in our behalf.'

3 ἔδωκεν ἑαυτόν. 參：提前二 6（ὁ δοὺς ἑαυτόν），加一 4（τοῦ δόντος ἑαυτόν）。新約另外的講法有**捨命**（可十 45 ‖ 太二十 28：δοῦναι τὴν ψυχὴν αὐτοῦ）和「捨身」（路二十二 19：τὸ σῶμά μου τὸ . . . διδόμενον）。「捨己」、「捨命」這種講法 'is traditional for the death of martyrs among the Jews and soldiers among the Greeks'（F. Büchsel, *TDNT* 2.166），例：「厄肋阿匝爾」（Eleazar）「為了拯救百姓……決意犧牲自己（ἔδωκεν ἑαυτόν）」（次經《馬加比一書》〔思高瑪加伯上〕6.44）；「瑪塔提雅」（Mattathias）臨終時告訴兒子們，「應為我們祖先的盟約捨生致命（δότε τὰς ψυχὰς ὑμῶν ）」（同上，2.50）。

4 參《羅》2.63；《加》752；《弗》708-9；《西・門》911-12 註 13 之（3）；《帖前》410-11。See also Simpson 110-12; Lau 151; Zerwick §91: 在 'ὑπέρ = ἀντί' 這標題下，作者說：'Ὑπέρ . . . not rarely covers also "for" in the sense "in place of", e.g. . . . Tit 2,14'; Marshall 283: 'The preposition here is equivalent to ἀντί in Mk 10.45'; Collins 354: 'The formulaic expression "for us" expresses the vicarious nature of the death of Jesus Christ'; Laansma 270: 'The force of "for" . . . is both substitution ("in the place of") and representation ("for the benefit of")'; Towner II 248: 'the phrase *for us* reveals that this offering was both representative and substitutionary'; Towner III 760: 'Jesus died as a representative and a substitute' =「耶穌是以代表者和替代者的身分而死的」（唐 1108）。

5 （**i**）基督在我們還作罪人的時候為我們死（羅五 8），他為我們死了（帖前五 10，思高），為我們捨了自己（弗五 2），為我們成了詛咒（加三 13），如今在上帝的右邊為我們祈求（羅八 34，新普）；（**ii**）上帝為我們眾人捨了祂自己的兒子（羅八 32）；上帝使無罪的基督為了我們成為罪（林後五 21，現修）；上帝若為我們，誰能敵我們呢？（羅八 31，呂譯）；（**iii**）保羅告訴哥林多人，要為我們的緣故用祈禱相支持，這樣……就必有這麼多人……為我們感謝上帝（林後一 11，呂譯）；他要給哥林多

們在文理中是指所有被救贖脫離罪惡、又被潔淨成為上帝的子民（14b～c 節）的人，即是所有信徒。[6]

對應著上帝的恩典教導信徒的內容分為消極的（12b 節）和積極的（12c～13 節）兩方面，**基督為我們的緣故捨己**也是為了雙重（正負兩面）的目的，[7] 兩個目的子句構成希伯來詩歌的「綜合平行體」。[8] **（甲）為了要贖我們脫離一切罪惡**[9]（故此我們〔要〕棄絕不敬

人有為我們誇口／誇耀的機會（林後五 12，呂譯／思高）；他曾寫信使哥林多人憂愁，但那是為要把你們對我們的熱情在上帝面前對他們顯明（林後七 12，思高）。

6 Fiore II 212 則認為，我們主要指接受了救恩的信徒，但至終包括所有的人，上帝想要他們都得救（二 11）。Cf. Wall 377: 'The antecedent of "for us" must be "for all people" (2:11)'.

7 Fee 194-95.

8 Collins 353: 兩個目的子句（14b 節，14c 節〔減去熱心為善〕）反映閃族風格的綜合平行（'the Semitic style of synthetic parallelism'）。綜合平行體是「平行體的一種，希伯來詩普遍的文學特色。在格式上後一句作前一句的伸展、補充或解釋，前後兩句綜合成整個意思，第二行通常補足第一行所未盡表達的意思」（《聖神》495*a*）。Wieland 208 則認為，'καθαρίσῃ [is] attached to λυτρώσεται [*sic*, λυτρώσηται] by the exegetical καί'，意即潔淨解釋了贖的意思。

9 此句原文可能得自詩一三〇8 = LXX 一二九 8（so Blaiklock 85; Guthrie I 201; Guthrie II 213〔古特立 215〕; White 196*b*）。Cf. F. Büchsel, *TDNT* 351 n.14: 'There is no doubt that Tt. 2:14 is based on Ψ 129:8'; C. Brown, *DNTT* 3.200: 'Tit. 2:14 interprets christologically the thought of Ps. 130:8'，即是將他必救贖以色列……這思想解釋為基督救贖祂的子民。比較：

(詩) καὶ αὐτὸς λυτρώσεται τὸν Ισραηλ ἐκ πασῶν τῶν ἀνομιῶν αὐτοῦ
他 必救贖 以色列 脫離 切的 罪孽
(多) ὃς ἔδωκεν ἑαυτὸν . . . ἵνα λυτρώσηται ἡμᾶς ἀπὸ πάσης ἀνομίας
他捨 己…… 為了要贖 我們 脫離 一切 罪惡

'The contact points suggest that the primary scriptural echo is the Greek text of Ps. 129:8 (130:8 ET)'（Towner IV 913*b*）。如此，在詩篇該節指耶和華的「他自己」（αὐτός），在本節直接應用到基督身上（祂捨己：ἔδωκεν ἑαυτόν），顯示了保羅的 'standard high Christology'（Fee, *Christology* 447）。亦參註 27 及所屬正文（下面 337）。**(1)** Beale（*Theology* 675）認為，保羅似乎認為詩一三〇8 這預言在教會身上開始獲得應驗（'finding its inaugurated fulfillment in the church'）。**(2)** Marshall（'Book of Titus' 808*b*）認為，「救贖」這字眼「頗刻意地呼應了詩篇一百三十篇 8 節和馬可福音十章 45 節的話」（〈提多書〉764*a*）。參註 22 之（4）= 下面 335。**(3)** Lappenga（'Repercussions' 707）則認為，作者的詞彙所取自的舊約經節亦包括 LXX 撒下七 23：上帝引導以色列 'to redeem a people for himself [λυτρώσασθαι αὐτῷ λαόν] . . . to work majesty and a manifestation [ἐπιφάνειαν] . . . before your people [λαοῦ σου] whom you redeemed for yourself [οὗ ἐλυτρώσω σεαυτῷ] out of Egypt.' Lau 152 更認

虔的行為和屬世的私慾〔12b 節，現修〕)。加拉太書一章 4 節表明，基督是**為我們的罪捨己**，意即基督捨己的目的是要處理我們所犯的罪，**為我們贖罪**（當代），或為我們的罪進行「補贖」；[10] 在提摩太前書二章 6 節，基督被描寫為**捨了自己作萬人的贖價**（新譯）。**贖價**原文名詞與本節的動詞**贖**字同一字根，[11] 兩節所用的詞彙所提示的，都只是「贖罪」的觀念而不是更明確的「使上帝息怒」的觀念。[12] 不過，兩個觀念的關係十分密切：罪是惹動忿怒的（羅四 15），[13] 因此：(i) 贖罪之所以為必須，是由於上帝與人之間的關係要求人的罪必須被處理好；(ii) 如果罪藉著贖罪的行動獲得赦免，即是上帝對罪（和罪人）的忿怒亦告止息；換言之，「贖罪」的結果就是「使上帝息怒」，兩者（「贖罪」和「使上帝息怒」）都是「補贖」工作的一方面。[14] 本節的著眼點在於基督**救贖我們脫離一切罪惡**（思高），[15] **一切罪惡**原文直

為，撒下七 23 類似的主題和詞彙在多二 11～14 出現，這表示範例性的出埃及事件（'the paradigmatic Exodus-event'）就是解釋上帝在基督裏的救贖之舉的鑰匙（cf. 254: 'the Pastor has consciously alluded to the paradigmatic Exodus-event and assigned to Christ the work of redemption and purification otherwise belonging to Yahweh in the OT'）。

10 《加》227-28。按筆者的用法，「贖罪」是英文的 'to expiate / expiation' 的翻譯，「補贖」= 英文的 'to atone for / atonement'. 參《羅》1.516-17 註 2。

11 原文依次為：**ἀντίλυτρον**（名詞），**λυτρόω**（動詞〔λυτρώσηται 是中間語態假設式語法〕)。**(1)** 前者在希臘文聖經不再出現；後者僅再出現兩次，分別指耶穌的門徒**素來所盼望要救贖以色列民的就是他**（路二十四 21：λυτροῦσθαι, 中間語態不定詞），以及信徒得以**從虛妄的行為中救贖出來**（彼前一 18：ἐλυτρώθητε, 被動語態）是憑著基督的寶血（19 節）。**(2)** 同字根的人物名詞 λυτρωτής 在新約只出現一次，指摩西是上帝所差派的**解救者**（徒七 35）；在 LXX 則出現四次，其中兩次詩人稱耶和華為**我的救贖主**和**他們〔以色列人〕的救贖主**（詩十八 15〔十九 14〕／七十七 35〔七十八 35〕)，另見利二十五 31、32。

12 「使上帝息怒」即是英文的 'to propitiate / propitiation'（參上面註 10）。

13 全節的意思可表達如下：「律法存在，有罪的人違犯律法，違法的行為激起上帝的忿怒」《羅》1.616）。

14 《羅》1.526-27。

15 See also KJV, RSV, NRSV: 'all iniquity'; NIV, TNIV, NIV2011: 'all wickedness'; NLT: 'every kind of sin'. NJB 的 'all our faults' 是太弱的意譯。**(1)** Quinn 27, 150 的翻譯（'to set us free from every wrong'）有兩個疑點：(**i**) ἀνομία 不應減弱為 'wrong'; 見正文。See also Marshall 284: 'ἀνομία is "lawlessness, iniquity", the opposite of

譯作一切不法之行為／不法之事（呂譯[16]／新譯）；[17] 按約翰一書三章 4 節的定義，罪就是不法。馬歇爾認為，鑑於文理提到基督的再來（因而間接提到審判），[18] 脫離一切罪惡的意思是脫離罪的力量（單數）以及罪所帶來的結果（複數）。[19] 不過，基督的再來對信徒而言是福樂的盼望（13 節），故此審判的意思在這裏並不明顯；脫離一切罪惡

righteousness and synonymous with sin.'（**ii**）λυτρόω 的意思不僅是 'set free', 而是 'redeem'; 後者暗示，基督成就救贖，是要付出高昂代價的——不是要繳付「贖金（ransom）」（*pace* Guthrie, *Theology* 478: 'Christ's self-giving is the ransom price'; Hendriksen 376: 'The ransom-price was his own precious blood'; Hinson 283: 'Christ's death furnished the ransom price needed to free us from evil'; Ladd, *Theology* 433: 'This . . . includes specific mention of the ransom price: he gave himself'; F. Büchsel, *TDNT* 4.351: 'it would be quite wrong to say of Tt. 2:14 and 1 Pt. 1:18 that . . . the idea of ransom . . . is not contained in these passages'），而是要付出代價（at cost to Himself）；* 參彼前一 18～19（上面註 11 之〔1〕）。亦參《加》739-40。（* 'The idea that God has to pay anything to anybody as the price of setting his people free is rejected (Isa 45.13; 52.3)' [Marshall 284].）（**2**）第（ii）點評語同樣適用於 Banker 75, 85*a* 的翻譯：'in order that he might cause us(inc) to be free from all sin, (that is, in order that he might enable us(inc) not to sin at all').

16 See also NKJV, NAU: 'every lawless deed'; ESV: 'all lawlessness'; *Paraphrase* 293: 'lawlessness of every kind'; BDAG 85*b* (s.v. ἀνομία, 2): 'the product of a lawless disposition, *a lawless deed*'.

17 （**1**）名詞 **ἀνομία** 在保羅書信另外出現六次（羅四 7：複數的不法行為〔呂譯〕；單數的不法：羅六 19a、b；林後六 14〔呂譯、思高、新譯〕；帖後二 3、7），新約另外八次，詳見《帖後》170-71；BDAG 85*a-b* (s.v.);《新希》30*a*（s.v.）。這字是複合名詞（from νόμος + α-privative [Vine 2.260]）；名詞 νόμος（律法、法則）沒有在本書出現，但在提前一 8、9 出現各一次，監獄書信四次，哥林多前書九次，加拉太書 32 次，羅馬書 74 次（保羅書信合共 121 次 – 新約全部 193 次的 62.7%）！（**2**）同字根的形容詞 ἄνομος 在保羅書信出現六次，新約另三次，分別指沒有律法的人（林前九 21a、b、d），保羅並非沒有律法（九 21c）；不法的人到了時候就要出現（帖後二 8）；律法是為不法的人制定的（提前一 9）；聖經預言耶穌要被列在不法者之中（路二十二 37，新譯），以色列人藉著不法之人的手把耶穌殺了（徒二 23）；羅得因不法的事而傷痛（彼後二 8）。（**3**）同字根的副詞 ἀνόμως 在新約僅出現兩次（羅二 12：凡在律法之外犯了罪的，將在律法之外滅亡〔參《羅》1.364〕），在 LXX 僅出現一次（次經《馬加比二書》8.17: 'lawless outrage' [RSV, NRSV]）。

18 屈梭多模認為，基督的再來意味著審判：'He speaks here of two appearings: the first of grace, the second of retribution and justice'（Gorday 298*a*）。但是如 Bassler（'Christology' 211）所指出，'There are . . . no allusions to an associated judgment (cf. 2 Tim. 4.1, 8).'

19 Marshall 285. Griffin 315 則認為，'This phrase ["from all wickedness"] suggests deliverance from both the power of sin (cf. Rom 6:17-18, 22) and the penalty of sin (cf. Rom 6:23; 8:1).'

可能僅指脫離罪的力量。[20]

（乙）為要潔淨[21] 我們作他自己的子民，熱心為善（故此我們要在今世過克己、正直、敬虔的生活〔12c 節〕)。如果脫離一切罪惡是指脫離罪的力量，潔淨我們是指除去罪的污染。[22] 自己的子民原文

---

20 Knight II 328: 'λυτρώσηται speaks of removing Christians from the control of sin'. See also Towner I 76: 'in every NT passage that describes Christ as Savior the primary thought is that of deliverance from sins (2 Tim 1.10; Titus 1.4; 2.13; 3.6); Knight II 328: 'Christ liberates us from control by every kind of sin'; Towner III 761（唐 1110）：'the effects of Christ's self-offering are interpreted in terms of redemption from sin's enslavement'; Towner IV 914*a*: 'To this point, the effects of Christ's self-offering are interpreted in terms of redemption from sin's enslavement'. **(1)** Lock 146 也認為，基督救贖我們脫離一切罪惡，就如上帝在過去救贖以色列民脫離埃及的奴役（出十五 13），又救贖他們脫離巴比倫（賽四十四 22～24）；因此，這裏的主要思想是獲救脫離罪惡的力量，而不是脫離罪咎。**(2)** 參較 Towner III 760（唐 1108）：'his self-offering accomplished the removal of "us" from the <u>sphere</u> of sin'; 760-61（唐 1109）：'from all wickedness' names 'the <u>environment</u> from which people are "redeemed"'; Jeon I 85: 'The preposition "from" . . . indicates that Christ's death has removed the "elect of God" (1:1b) from the "<u>sphere</u>" <u>or</u> "<u>power</u>" of "lawlessness."'

21 DC 142*a*, 143*b* 則翻譯為 'consecrate',「使之聖化」。**(1)** 動詞 **καθαρίζω** 在保羅書信僅再出現兩次（新約全部 31 次），分別指信徒應該<u>潔淨</u>自己（林後七 1）以及基督以水藉著道把教會<u>洗淨</u>(弗五 26〔參《弗》854-59〕)。**(2)**在 καθαρίσῃ ἑαυτῷ λαὸν περιούσιον 這子句內的 ἑαυτῷ 一字（= 'unto himself / for Himself / for himself' [KJV / NKJV, NAU / RSV, NRSV, NIV, TNIV, NIV2011, ESV]），可能並無 'for his own service'（Lock 137）之意，而只是加強 λαὸν περιούσιον, 所得出的意思就是 'to purify a people to be his very own'（NJB），'to . . . purify a people for His very own'(*Paraphrase* 293)，'to make us his very own people'(NLT)。See Banker 86*b*.

22 Knight II 328: 'καθαρίσῃ speaks of removing the defilement of sin from Christians.' 參：林後七 1：既然我們有這樣的應許，就當潔淨（καθαρίσωμεν）自己，除去身體和靈魂一切的污穢。

(1) 保羅可能自覺地或不自覺地想到 LXX 結三十七 23（Blaiklock 85; White 196*b*; see also Karris 117）。比較：

多二 14b： ἵνα λυτρώσηται ἡμᾶς ἀπὸ πάσης ἀνομίας
為了要贖 我們 脫離 一切 罪惡

結三十七 23b：καὶ ῥύσομαι αὐτοὺς ἀπὸ πασῶν τῶν ἁμαρτιῶν αὐτῶν
我也要救 他們 脫離他們一切的罪惡

多二 14c 上：καὶ <u>καθαρίσῃ</u> <u>ἑαυτῷ</u> <u>λαὸν</u> περιούσιον
又 潔淨 我們 作他自己的子民

結三十七 23c：καὶ <u>καθαριῶ</u> αὐτοὺς καὶ ἔσονταί <u>μοι</u> <u>εἰς λαόν</u>
我要潔淨 他們…… 他們要作我的子民

上帝在該節的應許（我……要救他們……我要潔淨他們）藉著基督的工作（贖我們

脫離一切罪惡，又潔淨我們）應驗了。誠如 Kidd（'Titus' 202）所言，'What Israel's God promised to do, Jesus has done: he has redeemed, he has purified, he has taken a people to himself for possession.'

（**2**）對唐書禮而言，潔淨的圖像使人也想起（除了結三十七 23）另三節經文：結三十六 25：我必灑清（καθαρόν）水在你們身上，你們就潔淨了（καθαρισθήσεσθε）。我要潔淨（καθαριῶ）你們，使你們脫離一切的污穢（τῶν ἀκαθαρσιῶν），棄絕一切的偶像；三十六 29：我要救你們脫離一切的污穢（τῶν ἀκαθαρσιῶν）；三十六 33：主耶和華如此說：我潔淨（καθαριῶ）你們，使你們脫離一切罪孽（ἐκ πασῶν τῶν ἀνομιῶν ὑμῶν）的日子，必使城鎮有人居住，廢墟重新建造（Towner III 761-62〔唐 1111〕；Towner IV 914*a*）。（**3**）愛華斯則聲稱，同一位作者根據賽四十二 6～7 和四十九 6～8 來理解多二 14 和提前二 6 這兩節的救贖語錄（Edwards, 'Titus 2,14' 266: 'the same author reads the ransom logion in 1 Tim 2,6 and Titus 2,14 in light of Isa 42,6-7; 49,6-8' [cf. 264]）。就多二 14 本節而論，愛華斯（264-65 [repeated in idem, 'Christology' 145]）認為兩個目的子句（14b、14c 節）的背後是賽四十二 6～7 和四十九 6～7 這兩段；他的理由是，這兩個目的子句跟早期教會文獻《巴拿巴書信》14.6 幾乎完全一樣（'almost completely parallel'），而《巴拿巴書信》14.6 只是作者對賽四十二 6～7 和四十九 6～7（這兩段引於《巴拿巴書信》14.7-8）的撮要。愛華斯因此認為，多二 14b、14c 像《巴拿巴書信》14.6a、6b 一樣，也是賽四十二 6～7 和四十九 6～7 的撮要。筆者沒有被他的辯證說服（見下面之〔4〕〔5〕）。

（**4**）可能得多的是，在多二 14（和提前二 6）的背後，是類似可十 45c 的耶穌語錄（Edwards ['Titus' 264] 指出，學者們皆認為前者受後者影響〔e.g., Marshall, 'Christology' 172: 'Behind the author's statements lies the tradition found in Mark 10:45'; Wolfe, 'Use of Scripture' 210: 'The passage reflects the saying of Jesus in Mark 10:45b and Matt 20:28b'〕；愛華斯在另一文中承認，在多二 11～14 和提前二 1～7 這兩段之間，'Perhaps the most important similarity is the dependence on a tradition that is similar to Mark 10:45' [Edwards, 'Christology' 142, see also 146]）：

可十 45c	καὶ δοῦναι	τὴν ψυχὴν αὐτοῦ	λύτρον ἀντὶ πολλῶν
多二 14a～b	ὃς ἔδωκεν	ἑαυτὸν ὑπὲρ ἡμῶν	ἵνα λυτρώσηται ἡμᾶς
提前二 6a	ὁ δοὺς	ἑαυτὸν	ἀντίλυτρον ὑπὲρ πάντων

愛華斯的理論卻捨顯（可十 45c）取晦（賽四十二 6～7，四十九 6～7），捨易（多二 14 和提前二 6 與可十 45 有直接關聯）取難（透過二世紀的《巴拿巴書信》〔見下一段〕來建立多二 14 和提前二 6 與賽四十二 6～7，四十九 6～7 的關聯）。

（**5**）愛華斯抱怨說：'The connection between Titus 2,14 and Isa 42,6-7; 49,6-7 is almost completely missed in modern scholarship because the connection between Titus 2,14 and *Barn* 14,6 is never appreciated'（265 n.3），但這種 lack of appreciation of the latter connection leading to the former connection being 'almost completely missed' 豈是沒有原因的呢？對筆者而言，這些原因就是：（**i**）多二 14b、14c 和《巴拿巴書信》14.6a, 14.6b 並非（如愛華斯所聲稱）'almost completely parallel'，如下表所示：

多二 14b	ἵνα λυτρώσηται	ἡμᾶς	ἀπὸ πάσης ἀνομίας
《巴拿巴書信》14.6a	λυτρωσάμενον	ἡμᾶς	ἐκ τοῦ σκότους
多二 14c	καὶ καθαρίσῃ	ἑαυτῷ	λαὸν περιούσιον
《巴拿巴書信》14.6b	ἑτοιμᾶσαι	ἑαυτῷ	λαὸν ἅγιον

有「特殊的」、[23] **屬他自己的**子民（新普）[24] 之意。這詞採用了舊約聖經**屬我的子民**（出十九 5）／**自己**／**他寶貴的子民**（申七 6，十四 2／二十六 18）一詞，[25] 暗示教會就是上帝的新以色列，即是新

愛華斯認為兩節共享了 'the same concepts and unbroken word order'（265）；但真正相同的詞彙其實只有動詞 λυτρόω（分別以限定動詞和分詞形式出現），以及十分普遍的名詞 λαός 和代名詞 ἡμᾶς, ἑαυτῷ 等字。(**ii**) 更為重要的，即使假設提多書為冒名之作，它的成書日期很可能仍是早過《巴拿巴書信》的（《聖神》83*b*：「130 年」）；那麼，就算《巴拿巴書信》14.6 確與賽四十二 6～7，四十九 6～7 有關聯，而《巴拿巴書信》14.6 亦與多二 14 有相似之處，為甚麼這就使在《巴拿巴書信》之前就已寫成的多二 14 亦與賽四十二 6～7，四十九 6～7 有關聯？簡單的事實可能只是：在後的《巴拿巴書信》14.6 與在先的多二 14 有相似之處（但有釋經者指出，'The *Epistle of Barnabas* . . . shows no signs of familiarity with Titus' [Lappenga, 'Repercussions' 708]）；在後的《巴拿巴書信》14.6 與賽四十二 6～7，四十九 6～7 有關聯；但在先的多二 14 與賽四十二 6～7，四十九 6～7 並無明顯的關聯（若有的話，必有釋經者在愛華斯之先就已把這〔些〕關聯指出來了）。

23 λαὸν περιούσιον = 'a peculiar people' (KJV). περιούσιος（新約聖經僅此一次）= 'pert. to being of very special status, *chosen, especial*' (BDAG 802*b* [s.v.]); 'peculiar, special' (LN §58.48). 'Peculiar' 在這裏的意思不是「奇怪的」，而是「特殊的」（參《牛津》838*b* [s.v.]）。See also *EDNT* 3.75*a* (s.v.): 'a pure people *that belongs to him as his special possession*.'（**1**）LN §57.5 提出另一可能的意思：'pertaining to being a special or a distinctive possession of someone . . . a pure people who belong to him alone'; 參《輔讀》528：「特別的，只屬於自己的」；《新希》262*b*（s.v.）：「一些實體所獨有或特別的，有『只屬於某人的』的意味。」（**2**）另有翻譯為 'precious'; 見下面註 25 之（2）。（**3**）名詞 **λαός** 在保羅書信另外出現十一次（新約全部 142 次〔包括約八 2〕），全部都是在舊約引句中：七次指上帝的**子民**／**百姓**（羅九 25a、25b、26，十五 10〔參《羅》4.536-38〕；林後六 16／羅十一 1、2），四次分別指以色列人（**百姓**：羅十 21；林前十 7，十四 21）和**萬民**（羅十五 11）。Quinn 160 認為：'All 11 Pauline uses are in quotations from the OT'. 惟一有商榷餘地的是羅十一 1；參《羅》3.457-58。（**4**）H. Thyen（*EDNT* 2.220*a* [s.v. καθαρός, 4 c]）聲稱，在本節和弗五 26，外邦人的教會 'has usurped the place of the "purified people of God"'.「篡奪了（has usurped）」是含有強烈貶義的講法，但（舉例說）保羅以教會為更新的以色列，舊約論更新的以色列的預言，應驗在新約的教會身上（羅九 25～26〔參《羅》3.221-33，尤其是 232-33〕）；對他而言，新約的教會就是**上帝的以色列民**（加六 16〔參《加》1425-26〕）。另見下文。

24 See also NLT: 'his very own people'; NKJV: '*His* own special people'; RSV, NRSV: 'a people of his own'; NJB / NIV, TNIV, NIV2011: 'a people to be / that are his very own'. 如 Fairnbairn 286 所指出，這詞實質上與彼前二 9「**屬於上帝自己的**（新普）子民（λαὸν εἰς περιποίησιν）」相同。

25 原文皆為 λαὸς περιούσιος；只是第一次是主格，其餘三次是直接受格。前者（主格）亦見於出二十三 22（LXX only）。（**1**）形容詞 **περιούσιος** 在 LXX 出現僅此五次。希臘文背後的希伯來文是 עַם סְגֻלָּה（申七 6，十四 2，二十六 18）；see BDF §113(1).

約時代的**上帝的選民**（一 1）。[26] 但是舊約屬上帝的子民在這裏變成**他**〔= 13 節的**耶穌基督**〕**自己的子民**。如此，通常被歸予上帝的功能（贖）和崇高地位在本節被歸予降世為人、在十字架上成就救贖的耶穌基督。[27] 克里特那些敵對者所關注的是禮儀上的潔淨（一 15），[28] 但是只有基督的救贖能夠帶來真正的、靈性和道德方面的潔淨[29]（參：徒十五 9：〔**上帝**〕**藉著信潔淨了他們的心**）。

熱心為善是子民的修飾語。[30] 善字在原文是二字片語，已在上

（**2**）Fiore II 212 翻譯為 'precious'. 他解釋說：'The meaning "precious" is based on the use of the word in the LXX for the Hebrew *segullah* (see Ps 134:4 [LXX 134:5]; Eccl 2:8), which means not just "one's own" but also "heaped up." The word seems to carry the connotation of a rich, prized possession.' 不過，上述 LXX 兩節所用的希臘字不是本節的形容詞 περιούσιος，而是名詞 περιουσιασμός，而 LXE 兩次都翻譯為 'peculiar treasure'〔單數和複數〕）。See also Quinn 160: περιουσιασμός = 'a private possession or a special treasure'.

26 Towner I 130.

27 Lau 159. 作者認為：'Such high estimation of Christ not only indicates that there is no essential difference between the attitude of the Father and the Son in redemption, and that the latter's role as Saviour is coextensive with God the Saviour (2.10; 3.4), but it also implies his pre-existence and divinity.' See also Fee, *Christology* 447-48; Matera, 'Pastoral Epistles' 170-71. 亦參註 9 Fee（上面 331）。

28 參一 15 註釋註 13 及所屬正文（上面 198-99）。

29 Van Neste 267-68.（**1**）Donelson I 145 從二 11～14 這一段看出基督論與倫理的關係如下：'Christology for the author lives in ethics. The argument is clearly stated. Jesus appeared in order to teach his people how to live ethically.' 'Jesus has appeared, "teaching (παιδεύειν)" us to live the ethical life.' 筆者加上底線的話有點言過其實：因為分詞「教導（παιδεύουσα）」（陰性）所形容的是上帝救眾人的**恩典**（χάρις，陰性）；本段的基督論更重要的部分是在 13b～14 節（基督的身分、祂的救贖工作，和祂的再來）。Cf. Matera, 'Pastoral Epistles' 281 n.96: 'The remark of Donelson [first quotation, endorsed by Malherbe, 'Paraenesis' 317] . . . overstates the case since it does not give sufficient attention to the theme of redemption'; Lau 255: 'we cannot reduce the epiphanic statements about Christ's earthly appearance to a functional Christology which, for instance, focuses simply on Jesus' role as a teacher and the moral or ethical effects of his teaching' (n.97 refers to Donelson I 145). 因此，（**2**）以下的講法較為正確：'In Greek terms, the appearance of God's grace "teaches" ("civilizes in") a new way of life; in terms of the biblical tradition, that very life of godliness, lived in the present age until hope has been fulfilled, has proved to be the goal of the Messiah's redemptive self-offering'（Towner III 765〔唐 1116〕）。

30 名詞 ζηλωτήν 與 λαόν 同等（in apposition with λαόν），兩個字都是單數直接受格。（**1**）名詞 **ζηλωτής** 在保羅書信僅再出現兩次，分別指哥林多人**切慕屬靈的恩賜**（林前十四 12），以及保羅歸主前比他的同輩為〔**他**〕**祖宗的傳統更熱心**（加一 14）。在新約另外出現五次，分別指**激進派的西門**（新譯：路六 15；徒一 13）、

文出現一次（二 7：提多要顯出自己是好行為的榜樣），在下文會再出現兩次（三 8、14）。[31]「好行為」是基督救贖和潔淨信徒作他自己的子民的目的，這目的的陳述同時是對信徒的勸勉。[32] 這裏的善或「好行為」可能不是特指能促進人們福祉的事，[33] 而是信徒應該過的生活的總結[34]（參：弗二 10，我們是……在基督耶穌裏創造的，為要使我們行善，就是上帝早已預備好要我們做的）。[35] 值得留意的是，「好

熱心於律法的人（徒二十一 20）、保羅熱心事奉上帝（二十二 3），和信徒熱心行善（彼前三 13：τοῦ ἀγαθοῦ ζηλωταί）。最後一節與本節（ζηλωτὴν καλῶν ἔργων）十分相似；不過，該節的重點是在行善（參三 17：因行善〔ἀγαθοποιοῦντας〕受苦），本節則指較籠統的「好行為」（cf. Lappenga, 'Repercussions' 709）。(**2**) 此名詞（ζηλωτής）在 LXX 出現八次，分別指耶和華是忌邪的神（出二十 5，三十四 14；申四 24，五 9，六 15；鴻一 2）；敖尼雅是「對律法熱心的人（ζηλωτὴν τῶν νόμων）」（次經《馬加比二書》4.2〔思高作「忠誠守法的人」〕）；以及「熱心者非尼哈（τὸν ζηλωτὴν Φινεες）」（偽經《馬加比四書》18.12）。

(**3**) Lappenga（art. cit. 712）認為，ζωλωτής 在本節至少含有「效法者」（'"imitator(s)" or "emulator(s)"'）之意，因為在希臘文獻中，當文理提及「教導」時（如在二 12：訓練），此字常有這個意思。作者認為二 7 好行為的榜樣（τύπον καλῶν ἔργων）和二 14 熱心為善（ζηλωτὴν καλῶν ἔργων = 'emulators of good works' [715]）的關聯支持他的理解。筆者倒認為，提多要做好行為的榜樣，信徒要效法提多的榜樣而在好事上熱心（呂譯），這並不使原文名詞的意思由「熱心者」變成「效法者」。(**4**)Lappenga（art. cit. 713-14）又認為，熱心（二 14）與嫉妒（三 3）構成對比，因為與 ζηλωτής 同字根的 ζῆλος（zeal）和 φθόνος（envy）常用作相反詞。他聲稱，'The contrast between those who are "zealous" for good works (2:14) and those who have mere φθόνος (3:3) seems to carry a similar* polemical edge in the Letter of Titus'（714. *參下面註 37）。因此，他的意譯包括這個意思在內：'. . . and purify for himself a special people who are, *in stark contrast with those among you who are* <u>*envious*</u> [3:3] *and teaching for shameful gain* [1:11], . . . "zealous for good works"'（717）。可是，三 3 並非明確地描寫假教師，而是籠統地描寫一切仍未歸信基督的人。

31 參二 7～8a 註釋註 5 及所屬正文（上面 259）。

32 Wendland, 'Discourse' 346: 'implied exhortation: ". . . do what is good"'.

33 Karris 114: 'conduct which promote human welfare in this world'; 93: 'acts of social concern'. Matera（'Moral Guides' 246）認為，在教牧書信裏，'"good works" refers to charitable deeds toward others.'

34 Collins 355: 'a summary description of the life they should live.' See also Towner I 153: 'the term accurately epitomizes the new existence from the standpoint of "doing"'; 154: 'the term "good works" describes the observable, horizontal facet of the Christian life'; Towner IV 915*a*: '"Good deeds" (1:16; 2:7[, 14]; 3:8, 14) is Pauline shorthand (particularly in these letters to co-workers . . .) for the visible, outward dimension of Christian existence (cf. Eph. 2:10).' 亦參張 359：「一切基督徒所當作的事」；彭編 29*a-b*：「可以讓人看見、與　神心意相符的好行為。」

35 弗二 10 的善（ἔργα ἀγαθά, good works）可理解為「美好的工作和美好的行為」；

行為」一詞在信上出現的其餘五次，多數都是在明顯爭論性的段落中出現，或是明確地與敵對者的行為構成對比：（1）〔他們〕根本做不出甚麼好事來（一 16，當代）將一章 10 至 16 節對假教師的描寫和定罪帶到高潮；（2）提多要顯出自己是好行為的榜樣（二 7）與那反對的人（二 8）構成對比；（3）預備行各樣善事（三 1）與隨後的惡行目錄（三 3）構成對比；（4）使那些已信上帝的人留心行善（三 8）與那些敵對者的行徑（三 9）構成對比；（5）我們的人也該學習行善（三 14）是「好行為」這個主題的摘要重述。[36] 由此看來，「好行為」是信徒與克里特的假教師主要的對照點，因而本節的熱心為善將本節（儘管只是間接地）連於那些明顯地是爭辯性的段落（一 10～16，三 9～11）。[37] 根據主耶穌的教導，凡好樹都結好果子，而壞樹結壞

更具體地說，就是第四至六章所描述的生活方式（詳參《弗》310-11）。

36 以上五次，原文分別用單數的 πᾶν ἔργον ἀγαθόν（一 16，三 1）和複數的 καλῶν ἔργων（二 7，三 8，三 14〔二 14 同〕）。ἀγαθός 和 καλός 可視為同義的；參三 8b～d 註釋註 17 之（3）= 下面 427；二 7～8a 註釋註 6 及所屬正文（上面 259）。

37 Lappenga, 'Repercussions' 710-11. 作者進一步辯證（715-17），'zealous for good works' 隱含了與 'zealous for the law' 的對比。（**i**）對一世紀的猶太人而言，ζηλωτής（熱心者）一字具有重大意義，因為熱心（ζῆλος）就是猶太人的象徵：在次經《馬加比一書》，「熱心」（尤其是對律法熱心）用來指猶太民族主義的激情（'Jewish nationalistic fervor, especially in regard to the law'）；舊約的非尼哈、以利亞，和兩約之間的瑪他提亞（即馬加比猶大的父親），都是為上帝的榮耀或律法大發熱心的表表者。在王上十九 14，以利亞自稱為耶和華……大發熱心（ζηλῶν ἐζήλωκα τῷ κυρίῳ），但在《馬加比一書》2.58，他是「因熱愛法律（ἐν τῷ ζηλῶσαι ζῆλον νόμου），纔被接升天」。瑪他提亞也是由於他對律法的熱心驅使他殺死危害猶太習俗的人而出名（《馬加比一書》2.24-28：「熱情勃發」〔ἐζήλωσεν [2.24]〕，「對於法律……熱誠」〔ἐζήλωσεν τῷ νόμῳ [2.26]〕；「凡熱心法律……的〔ὁ ζηλῶν τῷ νόμῳ〕，請跟我來！」[2.27]）；他臨終時對他的兒子們說，「你們對法律應熱誠服膺」（ζηλώσατε τῷ νόμῳ [2.50]）。非尼哈的熱心（民二十五 7～13）則名聞遐邇，他的名字本身就足以使人想起「為律法熱心」的意思（《馬加比一書》2.26：「他〔瑪他提亞〕對於法律這樣熱誠，完全像丕乃哈斯……所作的一樣」〔ἐζήλωσεν τῷ νόμῳ, καθὼς ἐποίησεν Φινεες〕；以上引句皆出自思高瑪加伯上）（715-16）。（**ii**）「對律法熱心」在一世紀繼續成為猶太人重要的標誌：例如，保羅提到為〔他〕祖宗的傳統更熱心（加一 14，參《加》304-7）；就熱心說，〔他〕是迫害教會的〔腓三 6，參《腓》350-51〕）（716）。（**iii**）假教師是以猶太詞彙來描寫的：他們是奉割禮的人（一 10），他們傳播猶太人無稽的傳說（一 14），又參與愚拙的辯論、家譜、紛爭和因律法而起的爭辯（三 9）（715）；正是他們與猶太傳統

果子。好樹不能結壞果子，壞樹也不能結好果子（太七 17～18）；由此可以推論，既然那些假教師根本做不出甚麼好事來（一 16，當代），他們就根本沒有經歷上帝的救贖和潔淨，因此，克里特的信徒最好不要被他們誤導而跟從他們！

的密切關係，使他們與保羅的使徒職事和教導對立起來（716-17）。因此，保羅「騎劫（hijacked）」了以縮壓方式表達猶太人身分的「對律法熱心（ζῆλος νόμου）」一詞，將它改為「對好行為熱心（ζηλωτὴς καλῶν ἔργων）」，他是用了充滿戰意（'combative'）的語言來對那些假教師發出一個衝擊他們的信息（'a jolting message'）（717）。Lappenga 的意譯這樣表達這個意思（717）：'. . . and purify for himself a special people who are . . . *not "zealous for the law" in the way that you opponents have twisted it, but* "zealous for good works" *in the sense that I have expounded in this letter*.' 筆者認為，上述（本註）的見解比作者的另一建議（見上面註 30 之〔4〕）理據較強，因而較為可取。

4.3 要旨的重述（二 15）

二 **15a** 這些事你要講明，要……勸勉人，責備人。

15b 充分運用你的職權

15c 不要讓任何人輕看你。

本節是二章 1 至 14 節一段的摘要；[1] 它重複了上文兩個命令式語法的鑰字（**講明**即 1 節的**講**；**勸勉**即 6 節的**勸**），因而本節和第 1 節首尾呼應。與此同時，本節也重拾一章 13 節命令式語法的**責備**一字[2]（**勸勉**和**責備**原文亦以不定詞的形式在一章 9 節出現過〔後者在該節翻譯為**駁倒**〕）；[3] 這字最可能的意思是「使他們認識自己的錯

---

1 （1）Classen（'Titus' 444, 'Epistle to Titus' 66）則以本節為 一 13～二 14 的摘要（'summary'）。無論如何，並無連詞將本節連於上文，說明了「無連詞現象（asyndeton）」是 '[s]ummaries of previous material' 的一個特色（Levinsohn, 'Constraints' 331）。（2）另一方面，Collins 355 以二 15 開始二 15～三 3 這一段，但並無提出理據。參導論第伍節註 13 之（乙）= 上面 33-34。

2 （1）λάλει καὶ παρακάλει καὶ ἔλεγχε 是 polysyndetic emphatic clustering 的例子（Genade 128, 64〔ἔλεγκε 是 ἔλεγχε 之誤〕）；參一 16 註釋註 2，二 12 註釋註 37 之（1）=（上面 207，297）。（2）Clark（'Structure' 113）從這三個動詞出現的次序看出交叉配置模式，並由此認為頭兩個動詞幾乎同義：

A	ἔλεγχε	（責備，一 13）
B1	λάλει	（講，二 1）
B2	παρακάλει	（勸，二 6）
B1	λάλει	（講明，二 15）
B2	παρακάλει	（勸勉，二 15）
A	ἔλεγχε	（責備，二 15）

筆者認為，是項有趣的觀察對釋經的幫助不大。（以上六次，就是信上到此為止所有的命令式語法；餘下三次是在三 1、9、10〔**提醒**、**遠避**、**拒絕跟他來往**〕。）（3）Wendland（'Discourse' 338）聲稱，（i）這三個命令式語法動詞簡潔地提出了全書的重要功能（'functional import'）；（ii）本節是全書的結構核心（'Compositional Core'; cf. 340: 'the structural pivot ("fulcrum" or "midpoint") of the entire epistle'）。

3 Clark, 'Structure' 112. Cf. F. Büchsel, *TDNT* 2.474 n.5: 'The ἔλεγχε of 2:15 cannot be

誤」，[4] 而「改正」[5] 可視為這個意思的含義。透過重複這詞彙，保羅顯示提多的職事和監督的職事之間有相似之處。[6] 更為重要的，本節從正反兩面重申，提多在克里特的工作是有保羅的授權的（參一 5）。

這些事回望本段的上文，即是二章第 1 至 14 節的教導，[7] 就如提摩太前書六章 2e 節用了類似的話（**你要教導和勸勉這些事**）[8] 來

---

construed differently from the ἔλεγχε of 1:13 or the ἐλέγχειν of 1:9, even though it is linked with ταῦτα.' 參註 20（下面 345）。

4 參一 13b～14 註釋末段開首，連註 21（上面 185）；《輔讀》528（第一解釋）：「指出錯誤」。

5 NLT, Banker 87, 88*a*: 'correct' (verb); 彭編 103*b*：「糾正」。REB 則翻譯為 'argue (them)'.

6 Genade 64. 簡內德甚至這樣聲稱：'The only way elders are going to know how to perform this ministry is by observing Titus.'

7 Towner III 766（唐 1117）。See also Arichea－Hatton 295: 'everything that is contained in this chapter'; Keener 630*a*: 'Paul encourages Titus to pass on the sound doctrine of 2:1-14.' Ταῦτα = 'anaphoric' (Clark, 'Structure' 113), i.e., 'backward-looking'（Towner III 766 n.1〔唐 1117 註 1〕）。**(1)**班約翰認為，**這些事**指一 10～二 14 的內容（Banker 14, 58*a*, 87, 88*a*, 88*b*）。See also Griffin 316: '"These [things]" . . . may refer to all of Paul's instructions to Titus from 1:10ff.'（方括號是原來的）；Fee 197: '**These things** refers at least to 2:2-14, perhaps to 1:10-16 as well'; cf. Towner II 250: '*these . . . things* refers at least to vv. 1-14, perhaps also to 1:5-16'. **(2)** Bassler 202 則認為**這些事**同時指上文（第二章）和下文（三 1～8）。**(3)** Mounce 432 甚至認為，'ταῦτα refers to the whole epistle', 從一 5 開始（cf. Ngewa 380）。Cf. Smith 120: 'the repetition of λαλέω in 2:15 with two other verbs used elsewhere in the letter for Titus' ministry (cf. παρακαλέω 1:9; 2:6; ἐλέγχω 1:9, 13) suggests the content of the two charges was the entire letter'; 286: 'ταῦτα is best understood as a reference to the entire body of the letter'; 336: 'ταῦτα more likely refers to the entire letter.' **(4)** 黃編 215 認為**這些事**僅「指神救恩的性質和目的（參 11～14 節）」。**(5)** Keegan II 100 則認為，**這些事**是指「二 1～10 的『家規』內容」（Keegan I 63 只作 'the things he [Titus] is told to say in 2:1-10'）。See also Guthrie I 202 / Guthrie II 214: 'all the practical exhortations contained in chapter ii/2'（endorsed by Levinsohn, *Discourse Features* 119）；古特立 216：「整個第二章所有實際的教訓。」**(6)** 但是鑑於二 1～10 和二 11～14 這兩段的緊密關係（參二 11～14 註釋引言〔上面 281-83〕），**這些事**大可以同時指這兩段的內容（Van Neste 259）。See Fiore II 212: 'The content of "these things" . . . includes both the community rules [2:1-10] and the core apostolic "preaching" . . . of Jesus' redemptive death and its effects [2:11-14].' **(7)** Marshall 297 指出，λάλει（二 1、15）兩次首尾呼應，他認為這提示**這些事**是指二 <u>2</u>～14（thus also Knight II 329; Spencer 53）全部。但為甚麼要撇除**你所講的總要合乎那健全的教導**（二 1）這麼重要的指示呢？

8 Ταῦτα δίδασκε καὶ <u>παρακάλει</u>. 比較多二 15a 的 Ταῦτα λάλει καὶ <u>παρακάλει</u> καὶ ἔλεγχε. M. A. Schmitz（*TDNT* 5.796 n.173）認為 παρακαλεῖν 的意思是 'urgently to impress on'（使

結束上文（五 1～六 1d）的勸勉。

職權的原文名詞已在一章 3 節出現過。祈勒克認為，它在該處指上帝所賦予保羅的權柄，如此，保羅本節是否暗示，提多分享了保羅自己所擁有的、上帝賦予的權柄呢？[9] 但較自然的看法是，這名詞在一章 3 節是指上帝的**命令**，在這裏則指提多的**職權**，[10] 因而並無暗示祈氏所提議的意思。不過，在這裏重複這字可能提示這樣的意思：就如保羅有上帝的授權，提多有保羅的授權。[11]

充分運用你的職權（15b 節）意即「運用你全部的權柄」，[12] 這權柄是使徒保羅的權柄之延伸，至終是來自上帝的。[13] 在原文，這介詞片語位於第 15a 節的末尾，而在此之前有三個命令式語法的動詞，當中所引起的問題是，這片語是哪個或哪些動詞的修飾語呢？（一）若把這片語只是連於最後一個動詞，所得出的意思就是：**用充分的職權來指責**（呂譯）或**用各等權柄責備人**（新和）。[14] 這種理解有時加

人明白其重要性），最好的翻譯是 'to admonish'（勸告、告誡、警告）。兩種意思似乎不盡相同。

9 Clark, 'Structure' 113. See also Banker 88*b*: 'this message . . . has been entrusted to Paul and now to Titus by the command of God.' 古特立斷言：'Here Paul no doubt means that the Christian minister is endowed with nothing less than a divine authority'（Guthrie I 202; Guthrie II 214〔古特立 216〕）。

10 ἐπιταγή = 'right / the right or authority to command' (BDAG 383*a* [s.v. 2] / LN §37.42);「權柄，職權」(《輔讀》528〔第二、三解釋〕)。

11 Genade 64-65. See also Towner III 767 n.6（唐 1118 註 6）。亦參曾 42：「對於受眾來說，這封信代表保羅的權柄……這信確認提多是代保羅行事的左右手。」Hinson 283 就認為，提多要運用的權柄是保羅的（'He must . . . act . . . with full authority, that is, Paul's'）。（**1**）提摩太是經由**眾長老**及保羅**按手**（提前四 14；提後一 6）而接受了委派作保羅的同工的（參《恩賜》126-27）；關於提多則並無類似的報導。（**2**）雖然如此，Fitzmyer（'Ministry' 587）認為提多擁有**職權**這事實暗示，他的權柄也是從按手得來的（'his "authority" comes from the laying on of hands'）。

12 μετὰ πάσης ἐπιταγῆς = 'with full authority' (Banker 87, 88*b*; Kelly 244, 247; Marshall 297), 'using your full authority' (LN §76.25). πᾶς here = 'full, greatest, all' (BDAG 783*b* [s.v. 3.a]).（**1**）Quinn 28, 177, 178 意譯為 'in as commanding a way as possible' =「以盡可能威嚴的方式」; cf. Fiore II 208: 'with complete insistence'.（**2**）Barrett 139 則認為，ἐπιταγή 'presumably stands for ὡς ἐπιτάσσων, "as if giving orders".'

13 Cf. Marshall 297. 參一 5 註釋註 37、38 所屬正文（上面 97-98）。

14 See also Ward 264: 'The phrase goes with *reprove*'; Mounce 432: 'μετὰ πάσης

上經文沒有明言的一個意思：<u>必要時可以</u>運用權力責備他們（當代）；<u>在必要的時候</u>，你可以行使你的權柄指正他們（新普）。[15]（二）《和合本修訂版》將這片語連於後兩個動詞而得要充分運用你的職權勸勉人，責備人，[16] 這做法所得出的意思更清晰地表達為：以全權規勸和指摘（思高），或充分運用你的職權來勸勉人或責備人（現修）。[17]（三）若把這片語視為「同時形容三個動詞」[18] 的修飾語，所得出的意思就是：「這些事你要以盡可能威嚴的方式講明，無論是在鼓勵人或駁斥人的時候（都要這樣做）。」[19]

從翻譯的角度而言，這些事（直接受格）既然是動詞的賓詞，它

ἐπιταγῆς . . . is appropriate only for the command to rebuke'; Griffin 316: 'the phrase . . . is a noteworthy addition to "rebuke"'; Ngewa 380: 'Paul is speaking of rebuking with authority.'（**1**）Lock 147-48 認為，一 13 你要嚴厲地責備他們（ἔλεγχε αὐτοὺς ἀποτόμως）這話提示，二 15 的 μετὰ πάσης ἐπιταγῆς 只是連於最後一個動詞 ἔλεγχε.（**2**）KJV（'These things speak, and exhort, and rebuke with all authority'）和 NKJV（'Speak these things, exhort, and rebuke with all authority'）似乎反映這種立場（除非這是立場〔三〕)。

15 NLT: 'You have the authority to correct them when necessary'; see also Mounce, 'Titus' 107: 'When necessary, rebuke them with full authority.'

16 參新譯：運用各樣的權柄去勸戒人，責備人。

17 See also NIV, TNIV, NIV2011: 'Encourage and rebuke with all authority'; RSV, NRSV / ESV: 'Declare these things; exhort and reprove/rebuke with all authority'（留意分號）。Cf. Wall 357: 'Talk about these things. Encourage and refute with complete authority'（留意句號）。

18 張 360。See also Knight II 329: 'μετὰ πάσης ἐπιταγῆς . . . probably modifies all three [verbs]'; Smith 335: 'All three activities were to be done "with full authority"'; cf. 285-86. 三個動詞由兩個 καί 字連起來。這現象稱為 'polysyndeton'（Spencer 52）；n.78 的解釋卻有欠準確，因作者說，'the same conjunction *kai* is used <u>between each verb</u>.' 但介系詞 'between' 之後不可能只有一個單數的賓詞。

19 Quinn 28: 'These are the things to speak of, Titus, in as commanding a way as possible, whether you are encouraging or refuting.' See also NAU: 'These things speak and exhort and reprove with all authority'; Young 78: 'these are the themes, the exhortations, the reproofs you must offer with all command'.（**1**）似乎反映立場（三）的英譯本還有 NJB: 'This is what you must say, encouraging or arguing with full authority'（除非這是立場〔二〕)。（**2**）DC 142*a* 則把 μετὰ πάσης ἐπιταγῆς 翻譯為 'with all impressiveness'（thus also BDAG 302*a* [endorsed by Ward 264, Marshall 297, and Saarinen 184]）。作者們認為這詞語應理解為命令（林前七 6：κατ' ἐπιταγήν, 'by command'）的加強版（146*a*）。如此，'with all impressiveness' 的意思到頭來與 'with all authority' 相近（see BDAG 383*a* [s.v. 2]: 'with all or full authority'）。

就不適宜作**勸勉**或**責備**的賓詞（「勸勉這些事」還勉強可以，但「責備這些事」是無意義的，因為**這些事**的內容都是正面的）；但是很難認為，保羅的意思是說，只在勸勉人或責備人的時候，提多才需要充分運用他的職權，講明這些事的時候則不需要。因此，討論中的介詞片語在意思上很可能是同時連於三個動詞的，但**這些事**則只是第一個動詞的賓詞，[20] 所得出的整個意思就是：「**要充分運用你的職權**（i）講明這些事，（ii）勸勉人，和（iii）使那些反對的人（一 9c）認識自己的錯誤」[21]（第一個賓詞是經文提供的，第二和第三個賓詞是根據文理而加上的）。[22]

不要讓任何人輕看你（15c 節）[23] 這句話，從反面重申提多具有

20 Thus also F. Büchsel, *TDNT* 2.474 n.5: 'This [2:15a] is a careless construction, since ταῦτα is correct only with λάλει'——儘管表面上 'ταῦτα is the object of all three following verbs'（Knight II 329）。

21 參黃編 216：「『責備』指藉暴露其錯誤使之歸正。」

22 Cf. Banker 87, 88*a*: 'Teach (the believers) these things . . . , urge (them to do them), and correct (those who do not follow them).' 利斐特 359 卻認為，「這裡的 "講論"、"勸戒"，和 "責備" 都是以人作其賓語〔Liefeld 341: 'all have people as their object'〕。」筆者加上底線的部分不能成立，因為經文明說 ταῦτα λάλει: 賓詞是**這些事**。由此看來，'object' 在這裏是否應改譯為「對象」呢？

23 對於這種翻譯，Clark（'Structure' 113）'from the translation point of view' 提出異議。祈氏聲稱，由於原文動詞（περιφρονείτω）是第三人稱的命令式語法動詞，因此本句（像三 14a 一樣〔該處也是用了第三人稱命令式動詞〕）是給克里特教會的其他會友（而不是給提多）的指示；'Let no one disregard you'（so *EDNT* 3.80*a* [s.v. περιφρονέω]）的意思是 'Other people must not disregard you', 而不是 'Don't let other people disregard you'. 他問道：'How could Titus stop them if they were determined enough?' 筆者認為祈氏的論證沒有說服力，因為：（**i**）'Other people must not disregard you'（cf. NJB: 'No one should despise you'）或 'No one is to disregard you'（筆者自譯）這話仍是對提多說的，因而它的實質意義仍然是〔**你**〕**不要讓任何人輕視你**（思高）。（**ii**）雖然三 14 的 μανθανέτωσαν οἱ ἡμέτεροι 的意思確是 'Let our people learn' (RSV, NRSV, ESV) = 'Our people must learn' (NIV, TNIV, NIV2011), 但不見得這話就是對教會的會友而不是對提多說的；因為這話是保羅對提多的指示（三 12～14）的一部分，因而其實質意義等於說，「你要使／教導我們的人學習」。（**iii**）二 15c（μηδείς σου περιφρονείτω）的第三人稱命令式語法動詞的意義，有別於加六 17（κόπους μοι μηδεὶς παρεχέτω）的第三人稱命令式語法動詞的意義：前者是保羅對提多（**你**）說的話，後者才是保羅對別人說的話；事實上，**不要有人再攪擾我**很可能是保羅對其敵對者的警告（參《加》1430-31）。

宣講、勸勉和責備的權柄（15a～b 節）。[24] **輕看**原文動詞的另一翻譯是「使（你的權柄）成為無效」。[25] 這句話使人想起保羅對提摩太同樣的囑咐：**不要讓人小看你年輕**（提前四 12，思高）。[26] 在該節，**你〔的〕年輕**是**小看**的賓詞，句子的意思自然是**不要讓人<u>因</u>你年輕<u>而</u>小看你**（新普）；在本節，**輕看**或**輕視**（呂譯、思高、當代）的賓詞是**你**。[27]（一）有釋經者認為，提多和提摩太二人，在教牧書信中都被描寫為保羅較年輕的伙伴，「在他們各自的崗位上被委任有權威的職位」。[28] 而保羅對他們的鼓勵（**不要讓……**）可能提示，有人抗拒

---

24 See Banker 89*b*: '2:15c is a negative restatement of 2:15a-b especially in reference to "with all authority."'

25 LN §76.25: 'let no one invalidate your authority'.

26 基里認為，提摩太也許是 'in his middle or late thirties'（Kelly 2）。保羅告訴哥林多人：**無論誰都不可藐視他**（林前十六 11，μή τις . . . αὐτὸν ἐξουθενήσῃ）。鮑維均認為，'the language of despising is frequently understood within the honor and shame framework, and therefore "let no one despise" a person should be considered a call to attribute honor to that individual within the structure of a particular community'（Pao, 'Church' 747）。'He is to be honored not because of his youthful energy and accomplishment, but because he represents ultimately the living God who alone deserves all "honor," "glory," and "power" (1:17; 6:16)'（752）。

27 比較：　Μηδείς σου τῆς νεότητος καταφρονείτω（提前四 12）
　　　　　μηδείς σου　　　　　　　　εριφρονείτω　（多二 15）

兩個動詞的意思相同（Carl Schneider, *TDNT* 3.633）。兩個動詞之後的賓詞皆為所有格（林前十六 11 的賓詞〔見上註〕則為直接受格）。新普／NLT 將本節原文的**你**意譯為**你所說的話**／'what you say'.（**1**）提前四 12 所用的動詞（καταφρονέω）在多二 15 以 περιφρονέω 之異文的形式出現（see BDAG 529 [s.v. 1]），可見兩個動詞是同義詞。'περιφρονεῖν forms a substitute, comparatively rare, for the common καταφρονεῖν' (Simpson 110).（**2**）多二 15 所用的動詞（**περιφρονέω**）在新約不再出現。它在偽經《馬加比四書》出現三次，所「輕看」的都是不同形式的痛苦（6.9 ἀνάγκη, 'punishment'; 7.16 βάσανος, 'torture'; 14.1 ἀλγηδών, 'agony' [see RSV, NRSV]）。在多二 15 本節，英譯本多作 'despise'（KJV, NKJV, NIV, TNIV, NIV2011, NJB; *Paraphrase* 293: 'despises'）、'disregard'（RSV, NAU, ESV, NLT）、'look down on'（NRSV; Fiore II 208）。See also Hendriksen 370, 377, Quinn 28, 177, 178, 181: 'slight'.

28 Keegan II 100（Keegan I 63）。Marshall 296 認為，二 7～8 很可能指向提多是年輕的。（**1**）關於提多，參導論第貳節首段（上面 23-24）；關於提摩太，參《西．門》104-5；詳參《帖前》47-48；《羅》4.787-88。（**2**）Fellows（'Titus'）提出「提多－提摩太論」（33），即這兩個（從不一起出現的）名字是屬同一人的；林後及加拉太書的**提多**只是提摩太所用的、非正式的名字（58），這與古代的做法一致（34-35）。釋經者普遍不接受此說（《加》382 註 20）。

（或至少不滿意）這種安排。[29] 不過，(二) 本節沒有提到提多是年輕的，這可能表示提多比提摩太年長。[30] **而不要讓任何人輕看你**這句話，可能與人們（尤其是那些假教師〔一 10：**不受約束**〕）反權威的自然趨勢有關。[31] 兩節的原文都使用第三人稱的命令式語法動詞；[32] 本節直譯的意思是「任何人都不可輕看你」，[33] 因此基里認為，保羅這句話是講給克里特的教會聽，多過是講給提多本人聽的。[34] 不過，當第三人稱的命令式語法動詞的主詞是「沒有人」[35] 的時候，對收信人來說，這動詞的語意功用就像第二人稱的命令式語法動詞一樣。[36]

---

29 Fiore II 19. Cf. Marshall 251: 這裏反映的問題是，'the youthfulness of appointed leaders was not acceptable to the older generation.' 但見二 7～8a 註釋註 9（中文部分）= 上面 260。

30 Fee 198. 再看二 7～8a 註釋註 9（中文部分）= 上面 260。**(1)** Witherington 74 認為，提多 'is called upon to be an example "to the younger men,"* 這顯然暗示 'he is older than they are'.（*但見二 7～8a 註釋註 9 及所屬正文〔上面 259-60〕。）**(2)** Ramsay 119 甚至認為，'Throughout Titus 2 it is evident that the person addressed must rank among the *presbyteroi*, for he is conceived as entitled to address both the elderly and the younger men and women in the same tone, and not like Timothy, who as a younger man was expected to use a different style to the elderly from what he used to those of vigorous age [see 1 Tim. 5:1-2].' 由此看來，藍賽的 '*presbyteroi*' 似乎不是指一 5 的**長老**（πρεσβυτέρους），而是指二 2 的老年人（πρεσβύτας）。

31 Cf. Bassler 202: 這句警告的話 'should . . . be linked to the letter's general concern over rebellion against authority (1:6, 10) and not taken as an allusion to Titus's age or inexperience'（Witherington 151: 'Bassler . . . may be right'）；Mounce 433: 'Why would Paul express concern for Titus? Perhaps because there was a natural opposition to authority, especially when that authority was demanding a change in behavior.'

32 見上面註 27。

33 NJB: 'no one should despise you.' See also Kelly 244: 'No one must underrate you.'

34 Kelly 248: 'the remark is intended <u>more</u> for the Cretan churches <u>than</u> for Titus himself.' 基里表示同意加爾文的見解；see Calvin 376: 'here he [Paul] is addressing the people <u>rather than</u> Titus.'

35 μηδείς, 如在本節、提前四 12，和以下各節：林前三 18、21，十 24；弗五 6；西二 18；雅一 13；約壹三 7。（但加六 17 不在此列；見註 23 之〔iii〕= 上面 345；參《加》1431。）

36 Banker 89*a*. 留意提前四 11～12a 和多二 15 都從第二人稱命令式語法動詞轉到第三人稱命令式語法動詞，但是提前四 12b 再回到第二人稱命令式語法動詞：

因此，這句話確是對提多說的。與此同時，這句話也是保羅對克里特信徒的警告，告訴他們不可輕視提多。總言之，雖然就原文動詞的形式而論，動詞的主詞是「沒有人（可以輕視你）」，但是從語意的角度來說，提多才是這命令的對象（不要讓人輕看你〔現修〕），[37] 而就保羅的用意而言，看來他也要克里特的信徒不可輕視提多，[38] 而是要尊敬提多，[39] 因他具有經由保羅而來的、上帝所賦予的權柄（一5，二 15a）。[40]

	第二人稱命令式語法	第三人稱命令式語法
提前四 11	你要囑咐（παράγγελλε）和教導（δίδασκε）這些事	
提前四 12a		不可叫人小看你年輕（καταφρονείτω）
提前四 12b	總要……作（γίνου）信徒的榜樣	
多二 15a	這些事你要講明（λάλει）……要……勸勉人（παρακάλει），責備人（ἔλεγχε）	
多二 15c		不要讓任何人輕看你（περιφρονείτω）

提前四 11～16 整段都明顯是對提摩太講的勸勉話，因此，四 12a 那個命令的執行者很不可能由提摩太改為別人；這一點進一步支持正文的論點，即是多二 15c 那個命令的執行者並沒有由提多改為別人。So Banker 89*b*.

37 See Marshall 298: 'the primary force of it is surely an appeal to Titus himself = "Don't let anybody despise you"'; Mounce, 'Titus' 107: 'Don't let anyone treat you with disrespect'; Towner III 767（唐 1119）：'the force of the command is personal; that is, "Titus, even if someone disrespects your authority, do not be dissuaded from your task."'

38 Banker 89*a-b*. See also Lock 148: 'It probably implies advice both to Titus and to his hearers.'
Hendriksen 377-81 n.193 詳細反駁「多二章含有許多只出現一次的字詞（*hapax legomena*），因而保羅不可能是提多書的作者」之說。

39 參註 26（上面 346）。

40 參註 13 所屬正文（上面 343），一 5 註釋註 37、38 及所屬正文（上面 97-98）。

伍　與福音相符的生活：之二（三 1～8）

5.1　做公民的義務（三 1～2）[1]

1 你要提醒眾人，叫他們順服執政的、掌權的，要服從，預備行各樣善事。
2 不要毀謗，不要爭吵，要和氣，對眾人總要顯出
溫柔。

在上一大段（二 1～15）結束時，末尾一節回到提多在開首一節的顯著地位，保羅以一連串的命令式語法動詞囑咐提多，這些事你要講明，要……勸勉人，責備人。不要讓任何人輕看你。三章 1 節的你要提醒眾人自然地延續了上一節那四個命令語法的動詞，與前三個的關係尤其密切，因為那三個動詞和這一個（提醒）都是關乎教導的。[2] 另外，雖然二章 15 節並無明確表示那三個動詞的賓詞是誰，但合乎邏輯的推論是，他們就是接受了上帝拯救之恩和基督的救贖（11～14 節）的人（責備則特別適用於那些反對的人〔一 9c〕和他們的跟隨者）；如此，可以推論本節的眾人也是指他們。由此可見，目前的兩節跟二章 15 節的銜接是順暢的。[3] 三章 1 至 2 節在原文只是一句，由一

1　參導論第伍節註 15（上面 34）。See also Van Neste, 'Message' 24*a*: 'Paul explains what Christian behavior looks like . . . in relation to the outside world (3:1-2)'; Towner III 769: 'Christian Living within Society (3:1-2)' =「基督徒活在社會中」（唐 1121）。Wild 894*a* 則以 'Christian Duties within Society' 為三 1～8 這一整段的標題。

2　Van Neste 260. Wendland（'Discourse' 340）認為，動詞提醒合併了「教導」和「鼓勵」兩個意思。

3　Van Neste 260.

個命令式語法的動詞（你要提醒）加賓詞（眾人），引進五個不定詞（構成六個項目）以及末尾的分詞片語。[4] 這兩節的教導是給眾人的，而不是給教會內某些組別的人（如在二 1～10）；這足以解釋為甚麼作者沒有將這些教導納入該段，而是在這裏重新開始。[5]

簡內德認為，這兩節的教導是關乎信徒應該對教外人（更明確地說，就是未得救的克里特人）顯出這兩節所列舉的正面行為。[6] 這些教導的目的，是避免外界懷疑或批評教會破壞社會秩序。[7]

---

4 Van Neste 246. 五個不定詞之所以構成六個項目，是由於第五個不定詞的前後都有屬於它的述語形容詞（predicate adjective）：ἀμάχους εἶναι ἐπιεικεῖς（不要爭吵，要和氣）。

5 Marshall 298.

6 Genade 87 ('outsiders'), 88 ('these unsaved Cretans'). 按簡內德的理解，三 4～7 的主要修辭目的就是要說服克里特的信徒，向那些被視為「不值得（undeserving）」的人行善，是與上帝行事的榜樣相符的（80, 115, 118, 120-21）。假教師似乎鼓勵他們的跟隨者把異教的鄰舍孤立起來甚或敵視他們，認為不值得跟他們來往；保羅在本段對這種思想迎頭痛擊（88 [see also 118]）。

7 Fiore II 217.

三 1 你要提醒眾人，叫他們順服執政的、掌權的，要服從，[1] 預備行各樣善事。

動詞**提醒**暗示，本節的教導對克里特的信徒來說不是新的，他們已經接受過這方面的口頭教導；只是，保羅認為有需要提醒他們。[2] **提醒**原文的現在時態提示繼續不斷的行動。[3] 籠統的**眾人**（原文作**他們**〔新譯〕）[4] 形式上是指上文提到的**老年人**（二 2）、**年長的婦女**（二 3）、**年輕人**（二 6）和**僕人**（二 9），[5] 但在意思上一定也包括**年輕的婦女**和她們的**丈夫**、**兒女**（二 4），以及僕人的**主人**（二 9）——如果這些丈夫、兒女和主人是信主的。《新普及譯本》在這裏就正確地意譯為**你要提醒<u>信徒</u>**。[6] 換句話說，這裏的**他們**是上述各組別的統

1 如 Banker 94*b* 所指出，原文的四個字可視為構成工整的對應：兩個無連詞的名詞（ἀρχαῖς ἐξουσίαις: **執政的**、**掌權的**）在先，隨後是兩個無連詞的不定詞（ὑποτάσσεσθαι, πειθαρχεῖν: **順服**、**服從**）。不過，班約翰的用詞自相矛盾（a contradiction in terms），他說：'two nouns <u>linked by asyndeton</u> immediately followed by two verbs <u>linked by asyndeton</u>'; 可是，'asyndeton' 所來自的形容詞（asyndetic, ἀ-σύν-δετος）的意思正是 'not bound together, <u>unconnected</u>'（Harris, *Colossians* 292）。

2 Marshall 300. 唐書禮認為，這需要是由於克里特的假教師的教導和行為與使徒傳統相左並造成破壞（Towner III 770〔唐 1122-23〕）。參 ·11。

3 See Wallace 485: 'With the *present* [imperative], the force generally is to *command the action as an ongoing process*'; Quinn 183: 'keep reminding'.「*hypomimneskō* [*sic*] . . . 此字在此處是 middle voice, 故有要甘心順服之意」（張 367 註 4）這話顯然有誤：後面的解釋應指隨後的不定詞 ὑποτάσσεσθαι（**順服**）而非動詞 ὑπομίμνησκε（**提醒**）。

4 αὐτούς, 不是 2 節／二 11 的「所有的人」：πάντας ἀνθρώπους / πᾶσιν ἀνθρώποις（和修皆作**眾人**）。

5 So Clark, 'Structure' 114.

6 NLT: 'Remind the believers'. See also NIV, TNIV, NIV2011: 'Remind the people'; Arichea－Hatton 296: 'Remind the Cretan Christians'. **(1)** 動詞 **ὑπομιμνῄσκω**（see BDAG 1039*b* [s.v.];《新希》341*a* [s.v.]）在新約另外出現六次，一次為被動語態，意思是「被提醒」= **想起**（路二十二 61）；五次為主動語態，意思是**提醒**（提後二 14；彼後一 12；猶 5 節），**使（你們）想起**（約十四 26），或**提起**（約叁 10 節），後者在文理中可意譯為「報告」（NLT: 'report'）或**揭發**（現修、新普）。**(2)** 這動詞在 LXX 出現四次，其意思分別為「記錄者」（王上四 3：**史官**）、「〔使人〕<u>想起</u>所犯的罪惡」（次經《所羅門智訓》12.2〔思高智慧篇〕）、無可指責的人「<u>提起</u>上主與祖先所發的誓」（18.22〔思高〕），以及七子之父在生時「<u>使</u>〔猶太人〕<u>想起</u>以

稱，[7] 所指的是教會的所有成員。[8] 他們被提醒要做或不要做的事，有以下七項（在原文由五個不定詞和一個分詞以無連詞的形式表達），前三項關乎他們與政府的關係，後四項則關乎他們與眾人的關係。[9]

（**#1**）動詞**順服**已在上文出現兩次，其對象分別是妻子的**丈夫**（二5）和僕人的**主人**（二 9）；這裏的對象則為**執政的**、**掌權的**，[10] 即是

賽亞的話」（偽經《馬加比四書》18.14）。

7 See Genade 67-68.

8 Scott 171: 'the Christians in Crete'; Hiebert 442: 'the members of the churches'; Marshall 300: 'all the members of the church'. Quinn 28, 177 則意譯為 'these Jewish Christians', 解釋為 'these Jewish-Christian opponents of an ethical commitment as well as of a creedal one'（183）。See Quinn 182-83:「他們（αὐτούς）」是指提多先前被指示**要嚴厲地責備**（一 13）的那些敵對保羅的福音的「猶太基督徒」。這見解被評為 'without much warrant'（Marshall 300 n.3）。

9 Marshall 300 按其內容將這七項歸納為四項基本要求，分為兩對：'subjection to authorities [##1-2] and readiness for good works [#3]; non-aggression [##4-6] and showing patience to everybody [#7].'

10 （**1**）比較這裏的 ἀρχαῖς ἐξουσίαις（複數間接受格）和路十二 11 的 τὰς ἀρχὰς <u>καὶ</u> τὰς ἐξουσίας（**官長和掌權的人**；複數直接受格）。前兩個字之間並無 καί 字（Lock 152 認為它是意外地被漏去），就如隨後的三個不定詞之間亦無 καί 字，可見兩次的 asyndeton（無連詞現象）都是刻意的（Classen, 'Titus' 440 n.41, 'Epistle to Titus' 60 n.48. BDF §460(1) 也認為，如果原來的讀文並無 καί 字，前一次的無連詞現象是因第二次的無連詞現象而導致的）。事實上，3 節的七個項目同樣沒有 καί 字把它們或最後兩項連起來（第四項之內則以 καί 字將兩個名詞 ἐπιθυμίαις 和 ἡδοναῖς 連起來）；〈公認經文〉（《聖神》508*a*）在 ἀρχαῖς 之後有 καί 字，但這是有抄寫員想要 'relieve the asyndeton' 的結果（*TextC* 586）。因此，沒有必要把這裏的 ἀρχαῖς 視為 ἐξουσίαις 的形容詞而得 'chief authorities'（Richards 70）、'governing/government authorities'（Smith 358 / Quinn 28, 177, 178, 182, 183, 209; also K. Weiss, *EDNT* 1.162*b* [s.v. ἀρχή, 3 c]）、'ruling authorities / the ruling authorities'（Jeon I 87, 89, 90, 91; Jeon II 28 / Aageson 54; Richards 87; Wild 895*b*）、'"authorities who rule" or "powerful rulers"'（Arichea－Hatton 296）或 'legitimate rulers'（Collins 357）等意思（so, correctly, Genade 70）。

（**2**）Ward 265 這樣區別**執政的**和**掌權的**：'The *rulers* means those who are actually ruling; *authorities* tells us that they have the right to do so.' See already Hendriksen 386: 'those . . . who not only actually *rule* but as such have also been invested with divine *authority*'. 此區別似乎亦適用於路二十 20 單數的 τῇ ἀρχῇ καὶ τῇ ἐξουσίᾳ τοῦ ἡγεμόνου, 'the rule and the authority [= right to rule] of the governor'（NAU），'the jurisdiction and authority of the governor'（NRSV, NJB）。（**3**）Marshall 300 則認為，兩個名詞一起 'are meant to cover all possibilities, and are probably not to be sharply distinguished.'

（**3**）名詞 **ἀρχή** 在保羅書信一共出現十一次（新約全部 55 次），除了兩次分別指保羅傳福音的**初期**（腓四 15，現修、新譯）和基督是**元始**（西一 18），另一次與**天**

政府當局。[11] 如在上兩次，動詞的中間語態提示自願順從的意思。[12] 如此，順服由家裏開始（當時的僕人是「一戶」的成員），亦應展現於世俗的社會中。[13] 順服政府當局這項要求亦見於新約其他的書信（羅十三 1～7；彼前二 13～17）；有認為克里特人的已知的騷動，使這項要求在這裏尤其適切，[14] 但是鑑於假教師是**不受約束的**（一 10，參一 6b），也許這裏的教導跟假教師的影響所造成的不順服的趨勢有

使和有權能的一起出現（羅八 38），其餘八次都與 ἐξουσία 連著出現；在其中，**執政的**、**掌權的**／**執政掌權者**／**執政者**、**掌權者**有七次指靈界的權勢（林前十五 24；弗一 21，三 10，六 12；西一 16／二 10／二 15），餘下一次則指地上的執政者（多三 1 本節）。參《西・門》216 註 15；BDAG 137*b*-38*b* (s.v.);《新希》46*b*（s.v.）。**（4）**名詞 **ἐξουσία** 在保羅書信一共出現 27 次（新約全部 102 次），呈現四個主要意思：（**i**）抉擇上的**自由**（林前八 9；參林前七 37〔呂譯**主權**〕），例如陶匠所擁有的**權力**（羅九 21），某些事情上的**權利**（林前九 4、5、6、12a、12b、18）；（**ii**）**權柄**（羅十三 1b；林前十一 10；林後十 8，十三 10；帖後三 9）；（3）之下的「其餘八次」亦屬於此處；（**iii**）**有權柄的**（羅十三 1a），即是**掌權的**（羅十三 2、3）；（**iv**）掌權者行使權力的範疇，例如黑暗的**王國**（西一 13，新普），惡者在其中行使他的權力的領域（弗二 2〔參《弗》271-73〕）。參《西・門》174；BDAG 352*b*-53*b* (s.v.);《新希》120*a*（s.v.）。

11 NEB, REB: 'the government and the authorities'; H. Bietenhard, *DNTT* 1.166: 'the civil powers and the authorities'; O. Becker, *DNTT* 1.593, K. H. Bartels, *DNTT* 3.243, Zehr 270: 'rulers and authorities'; Hiebert 443: '"Rulers and authorities," two abstract nouns, signifies not the individual rulers but the various forms of human government'; Marshall 301: 'Governmental officials, whether imperial, national or local, are in mind.' See also W. Foerster, *TDNT* 2.565: 'It [ἐξουσία] is . . . used, often in the plur., for the authorities, Lk. 12:11; R. 13:1; Tt. 3:1'; BDAG 353*a* (s.v. 5 a): 'bearer of authority—human *authorities*, *officials*, government'.

12 參二 4b～5a 註釋註 36 及所屬正文（上面 248-49）；二 9～10 註釋註 18 及所屬正文（上面 272）。1～2 這兩節所談論的都是信徒與別人（不是與上帝）的關係，因此**服從**並不是指對上帝的服從（Banker 94*b*）。

13 Genade 128 稱之為 'Thematic progression' 的例子：'Thus, submission starts in the home, then moves to the place of employment, and finally occurs within secular society.' 但見正文括號內的解釋（「一戶」即 'household'）；簡內德的講法較適用於現代的社會結構。

14 Hiebert 443. **（1）**古特立也認為，保羅在這裏顯然害怕，動蕩不安的克里特人會輕易地使教會牽連於政治騷動中，而這只會使福音受到懷疑（Guthrie I 202; Guthrie II 214〔古特立 216〕）。**（2）**按司各脫的理解，作者（不是保羅）這麼強調基督徒「公民順命（civil obedience）」的責任，一方面是由於克里特人「因他們的騷亂傾向是聲名狼藉的（notoriously inclined to turbulence）」；另一方面，對政權的任何抗爭都可能導致整個教會受到逼迫，因此，基督徒即使受到不公義的對待，但是為了使教會能繼續生存，對人類作出教會真正的貢獻，他們仍得讓步，避免一切的政治騷亂（Scott 171-72）。

關連。[15]

（**#2**）要服從，（**#3**）預備行各樣善事與一章 16 節對那些敵對者的描寫構成令人矚目的對比：[16] 他們……是悖逆的，不配做任何好事。服從與悖逆相對；[17] 預備行各樣善事和不配做任何好事相對，兩者在原文只是一字之差，[18] 加上第一項順服與一章 10 節的不受約束相對，[19] 這裏對信徒應有表現的描寫，似乎是刻意地與第一章對反對者的描寫構成對比的。從原文的結構來看，不定詞服從是獨立於順服執政的、掌權的，並無連詞將前者連於後者；白新港認為服從的對象比順服的對象（執政掌權者）更廣，卻沒有解釋那些更廣的對象是甚

15 Cf. Marshall 299: 'the teaching may have been called forth by a tendency towards insubordinate behaviour somehow associated with the influence of the errorists.' 參註 2（上面 351）。

16 Van Neste, 'Structure' 125. Genade 70/130 稱之為 'Implicit contrast/contrasting' 的修辭技巧。

17 原文依次為：形容詞 ἀπειθεῖς（一 16，from ἀπειθής），不定詞 πειθαρχεῖν（三 1，from πειθαρχέω）；這些字是同字根的。（**1**）動詞 **πειθαρχέω** 在新約僅再出現三次，分別指順從上帝（徒五 29、32）和聽保羅的話（二十七 21）。See BDAG 791*a* (s.v.);《新希》259*a*（s.v.）。（**2**）這字是複合動詞（from πείθομαι, 'to be persuaded', + ἀρχή, 'rule' [Vine 2.206]; *EDNT* 3.62*b* [s.v. πειθαρχέω] 認為其字面意義是 'obey an authority/power (ἀρχή)'）。動詞 πείθω 在新約一共出現 52 次，其中 22 次是中間或被動語態的 πείθομαι（see MGM 864*b*-65*b*），包括保羅書信的七次（順從：羅二 8；加五 7；深信：羅八 38，十四 14，十五 14；提後一 5、12）；名詞 ἀρχή 見上面註 10 之（3）。

18 原文依次為：πρὸς πᾶν ἔργον ἀγαθὸν ἑτοίμους, πρὸς πᾶν ἔργον ἀγαθὸν ἀδόκιμοι. πρός '[a]fter adjectives [as here and 1:16] and participles [=] *for*' (BDAG 874*b* [s.v. πρός, 3 c β]).（**1**）C. Brown（*DNTT* 3.197）認為，πᾶς 兩次的意思都是 'not all, in an absolute and inclusive sense, but all kinds of'（C. Brown, *DNTT* 3.197）。參一 16 註釋註 30 之（1）= 上面 212。（**2**）形容詞 **ἕτοιμος** 在保羅書信僅再出現三次（林後九 5，十 6、16），新約另外十三次：其意思分別是（**i**）要預備（太二十四 44；路十二 40）／作好準備（彼前三 15，新譯）；（**ii**）預備妥當（林後九 5；太二十二 4〔新譯〕；可十四 15〔新譯〕）／預備好了（林後十 6；太二十五 10；徒二十三 21）／已準備好（路二十二 33）／已經預備好（徒二十三 15；彼前一 5〔現修〕）／已經齊備了（思高：太二十二 8 ‖ 路十四 17）；（**iii**）他人……所成就的工作〔林後十 16，現修〕）；（**iv**）耶穌的兄弟隨時都方便（約七 6，現修）。

19 原文依次為同字根的動詞 ὑποτάσσεσθαι（from ὑποτάσσω）和形容詞 ἀνυπότακτοι（from ἀνυπότακτος）。Barrett 139 建議將 ὑποτάσσεσθαι 翻譯為 'respect the authority of'(cf. NEB at 2:5, 9)：'the Christian may and must recognize the (God-given) authority of the state, but without being submissive to it in a servile way.'

麼。[20] 本節提到順服和服從，也許是為要同時強調態度（順服）與行為（服從）。[21] 周天和正確指出，「保羅在此沒有提到政府的法例是否屬於公正的法例；也沒有討論，若政府的法例與基督徒的信仰相抵〔原文照錄〕觸時，基督徒當怎樣行。他所假定的原則是，政府的責任是維護正義，賞善罰惡，對這樣的政府，基督徒有責任做個奉公守法的好公民。」[22] 在羅馬書十三章 3 至 4

20 White 197*b*. Knight II 332 則認為，執政的、掌權的也是服從的賓詞。

21 Lock 152: ὑποτάσσεσθαι '[is used] of the general attitude', πειθαρχεῖν 'of obedience to particular commands', 例如納糧（羅十三 6；see also Towner I 196; Towner II 252）；Griffin 318: 'Christians [are] "to be subject" (in attitude) and "to be obedient" (in action)'; Hiebert 443: '"To be obedient" states the result and visible demonstration of their attitude of submission'; Bouwman 133: 'Obedience, then, is the daily face of "submission."' See also Barclay 258: 'to be duly subject to those who are in power and authority, to obey each several [= separate] command'; 馮譯：服從掌權的長官，遵守法令。(**1**) Johnson I 133 則這樣解釋：'an attitude of "submission" . . . is what Paul commands. In addition, he interiorizes and extends the meaning of that submission. It is . . . to be matched by a spirit of obedience.' 如此，順服指外在的態度，服從指內在的心態。See already Hendriksen 386: 'believers must not only in a general way *outwardly subject themselves* but must even be *inwardly obedient*'.(**2**) Wilson（*Luke* 41）認為這裏的兩個動詞一起使用 'reinforces the absolute nature of the command, and apparently no exceptions are envisaged.'

22 周 436-37。Cf. Marshall 299 n.2: 'only "normal" circumstances are in mind, and worship of the emperor was out of the question'; 302: 'A statement describing the ruler's responsibility to dispense justice is lacking (though probably assumed) in Titus.' See also Witherington 155: 'we must see this as a general exhortation that excludes any capitulation to clearly non-Christian conduct'; Oden 87: 'such powers are not to be obeyed when they are idolatrously opposed to the Creator. Then one must obey God rather than men (Acts 5:29)'; Mounce 444: 'as is true throughout Paul and the NT, obedience to God overrides all other concerns, especially the evil demands of an ungodly government'. (**1**) Witherington 155（引 Barrett 139-40）指出，順服……要服從這命令很可能寫於「帝國之內所有人都要敬拜皇帝」這命令被頒佈之前，即是在一世紀末、一定是在多米田（81-96）之前。(**2**) 特土良的一名對手聲稱，多三 1 的囑咐表示他們有責任遵照羅馬皇帝的諭令向偶像敬拜；特土良則指出，保羅所說的順服和服從並不包括偶像敬拜，* 而且對手忽視了但以理書清楚的見證：四個主角拒絕王要他們敬拜偶像的命令。'For Tertullian, Daniel is used to interpret Titus on the basis of what he saw as the clear scriptural injunction against idolatry, while his opponent had mis-read Titus on the basis of lax discipline'（Frisius, *Tertullian's Use* 79）。*69: 'For Tertullian, the natural sense of obedience did not include idolatry, or the deification of an emperor.' See also Gorday 302*b*. (**3**) 亦參黃編 220：「這個命令是針對一般正常情況而發的，並不適用於任何反常的情形，例如：（1）當違背神清楚而明確的話語和旨意時，便須採用『順從神不順從人』的原則（徒五 29）；（2）當違反道德規範時，便須採用『不要犯罪』的原則（林前十五 34；來十 26）；（3）

節，[23] 保羅同樣「假定了執政者正當地行使職權，維持正義。保羅沒有提出（更遑論討論）特殊情況（例如：政府迫害信徒）所引起的問題，他只是指出，在正常的情況下執政者是賞善罰惡的。」[24]

有釋經者指出，「初代教會『順服政府』的教導，需從〔當代〕的法律制度與社會現象來理解」;「就法律而言，羅馬本身的宗教與帝國內各民族的古老宗教，均受到羅馬法律的保障，但新興宗教則無法律的保障。就社會而言，新興宗教往往因其狂熱的儀式或反社會秩序的色彩，被羅馬帝國視為社會的亂源。……主後一世紀的基督教，為一新興的宗教現象，亦為當時社會中極端弱勢的群體，觸怒政府將危

當被迫放棄信仰的自由時，便須才〔原文照錄〕用『在主裏聽從』的原則（弗六 1；約壹二 6）。」但「被迫放棄信仰的自由」是否等於「被迫放棄信仰」？若是，這肯定是「違背神清楚……的……旨意」的。另外，「在主裏聽從」的原則是指甚麼呢？因此，對筆者而言，(3) 的意思並不清晰。

23 作官的原不是要使行善的懼怕，而是要使作惡的懼怕。你願意不懼怕掌權的嗎？只要行善，你就可得他的稱讚；因為他是上帝的用人，是與你有益的。你若作惡，就該懼怕，因為他不是徒然佩劍；他是上帝的用人，為上帝的憤怒，報應作惡的。

24 《羅》4.242。（這在彼前二 13～14 表達得更簡潔清晰：你們為主的緣故要順服人的一切制度，或是在上的君王，或是君王所派懲惡賞善的官員。）亦參辛惠蘭：〈從命？〉143：「保羅在羅馬書十三章 1 至 7 節並未要求信徒無條件和無區分地去順服掌權者。他的教導是以掌權者履行上主設立政權的原意，維持社會正常秩序，按著上主旨意賞善罰惡為前題〔原文照錄〕，其實並未處理當政權沒有按上主原先心意賞善罰惡時，信徒應有的回應。」**(1)** Fee 201 指出，多三 1 的指示跟羅十三 1～7（作者說 'Romans 13:1-8'）是一致的，它們反映在保羅當代，「國家／政府仍是善待基督徒的（the state was still a benefactor of Christians）」。**(2)** Horrell（'Ideologies' 117）稱羅十三 1～7 為 'a passage clearly echoed by Tit. 3.1'. Mounce 444 也認為，'This injunction [to be subject to the governing authorities] agrees with Paul's teaching in Rom 13:1-7 . . . although it is more cursory.' Krause II 609 說，'The rhetoric of Titus 3:1-2 stands as shorthand of the earlier argument of Rom. 13:1-7.' **(3)** 關於羅十三 1～7 這一段，筆者的理解可參《羅》4.203-79（278-79 總結）。薛霞霞指出，「羅馬書十三章 1 至 7 節並非保羅專門論述政教關係的經文，而是置於基督徒新生活的倫理框架之下的一個片段，即教會信徒如何彼此對待及處理與外部群體關係的論說中的一個片段」(〈上文下理〉074，參 076)；她的結論是（076），「保羅在向外邦人宣教的處境之下，藉羅馬書十三章 1 至 7 節特別重申外邦政權在神救贖計劃當中的作用，所提到的要順服掌權的，在當時是為了勸勉信徒順服神及其救贖計劃。」筆者同意她所指出的事實（參《羅》4.215-17），但是對她的結論有保留：「外邦的執政者也可以為神所用，成為神救恩救贖〔原文照錄〕計劃的一部分，使福音可以廣傳至列邦列國當中」(076) 這思想在該段經文（及其文理）中真的顯著嗎？保羅在該段對羅馬信徒的勸勉是否只有在「當時」才是適切的呢？

及其存續，順服政府則可使其有空間，在所處的社會中以行善的方式，為所信的福音作見證。但順服政府，熱心行善，不僅是教會求生存的策略，也與福音是 神與人和好，並帶來和睦的信息有關（參如太五9；弗二 12～18）。」[25]

昆謝隆將**預備行各樣善事**理解為（一）「準備好接受任何誠實的工作」。[26] 班約翰則認為，（二）**善事**是籠統意義的助人之事，而不是好的行為，因文理並無任何線索，表示作者在這裏想到的是好行為。[27] 另有認為，（三）**行各樣善事**指積極地履行各種公民義務，[28]「參與一切有益於社會人羣的善舉。」[29] 信徒「熱心公益」，就證明基督教是社會上一種具建設性的力量。[30] 費歌頓認為（四）**善事**包括但並非限於公民義務；**預備行各樣善事**較可能是籠統的命令，為第 2 節的各項鋪路。[31] 也許更為可能的解釋是，（五）**預備行各樣善事**緊隨「要服從在位者」，可能是由於保羅想到，為官者的責任是壓制邪惡和鼓勵行

---

25 彭編 104*b*-5*a*（底線是原來的）。（**1**）Collins 357 認為，作者（不是保羅）很可能要提醒收信人 ‘that Christians should avoid any kind of civil disobedience that would render them suspect in the eyes of governmental authorities and perhaps lead to violence or some other form of persecution (see 1 Pet. 2:13-15).’（**2**）Genade 69 同樣認為，信徒必須避免某些行為——‘conduct that would make them appear separatist, exclusivist, and insurrectionary’——免得引起政府當局和社會上其他人士的負面反應。

26 Quinn 28, 177, 180, 182, 185: ‘to be ready to take any honest work’. Cf. REB: ‘to be ready for any honourable work’; Neyrey 1217*a*: ‘to be open to every good enterprise’ (referring to ‘full employment’).

27 Banker 95*b*. 班約翰早前曾認為，這裏的**善事**很可能 ‘refers either to doing good deeds to benefit others, or good work done for those in authority’（56*b*），但其後的討論表明，他認為前一種解釋較可取，儘管後一種解釋 ‘has considerable merit’（95*a-b*）。See also Arichea－Hatton 297: ‘any good deed that is done for the benefit of others.’

28 Johnson I 133: ‘the positive performance of civic obligations’; Kelly 249: ‘The reference is . . . to the activities of whatever kind which go with good citizenship.’ See also Scott 172: ‘Christians should be among the foremost in showing public spirit’; Kelly 249: ‘Christians should be to the fore, as far as possible, in showing public spirit in their district.’

29 周 437。Cf. Mounce, ‘Titus’ 107: ‘be available to help in every good cause.’

30 Hiebert 443: ‘They must . . . show good public spirit, thus proving that Christianity is a constructive force in society.’ 引句出自《串釋（增簡）》1755*a*。

31 Fee 201: ‘this is a generalizing imperative that prepares the way for the rest of the list.’ 由於 2 節那些項目屬於「好行為」的範疇，費氏的解釋可說是回應了（二）和包括了（三）。

善（羅十三 3）。[32] 該節兩次提到行善：作官的原不是要使行善的懼怕……只要行善，你就可得他的稱讚（3a、3c 節）；第一次是指奉公守法的行為，第二次則除了奉公守法的行為外，還包括那些本身有價值、在道德意義上是好的事（羅十二 2c、9c、21）。[33] 如此，預備行各樣善事便可理解為隨時準備行美善的事（新普），包括各種公民義務（上面之〔三〕）、[34] 助人之事（上面之〔二〕），以及名副其實的基督徒行為（＝好行為〔二 7〕[35]）。[36]

32 Fairnbairn 288.

33 參《羅》4.241-42、244。

34 張 368 認為，預備行各樣善事「大概指信徒要隨時隨地與政府合作，作知法守法的良好公民。」Stott 199 更詳細地解釋如下：根據保羅（羅十三 3～4）和彼得的教導，政府有懲惡賞善（彼前二 14）的雙重責任；因此，上帝的子民應準備好在這兩方面與政府合作。行各樣善事不但澄清我們的責任，同時亦加以限制：'We cannot cooperate with the state if it reverses its God-given duty, promoting evil instead of punishing it, and opposing good instead of rewarding and furthering it.' Cf. Davies I 106: '*to be ready for any good work* . . . could exclude believers' obedience to any ruler's demand for bad actions. Apostasy, for example, or murder could not be justified by appeal to a ruler's orders.'

35 參二 7 註釋註 8（上面 259）。

36 Cf. Bassler 205: 'the author is clearly referring to Christian life in its fullness and not simply to political obedience'; Knight II 333: 'the immediate connection is with the government but the statement is not meant to be confined to that'; Collins 357: πᾶν ἔργον ἀγαθόν (every good work) 'is the Christian life in its totality'; Marshall 302: 'according to the meaning of the term in the PE, "readiness to do 'good works'" is a call to live in such a way that the fruit of the new life in Christ is manifested in tangible ways in this mundane context'.

三　**2**　不要毀謗，不要爭吵，要和氣，對眾人總要顯出溫柔。

信徒除了對政府當局有義務之外，對不信主的鄰舍亦有義務。（**#4**）不要／不可毀謗（同呂譯、當代、新和、現修／新譯、新普）[1] 的另一種翻譯是不要辱罵（思高）。[2] 不過，雖然原文動詞的意思有時確是辱罵（路二十二 65），但在新約裏，這個意思通常是用另兩個動詞表達的。[3] 因此，本節的動詞在這裏的意思較可能是毀謗，即是說別人的壞話，以不真實的話使別人的名譽受損。[4]

（**#5**）不要爭吵（同呂譯、思高、當代、現修）[5] 即是要避免與人爭吵（新普）；[6] 另有翻譯為不要爭競（新和）、要與人無爭（新譯）或「和平的」。[7] 這一項跟敵對者牽涉於因律法而起的爭辯（9 節）構成對比，但與提摩太前書三章 3 節所要求於監督的一項資格相同：不

---

1 Laansma 280 認為，'the focus is on the response of Christians toward those in government', '[t]he believers are called upon to avoid slandering the government'（281）。但本節開首的 μηδένα（no one）表示，毀謗不是僅指對執政掌權者的毀謗（Towner III 772 n.13〔唐 1126 註 13〕）。

2 See also Quinn 28, 177, 180, 185: 'insult'. H. W. Bayer（*TDNT* 1.625）聲稱，即使在這籠統的命令中，'The predominantly religious connotation [of the word group βλασφημ-]* is present'.（*622: 'In the NT the concept of blasphemy is controlled throughout by the thought of violation of the power and majesty of God.'）筆者認為很難在這裏看出這種宗教意義來。

3 ὀνειδίζω（例：太五 11；路六 22；羅十五 3；彼前四 14）和 λοιδορέω（例：約九 28〔呂譯、思高、現修〕；徒二十三 4；林前四 12〔呂譯〕；彼前二 23）。亦參和後者同字根的抽象名詞 λοιδορία（提前五 14；彼前三 9）和人物名詞 λοίδορος（林前五 11，六 10）。

4 See KJV, NKJV, RSV, NRSV, ESV, *Paraphrase* 293, LN §88.63, BDAG 178*a* (s.v. βλασφημέω, a): 'speak evil of'; NAU: 'to malign'; REB, NIV, TNIV, NIV2011 / NJB: 'to slander / go slandering'; NLT/LN §33.400: 'slander/defame'. 原文動詞已在二 5 出現過；參二 5b 註釋註 12 之（1）= 上面 252。

5 See also KJV: 'to be no brawlers'; Quinn 28, 177, 180: 'not to be argumentative'.

6 See also RSV, NRSV, ESV: 'to avoid quarreling'; NLT: 'they must avoid quarreling'. 黃編 220-21 則解釋為「基督徒不但決不惹事生非，也決不反擊。」

7 NKJV, RSV, NRSV, NAU, NIV, TNIV, NIV2011, NJB, *Paraphrase* 293: 'to be peaceable'. I.e., ἄμαχος = 'peaceable'（BDAG 52*a* [s.v.]; A. Ringwald, *DNTT* 1.646; G. Schneider, *EDNT* 1.69*a* [s.v.]; Mounce cvii），'"peaceable" in the sense of "uncontentious"'（Knight II 334），'peaceful'（O. Bauernfeind, *TDNT* 4.528），「不愛爭吵的；和平的」（《新希》18*b* [s.v.]）。

好鬥，即是「避免爭吵」。[8] 同樣，提摩太後書二章 24 節使用同字根的動詞，[9] 說：**主的僕人……不應該好爭吵**（呂譯），或**不可／不應當爭吵**（現修／思高），即是**不可與人爭執**（當代、新普）。

（**#6**）**要和氣**（新和：**要和平**）的另一些翻譯是**和氣友善**（現修）、[10] **溫良和藹**（呂譯）、**溫柔**（新普）、[11] **謙讓**（思高）、**謙恭有禮**（新譯）。[12] 原文形容詞可以有「讓步、溫柔、仁慈、有禮、寬容」等多種意思，[13] 但是由於隨後一項正是**對眾人總要顯出溫柔**，目前一項就可能不是「溫柔」；又由於這一項和前一項（**不要爭吵**）構成對比，

---

8 這字（**ἄμαχος**）在新約僅此兩次，在希臘文聖經不再出現。原文是複合形容詞（from μάχη + α-private; literally 'not fighting' [Vine 1.146]; 三世紀的一個墓碑這樣說：'I lived without fighting [ἄμαχος] with friends and relatives' [Quinn 180, with reference to MM (25*b*, s.v.)]）；名詞 μάχη 見三 9 註釋之（**#4**）= 下面 437。

9 μάχομαι. 這動詞在新約僅再出現三次，分別指摩西遇見有人在**打架**（徒七 26），猶太人就耶穌所說的話而彼此**爭論**（約六 52），以及信徒之間**起爭執**（雅四 2）。See BDAG 622*b* (s.v.);《新希》211*b*（s.v.）。

10 Cf. NIV, TNIV, NIV2011: 'to be . . . considerate' (= kind and helpful).（**1**）Kelly 248, 249 則譯作 'conciliatory'（endorsed by Fee 201; also Marshall 303）=「有助於或可能促進修好的」(《牛津》240*b* [s.v. 'conciliate']）。（**2**）Sewakpo（'Titus' 14）從政治領袖的角度將 εἰπιεικής 解釋為 'the quality which rectifies and redresses the injustice of justice', 因為 'justice may become utterly unjust when the law is applied [merely] according to the letter'.

11 See also KJV, NKJV, NAU, NJB, *Paraphrase* 293: 'to be . . . gentle'; RSV, NRSV, ESV, Quinn 28, 177, 180: 'to be gentle'; NLT: 'be gentle'; H. Preisker, *TDNT* 2.590: 'meek' (endorsed by H. Giesen, *EDNT* 2.26*b* [s.v. ἐπιεικής, 2 b]).

12 三 2 在當代譯作**不要毀謗，不要爭吵，待人總要謙恭有禮**。但原文共有四個項目，而**待人**顯然是本節末尾的 πρὸς πάντας ἀνθρώπους 的翻譯；因此，除非當代漏譯了第三項，不然的話，就是把第三項 ἐπιεικεῖς 翻譯為**謙恭**（新譯作**謙恭有禮**），把第四項的 πᾶσαν ἐνδεικνυμένους πραΰτητα 翻譯為**有禮**。

13 BDAG 371*a* (s.v. ἐπιεικής): 'yielding, gentle, kind, courteous, tolerant'.（**1**）這形容詞（**ἐπιεικής**）在保羅書信僅再出現兩次，新約另外兩次，分別指信徒要讓大家看出他們的**謙和**（腓四 5，新譯〔參《腓》434〕）；作監督的一項資格就是**要溫和**（提前三 3）；從天上來的智慧是**謙和的**（雅三 17，現修）；以及信主的奴僕要順服主人，不管他是**溫和的**或是乖僻的（彼前二 18）。參《新希》126*a*（s.v.）。（**2**）同字根的抽象名詞 ἐπιεικεία 在新約出現兩次，分別指受僱控告保羅的律師請求總督腓力斯在聆聽時顯出的**寬容**（徒二十四 4），以及基督所顯的**溫柔／慈祥／仁慈**（林後十 1，新譯／現修同／新普）。參張略：《雅各書》222 的討論。（**3**）同字根的複合動詞 ἐπιεικεύομαι 在希臘文聖經僅出現一次，指耶和華向祂的子民**施恩**（拉九 8）。

文理似乎支持「謙讓、寬容」等意思。[14]

（**#7**）**對眾人總要顯出溫柔**原文直譯是**向所有的人表現出**（新普）**極其溫和**（思高）。[15] 原文的次序（見註 15：極其｜顯出｜溫柔）表示形容詞「極其」受到強調。[16] **總要顯出溫柔**[17] 這種翻譯不必要地將原文的形容詞化為副詞。這裏的原文結構跟二章 10 節**顯出完美的忠誠**十分相似；就如該節勸喻奴僕要對主人**表現出自己是絕對可靠……的**（新普），本節勸勉信徒要對眾人**表現充分**〔或：極其量的〕**溫柔**（新譯〔原文並無**的心**二字〕）。[18] **溫柔**（同新和）原文另有翻譯為**謙卑**（新

---

14 See LN §88.63: 'to be forbearing' (= patient and forgiving); REB: 'show forbearance';《輔讀》529（第二解釋）：「謙讓的」；黃編 221：「對人性的弱點抱持寬容同情的心態」。亦參《腓》433-34 較詳細的討論。

15 πᾶσαν ἐνδεικνυμένους πραΰτητα πρὸς πάντας ἀνθρώπους = 'shewing all meekness unto all men' (KJV).（**1**）「πᾶς + 抽象名詞」是典型的保羅用語（Simpson 113）；參：πάσῃ σπουδῇ（林後八 7），ἐν πάσῃ μακροθυμίᾳ καὶ διδαχῇ（提後四 2），ἐν πάσῃ ὑπομονῇ（林後十二 12），μετὰ πάσης σεμνότητος / ταπεινοφροσύνης（提前三 4／徒二十 19）。（**2**）動詞 ἐνδείκνυμι 已在二 10 出現過；見二 9～10 註釋註 32 之（4）= 上面 275。（**3**）名詞 **πραΰτης**（= 'the later form of the classical πραότης' [Simpson 113], 後者在希臘文聖經只見於次經《便西拉智訓》1.27）在保羅書信另外出現七次（林前四 21；林後十 1；加五 23，六 1；弗四 2；西三 12；提後二 25），在新約僅再出現三次（雅一 21，三 13；彼前三 16）；詳見《西‧門》594。See BDAG 861*a*-61*b* (s.v.);《新希》280*a*（s.v.）。

16 類似的情形（名詞在分詞之前，表示受到強調）見猶 3 節（πᾶσαν σπουδὴν ποιούμενος, **很迫切地**）；彼後一 5（σπουδὴν πασαν παρεισενέγκαντες, **竭盡所能**〔新普〕）。

17 See Banker 95*b*: 'Believers should *invariably* exhibit a considerate attitude toward all others'; NJB: 'to be . . . always polite to people of all kinds'; TNIV, NIV2011: 'always to be gentle toward everyone'; REB: 'always to show . . . a gentle disposition to all.'

18 比較：

二 10	πᾶσαν πίστιν ἐνδεικνυμένους ἀγαθήν	
	'displaying the utmost trustworthiness' (White195*b*)	
三 2	πᾶσαν ἐνδεικνυμένους πραΰτητα	
	'[displaying] the greatest possible meekness' (White 197*b*)	

'πᾶς is elative' (Marshall 304 n.16); 'πᾶς calls for the highest degree of meekness to be exhibited'（Towner III 773 n.15〔唐 1127 註 15〕）。如 Hendriksen 387 所指出，這一項要求難度極高：'Showing *some* mildness toward *some* people might not be so difficult. Nor showing *all* (that is, *complete, thorough-going*) mildness to *some* people, or *some* mildness to *all* people. But to *show all* mildness to *all* people, even to those Cretan "liars, evil brutes, and lazy bellies," [1:12] was an assignment impossible of fulfillment apart from God's special grace!'

普）[19] 或謙讓的態度（現修）；[20] 但保羅書信通常用另一個字來表達「謙卑」之意，[21] 而「謙讓」的意思已包括在上一項美德裏，因此溫柔是較合適的翻譯，所指的是對人的柔和（呂譯）、為他人著想。[22] 保羅強調，收信人要以〔這種〕態度對待所有的人（現修），包括（尤其是）他們信奉異教的鄰居，因為（他即將指出）我們從前也像他們現今那樣（三 3）。[23] 就如上帝的恩典……為所有人帶來拯救（二 11，新普），[24] 他願意所有的人都得救（提前二 4，思高），照樣，信心的羣體要以〔這種〕態度對待所有的人，彰顯與上帝的拯救相符的品格特質，藉以示範福音的健全的教導（二 1）。[25]

---

19 See NLT / NIV*: 'show true humility to everyone / toward all men'; NKJV: 'showing all humility to all men'.（*但見上面註 17 之 TNIV, NIV2011: 'to be gentle'.）

20 Cf. RSV/ESV: 'show perfect courtesy toward all men/people'; NRSV / *Paraphrase* 293: 'show every / showing perfect courtesy to everyone'; Wall 357: 'showing complete civility toward everyone.'

21 名詞 ταπεινοφροσύνη: 弗四 2；腓二 3；西三 12（在二 18、23 則指「假謙卑」〔參《西・門》450-51、494〕）；參：徒二十 19；彼前五 5。

22 See Banker 93, 94*b*, 95*b*: 'act considerately'; Quinn 28, 177, 180, 185, 209: 'show every consideration'; Fiore II 216, 217: 'exhibiting total consideration'; NAU: 'showing every consideration for all men'; Mounce, 'Titus' 107: 'treat the other person with consideration.'（1）基里將 πραΰτης 翻譯為 'gentleness'（Kelly 248, 249），但解釋為 'courteous consideration'（249）。Dunn 876*a* 的解釋涵蓋上述數個意思：'showing all "gentleness, humility, courtesy, considerateness"'; cf. Mounce 445: '[the word] denotes a humility, a courtesy . . ., a consideration of others without being servile.' Griffin 319 甚至聲稱，πραΰτης 的定義 'embraces some aspect of each of the verbal infinitives preceding it in this context (i.e., "in subjection," "obedient," "ready to do good works," "speaking no evil," "peaceable," and "considerate" [author's translations])'（方括號是原來的）。（2）留意這字（#7）和 #6（ἐπιεικής）在林後十 1 按相反的次序用於基督身上：我保羅要本着基督的溫柔〔πραΰτητος〕和仁慈〔ἐπιεικείας〕向你們呼籲（新普）。Griffin 319 認為，保羅在這裏使用此二字可能表示，他預期耶穌所展現的態度和行為要成為基督徒與執政掌權者和與眾人的關係之標準。

23 See Kelly 249-50, endorsed by Banker 98*b*. Knight II 331 認為，2 節的眾人（僅）指非基督徒，因為保羅說，他們現在的情況，就是基督徒從前的狀況（3 節）。Cf. Towner I 197: 'The places where believers will encounter "all men" are the various social institutions that form the social structure.'

24 參二 11 註釋首段之（乙）＝ 上面 285-87。

25 See Johnson I 133-34. Goodwin 1757*b* 這樣總結這兩節的教導：'In short, Christians should devote themselves as good citizens to the welfare of the city in a spirit of gentleness and kindness.'

巴思樂認為，作者的教導與行為並不一致：一方面，提多要提醒信徒要向所有的人表現出（新普）極其溫和（思高），所有的人應包括那些不受約束的敵對者（一 10）；另一方面，作者對假教師的描述並不禮貌（一 10～16），要堵住他們的口（一 11）和嚴厲地責備他們（一 13b）這些指示也絕不溫柔。也許本節的眾人僅指未信主的人，作者的用意是要鼓勵信徒以良好的行為在希羅社會中促進福音的傳播；但是當真理和基督羣體的合一受到危害時，較嚴厲的方法是作者暗中贊同的。可是，提摩太後書二章 25b 節明言，提摩太要用溫柔勸導反對的人。如此，教牧書信發出混雜的倫理信息；在提多書本身，信息的一面是以上帝的恩典為根據，另一面則由異教的先知支持（一 12）。[26] 不過，在「疑點歸於被告」這原則下，我們應假定作者（保羅）的立場是一致的：如果嚴厲地責備他們（一 13c）的意思是「嚴緊地、縝密地」使他們知道自己的錯誤，[27] 這與用溫柔勸導反對的人並非必然相違背的，[28] 使他們在信仰上健全（一 13c）這目的，以及警戒過一兩次後才拒絕跟〔分門結黨的人〕來往（三 10）的做法，亦與也許上帝會給他們悔改的心能明白真理（提後二 25a）的盼望相符。我們也不可忘記，「溫柔並不使人不能發（義）怒，耶穌和保羅都說明此點：心裏柔和謙卑的主（太十一 29）曾在會堂裏含怒環視眾人（可三 5，思高）；保羅以基督的謙遜溫柔勸哥林多人（林後十 1，新譯），卻對傳假福音者宣告咒詛（加一 8～9，參五 12）。」[29] 照樣，對眾人總要顯出溫柔的勸勉，和作者對假教師的描述和譴責（一 10～16）可以並存不悖。[30]

---

26 Bassler 209-10.
27 參一 13 註釋註 25 及所屬正文（上面 186）。
28 英文就有 'gently but firmly' 這講法。
29 《加》1282。（「林後十 1」改正了原來的「林後十一」。）
30 Cf. Mounce 445: 'There is no contradiction with 1:10-16 . . . . A refusal to blaspheme a person does not negate the need to confront sin and error. Jesus himself showed a balance between gentility and righteous angers.' 利斐特 340-41（Liefeld 323）說：「第

本小段從**順服執政的、掌權的**（1 節）過渡到**對眾人總要顯出溫柔**（2 節）。這裏的兩個元素（執政者和眾人）在新約另兩段經文同樣被放在一起：在彼得前書二章 13 至 17 節，彼得告訴信徒不但要**尊敬君王**（17c 節）並**順服**他和他**所派懲惡賞善的官員**（13～14 節），也要**尊重眾人**（17a 節）；保羅在羅馬書十三章 1 至 7 節教導信徒對執政者的責任，但在此之前他發出了以愛為首的一連串勸勉（十二 9～21），包括**眾人以為美的事要留心去做**（17 節）和**若是可行，總要盡力與眾人和睦**（18 節），而在此之後又闡釋愛人如己就成全了律法（十三 8～10）。[31] 因此，這裏從**執政的、掌權的**迅速地轉到**眾人**，不應被視為奇怪的事。[32]

---

10 至 16 節需要強烈實行。雖然保羅的勸告（特別針對提摩太〔原文照錄〕）是在改正時要溫和，有些時候卻需要嚴格的紀律處分和公開譴責，特別是針對那些“不服約束”和“欺哄人”（10 節），“因貪不義之財”“敗壞人的全家”（11 節），“污穢”（15 節〔英文原作 ‘corrupted’〕），否認神，“可憎惡”，以及“悖逆”（16 節）的人。倘若教會沒有強力和認可的領導層，實在是很難應付這些人。」

31 參《羅》4.6。**眾人以為美的事要留心去做**（羅十二 17）的意思是：基督徒生活在不信福音的人當中，必須留心自己的生活行為，務要使不信者也可以看見，他們行事的目標是高尚可敬的（參《羅》4.176-79，尤其是 178）。

32 Correctly, Knight I 80 n.1.

5.2 教義性的動機（三 3～7）[1]

3 我們從前也是無知、悖逆、受迷惑，作各樣私慾和宴樂的奴隸，在惡毒、
嫉妒中度日，是可恨的，而且彼此相恨。

4 但到了我們救主上帝的恩慈和慈愛顯明的時候，

5c 他救了我們……藉著重生的洗和聖靈的更新。

5a 並不是因我們自己所行的義，

5b 而是照他的憐憫，

6 聖靈就是上帝……厚厚地澆灌在我們身上的，
藉著我們的救主耶穌基督

7a 好讓我們因他的恩得稱為義，

7b 可以憑著永生的盼望成為後嗣。

---

1 三 3～7 在原文只是一句（參 NRSV 的標點符號）；Nestle-Aland 則以 3 節為一句，4～7 節為另一句（並且將此句以詩的形式印出）。但是祈勒克認為，'the period at the end of 3.3 in UBS4 is questionable'（Clark, 'Structure' 114）。（**1**）Ellis（'Traditions' 238 n.11）認為，4～7 節 'combines (implicit) midrash* and a hymnic form'; cf. Ellis, 'Pastoral Letters' 664*a*: 'One passage combines midrash* and a hymnic form (Tit 3:3-7)'（《辭典》961*b*）。*'Titus 3 includes an implicit midrash on Joel 2:28f. (=3:1f.), understood as fulfilled at Pentecost'（'Traditions' 242; 'midrash' =「米人示」，參《弗》554 註 3 之〔1〕)。艾利斯以這幾節為一首詩歌（238 with 239 n.12）。Martin（*Foundations* 262）將三 4～7 列於 'sacramental hymns' 之中。（**2**）Fee 208 指出，新約學者太容易稱一些經文為 'hymnic or liturgical fragment . . . even when the barest poetic requirements (structure and meter) are missing. No poetic elements appear in this sentence'. *Contra* Thurston, 'Titus' 181: 'I have become convinced that it is, indeed, a hymn fragment with a Trinitarian structure'; Karris, *Symphony* 131: 'it is my judgment that Titus 3:4-7 is a hymn because of reasons external to the text, but especially because of internal reasons'（詳見 127-31）。卡羅拔所用的一個理由是：'in the other Pauline letters there is no clear reference to the Trinity as one finds in Titus 3:4-7: God our Savior, Holy Spirit, Jesus Christ our Savior'（129）。可是，以下的經文都清晰地顯示保羅神學的「三一」性質：羅一 1～4（參《羅》1.186）；羅八 9～11（參《羅》2.597）；林後十三 14。另見羅十五 16（參《羅》4.572 註 37）；羅十五 30（參《羅》4.654）；林前六 11（see Fee, *Presence* 128-29）；弗一 3～14（參《弗》204-6）；弗一 17（參《弗》223）。不過，卡羅拔的重點可能是在於「不像在本段那麼清晰」。

三章 3 節開首原文有**因為**（呂譯、思高）一字，[2] 這表示本段為上一小段（三 1～2）的勸勉提供了教義性的基礎，[3] 就如二章 11 至 14 節為之前的一段（二 1～10）提出教義性的基礎。[4] 這兩段（二 11～14，三 3～7）所談論的都是上帝的救恩，其中有不少相同或意義相近的詞彙，[5] 如下表所示：

---

2 γάρ = 'For' (KJV, NKJV, RSV, NRSV, NAU, ESV).

3 見導論第伍節註 16（上面 34）。參《串釋（增簡）》1755*a*：「謙和待人的信仰根據」；Banker 93*a*: 兩小段的語意關係是 '*exhortation-grounds*'; 98*a*: '3:3-7 . . . is . . . grounds for 3:1-2'. **(1)** Ward 267 則認為，**因為**所解釋的不是 'the exhortations themselves' 而是 'the reasonableness of the exhortations'. **(2)** White 197 認為**因為**提示這樣的關聯：你（提多）不必認為這些不受控制的克里特人是無法挽回的；我們就是上帝恩典之大能的明證。

4 Malherbe, 'Soteriology' 350: 'Each passage begins with paraenesis (2:1-10; 3:1-2), for which the soteriological passage then provides the theological ground (2:11-14; 3:3-7), in each case provided by γάρ.' 兩段（三 1～7，二 1～14）都是以 the gift of salvation（indicative）作為 the task of ethics（imperative）的根據，'[each] providing a paradigm case of the Pauline hortatory style'（Madsen, 'Ethics' 221-23 [quotation from 222]）。**(1)** Lamp（'Titus' 104）聲稱，這兩段（三 3～7，二 11～14）分別只是之前的實際應用（三 1～2，二 1～10）之神學理據（'that the relationship is simply that of theological justification for practical application'），這種假設是未經深思熟慮（'somewhat facile'）的；這樣評論的理由是，'Within the theological passages themselves is found an appeal to practical application, albeit at a more general level than the more specific exhortations of the paranetic [*sic*] sections.' **(2)** 但是按作者自己的描述，「訴諸實際應用」的每一部分（二 12、14b～c，三 7），所表達的都是 '[the] desired effect of salvation'（96, 98, 101），即它們仍然是有關救恩的神學性陳述的一部分；若把上述的每一節都視為 'an appeal to practical application', 那也最多只是 'an <u>implied</u> appeal', 無損其本身「神學理據」的基本性質。故此，「未經深思熟慮」的批評似乎並不公允。事實上，作者本身（不自覺地？）將二 1～10 和二 11～14 的關係視為「勸勉」與「根本原因」（108: 'The paranesis found in 2:1-10, for which 2:11-14 is given as the rationale . . .'），這跟將兩段的關係視為「勸勉」與「神學理據」有甚麼重要的分別呢？

5 See Banker 76*a*.

二 11～14	三 3～7
11 節　上帝救眾人的恩典 （由 10c 節我們救主上帝的教導引入）	4 節　我們〔的〕救主上帝 5c 節　他救了我們[6] 7a 節　因他的恩＝ 4 節　〔因〕上帝的恩慈和慈愛[7]
13b 節　我們的救主耶穌基督	6 節　我們的救主耶穌基督
14a 節　為我們的緣故捨己 14b 節　為了要〔救〕贖我們	7a 節　好讓我們……得稱為義 7b 節　可以……成為後嗣

與此同時，這兩段在其文理中的功用是略為不同的：第二章該段的功用是要從救恩歷史的角度解釋，上帝的救贖行動之目的是要創造一個熱心為善的子民；第三章本段則以個人歸主及得救的詞彙來解釋，信徒有能力行善，因為上帝拯救了他們。雖然如此，兩段的分別不應被誇大：在前一段，上帝的救贖行動包括個人的救贖；在後一段，個人歸主是上帝整個救贖行動的一部分。[8]

另一方面，本段延續了上一小段（三 1～2）的倫理性詞彙：（i）第 3 節的惡行目錄跟第 1、2 兩節的美德目錄（各有七個項目）構成對比。[9] 其中的悖逆（3 節）和順服（1 節）字詞上

6　二 11 的救字原文為形容詞 σωτήριος，三 5 的救字則為動詞 σῴζω.

7　7 節的恩和 4a 節的恩慈、慈愛原文依次為 χάρις, χρηστότης, φιλανθρωπία.

8　Marshall 305. Mounce 437-38 則強調 'the corporate nature of the creed'. 有趣的是，作者在解釋 6 節時卻用了「個人」的講法：'What was true then [at Pentecost] of the early church is true for every believer in salvation.'

9　關於信上的「美德目錄」，參一 6 註釋註 7（上面 101-2）。關於信上的「惡行目錄」，參一 16 註釋註 22 之（3）= 下面 211。（**1**）留意 Johnson II 31 的觀察：'For fellow workers of Greek education [Titus was of Greek background, Gal. 2:3; Timothy had a Greek father, Acts 16:1], we might well expect . . . ethical teaching that stressed the pursuit of virtue and the avoidance of vice.'（**2**）美德目錄和惡行目錄在保羅書信的各種功用中，最顯著的用途就是用以「鼓勵信徒消除（avoid）惡行並實踐美德」（C. G. Kruse,《辭典》1376*b*〔*DPL* 962 (§1.2)〕）；參《西．門》529 註 32。（**3**）關於新約

的聯繫[10] 加強了這籠統的對比。(**ii**)有關救恩的陳述強調倫理性的改變：**重生的洗和聖靈的更新**(5c 節)指向救恩所帶來的屬靈潔淨和新的生活方式。如此，本段的倫理關注與上一小段的倫理指引之銜接是順暢的。從邏輯的角度而言，第 3 至 7 節表明**我們**<u>能夠</u>按照第 1、2 兩節的指示來生活的原因：因為上帝的救恩帶來了改變。或許，上帝的救恩特別是**對眾人總要顯出溫柔**(2 節)的基礎：[11]「我們曾經是他們現在仍然是的那個樣子，但是我們藉著上帝的仁慈得了釋放，因此，我們<u>應當</u>以仁慈對待我們曾經像他們一樣的那些人。」[12]

的美德及惡行目錄的背景和特色，可參《西・門》529-30。

10 原文二字(同字根)依次為 ἀ<u>πειθ</u>ής, <u>πειθ</u>αρχέω.

11 See Fiore II 224: 'The conjunction "for" . . . introduces the explanation of the call to demonstrate humility to all.'

12 以上一段參 Van Neste 261. 末後的引句取自 Marshall 305(譯自 Holtzmann)。(**1**) Towner II 253 認為，本段也許同時回答 'why we *ought* to live this life' 和 'why we *can* live it' 這兩個問題。但他稍後對 8 節的註釋則表示，所回答的是後者：'Here Paul attaches a strong motive for living the life described in verses 1-2, the <u>possibility</u> of which verses 3-7 subsequently demonstrate'(259)。(**2**) Stott 200 則從代名詞的轉變([1] 要提醒……<u>他們</u>……[3] 因為<u>我們</u>從前也是無知……[4] 但……[5] <u>他</u>救了我們)看出這樣的意思來：'the only reason we dare instruct others in social ethics is that we know what we were once like ourselves, that God nevertheless saved us, and that he can therefore transform other people too.' 不過，嚴格地說，「因為(γάρ)」所引介的，並不是提多要提醒眾人的原因，而是提多要叫他們順服……對眾人總要顯出溫柔的原因。

5.2.1 信徒從前的景況（三 3）

三 3 我們從前也是無知、悖逆、受迷惑，作各樣私慾和宴樂的奴隸，
在惡毒、嫉妒中度日，是可恨的，而且彼此相恨。

我們籠統地指保羅、提多和克里特的基督徒，[1] 同時亦表示保羅與聽眾認同（儘管這裏的描述與保羅歸主前的生活並不完全吻合[2]），這種認同使隨後嚴厲的描寫變得較易接受。**也**字的含義是，「就像現今仍未歸信基督的人一樣」。[3] **是**字原文是過去未完時態，表示隨後所描述的是一種持續的狀況。這裏七個負面的項目，和上兩節那七個正面的項目相對。[4] 這裏的七個項目[5] 把他們的意（##1、3）、情（##4、7）、志（##2、5）各方面都包括在內；**是可恨的**（#6）描寫了他們的客觀

---

1 Jeon II 29: 'Paul, Titus, and the audience members'. 這裏所描寫的是「革哩底* 的生活品質」（唐 92〔Towner III 65〕）。（*和合；新和、和修：克里特。）（**1**）本節和 5 節的 ἡμεῖς 都是 'inclusive *we*', 即是包括作者和聽眾（Wallace 397, 398）。（**2**）Quinn 200 則認為，**我們**指 'We Jewish Christians', 也許暗地裏與外邦基督徒提多成為對比。

2 （**1**）Young 127 斷言，'Paul would certainly not have identified himself as a slave to desires and pleasures, living in wickedness . . .'. Hagner（'Titus' 555 n.21）正確指出，'There is no need to conclude that Paul identifies himself with every sin that is listed here. . . . He *is* happy, however, to identify himself as a sinner in need of the same redemption as the Cretans.' Mounce 446 指出，'These sins are . . . the sins of humanity in general . . . . It is an accurate picture of the world as seen through God's eyes and those of the redeemed.'（**2**）威瑟靈頓則認為，'Unless this is rhetorical hyperbole, it sounds much more plausible coming from Luke, a Gentile, than from the Paul, [*sic*] who wrote Philippians 3:5-6 and 2 Corinthians 11:22-23'（Witherington 156 n.234）。

3 Banker 96, 98*a*; Marshall 309.

4 See Hendriksen 387-88; Classen, 'Titus' 441 n.42, 'Epistle to Titus' 60 n.49. 簡內德認為，本節的修辭目的是要讓聽眾對他們從前的景況產生厭惡（Genade 75: 'The overarching rhetorical objective in 3:3 is to fill the audience with disgust, to show them up' (see also 115, 118)）。簡內德稱本節所用的修辭技巧為「自我詆毀（self-vilification）」（77, 79, 87, 118, 129）。

5 Stott 202 則把**惡毒**和**嫉妒**（#5）視為兩項，從而得出八項，構成四對（'four couplets'）。但在**惡毒**、**嫉妒**中**度日**顯然是一項而非兩項。

狀況。[6]

（**#1**）無知（同呂譯、新和、現修、新譯）[7] 指他們因為不認識上帝，缺乏屬靈的理解，以致他們的思想和行動都是愚蠢（新普；思高昏愚）[8] 的。[9]

（**#2**）悖逆（同呂譯、思高、新和、現修，新普同）是假教師目前的情況（一 16）；但信徒要服從（三 1），與他們從前和假教師目前的情況相反。[10] 因此，信徒現今若有任何不順服（新譯）[11] 的表現，等於走了回頭路，並且變成與假教師同夥！[12] 由於本節是對未信主的

---

6 Marshall 309 這樣分析這七項：頭三項屬於同一組（'Wandering in ignorance'），導致被私慾奴役的狀況（#4）；最後三項 'have to do with antisocial sins'. 參較唐 1130（Towner III 775）：「這清單可分為三部分：第一部分的惡行聚焦於無知；第二部分用了奴役的意象；第三部分則集中在低劣且傷害人際關係的缺陷上。」Köstenberger 622*a* 則認為這七項呈現 'a 2-3-2 pattern'.

7 See also NJB: 'ignorant'.（**1**）原文 **ἀνόητος** 在新約另外出現五次，除了一次指沒有學問的人／沒受過教育的（羅一 14，現修／新普），其餘四次的意思都是無知（路二十四 25；加三 1、3；提前六 9）。See BDAG 84*a* (s.v.);《新希》29*b*（s.v.）。（**2**）這字是複合形容詞（from νοέω + α-privative）；動詞 νοέω 在保羅書信出現五次（羅一 20〔了解〕；弗三 4〔知道〕、20〔想〕；提前一 7〔明白〕；提後二 7〔考慮〕），新約另外九次（福音書八次；來十一 3〔明白，新譯、新普〕）。

8 I.e., ἀνόητοι = 'foolish' (KJV, NKJV, RSV, NRSV, NAU, NIV, TNIV, NIV2011, ESV, *Paraphrase* 293).

9 Banker 98*b*. See also Guthrie I 203, Guthrie II 215: 'without spiritual understanding' (endorsed by Knight II 336); 古特立 217：「缺少屬靈的認知」; White 197*b*: 'without understanding of spiritual things'; Witherington 156: 'foolish with regard to spiritual matters'. Cf. Laansma 283: 'the statement ultimately relates to what theologians call noetic depravity (noetic = relating to the mind), the effects of sin on human rationality, especially in its response to God and the world as God's.'（**1**）黃編 222 則以無知為不認識上帝的原因：「『無知』指缺乏屬靈的理解力和識別力，因此不認識神，也不明白真理」。（**2**）但羅一 21 支持正文所提出的因果關係，該節說：他們〔外邦人〕雖然知道神，卻不尊他為神……反而心思變為虛妄，愚頑〔ἀσύνετος〕的心就迷糊〔ἐσκοτίσθη〕了（新譯）。若把這個反而視為「反（因此）而」之意，後半節所說的情況，便是人們拒絕了上帝在其創造中的自我啟示的結果（《羅》1.295）。

10 這裏的 ἀπειθής 和 1 節的 πειθαρχεῖν 構成 paronomasia（參一 1～2a 註 25 之〔2〕= 上面 53）。ἀπειθής 也是複合形容詞（見一 16 註釋註 22 之〔2〕= 上面 211），像 ἀνόητος（#1）一樣（見上面註 7 之〔2〕）。

11 See also KJV, NKJV, RSV, NRSV, NAU, NIV, TNIV, NIV2011, NJB, ESV, *Paraphrase* 293: 'disobedient'.

12 Genade 77.

人籠統的描述，這個項目也應視為籠統的，包括對上帝的和對人的悖逆／不服從。[13]

（**#3**）受迷惑（同新和）、易受迷惑（當代）或受了迷惑（呂譯、新譯）這種翻譯，將原文分詞視為被動語態。[14] 另一種翻譯則把它視為中間語態，具主動意思，即是迷途（思高）或迷失（現修）。[15] 原文分詞在提摩太後書三章 13 節與主動語態的分詞一起出現，將作惡者描寫為迷惑人也被人迷惑；[16] 這提示在提多書本節，前一種翻譯（將分詞視為被動語態）是正確的。這裏的意象是不識路的人任由假的嚮導擺佈。[17] 洛窩特認為，受迷惑解釋無知（#1），就如作……奴隸（#4）

---

13 Banker 98*b*-99*a*. See also Montague 245: '**Disobedient** refers to an attitude of rebellion —against God and against earthly authorities, whether parents (Rom 1:30; 2 Tim 3:2) or the state.' (**1**) Kelly 250 認為這一項是指對上帝輕蔑和（鑑於 1 節）對掌權者不耐煩。See also Hiebert 444: 'refusing obedience to God's law and fretting under human authority'; Knight II 336: 'This disobedience to God may be shown . . . by one's attitude and actions to those in authority'; Marshall 309: 'The disobedience . . . is clearly towards God or his agents'.（**2**）唐書禮認為是指 'a conscious rejection of God and perhaps also Paul, his servant'（Towner III 776〔唐 1130〕）。（**3**）Fee 202 只解釋為對上帝悖逆。See also Arichea—Hatton 299: 'Here the focus is on not obeying God'; Griffin 320: 'We were "disobedient" to God and his will for our lives'; Köstenberger 622*a*: 'rebellious against God'; Mounce, 'Titus' 107: 'disobedient to God'. (**4**) Saarinen 190 則認為，悖逆 'refers to the lack of obeying authorities (Titus 3:1), but it also alludes to the incapacity to obey reason.'

14 I.e., πλανώνενοι = 'deceived'（KJV, NKJV, NAU, NIV, TNIV, NIV2011; Fiore II 216），'deluded'（Quinn 28, 187, 200, 202 ）=「受騙的」，'led astray'（RSV, NRSV, ESV），'misled/misguided'（NJB, NLT / Mounce, 'Titus' 107），被他人誤導（新普）。

15 See also Fairnbairn 57, 290, Barrett 140: 'going astray'; O. Böcher, *EDNT* 3.99*b* (s.v. πλανάω, 3): 'have gone astray'; 馮譯：誤入歧途。動詞 **πλανάω** 在保羅書信另外出現五次（新約全部 39 次），其中三次是在不要自欺一語中（林前六 9，十五 33；加六 7〔參《加》1352〕；另見雅一 16），其餘兩次指作惡者和騙人者迷惑人也被人迷惑（提後三 13）。See BDAG 821*b*-22*a* (s.v.);《新希》268*a*（s.v.）。

16 πλανῶντες [active] καὶ πλανώμενοι [passive].

17 Scott 173: 'the image is that of one ignorant of the road and at the mercy of every false guide'; Chapell 358: 'the word suggests a false guide leading us astray.' (**1**) Fee 202, Stott 202, Witherington 156, Liefeld 350（利斐特 367）明確地解釋為受撒旦欺騙（參：提前四 1～2；林後四 4）。See also Griffin 320: 'misled, perhaps by Satan'; Ngewa 398: 'probably Satan'; Arichea—Hatton 299: 'Perhaps the deceivers here are spiritual forces, as, for instance, those mentioned in 1 Tim 4.1.' (**2**) 張 370 則認為受迷惑「大概是罪人為罪所困的苦境。」但「被困」是與「受惑」不同的意象。

解釋悖逆（#2）。[18] 不過，無知（不認識神、缺乏屬靈的理解）更可能是受迷惑的原因，而人們對上帝的悖逆更可能是他們被私慾奴役的原因（參：羅一 22～24、25～26、28）。

（**#4**）作各樣私慾和宴樂的奴隸和（#5）在惡毒、嫉妒中度日在原文呈現交叉配置模式。[19] 動詞作……奴隸[20] 在這裏是比喻用法，且有完全負面的意思。真正的奴隸不是那些服事地上的主人的奴隸（二 9，思高），而是服事罪的人（參：羅六 16～18；約八 34）。[21] 保羅從

---

18 Lock 153（「解釋」英文原作 'explains'）。

19 [A] δουλεύοντες [B] ἐπιθυμίαις καὶ ἡδοναῖς ποικίλαις, [B'] ἐν κακίᾳ καὶ φθόνῳ [A'] διάγοντες. Quinn 201/206 稱之為七個項目中的 'central chiasmus / chiastic centerpiece'.（**1**）首末二字是 'alliteration/Alliteration and rhyme' 的例子（Witherington 160 / Genade 128）。（**2**）δουλεύειν ταῖς ἡδοναῖς 是希臘倫理的常用詞語（Simpson 113; cf. Towner III 776 n.23〔唐 1131-32 註 8〕）。（**3**）[B] 的兩個名詞（ἡδονή 和 ἐπιθυμία）常在希臘化時期的文獻中連著出現，但本節是聖經裏惟一的一次（Mott, 'Ethics' 36）。

20 動詞 **δουλεύω** 與名詞 δοῦλος（奴隸）同字根，具有「以奴僕的身分、像奴僕般服事」的意思。參以下英譯：'enslaved to/by' (NAU / NIV, TNIV, NIV2011; NJB); 'became slaves to' (NLT); 'slaves to' (RSV, NRSV, ESV); 'slaving for' (Quinn 28, 187, 188, 200).（**1**）這動詞在保羅書信另外出現十六次（新約全部 25 次），其中（**i**）五次並無指明服事的對象，但文理提示對象是上帝（羅七 6〔參 4c 節〕）、耶穌基督（腓二 22〔參 21 節〕；參《腓》306-7）、「律法」（加四 25〔參《加》1081-83〕），和奴僕的主人／信主的主人（弗六 7〔參 5 節〕／提前六 2b〔參 2a 節〕）；（**ii**）五次為上帝（帖前一 9）、主（羅十二 11〔參《羅》4.143-46〕）、基督（羅十四 18）或主基督（羅十六 18；西三 24）；（**iii**）另四次的對象分別是罪（羅六 6）、與罪的律相對的上帝的律法（七 25，新普〔參《羅》2.501-3〕）、那些本性不是神的（加四 8，呂譯〔參《加》969〕），和那懦弱無用的粗淺學說（四 9〔參《加》976-91〕）；（**iv**）餘下兩次是人（羅九 12〔雅各〕；加五 13〔信徒〕）。（**2**）同字根的抽象名詞 δουλεία 在新約出現五次，分別指奴役之靈（羅八 15，呂譯〔參《羅》2.623-24〕），與兒子名分的靈相對；敗壞的奴役／朽壞的枷鎖（八 21，新譯／現修）；西乃之約不斷地生子為奴（加四 24〔參《加》1069-71〕）；律法的奴役（加五 1，新譯〔參《加》1126-27〕）；以及對死亡的恐懼所造成的奴役（來二 15，現修、新普〔參《來》2.173-74〕）。See BDAG 259*b*-60*b* (s.v.);《新希》88*b*-89*a*（s.v.）。

21 Stott 202 認為保羅在這裏（多三 3）無疑暗指那大暴君（'the arch-tyrant'）魔鬼，他把人擄去（提後二 26）做他的奴隸。不過，雖然被……擄去（ἐζωγρημένοι [from ζωγρέω]）和被……奴役（δεδουλωμένας [from δουλόω]: 多二 3，新譯）的意思相近，但這裏所用的畢竟是主動語態的另一個字——作……奴隸（δουλεύοντες [from δουλεύω]），而且所服事的對象是私慾和宴樂，不是魔鬼。因此，不宜認為這裏的作……奴隸暗指魔鬼，儘管魔鬼的確與人的私慾「裏應外合」（參：弗二 2～3；《弗》269、277、283）。

前也置身於這些人當中（**我們從前**），但如今他已成為上帝的「奴隸」（一 1，原文直譯）。[22] **私慾**原文只是**慾望**（新普），這名詞（一如其同字根的動詞）是中性的，[23] 即它本身並無肯定是好或是壞的含義；它事實上所表達的意思是好或是壞，端視乎文理而定。這裏明確地將這些慾望視為奴役人的，因而（像二 12 的**世俗的情慾**）肯定具負面意義。**宴樂**原文較好的翻譯是**享樂**（現修、新普）。[24] 希臘雅典哲學家伊壁鳩魯（公元前 341～270）「以獲取快樂為人生所追求的目標」，他所發展的思想（「伊壁鳩魯主義」）亦可稱為「享樂主義」；[25] 但在新約裏，享樂是個負面的概念，**愛享樂卻不愛／過於愛上帝**（提後三 4，新普／現修）更是末世人性的特徵之一。[26] 在斯多亞派的文獻中，**享樂**原文有時與**私慾**原文平行，因而有「熱烈的渴望」之意；在斐羅的著作裏，前者有時等同「渴望」；因此，**享樂**與**私慾**在本節連著出現，前者很可能也是（如在雅四 3）指**享樂的慾望**（雅四 3，新普）。[27]

---

22 Genade 78.

23 原文二字依次為（名詞）ἐπιθυμία,（動詞）ἐπιθυμέω. 前者已在二 12 出現過。參該節註釋註 33、34（上面 297）。

24 《輔讀》529（第一解釋）同。ἡδοναῖς = 'pleasures' (KJV, NKJV, RSV, NRSV, NAU, NIV, TNIV, NIV2011, ESV, NLT). F. Büchsel（*TDNT* 3.171 n.36）這樣描寫**私慾**與**享樂**的關係：'when ἐπιθυμία is satisfied we have ἡδονή, and when ἡδονή is sought we have ἐπιθυμία.' **(1)** 名詞 **ἡδονή** 在新約僅再出現四次，分別指**生活上的……享樂**（路八 14，現修）、**在〔人〕裏面交戰的邪惡慾望**（雅四 1，新普）、**享樂的慾望**（四 3，新普），以及假教師**在白晝縱情作樂**（彼後二 13，新譯）。**(2)** 形容詞 **ποικίλος**（《新希》274*a* [s.v.]：「有不同種類的；多樣化的」）在保羅書信僅再出現一次，同樣是指**各樣的私慾**（提後三 6）。此字在新約另外出現八次，分別指**各樣**／**各種**疾病（太四 24；可一 34／路四 40〔新普〕）、**各種**異能（來二 4，呂譯、思高）、**各樣**怪異的教訓（十三 9，新譯）、**各種**試煉（新譯：雅一 2；彼前一 6），以及**各種**恩賜（彼前四 10）。同字根的複合形容詞 πολυποίκιλος 在希臘文聖經僅出現一次，指上帝**那豐富多樣的智慧**（弗三 10，新普）。參《弗》448-49。

25 《聖神》191*b*（s.v. 'Epicurus'）。亦參《宗教》97*a*（s.v. 'Epicureanism'）。

26 Fiore, 'Pastoral Epistles' 276. 原文用了與 ἡδονή（見上面註 24 之〔1〕）同字根的複合形容詞 φιλήδονος, 與 φιλόθεος 相對（兩個字都在新約不再出現）。誠如 E. Beyreuther（*DNTT* 1.460）所言，'*hēdonē* as the drive to self-expression can be conquered only by the power of God.'

27 G. Stählin, *TDNT* 2.910-11; cf. 918-19: '"desire for joy," "lust for pleasure"'; *TDNTA* 304: 'the "desire for pleasure"'. 不過 Marshall 311 認為，'the line between the longing for pleasure and the actual enjoyment of it is a thin one.'

（#5）在惡毒、嫉妒中度日即是生活在惡毒和嫉妒中／之中（現修／新譯）。[28] 惡毒[29] 另有譯為邪惡（思高、新普）。[30] 原文名詞在新約另外出現十次，除了一次指日常生活上的難處（太六 34），五次具有籠統的邪惡之意，[31] 其餘四次則（如在本節）於「惡行目錄」中出現，可能有較明確的（內心的）惡毒之意，指傷害他人的意願。[32] 嫉妒在羅馬書一章 29 節與兇殺連著出現，不僅在原文構成諧音現象，[33] 更在意思上有邏輯關係：嫉妒可能是謀殺（同上，思高）的動機（太二十七 18 ‖ 可十五 10）。[34] 惡毒和嫉妒是破壞人際關係的「十分醜陋的雙胞胎」：[35] 前者想要傷害別人，後者則「以惡意看別人之所是或

---

28 (1) διάγειν（度日）在此單獨使用，其意思與 βίον διάγειν（提前二 2：過……生活）相同，即是在此省略了賓詞 βίον（BDF §480(2); G. Schneider, *EDNT* 298*b* [s.v. διάγω]）；動詞 **διάγω** 在新約出現僅此兩次。(2) Quinn 205 則認為，作者刻意使用單字 διάγοντες, 因他不能用 ζῶντες（參二 12 的 ζήσωμεν），也不能用 διάγοντες βίον（參：提前二 2），因為二者皆指基督徒的生活；而對作者而言，在基督裏的生活才堪稱為「生活」，在惡毒、嫉妒中度日不能稱為「生活」。

29 See KJV, NKJV, RSV, NRSV, NAU, NIV, TNIV, NIV2011, ESV: 'malice'.

30 《輔讀》529（第一解釋）同。See also NJB, Spencer 58, 59: 'wickedness'; NLT, Witherington 153, M. Lattke, *EDNT* 2.237*b* (s.v. κακία, 4): 'evil'. Cf. Witherington 160: 'malice manifesting inward moral wickedness.'

31 行邪術之西門的邪惡（徒八 22，現修、新普），就是他欲以金錢換取藉著按手授予聖靈的能力；信徒應在<u>邪惡</u>上做嬰孩（林前十四 20，思高），要除去……一切……<u>邪惡</u>（雅一 21，新普），不要用自由來掩飾<u>邪惡</u>（彼前二 16，新譯）；<u>惡毒</u>、邪惡（林前五 8：<u>κακίας</u> καὶ πονηρίας）與純潔和真理（現修）相對，前二者幾乎同義，合起來可以涵蓋各種罪惡。

32 「其餘四次」為：羅一 29；弗四 31；西三 8；彼前二 1。在這五次，**κακία** = 'a mean-spirited or vicious attitude or disposition, *malice*, *ill-will*, *malignity*' (BDAG 500*a*, s.v. 2). 參《西・門》551-52；《新希》170*a-b*（s.v.）。

33 φθόνος, θόνος.

34 (1) 名詞 **φθόνος** 在新約另外出現五次（即新約共九次）：兩次在另一「惡行目錄」中（加五 21；彼前二 1）；兩次與 ἔρις 連著出現（腓一 15：有些人宣講基督……是出於嫉妒和競爭〔思高；參《腓》122〕；提前六 4：嫉妒、紛爭）；另一次在 πρὸς φθόνον 這介詞片語中（雅四 5〔參張略：《雅各書》241-44 的討論〕）。(2) 這字在 LXX 出現四次，分別指羅馬人中「沒有<u>嫉妒</u>，也沒有競爭」（οὐκ ἔστιν <u>φθόνος</u> οὐδὲ ζῆλος: 次經《馬加比一書》8.16，思高）；但以理是被 'envious slanders' 所害（διαβολαῖς φθόνου: 偽經《馬加比三書》6.7〔RSV, NRSV〕）；死亡進入了世界，是「因魔鬼的嫉妒」（φθόνῳ διαβόλῳ: 次經《所羅門智訓》2.24〔思高智慧篇〕）；智者「決不與使人消沉的嫉妒同行」（φθόνῳ τετηκότι: 6.23〔思高〕）。

35 Stott 202: '[they] are very ugly twins. . . . Both disrupt human relationships.'

所有，因看見別人擁有自己所沒有的而大為不悅，卻不想自己也努力得到別人所擁有的，而是竭力使別人也沒有自己所缺少的。」[36]

（#6）**是可恨的**意即行為舉止引起別人的憎恨或厭惡。[37] 可能這是**惡毒**和**嫉妒**的人所引發的、別人對他們的回應，即是別人認為他們**是可恨的**。[38]

（#7）**彼此相恨**。[39] 有釋經者認為，「按下一項的授意，此處〔**是可恨的**〕大概是指充滿憎恨的。」但這不必要地使這兩項成為「同義詞」。[40] 較可取的是斯托得的解釋：「我們被憎恨，**而且彼此相恨**」意即我們在人際關中所經歷的敵意是相互的。[41]

保羅可能刻意以**惡毒**、**嫉妒**、**彼此相恨**（##5-7）等反社會的行為結束本節的惡行目錄，為要與下一節**上帝的恩慈**和**慈愛**這些與人為善的美德構成對比。[42]

---

36 《加》1257-58。

37 馮譯作**面目可憎**！（**1**）原文形容詞（**στυγητός**）在希臘文聖經不再出現。它的意思是 'loathsome, despicable'（BDAG 949*b*, s.v.）。英譯多作（**i**）'despicable/detestable'（NRSV / Hendriksen 385, 387; Mounce 435, 445-46; Simpson 113）或 'hateful'（KJV, NKJV, NAU, REB, NJB, *Paraphrase* 293〔後三者加上 'ourselves' 一字〕; O. Michel, *TDNT* 4.692; DC 148*a*; Hanson III 190; Fiore II 216; Wall 357, 360）;（**ii**）'hated by men/others/people'（RSV / ESV; Jeon I 95 / *EDNT* 3.281*a* [s.v.]）或 'being hated'（NIV, TNIV, NIV2011）; see also Quinn 28, 187, 200: 'detested'. 參《新希》310*b*（s.v.）：「被人厭惡的〔ii〕或被認為足以惹人討厭的〔i〕。」（**ii**）可視為表達了（**i**）的含意。（**2**）Arichea－Hatton 300 則理解為主動意義的 'full of hate'.（**3**）Neyrey 1217*a* 不知從哪裏看出 'hatred of self' 的意思來。Similarly, Oden 36: 'detesting ourselves'.（**4**）同字根的複合形容詞 θεοστυγής 在希臘文聖經亦僅出現一次，意思是**憎恨神**／**上帝**（羅一30，新譯／現修、新普〔參《羅》1.323-24〕）。

38 Towner III 777（唐 1133）。

39 μισοῦντες ἀλλήλους = 'hating/detesting one another' (KJV, NKJV, RSV, NRSV, NAU, NIV / Fiore II 216).（**1**）類似的詞語見於太二十四 10：**彼此陷害**，<u>**彼此憎恨**</u>。原文呈現 ABB'A' 的交叉配置模式：ἀλλήλους παραδώσουσιν καὶ <u>μισήσουσιν ἀλλήλους</u>.（**2**）動詞 **μισέω** 在本書出現僅此一次，在保羅書信僅再出現三次（羅七 15，九 13；弗五 29），新約全部則為四十次。See BDAG 652*b*-53*a* (s.v.);《新希》220*a*（s.v.）。

40 二引句依次見張 370、370-71。

41 Stott 202. Marshall 311 解釋如下：'Malicious and envious people [#5] are odious; they cause other people to react with hatred [#6], and they respond in kind [#7].'

42 Mott, 'Ethics' 36.

5.2.2　如今享受的救恩（三 4～7）

溫德蘭根據原文的次序從這一小段看出以下的模式：

第 4 至 5 節	第 6 至 7 節
（甲）但到了……恩慈和慈愛顯明的時候	（己'）聖靈就是上帝……厚厚地澆灌在我們身上的
（乙）我們救主上帝的	（乙'）藉著我們的救主耶穌基督
（丙）並不是因我們自己所行的義	（丙'）好讓我們……得稱為義（＝ 上帝的、義的工作）
（丁）而是照他的憐憫	（丁'）因他的恩
（戊）**他救了我們**	（戊'）可以……成為後嗣（＝得救）
（己）藉著重生的洗和聖靈的更新	（甲'）憑著永生的盼望（在基督末日再臨之時）[1]

明顯地，這並不是真正的交叉配置模式，因為右欄中央四項的次序，並不是和左欄中央四項的次序相反，而是相同；因此，這裏所呈現的是一種混合的模式，既有交叉配置（首末兩行），亦有平行排列（中央四行）。[2] 就其內容而論，這四節分別提出他救了我們（5c 節上）這行動的

1　Wendland, 'Discourse' 348. 作者指出，'This bipartite construction . . . is marked by a significant chiastic shift . . . at the middle boundary'（347），指由（己）轉到（己'）。

2　Wieland 216 從三 3～7 看出以下的交叉配置模式：

A　The condition out of which we are saved（3 節）
　B　The source of salvation: operation of God's graciousness（4 節上：但到了……恩慈和慈愛顯明的時候）
　　C　The saviour: God（4 節下：我們救主上帝）
　　　D　Explanation of salvation: why?（5a～b 節：並不是因我們自己所行的義，而是照他的憐憫）

- 時間——到了我們救主上帝的恩慈和慈愛顯明的時候（4 節），
- 基礎——並不是因我們自己所行的義，而是照他的憐憫（5a～b 節〔原文次序〕），

他救了我們（5c 節上）

- 方法——藉著重生的洗和聖靈的更新。聖靈就是上帝藉著我們的救主耶穌基督厚厚地澆灌在我們身上的（5c 節下～6 節），
- 目的——好讓我們因他的恩得稱為義，可以憑著永生的盼望成為後嗣（7 節）。[3]

E The saving act（5c 節上：他救了我們）

D' Explanation of salvation: how?（5c 節下～6 節上：藉著重生的洗和聖靈的更新。聖靈就是上帝……厚厚地澆灌在我們身上的）

C' The saviour: Jesus Christ（6 節下：藉著我們的救主耶穌基督）

B' The source of salvation: operation of God's grace（7a 節：好讓我們因他的恩得稱為義）

A' The condition into which we are saved（7b 節：可以憑著永生的盼望成為後嗣）

這裏惟一的問題是，我們〔的〕救主上帝（C）是直接地連於他〔上帝〕救了我們（E）這主要的拯救行動，但我們的救主耶穌基督（C'）並不是直接連於（E）的拯救行動，* 而是連於上帝把聖靈厚厚地澆灌在我們身上那個行動（D'）；在這個意義上，C' 和 C 的對應並不十分工整。*Wieland 228-29 則認為藉著我們的救主耶穌基督這片語 'qualifies the whole unit which explicates the statement ἔσωσεν ἡμᾶς', 所得出的意思就是：'God our saviour saved us in the manner described in vv. 5-6a through Jesus Christ our saviour: Christ is the agent through whom God saves.' 但見三 6 註釋末段（下面 401-2）。

3 Marshall 307. Cf. Fee 203; Hiebert 444; Laansma 285. Stott 201-6 從三 3～8 看出救恩的六個成分（'ingredients'）：（**i**）'its need (why it is necessary)' = 未重生者的狀況（3 節）；（**ii**）'its source (where it originates) = 上帝的恩慈和慈愛（4 節）；（**iii**）'its ground (what it rests on)' = 他的憐憫（5b 節）；（**iv**）'its means (how it comes to us)' = 藉著重生的洗和聖靈的更新（5c 節）；（**v**）'its goal (what it leads to) = 可以憑著永生的盼望成為後嗣（7 節）；（**vi**）'its evidence (how it proves itself)' = 留心行善（8b 節）。See also 207. 但見三 8b～d 註釋註 6 之（2）= 下面 425。

三 **4** **但到了我們救主上帝的恩慈和慈愛顯明的時候，**

但字引進信徒從前的景況（3 節）和他們現今所享受的救恩（4～7 節）的對比。[1] 上一節以主詞形式出現的**我們**，在第 5、6 兩節以受詞的形式出現；[2] 現在主詞變成了**上帝的恩慈和慈愛**，[3] 以及拯救我們的**他**（5c 節）；這種改變突出了上帝在救恩上採取主動，人只是接受者。[4] **我們救主上帝的恩慈和慈愛顯明的時候**回望二章 11 節**上帝救眾人的恩典已經顯明出來**，[5] 兩次都是指上帝拯救的恩典藉著基督的首次降臨而顯明出來。[6] 不過，第 5 至 7 節的內容顯示，這裏的重點是在於信徒對**上帝的恩慈和慈愛**的主觀體驗，即是藉著**聖靈所施重生和更新的洗**（5 節〔現修〕，見下文）而得救，並且憑著**永**

1 Genade 90 則認為，作者是在頌揚上帝的榜樣之卓越，與歸主前的人類之貧乏狀況相對。

2 ἔσωμεν ἡμᾶς（**他救了我們**〔5c 節〕），ἐξέχεεν ἐφ' ἡμᾶς（**他澆灌在我們身上**〔6 節〕）。雖然主格的 ἡμεῖς 仍在 5a 節出現，但那是一項否定陳述，指出**我們所行的義**並不存在。

3 Collins 361-62 舉例指出，χρηστότης（**恩慈**）和 φιλανθρωπία（**慈愛**）是 'a classic pair'. '[They] are qualities which were specially praised in Hellenistic rulers, but are here transferred to God' (J. Schneider, C. Brown, *DNTT* 3.220).

4 Van Neste, 'Message' 26*a*.

5 **(1)** Genade 92 聲稱，本節（誤作三 5）的動詞 ἐπιφαίνω（**顯明**）與二 13 同字根的名詞 ἐπιφάνεια（**顯現**）構成 paronomasia 的另一例子。問題是，二字可否視為 '[being] in close proximity'（參一 1～2a 註釋註 25 之〔2〕= 上面 53）。**(2)** 雖然動詞 ἐπεφάνη 是被動語態，但其意思仍是主動的 'show oneself, make an appearance'（BDAG 385*b* [s.v. ἐπιφαίνω, 4]），即是「出現；顯現」(《新希》130*b* [s.v. I.2])，而不是被動的 'were revealed'（NJB），即是「被顯出來」（張 371）。**(3)** 'It should be noted that this is the third of three "appearings" in Titus: (1) the grace of God (2:11), (2) the glory of God (2:13), (3) the goodness of God (3:4)'（Akin, 'Mystery' 145）。中文無法複製這種頭韻現象（g, G）。

6 見二 11 註釋第二段（上面 288）。**(1)** 兩個詞語（**上帝……的恩典**和**上帝的恩慈和慈愛**）都是 'circumlocutions for the redemptive Christ-event'（Towner I 68）。Cf. Goulder, 'Wolves' 252: 'Twice the incarnation is described in a periphrasis'. **(2)** 但若**上帝的恩慈和慈愛顯明**是藉著基督的首次降臨，為甚麼保羅不明確地這樣說呢？Knight I 91-92 解釋，這是由於本段的要旨是述說上帝為我們信徒作了甚麼，並以此作為我們應當怎樣行（1～2 節）的榜樣和動機；基督如何成就救贖，以及信徒必須以信心回應等事情，都不在本段的考慮範疇之內。

生的盼望成為後嗣（7 節）。[7]

恩慈這名詞[8] 在新約另五次用於上帝時，其文理提示，這字總是有救贖意義，指上帝對罪人那滿有恩典的態度和行動。在羅馬書二章 4 節，[9] 上帝的恩慈，即是祂的寬容和恆忍，[10] 是以罪人的悔改為其目標的。在以弗所書二章 7 節，他極豐富的恩典顯明於他在基督耶穌裏向我們——這些生來是可怒的兒女的人（3 節）——所施的恩慈。[11] 在羅馬書十一章 22 節，上帝的恩慈與祂的嚴厲相對；是上帝的恩慈使信主的外邦人得以被接在好橄欖上（24 節）。[12] 在前兩節，上帝的恩慈與祂的另一或另兩項屬性一起出現：他的……寬容、忍耐（羅二 4）、他……的恩典（弗二 7）；照樣在本節，顯明的是上帝的恩慈和慈愛。[13]

---

7 Fee 203. 參二 11 註釋註 21 所屬正文（上面 288-89）。

8 （**1**）χρηστότης 另有譯為「慷慨」：'generosity' (Kelly 251; Fiore II 216, 218). Simpson 115 認為 '*Benignity* is the nearest English equivalent'，意即「仁慈、和善」。Johnson I 135 甚至聲稱，'it is really the "sweetness" of God which is revealed'（參：彼前二 3：你們已嘗到了『主是何等的甘飴』〔思高；ἐγεύσασθε ὅτι χρηστὸς ὁ κύριος〕）。（**2**）Köstenberger 623*a* 認為，'It is possible that the term *chrēstotēs* is intended to convey a wordplay with "Christ" (*Christos*).' 筆者認為可能性不大。參《西‧門》899-900 註 8 之（3）（4）。（**3**）這字（**χρηστότης**）在新約另外出現九次，全部是在保羅書信裏（參《加》1277-78；《西‧門》591-92）；其中四次用於人（羅三 12；林後六 6；加五 22；西三 12），五次用於上帝（羅二 4，十一 22a、22c、22d；弗二 7）。

9 還是你藐視他豐富的恩慈（της χρηστότητος）、寬容、忍耐，不知道他的恩慈（τὸ χρηστόν）是領你悔改嗎？第二個恩慈原文是與第一個恩慈同字根的形容詞加冠詞用作名詞，第二個恩慈顯然重複了第一個恩慈的意思。

10 保羅談到上帝豐富的恩慈、寬容、忍耐之後，隨即以他的恩慈概括剛提到的三個項目；這提示上帝的恩慈就是祂的寬容與恆忍（呂譯），即是祂以慈悲為懷，約束自己不降罰、不施行祂的義怒（參《羅》1.345）。

11 參《弗》296-97。在基督耶穌裏表達了上帝的恩慈所在的範疇。

12 好橄欖指整個得救的社羣、上帝的真子民整體，包括外邦人和猶太人。參《羅》3.564、594。

13 See Knight I 87.（**1**）Genade 89 聲稱，χρηστότης（恩慈）和 φιλανθρωπία（慈愛）二字是稱為 'anthropopathism' 這修辭技巧的例子（See 97-98, 128）。筆者認為此見解不可取，因為恩慈和慈愛是上帝本身具有的素質，而不僅是被歸給上帝的、人的感情（human emotions ascribed to God）。（**2**）ἡ χρηστότης <u>καὶ</u> ἡ φιλανθρωπία 這有連詞（syndetic）的結構，比對於 3 節無連詞的七個項目，使上帝的正面素質和信徒從前負面的表現之間的對比更為突出（Genade 89）。（**3**）昆謝隆將 ἡ χρηστότης καὶ ἡ φιλανθρωπία（'conceived to be a unit' [Quinn 213]）翻譯為 'humane

慈愛原文[14] 在新約出現惟一的另一次，是指馬耳他島上的居民對保羅等人的**友善**（徒二十八 2，思高、當代、現修、新譯、新普），在這裏則指上帝**對人的慈愛**（思高）。[15] 原文名詞在次經《馬加比二書》14 章 9 節指統治者「對天下所懷的仁德」（思高瑪加伯下）。在希臘化時期，「這是統治者被稱譽的普通美德中最被珍惜的一樣」；保羅可能刻意使用了當代君王崇拜的詞彙，為要使人對基督教的宣稱留下更深刻的印象。[16] 上帝對人的慈愛就是上帝對人們**彼此相恨**（3 節）的答案，也是信徒要**對眾人……顯出溫柔**（2 節）的理由。[17]

恩慈和**慈愛**在聖經以外的希臘文獻常一起出現。[18] 在本節，兩

---

munificence'（28, 187, 192, 210, 215, 220），這等於把原文視為重言法，兩個名詞是主（前者）從（後者）關係。參一 4b 註釋註 2 之（2）= 上面 80。

14 **φιλανθρωπία** 是複合名詞（from φίλος + ἄνθρωπος [Vine 2.292]）。形容詞 φίλος 見一 8 註釋註 5 之（1）= 上面 132。名詞 ἄνθρωπος 見一 14 註釋註 16（上面 192）。**(1)** 與複合名詞同字根的副詞 φιλανθρώπως 在新約只出現一次，指羅馬百夫長猶流**以仁慈**待保羅（徒二十七 3，呂譯），即是**寬待**他（和修、現修、新譯）或對他**十分友善**（新普）。這副詞在 LXX 出現兩次，也是「仁慈地」之意（次經《馬加比二書》9.27／偽經《馬加比三書》3.20 [RSV, NRSV: 'with . . . kindness / with benevolence'）。**(2)** 這副詞衍生自同字根的形容詞 φιλάνθρωπος, 此字沒有在新約出現，但在 LXX 出現六次，分別指智慧是「愛人的」（次經《便西拉智訓》= 思高智慧篇 1.6 / 7.23；NJB: 'friendly to humanity / human beings'）；義人必須「憐愛眾人」（12.19; NJB: 'kindly to his fellows'）；波斯王亞達薛西「仁慈的」決定（次經《以斯得拉一書》8.10；RSV, NRSV: 'my gracious decision'）；諸王賜予猶太人的種種「特權」（次經《馬加比二書》4.11〔思高瑪加伯下〕；NJB / RSV, NRSV: 'liberties/concessions'）；以及「仁慈的」忠告（偽經《馬加比四書》5.12；RSV, NRSV: 'humane advice'）。

15 φιλανθρωπία = 'affectionate concern for and interest in humanity, *(loving) kindness*' (BDAG 1055*b*, s.v.), 'affection for mankind' (LN §25.36), 'love for/of humanity / Love of Humanity' (Witherington 153/158/156);「（神）向人類的慈愛」（《輔讀》529）;「對世人的愛」（《新希》347*a* [s.v.]）。See also Knight I 87: 'It is not love in the abstract but love that focuses upon man as man'. REB 則翻譯為 'generosity'. 孟威廉直譯為 'philanthropy'（Mounce cix, 435, 436, 438, 447; also Malherbe, 'Paraenesis' 306, 311）。窩羅伯則譯作 'friendship'（Wall 357, 360, 378, 379, 384, 385, 386, cf. 14）。

16 Kelly 251 (endorsed by Marshall 313). 引句英文原作 'it was the most prized of the stock virtues acclaimed in rulers.' Cf. Towner IV 916*a*: 'typically a virtue to be found in rulers'.

17 See Fairnbairn 291.

18 See BDAG 1056*a* (s.v. φιλανθρωπία); Knight I 88; Wall 361; White 198*a*; Bassler 207: 'goodness and loving-kindness . . . were widely used by contemporary writers to

個名詞在原文各有冠詞，因而構成一個複數的主詞，但動詞顯明卻是單數的，這表示上帝的恩慈和慈愛被視為一個（不是兩個）概念；[19] 事實上，上帝的恩慈和慈愛與上帝……的恩典（二 11）是相同的思想，[20] 前者只是以較為希臘化的方式表達了後者的思想。兩者的相似更由另一事實證明了：兩者的顯明都帶來救恩（二 11，三 4、5）。兩者所表達的都是上帝以救主的身分對罪人的態度和行動。[21] 正是由於我們從前也是（3 節）像他們一樣的時候，我們〔的〕救主上帝[22] 向我們顯明了祂的恩慈和慈愛，因此保羅要提多勉勵信徒，要和氣，對眾人總要顯出溫柔（三 2）。[23]

---

describe the actions of humans . . . and in hellenistic Judaism to describe both God and humans.'

19 Cf. Mounce 447: 'the repeated articles (ἡ . . . ἡ) emphasiz[e] their identity.'

20 'Tt. 3:4-7 shows that χάρις can be replaced with χρηστότης, φιλανθρωπία' (H. Conzelmann, *TDNT* 9.398). 'Two nouns express the grace shown by God' (Marshall 312).

21 Cf. Collins, 'Theology' 67: 'It [φιλανθρωπία] is both attitudinal and concrete.' 如 Kidd（'Titus' 203）所指出，（i）這兩節（二 11，三 4）使用抽象名詞並不表示上帝沒有真正參與人間（'does not indicate that God's involvement with humanity is problematic, much less docetic'*），而只表示上帝的這些屬性就是人的救恩所最需要的；（ii）這兩節使用抽象名詞，因為基督的來臨要複製到人（信徒）的生命中的，就是這些屬性（見下文）。（* = 與 'docetism' 同字根的形容詞；名詞「幻影說」是「基督論的異端理論，以物質是邪惡的，認為基督的身體不是真實的，而只是幻影。故此，基督並沒有真正受苦、死亡和復活。這理論成為公元 2 世紀諾斯底主義與 4 世紀摩尼教的基督論解釋，其論點早於約翰書信中已受到警告（約壹四 2；約貳 7）」〔《聖神》169*b*〕。）

22 這詞（τοῦ σωτῆρος ἡμῶν θεοῦ）已在上文出現兩次（一 3，二 10）；參一 3b 註釋註 3 之（2）= 上面 73。

23 See Knight I 88. Cf. Bassler 207: 'in hellenistic Jewish writings, heavenly goodness and loving-kindness are presented as models for human actions . . . and that is the intended application here.'

三 5c 他救了我們……藉著重生的洗和聖靈的更新。

5a 並不是因我們自己所行的義，

5b 而是照他的憐憫，

留意本節在原文並不是以他救了我們開始，而是以 5a 節和 5b 節的對比（並不是……而是）開始，然後才是主句他救了我們（5c 節）；[1] 這種鋪排將重點放在那個對比上，尤其是在對比中積極的一面。我們在原文是獨立代名詞，而不僅是隱含於動詞內，因而有強調之意；[2] 中譯加上自己二字，正是要表達此意。[3] 我們指基督徒羣體。[4] 所行的義原文直譯作「在義中的行為」，[5] 大抵意即「我們生活在義的狀況或範疇中所作的行為」，[6] 簡化為「義的行

1 救字原文動詞（σῴζω）在本書僅在這裏出現，但在保羅書信另外出現 28 次，新約全部 106 次（see BDAG 982*a*-83*a* [s.v.];《新希》322*a*）。

2 ἃ ἐποιήσαμεν ἡμεῖς. (**1**) 關係代名詞 ἅ 的前述詞是所有格的 ἔργων（見註 5）；前者沒有受到後者的影響而變成所有格的 ὧν, 是 'non-attraction of the relative' 的例子（BDF §294(1)）。(**2**) 動詞 **ποιέω** 在保羅書信出現 83 次（新約全部 568 次）；詳參《帖後》304-7。

3 Genade 91 認為，很可能克里特的假教義強調自己所行的義，或是克里特的信徒當中有傾向寬容地對待這種教導，因而保羅對此嚴詞否定。簡內德稍後更明確地認為，5 節的刻意鋪排提示，這裏嵌入了針對靠行為（尤其是藉著遵行律法）稱義或憑己力得救的爭辯（93）。

4 Marshall, 'Salvation' 348: 'the community of Christians'; Towner III 781 n.46:「ἡμᾶς……代表教會整體，直接所指的就是讀者們」（唐 1138 註 31）。

5 ἔργων τῶν ἐν δικαιοσύνῃ = 'deeds/works . . . in righteousness' (NAU, RSV / ESV). 參呂譯：本於義的行為。名詞 **δικαιοσύνη** 在新約一共出現 92 次：福音書 10 次，使徒行傳 4 次，普通書信 18 次，啟示錄 2 次；其餘 58 次都是在保羅書信，尤其是羅馬書（34 次 = 保羅書信以外的次數之總和），其中多次用於「上帝的義（[ἡ] δικαιοσύνη [τοῦ] θεοῦ）」（羅一 17，三 5、21、22，十 3；林後五 21）、「他的義（ἡ δικαιοσύνη αὐτοῦ）」（羅三 25、26）、從上帝而來的義（ἡ ἐκ θεοῦ δικαιοσύνη）」（腓三 9），和「信心的義（[ἡ] δικαιοσύνη [τῆς] πίστεως）」（羅四 11、13）、「出於信心的義（ἡ ἐκ πίστεως δικαιοσύνη）」（羅九 30，十 6）、「基於信心的義（ἡ δικαιοσύνη ἐπὶ τῇ πίστει）」（腓三 9）等詞語中。See BDAG 247*a*-49*a* (s.v.);《新希》84*b*-85*a*.

6 Fairnbairn 292. See also Hendriksen 385, 390: 'in (a state of) righteousness'; Ward 228: 'our deeds in the sphere of righteousness'; 269: '*deeds in* the sphere of *righteousness* which we did.' (**1**) 按 Jeon I 104 的解釋，'The phrase "works that we did in

為」。[7] 有認為義在這裏是特指遵行上帝的命令，[8] 但保羅在這裏是要將一切（不論是按猶太人的理解或是按外邦人的理解）的「義」行都摒諸門外，故此所行的義較可能是籠統地指一切的「義的行為」。[9] 這話並不確認我們實在有「義的行為」，因為在上帝的眼中，信主之前的人並無「義的行為」可言（見 3 節；參〔例如〕羅三 10～12、19、23）。[10] 這裏強調「行為」不能使人得救，為要襯托出他的憐憫（5b 節）作為我們得救的基礎；[11] 這樣全然否定「行為」能使人得救，清楚表

---

righteousness" refers to "works" . . . done "in" . . . the sphere or state of "righteousness" (δικαιοσύνῃ), i.e., "works" done while living "sensibly and righteously (δικαίως) and godly in the present age" (2:12).' 可是，我們從前（三 3）是這樣生活的嗎？（**2**）ἐποιήσαμεν 可視為 'constative [aorist], summarizing all our deeds before God acted on our behalf'（Ngewa 463 n.172）。

7 KJV, NKJV, NRSV / Wall 357, 361, 368, 370, 401: 'works of righteousness / moral rectitude'. Knight I 93 n.50 指出，多三 5 以較籠統的用詞來表達腓三 6、9 以較希伯來式的詞彙表達的意思；該二節談到律法上的義（6 節：δικαιοσύνην τὴν ἐν νόμῳ）和自己因律法而得的義（9 節：ἐμὴν δικαιοσύνην τὴν ἐκ νόμου），而保羅表明他並不是靠自己努力遵行律法而獲得稱義和救恩的（參《腓》351-52、362）。

8 Quinn 216: 'The righteousness in question is biblical, that is to say, righteousness as the OT and first-century Judaism conceived it, an obedient performance of the commands of the one God'; Marshall 314: 'conduct in accordance with God's requirements or laws'; 315: 'the deeds are those done in observance of the righteousness required by the law'; K. L. Onesti & M. T. Brauch（*DPL* 827）：「義在此指遵行律法」（《辭典》1193*a*）。Fiore II 219 也認為，'The works were considered as done in accordance with God's law', 儘管這裏沒有使用律法的行為（[ἐξ] ἔργων νόμου: 羅三 20、28；加二 16a、c、d，三 2、5、10）一詞（參《羅》1.467-70；《加》526-45〔結論於 533-34、545〕）。

9 Towner III 780（唐 1137）。See also Kelly 251: 所行的義是指「一般的正直道德行為（upright moral conduct in general）」（followed by Wieland 223）。Marshall 46 同樣認為，'This rejection is of human works in general . . . . It seems unlikely that a specific application would not have been made if Jewish works were being made a condition or essential accompaniment of salvation.' Cf. 102: 'The concept of "not by works of the law" is enlarged to make it clear that human works in general do not contribute to justification. The reason for this stress must lie in some kind of limitation of salvation on the part of the opponents, although just exactly what kind of limitation is not apparent.'

10 Knight I 93-94. Cf. Towner I 114: 'the notion of a righteous deed (in the Pauline sense of *dikaiosynē*) may here be only rhetorical . . . (because we can do nothing righteous)'. Calvin 381 指著 3 節所描述信徒從前的景況問道：'what good work could proceed from such a mass of corruption?'

11 Knight I 94.（**1**）單此一點足以使 Donelson II 178 的聲稱成疑，他說：'the Pastoral Epistles . . . insist over and over again that we must flee the vices and practice the virtues in order to obtain salvation'. 按他的理解，教牧書信的教導是：'Reliable apostolic

明對恩典惟一可能的回應就是信心（信靠）。[12] **與此同時**，好行為是上帝救贖和潔淨信徒作祂自己的子民的目的（二 14c），因此，信了上帝的人要留心行善（三 8c，參 14 節），信徒要隨時準備行美善的事（三 1，新普），提多更要顯出自己是好行為的榜樣（二 7）；假教師則根本做不出甚麼好事來（一 16c，當代），他們在行為上否認上帝（16b 節）。[13] 如此，雖然人不能靠行為得救，但好行為卻是信了上帝和已經得救的重要指標；缺乏好行為則是不認識上帝的標誌，也是尚未經歷重生的洗和聖靈的更新（5c 節）的標誌。[14]

而是照他的憐憫這片語內的所有代名詞他字，在原文的位置表示它是受到強調的，[15] 越發突出了他的憐憫和我們自己所行的義的對

---

teachings, taken on with the power of the Spirit, produce virtue and, in turn, salvation'（180）。但見正文下文的「與此同時」。
（2）不是因我們自己所行的義，而是照他的憐憫這種對比，可能源自申命記的教導（Marshall, 'Salvation' 350-51）：上帝揀選以色列，並非因〔他〕們人數比任何民族多（其實他們的人數在各民族中是最少的），而是因為上帝愛他們，又因要遵守他向〔他〕們列祖所起的誓（申七 7～8；參四 37～38）；他們得進迦南地，也不是因他們的義（九 4～6）；那裏的城鎮不是他們建造的，裝滿各樣美物的房屋不是他們裝滿的，水井不是他們挖成的，果園不是他們栽植的（六 10～11）；他們不可心高氣傲（八 14），以為所擁有的財富是自己的力量和能力得來的，而是要切記得財富的能力來自上帝（八 17～18）。**（3）** Wieland 223 指出，同樣的對比見於但九 18：我們在你面前懇求，不是因自己的義（οὐ . . . ἐπὶ ταῖς δικαιοσύναις ἡμῶν），而是因你豐富的憐憫（ἀλλὰ διὰ τὸ σὸν ἔλεος）。**（4）** Towner IV 916*a* 也認為，'the structure and theme of Deut. 9:5 may have influenced the presentation of 3:5a (as well as Paul's theology of justification)'. 比較：

申九 5：你能進去得他們的地，並不是因你的義（οὐχὶ διὰ τὴν δικαιοσύνην σου）……
而是（ἀλλά）……
多三 5a：他救了我們，並不是因我們自己所行的義（οὐχ ἐξ ἔργων τῶν ἐν δικαιοσύνῃ），
而是（ἀλλά）……

12 Marshall 216: 'The total disqualification of works is a clear indicator that the only possible response to grace is faith.'

13 以上八次（包括本節），原文都使用 ἔργον 一字。如唐書禮所言，'"Good deeds" (1:16; 2:7[, 14]; 3:8, 14) is Pauline shorthand (particularly in these letters to co-workers . . .) for the visible, outward dimension of Christian existence (cf. Eph. 2:10)'（Towner IV 915*a*）。參二 14 註釋註 34 及所屬正文（上面 338-39）。

14 See Genade 93-94.

15 κατὰ τὸ αὐτοῦ ἔλεος = 'Emphatic αὐτοῦ in attributive position' (BDF §284[3]; see also

比。[16] 照他的憐憫一方面表示，上帝的救恩與上帝的憐憫相符，彷彿上帝的憐憫定下了標準，而上帝的救恩達到這標準；[17] 與此同時，介系詞照字亦表示原因：上帝拯救了我們……是因為他憐憫我們（現修）。[18] 憐憫指上帝對不配得的人所顯出的恩惠（另見羅九 23，十一 31，十五 9；加六 6；弗二 4），可見憐憫相當於恩典（二 11），只不過憐憫著眼於領受者十分有需要的狀況（見下文），恩典的重點則在於上帝的恩惠為罪人所不配得的性質；[19] 而上帝……的恩典（二 11）與上帝的恩慈和慈愛（三 4）是同義的，故此他的憐憫在此總結了句子開首的上帝的恩慈和慈愛。[20]

驟然看來，他救了我們（5c 節）是在我們救主上帝的恩慈和慈

MHT 3.190: 'emph.'). Simpson 114 把它讀成 αὑτοῦ（= ἑαυτοῦ），即是「他自己的」。(**1**) White 198*b* 認為，這原文片語得自詩一〇九（LXX 一〇八）26：照你的慈愛拯救我（κατὰ τὸ ἔλεός σου）。更為接近本節這介詞片語的，是彼前一 3 的講法（只是多了一個字）：他曾照自己的大憐憫（κατὰ τὸ πολὺ αὐτοῦ ἔλεος）……重生了我們。(**2**) 名詞 **ἔλεος** 在保羅書信另外出現九次，分別指：蒙〔上帝〕憐憫……的器皿（羅九 23〔參《羅》3.212〕）、〔上帝〕施給〔外邦人〕的憐憫（十一 31a〔參《羅》3.673-76〕）、外邦人因他的憐憫，榮耀上帝（十五 9〔參《羅》4.524-25〕）；上帝有豐富的憐憫（弗二 4）；憐憫（和恩惠與平安）是卷首問安的內容（提前一 2；提後一 2），憐憫（和平安）也是信末祝福的內容（加六 16）；主的憐憫是保羅祈願的內容（提後一 16、18）。這名詞在新約另外出現十七次（新約全部 27 次）；詳見 BDAG 316*a*-16*b* (s.v.);《新希》109*a*（s.v.）。

16 Knight I 94; Fiore II 219.

17 Ward 270.

18 See BDAG 512*b* (s.v. κατά, B 5 a δ): 'Oft. the norm is at the same time the reason, so that *in accordance with* and *because of* are merged'（所例舉的例子包括多三 5）。Scott 175 則這樣解釋 'in accordance with': 'God's action . . . was simply in keeping with His Divine nature. Being the merciful One, He could not but show mercy.'

19 《加》1414。

20 Marshall 314. 如 Knight I 94 所指出，他救了我們，並不是因我們自己所行的義，而是照他的憐憫這話在其文理中的意思，由弗二 3～5 節闡釋了。該段以鮮明的對比陳述了憐憫的意思：我們從前也都生活在他們當中〔參多三 3：我們從前也是無知……〕，放縱肉體的私慾，隨著肉體和心中的意念去做，和別人一樣，生來就是該受懲罰的人。(4)然而，上帝有豐富的憐憫，因著他愛我們的大愛，(5)竟在我們因過犯而死了的時候，使我們與基督一同活過來——可見你們得救是本乎恩。上帝的憐憫（i）臨到人，是當他陷於這種悲慘的景況中：生活在私慾和悖逆之中，並因自己的過犯而在靈性上死亡；（ii）上帝的憐憫使我們脫離這種可憐的光景。上帝的憐憫（iii）表達了祂白白的無條件的愛，（iv）祂使我們與基督一同活過來，我們因祂的恩典得救。

愛顯明的時候（4 節），但即使對保羅而言，事實亦並非如此：上帝的恩慈和慈愛藉著基督的首次降臨而顯明了，但保羅並沒有立即歸信基督；克里特的信徒則比保羅更遲信主。由此可見，保羅在這裏並沒有想到顯明和救了這兩個行動的時間之間的準確關係。[21] 事實上，**他救了我們是藉著重生的洗和聖靈的更新**（5c 節），這是指基督所成就的救贖，是透過聖靈的工作成為信徒的主觀經歷。由此可見，**他救了我們**包含兩方面的意思：一方面，**我們的救主上帝的恩慈和慈愛顯明的時候**（4 節），即是基督首次降臨的時候，救恩（在客觀意義上）就完成了；[22] 另一方面，信徒要藉著相信使徒（及其後的傳福音者）所**傳揚**的福音（一 3），並經歷**重生的洗和聖靈的更新**，基督所成就的救恩才對他們成為真實的。[23]

藉著重生的洗和聖靈的更新原文是七個字的介詞片語，直譯可作「藉著洗｜重生的和更新的｜聖靈的」。[24]（甲）大多數譯本將「重生的」連於在前的「洗」，將「更新」連於隨後的「聖靈的」，所得出的意思就是，上帝**救了我們**的方法是**藉著**〔1〕**重生的洗**和〔2〕**聖靈**

---

21 Banker 99*b*. 'Here Paul is thinking without reference to exact time relationship.'

22 Towner I 114: 'the aorists [ἔσωσεν, δικαιωθέντες] (in conjunction with *epephanē*, v. 4) regard salvation and justification from the perspective of God's redemptive history: through the appearance of Christ, these things have affected the corporate *hēmas* and imply a new present state of affairs for God's people.'

23 See Knight I 90-91, 95.（**1**）Barrett 141 則認為意思只是後者：'It is clear from the context that here "saved" refers to the inward application to particular men of the universal act of redemption.'（**2**）Mounce 438 則持相反的意見，認為**他救了我們**……**澆灌在我們身上**……**得稱為義**……**可以成為後嗣**這些陳述，都不是在談及 'the individual's appropriation of salvation'; 複數的代名詞**我們** 'personalize God's intentions, spelling out why he did what he did, but the focus is still on God and his labors and intentions.'

24 διὰ λουτροῦ | παλιγγενεσίας καὶ ἀνακαινώσεως | πνεύματος ἁγίου = 'through [the] washing | of regeneration and renewal | of [the] Holy Spirit'. Fee（*Presence* 777-78 n.108）指出，有幾份古卷在**聖靈**之前加入了 διά, 這可能反映一種很早期的理解，即是這個片語有兩部分，其一指洗禮（διὰ λουτροῦ παλιγγενεσίας = 'through washing of regeneration'），其二指聖靈（ἀνακαινώσεως [διὰ] πνεύματος ἁγίου = 'renewal through the Holy Spirit'）。

的更新（新和、新譯同）。[25]（乙）但若不把「重生的和更新的」分拆，而把整個詞語視為形容「洗」字，[26] 又把末後的「聖靈的」也視為形容「洗」字，[27] 所得出的意思就如《現代中文譯本修訂版》的翻譯：

---

25 （1）參以下翻譯：藉着〔1〕再生之洗和〔2〕聖靈之再生力（呂譯）；

‘by/through [1] the washing of regeneration, and [2] renewing of the Holy Ghost/Spirit’ (KJV/NKJV);
‘by [1] the washing of regeneration and [2] renewal of / in / renewing by the Holy Spirit’ (ESV / RSV / NAU);
‘by means of [1] the cleansing water of rebirth and [2] renewal in the Holy Spirit’ (NJB);
‘through [1] the water/washing of rebirth and [2] renewal by the Holy Spirit’ (NRSV / NIV, TNIV, NIV2011);
‘through [1] the water of rebirth and [2] the renewing power of the Holy Spirit’ (REB)
‘through [1] the washing which brought us new birth and [2] the renewal which the Holy Spirit imparted’ (*Paraphrase* 295).

（2）Knight II 343 認為 διά 之後的四個名詞呈現交叉配置模式：through the [*a*] washing of [*b*] a new beginning and [through] the [*b*’] renewal of [*a*’] the Holy Spirit. 祈勒克也認為，重生的洗和聖靈的更新在原文可能呈現交叉配置模式：[διὰ] [A] λουτροῦ [B] παλιγγενεσίας* καὶ [B’] ἀνακαινώσεως [A’] πνεύματος ἁγίου（Clark, ‘Structure’ 115: ‘possibly chiastic’）。如此，重生與更新互相對應，洗與聖靈互相對應（張 375 同）。（3）持立場（甲）的釋經者還包括：Aageson 48, 55; Donelson I 185; Guthrie I 206; Guthrie II 217-18（古特立 219）；Hiebert 445-46; Karris 122; Mounce 442-43, 448; Ward 229, 270; White 199*a*.（4）Hanson III 191 認為，重生的洗和聖靈的更新指同一件事。Cf. Dunn 877*a*: ‘the spiritual cleansing is also renewal by the Spirit’; P. Trummer, *EDNT* 3.8*b* (s.v. παλιγγενεσία): ‘the bath of rebirth . . . is in essence . . . a renewal’. Collins 365 明確地說，καί（和）字是 ‘an epexegetical *kai*’, 即聖靈的更新是解釋重生的（see also Jeon I 105: ‘the conjunction . . . καί . . . is epexegetical’）。（5）馮譯則把二者的關係視為途徑與目的：藉着洗濯復起（夾注：「洗禮應許復活」），進入聖靈所賜的新生。

26 E.g., Hendriksen 391: ‘The washing . . . is that of *regeneration and renewing*, regarded as one concept’.

27 Dunn, *Baptism* 168: ‘the washing, of regeneration and renewal, which the Holy Spirit effects’; Köstenberger 623*b*: ‘“Rebirth” . . . and “renewal” . . . are jointly tied to the metaphor of “washing” . . . by the Holy Spirit’; Towner I 56: ‘Titus 3.5 describes the Holy Spirit as the agent whose “washing” (*loutron*) results in “regeneration” (*palingenesia*) and “renewal” (*anakainōsis*)’, 117: ‘the whole activity of “washing” which produces “regeneration and renewal” is to be attributed to the agency of the Holy Spirit’; Towner II 257: ‘it is probably best to understand verse 5 as referring to one event of washing by the Spirit which produces two closely related effects, rebirth and renewal’; Towner, ‘Pastoral Epistles’ 333*b*: ‘the Holy Spirit [is] the agent whose “washing” brings about “regeneration” and “renewal”’（thus also Towner III 56〔唐 80〕）; Chapell 362: ‘the “washing” along with the resultant rebirth and “renewal” are the work of the Holy

上帝……藉着〔1〕聖靈所施〔2〕重生和更新的洗……拯救了我們。[28]
後一種理解可取，[29] 理由如下：

（1） 整個片語以一個介系詞藉著帶領著；這表示作者將這裏所談及的看為一件（不是兩件）事件。即使一件事件可視為包含兩部分，但若是這樣，合理的預期仍是原文應有兩個介系詞。[30]

（2） 重生和更新的意義相近，因此很難明白為甚麼保羅會將二字用在不同的片語中，一個居於從屬的位置（重生的洗），另一個則居於主導的位置（聖靈的更新）。[31] 換一個講法，在重生的洗和聖靈的更新這兩個平行詞語中，與重生平行的是聖靈，與洗平行的是更新（即重生和更新不再是平行的），而所有格（即從屬）的兩個名詞則有完全不同的功能：第一個是受詞所有格（重生的洗＝由洗作成的重生）[32]

Spirit'. See also（i）Fee, *Presence* 778 n.111: 'through washing by the Holy Spirit'; 780-81: 'through the spiritual washing effected by the Holy Spirit'; 費歌頓稱 'through washing of regeneration and renewal' 為上帝救了我們（5a 節）所用的 'means', 'by the Holy Spirit' 為所用的 'agent'（778-79）;（ii）Fee 204-5, esp. alternative (3).

28 參思高：藉着聖神所施行的〔1〕重生和更新的〔2〕洗禮。新普則以上帝為「洗」的行事者，又以聖靈為「重生和更新」的行事者：上帝洗淨我們的罪，又藉着聖靈使我們重生，得着新生命。See also NLT: 'He washed away our sins, giving us a new birth and new life through the Holy Spirit.'

29 See also DC 147*b*: 'through the bath of rebirth and renewal, (as it is worked by) the holy spirit [*sic*]'. **（1）** 持立場（乙）的釋經者還包括：Arichea－Hatton 303; Griffin 323; Hendriksen 391; Jeon I 105; Kelly 251-52; Knight I 96-97; Towner I 115-16; Witherington 158; Trebilco, 'Significance' 251. **（2）** 基里認為，'the genitive in the original [πνεύματος ἁγίου] is causative'（Kelly 253）。但它較可能是主詞所有格，因為根據「文化變換法（transformational grammar）」，λουτροῦ . . . πνεύματος 的「核心構造（'kernel' construction）」（此二詞請參《羅》1.483 註 25）是 'the Spirit washes'. 若按立場（甲）將聖靈連於更新，ἀνακαινώσεως πνεύματος 的核心構造是 'the Spirit renews'.

30 Fee, *Presence* 781 (point 1). 不過，Mounce 443 認為，'It is characteristic for Paul to omit the second preposition in a construction where a preposition governs a series of phrases connected by καί'; 作者引 MHT 3.275 的觀察指出，'[of] twenty-four opportunities in the PE . . . the preposition is repeated in only four of them.'

31 Banker 102*a*. διὰ λουτροῦ παλιγγενεσίας（從屬位置）καὶ ἀνακαινώσεως（主導位置）πνεύματος ἁγίου.

32 參較張 373 註 49：「『重生』（*palingenesias*）是 objective genitive; 即因着罪的洗淨，產生了重生」。其實，不論是按正文括號內的解釋，或是本註下文的解釋，παλιγγενεσίας 都不能稱為受詞所有格，因為此字所屬的 head noun（λουτρόν）所

或形容所有格（以重生為特色的洗），第二個則為主詞所有格（聖靈的更新＝由聖靈作成的更新）。如此，這些詞語顯然並不彼此平衡。因此，重生和更新不大可能是指兩件事。但若重生和更新都是形容洗字，前兩個字便是同等和平行的（「重生和更生的洗」），所得出的意思（不是「由洗作成的重生和更新」，而是「以重生和更新為特色的洗」）亦更為清晰。[33]

(3) 在《七十士譯本》的以西結書三十六章 25 至 27 節，耶和華應許會用清水潔淨祂的子民，而這隨即等同為脫離一切污穢和偶像敬拜；耶和華又應許將新的靈（就是上帝的靈）賜給他們。以西結先知不可能是在想到兩件事（潔淨和賜靈）；相反，上帝的靈就是潔淨他們的罪的方法。這段經文很可能是在提多書本節的背後；[34] 這進一步支持第（2）點。[35]

(4) 第 6 節顯示，第 5、6 兩節的焦點在於聖靈的工作：句子的重點不是落在洗的比喻上，而是落在聖靈身上，聖靈就是上帝……厚厚地澆灌在我們身上的。因此，聖靈不僅更新（聖靈的更新，和重生的洗分開）；在保羅的神學裏，祂洗除罪惡、使人重生，並且更新信徒的生命（聖靈所施重生和更新的洗，現修）。[36] 第 4 至 7 節整句

隱含的動詞是 λούω（洗），若以重生為其賓詞（object），所得出的意思（'to wash regeneration'!）是無意義的。故此，如果「重生的洗＝「由洗作成的重生」或「由罪的洗淨產生的重生」，παλιγγενεσίας 都可能是 genitive of product（此詞詳參 Wallace 106-7）。筆者認為，將這字視為（正文即將提到的）形容所有格（以重生為特色的洗）顯然是較佳的選擇。

33 Fee, *Presence* 781-82 (point 2). Cf. Towner III 783（唐 1141）：'The conceptual similarity of the metaphors "rebirth" and "renewal" suggests unity.'（甲）的理解引起重生的洗和聖靈的更新二者的關係的問題；這問題的答案應該是，二者不是因果關係（前者導致後者），也不是先後的關係（重生的洗在先，聖靈的更新在後）；水禮所象徵的屬靈潔淨和聖靈的更新都是歸信基督這經歷的一方面，二者應視為同時發生。但是按（乙）的理解，這問題根本不存在。

34 Thus also Towner IV 916*b*.

35 Fee, *Presence* 782 (point 3). See also Akin, 'Mystery' 146.

36 Mounce 443 則認為，若聖靈的（πνεύματος ἁγίου）是形容重生和更新的洗（λουτροῦ παλιγγενεσίας καὶ ἀνακαινώσεως）的話，'one might expect τοῦ, "the," or ὑπό, "by," before πνεύματος ἁγίου . . . in order to set it off from ἀνακαινώσεως . . . thereby

的三一性質[37] 支持這兩節的焦點是在聖靈的工作。[38]

雖然名詞**更新**（羅十二 2）和動詞**更新**（林後四 16〔現修〕；西三 10[39]）在上述經文都是指一個過程，但是在提多書本節，**更新**是上帝施行拯救的方法，而上帝**救了我們**是已完成的行動，這就提示，這裏的**更新**不是指更新的整個過程，而是指這個過程的起點。[40] 保羅稱

---

joining παλιγγενεσίας . . . and ἀνακαινώσεως . . . more closely.' 不過作者承認，'it is dangerous to say what an author should have written to make himself clear'.

37 Wall, 'Salvation's Bath' 205: 'the shared responsibility of "God our Savior" who "pours out" the Holy Spirit "by Jesus Christ our Savior" coheres closely to a Trinitarian conception of salvation.' 詳見三 7 註釋倒數第二段（下面 414-15）。Bailey（'Theology' 353）指出：'This is the only passage in the Pastorals where all three members of the Trinity are referred to together.'

38 Fee, *Presence* 782 (point 4). **(1)** 名詞 **πνεῦμα** 在保羅書信出現 146 次（新約全部 379 次），詳見《帖前》461-63。這字常出現在以下的詞語中（see MHM 898*b*-903*b*）：

(i) **上帝的靈**（羅八 9b、14，十五 19〔參《羅》4.579 註 15〕；林前二 11、14，三 16，六 11，七 40，十二 3a；林後三 3；腓三 3）；
從上帝來的靈（林前二 12b）、**上帝的聖靈**（弗四 30〔原文有聖字〕）；
基督的靈（羅八 9c）、**耶穌基督的靈**（腓一 19）；
聖靈（原文有聖字：羅五 5，九 1，十四 17，十五 13、16；林前六 19，十二 3b；林後六 6，十三 13；弗一 13；帖前一 5、6，四 8；提後一 14；多三 5 本節）；

(ii) **聖靈**與**儀文／文字**相對（羅二 29，七 6／林後三 6a、6b），又與**肉體**（羅八 4、5、6、9a、13；加三 3，四 29，五 17a、b〔原文〕，六 8）及**身體**相對（羅八 10〔參《羅》2.599-602〕；林前五 3〔參新普；Fee, *Corinthians* 204〕）；

(iii) **靈魂／靈**與**肉體／身體**（林前五 5／帖前五 23）相對，**心靈**與**肉體**相對（林後七 1〔呂譯、思高〕），又與**身體**相對（林前七 34）。

(2) 形容詞 **ἅγιος** 在保羅書信出現 76 次（新約全部 233 次），十五次出現在**聖靈**一詞（見上面之〔i〕末項）；更多的時候（40 次）用作名詞，其中一次指天使（參《帖前》271-75），其餘皆指**聖徒**（羅一 7，八 27，十二 13，十五 25、26、31，十六 2、15；林前一 2，六 1、2，十四 33，十六 1、15；林後一 1，八 4，九 1、12，十三 12；弗一 1、15、18，二 19，三 8、18，四 12，五 3，六 18；腓一 1、四 21〔單數〕、22；西一 2、4、12、26；帖後一 10；提前五 10；門 5 節、7 節）。

39 原文依次為 ἀνακαίνωσις（名詞）和 ἀνακαινόω（動詞）；弗四 23 用同義（動）詞 ἀνανεόω.

40 See Banker 102*a*: 'The *anak.* is described here as to its beginning point and not as a continual process as elsewhere'; J. Behm, *TDNT* 3.453: 'The saying in Tt. 3:5 . . . refers to the unique and basic beginning which the Spirit makes in man'（筆者省略了隨後的 'at baptism' 二字）。這一點足以回應 Fairnbairn 296-97 的異議，他說：**更新**是個過程（= 'progressive sanctification'），故此，這裏較可能提到兩件事：**重生的洗**，和

這「重生和更生的洗」為**聖靈的**，表明這洗是聖靈的工作；信徒在基督徒生命的開端，經歷了聖靈所施行的屬靈潔淨和祂所賜的新生命。如此，（甲）**他救了我們……藉著重生的洗和聖靈的更新**（5c 節）[41] 原文的意思其實是，（乙）上帝藉著聖靈所施的洗同時重生和更新了我們。[42] 以下討論這句話的一些細節。

（一）**重生的洗**可能隱含與猶太人所著重的禮儀潔淨（參一 14～15）的對比：我們確實需要潔淨，但猶太人的禮儀潔淨遠不達到我們的需要，我們所需要的是能使我們獲得新性情的潔淨。[43] 洗字原文名詞在新約僅再出現一次，指基督**以水藉著道把教會**洗淨（弗五 26），即是以**水的洗**（呂譯）＝水禮來象徵屬靈的潔淨。[44] 在提多書

聖靈的更新。*Pace* Trench 64-65 (§28); 作者將**聖靈的更新**視為**重生的洗**之後的另一階段。

41 昆謝隆的翻譯作 '[God] saved us through a washing of regeneration and of renewal by/from the Holy Spirit'（Quinn 28, 194, 217 / 187, 210），即是**重生**和**更新**同屬於洗字之下。（Thus already Vos, *Eschatology* 49: 'the *washing* of palingenesia and of anakoinosis [*sic*] (which are both) of the Holy Spirit.'）他的解釋如下（219）：'the process of "washing" produces or effects "regeneration and renewal," which in their turn belong to the Spirit (thus "from" in another sense).' 這就是說，一方面「洗」帶來「重生和更新」；另一方面，「重生和更生」是聖靈的工作。

42 See Fee, *Presence* 857. See also Genade 84: 'through the *washing* by the Holy Spirit that brings rebirth and renewal'（παλινγγενεσίας 在 Genade 82-84 以 παλιγγενεςίας 的形式出現，不下六次〔另見 89〕；正確的形式終於在 94 出現）；Wall 364-65: 'The single preposition *dia* indicates a single Spirit baptism, but with a pair of effects: παλιγγενεσίας (*palingenesias*), "rebirth," and ἀνακαινώσεως (*anakainōseōs*), "renewal"'; Bailey, 'Theology' 353: 'The "rebirth and renewal" are a work "done by the Holy Spirit." . . . It seems most consistent to take "washing" as a reference to the spiritual cleansing which is effected through the ministries of the Holy Spirit.' 這種理解將原文分析為 διὰ [a] λουτροῦ [b] παλιγγενεσίας καὶ ἀνακαινώσεως [c] πνεύματος ἁγίου（[b] 的兩個名詞同屬 [a] 的名詞之下；[c] 則形容 [a]）。馬歇爾認為，這種理解 'is not an obvious rendering of the Greek'（Marshall 217; 他認為原文的意思是 'Through [a] a washing [b] of rebirth and [c] of renewal which is associated with the Holy Spirit'）。有趣的是，他最後的解釋卻和這種理解相符，他說（321）：'v. 5b depicts [c] the Holy Spirit as the source of [a] the "washing" which results in [b] a transformation characterised here from the dual perspective of "regeneration" and "renewal".'

43 Lock 154, endorsed by Banker 100*b*.

44 參《弗》854-59，尤其是該段之（2）= 854-58。**(1)** 洗字原文（**λουτρόν***）在 LXX 出現三次：歌四 2，六 6（**洗淨**）；次經《便西拉智訓》34.25（思高德訓篇 34.30：

本節，洗字很可能不是指水禮，[45] 理由如下：（1）原文名詞的基本

「人摸了死屍就去沐浴〔βαπτιζόμενος〕，以後再去摸它，他的沐浴〔ἐν τῷ λουτρῷ〕有甚麼用處？」）。（*在 Fee, *Presence* 779-80 誤作 λούτρον〔四次〕。）（**2**）同字根的動詞（λούω**）在來十 22 指信徒身體〔既〕用清水洗淨了，……就應該懷著真誠的心……進到神面前（新譯）。Banker 100*b* 認為，用清水洗淨亦是指水禮。但這詞語較可能是暗指結三十五 25 的比喻用法，指他們的罪已蒙赦免（參《來》2.184-86）。（**這動詞在新約另外出現四次，皆指字面意義的洗過澡〔約十三 10〕、清洗死者〔徒九 37〕、洗……傷〔十六 33〕，和豬洗淨了，又回到爛泥裏打滾〔彼後二 22〕。）

45 儘管很多釋經者認為洗字（λουτρόν）指水禮：（**1**）See e.g. J. Guhrt, *DNTT* 1.185: 'The picture suggests baptism'; H. Balz, *EDNT* 2.361*b* (s.v.): 'baptism is effective as a λουτρὸν . . .'; Calvin 382: 'I have no doubt that there is at least an allusion to baptism'; DC 148*a*: '"Bath" (λουτρόν) refers to baptism'; Bassler 208: 'a reference to baptism'; Drury 1233*a*: 'baptism [is] here described as the water of rebirth and renewal'; Johnson II 243: '*loutron* . . . seems without question to be a reference to baptism'; Montague 247: '**the bath of rebirth**, obviously baptism'; Oden 36: 'God saved us by a renewing bath (baptism)'; Quinn 220: 'this tradition in Titus calls the Christian baptismal rite a *loutron*'; Saarinen 192: 'In 3:5b-7 a brief theology of baptism and the Holy Spirit is outlined'; Collins, 'Theology' 68: 'through the Spirit the baptismal washing prepares for final resurrection and a newness of life'; Hagner, 'Titus' 551: 'the ceremonial washing (*loutron*) of baptism'; Malherbe, 'Soteriology' 354: 'a washing, that is, baptism, viewed here under two aspects, that of regeneration or rebirth, and renewal'; Stott 204: 'almost certainly a reference to water baptism'; LN §53.43: 洗的意思是「禮儀之洗，指洗禮（ceremonial washing referring to baptism）」；Leaney 127 甚至認為：'The Greek word . . . means literally "bath" . . . and probably implies total immersion in a sufficiently large cistern.'（**2**）張 374 部分根據此處的洗（λουτρόν）與來十 22 身體用清水洗淨了（新和）的動詞洗淨（λούω）為同一字根而認為，「此處是指洗禮的可能性是存在的」。不過，來十 22 的洗淨了很可能並非暗指洗禮：清水可能暗指結三十六 25（我必灑清水在你們身上，你們就潔淨了），身體用清水洗淨了（新和）是比喻性用法，指信徒的罪已蒙赦免（詳見《來》2.185-86）。

（**3**）Johnson I 136 認為，重生的洗指水禮（'by baptism they are reborn'）；also Malherbe, 'Soteriology' 333; Titus 893*a*: '**Washing of regeneration** refers to baptism'; DC 148*b*: 多三 5 及後將洗禮理解為重生（Quinn 50 / Collins 358 [also Hultgren, 'Pastoral Epistles' 151] 談到 'baptismal rebirth/regeneration'; cf. R. T. Beckwith, *DNTT* 1.158: 'regeneration is said to come through baptism'）；Karris 122: 使信徒由從前的光景（3 節）改變為現今的情況（4～7 節）的，是水禮；Kelly 252: 'The reference is clearly to baptism'; Stern, *Comm.* 657: 'The reference is clearly to immersion (baptism)'; Young, 'Ethics' 116: 'clearly referring to baptism'; 周 439-40：「這顯然是指洗禮而言。……在領受洗禮時，我們也便藉着聖靈的力量，得着重生的新生命，成為新造的人」。（**4**）Quinn 220-21 甚至認為，在羅馬的環境中，παλιγγενεσία 的通俗意思就是 'a return after death to one's own bodily life, a "resurrection"'; 因此，重生的洗可能指 'a bath that effects bodily resurrection, in other words, a rite through which the merciful God brings believers into the mystery of the death and resurrection of Jesus and sets them on a course that culminates at last in the bodily resurrection of all human beings, with its accompanying judgment.'

意思不是「洗禮」，而是「洗滌，潔淨」；[46] 在一份蒲草紙文獻（福音書殘篇）裏，同字根的動詞用來指進入聖殿之前必須進行的潔淨之舉。[47]（2）如果名詞洗字隱含與猶太人「齋戒沐浴」的對比，那麼，保羅的焦點就不在水禮本身，而在清洗和潔淨這思想。（3）得救的途徑不是外在的潔淨，而是裏面的潔淨。（4）保羅若有意聚焦在水禮，他大可以用動詞「洗」字來清楚表明他的意思。[48]（5）保羅並不常常

（**5**）Collins 300, 359 以三 4～8a 為 'A Baptismal Hymn'. Quinn 10 稱三 4～7 為 'a didactic baptismal oration'; Richards 90, 93 稱之為 'Hymn for the Newly Baptised'. Goodwin 1753*b* 說，'3:4-7 speaks of baptism as that which transforms and motivates a life fruitful in good works.' Quinn 49 給三 3～8a 這一小段的標題是 'The Baptismal Event'; Goodwin 1757*b* 的標題是 'Theological Premise: Baptismal Grace as the Motive for Good Works'. Hanson I 105 稱三 4～7 為 'An extract from a Baptismal Service'（also 120: 'we are here dealing with an extract from a baptismal liturgy'; see also Pietersen 107 with n.1; cf. Long 272-73: '[3:3-7 =] probably a hymn borrowed from the baptismal liturgy'）。Hanson III 191 甚至認為，提多書作者在三 4～5 這兩節指向上帝的救贖行動，他在這裏一定是想到 'some sort of archetypal baptism as having taken place during that redemptive action. . . . Christ is regarded as having undergone an archetypal baptism on behalf of all Christians in the waters of death.'（**6**）Scott（'Profit' 212）聲稱，'everything that Paul says here in 3:1-7 is to be seen . . . through the lens of baptism.'（**7**）'The washing is the means of God's saving action / baptism was a saving event for those who received it (3:5)'（Fiore II 220/13）這些講法（DC 145*a* 甚至聲稱，本節的救字 'refers to salvation through baptism'; see also Malherbe, 'Paraenesis' 314: 'God saved in a single, past event, through baptism'; White 198*a*: 'God saved by baptism'; Scott 175: 'By means of the rite of baptism the Spirit effects its work [of re-birth and renewal]'〔儘管司各脫認為這並非保羅的看法〕）值得商榷，至少必須加以解釋（水禮在何意義上可被稱為 'a saving event' 或 'the means of God's saving action'）。幸而作者的另一句話——'The saying refers to the initial, inner change in the believer that baptism symbolizes'（220）——正確地指出洗禮是內在改變的表徵（參《西・門》398）。Cf. Hughes, *Hebrews* 219: 'Reduced to a single phrase, baptism is "the washing of regeneration." The external element of this washing is water, but the water is a sacramental symbol which graphically points to an internal reality, "renewal in the Holy Spirit," who effectively applies to the believing heart cleansing from sin by the blood of Jesus Christ'.「外在的洗禮行動，催生了內在生命的重生和更新」（張 52）這話值得商榷。

46 《簡明》104*a*（s.v. λουτρόν）；《輔讀》529。See also G. R. Beasley-Murray, *DNTT* 1.153: 'it denotes the act rather than the place of washing.' 'For the active sense of washing there is abundant evidence throughout Greek literature' (Simpson 114).

47 BDAG 603*b* (s.v. λούω, 2 a): 'of the act of purification necessary before entering the temple'.

48 以上四點見 Banker 100*b*-1*a*. 第（4）點的「洗」字即 βαπτίζω.（保羅亦有名詞 βαπτισμός 和βάπτισμα 可用；見下註。）（**1**）Guthrie（*Theology* 756）也認為：'since the word "baptism" is not used, it would be precarious to argue for a connection between

提到洗禮，[49] 更少在有關歸信基督的經文中提到洗禮，而且他在一連六次提到洗禮的一段經文中（林前一 13～17），將**施洗**和**傳福音**清楚區別（17 節），其對水禮相對貶抑的態度溢於言表，因此在保羅的書信中，很難看到洗禮與聖靈的聯繫，亦難看到洗禮與歸主本身的聯繫。故此，提多書本節的**洗**應理解為比喻用法，所指的不是洗禮，而是聖靈所施的屬靈潔淨。[50]

---

the act of baptism and the actual experience of regeneration, in view of the fact . . . that in Romans 6:1-4 baptism is not thought of as a cleansing operation.'（**2**）有趣的是，動詞 βαπτίζω 在新約一共出現 77 次，大部分（64 次）是在四福音和使徒行傳，餘下的 13 次則全部在保羅書信裏；而除了羅六 3 的兩次和加三 27 的一次，其餘十次都是在林前（一 13～17〔六次〕，十 2，十二 13，十五 29〔兩次〕）。常見的結構是「受洗歸入（βαπτισθῆναι εἰς）」——**基督耶穌／基督**（羅六 3a／加三 27）、**他的死**（六 3b）、**保羅的名下**（林前一 13〔新譯，參呂譯、思高〕，參一 15）、**摩西**（十 2）、**一個身體**（十二 13）。一個特別的講法是**為死人／替他們受洗**（βαπτίζεσθαι ὑπέρ: 林前十五 29a／29b）。See BDAG 164*a*-65*b* (s.v.);《新希》55*b*-56*a*（s.v.）。

49 在保羅書信，（1）動詞 βαπτίζω 出現十三次（見上註）；（2）名詞 βάπτισμα（新約共十九次）僅出現兩次（羅六 4；弗四 5）；（3）另一名詞 βαπτισμός（新約共四次）僅出現一次（西二 12）。

50 Fee, *Presence* 780. See also Knight II 342: 'λουτρόν . . . is used here as a metaphor for spiritual cleansing'; Lau 166: λουτρόν 'is in fact used as a metaphor for spiritual cleansing … as in the only other NT occurrence (Eph. 5.26)'; Towner III 781（唐 1139）: 'here, as in Eph 5:26, the term falls into the metaphorical sphere, with the image of washing referring to a spiritual cleansing'（cf. Towner I 116-17）; Mounce 439: 'To interpret διὰ λουτροῦ παλιγγενεσίας . . . as the inner cleansing effected in conversion is a . . . natural reading of the text'. Cf. Marshall 318: 'the term refers primarily to that spiritual cleansing which is outwardly symbolized in baptism with water'; idem, 'Holy Spirit' 258: 'Whether or not an allusion to water baptism is intended, the primary referent is the inward, spiritual process of cleansing and renewal'; Wieland 229: 'this picture of washing, especially when associated with the Holy Spirit, is a natural metaphor for spiritual cleansing'.（**1**）不過，費歌頓隨即認為（*Presence* 781），'the richness of the imagery makes it difficult to imagine that Christian baptism is not lying very close to the surface in such a metaphor.' Hendriksen 392 也認為，'there is an implied reference to this sacrament [of baptism].' Similarly, Marshall 56: 'The practice of baptism is implied (Tit 3.5)'（cf. idem, 'Congregation' 109）。班約翰更認為，保羅可能想到兩個行動：'the washing of physical baptism which is itself the figure [for removal of sin] and the actual event of [removing sin and] making us holy'（Banker 101*a*）。NRSV 甚至將 λουτροῦ 翻譯為 'water', 頁邊註才註明原文作 'washing'; see also NJB: 'the cleansing water of rebirth'.（**2**）重要的是，即使這裏暗指洗禮，重生的媒介仍然不是洗禮而是聖靈；洗禮只是重生的表徵。See Fee, *Presence* 858: 'Salvation is not appropriated through baptism . . . but through the work of the Spirit';

（二）重生的原文複合名詞[51] 在希臘文聖經僅再出現一次，指萬物的更新（太十九 28）或世界被更新（新普），即是將來的新時代（現修）；它在這裏則指個別信徒靈性上的再生、內在的改變。[52] 在新約有別的方式表達這屬靈事實：[53]（i）以同字根的複合動詞來指上帝重生了信徒（彼前一 3），因而他們是蒙了重生的（一 23）；[54]（ii）以同字根的簡單動詞生字加上副詞，指人必須重生（約三 3、7）或從上面出生（新普頁邊註）；[55]（iii）以這簡單動詞加上介詞片語，稱信徒為從上帝生的（約一 13／約壹三 9a，五 18a／三 9b，五 1／五 4／五 18b）[56] 或由上帝而生（約壹四 7）。[57] 在上述這些經節，作者欲強調上帝

G. W. Bromiley, *ISBE* 1.428*b*: 'there is no particular danger in seeing a connection between the sign [baptism] on the one hand and the thing signified [regeneration] on the other so long as this is not conceived in causal or instrumental terms. . . . Christian regeneration is that which is signified in baptism, and baptism is that which signifies regeneration.'（**3**）彭編 107*a* 也認為，「無論採用〔對本節希臘文結構兩種可能的〕何種理解，此處的『洗』不宜理解為『洗禮』。」

51 παλιγγενεσία, from πάλιν + γένεσις (Vine 3.267). Cf. Marshall 320: 'etymologically the term is connected with γίνομαι and γένεσις, not with γεννάω'; Laansma 282.

52 Cf. Towner III 782: 'the new birth associated with conversion' =「與悔改歸正……有關的新生」（唐 1140）；Knight II 342: 'λουτροῦ παλιγγενεσίας might better be translated "the washing of a new beginning" or "the washing of conversion"'. F. Büchsel（*TDNT* 1.688）認為，παλιγγενεσία 同時含有 'attainment to a new life' 和 'moral renewal' 兩個意思，但本節的救了和 7 節的後嗣表示，前一個意思較為重要（cf. *TDNTA* 119: 'with a stress on the [former]'）。（**1**）Knight I 98 指出，太十九 28 本身及其文理同時含有個人的一面：耶穌和門徒的談話是關乎進天國／上帝的國（23／24 節），因而涉及他們個人得救（25 節）的問題。耶穌向門徒保證他們必定得救，祂說：到了萬物更新的時候，他們要坐在寶座上審判以色列（28 節），他們將要承受永生（29 節）。不過，就 παλιγγενεσία 一字的用法而論，正文所指出的區別仍然成立。（**2**）J. Guhrt（*DNTT* 1.186）將太十九 28 和多三 5 的不同觀點這樣連繫起來：'The NT is bounded by the horizon of the new creation (. . . 2 Pet. 3:13; Rev. 21:5) and the restoration of all things (Acts 3:21).* With regeneration the reality of this salvation enters this world and human existence.' 意即個人的重生是萬物更新／復興的開始。（*徒三 21 的復興原文為 ἀποκατάστασις〔在新約僅此一次〕。）

53 See Fiore II 220.

54 原文依次為 ἀναγεννήσας, ἀναγεγεννημένοι（from ἀναγεννάω, 新約僅此兩次）。

55 原文依次為 γεννηθῇ/γεννηθῆναι (from γεννάω) ἄνωθεν.

56 原文依次為 ἐκ θεοῦ ἐγεννήθησαν / γεγεννημένος ἐκ τοῦ θεοῦ / ἐκ τοῦ θεοῦ γεγέννηται / γεγεννημένον ἐκ τοῦ θεοῦ / γεννηθεὶς ἐκ τοῦ θεοῦ. 參：約三 5（從……聖靈生，γεννηθῇ ἐξ . . . πνεύματος）、6／8（從聖靈生，γεγεννημένον/γεγεννημένος ἐκ τοῦ πνεύματος）。

57 原文也是 ἐκ τοῦ θεοῦ γεγέννηται（上註第三個片語）。（**1**）雅各則用另一個動詞

的行動，因而選用主動語法的動詞（彼前一 3）或用被動語法動詞加上從上面／從上帝／由上帝等修飾語，這些修飾語聚焦在上帝身上；提多書本節則以較簡要的方式表達或宣認信仰，因而選用複合名詞重生一字。[58]

（三）更新原文名詞也是在希臘文聖經僅再出現一次：保羅告訴羅馬的信徒，「要讓上帝藉著心意的更新而改造你們」（羅十二 2）。[59] 但同字根的動詞[60] 在希臘文聖經再出現兩次：保羅的宣告是，雖然我們外在的軀體漸漸衰敗，我們內在的生命卻日日更新（林後四 16，現修）；信徒已穿上了新人，這新人照著造他的主的形像在知識上不斷地更新（西三 10）。[61] 與這動詞同義的另一動詞在新約僅出現一次，[62] 同樣是指信徒的「心思之靈」的更新：你們要把心靈更換一新（弗四 23，新譯）原文的意思其實是，要讓聖靈更新你們的思想和心態（新普）。在以弗所書該節，心靈一詞內的靈字並非指聖靈；讓聖靈只是表達了原文被動語態不定詞的含意。[63] 提多書本節的更新，按上述（甲）的理解，則明言為聖靈的更新，意即這更新是由聖靈造成的，更新者是

生字（ἀποκυέω: 雅一 18，參一 15b〔此字在希臘文聖經僅再出現一次：偽經《馬加比四書》15.17: 'O woman, who alone gave birth [ἀποκυήσασα] to such complete devotion [RSV, NRSV]〕)。(**2**) 為甚麼提多書本節不用與 γεννάω 或 ἀναγεννάω 同字根的名詞，而用另一個名詞 παλλινγενεσία 呢？Knight I 99 認為答案可能在於：'a noun form of ἀναγεννάω is virtually lacking in the common vocabulary of the day, and when it does occur it refers to the regeneration of the world, and . . . παλιγγενεσία was widely used and recognized and moreover expressed the thought in view. Further, the noun form of γεννάω is not fully appropriate to express the concept because without a prefix or some qualification such as a propositional phrase it would not convey the thought of a *re*birth or a *new* birth.'

58 See Knight I 99-100. See also Wieland 225-27.

59 參《羅》4.65。原文名詞為 ἀνακαίνωσις.

60 ἀνακαινόω.

61 關於新人、在知識上和造他的主（= 基督）的形象這些詞語的詳細討論，可參《西・門》564-65、566-67、567-70。

62 ἀνανεόω. 同字根的名詞（ἀνανέωσις）在希臘文聖經亦只出現一次，指猶太人大祭司約拿單寫了一封「關於重建我們之間弟兄友誼的書信」給斯巴達人（次經《馬加比一書》12.17〔思高瑪加伯上〕)。

63 詳參《弗》653-55。

聖靈。[64] 這是保羅書信一貫的教導：在心意更新（羅十二 2）、內在的人……日日更新（林後四 16），和信徒的新我不斷〔被〕更新（西三 10〔新普〕）的背後，更新者同樣是聖靈。[65] 按上述（乙）的理解，更新形容洗字，這「更新的洗」是聖靈所施的（現修），因而更新仍是聖靈的工作，就像（甲）的理解一樣。值得留意的是，更新的意思不是「回復先前的狀況」，而是「成為新的」，因為透過聖靈的工作，信徒如今生活在較前更高的平面上。[66]

64 I.e., (ἀνακαινώσεως) πνεύματος ἁγίου = 主詞所有格（Fiore II 220）。

65 參《羅》4.64-65；《西・門》565。

66 Guthrie I 205: '"Making new" rather than *renewing* [KJV] is implied, since the latter might erroneously suggest the restoration of former powers . . . whereas through the work of the Spirit the believer lives on a higher plane than before'（cf. Guthrie II 217〔古特立 219〕）。

三 6 聖靈[1] 就是上帝……厚厚地澆灌在我們身上的，藉著我們的救主耶穌基督

「將聖靈澆灌在某人身上」這種講法源自舊約：約珥預言，耶和華要將祂的靈**澆灌凡有血肉之軀的**，包括祂的**僕人和婢女**（珥二 28、29）；[2] 撒迦利亞談到，上帝**要將那施恩與懇求的靈，澆灌大衛家和耶路撒冷的居民**（亞十二 10），導致他們「真心痛悔」。[3] 彼得在五旬節的講道引用約珥的預言，表示聖靈的降臨應驗了先知的預言（徒二 17、18）。[4] **澆灌**（同新和、新譯）的另一翻譯是**傾注**（呂譯、思高、當代、現修）；這動詞本身已含有「豐富、充足、大量」等意思，加上

---

1 原文是關係代名詞 οὗ 字，其前述詞是 5 節末的 πνεύματος ἁγίου（**聖靈**）。後者是所有格，緊隨其後的關係代名詞受了它的影響（'by attraction': Fairbairn 298; Fiore II 221; Simpson 115; Towner III 784 n.60〔唐 1143 註 45〕）亦變成所有格，儘管這代名詞（作為動詞**澆灌**的賓詞）應該是直接受格的 ὅ.

2 （**1**）珥二 28b 在 LXX（珥三 1b）作：ἐκχεῶ <u>ἀπὸ</u> τοῦ πνεύματός μου ἐπὶ πᾶσαν σάρκα. 留意介系詞 ἀπό 改變了 MT 的講法（**我的靈是賓詞**）：不是 'I will pour out my Spirit upon all flesh', 而是 'I will pour out <u>of</u> my Spirit upon all flesh'（LXE）。'This is a partitive expression'（Ward 273）。不過，從神學角度而言，LXX 的講法比 MT 更為正確。（**2**）Towner IV 916*b* 指出，不能確定 'whether Paul draws directly from the OT text of Joel or rather accesses it as it has already been incorporated into the early church's paradosis'.

3 盧玉音：《小先知書》379。

4 徒二 17c 的引句是 LXX 珥三 1b 的原文照錄，徒二 18b 的引句是 LXX 珥三 2b 的原文照錄；全部包含 ἐκχεῶ <u>ἀπὸ</u> τοῦ πνεύματός μου 這些字眼。在徒二 33，動詞**澆灌**的賓詞是直接受格的 τοῦτο（'this'），指聖靈及其彰顯。（**1**）Holman（'Window' 54）說，除了徒二 17、18，'[t]he only other time that we find ἐκχέω with ἐπί in the New Testament is in Tit. 3.6.' 這話不確；見啟十六 8、10、12、17。（**2**）除了本註開首的上述三次（連同多三 6 就是四次），**澆灌**和**聖靈**連著出現，在新約還有兩次（但所用的動詞是 ἐκχύννομαι），都是被動語態（ἐκκέχυται: 徒十 45：**聖靈的恩賜……澆在外邦人身上**；羅五 5：**上帝的愛……已藉著……聖靈，澆灌在我們心裏**）。（**3**）前一個動詞（**ἐκχέω**）在新約（全部十六次）另外出現十二次（太九 17〔被動語態：**酒就<u>漏出來</u>**〕；約二 15〔**耶穌<u>倒出</u>兌換銀錢之人的銀錢**〕；羅三 15〔**殺人<u>流</u>血**〕；啟十六 1、2、3、4、6、8、10、12、17〔**傾倒**〕）。「十六次」這數目得自 *Concordance* 598*a*-98*b*; MGM 335*b*.《新希》107*b*-8*a*（s.v. ἐκχέω）的「(27)」次是由於這詞典，像 BDAG 312*b* (s.v. ἐκχέω) 一樣，將 ἐκχύν(ν)ω/ἐκχύννομαι（新約十一次）包括在 ἐκχέω 這詞條之下。

副詞厚厚地、豐富地（呂譯、思高）或慷慨地（新普），[5] 使這種意思更為突出。動詞澆灌原文為過去不定時時態，像上一節的救字一樣；兩個行動是同時發生的：[6] 上帝藉著聖靈的重生和更新救了我們（5c 節），這聖靈是上帝澆灌在我們身上的。兩個動詞都可以理解為個別信徒（包括保羅和克里特的信徒）得救的時候。如此，上帝把聖靈厚厚地澆灌在我們身上是在我們歸信時就已發生的。[7]

與此同時，由於聖靈並不是可量度之物，上帝把聖靈豐豐富富地傾注在我們身上（現修）可進一步理解為：（1）上帝（在我們歸信時）慷慨地把聖靈賜給我們，（2）這位聖靈在我們（當時及其後）的生命中豐富地動工，[8] 例如：

- 聖靈將上帝的愛澆灌在我們心裏（羅五 5，新和），即是聖靈在我們心中工作，使我們確實知道上帝的愛；[9]
- 聖靈幫助信徒稱上帝為父（羅八 15c；參：加四 6），見證他們是上

---

5 πλουσίως = 'abundantly' (KJV, NKJV), 'richly' (RSV, NRSV, NAU, ESV, *Paraphrase* 295), 'generously' (NIV, TNIV, NIV2011, NJB, NLT); 'richly, abundantly' (BDAG 831*b* [s.v.]). 這副詞在新約僅再出現三次，分別指信徒要讓基督的話豐豐富富地住在（西三 16，呂譯）他們當中（參《西・門》617-19），上帝把萬物豐豐富富地賜給我們享受（提前六 17，現修），和在某種情況下，信徒就可以豐豐富富地……進入我們主－救主耶穌基督永遠的國度（彼後一 11）。參《新希》271*a*（s.v.）。

6 Fiore II 221: 'The occasion of the pouring is the same as that of the saving act of God'.

7 Banker 104*b*. 班約翰認為這一句的焦點是 'on the beginning point of our Christian life.' See also Trebilco, 'Significance' 245: 'The Pastor affirms that all Christians receive the Spirit at conversion in Tit. 3:6-7.' Hiebert 446 則這樣解釋：澆灌原文動詞（過去不定時時態）首先指五旬節的經歷，但在我們身上則標誌著個別信徒歸主時的經歷。'The Spirit's work in each believer as a member of the Body is a continuation of the Pentecostal outpouring.'

8 See Banker 104*b*. 班約翰的原句是：'"whom he poured out upon us abundantly" would refer to (1) the giving of the Holy Spirit, and (2) the fact that this giving is one which resulted in the Holy Spirit "abundantly" working on our behalf, i.e., he acted mightily on our behalf.' 留意 'acted' 為過去時態；筆者則把「聖靈豐富地運行」理解為 'both at regeneration and ever afterward'. Cf. Arichea－Hatton 304: 'This [means] that the Holy Spirit was given to us freely and generously, and that the Holy Spirit is always available to help us.'

9 參《羅》2.50-52。

帝的兒女（羅八 16）；

- 聖靈幫助信徒敬拜上帝（腓三 3：靠神的靈來敬拜〔新譯〕）；[10]
- 聖靈幫助信徒承認「耶穌是主」（林前十二 3，現修）；
- 聖靈使上帝藉著基督所成就的救恩在信徒身上產生功效，使他們獲得新生命和新的行為模式（林前六 11）；[11]
- 聖靈引導信徒（羅八 14）把身體的惡行處死（羅八 13）；[12] 隨從聖靈去行就是成聖的關鍵（羅八 4；參：加五 16：「靠聖靈行事」，五 18：被聖靈引導）；[13] 事實上，聖靈的工作就是使人成為聖潔（帖後二 13：聖靈成聖的工作〔現修、新譯〕、使你們成聖的聖靈〔新普〕）；[14]
- 聖靈是改變生命的能力，在信徒身上所產生的倫理特性稱為聖靈的果子（加五 22～23；參：西一 8：聖靈賜給你們的愛意即「你們那由聖靈產生的愛」；[15] 帖前一 6：聖靈使帖撒羅尼迦人在大患難中仍有喜樂，故此這喜樂稱為聖靈的喜樂〔新譯〕，即是聖靈所賜的喜樂〔新和、現修〕或從聖靈而來的喜樂〔新普〕）；
- 聖靈讓我們有能力、愛心和自律（提後一 7，新普）；信徒內在的生命若要強壯起來，有賴聖靈賜給〔他〕們力量（弗三 16，現修）；聖靈給予保羅充足的支持（腓一 19：耶穌基督的靈的幫助）；[16]

---

10 參《腓》340-42。

11 See Fee, *Presence* 129-32. 參三 7 註釋註 16 之（1）= 下面 406。在宏觀的救恩層面上，基督成就及宣告了和平（弗二 14～17），聖靈則把基督所成就的撥歸信徒，使猶太信徒與外邦信徒藉著他一起進到神的面前（二 18；參《弗》371-74）。

12 參《羅》2.620-21。

13 依次參《加》1222-24、1238-39。事實上，聖靈不僅是信徒新生命的創始者（加五 25a：聖靈賜給我們新生命〔現修〕）、引導者（五 18），以及過新生活的能力（五 16），祂也是這新生活所應遵照的標準（五 25b：πνεύματι καὶ στοιχῶμεν〔參《加》1302-3〕）。

14 參《帖後》260-63。

15 參《西・門》141-42。

16 參《腓》137-39。

- 聖靈將不同的恩賜給予信徒，使他們參與事奉（林前十二 4～11）；聖靈將宣講福音的能力給予傳道者（帖前一 5a：**當我們把福音傳給你們的時候，……是靠着能力**〔新普〕），並使他們「**帶著對福音的確信**〔現修〕」（一 5b）來宣講；[17]
- 聖靈使信徒**大有盼望**（羅十五 13），確信必會獲得末日的救恩、身體得贖，並獲得榮耀（五 2、5，八 18、21、23～25，十二 12，十五 4）；他們**靠著聖靈……等候所盼望的義**（加五 5），聖靈就是這末日盼望的保證。[18]

正因為聖靈是**厚厚地**澆灌在我們身上的，即這位聖靈在我們的生命中**豐富地**（呂譯、思高）動工，一切信賴上帝而獲得救恩的人都能夠履行第 8 節的命令：**已信上帝的人〔要〕留心行善**。[19]

我們的救主耶穌基督和第 4 節的**我們〔的〕救主上帝**在原文呈現交叉配置模式。[20] 但上帝__藉著__**我們的救主耶穌基督**把聖靈澆灌在信徒身上[21] 是甚麼意思呢？（一）**藉著……耶穌基督**的意思可能是，耶穌基督**為我們的緣故捨己**（二 14）就是**上帝慷慨地將聖靈傾注在我們身上**（新普）的基礎。[22]（二）它的意思也許是，基督徒獲賜聖靈，

---

17 依次參《帖前》76-80、80-82。

18 參《加》1149-52。

19 Fee, *Presence* 784.

20 三 4 [A] τοῦ σωτῆρος ἡμῶν [B] θεοῦ
三 6 [B’] Ἰησοῦ Χριστοῦ [A’] τοῦ σωτῆρος ἡμῶν

相同的現象（除了 [B’] 的字序）已在一 3、4 出現過。參一 4b 註釋註 12（上面 82）。**（1）** Genade 127 同樣將首行分拆為 [A] τοῦ σωτῆρος [B] ἡμῶν θεοῦ. 見一 4b 註釋註 12 之（2）= 上面 83。**（2）** Akin（‘Mystery’ 142-43）說，‘It is quite normal and natural [in the Pastoral Epistles] for Paul to ascribe Saviorhood to God or Jesus. Paul sees no conflict and he feels no tension. To know Jesus as Savior is to know God as Savior and vice versa.’ 筆者認為，加上方括號內的字，作者的話才是準確的。參一 3b 註釋註 3 之（2）= 上面 73；一 4b 註釋註 11（上面 82）。

21 「在教牧書信中，這是第一次明顯地把父、子、聖靈聯在一起，雖然在保羅其他書信中我們較常見到這說法」（周 440）。

22 Towner II 257: ‘it was this Person and his work that made possible the gift of the Holy

乃是信徒藉著信與基督聯合的結果。[23] 較可能的解釋是，（三）介系詞**藉著**表示，耶穌基督本身就是上帝傾注聖靈的媒介，這就是說，上帝傾注聖靈的方法，就是藉著「耶穌基督把聖靈傾注在信徒身上」，[24] 就如彼得在五旬節的講道中所宣告的：**他〔耶穌〕既然被高舉到神的右邊，從父領受了所應許的聖靈，就把他澆灌下來，這就是你們所看見所聽見的**（徒二 33〔新譯〕；參：約十五 26，十六 7）。[25]

Spirit (Jn 16:7; Acts 2:33)'; Hiebert 446: 'That bestowal was based on the finished work of Christ as Savior'; Jeon I 107: 'through the appearance of the God-man in [*sic*] "Jesus Christ" Paul and the audience have received the full outpouring of the Spirit'; 曾 92：「『藉著耶穌』很可能是論到基督的救贖工作。」Lau 168 則認為，這介詞片語所表達的是 'the channel through which the recreating and renewing of the Spirit comes', 就如在徒二 32～33 基督的救贖工作是聖靈澆灌的先決條件。但這介詞片語分明是動詞**澆灌**（不是名詞**重生**和**更新**）的修飾語，就如作者自己稍後所說的（'the role of Christ as the personal agent through whom God has acted (poured out the Spirit) is never diminished'）。Lau 251 又說，'God's goodness and love for men . . . comes "through Jesus Christ our Saviour"'. 筆者認為，從文法的角度而言，只有第二引句（括號內的一句）才是正確的。

23 Kelly 253.

24 Cf. A. Oepke, *TDNT* 2.67: 'The formula "through Christ" . . . is [here] to be taken . . . in the sense that Christ mediates the action of another, i.e., the action of God, namely . . . the impartation of the Spirit'. Karris（*Symphony* 137）以林前十五 45（**末後的亞當成了賜生命的靈**）為這裏的思想的背景：'the risen Lord Jesus has become a life-giving Spirit. That is, Jesus, crucified and risen, is the giver of God's Spirit.' 值得留意的是，'[Paul] does not intend to say that Christ became *the* life-giving Spirit, but a life-giving spirit. Christ is not *the* Spirit'（Fee, *Presence* 266-67）。

25 Banker 103*b*; see also Knight II 345-46; Fee, *Presence* 783-84; idem, *Christology* 448; Holman, 'Window' 54. 班約翰認為**藉著……耶穌基督**是指（二）耶穌基督是上帝傾注聖靈的代理人，但同時稍微暗指（一）基督為我們捨己：'[διά relates] to the mediate agency of Christ in pouring out the Holy Spirit, with a more remote reference to Christ's death on our behalf'（Banker 103*b*）。Cf. Laansma 288-89: 'That the Spirit is poured out through Jesus alludes to [*a*] his direct role in bestowing the Spirit . . . and to [*b*] his work as the basis for the reception of the Spirit.'

三 **7a** 好讓我們因他的恩得稱為義，

7b 可以憑著永生的盼望成為後嗣。

連接詞好讓表達了上文某一個行動的目的；[1] 理論上，這個行動可能是（甲）第 5 節的他救了我們，[2] 也可能是（乙）第 6 節的澆灌在我們身上。[3] 班約翰力證後一種理解較前者可取，他的理由如下：[4]（**1**）新約別處從來沒有將目的子句繫於動詞「拯救」或名詞「救恩」。（**2**）聖靈的賜予和成為上帝的後嗣二者的聯繫，在羅馬書和加拉太書亦有論及。在羅馬書八章，聖靈被稱為兒子名分的靈（羅八 15b），祂幫助信徒稱上帝為阿爸，父！（八 15b），[5] 見證他們是上帝的兒女

---

1 （**1**）Lock 151 的意譯作 'All this He did that . . . we might become heirs . . . of eternal life.' Similarly Barclay 260: 'the aim of all this was that . . .'. 'All/all this' 似乎是指 5、6 兩節的內容。Montague 248 明確地說，'The aim or purpose of this entire process'（5－6 節）就是 'So that we might be justified by his grace'.（**2**）DC 147*b* 則把 ἵνα 翻譯成 'thus', 即是視之為表達結果。（**3**）Marshall 323 認為，ἵνα 表達 'the ultimate purpose, and, in effect, the result of God's act.'

2 Guthrie I 206 / Guthrie II 218: '[on] the previous statement *he saved us* (verse 5) . . . the telic clause / the clause introduced by *hina* . . . must depend'（古特立 220「這子句以 *hina* 開始（好叫我們成為後嗣）」完全漏去了作者欲表達的意思）; Barrett 143; Lamp, 'Titus' 103; Zehr 303. 所得出的意思就是：'God *saved us* . . . in order *that*, having been *justified by his grace*, *we might become* heirs . . .'（Ward 275）。See also Knight I 104-5: 'The balance and thrust of the whole sentence would seem to demand that the ἵνα refers back particularly to ἔσωσεν, although it must also be acknowledged that it takes into its purview the words intervening.' 這等於說，7 節表達了 5c～6 節的目的；這看法與上註之（1）的解釋相近。

3 Arichea－Hatton 304: 'it explains the purpose for the giving of the Holy Spirit'; 周 441：「在此所着重的是上帝把聖靈豐豐富富地澆灌在我們身上的目的」。See also Aaegeson 48; Kelly 253.（**1**）白新港認為，'[This] connexion brings out best the climax of the passage'; 成為後嗣是人在今生所能達到的頂點（White 199*b*）。不過，將好讓連於 5 節的他救了我們並不影響這事實：成為後嗣仍然是他救了我們 —— 我們得稱為義 —— 我們成為後嗣這進程的頂點。（**2**）Ziesler（*Righteousness* 155）甚至聲稱：'God accepts, or acquits us, purely by his grace. This justification seems to depend on baptism and the "regeneration and renewal in the Holy Spirit" which it represents (vv. 5f). Thus, justification is not simply of the ungodly, but of the baptized or converted ungodly.'

4 以下（1）-（4）參 Banker 102*b*.

5 參《羅》2.629-32。

（八 16）；[6] 他們既然是上帝的兒女（八 17，現修），便是……上帝的後嗣（呂譯）。在加拉太書四章，信徒領受聖靈（加四 6b：上帝就差他兒子的靈進入我們的心，呼叫：「阿爸，父！」）是他們獲得兒子的名分（四 5b）、因為〔他〕們是兒子（四 6a）的結果；[7] 他們既然是兒子，就靠著上帝也成為後嗣了（四 7b）。[8] **(3)** 保羅可能用了兩句平行的話（三 4～5、6～7）來強調這一小段的重要真理。[9] 如此，第 7 節就不是連於第 5 節，而是連於第 6 節。**(4)** 二章 14 節以關係代名詞他字（其前述詞是 13 節的耶穌基督）開始，第 14b 節隨即提到他為我們的緣故捨己（14a 節）的目的（為了要贖我們脫離一切罪惡……）。三章 6 至 7 節很可能是同樣的結構：第 6 節以關係代名詞「他」字（其前述詞是 5 節的聖靈）開始，第 7 節隨即提到上帝把聖靈厚厚地澆灌在我們身上的目的（好讓我們……）。基於上述理由，班約翰認為本節的連接詞好讓應視為從屬於上一節的動詞澆灌，而不是第 5 節的救了。

這些理由不是決定性的。第 **(1)** 點所指出的是事實，但不能排除本節正是個例外。第 **(4)** 點提出一個可能，但三章 6 節和 7a 節的關係，不一定要按照二章 14a 節和 14b 節的關係來理解，因為：

6　參《羅》2.638-40。
7　參《加》949、950-51。
8　參《加》961-64。
9　Banker 102*b* 以圖表表達如下：

	三 4～5	三 6～7
救主	我們救主上帝	我們的救主耶穌基督
救恩的基礎／永生的盼望的基礎	上帝的恩慈和慈愛、他的憐憫	他的恩、〔我們的〕得稱為義
途徑／方法	重生和更新的洗	聖靈……澆灌在我們身上
結果	他救了我們	成為後嗣承受永生

二章 14b 節的目的子句明顯地只能夠是連於 14a 節（他為我們的緣故捨己，為了要贖我們脫離一切罪惡），三章 7a 節的目的子句卻可能是連於第 6 節的動詞澆灌或第 5c 節的動詞救了。第（**2**）點所引自羅馬書和加拉太書的那些經文，所顯示的是：獲得聖靈是擁有兒子名分的證明或結果，卻不是：聖靈的賜予之目的是要使信徒成為上帝的後嗣。第（**3**）點的問題在於，它以聖靈……澆灌在我們身上作為成為後嗣承受永生的途徑或方法（見註 9 圖表）；換一個講法，按班約翰的理解，上帝將聖靈厚厚地澆灌在我們身上（6 節）的目的是讓我們……成為〔他的〕後嗣（7b 節），即是將領受聖靈視為成為後嗣的基礎。但是按保羅在加拉太書更詳細的闡釋，領受聖靈是獲得兒子名分（相當於成為後嗣）[10] 的憑據。[11] 基於上述理由——尤其是對（**2**）（**3**）兩點的回應——筆者認為本節的目的子句不是連於第 6 節的聖靈……厚厚地澆灌在我們身上（全節是對 5c 節末尾的聖靈二字的擴充描述），而是連於第 5c 節的他救了我們。[12]

（一）好讓（新和：好叫）我們因他的恩得稱為義這種翻譯，將分詞片語我們因他的恩得稱為義看為目的子句所表達之目的的一部

---

10 得兒子名分是成為後嗣的先決條件：見羅八 16～17；加四 6～7。

11 詳見「三章 7 節註 11 附錄」（下面 417-19）。Pfleiderer（*Paulinism* 2.209）早就指出這種不協調的情況：'justification by the favour of God, and the hoped-for inheritance of eternal life, are said to be the purposed consequence of the abundant pouring out of the spirit [*sic*] . . . . According to Paul, on the contrary (cf. Gal. 4:6), the imparting of the spirit [*sic*] is a consequence of the presupposed sonship, in which justification and the heritage of the eternal life are put together, so that the two latter are not conditioned by the renewing work of the spirit, but, on the contrary, precede and condition it.'

12 持此立場的釋經者包括 Barrett 143; Lau 169; Griffin 325 (Paul asserted that "he saved us" (v. 5) "so that . . . we might become heirs" (v. 7).' Dunn（*Baptism* 167）聲稱，'the ἵνα-clause describes the purpose of the Pentecostal outpouring as well as of the ἔσωσεν. The saving purpose of God, which is that we might be justified and become heirs, is effected by the baptism in the Spirit.' 然而，筆者加上底線的部分清楚表示，鄧雅各其實也是將好讓連於動詞救了。這一點由他進一步的解釋證實了，他說（同上）：'God's purpose in the act of salvation is our justification and adoption; the means by which he achieves that purpose is "the washing of regeneration and renewal in the Holy Spirit . . ."'.

分。[13] 可是，雖然這分詞片語緊接著連接詞**好讓**，但這不等於必須將這片語看為目的子句所表達之目的的一部分。[14] 事實上，（甲）如果這目的子句是連於第 5 節的主句**他救了我們**，則這目的子句（**好讓我們因他的恩得稱為義**）和主句（他照他的憐憫救了我們）在意思上是重疊的。[15]（乙）如果將**好讓我們因他的恩得稱為義**視為上帝將**聖靈厚厚地澆灌在我們身上**（6 節）的部分目的，所得出的意思（聖靈澆灌的部分目的是讓我們得稱為義）就更不合適，不單因為新約對聖靈在信徒得稱為義這事上所扮演的角色並無著墨，[16] 更因為「上帝以聖靈澆灌我們，好讓我們得稱為義」這思想，跟羅馬書八章 10 節的思想背道而馳。該節表明，聖靈在信徒身上的工作是以他們的稱義為基礎的：**基督若在你們裡面，〔雖然〕你們的身體因著罪的緣故是死的〔**新普：**你們的身體會因着罪而死去〕，⋯⋯聖靈卻因著義的緣故**〔因基督

---

13 See also RSV: 'so that we might be justified by his grace and become heirs in hope of eternal life.' 亦參思高：**好使我們因他的恩寵成義，本着希望成為永生的承繼人。**筆者加上底線的部分在原文為分詞片語：δικαιωθέντες τῇ ἐκείνου χάριτι.

14 在林後十三 10（ταῦτα ἀπὼν γράφω, ἵνα παρὼν μὴ ἀποτόμως χρήσωμαι），原文的意思是**我不在你們那裏的時候，把這些話寫給你們，好使我見你們的時候**〔παρών〕**不用⋯⋯嚴厲地待你們**，而不是「⋯⋯好使我可以見到你們（παρών），並且不用⋯⋯嚴厲地待你們」。這就是說，緊接著連接詞 ἵνα 的分詞 παρών 並不是目的子句所表達之目的的一部分；換一個講法，這裏只有一個目的（**好使我⋯⋯不用⋯⋯嚴厲地待你們**），不是兩個目的（好使我可以⋯⋯並且不用⋯⋯）。See Banker 105*b*.

15 As in, e.g., Knight II 341: 'One reason that God saved Christians is so that he might declare them righteous . . .'

16 Banker 106*a*: 'we do not elsewhere find the Holy Spirit's actions as prominent in justification.'（**1**）林前六 11（**你們奉主耶穌基督的名，並藉著我們上帝的靈，已經洗淨，已經成聖，已經稱義了**）表示，稱義和聖靈的工作有關聯，但二者的準確關係卻並不明顯，這裏所表達的只是一種籠統的意思：'the reference to the Spirit reflects Paul's understanding of the Spirit as the means whereby God in the new age effects the work of Christ in the believer's life. Together . . . the two propositions〔**奉**、**藉著**〕refer to what God has done *for* his people in Christ, which he has effected *in* them by the Spirit'（Fee, *First Corinthians* 247）。（**2**）**被聖靈稱義**（提前三 16）／**在聖靈裡稱義**（新譯）這句話是指著基督（而不是信徒）說的。費歌頓認為，ἐν πνεύματι 與前一句的 ἐν σαρκί 相對；**在肉身**意即 'in the sphere of humanity',「在靈裏」則指 'the spiritual/supernatural realm, the realm of the Spirit'（Fee, *Presence* 766）。

已為你們取得義者的地位〕賜給你們生命（新譯，亦參現修）。[17]

因此，另一種翻譯較為可取：（二）好叫我們既因他的恩得稱為義，便可憑着盼望而承受永生（呂譯）。[18] 按這種理解，因他的恩得稱為義是已發生的事，是信徒可以……成為後嗣的理由或根據。[19] 第 5 節曾以強烈的對比表明，救恩的基礎不是……我們自己所行的義，而是……他〔上帝〕的憐憫；第 7 節延續這個思想，表明信徒得以成為後嗣是由於他們已經得稱為義，而他們得稱為義是因他〔上帝〕的恩典（其含義即是，不是因自己所行的義〔5a 節〕）。[20]

---

17 參《羅》2.598-602。因此，黃編 225 以「我們得以稱義」為「聖靈澆灌在我們信徒身上（參 6 節）」所產生的「三個後果」之一，這見解不可能是正確的。Wieland 236 的陳述亦不可取，他說：'the Holy Spirit has been poured out to effect rebirth and renewal, which are the means whereby sinful people are justified'.

18 See also NKJV: '[so] that having been justified by His grace we should become heirs . . .'; NRSV, NIV, TNIV, NIV2011; Hagner, 'Titus' 550 / Mounce 453, 450: 'so that, / in order that having been justified by his grace, we might become heirs . . .'; NJB/REB: 'so that, justified [= having been justified] by his grace, we should become heirs / we might in hope become heirs'. Marshall 323 則認為，分詞 δικαιωθέντες 'is coincident in time with the main verb "become heirs"'（thus also Towner III 787〔唐 1148〕; Dunn, *Baptism* 167: 'a coincident aorist participle'），即是稱義與成為後裔同時發生。從神學的角度而言，這種理解無疑是正確的；但是從這裏的文法和邏輯的角度，稱義可能應視為先於成為後裔。事實上，Marshall 324 就反映這種理解：'The consequence of being saved and justified is that believers become heirs of God's promises'.

19 羅四 13 顯示類似（但並非一樣）的關係：神給亞伯拉罕和他後裔承受世界的應許，並不是因著律法，而是藉著因信而來的義（新譯）。因著和藉著原文是同一個介系詞（διά），所表達的是一種伴隨的情況（如在羅二 27）；該節的意思是，上帝對亞伯拉罕的應許（他和他的後裔要作世界的承繼者〔思高〕）不是在律法的情況下，而是在因信而來之義的情況下賜給他的。如此，亞伯拉罕稱義在先，他獲賜「作世界的承繼者」的應許在後。不過，該節並沒有像多三 7 那樣，明說稱義是作承繼者的基礎，因那並非保羅當下的關注。詳參《羅》1.608-12。

20 5a、5b 和 7a 節的行事者在原文都受到強調：不是因我們自己（ἡμεῖς, 獨立代名詞）所行的義，而是照他的憐憫（τὸ αὐτοῦ ἔλεος）；我們是因「那一位」的恩典（τῇ ἐκείνου χάριτι）而得以稱義的。在後兩個片語，被強調的代名詞居於冠詞和名詞之間。See Banker 105*b*-6*a*. (**1**) ἐκείνου 最接近的前述詞是 6 節的耶穌基督（因此 H. Seebass [*DNTT* 3.365] 作 'our being "justified by his [Christ's] grace"'〔方括號是原來的〕; see also Fee, *Christology* 448-49），但它真正的前述詞較可能是 6 節的動詞澆灌所隱含的主詞上帝，理由如下（see Banker 107*b*-8*a*）：（**i**）他的恩使人自然地想到二 11 的上帝……的恩典；（**ii**）恩慈和慈愛（4 節）、憐憫（5 節）這些構成我們得救基礎的屬性，都是上帝的／他的，使我們得稱為義的恩也應是上帝的；（**iii**）5b 節照他的憐憫（κατὰ τὸ αὐτοῦ ἔλεος）和 7a 節因他的恩（τῇ ἐκείνου χάριτι）提示，兩個他字指同一人，即是 4 節的上帝；(**iv**) 在新約裏，使人稱義的是上帝（羅三 26、30，八 30、33；加三 8），因而得稱為義是因著神的恩典（羅三 24，新譯）。White 199*b* 指出，正是由於使人稱義的恩典是上帝的恩典，因此這裏使用 τῇ ἐκείνου χάριτι 而不是 τῇ αὐτοῦ χάριτι；即是不用 αὐτοῦ（他的）來指向最接近的前述詞救主耶穌基督（6 節），而是用 ἐκείνου（那人的）來指向距離較遠的前述詞救主上帝（4 節）。Similarly, Lau 170: 'the use of ἐκείνου instead of αὐτοῦ seems to point to the more remote antecedent (God)'. *Pace* Towner III 787（唐 1147）：'Paul's choice to employ the emphatic demonstrative pronoun (*ekeinou* . . .) suggests that Christ, the nearest antecedent, is meant'.

(**2**)班約翰聲稱，'Grace is much more often used in connection with God the Father than with Christ in the New Testament.' 他以此支持本節他的恩是指上帝的恩（Banker 107*b*）。筆者不認為這是很強的理由，但他的聲稱是成立的。從以下（筆者自製）的圖表可見，在新約有註明恩典屬誰的一共 50 次中，「上帝的」和「基督的」分別為 34 和 16 次（即 2.125 與 1 之比）：

	上帝的恩典	基督的恩典	次數
主格（1）	χάρις **θεοῦ**（路二 40） ἡ χάρις **τοῦ θεοῦ**（羅五 15a；林前十五 10c；多二 11） ἡ χάρις **αὐτοῦ**（林前十五 10b） ἡ χάρις **τοῦ κυρίου** ἡμῶν（提前一 14）		1 + 3 + 1 + 1 = **6**
主格（2）		ἡ χάρις **τοῦ κυρίου** Ἰησοῦ（林前十六 23；啟二十二 21） ἡ χάρις **τοῦ κυρίου** ἡμῶν Ἰησοῦ（羅十六 20） ἡ χάρις **τοῦ κυρίου** Ἰησοῦ Χριστοῦ（林後十三 13；腓四 23；門 25 節〔羅十六 24 不屬原著，見《羅》4.803-6〕） ἡ χάρις **τοῦ κυρίου** ἡμῶν Ἰη. Χρ.（加六 18；帖前五 28；帖後三 18） ἡ χάρις **μου**（林後十二 9）	2 + 1 + 3 + 3 + 1 = **10**

動詞「稱義」在本書出現僅此一次，[21] 在教牧書信另外出現一次（提前三 16），在其他的保羅書信一共出現 25 次（羅 15，林

直接受格（1）	τὴν χάριν **τοῦ θεοῦ**（林前三 10；林後六 1，八 1；加二 21；西一 6） τὴν χάριν [τὴν] **τοῦ θεοῦ**（徒十一 23） κατὰ τὴν χάριν **τοῦ θεοῦ** ἡμῶν κ.τ.λ.（帖後一 12a） διὰ τὴν ὑπερβάλλουσαν χάριν **τοῦ θεοῦ**（林後九 14） ἀληθῆ χάριν **τοῦ θεοῦ**（彼前五 12） τὴν **τοῦ θεοῦ** ἡμῶν χάριτα（猶 4 節）		5 + 1 + 1 + 1 + 1 + 1 = **10**
直接受格（2）		τὴν χάριν **τοῦ κύριου** ἡμῶν Ἰησοῦ Χριστοῦ（林後八 9） κατὰ τὴν χάριν . . . **κυρίου** Ἰησοῦ Χρ.（帖後一 12b；參《帖後》133-34）	1 + 1 = **2**
所有格（1）	χάριτος **θεοῦ**（彼前四 10） τῆς χάριτος **τοῦ θεοῦ**（徒二十 24；弗三 2、7；來十二 15） τῆς χάριτος **αὐτοῦ**（加一 15；弗一 6、7，二 7）		1 + 4 + 4 = **9**
所有格（2）		διὰ τῆς χάριτος **τοῦ κυρίου** Ἰησοῦ（徒十五 11）	**1**
間接受格（1）	τῇ χάριτι **τοῦ θεοῦ**（徒十三 42，十四 26；林前一 4） χάριτι **θεοῦ**（林前十五 10a；林後一 12；來二 9） τῇ χάριτι **τοῦ κυρίου**（徒十五 40） τῇ **αὐτοῦ** χάριτι（羅三 24） τῇ **ἐκείνου** χάριτι（多三 7）		3 + 3 + 1 + 1 + 1 = **9**
間接受格（2）		ἐν χάριτι **τοῦ** ἑνος ἀνθρώπου **Ἰησοῦ Χριστοῦ**（羅五 15b） ἐν χάριτι **[Χριστοῦ]**（加一 6） ἐν χάριτι . . . **τοῦ κυρίου** ἡμῶν（彼後三 18）	1 + 1 + 1 = **3**

21 這裏的分詞 δικαιωθέντες（得稱為義）和 5 節的名詞 δικαιοσύνη（義）是 paronomasia 的另一例子；參三 3 註釋註 10，三 4 註釋註 5（上面 370，378）。

前後 2，加 8），常見於以下的詞語：（**1**）因律法的行為稱義（羅三 20；加二 16c，參 16a），[22] 靠著律法……稱義／靠律法稱義（加三 11／五 4）；[23]（**2**）因信稱義（羅五 1；加三 24），因信基督稱義（加二 16b）；[24]（**3**）靠著他〔基督〕的血稱義（羅五 9），奉主耶穌基督的名……稱義（林前六 11），在基督裏稱義（加二 17）；[25]（**4**）本於信稱（那受割禮的）為義（羅三 30a），藉著信稱（那未受割禮的）為義（羅三 30b），基於（外族人的）信心，宣佈他們為義（加三 8，新普）。[26] 回到本節，《思高聖經》翻譯為因他的恩寵成義，[27] 但多數

---

22 原文的結構皆為 ἐξ ἔργων νόμου + 動詞 δικαιόω 的**被動**語態（加二 16a 的次序相反）。參雅二 21、25 的「因行為稱義」（原文皆為 ἐξ ἔργων + δικαιόω 的被動語態）。

23 原文的結構皆為 ἐν νόμῳ + δικαιόω 的被動語態。

24 原文的結構首末二節為 δικαιόω 的被動語態 + ἐκ πίστεως 或 ἐκ πίστεως Χριστοῦ，中間一節為 ἐκ πίστεως + δικαιόω 的被動語態。

25 原文的結構皆為 δικαιόω 的被動語態 + 介系詞 ἐν 字。

26 原文的結構依次為 δικαιόω 的**主動**語態 + ἐκ πίστεως / διὰ τῆς πίστεως 和 ἐκ πίστεως + δικαιόω 的主動語態。以上出自羅馬書及加拉太書的各段，可參《羅》及《加》的有關討論。

27 See also Quinn 28, 187, 198, 226, 228: 'God's was the grace that made us upright'; Jeon I 111, 126: 'made righteous by his grace'; Johnson II 142, Karris, *Symphony* 133 / Wall 357, 366, Wall, 'Salvation's Bath' 208: 'having been made righteous by his/that grace'; Malherbe, 'Soteriology' 354: 'Justification here is . . . to be understood . . . in a moral sense, a just life by virtue of Christ's grace'; Genade 94: 'In 3:7, the . . . explanation is given as to how a believer comes to manifest this quality [of righteousness, 3:5]: they are *made* righteous by divine grace.' 簡內德稍後的陳述（95）較為正確：'they are passive in the act of acquiring the status of righteousness.'（**1**）Houlden 154 認為，鑑於作者（不是保羅）對道德強烈的關注（'strong moral concern'），得稱為義這保羅式的詞彙可能隱藏著道德上正直之意：'having been made morally upright by his grace . . .'（**2**）費阿利將 δικαιωθέντες 翻譯為 'being rendered righteous'（Fiore II 216, 221），然後解釋為包括兩方面的意思：'the sinner [is] declared righteous, the believer is also transformed within by the Holy Spirit'（221）。Similarly, Witherington 161: 'The verb *dikaioō* means "to set right" or "to make upright." . . . we cannot take *dikaioō* to have a purely forensic sense here – "to count as righteous." There is enunciated a connection between the internal transformation and the being set right or made upright before and with God.' 筆者認為這種解釋把稱義和成聖混為一談；* 關於稱義在保羅書信（筆者認為）正確的解釋，詳參《加》522-26；亦參《羅》1.366-67。

*「跟隨路德的語言，加爾文採用法庭式的概念（forensic notion）來表述上帝如何看待罪人的狀況。改革家巧妙地把『算為義』（imputed [*sic*] or reckoned righteous）和『成為義』（made righteous）區分開來。每當他們論及稱義時，他們只會採用前者，而把後者留給成聖的領域」（李耀坤：《加爾文》87；亦參 149）。

的中譯本都正確地將原文動詞翻譯為**得稱為義**（同呂譯、新和、新譯），即是**被稱為義人**（當代），全句的意思就是，上帝**出於他的恩典，宣佈我們是義人**（新普）。[28] 這裏的**恩典**就是上帝拯救的恩典（二 11），實質上與**上帝的恩慈和慈愛**（三 4）同義。

如上所言，上帝**救了我們**信徒的目的，[29] 是要讓他們**成為後嗣**（7b 節）。簡內德聲稱，**成為**原文的被動語態重申第 4 至 7 節這句子內一貫的重點，即是在救恩這事上，人是被動的，上帝則完全是主動的。[30] 其實，這形式上是被動語態的動詞，[31] 在意思上只是**成為**（同思高、新和、新譯），並無「被（上帝）使之成為」之意。[32] 第 7b 這半節[33] 有兩種主要的翻譯：（一 A）**憑著**〔按照〕**永生的盼望成為後嗣**（同新和、新譯），[34] 即是**永生的盼望**是一個單元，**後嗣**則單獨使用（沒有指明所「繼承」的是甚麼）。（一 B）「成為後嗣，懷著永生的

---

28 δικαιόω =「宣告為義」（《輔讀》529）。這裏用的是被動語態分詞（δικαιωθέντες = 'Having been declared righteous' [Jeon II 30]; 但 Jeon II 31 卻說 'we have now been made righteous'）。

29 新譯**使我們既然因著他的恩典得稱為義**的**使**（而不是「好使」）字，可被理解為表達結果（而不是目的）；但原文的 ἵνα 應是表達（從上帝**救了我們**的角度來看這行動之）目的的（參註 1 及所屬正文〔上面 403〕）。

30 Genade 96. See also NAU / Knight I 104, 138, 141: 'we would/might be made heirs'.

31 See BDF §78: 'The later language preferred the aorist passive in the case of deponents (where a real passive meaning is at best a possibility . . .)'; §307: 'deponents in the future and aorist prefer passive forms'; MHT 3.54: 'deponent* verbs prefer passive forms, and . . . ἐγενήθημεν (*we were*, not *we were made*) displaces ἐγενόμεθα'.（*'Used to describe certain verbs that have middle or passive forms but active meanings. They seem to have laid aside (Lat. *Depono*, lay aside) their active forms (rather than their middle or passive meanings) [Harris, *Colossians* 296].）此動詞（**γίνομαι**）在新約一共出現 669 次。

32 See Wallace 441: 'A verb that has no active *form* may be active in meaning though passive in form. Two of the most common deponent passives are ἐγενήθην and ἀπεκρίθην.' NKJV 正確地把 KJV 的 'we should be made heirs' 修正為 'we should become heirs'.

33 κληρονόμοι γενηθῶμεν κατ' ἐλπίδα ζωῆς αἰωνίου, literally 'heirs we-might-become according-to hope of-life eternal'.

34 See also NKJV, NRSV, ESV: 'become heirs according to the hope [κατ' ἐλπίδα] of eternal life'; B. Mayer, *EDNT* 1.440*a* (s.v. ἐλπίς, 3 d): 'heirs in accordance with the *hope* . . . of eternal life'; Marshall 324-25; Mounce 435, 451; Towner III 788 n.73（唐 1149 註 58）。這可以理解為 'Our standing as heirs is "according to" (*kata*), in full harmony with, "the hope of eternal life"'（Hiebert 446）。

盼望／成為懷著永生盼望的後嗣」。[35] 另一種翻譯則指明所承受的是永生：（二 A）憑着盼望而承受永生（呂譯），本着希望成為永生的承繼人（思高），[36]「成為『在盼望中的』永生的承受者」。[37]（二 B）「按照基督信仰的盼望，成為永生的承受者」。[38]

筆者認為第（一）種翻譯勝於第（二）種，[39] 理由如下：（1）消極方面，第二種翻譯將原文子句末尾的永生二字，越過在永生之前的名詞盼望而連於開首的名詞後嗣，這不是最自然的做法。這做法又使介詞片語本着希望（思高）／憑着盼望（呂譯）受到強調（因這片語被置於開首的承繼人和末尾的永生之間），但強調這介詞片語的原因並不明顯。（2）積極方面，第一種翻譯自然地反映了原文的次序，而且永生的盼望一詞已在一章 2 節出現過，這事實有力地提示不應在本節將盼望和永生分開。[40] 在（一 A）和（一 B）之間，前者比後者更

35 See RSV, NJB / NIV, TNIV, NIV2011: 'become heirs in hope [κατ' ἐλπίδα] / having the hope of eternal life'; Quinn 28, 187, 198, 226, 228: 'become heirs with a hope of life eternal' (199: 'literally, "with the goal/purpose of hope" as in 1:1'); Karris, *Symphony* 127: 'might become heirs in hope of eternal life'.

36 See also NEB, REB / Kelly 248, 253: 'so that . . . we might in hope become heirs to/of eternal life'; Johnson II 217, 242: 'we might on the basis of hope become heirs of eternal life'; Hinson 284: 'we may become heirs of eternal life'. 這種翻譯將 7b 節的 κατ' ἐλπίδα 連於之前的動詞 γενηθῶμεν, 又將句末的 ζωῆς αἰωνίου 連於句首的名詞 κληρονόμοι. 但見下一段之（1）。

37 Hendriksen 385, 392: 'become heirs-in-hope of life everlasting.' See also 393: 'we are . . . heirs-in-hope, hoping heirs.' 這種翻譯將 κατ' ἐλπίδα 和 ζωῆς αἰωνίου 都連於名詞 κληρονόμοι. 但見下一段之（2）。

38 *Paraphrase* 295: 'become heirs of eternal life, in conformity with the Christian hope.' 這種翻譯將 κατ' ἐλπίδα 視為這子句其餘部分的修飾語。Wall 357/366 的翻譯 'we may become heirs of the hope of /for eternal life' 不可取，因 κατ' ἐλπίδα 不可能翻譯成 'of the hope'.

39 彭編 107*b* 也認為，「不宜作『可以憑著盼望承受永生』〔= 正文之（二 A）〕。」

40 See BDAG 320*a* (s.v. ἐλπίς, 1 b β): 'ἐ. ζωῆς αἰωνίου **Tit 1:2; 3:7**'（永生的盼望是一個單元）。Denton（'Hope' 24*b* n.39）提出另一理由：保羅的習慣是不在 κληρονόμος 之後加上所有格的字（'only once out of six occurrences of the word, viz. Rom. 4:13）。不過，較準確的數字應是（本節不算在內）七次之中有兩次是這樣：羅四 13（κληρονόμον . . . κόσμου），八 17b（κληρονόμοι . . . θεοῦ）；其餘五次均無所有格的字緊隨其後（羅四 14，八 17a；加三 29，四 1、7）。

能保存「介系詞加直接受格」常見的意思（「按照」[41]）。按這種理解，信徒可以〔按照〕永生的盼望成為後嗣的意思就是，他們成為後嗣是與永生的盼望相符的；保羅作使徒的目的就是要使上帝的選民獲得永生之盼望（一 2，呂譯），而上帝將聖靈傾注在信徒身上的目的，就是讓他們按照這盼望成為後嗣。[42] 嚴格地說，「後嗣」是從已死的人有所繼承的人，[43] 但是按新約的用法，「後嗣、繼承」這組字彙往往不含「從死者」之意而只有「獲得從而擁有」的意思。[44] 這裏的後嗣可理解為上帝的後嗣，因為保羅告訴我們，由於信徒是上帝的兒女，他們也就是後嗣，是上帝的後嗣（羅八 16、17a、17b；參：加四 7：既然是兒子，就……也成為後嗣了）。[45] 而既然他們所盼望的是永生，

---

41 See BDAG 548*a* (s.v. κληρονόμος, 2 b): '*that we might become heirs in accordance w. the hope of eternal life*'.

42 Jeon I 108 則解釋為 'they [the audience] have "become heirs according to" the plan of salvation that is outlined in 1:2a-3'; 永生的盼望則被視為不但提供了 'the motivation for living as a "slave of God and apostle of Jesus Christ" (1:2a), but also a specific framework－bracketed by the first and second appearance of God's grace [2:11, 13b]－for righteous living.' 這解釋不必要地將 'according to the hope of eternal life' 這一個單元拆開，並使它的意思變得複雜。

43 彭編 107*a*：「『後嗣』指擁有合法繼承權的人。」

44 See BDAG 547*b* (s.v. κληρονομέω, 2): 'acquire, obtain, come into possession of τὶ *someth*.'; BDAG 548*a* (s.v. κληρονόμος, 2): 'one who receives someth. as a possession, *beneficiary*'.

45 亦參：加三 29：屬〔於〕基督的人既然是亞伯拉罕的後裔，他們也就是照應許做〔上帝的〕後嗣（呂譯）的人（參《加》903-5）。除了多三 7、羅八 17a、17b、加四 7 和加三 29，名詞 **κληρονόμος**（後嗣）在保羅書信另外出現三次，新約另七次。四次指字面意義的承受產業的（太二十一 38 ∥ 可十二 7 ∥ 路二十 14；加四 1），另外的六次為比喻用法，其中一次指基督被上帝立為萬有的承繼者（來一 2〔思高〕；參《來》1.40-42），其餘五次皆指基督信徒或信上帝的人：（i）亞伯拉罕在因信稱義的基礎上領受了上帝的應許，使他作世界的承繼者（羅四 13〔思高〕；參《羅》1.608-12）；（ii）假使本着律法〔而活〕的人纔是承受產業的，那麼信就落了空，應許也就失效了（羅四 14〔呂譯〕；參《羅》1.612-15）；（iii）上帝定意向繼承應許的人，充分顯示自己不可更改的旨意，就以起誓來自作擔保（來六 17〔思高〕；參《來》1.395-98）；（iv）挪亞藉著信（造方舟）而成了由信德得正義的承繼者（來十一 7，思高），意即挪亞是由於他的信心（他的信心引致正義的生活，尤其顯明於造方舟一事）而獲得聖經稱他為義人（參《來》2.257）；（v）上帝……揀選了世人以為窮的……，以承受他所應許給愛他之人的國（雅二 5，呂譯）。See BDAG 548*a* (s.v.)；《新希》187*a*（s.v.）。

那麼，他們作為後嗣所承受的亦可理解為永生。[46] 因此，成為後嗣可意譯為「成為（上帝的）後裔（可以承受永生）」。

本節永生的盼望亦回望二章 13 節信徒所等候的福樂的盼望以及至大的上帝和我們的救主耶穌基督的榮耀顯現。這三重的提說（一 2，二 13，三 7）強調了這盼望的確定性：[47] 保羅作使徒的基礎是永生之盼望（一 2，呂譯）；信徒可以按照永生的盼望成為上帝的後裔（三 7）；信徒所等候的福樂的盼望，將會在基督再臨的時候成為事實（二 13）。[48]

第 4 至 7 節這一小段，充分顯示了保羅神學（尤其是救恩論）的三一性質。**(1)** 救了我們的是上帝（5c 節）——我們〔的〕救主上帝（4 節）；祂的拯救的根據是他的憐憫（5b 節）、恩慈和慈愛（4 節）；祂拯救的方法是藉著聖靈所施重生和更新的洗（5c 節）；我們……得稱為義是由於他的恩典（7a 節，現修）；[49] 祂的拯救的目的是使得稱為義的人可以憑著永生的盼望成為後嗣（7b 節）。**(2)** 我們的救主耶穌基督是上帝把聖靈厚厚地澆灌在我們身上的渠道（6 節）。**(3)** 聖靈是上帝澆灌在信徒身上的（6 節），聖靈的重生和更新就是上帝拯救他們的方法（5c 節）。[50] 如此，信徒若沒有敬虔的行為等於否定了三一

---

46 W. Foerster, *TDNT* 3.783: 'the content of the inheritance [is] eternal life'.

47 Genade 98.

48 ἐλπίς 在三 7 和一 2 指主觀的期望，在二 13 則指客觀的所盼望之事。參二 13 註釋註 14（上面 305-6）。

49 他（ἐκείνου）字的前述詞是上帝而非基督，此點見註 20 之（1）= 上面 407-8。

50 Cf. Akin, 'Mystery' 146: 'As a united work of our triune God, the Father (vv. 4-5), the Son (v. 6), and the Holy Spirit (v. 5), our inheritance is a signed, sealed, and settled issue. Once more [as in 2:11-14] Paul has wed soteriology to Christology to eschatology, this time in the context of Trinitarianism.' 在救贖與三一上帝這課題上，「加爾文把改教的恩典神學加以擴充，並將其與三一神在歷史中的活動融合起來：

> 我們得救的起始因（effectum）在於父上帝的慈愛，質料因（materiam）在於聖子的順服，工具因（instrumentum）在於聖靈的啟迪，目的因（finem）在於榮耀上帝如此浩大的善意」（李耀坤：《加爾文》148）。

真神在他們身上所施行的拯救。[51] 值得留意的是父、子、聖靈在本段出現的次序：雖然聖靈是上帝藉著救主耶穌傾注在我們身上的（6 節），但是聖靈的工作比基督的工作更早提及，這表示這裏的重點首先是在上帝的憐憫（5b 節），那是救恩的基礎；然後是在聖靈所施重生和更新的洗（5c 節）——這絕對重要的事件一方面將我們從前生活在其中的罪惡（3 節）洗除，同時更新我們，使我們可以行上帝要求於其子民的善（1～2、8 節）。[52]

第 4 至 7 節這四節也表明，救恩包括我們的過去（獲得聖靈所

---

51 Genade 94.

52 Fee, *Presence* 779. 坡特稱多三 4～6 及保羅書信其他的段落——羅一 1～4，八 1～3、9～11（參《羅》1.186，《羅》2.566）；加四 6；弗一 13～14（參《弗》204-7）、17，二 18、22，三 15～17（參《弗》479），四 4～7；腓三 3；西一 6～9；帖前一 4～6——為 'prototrinitarian passages'（Porter, *Analysis* 379 n.8），意即這些經文反映一種「原始的三位一體觀」。（除了坡特列出的上述經文外，這類經文還包括：羅五 1～8，十五 16，十五 30〔參《羅》2.65 註 21，《羅》4.572 註 37，4.654〕；帖後二 13～14。）坡特（i）利用語言學「下義關係（hyponymy）」的概念——「鬱金香（tulip）」、「紫羅蘭（violet）」、「玫瑰（rose）」、「雛菊（daisy）」都是「花（flower）」這「上級詞（superordinate term）」的「下級詞（hyponyms）」，就如「陸軍（army）」、「海軍（navy）」、「空軍（air force）」、「海軍陸戰隊（marines）」都是「軍隊（military）」這「上級詞」的「下級詞」（378-79）——辯證，保羅認識到「上帝」、「主」、「耶穌基督」、「聖靈」這些字詞之間的關係（也許甚至是這些個體之間的「本體性〔ontological〕」關係）是密切的，足以把它們放在一起，儘管他沒有一個「上級詞」來蓋括這些「下級詞」（380-81）。坡特（ii）進一步認為，由於一個「下級詞」可同時用作一個「上級詞」——例如，「公鴨（drake）」、「母鴨（duck）」都是「鴨子（duck）」這「上級詞」的「下級詞」——因此，「上帝（God）／父上帝（God the Father）」、「聖子（Son）」、「聖靈（Holy Spirit）」可視為「上帝（God）」（指 'the Godhead'）這 'inclusive superordinate term for God, which includes the three persons' 的「下級詞」（382-83）（我們現今就區別「三位一體的上帝（the Trinitarian God）」和「父上帝（God the Father）」〔384〕）。最後，坡特（iii）指出 'using hyponymy as a model of the Trinity' 的數點好處（383-84），其中的第二點是（384）：'hyponymy can help us to understand the evolution of thought regarding the Trinity. It is entirely plausible that Paul himself may well have deeply understood what is now called the Trinity, as evidenced through his conscious use of tripartite formulas that conform to the superordinate and hyponymous lexical pattern. This, then, places the concept of the Trinity early in Christian understanding much earlier than often posited, even if there was not a specific or single term for it. To put it another way, there is no critical objection to the early formulation of the concept of the Trinity, since prototrinitarian formulas undoubtedly appear in the Pauline Letters, and there is linguistic precedent for such an understanding.'

施的**重生**和**更新**的洗〔5c 節〕、**得稱為義**〔7a 節〕)、現在(有聖靈的同在和能力〔6 節〕),和未來(承受永生〔7b 節〕)。

三章 7 節註 11 附錄

如果因他〔基督〕的恩得稱為義（三 7a）是成為後嗣的基礎，而上帝又將聖靈厚厚地澆灌在我們身上（6 節），那麼這三者（獲賜聖靈、成為後嗣、因信稱義）之間的關係是怎樣的呢？由於成為後嗣的先決條件是得兒子的名分（見羅八 16～17；加四 6～7），這問題亦可改寫為：因信稱義、得兒子名分，和獲賜聖靈這三者的關係是怎樣的？加拉太書第三、四兩章的教導對這問題極具啟發性，以下節錄筆者所得到的答案最重要的有關部分：[1]

（一）從三章 1 至 6 節可見，「保羅把領受聖靈看為與稱義有十分密切的關係，二者在某意義上是同義的，以致加拉太人領受聖靈的事實同時隱含了他們的稱義。說得更清楚一點，對保羅而言，信徒現今經歷聖靈**見證了**與〔上帝〕的正當關係；獲賜聖靈表示被算為義已經發生；領受聖靈與被算為義彼此牽涉，保羅無法想到其中一樣而不同時想到另外一樣。」[2]

（二）三章 7 至 14 節顯示，「因信稱義與作亞伯拉罕的兒女有著密切的關係，因為與亞伯拉罕同得因信稱義之福（9 節）等於作了亞伯拉罕的兒女（7 節）。因信稱義和領受聖靈也是緊密相連的：領受了聖靈是因信稱義的**印證**（14 節）。[3] 由此可以確定，這三個觀念之間存在著緊密的關係：藉著信稱義、藉著信成為亞伯拉罕的兒女、藉

---

1 參 Fung, 'Sonship'; 馮蔭坤：〈因信稱義〉;《加》907-8 之（二）、965 之（二）。修正：筆者不再認為可以從加四 1～7 獲得以下這個結論：'adoption to sonship to God (vv. 5b, 7) . . . provides the logical basis for [reception of the Spirit, v. 6]'（'Sonship' 91 [see also 95: 'sonship = basis for Spirit-reception']）=「這兒子身份就是我們得以領受聖靈的邏輯根據」(〈因信稱義〉106)；這是由於筆者對加四 6a 的理解有所改變（參《加》965 註 6、950-51）。

2 《加》665。黑體為筆者所加。

3 參《加》767-68。黑體為筆者所加，下同。

著信領受聖靈。三者的共通點顯然是信：就形式而言，以信為本的人就是亞伯拉罕的兒女；實質上說，他們是被稱為義，並且領受了所應許之聖靈的人。這裏將領受聖靈視為因信稱義的**印證**，是重複和確定了上一小段（1～6 節）同樣的結論」。[4]

（三）從三章 23 至 25 節可見，「就如因信（24b）與因信耶穌基督（22b）彼此對應，同樣，使我們可以因信稱義（24b，新譯）與「使那應許……可以賜給相信的人」（22b）彼此對應。這就有力地提示，保羅將第〔22〕節所論的得地為業之應許，理解為因信稱義之應許……。[5] 由此可見，信徒藉著信稱義，兌現了〔上帝〕給亞伯拉罕的應許，就如上文從三章〔8〕節看見，〔上帝〕對亞伯拉罕的應許，隱含並預告了因信稱義之理。」[6]

（四）從三章 26 至 29 節可見，「信徒個別地是〔上帝〕的兒子（26 節），集體地是亞伯拉罕（真正）的後裔（29b）。他們是〔上帝〕的兒子，因為他們藉著信已被納入〔上帝〕的兒子基督裏（27 節、29a）；他們集體地是亞伯拉罕的真後裔，因為他們藉著信與基督聯合，就在亞伯拉罕的真後裔基督（參 16 節）裏成為一體（28 節）。因此，實質上，〔上帝〕的兒子（複數）亦是亞伯拉罕的真後裔，而做亞伯拉罕的兒子與做〔上帝〕的兒子同義；既然成為亞伯拉罕的兒子兌現了〔上帝〕給亞伯拉罕的應許（29c），成為〔上帝〕的兒子也是這應許的兌現。但我們剛在上一段〔三 23～25〕看到，這應許亦兌現於因信稱義一事上；又由於領受聖靈是得稱為義的**印證**，二者是一體的兩面，[7] 因而在這間接的意義上，領受聖靈亦可說是〔上帝〕給亞伯拉罕的應許之兌現。由此可見，因信稱義、藉著信領受聖靈、藉著信成

---

4 《加》769。

5 參《加》841-42：22 節的應許是關乎 21 節所提及的義的問題的。

6 《加》906-7。

7 參上面註 3 及所屬正文，亦參上面第**（一）**點。

為〔上帝〕的兒女，此三者有十分密切的關係，它們以不同的方式表達了應許的兌現。[8] 我們可由此推論，此三者不是分開的不同的經歷，而是藉著信與基督聯合這單一的經歷之中彼此交織的幾方面。從主觀經歷的角度而言，此三者同時發生，兌現了同一個應許；但是就邏輯來說，它們可被分開……。」[9]

（五）四章 1 至 7 節進一步讓我們看見上述三者之間的一些邏輯關係：「信徒藉著基督的救贖得以脫離律法的約束（1）、被收納為〔上帝〕的兒子（2），並且領受聖靈（3），此三者構成一個連結的系列：（1）是（2）的基礎，因為（1）使（2）成為可能，（2）是（1）的目的（4～5 節）；（3）是（2）的**憑據**（6 節）。但〔是由於（1）〕脫離律法的含義就是因信稱義（三 23～24），[10] 因此我們可以說，因信稱義（1）、成為〔上帝〕的兒子（2）及領受聖靈（3）此三者之間，有著緊密的邏輯關係。」[11] 此三者不僅都（直接或間接地）是上帝給亞伯拉罕的應許得應驗的方式，是信徒同一個經歷的三方面（三 26～29）；本段進一步讓我們看見，**（甲）**因信稱義是被收納為上帝兒子的基礎，而**（乙）**領受聖靈是獲得兒子名分（及得稱為義）的**憑據**。

---

8 （筆者以底線取代了原來的楷體。）上文曾指出因信稱義、藉著信領受聖靈、藉著信成為上帝的兒女此三者之間的密切關係（參上面第**〔二〕**點）；這裏讓我們進一步看見，做亞伯拉罕的兒女實質上等於做上帝的兒女。

9 《加》907（黑體為筆者所加）。這第**（四）**點可以用圖表展示（908）。

10 參《加》856-57、864-65。

11 《加》965。底線及黑體皆為筆者所加。

5.3 總結性的勸勉（三 8）

8a 這話是可信的。

8b 我願你堅持這些事，

8c 使那些已信上帝的人留心行善。

8d 這都是美好且對人有益的。

三 **8a** 這話是可信的。

這是信上最短的一句。[1] 原文的次序表示，位於句首的述詞可信的是受到強調的。[2] 這話（像一 13 的這個見證）顯然是回指上文的。[3] 簡內德認為這話是指「到目前為止所說的一切」，這一切構

1 Πιστὸς ὁ λόγος, 三個字，五個音節。沒有表達出來的動詞是 ἐστίν（是）；這一點由帖後三 3（πιστὸς δέ ἐστιν ὁ κύριος = 主是信實的）表明了。信上另有五個短句，其中三句是在信末：

二 15b	μηδείς σου περιφρονείτω	三個字，八個音節
三 15c	Ἡ χάρις μετὰ πάντων ὑμῶν	五個字，九個音節
一 13a	ἡ μαρτυρία αὕτη ἐστὶν ἀληθής	五個字，十二個音節
三 15a	Ἀσπάζονταί σε οἱ μετ' ἐμοῦ πάντες	六個字，十一個音節
三 15b	ἄσπασαι τοὺς φιλοῦντας ἡμᾶς ἐν πίστει	六個字，十二個音節

2 πιστὸς ὁ θεός（林前一 9）、πιστὸς δὲ ὁ θεός（林前十 13；林後一 18）、πιστὸς δέ ἐστιν ὁ κύριος（帖後三 3）、πιστὸς ὁ καλῶν ὑμᾶς（帖前五 24）是同樣的情形。在這五節如在多三本節，'πιστός is a predicate adjective before the articular noun', 並且受到強調（Knight I 21-22）。形容詞 πιστός 已在上文出現兩次（一 6、9）；參一 6 註釋註 50 第二段（上面 114）。

3 Clark, 'Structure' 115; Wallace 221. 不過，一 13a 原文有這字（ἡ μαρτυρία αὕτη），這裏則沒有，只說 'The saying is sure' (RSV, NRSV): Πιστὸς ὁ λόγος（此句在 Genade 100 以 Π/πιστός ὁ λόγος 的形式出現，不下三次。）

成合法的教導，即是由保羅授權、得到保羅認可的教導。[4] 但這話較可能是指第 4 至 7 節（在原文只是一句）。[5]

---

4 Genade 100-1. Ward 277 直言，'No precise *saying* can be identified.' 褒文則力辯，原文的意思是 'the Word is faithful'（Bouwman 137-39）—'an exclamation of Paul's confidence in the Word (i.e., the gospel)'（139）。

5 Aageson 48-49; Arichea－Hatton 305; Collins 367; Dunn 876*b*（875*a* 卻說這話是 '3:4-8*a*'）; Fairnbairn 300; Fee 207; Fiore II 221; Goodwin 1758*a*; Griffin 326; Guthrie I 207; Guthrie II 219（古特立 221）; Hendriksen 393; Hiebert 446; Knight I 86, 138; Köstenberger 622*b*-23*a*; Laansma 290; Liefeld 353（利斐特 370）; Montague 249; Ngewa 403; Simpson 117; Towner I 112; White 200*a*; Witherington 161-62; Zehr 303; Collins, 'Theology' 66-67; Hagner, *New Testament* 630; Haykin, 'Spirit' 301-2; Köstenberger－Kellum－Quarles, 'Titus' 284; Lamp, 'Titus' 101-2; 侯嘉文 160；周 442；張 378-79；彭編 107*a*；黃編 226。REB 和 Quinn 28, 187 都把 4～7 節放在引號內，表示這話是指該四節。參 Nestle-Aland 的排列法。
(1)班約翰則認為這話所指的與這些事（8b 節）所指的都是 3～7 節的內容（Banker 90*b*, 108, 108*b*）。See also DC 28*b*: 'a quotation is contained in the section beginning with 3:3'（thus also Wild 895*b*; 艾利斯認為這話是指 'Tit 3:3-8a' [Ellis, 'Traditions' 241 with n.25; 'Pastoral Letters' 664*b* =《辭典》962*a*]）。但勵佐治針對 Dibelius 的論證指出，（**i**）3 節使用複數的我們並不足以支持該節是這話的一部分；'[its] use in v. 3 may be influenced by the following verses and adapted to them';（**ii**）3 節以 γάρ（因為）一字開始，表示 3 節與 2 節的關係密切，因而不宜視為 3～7 節的一部分；（**iii**）若把 3 節視為這話一部分，這話便有兩句（3 節是一句，4～7 節是另一句），但其他的「可信的話」（見下面註 7）全都（在原文）只有一句（Knight II 348; see also Knight I 82）。因此，3 節不屬於這話。**(2)** Lock 155 認為，這話或是指 5～7 節，或是指其中一部分（例如，僅指 5 節，6～7 節是作者自己的擴充）。布魯斯（*Paraphrase* 295 n.1）則認為，這話也許是指 6～7 節（聖靈就是……成為後嗣）。**(3)** Kelly 254 將這話限於 '[vv.] 5b-6, i.e. the specifically baptismal section'（即筆者的 5c～6 節）。但見 Knight I 83-85, Knight II 348-49 的反駁。**(4)** 構成這話的是 4～7 節而不僅是 5～7 節，理由包括（Knight I 85-86）：（i）4～7 節在原文是一句；（ii）這一句的主旨在於「我們〔的〕救主上帝〔4 節〕救了我們〔5 節〕」，而這發生於我們也是無知……（3 節）的時候；因此，是這一整句（包括 4 節）提供了「我們應按照 1～2 節的囑咐而行」的理由；（iii）4 節的慈愛（φιλανθρωπία）一字在新約僅再出現一次，指馬耳他島上的居民對保羅等人的友善（徒二十八 2），在這裏則指上帝的慈愛；也許（若 4 節不是這話一部分）保羅在這裏使用了他在其他的書信從未使用的一個字，但較可能的解釋是，這字得自保羅所引用的這話。**(5)** Spencer（65 n.62）認為這話是指 8b 節（筆者的 8b～d 節）。她的理由是：'the saying follows a conjunction as in 1 Tim 1:15 and 4:9; in the other four sayings, the saying most likely follows the phrase *pistos ho logos* and 3:8b is more pithy than 3:4-7.' 但見下文的（**6**）之（**iv**）。**(6)** Campbell（'Sayings' 78-79）則辯證，這話是已信上帝的人〔必須〕留心行善（8c 節〔similarly Scott 178〕），開首的 ἵνα + subjunctive φροντίζωσιν 相當於命令式語法動詞（像弗五 33b 的 ἵνα φοβῆται 一樣〔參《弗》892-93〕）。他把 8 節分析如下：

這話是可信的（同提前三 1；提後二 11）原文在教牧書信再出現四次，其中兩次在**這話可信**之後，還加上**值得完全接受**（提前一 15，四 9）。[6] 馬歇爾指出，這公式（有或沒有加上的一句）的作用不在於

引介公式（8a 節：**這話是可信的**）；
強化插句（8b 節，'Parenthetical Reinforcement': 'and on this I desire you to insist'）；
這話（8c 節）；
進一步的修飾（8d 節，'Further Qualification': '*that is* [ταῦτά ἐστιν], good and profitable to humankind'）。

可是，（**i**）將 8b 節視為介乎引介公式（8a 節）和**這話**（8c 節）之間的插句並不自然，儘管坎伯爾認為（77-78）這現象已在提前四 9～10 出現過：引介公式（9 節）；強化插句（10a 節：**我們勞苦，努力正是為此**）；**這話**（10b 節：**我們的指望在永生的上帝。他是人人的救主**）；進一步的修飾（10c 節，**更是信徒的救主**）。（**ii**）更不合理的是將複數的 περὶ <u>τούτων</u>（**這些事**）化為單數的 'on <u>this</u>'（指 'this [saying]'）。（**iii**）ταῦτά ἐστιν 在新約僅再出現一次（太十五 20），意思是 'These are'（e.g., NKJV, RSV, NRSV, NAU, NIV, TNIV, NIV2011, NJB）；在 LXX 出現十四次，它的意思沒有一次是 'that is', 而總是 'these things are'（創三十八 25，LXE〔下同，除非另外註明〕；賽二十二 14；哈二 13〔問句〕）或 'these are'（出二十九 1、38；利十一 35；申十四 19〔沒有譯出 ταῦτα〕；伯五 27；結十六 44，四十七 20；何二 14；亞六 5；次經《便西拉智訓》27.30 [NJB]；參：箴三十 24〔ταῦτα δὲ ἐστιν〕）；有一次意譯為 'this lot belongs'（詩一四三〔一四四〕15）。常用來表達解釋性的 'that is' 之意的是單數的 <u>τοῦτ'</u> ἔστιν（太二十七 46；可七 2；徒一 19，十九 4；羅七 18，九 8，十 6、7、8；門 12 節；來二 14，七 5，九 11，十 20，十一 16，十三 15；彼前三 20）。（**iv**）Marshall 329（endorsed by Towner III 790 n.75〔唐 1152 註 1〕）斷言，8b 節開首的 καί 字使討論中的見解（8a 節的**這話**指向下文）不能成立（'the following καί prevents this'）。

（**7**）Jeon I 109 認為，'"Word" in 3:8a . . . is a reference to the "word of God" (2:5) concerning "eternal life" [3:7] that was "revealed . . . in the proclamation" and entrusted first to the apostle (1:3) and now to Titus (2:8) and the elders (1:9b).' 借用作者對 Campbell 的立場（〔6〕）的評語，'This position is unpersuasive'（n.24）。（**8**）勵佐治認為，這幾節可能是在洗禮場合中（由受洗者或受洗者和會眾一起）宣認信仰的話（Knight I 109-11）。但見下面註 7（Towner）。

6 （後一句的作用只是加強前一句〔Marshall 327, 397〕。）上述的事實構成保羅書信（及新約）的獨特現象。Knight I 就是針對這現象的專題研究。（**1**）連同多三 8 以外的這四節，**這話**分別是：（**i**）隨後的「**基督耶穌到世上來是要拯救罪人**」（提前一 15b；see Knight I 32, 138; Marshall 397）；（**ii**）隨後（原文次序）的「**若有人想望監督的職分，他是在羨慕一件好事**」（提前三 1b；see Knight I 52-55, 138; Marshall 475〔另有認為，**這話**是提前二 15：e.g., Bassler, 'Epiphanies' 323-24; Campbell ['Sayings' 80-84] 甚至認為**這話**是提前三 16，'but his argument . . . is unconvincing [Marshall 328]〕）；（**iii**）<u>之前</u>的**操練身體有些益處；但敬虔在各方面都有益，它有現今和未來的生命的應許**（提前四 8；see Knight I 62-65, 138; Marshall 554）；（**iv**）隨後的**我們若與基督同死，也必與他同活；我們若忍耐到底，也必和**

引入或結束一引句（一個引介公式不能結束一個引句），而是在於確定所說的話是真的；這公式以嚴肅的口氣強調所說的話的真確性和重要性。雖然所說的話可能至終是基於傳統資料，但一般而言作者是用了他自己的方式來表達的，因而不能認為他是在「引用傳統」。[7] 作者使用這公式的明確目的，就是要推薦他欲強調的教導；這公式的用法是靈活的，所指的教導通常是基於傳統，並且與救恩及隨之而來的實際行為有關。[8] 這些「可信的話」之所以為**可信的**，是由於它們是上帝認可的教導的一部分。以下數點支持這看法：第一，在啟示錄，上帝稱祂自己所說的話為**可信靠的**和**真實的**（啟二十一5，二十二6）；第二，監督要堅守的**可靠之道是合乎教義的**（多一9），即是合乎那被認可的使徒教義；[9] 第三，保羅被委派服事基督，是因基督認為他**忠誠可靠**（提前一12〔新普〕）。[10]

他一同作王。我們若不認他，他也必不認我們；我們縱然失信，他仍是可信的，因為他不能否認自己（提後二 11b～13；see Knight I 112-15, 138; Marshall 739, 733〔Campbell [‘Sayings’ 80, 84] 則把因為他不能否認自己視為 ‘Further Qualification’ 而非這話的一部分〕）；（**v**）之前的多三 4～7（減去開首的但字）。（**2**）對比於（1）——這話三次指隨後、兩次指之前的話——G. Kittel（*TDNT* 4.118 n.199）則認為，‘In most cases πιστὸς ὁ λόγος does not refer . . . , or does not refer only, to the sentence which follows. It is a confirmation of that which precedes.’（**3**）Riesner（‘Once More’ 250 n.64）相信，除了提前三 1，‘all the other examples of the formula πιστὸς ὁ λόγος point backwards or forwards to traditions’：（**i**）提前一 15a（一 15b；參：路十五 2，十九 10〔誤作十九 19〕）；（**ii**）提前四 9a（四 8b 參：可十 30 ‖ 路十八 30；四 10c 參：可十六 15～16；路一 47；多二 11）；（**iii**）提後二 11a（二 11b～13；參：路二十二 28～30；路十二 9 ‖ 太十 33；路二十二 31～34）；（**iv**）多三 8（三 4～7；[parallelisms] 三 4 參：路一 47；三 5 參：太十九 28；約三 5；三 6 參：路二 11；約四 42；徒二 4、17；三 7 參：太十九 29；可十 17 ‖ 路十 25；路十八 18；加四 4～7）。

7 按 H. Ritt（*EDNT* 2.359*b* [s.v. λόγος, 7 d]）的理解，‘The characteristic formula of the Pastorals, “faithful is the *word*” . . . refers to the kerygmatic, liturgical, and institutional faith tradition of the Christ-event.’ Towner III 790（唐 1151）則認為，8a 節這話 ‘does not imply that traditional material has been cited, for Paul seems clearly to have given the material its present form, but rather to guarantee the veracity of this articulation’.

8 Marshall 328-29.「引用傳統」英文原作 ‘a *citation* of tradition’.

9 參一 9 註釋第二段（上面 142-44）。

10 Marshall 328. 加上底線的三個形容詞在原文皆為 πιστός, 即本節的可信的。

三 **8b** 我願你堅持這些事，

8c 使那些已信上帝的人留心行善。

8d 這都是美好且對人有益的。

我願你堅持在形式上是一項陳述，但直說式語法的願字加上不定詞堅持，實質意義相當於「你要堅持」；願字在提摩太前書另兩次（二 8，五 14）同樣有這種果效。[1] 堅持原文在希臘文聖經僅再出現一次（提前一 7），指一些人堅確講論／肯定主張連自己都不清楚的事（呂譯／現修）。[2] 本節的原文以關於這些事（呂譯）開始，即這些事並不是動詞的賓詞（如在堅持這些事），因此，動詞的意思可能同樣是堅確地講論（呂譯），全句意即關於這些事，我願你堅確地講論（8b 節，呂譯），[3] 而這個意思可以被簡化為我願（思高願意）你堅持這些事。[4] 類似的翻譯是我希望你特別強調這些事（現修），希望你強調這

1 Clark, 'Structure' 115. See also H.-J. Ritz, *EDNT* 1.225*b* (s.v. βούλομαι, 2): 'It has an imperative ring in . . . Titus 3:8, where Paul . . . *commands* a certain behavior . . . of Titus'; Marshall 330-31: 'used with acc. and inf. to express a strong command (1 Tim 2.8; 5.14)'; G. Schrenk, *TDNT* 1.632: 'Three times βούλομαι is used in the Past. with reference to ordering by apostolic authority.'（1）Fiore II 216, 221 把動詞 βούλομαι 翻譯為 'it is my decision'. 筆者認為這種意思較適合來六 17：神定意向那些承受應許的人，更清楚地表明他的旨意是不更改的，就用起誓作保證（新譯）；參《來》1.395。（2）這動詞（**βούλομαι**）在保羅書信另外出現八次（新約全部 37 次）：林前十二 11；林後一 15、17；腓一 12；提前二 8，五 14，六 9；門 13 節。See BDAG 182*a-b* (s.v.);《新希》62*a*（s.v.）。

2 參新普：儘管他們講話很有自信，其實對所講的內容一竅不通；Mounce cv: 'to assert dogmatically'.

3 See also Banker 109*a*: 'speak confidently about these things'. Cf. DC 151*b*: 'speak firmly'; Knight I 107: 'affirm confidently'; Vine 1.37: '*dia*, intensive, and *bebaioō*, to affirm, make sure, denotes to assert strongly, "affirm confidently"'.

4 BDAG 226*a* (s.v. διαβεβαιόομαι*): '*speak confidently*, *insist* περὶ τινος'.（*此字在 Genade 101 兩次皆以 διαβεβαιοόμαι 這形式出現。）See also RSV, NRSV, ESV, NLT, *Paraphrase* 295, LN §33.322, G. Schneider, *EDNT* 1.297*a* (s.v.), Quinn 28, 233, 241: 'insist on';《新希》77*a*（s.v.）：「堅持——有把握、又有信心地陳述事情。」Cf. Mounce 435, 451-52: 'insist emphatically on'; Towner III 791: 'insist confidently on' =「滿有信心地堅持」（唐 1153）; Davies I 109: 'Titus is exhorted to *insist on* the acceptance of the teaching contained in the epistle, in the sense that he is to speak confidently about those matters.'

些教導（新普）；[5] 我願你確實地強調這些事（新譯）則似乎合併了「堅確地講論」和「強調」這兩個意思。

范尼斯認為，這些事可能不僅指第 1 至 7 節的這些教導（新普），[6] 也包括第二章的那些教導（參二 1、7、10），即這些事是指二章 1 節至三章 8a 節的全部教訓。[7] 與此同時，二章 1 節的你所講的總要合乎那健全的教導，大可以包括二章 2 節至三章 8a 節的內容；三章 1 節並無過渡性陳述，而只是繼續上文的勸勉。如此，二章 1 節<u>和</u>三章 8 節一起提示，二章 1 節<u>至</u>三章 8 節可以看為合一的大段落，細分為平行的兩段（二 1～15 ‖ 三 1～8）。[8] 在這包含了信上的主要教導的一大段落的前後，就是信上較詳細地討論反對的人的兩段（一 10～16 在前，三 9～11 在後）；[9] 這結構上的鋪排可能提示，這

---

5 See also NLT, NIV, TNIV, NIV 2011: 'stress'. 類似的意思是 'maintain strongly'（Fiore II 216），'affirm constantly'（KJV, NKJV），和「毫不妥協地教導（be quite uncompromising in teaching）」（NJB）。

6 Fee 207: 'the content of vv. 1-7, but esp. of 4-7'（cf. White 200*a*: 'the various topics indicated in that statement [vv. 4-7]'; 黃編 226：「四至七節所記的救恩真理」）。**(1)** 班約翰則認為，這些事是指 3～7 節有關福音的真理（Banker 90, 90*a*, 90*b*, 111*a*, 111*b*-2*a*）。**(2)** Stott 206 認為是指 3～8 節那些 'essential ingredients of salvation'（見三 4～7 註釋引言註 3〔上面 377〕）。可是，按斯托得的理解，那些「救恩的基本成分」包括 8b 節的留心行善（那是獲得救恩的證據），但是按本節的講法，使那些已信上帝的人留心行善，乃是提多要堅持這些事的目的。因此，這些事應該不包括留心行善。

7 See Lock 156. Cf. Johnson II 250: 'the instructions just given in 2:1-3:7 together with their theological backing'; Malherbe, 'Paraenesis' 302: 'the things he [Titus] had detailed in 2:1-3:7'. **(1)** 祈勒克認為這些事至少指二 1～三 8a，可能指一 13b～三 8a 的全部（Clark, 'Structure' 116）。不過，一 13b～16 是關乎提多應如何對付克里特的假教師，但三 8c 表示，提多應堅持這些事的目的，是為要使那些已信上帝的人留心行善。因此，這些事不大可能包括一 13b～16 的指示。**(2)** Genade 101 甚至認為，8b 節的這些事 'refers to everything that has gone before till now'. 如此，τούτων 所指的便與 8a 節 ὁ λόγος 所指的相同（參三 8a 註釋註 4 及所屬正文〔上面 420-21〕）。但簡內德稍後又說，8d 節的這是指 'all the teaching contained in chapter 3'. 但 8b 節的 τούτων 和 8d 節的 ταῦτα 有不同的內容嗎？參註 25 及所屬正文（下面 428-29）。**(3)** Wendland（'Discourse' 341）認為這些事是指 'whatever I am telling you in this letter', 但也許特指 3～7 節那可信的話。

8 Van Neste, 'Structure' 129-30. 參一 9 註釋註 56 及所屬正文（上面 151）。

9 這兩小段之間亦有題材上的相似之處：一 10 的不受約束的人很可能包括三 10～11 的分門結黨的人；那些與猶太人的傳說和人的命令（一 14）有關、並且關心禮儀

些反對的人是在教導部分的視野之內，這些教導可能就是因他們而引起的。[10] 不過，正因為二章 1 至 15 節和三章 1 至 8 節是平行的兩段，而三章 8b 節（我願你堅持這些事）重複了二章 15 節的命令（這些事你要講明），因此，就如二章 15 節重述了之前一段的要旨，即是該節的這些事回望二章第 1 至 14 節的教導，照樣，三章 8 節總結了第 1 至 7 節的教導，即是三章 8b 節的這些事（僅）回望第 1、2 兩節的勸勉以及支持這勸勉的神學基礎（3～7 節）。[11]

使那些已信上帝的人留心行善（8c 節）表達了提多要堅確地講論（呂譯）這些事的目的。[12] 留心於／留心（呂譯／同新和）或常常留心（新譯）原文[13] 在新約聖經僅見於此處；[14] 另一些翻譯是

潔淨（一 15）的奉割禮的人（一 10），跟那些關心家譜以及因律法而起的爭辯的人（三 9）相符（Van Neste, 'Structure' 130 n.2）。

10 Van Neste, 'Structure' 130.

11 Towner III 791 with n.81（唐 1153 連註 7）。See also Towner II 259; Malherbe, 'Soteriology' 350: 'the precepts and their justification given in vv. 1-7'; Arichea－Hatton 307; Fiore II 221: 'these matters' 指 1～7 節整個勸勉單元的內容（thus also Hiebert 447）；Knight II 350: 'τούτων . . . refers to . . . 3:1-7'; Marshall 330 (endorsed by Köstenberger 624*a*): 'all that is included in the previous section of the letter [i.e., 3:1-7]'; Mounce 452: 'all of chap. 3 [thus far]'; Smith 307; 陳 47；張 379。

12 Hanson III 193 則認為，不應照足使字的字面意義來了解這一句，作者只是從禮儀性的一段過渡到勸勉性的一段，也許我們應這樣翻譯：「要堅持這些事；讓已信上帝的人……」。See also Quinn 234: '"So that" formally opens a result clause . . . which may be construed imperatively both here and in 3:13-14'.

13 φροντίζωσιν = 'be careful to'（KJV, NKJV, RSV, NRSV, NAU, NIV, TNIV, NIV2011, ESV, *Paraphrase* 295; *EDNT* 3.440*a* [s.v. φροντίζω]），'pay attention to'（BDAG 1066*b* [s.v.]），'devote themselves (in concert) to'（B. Reicke, *TDNT* 6.703），'take thought / take care to'（Fiore I 217 / II 217, 222），'keep their minds constantly occupied in'（NJB），'fix their attention on'（LN §30.20, §35.12），'be intent on'（Quinn 28, 233, 234, 241; Mounce 435, 452），'taking trouble over'（L. Coenen, *DNTT* 1.197），'think of, be mindful of, care for'（J. Goetzmann, *DNTT* 1.277），「老是想着；不斷考慮；專注於……——不斷地認真考慮事情」（《新希》350 [s.v.]）。

14 在 LXX 則出現十五次，呈現多個意思：**(i)** 掛慮（撒上九 5，思高）、擔心（箴三十一 21）；**(ii)**「照顧」（詩四十 17〔LXX 三十九 18；LXE 'take care of'〕；次經《便西拉智訓》32.1〔RSV/NRSV: 'take good care of / Take care of'〕，50.4〔思高德訓篇〕）；**(iii)**「思想」（伯三 25〔cf. LXE: 'meditated [on]'〕）、「想到」（伯二十三 15〔LXE: 'thought of'〕）、「思量」（次經《所羅門智訓》8.17〔RSV/NRSV: 'thought upon / pondered'〕）；**(iv)**「注意（你的名譽）」（《便西拉智訓》41.12 = 思高德訓篇

專心（當代、新普）和**熱心**（思高、現修）。[15] **留心行善**的原文結構將「好行為」放在動詞**留心**和不定詞行字[16] 之間，使賓詞「好行為」受到強調。[17] 主詞**那些已信上帝**[18] **的人**[19]（指基督

41.15〔cf. NJB / RSV, NRSV: 'Be careful of / Have regard for'〕)；(**v**)「料理〔事務〕」(次經《馬加比一書》16.14〔思高瑪加伯上〕)；(**vi**)「以之為目標」(次經《馬加比二書》2.25〔RSV, NRSV / NJB: 'we have aimed to/at'〕，11.15〔NJB / RSV, NRSV: 'thinking only of / having regard for'〕)；(**vii**)「籌算／安排」(《馬加比二書》4.21〔NJB / RSV, NRSV: 'began thinking about / took measures for'〕，9.21〔RSV, NRSV / NJB: 'take thought for / make provision for〕)；(**viii**)「準備好」(《便西拉智訓》8.13〔NRSV, NJB: 'be prepared'〕)。

15 亦參《輔讀》530：「專心，熱心(做某事)」。Spencer 65 則翻譯為 'to stand forth with good deeds' = 'stand forth marked by *good deeds*'（n.56）。

16 **προΐστημι** 在下文再出現一次(三 14：**行善**)，兩次的意思都是 'apply oneself to'（*EDNT* 3.157*a* [s.v.]）。這字在保羅書信另外出現六次（羅十二 8：**治理的**〔參《羅》4.113-16〕；帖前五 12：**治理**〔新和、新譯；參《帖前》422-23〕；提前三 4、5、12〔當代、新和、思高、新普〕：**管理**；提前五 17：**管理**〔當代、新和〕、**領導**〔現修〕、**督導**〔呂譯、思高、和修〕)，在新約不再出現。

17 ἵνα φροντίζωσιν καλῶν ἔργων προΐστασθαι, literally 'so that they may be intent on | good works to engage in'. 正常的字序應該是 'be intent on the doing of good works'; cf. NLT: 'devote themselves to doing (good)'. (**1**) Quinn 28, 233, 234, 241 將 προΐστασθαι 翻譯為 'taking the lead in fine deeds'（see also Lock 124: 'take the lead in good works'; Simpson 117: '*to be forward* or perhaps *foremost* in good works'; Hiebert 447: 'taking a lead in the performance of excellent deeds'）。(**2**) LN §35.12 認為 προΐσταμαι (*sic*) = 'to be active in helping, to be involved in giving aid'（參《新希》283*a* [s.v. I.2]:「參與幫忙或援助」)。DC 151*b*, 151*a* 則認為其意思是 'to be concerned with'. 馬歇爾認為（1）（2）兩種看法都是 'improbable'（Marshall 331 n.97）。(**3**) NEB 的翻譯（'engage in honourable occupations' [accepted by Hanson I 121; cf. Scott 177, 178: 'practising honourable occupations']）將 προΐστημι 按其聖經以外希臘文獻的專門意義理解為「從事一項職業」之意；亦參三 14 註 15 之(3) = 下面 465。這翻譯同樣值得商榷，因為 καλὰ ἔργα 在本書另外三次（二 7、14，三 14）及 ἔργα καλά / τὰ ἔργα τὰ καλά 在提前三次(提前五 10a，六 18／五 25)——亦參同義詞 ἔργον ἀγαθόν / ἔργα ἀγαθά（多一 16，三 1；提前五 10；提後二 21，三 17／提前二 10)——皆指籠統意義的「好行為」(see Banker 109*b*)。Cf. Mounce 452: 'Paul's concern is for their behavior in general and not merely one aspect such as a profession.' (**4**) 同理，將**留心做正經事業**（新和；曾 98）理解為「留心作主的聖工」(陳 48）也不可取。(**5**) Collins 373 則認為：'In the exhortation of 3:8, the good deeds are clearly that－namely, deeds that are beneficial for human beings.'

18 M. J. Harris（*DNTT* 3.1214）指出：'The fact that God is (relatively speaking) so infrequently held up as the object of faith . . . and Christ so frequently, indicates that it is in Christ that God meets the individual in salvation. There are not two competing personal objects of human faith.'

19 οἱ πεπιστευκότες θεῷ(主格)= 'those who have come to believe in God' (NRSV, NEB, REB). (**1**) Johnson II 251 認為，這動詞的完成時態提示他們剛信主不久（thus also

徒[20]）在原文居於句子的末尾，因而也是受強調的。[21] 這雙重的強調突出了**信上帝**和「好行為」的密切關係：前者是根，後者是果；[22] 信靠[23] 上帝的人應該展現好行為（亦參 1 節），不像那些**宣稱認識上帝，卻在行為上否認他**，並且無法表現甚麼好行為（一 16）的假教師！[24]

末句（8d 節）的**這**字原文是**這些事**（呂譯、現修），與第 8b 節開首的**這些事**是同一個字（只是不同格），因而它的意思可能也是**這些教導**（新普）。[25] **這些事**的述語有兩部分：**（一）是美好的**（現

Witherington 162）。但是唐書禮正確指出：'This newness of their faith . . . is better determined from other factors in the context of the letter than from the perfect tense'（Towner III 791 n.82〔唐 1154 註 8〕）。(**2**) πεπιστευκότες 可能是 intensive perfect（往往最宜翻譯為英文的現在時態），所強調的是他們現在的狀況是「信上帝的」（see Wallace 574-76）; thus NJB: 'those who now believe in God'; NLT: 'all who trust in God'. (**3**)（**i**）單數的 πεπιστευκὼς τῷ θεῷ 在徒十六 34 指腓立比獄警全家**信了上帝**，又在偽經《馬加比四書》7.21 指「信神」的哲學家。(**ii**) 複數直接受格的 τοὺς πεπιστευκότας 在約八 31 指那些**信了他〔耶穌〕的猶太人**，又在次經《馬加比二書》3.12 指「那些信賴聖所〔之〕神聖的人」（思高瑪加伯下）。(**iii**) 所有格的 τῶν πεπιστευκότων 在徒十九 18，二十一 20 和二十一 25 分別指 **已經信的人**、**猶太人中⋯⋯的信徒**，和**信主的外邦人**。(**iv**) 間接受格的 τοῖς πεπιστευκόσιν 在徒十八 27 指**那些蒙恩信主的人**，又在次經《馬加比二書》3.22 指「存款的人」（思高瑪加伯下）。

20 Fee 207: 'Christian believers'. Hagner（'Titus' 548）指出，**已信上帝的**（'those who have come to believe in God'）這描述清楚顯示，克里特教會的信徒大部分是外邦人。Quinn 111-12 卻認為這些 'believers in God'（234）是 'the Jewish Christians'（反對使徒傳統的猶太基督徒），他們被膚淺的**愚拙的辯論、家譜、紛爭和因律法而起的爭辯**（9 節）所捆綁。

21 主詞通常緊隨動詞之後。See BDF §472: 'The verb . . . stands immediately after the conjunction (the usual beginning of a sentence); then follow in order the subject, object, supplementary participle, etc.'

22 Calvin 385: 'It is those who believe in God who are told to be careful for good works, and by this he means that faith must come first, so that the good works will follow.'

23 Marshall 215: 'the element of trust appears to be present [in πιστεύω]'.

24 參三 5 註釋首段「**與此同時**」開始（上面 384）。

25 Mounce 453: 'the twofold repetition of "these" in one verse suggests the former [ταῦτα referring back to τούτων].' See also Calvin 385: 'I take this to refer to the teaching rather than to the works'; Chapell 363: 'the duties he has enjoined'; Jeon II 35: 'sound doctrine and the appropriate lifestyle that should follow'; Ngewa 406-7: 'The things Titus is to teach . . .'. (**1**) Marshall 332-33 則認為，'it is the activity of sound teaching which is being commended', 儘管他同時指出，'the act and the content of teaching cannot be separated'. (**2**) Quinn 28, 233, 241, 243 把**這些事**理解為 'Activity like that', 指信徒 'taking the lead in fine deeds'. Cf. Köstenberger 624*a*: 'i.e., doing good deeds';

修）。[26] 這形容詞拾起了上一句的「好行為」一詞內的「好」字，因而提示這樣的意思：這些教導之所以為美好，至少部分的原因是，這些教導要求、從而導致信徒有好行為。[27]（二）是對人有益的（現修、新譯）。[28] 對人使人想起二章 11 節的「向眾人」（亦參三 2：對眾人）：

Bouwman 130: 'doing good works "are [*sic*, is] excellent and profitable for people"'.（3）Fiore II 224 將 ταῦτα 理解為 8c 節的 'good works'（thus also Arichea－Hatton 307; Dunn 877*b*; Griffin 326; Laansma 290; Montague 249; Spencer 62; Towner I 197; Towner II 260; Matera, 'Moral Guides' 243; Ridderbos, *Paul* 434; Winter, *Roman Wives* 165），這些善行之所以為有用，是因它們說明了耶穌和聖靈的拯救之工（5～6 節），那是為所有的人的（二 11）。Fee 208 用來支持「這些事是指信徒的好行為」的理由是，與有益（ὠφέλιμα）相對應的無益（ἀνωφελεῖς〔9b 節〕）是指假教師的 'evil works'; 因而有益的較可能是指信徒的 'good deeds'. 可是，無益所形容的其實不是倫理意義的 'evil works', 而是屬於「教導」範疇的辯論、家譜、紛爭和因律法而起的爭辯，後者與正確的教導（這些事）構成更好的對比。

（4）窩羅伯將這些事理解為<u>隨後的</u>指示：'These practices are good and useful for people: avoid foolish controversies . . .'（Wall 370, 留意冒號）; 'A third and preferable <u>antecedent</u> is the concluding catalog of ecclesial practices in 3:9-11'（371）。但稱<u>隨後的</u>指示為 ταῦτα 的<u>前述詞</u>是奇怪的。（5）若 8d 節的 ταῦτα 是指 8c 節的 καλῶν ἔργων, 為甚麼保羅在 8d 節隨即重複「好」字，稱這些事為 καλά 呢（Banker 91*b* [see also 112*a*: 'that would be <u>over</u>redundant'!]）？Towner III 793（唐 1156）這樣回答：'"good deeds" (*kala erga*) is heavily coded language for authentic Christian living . . . and it is therefore not a tautology to affirm the concept as "good" or "excellent." On the contrary, such wordplay might be an example of *paronomasia** employed to create a subtle emphasis.'（* '*Paronomasia* is the name given to the recurrence of the same word or word stem in close proximity' [BDF §488(1)].）筆者沒有被這論證說服。（6）Knight II 352 則認為這些事指 1～7 節的全部，因而同時指教導和「好行為（good deeds）」。勵佐治又認為，美好是指有關上帝的救恩之教導（4～7 節）可稱讚（見下註）的性質，對人有益則指 'good deeds' 所帶給非信徒（2 節的眾人）的好處。

26 Fiore II 217 則意譯為 'praiseworthy'.

27 Marshall 333: 'Such teaching is "good", in that it gives rise to good deeds.' REB 則翻譯為 'These precepts are good <u>in themselves</u>'.

28 呂譯將 τοῖς ἀνθρώποις 理解為形容 καλὰ καὶ ὠφέλιμα 這整個片語，因而翻譯為這些事對於人都是美好而有益的。See also *EDNT* 3.512*b* (s.v. ὠφέλιμος): 'good and *profitable* for people'; Banker 110: 'beneficial and profitable for (all) people'.（1）班約翰引林前七 1（男人不親近女人倒好：<u>καλὸν</u> ἀνθρώπῳ γυναικὸς μὴ ἅπτεσθαι）來表明，將多三 8 的 καλὰ . . . τοῖς ἀνθρώποις 理解為「對人是好的」並無不妥。不過，班約翰的翻譯不必要地使兩個形容詞變成同義字（'beneficial', 'profitable' =「有益的」）。（2）形容詞 **ὠφέλιμος** 在希臘文聖經僅再出現三次，意思也是有……益處／有益（提前四 8a／四 8b；提後三 16）。

就如帶來拯救的、上帝的恩典是向眾人顯明的，[29] 照樣，信上的**這些教導也對每個人都有益處**（新普），即是靈性上有益處。[30] 關於**這些事**的上述兩點，就是提多要**堅持這些事**的原因。[31]

29 參二 11 註釋首段（上面 285-87）。

30 Marshall 333: 'profitable spiritually'. REB 理解為 'useful to society'. Lau 173 則把 καλὰ καὶ ὠφέλιμα τοῖς ἀνθρώποις 視為形容 8c 節的「好行為」："“Good works” are . . . done . . . for the benefit of men . . . , that is, for the sake of those who have not believed in God's goodness and love in Christ.' 如此，「好行為」(即是可見的、具吸引力的基督徒生命／生活)的主要目標，就是向未信者指向上帝，叫他們接受福音。See also, already, Towner II 260; and Mounce, 'Titus' 107: '. . . a life of good works, which will . . . attract others to the truth.'

31 Van Neste 249: '[the] clause [v. 8c = my v. 8d] appears to provide a grounding or rationale for the exhortation'. 因此，8d 節開首的「無連詞（asyndeton）」現象，並不構成 8d 節應連於下文的有力理由（*pace* Banker 91*b*）。參導論第伍節註 17 之（5）= 上面 35。

陸 如何對付反對的人：之二（三 9～11）

9a 要遠避愚拙的辯論、家譜、紛爭和因律法而起的爭辯，
9b 因為這都是虛妄無益的。
10 分門結黨的人，警戒過一兩次後就要拒絕跟他來往；
11a 因為你知道這樣的人已經背道，
11b 常常犯罪，自己定自己的罪了。

本小段延續了第 8b 節的勸勉（願你堅持相當於命令語法的「要堅持」；參當代：你要認真教導人）。保羅在這裏再次（參一 10～16）指導提多要怎樣對付那些反對的人。本段在原文由兩個句子構成。兩個命令式語法的動詞——第 9a 節的遠避，和第 10 節的拒絕——隨後都各有支持的理由（9b 節，因為；11a 節，因為你知道），而兩個理由都各含雙重的描述（9b 節，無益、虛妄；11a、b 節，背道、犯罪）。[1]

信上討論敵對者的這兩段（三 9～11，一 10～16）有很強的連貫性。**第一**，這些從事虛妄之爭辯的人（三 9b）與一章 10a 節那些說空話的人相似。**第二**，在這裏，他們參與有關律法（幾乎可以肯定是指猶太人的妥拉）的爭辯（三 9a）；在第一章，他們是屬割禮派的人（10b 節），他們附從猶太人的傳說（14a 節），並且關注禮儀潔淨的問題（15 節）。**第三**，兩段都指他們在擾亂教會，因他們不受約束（一 10a）、敗壞人的全家（11b 節），並且可被稱為分門結黨的人（三 10）。**第四**，兩段都把他們描寫為大體上是有罪的，又在結束時都

1 本段參 Van Neste 250.

提到他們是被棄絕的（一 16c，三 10～11）。**最後**，兩段都是尾隨剛提到的可靠之道／可信的話（一 9a／三 8a）。[2]

三章 9 節提出的方法——遠避敵對者無益的爭論——似乎有別於一章 11 節：這些人的口必須堵住。[3] 但一章 14 節同樣提出了不要聽猶太人無稽的傳說。其實兩者並非互不協調；避免參與他們的爭論可能是使他們住口的有效方法，如果要使他們住口（新普）可以解釋為「不要再給他們機會散播他們的謬誤」，[4] 就更是這樣。三章 10 節提到的一兩次的警戒，與嚴厲地責備他們（一 13b）[5] 一致；而拒絕跟他來往（三 10）的對抗意味，不亞於一章 10 至 16 節。因此，兩段的氛圍並非顯著不同。[6] 雖然本段含有新的資料，但本段與一章 10 至 16 節是連貫一致的。[7]

---

2 本段參 Van Neste 276.

3 Banker 111*a* 認為，遠避必須解作「不與之有任何瓜葛（have nothing to do with whatever）」，而不是「不要制止但要避開他們」，因為保羅在上文曾告訴提多，必須堵住那些假教師的口（一 11），也要嚴厲地責備跟隨他們的人（一 13）。基於相同的理由，班約翰稍後將動詞解釋為 'don't allow these things to happen wherever you have influence and authority'（114*a*）。

4 Van Neste, 'Message' 23*a*.

5 解釋見一 13b～c 註釋末段（上面 185-86）。

6 *Pace* Quinn 244: 'The atmosphere in the two sections is markedly different.' 昆謝隆甚至認為可以想像，'two different sources have been reproduced but not brought into harmony.'

7 以上一段參 Van Neste 277.

三　**9a**　要遠避愚拙的辯論、家譜、紛爭和因律法而起的爭辯，[1]
　　9b　　　　因為這都是虛妄無益的。

本節開首在原文有「但」字，[2] 一些中譯本意譯為至於（呂譯、思高、當代），二者同樣提示與上文的對比。簡內德認為這字延續了信上一貫的對比，就是健全的教義和假教義的對比。[3] 不過，最接近的文理提示，「但」字所引入的是保羅要提多堅持這些事（8b 節）和保羅要提多遠避另一些事（9a 節）的對比；[4] 而這對比最重要的一點就是，這些事是對人有益的（8d 節），這「另一些事」卻是無益

1　（1）Clark（'Structure' 116）認為，9a 節可能呈現交叉配置模式：

形容詞 + 名詞	μωρὰς δὲ ζητήσεις	（愚拙的辯論）
名詞	καὶ **γενεαλογίας**	（和家譜）
名詞	καὶ **ἔρεις**	（和紛爭）
名詞 + 形容詞	καὶ μάχας νομικάς	（和因律法而起的爭辯）

祈勒克問道，如果可以將愚拙的辯論與因律法而起的爭辯等同，那麼中央的兩項是否可以視為重言法，意即「關於家譜的紛爭」呢？（關於重言法〔hendiadys〕，參二 13 註釋註 13 之〔2〕= 上面 305。）（**2**）祈氏又認為，如果將上表的前兩項和後兩項分別視為重言法，所得出的意思就是「關於家譜的愚拙的辯論」和 'dissensions over legal disputes'，即是「關乎律法之爭辯（presumably different interpretations of the Jewish law）的紛爭」。他認為並無決定性的證據可藉以作出取捨。筆者認為（2）比（1）可取；參註 35 之（2）= 下面 439。（**3**）無論如何，這些詞語所指的可能都是 'specifically Jewish matters'（Classen, 'Titus' 442, 'Epistle to Titus' 62）。（**4**）在提後二 23 對提摩太類似的勸勉中，上面加上底線的三個字亦有出現：要棄絕那愚拙（μωρᾶς）無知的辯論（ζητήσεις），因為你知道這等事只會引起爭辯（μάχας）；加上黑體的兩個字，卻並非本節獨有的新元素：γενεαλογία 見提前一 4（家譜），ἔρις 見提前六 4（紛爭）。

2　δέ = 'But' (KJV, NKJV, RSV, NRSV, NAU, NIV, TNIV, NIV2011, NJB, ESV, *Paraphrase* 295).

3　Genade 103. Mounce 453 則認為這裏的對比是 'between the people of vv 1-8 and the opponents'.

4　Towner III 795（唐 1159）；Aageson 54-55. 遠避（περιΐστημι）亦與 8c 節的留心（προΐστημι）構成對比及文字遊戲。（**1**）遠避的意思是不要個人參與其中；Marshall 336-37 認為也許亦包括制止（參一 11）之意。（**2**）前一個字（**περιΐστημι**）在新約僅再出現三次，兩次為主動語態，意思是站著（約十一 42；徒二十五 7），另一次（提後二 16）為中間語態，意思也是遠避（如在多三 9 本節）。後一個字（προΐστημι）見三 8b～d 註釋註 16（上面 427）。

的（9b 節）。[5] 這「另一些事」包含四個項目，由三個「和」字連起來。[6] 原文的次序是構成賓詞的四個項目在前，動詞在後，因而賓詞和動詞同樣受到強調。[7]

（#1）辯論（同呂譯、思高、新和、現修、新譯）[8] 或討論（新普）[9] 原文在教牧書信另外出現兩次：一次指辯論的活動（提前六 4：專好爭辯），另一次除了愚拙還有無知作為另一個修飾語（提後二 23：愚拙無知的辯論），[10] 所指的應是同一類的事

---

5 二字是同字根的：ὠφέλιμος, ἀνωφελής, 很可能是刻意的文字遊戲。

6 見上面註 1 之（1）。這個修辭技巧稱為 'polysyndeton'（Genade 104, 126; polysyndeton '[is used] for abundant expressiveness' [Quinn 6]）。簡內德沒有把它放在 polysyndetic emphatic clustering 的例子之列，是由於後者* 被定義為 'the grouping together or clustering of related concepts or words in groups of three'（Genade 128）。* 參一 16 註釋註 2（上面 207），二 12 註釋註 37 之（1），二 15 註釋註 2 之（1）= 上面 297，341。
卡羅拔認為辯論和紛爭（##1、3）是希臘哲學家對「詭辯派」常見的批評（Karris, 'Polemic' 553）；* 本節獨特之處在於它提到家譜和因律法而起的爭辯（562）。*參一 11 註釋註 26 之（2）= 上面 170。

7 參三 8b～d 註釋註 21 所引之 BDF §472（上面 428）。

8 See also *Paraphrase* 295: 'debates'; NKJV, Marshall 334: 'disputes'; RSV, NRSV, NAU, NIV, TNIV, NIV2011: 'controversies'. **（1）** DC 151*b* 翻譯為 'investigations'（cf. Stegemann, 'Prejudices' 279: 'discussions or investigations'; 參下面註 11 之〔2〕所提到的徒二十五 20）。E. Larson（*EDNT* 2.103*b* [s.v. ζήτησις, 2]）正確指出，'the tr. "investigation" is possible, but the context speaks for the meaning *debate*.' **（2）** Hendriksen 394 則翻譯為 'inquiries'（also Jeon I 99, 112; Johnson II 249; cf. Calvin 386: 'questionings'; Towner III 795: 'inquiry'〔唐 1159：「詢問」〕），解釋為 'investigations into genealogical lore'. H. Greeven（*TDNT* 2.894）指出，文理提示 ζήτησις 必須理解為 'enquiry' 之意的，就只有徒二十五 20 那一節。

9 NLT: 'discussions'. 另有翻譯為 'questions'（KJV; 參當代：問難）、'researches'（Murphy-O'Connor, '2 Timothy' 416），或 'speculations'（NJB; Barclay 264; Kelly 248; Quinn 28; Stott 210; Mounce, 'Titus' 107）。**（1）** 基於 'speculation'（also Mounce cv）這翻譯，Mounce 453 認為這解釋了為何保羅沒有從神學的角度來處理克里特的異端：敵對者的教導 'lack[s] substance . . . . It is vacuous, a quibbling about words.' **（2）** 但是在 Thayer 272*b* (s.v. ζήτησις), BAGD 339*a-b*, BDAG 428*b*-29*a* (s.v.), LN vol. 2, p. 113 (s.v.) 這些辭典，都找不到 'speculation' 這個意思。Cf. Banker 112*b*: '*zētēsis* cannot be definitely shown to mean "speculation" anywhere else in the New Testament.'

10 除了本節和提後二 23，形容詞 μωρός 在保羅書信另外出現四次，分別指神的愚拙／世上愚拙的（林前一 25／27〔形容詞 + 冠詞 = 名詞〕），自以為在今世有智慧的倒不如變為愚拙（三 18），以及使徒們為基督的緣故成為愚拙的（四 10）；

情。[11] 根據提摩太前書六章 4 節，爭辯（#1）和舌戰生出……紛爭（＝#3）；又根據提摩太後書二章 23 節，愚拙無知的辯論（#1）……只會引起爭辯（＝#4）。由此看來，這裏提到要遠避的首先是愚拙的辯論，不是沒有原因的。此等辯論之所以稱為愚蠢（新普）的，大抵是由於它們對敬虔（一 1）毫無貢獻，因而是無意義的。[12]

（#2） 家譜／祖譜／族譜（同新和、新譯／思高[13]／呂譯、當代）、[14] 族譜名錄（現修）或宗教家譜（新普）[15] 原文[16] 在希臘文聖經僅再出現一次（提前一 4）：提摩太要囑咐某些人勿聽從無窮的家譜／族譜（新和、新譯／呂譯）、無窮盡的祖譜（思高）或冗長的家

在新約另外六次（太五 22：罵弟兄是白痴；太七 26／二十三 17：無知的人／文士和法利賽人；太二十五 2、3、8：愚拙的童女）。See BDAG 663*b* (s.v.);《新希》223*b*（s.v.）。

11 **（1）** Quinn 112 認為，本節愚拙的辯論（ζητήσεις）、家譜和提前一 4 無稽的傳說（μύθοις）和冗長的家譜平行，因而辯論似乎是指與保羅對聖經（＝ 舊約）之解釋相違的 'haggadic midrash . . . on the OT'（哈加達米大示＝哈加達式的解經〔參《聖神》362*b*〕）。Similarly, Mounce lxix-lxx: '"Myths and genealogies" (1 Tim 1:4; Titus 3:9) are probably haggadic midrash: allegorical interpretations of the OT, perhaps as fanciful interpretations of the OT genealogies . . . , especially of the patriarchs and their families'. Cf. Quinn 245: 'The authority of the Pauline hermeneutic of the OT and its application to Christian living is being prescribed by some Christians and proscribed by others'; 對教牧書信的作者而言，'speculations that ignore or attempt to discredit Paul are "foolish."' **（2）** 此字（**ζήτησις**）在希臘文聖經再出現四次，分別指有關潔淨的禮儀的辯論（約三 25），有關外邦基督徒是否必須受割禮才可以得救的辯論（徒十五 2、7），以及關於已死的耶穌是否仍然活著的究問／調查（徒二十五 20，思高、新和／新普）。See BDAG 428*b*-29*a* (s.v.);《新希》145*b*（s.v.）。

12 Marshall 334: 'they are pointless precisely because they are inane. They do not contribute to godliness'.

13 胡國楨認為，這裏的祖譜是假教師所關心的「眾先祖」的族譜（Keegan II 103 註 1「審訂者註」）。

14 See also KJV, NKJV, RSV, NRSV, NAU, NIV, TNIV, NIV2011, NJB: 'genealogies'; C. Brown, *DNTT* 36: '[γενεαλογία] alludes specifically to the practice of searching back through one's family tree in order to establish ancestry.'

15 NLT: 'spiritual pedigrees'. 新普頁邊註／NLT margin 作宗教譜系／'spiritual genealogies'.

16 γενεαλογία, 'an account of ancestry' (BDAG 192*a* [s.v.]),「記載一家世系的記錄」(《新希》66*a* [s.v.])。這字是複合名詞（from γενεά + λόγος）。γενεά（新約共 43 次）在保羅書信出現四次，其意思都是世代（弗三 5、21；腓二 15；西一 26）；λόγος（新約共 330 次）在保羅書信出現 84 次，包括提多書的五次（一 3、9，二 5、8，三 8），此字的意思之一就是「帳（account）」(例如：羅十四 12〔現修〕; see Vine 1.25)。

譜／族譜（現修）。既然家譜與無稽的傳說關係密切（提前一 4），而本書一章 14 節明言那些無稽的傳說是猶太人的，因此可以推論，這些家譜的內容也是關於猶太人的。[17] 由於提摩太前書一章 4 節的無稽的傳說和……家譜可以理解為「那些無稽傳說的主題就是家譜」，班約翰將提多書本節的家譜理解為「關於家譜的無稽傳說」。[18] 本節的這兩項（辯論和家譜）亦以因果關係的形式——不要聽從無稽的傳說和冗長的家譜；這樣的事只會引起爭論——在提摩太前書一章 4 節出現；[19] 這表示克里特和以弗所的處境有明顯相似之處。[20] 家譜很可能指在聖經、拉比文獻和死海古卷等處所見的猶太人家譜。[21]

（#3）紛爭／爭執（同呂譯、新和、新譯／思高、現修）[22] 原

---

17 F. Büchsel, *TDNT* 1.664. Blomberg（'Titus' 356）認為，'The use of "genealogies" could imply Gnostic-like speculation about the evolution of the Godhead or Jewish concerns over tracing one's ancestry to determine what privileges might come with it.'

18 Banker 110, 112*b*: '(myths about) genealogies'. See also Vine 2.143: 'Probably Jewish genealogical tales crept into Christian communities.' Cf. F. Büchsel, *TDNT* 1.664-65: 'it is probable that the expression [μῦθοι καὶ γενεαλογίαι, 1 Tim. 1:4] denotes the biblical history enriched by interpretations and additions. If so, the γενεαλογίαι of Tt. 3:9 are the same as the μῦθοι καὶ γενεαλογίαι of 1 Tm. 1:4.'

19 Cf. Pietersen 121: 'It would appear therefore that, whatever the preoccupation with genealogies precisely means, it gave rise to intense debate and speculation.' 多三 9 的辯論原文是簡單名詞 ζητήσεις（ζήτησις 之複數直接受格），提前一 4 的爭論則為同字根的複合名詞 ἐκζητήσεις（ἐκζήτησις 之複數直接受格）。

20 Guthrie I 208; Guthrie II 220（古特立 222）。Cf. Marshall, 'Timothy and Titus' 193*b*: 'There were speculations based on weird interpretations of passages from the Jewish Scriptures – the "myths and genealogies" (1 Tim. 1:3-4; Titus 1:14; 3:9).' Sumney（*Opponents* 295）則認為，提多書此處 'these rather general accusations, which include stock polemical charges, are too vague and too common to make a connection with 1 Timothy.'

21 Collins 368. See also V. Hasler, *EDNT* 1.242*a-b* (s.v.): 'OT and Essene or rabbinic lists'; Murphy-O'Connor, '2 Timothy' 416: 'allegorical speculations on the pedigrees of the patriarchs'; Towner III 795: 'a Jewish type of interpretation based on OT and extra-canonical stories of the biblical heroes and speculation based on family trees'（唐 1159-60：「猶太人根據舊約聖經、正典外聖經英雄人物的故事建立的解經方式，以及根據家譜所作的揣測」）。

22 參以下英譯：（**i**）'dissensions' (RSV, NRSV, ESV), 'quarrels' (REB, NLT), 'strife' (NAU);（**ii**）'contentions' (KJV, NKJV), 'disputes' (*Paraphrase* 295), 'arguments' (NIV, TNIV, NIV2011), 'quibbles' (NJB), 'controversies' (Quinn 29), 'rivalries' (Witherington 153, 162). See also BDAG 392*b* (s.v. ἔρις): 'Engagement in rivalry, esp. w. ref. to positions taken in a matter, *strife*, *discord*, *contention*'; 亦參《輔讀》530：「爭鬥，(自

文在新約另外出現八次，都是在保羅書信中。[23]

(#4) **爭辯／爭論**（呂譯、思高、當代）或**爭吵／爭執**（新普／現修、新譯）原文原指「戰爭」（每邊一人即可構成），在新約僅再出現三次，都是（如在本節）複數並指不涉及真正武器的[24] **爭戰／爭鬥／鬥爭**（林後七 5，新和、新譯／思高／新普）、**爭辯／爭論／爭吵／爭執**（提後二 23，和修／新譯／呂譯、思高、現修／新普），和**打鬥／鬥毆／鬬毆／爭鬥**（雅四 1，新譯／呂譯、新和／當代／新普）或**爭吵／爭執**（現修／和修）。但保羅要提多提醒眾人，叫他們**不要爭吵**（三 2）。[25] 這裏的爭論跟猶太人的律法有關，[26] 可能是「與食物條例、禮儀等律法細節有關的爭論」。[27]

私的）競爭」。有古卷作單數的 ἔριν, 但外證及文理皆支持複數的 ἔρεις 才是原來的讀文（*TextC* 586; see also Quinn 236-37; MHT 2.131）。

23 一次為複數（林前一 11：ἔριδες），如在本節（ἔρεις），其餘七次為單數（羅一 29，十三 13；林前三 3；林後十二 20；加五 20；腓一 15；提前六 4），和修皆譯作**紛爭**。參《加》1253-54；《新希》133*a*（s.v.）。**(1)** 此字（ἔρις）在 LXX 出現三次，分別指「輕率／突然的口角」（次經《便西拉智訓》28.11〔RSV, NRSV / NJB: 'hasty/sudden quarrel'〕）；人生的痛苦包括「爭論的事」（40.4〔思高《德訓篇》〕）和「鬥爭」（40.9〔思高〕）。**(2)** H. Giesen（*EDNT* 2.52*b* [s.v.]）聲稱：''Ερις is always used of *disputes* that endanger the Church'. 但至少在羅一 29，**紛爭**是異教社會的一個特徵。

24 BDAG 622*a* (s.v. μάχη): 'in our lit. only in pl. and only of battles fought without actual weapons *fighting*, *quarrels*, *strife*, *disputes*'; C. Brown, *DNTT* 3.963: 'strife and quarreling'. MHT 3.27-28 認為，複數的 μάχαι 是新約有時使用 'the Pluralis Poeticus for abstract subjects in a class. way' 的例子。這些複數的例子 'may imply *cases of* . . .'. 複數的 ζητήσεις（#1）和 ἔρεις（#3）大抵可以同樣理解。

25 三 2 的 ἄμαχος（**不要爭吵**）和三 9 的 μάχη（**爭辯**）是同字根的形容詞和名詞。

26 See DC 151*b*, 151*a* (order correct) / Quinn 29, 233, 237: 'disputes/wranglings about the Law'; Donelson I 121 / REB; H. Hübner, *EDNT* 2.471*a* (s.v. νομικός, 1) / Fiore II 217, 222: 'battles/controversies/disputes over the law'; Witherington 153: 'legal wrangles'; H. Balz, *EDNT* 2.398*b* (s.v. μάχη): '*disputes* over questions of the law'; Aageson 66: 'on the literary level of the text, it is clear that the core of the opposition revolves around Jewish issues and disputes about the Jewish law.'

27 彭編 107*b*。**(1)** DC 151*a* 則認為，這裏的爭論可能是關於禁慾的誡命（而非明確的猶太人誡命）。**(2)** Quinn 247 認為，形容詞**律法的**提示，這些爭論是關乎 'the interpretation of the Law par excellence, the five books of Moses', 但亦可理解為指舊約聖經整體。Witherington 163 也認為，'Here the false teaching seems to have focused on the Pentateuch, since we hear about genealogies and laws [*sic*].' Guthrie（*NTI* 628）認為，這些有關律法的爭論以猶太人對五經中的家譜之臆測的形式出現：'The

以上的四個項目由三個「和」字連起來。(一)《新耶路撒冷聖經》將最後兩項連起來成為一個意思，即是四個項目構成三個意思。[28](二)另一些譯本將第二、三兩項連起來成為一個意思，第四項為另一意思（一共也是三個意思）：例如，《呂振中譯本》作**愚拙的辯論**（#1）**和族譜之空談跟紛爭**(合併了 #2 和 #3)、**以及律法上的爭論**(#4)。《現代中文譯本修訂版》的翻譯(**有關族譜名錄以及法律上的爭執**)，其實包含了**有關族譜名錄……的爭執**（合併了 # 2 和 #3）和**法律上的爭執**（#4）這兩個意思。[29]（三)《新普及譯本》將首兩項連起來，又把末後兩項連起來，[30] 從而得出兩個意思：[31] **不要捲入那些關於宗教家**

absorbing interest in genealogies gives some indication in view of contemporary Jewish speculations centred mainly around the Pentateuchal genealogies.'（**3**）Keener 630*b* 認為，**因律法而起的爭辯**包括 'arguments of Jewish legal scholars over spellings or vocalizations of Hebrew words' 這些瑣碎的事。(**4**) Neyrey 1217*b* 認為，這些爭論是關乎 'the issue of law vs. grace'，即是克里特的假教師延續了保羅當年所遇到的問題（1215*b*），'whereby new converts were required to be circumcised and otherwise made to live like Jews'(加五 1～2，二 14)。Dunn 878*a* 同樣認為：'One of the issues, if not the issue, presumably was the continuation of the earlier question: To what extent do Gentile converts have to observe all of the law's injunctions? . . . the implication of v. 9 is of tensions between Jewish and Gentile members of the same congregations.' Wild 895*b* 解釋為，保守的猶太基督徒繼續迫切要求將律法全面地應用到基督徒身上（'[they] continued to press for the full applicability of the law'）。

28 NJB: 'But avoid [*a*] foolish speculations, and [*b*] those genealogies, and [*c* + *d*] the quibbles and disputes about the Law'. See also Mounce, 'Titus' 107: 'Avoid [*a*] foolish speculations, [*b*] disputes about ancestry, [*c* + *d*] arguments and quarrels about Jewish law.' 亦參註 1 之（1）= 上面 433。留意 NJB（和 Mounce）將 ζητήσεις 翻譯為 'speculations'; 但見註 9 之（2）= 上面 434。

29 νομικός = 'about the law, about laws' (LN §33.337), 可理解為特指 'the Jewish Law' (ibid.). Cf. BDAG 676*a* (s.v. 1): '*about the law* (i.e. the validity of the [Mosaic?] law'（方括號是原來的）。(**1**) 此字（**νομικός**）在下文再出現一次（三 13：**律師**），新約另外七次，全部都是指精通摩西律法的**律法師**(太二十二 35；路十 25，十一 45、46、52)，其中兩次和**法利賽人**一起提及(路七 30，十四 3)。See BDAG 675*b*-76*a* (s.v.);《新希》227*a*（s.v.）。(**2**) **律法師**更準確的描寫是**律法教師**（νομοδιδάσκαλος: 提前一 7；徒五 34；路五 17〔新約僅此三次〕)。

30 *Paraphrase* 295 只將首兩項連起來，因而得出三個意思：'avoid [*a* + *b*] foolish debates and genealogies, [*c*] disputes and [*d*] quarrels about the law.'

31 Cf., already, Banker 110, 112*a*: 'but (when people) foolishly [*a* + *b*] dispute about senseless (myths about) genealogies and foolishly [*c* + *d*] argue and quarrel about the (Jewish) law, have nothing to do with that'. 留意 'foolishly' 出現兩次；見下面註 35 之（1）(2)。

譜的愚蠢討論，也不要為遵守猶太律法的事與人辯論、爭吵。[32] 如此，這裏所指的辯論和爭辯是環繞著兩個問題的：（猶太人的）家譜[33] 和（猶太人的）律法。有兩點特別支持這種理解：第一，保羅在提摩太前書一章 4 節說，無稽的傳說和……家譜（#2）……引起爭論（#1），[34] 這使合併第一、二兩項而得「關於家譜的辯論」之意顯得合理；第二，「關於家譜（或由家譜引起）的辯論」和「關於律法（或因律法而起）的爭辯」彼此平行。[35] 幾乎可以肯定，形容詞「律法的」所隱含的名詞律法指猶太〔人的〕律法（新普），[36] 即是摩西的律法，[37] 因為克里特的假教師是奉割禮的人

---

32 NLT: 'Do not get involved in [*a* + *b*] foolish discussions about spiritual pedigrees or in [*c* + *d*] quarrels and fights about obedience to Jewish laws.' NAU / NIV, TNIV, NIV2011 的翻譯有點模稜兩可；或是理解為四個項目：'But avoid [*a*] foolish controversies and [*b*] genealogies and [*c*] strife/arguments and [*d*] disputes/quarrels about the Law/law', 或是理解為兩個單元：'But avoid [*a* + *b*] foolish controversies and genealogies and [*c* + *d*] strife and disputes about the Law / arguments and quarrels about the law'. 後者似較自然。

33 見註 21 及所屬正文（上面 436）。

34 爭論原文（ἐκ-ζητήσεις）是與多三 9 的 ζητήσεις（辯論）同字根的複合名詞。

35 以上兩點見 Banker 113*b*.(**1**)班約翰（同上）又認為，位於本節開首的形容詞 μωράς（愚拙的）同時形容隨後（由三個 καί 字連起來）的全部四個名詞。Spencer 66 同樣認為，'the adjective **foolish** precedes and modifies the four nouns that follow (**arguments, genealogies, contentions, battles**).' 這見解不可取，因(**i**)在提後二 23，愚拙只形容辯論（見註 1 之〔4〕= 上面 433），在本節很可能也是一樣。(**ii**)'battles' 本身已有形容詞 '**pertaining to the law**'（νομικάς）。(**2**)筆者認為，將開首的 μωράς 視為只形容第一、二兩項，將末尾的 νομικάς（律法的）視為形容三、四兩項，會得出更工整的平行及交叉配置模式，如下：

[A] μωρὰς δὲ　[B] ζητήσεις καὶ γενεαλογίας καὶ [B'] ἔρεις καὶ μάχας [A'] νομικάς
（甲）愚蠢的（乙）辯論和家譜　　　　及（乙'）紛爭和爭辯（甲'）律法的

參註 1 之（2）= 上面 433。(**3**) 按這種理解，加上底線的三個名詞就不必視為 'seem[ing] to be in intensifying sequence . . . arguments necessitating resolution (*zētēsis*) become jealous contentions that incite people (*eris*) to full battles (*machē*)'（Spencer 67）。

36 留意 NLT: 'Do not get involved . . . in quarrels and fights about obedience to Jewish laws.' 複數的 'laws' 是否暗指猶太律法眾多的規條呢？

37 一些英譯本用大寫的 L 字表明此點：NAU, NJB: 'disputes about the Law'. Cf. Köstenberger 610*b*: 'it appears that the heretics focused on certain minutiae of the OT law.'

（一 10），[38] 他們推銷的是猶太人無稽的傳說（一 14）。[39]

下半節（9b 節）指出提多要遠避上述的辯論和爭辯的雙重原因：因為這都是虛妄無益的（同新和、新譯）。原文的次序與此相反。[40]（甲）無益與同字根的對人有益（三 8d）相對。[41]（乙）虛妄回望一章 10 節：那些假教師是說空話的人，他們從事於無用的、無益的閒談！[42] 虛妄原文較好的翻譯是徒勞（呂譯、新普），[43] 但它可能包括「無用、[44] 沒有結果、[45]（因而）沒有價值[46]」

---

38 參一 10 註釋末段（上面 160-64）。

39 Cf. Dunn 783 (= Dunn, 'Titus' 278*b*): 'the reference to "Jewish myths" (Titus 1:14) and the association of "genealogies" with "fights over the law" (Titus 3:9) . . . indicate an opposition more likely to be rooted in the local synagogues than anywhere else.'

40 參呂譯：因為那是無益而徒勞的；思高：因為這些都是無益的空談；BDAG 621*a* (s.v. μάταιος) / Fiore II 217: 'useless and fruitless/futile'; REB, H. Balz, *EDNT* 2.396*b* (s.v. μάταιος): 'unprofitable and futile/*futile*'. μάταιοι 是陽性形容詞，但它所形容的那四個名詞（9a 節：ζητήσεις, γενεαλογίας, ἔρεις, μάχας）皆為陰性；不過，這做法不算違規（so Quinn 248; see BDF §134(2)）。

41 ἀνωφελής vs. ὠφέλιμος. 前者的另一意思是 'harmful'（BDAG 93*a* [s.v. 2]; Marshall 337; Mounce cvi）。(**1**) 形容詞 **ἀνωφελής** 在新約僅再出現一次（來七 18），指律法的無能（同現修）、無益（呂譯、新和）或無用／沒有用處（思高、新普／新譯）；解釋見《來》449-50。這字在 LXX 出現五次，分別指「無益有害的」雨（箴二十八 3）；人所鑄造的「無益的東西」（賽四十四 10），先知所隨從無益的東西（耶二 8）；「無益的」怨言（次經《所羅門智訓》1.11〔思高智慧篇〕）；「無用的」罪惡（偽經《所羅門詩篇》16.8）。(**2**) 這字是複合形容詞（from ὠφελέω + α-privative; the ν is 'euphonic' [Vine 4.173], 即是 *an-ô* 比 *a-ô* 讀起來更悅耳）；動詞 ὠφελέω 在保羅書信出現四次（新約另外十一次），意思都是「對人有益」（羅二 25；林前十三 3，十四 6；加五 2）。

42 原文二字依次為 μάταιος 和同字根的 ματαιολόγος. 後者參一 10 註釋首段之（#2）= 上面 158-59。(**1**) 前一個字（**μάταιος**）在新約另外出現五次，分別指：偶像是無用的東西（徒十四 15，新普）；聰明人的心思毫無價值（林前三 20，新普）；基督若沒有復活，你們〔基督徒〕的信就是徒然（林前十五 17），即是沒有效用的（你們仍在你們的罪裡〔新譯〕）；某一種的虔誠是毫無價值的（雅一 26，現修、新普）；信徒已從他們祖傳徒勞無效的生活被贖出來（彼前一 18，呂譯）。See BDAG 621*a-b* (s.v.). (**2**) Quinn 248 則認為，就如這裏的無益與 8d 節的有益相對，虛妄與 8d 節的美好相對。若是這樣，這四個字便呈現交叉配置模式：[A] καλὰ καὶ [B] ὠφέλιμα τοῖς ἀνθρώποις . . . [B'] ἀνωφελεῖς [A'] καὶ μάταιοι.

43 See also KJV: 'vain'; RSV, NJB, *Paraphrase* 295: 'futile'. NLT 意譯為 'a waste of time'.

44 See NKJV, NIV, TNIV, NIV2011: 'useless'.

45 See Quinn 29: 'fruitless'.

46 See NRSV, NAU, ESV: 'worthless'; 現修：沒有價值。

之意。[47]

費歌頓認為，本節連同一章 10 節就是確實的證據，表示克里特眾教會內的謬誤，基本上來自希臘化時期的猶太教。當時的情況似乎是這樣：克里特島上一些「接受了基督」的說希臘語的猶太人，鼓吹繼續——尤其是以「基於臆測的教導及嚴守規條」的方式——與猶太教保持聯繫。如此，使保羅感到苦惱的，不僅是假教師的神學謬誤（一10～16），還有他們那些無益和沒有價值（現修）的行徑。[48]

47 BDAG 621*a* (s.v. μάταιος): 'pert. to being of no use, *idle*, *empty*, *fruitless*, *useless . . .*';《新希》211*a*（s.v.）：「因為無益和缺乏實質內容，所以是無價值的。」亦參上面註 42 之（1）。詳參《弗》2.626-27 連註 28-30 的討論。

48 Fee 211. 第二引句英文原作 'speculative teaching and rigorous devotion to rules and regulations'.

三 **10** 分門結黨的人，警戒過一兩次後就要拒絕跟他來往；[1]

分門結黨／拉幫結夥／好分宗派（同新和、新譯／馮譯／呂譯）[2] 原文（希臘文聖經僅此一次）的意思是引起分裂（新普）[3] 或「製造分裂」。[4] 這裏以單數的分門結黨的人代表了一章 9 節複數的反

---

1 （**1**）Clark（'Structure' 115）留意到，9a 節的命令動詞 περιΐστασο（遠避）和 10 節的命令式動詞 παραιτοῦ（拒絕跟〔他〕來往）居於所屬子句的較後位置，有別於一 13b 的 ἔλεγχε（責備）、二 1 的 λάλει（講），和三 1 的 ὑπομίμνησκε（提醒），後三者居於所屬子句或主句較前的位置。祈勒克問道：'is this perhaps a way of toning down the authoritarian aspect of a command?' 他認為也許 'Paul is addressing Titus less peremptorily than he expects Titus to address the Cretan congregation.' 筆者認為這提議不可取，因為上述後三個命令式語法動詞也都是保羅對提多發出（而不是提多對克里特人發出）的命令。（**2**）Genade 105 聲稱 'there is progression: from confrontation or ἐλεγχειν [*sic*] (1:9), to censuring, ἐπιστομίζειν (1:11), to avoidance of the doctrine (3:9), and, finally, shunning of the person, παραιτέομαι (3:10).' 可是，一 11 那個動詞的意思並不是「譴責」，而是禁止（這些人）說話（現修），使（他們）住口（新普）；參該節註釋首段開首（上面 165）。

2 參以下英譯：（**i**）'factious'（RSV, NAU, *Paraphrase* 295, Davies II 73; DC 151*b*, 151*a* (order correct); Fiore II 217, 222; Goodwin 1753*a*, 1758*b*; Hendriksen 394, 395, 400; Johnson II 249; Laansma 292; Maloney 375; Mounce cvi, 435, 454; Oden 86; Hagner, 'Titus' 548; Malherbe, 'Medical Imagery' 124; Sumney, *Opponents* 296）；（**ii**）'*capable of choosing* (Plato) and so *factious*'（MHT 2.379）。（**iii**）Houlden 155 則認為，這字 'is on the edge between "factious" and "heretical".'

3 NLT, Zehr 311: 'causing divisions'; NRSV: 'anyone who causes divisions'; LN §34.41 / §39.17: 'the man/person who causes divisions'. See also NKJV, NIV, NIV2011, Jeon II 46, Oden 86, Quinn 29, 233, 238, 248, Spencer 68, Wall 370, 372, Zehr 310, 311: 'divisive'.

4 《新希》10*a*（s.v. αἱρετικός）；參《輔讀》530：「製造分裂的」；利斐特 371：「分裂分子」（Liefeld 354: 'divisive person'）。See also BDAG 28*a* (s.v.): 'pert. to causing divisions, *factious*, *division-making*'; 現修：製造紛爭（現修）。Cf. G. Bertram, *TDNT* 7.719 n.6: 'a sectarian who will not be corrected'. Johnson I 114（誤？）作 'the "fractious* person"'; see also Jeon II 36: 'Paul . . . commands the community to break fellowship with such a fractious person' (also 42: 'a fractious person'); cf. Calvin 387: 'there is no lack of men who are . . . fractious'.（*易怒的、暴躁的。）（**1**）思高則譯作異端人；see also KJV: 'an heretick'; H. Schlier, *TDNT* 1.184: 'the "adherent of a heresy"'; G. Baumback, *EDNT* 1.40*b* (s.v. αἵρεσις, 2): 'the *heretic* who has turned aside from "true doctrine"'; Fairnbairn 57, 301 / Jeon I 2 / Jeon I 114, 121: 'A heretical man / a heretical person / a "heretical human being"'（但第一位作者隨即正確地補充說：'perhaps *schismatical* or *factious* would more nearly approach to [the word αἱρετικός]' [301]; cf. Witherington 153-54: 'schismatic persons'; 163: 'we should probably translate it "schismatic" or "factious"'）。Saarinen 194 聲稱，'here it clearly means "heretic."' Lock 157 認為，'heretical' 這個意思更符合文理（9、10 節）。NJB 理解為 'disput[ing]

對的人（現修、新譯、新普）。[5] 由於分門結黨的人若堅持自己的道路就是已經背道的（三 11），他們被稱為引起分裂或「製造分裂」，大抵是由於他們拒絕真正的救恩信息以及獲授權之教會領袖（如提多）的權柄，[6] 欲在純正信仰的羣體之外另起爐灶，[7] 而他們所教導的是假的教義！[8]

警戒（同呂譯、新和、新譯）原文是個名詞，[9] 在這裏的意思可能不是譴責（思高），而是警告（現修、新普），[10] 包括教導。[11] 警告的目的是要他們停止「製造分裂」的行為。[12] 一兩次原文直譯是「一

---

what you teach'（因而有異端的含意）。(**2**) 當代合併兩個意思：傳講異端，製造紛爭。See Banker 110*a*: '*hairetikon* . . . in New Testament times still had the primary meaning of "factious," but had a component or connotation of "heretical," as shown by the fact that not too much later its primary meaning became "heretical."' (**3**) Richards 91 作 'the "mavericks"'（特立獨行者），大抵是由於那些假教師被形容為不受約束（一 10）。

5 Genade 105 (see also 128).

6 Van Neste 273.

7 Fairnbairn 301: 'The word αἱρετικὸς [*sic*] . . . denoted one who set himself to make a αἵρεσις or party, separate from the community of the faithful.' (**1**) Kelly 248, 255 就翻譯為「分離主義者（a separatist）」。(**2**) 名詞 αἵρεσις 在新約一共出現九次，包括保羅書信的兩次（林前十一 19：分黨結派／結黨分派〔新譯／新普〕；加五 20：結黨）；詳見《加》1257；BDAG 27*b*-28*a* (s.v.);《新希》10*a*（s.v.）。

8 See Banker 114*b*: 'teaching false doctrine is the main reason behind the divisions being caused.'

9 **νουθεσία**, (**i**) 在新約僅再出現兩次，分別指發生在曠野漂流的以色列人身上的事被記錄下來，是為了警告我們這些活在末世的人（林前十 11，新普），和父親對兒女所施口頭的訓誡／警戒／儆戒（弗六 4，思高／呂譯、新和／馮譯）或「糾正」（參《弗》910-12）；(**ii**) 在 LXX 只出現一次（次經《所羅門智訓》16.6），指以色列人「受到了猛獸的殘害，和毒蛇的咬傷」（16.5）只是上帝「警戒他們，使他們暫時驚惶，獲得救援的標記」（思高智慧篇）。See BDAG 679*b* (s.v.);《新希》227*b*（s.v.）。

10 See also NAU, NJB, NLT, *Paraphrase* 295 / ESV / NIV, TNIV, NIV2011: 'warning [noun] / warning [verb] / warn'. Cf. KJV, NKJV, NRSV / RSV: 'admonition / admonishing'; G. Schneider, *EDNT* 2.478*a* (s.v.): 'of the admonition of heretics'（但見上面註 4）。

11 Knight II 354: 'νουθεσία . . . includes both "instruction" and "warning" but with emphasis on the latter'; Towner III 797（唐 1162）: 'This includes instruction, correction, and warning with a view to regaining the offender (as in 2 Tim 2:25-26).' See also J. Behm, *TDNT* 4.1022: 'νουθεσία is the attempt to make the heretic aware of the falsity of his position'.

12 Banker 115*a*.

次和第二次」，[13] 即是混合了表示數目的「一」[14] 和表示次序的「第二」；不過，這種做法不算反常。[15] 兩次的警告表示，保羅對於這些人的回轉仍然抱持盼望（參：提後二 25～26）。[16]

但若警告無效，就要**拒絕跟他來往**[17] 或**拒絕交往**（呂譯），意即**和他絕交／斷絕來往**（新譯／當代），**不再跟他／與他們來往**（現修／新普），[18] 等於**遠離他**（思高）。[19] 有認為原文動詞的意思只是「不要再見他」[20] 或**不必理睬**（馮譯）、「不予理會，避免與他們接觸」，[21] 或是「讓他感到雖然名義上仍是教會成員，但其實並非這個基督徒團契

---

13 μίαν καὶ δευτέραν literally = not 'the first and second' (KJV, NKJV), 'a first and second' (NRSV, NAU, NJB), 'a first and a second' (NJB), but 'one and a second' (Quinn 239). G. Stählin（*TDNT* 1.381）翻譯為 'after more than one admonition'.（**1**）前一個字（**εἷς**）在新約一共出現 344 次，這數字並不包括路十七 36，二十三 17（see *Concordance* 555*a-b*; *TextC* 142-43, 153）。See BDAG 291*b*-93*b* (s.v.);《新希》99*b*-100*b*（s.v.)(345 次)。(**2**)後一個字(**δεύτερος**)在新約一共出現 43 次。See BDAG (s.v.) 220*b*-21*a*;《新希》75*b*（s.v.）。

14 用表示數目的「一」字來表達次序「第一」的例子在新約還有八次（全部為陰性的 μία）：太二十八 1 ‖ 可十六 2 ‖ 路二十四 1 ‖ 約二十 1；約二十 19；徒二十 7；林前十六 2；啟九 12。See BDAG 293*a* (s.v. εἷς, 4);《新希》100*a*（s.v. I.4, 5d）。

15 Quinn 239: 'the shift from the cardinal *mia* to the ordinal *deutera* . . . is not anomalous'.

16 Fee 211. 對比特土良的做法：'Tertullian allows for a single admonition, based solely on Titus 3:11 [*sic*], before a Christian is prohibited from engaging with a heretic'（Frisius, *Tertullian's Use* 88）。參三 11 註釋註 11（下面 448）。亦參安波羅修的評語：'he [Paul] . . . rejects immediately after a single admonition a heretic from the fold entrusted to him'（Gorday 306*a*）；安波羅修這樣引述保羅的話：'One who is a heretic, avoid after the first reproof'（Gorday, 306*b*）。

17 Cf. NKJV, NAU / KJV; Mounce cvi; *EDNT* 3.23*a* (s.v. παραιτέομαι): 'Reject/reject'. 第 9a 節的**遠避**（περιΐστασο）和 10 節的**拒絕……來往**（παραιτοῦ）是信上最後兩個命令式語法的動詞（參二 15 註釋註 2 之〔2〕末〔上面 341〕）。這些分佈於全書的命令式語法動詞表明，提多書是 'a letter with instructions, mandates, injunctions, admonitions and warnings'（Classen, 'Epistle to Titus' 65 [see also Genade 7]）。

18 See also NJB / RSV, ESV / NIV: 'have no more / have nothing more / have nothing to do with him'（TNIV, NIV2011: 'with them'）。

19 See also Bassler 211: 'Avoid them'; Mounce lxxxi: 'stay away from them'; Oden 86: 'Hold yourself aloof'.

20 Quinn 29, 233, 238, 248: 'Don't see him again'.

21 周 443。Cf. Murphy-O'Connor, '2 Timothy' 411: 'Offenders are to be given two chances and then ignored'. 班約翰認為，動詞的意思是 'no (longer) allow (him to influence the believers)'（Banker 110, 114*b*, 115*a*）。

真正的一分子」。[22] 亦有認為可能涉及「執行教會紀律」，[23] 將他革除會籍。[24] 原文動詞在本節的意思很可能就是「趕出去」。[25] 保羅的關

22 Scott 179: 'He must be made to feel [that] while he was still nominally a member he had no real part in the Christian fellowship.' Cf. Arichea – Hatton 309: 'The expression may simply mean not to have any more dealing with the person so as to make them feel that they are no longer part of the Christian community'. Cf. Malherbe, 'Paraenesis' 299: '[Titus] should ostracize refractory members'.

23 張 382（參 46：「執行紀律，驅逐他們」）。See also G. Nordholt, *DNTT* 1.535: 'In Tit. 3:10 we see the church's procedure for disciplining heretics, following Matt. 18:15 ff. and 2 Jn. 10.' 不過，αἱρετικός 在這裏的意思並非 'heretic'（參註 4〔上面 442-43〕）。Mounce 454 則認為，'Paul is not spelling out in detail how to deal with the issue of church discipline'.

24 Van Neste 277 n.126. See also Collins 369: 'Repudiation may entail the excommunication of the recalcitrant person'; Fiore II 222: 'The result of the process of proven and persistent misconduct is expulsion'; Hagner, 'Titus' 555: 'they are to reject . . . this person from the community'; Hendriksen 395: 'Official exclusion from church-membership is probably indicated'; Richards 94: 'excommunicating'; Wall 372: 'two warnings . . . prior to . . . excommunication'; F. Selter, *DNTT* 1.569: 'total rejection'; J. Jeremias, *TDNT* 3.752: 'it is the authorized apostle rather than the congregation who excommunicates'; 752-53: 'Excommunication . . . took place . . . when the Gospel was falsified (Gl. 1:8-9; Tt. 3:9f.).'（**1**）參提前一 20：保羅把許米乃和亞歷山大**交給撒但**（οὓς παρέδωκα τῷ σατανᾷ）；林前五 5：保羅要哥林多教會把上文提及的那人**交給撒但**（παραδοῦναι τὸν τοιοῦτον τῷ σατανᾷ）。（**2**）White 201*a* 則反對「革除會籍」之說。他認為這舉措既非必須，亦無效用；'Excommunication has no terrors for those who deliberately separate themselves.' Bouwman 148-49 的反對理由是，「革除會籍」必須由教會執行（參：太十八 17；林前五 5），但保羅這句話是對提多個人說，而不是對長老們說的。可是，保羅對提多的這項指示，大可以由提多聯同長老們執行。褒文自己說，'these elders have the task to address the divisive brother'（151）。（**3**）本節可能暗指耶穌在太十八 15～17 的指示（so, e.g., Robertson, *Pictures* 4.608; Ridderbos, *Paul* 472）。後一位作者認為，'A further background is very likely to be sought in the synagogical disciplinary practice, where likewise the practice was not to proceed to excommunication before repeated warnings had been given.'

25 BDAG 764*b* (s.v. παραιτέομαι, 2 b α): 'here the word prob. has the sense *discharge, dismiss, drive out*'; Knight II 355: '"reject" or "dismiss," i.e., remove from the fellowship of the Christian community'; Goodwin 1758*b*: 'if there is no repentance the agitators should be removed from the community'; Marshall 338: 'to dismiss, drive out' (cf. idem, 'Congregation' 111: 'to exclude them from fellowship'); Perkins 1445*b*: 'Individuals who resist correction are to be excommunicated'; Towner II 262: '*have nothing to do with him* must mean the same thing [as excommunication]'; Towner III 797-98（唐 1163）：'Probably the severest sense of "drive out, dismiss, discharge" is meant, with excommunication from the church in view'; G. Stählin, *TDNT* 1.195: 'expulsion in the sense of putting out disruptive elements and possibly of excommunication'. 參《輔讀》530（第一解釋）：「棄絕」。Banker 115*a* 則認為，若保羅的意思是「把他趕出去」，他大抵會用較強的字（例如 ἐκβάλλω〔加四 30〕）。（**1**）παραιτέομαι + accusative of person 這結構在新約亦見於提前五 11（**拒絕**登記年輕的寡婦）和來十二 25a/b（**拒絕**那向你們說話的／**拒絕了**在地上

注似乎是，不要提多或任何其他的教會成員牽涉於這樣堅持犯罪的人的罪行之中[26]（參較提前五 22：不可在別人的罪上有分）。

警戒他們的）；παραιτέομαι + accusative of thing 這結構則見於徒二十五 11（逃避〔現修〕死刑），提前四 7（要棄絕／應該避免〔現修〕世俗的無稽傳說）和提後二 23（要棄絕／務要躲避〔思高〕愚拙無知的辯論）。**(2)**這動詞（**παραιτέομαι**）在新約另外出現五次（全部合共十二次），分別指民眾所請求的一個囚犯（可十五 6，呂譯）；獲邀宴的客人推辭（路十四 18a）並請〔主人〕原諒（18b、19a 節〔思高、現修、新譯、新普〕）；以及以色列人求〔上帝〕不要再向他們說話（來十二 19）。See BDAG 764*a-b* (s.v.);《新希》250*b*（s.v.）。

26 Fiore II 225. Quinn 251 則認為，雖然教會的領袖要和「製造分裂」的人斷絕關係，教會的會友卻沒有被指示要這樣做。

三 **11a** 因為你知道這樣的人已經背道，

11b 常常犯罪，自己定自己的罪了。

本節提出要拒絕跟他來往（10 節）的理由：因為你知道……。[1] 這樣的人指他引起分裂，並且經兩次警告仍然堅持自己的道路（10 節）。這人由三個修飾語形容：

（#1）已經背道／已經乖離正道／已背棄正道（同新和、新譯／呂譯／思高〔當代缺「已」字〕）[2] 原文動詞主動語態的意思是「使人偏離正路、使人墮落」，因而這裏的完成時態被動語態動詞[3] 意即「已經墮落＝走入了歧途」。[4] 在一章 14 節，假教師被形容為背棄真理之人，本節這樣的人是已經背道的，二者前後呼應。

（#2）常常犯罪（同新譯）這翻譯修正了先前的犯了罪（新和），因原文動詞是現在時態的。[5] 所指的大抵是這人堅持己見，不斷地拒

---

1 εἰδώς = causal participle (Wallace 631-32).

2 See also NLT: 'have turned away from the truth'. 參《輔讀》530（第一解釋）：「叛教」。

3 ἐξέστραπται.

4 BDAG 309*b* (s.v. ἐκστρέφω): 'such a man is perverted = he has gone the wrong way'; 「離開了正確的行為模式而變得墮落」(《新希》106*b* [s.v.])。See also RSV, NRSV, NAU, *Paraphrase* 295, Fiore II 217: 'perverted'. 周 444 則認為，「原文的意思〔只〕是『歪曲』或『偏離』，沒有向正確的目標瞄準。」**(1)** 另二種翻譯是「扭曲的（distorted/warped）」(BV / NKJV, NIV, TNIV, NIV2011, NJB, ESV; Jeon II 36; Mounce, 'Titus' 107）和是腐化的（現修）= 'has become corrupt'（LN §88.265; cf. Quinn 29, 233, 239, 248: 'has turned sour'）。Hiebert 448 認為，動詞的被動語態指向這狀況背後的 'satanic agency'. 筆者認為這是不確定的；原文只表達一種狀況，如在上述的「另二種翻譯」。**(2)** 背離真理去犯罪（新普）這翻譯將犯罪視為背離真理的目的，但這邏輯關係在原文並不明顯。**(3)** 這動詞（**ἐκστρέφω**）在新約不再出現；它在 LXX 出現五次，分別指乖謬／敗壞的（ἐξεστραμμένη, 也是完成時態被動語態）一代（申三十二 20〔和修／思高〕，偽經《所羅門頌歌》2.20 同），將公道／公平變為毒藥（摩六 12，思高／現修），使頸的關節脫臼（亞十一 16〔LXE: 'dislocate the joints *of their necks*'〕），使人的靈魂墮落（結十三 20〔LXE: 'their souls which ye pervert'〕）。

5 **(1)** 明知故犯，被罪奴役（當代）是 ἁμαρτάνει 一字的意譯：它在常常犯罪這簡單意思之外加入了另二個意思。不過，Fairnbairn 303 也認為 ἁμαρτάνει 的意思是 '[he] lives in sin, or errs knowingly and deliberately' =「明知故犯」；而「被罪奴役」

絕接受改正，[6] 繼續不受約束（一 10），並且將不該教導的事教導人，敗壞人的全家（一 11）。[7]

（#3）自己定自己的罪或自己給自己定了罪案（思高）原文[8] 在希臘文聖經出現僅此一次；[9]「被自己定罪」可能意即「被自己的行為定罪」，[10] 即是由於堅持著引起分裂的行為而被自己這種罪行定罪，將自己排拒於外，因而應被提多和教會和他絕交（10 節，新譯）。[11] 一些譯本將（#3）緊連於（#2）而得出這種意思：這種人……犯罪，就

可視為常常犯罪 =「生活在罪中」的含意。Cf. Marshall 339: 'the force is "and is [deliberately] sinning".'（方括號是原來的。）Mounce 455 則質疑「明知」之意。**（2）** **ἁμαρτάνω** 在保羅書信出現 17 次（在本書僅此一次），新約一共 43 次；其中八或九次是在「得罪（ἁμαρτάνειν εἰς）」這結構中（太十八 21；路十五 18、21，十七 4；徒二十五 8；林前六 18，八 12a、12b。太十八 15 的 εἰς σέ 不肯定是否原來讀文〔see *TextC* 36〕）。See BDAG 49*b*-50*a* (s.v.);《新希》18*a*（s.v.）。

6 Hiebert 448: '[he sins] by his persistent refusal to receive correction.'

7 Cf. Towner III 798（唐 1164）。

8 **αὐτοκατάκριτος** = 'self-condemned' (NKJV, RSV, NRSV, NAU, NIV, TNIV, NIV2011, NJB, ESV; BDAG 152*a* [s.v.]; Quinn 240). Jeon I 99, 115, 116 則翻譯為 'self-decided'; 意即 'the heretic's decision to remain sin [*sic*] is intentional and exhibits a sense of determination'（cf. Jeon II 36: 'willful'）。**（1）**這字是複合形容詞（'*auto*, self, *katakrinō*, to condemn' [Vine 1.223]）。**（2）**沒有 αὐτο- 作為前綴的形容詞 κατάκριτος（BDAG 519*a* [s.v.]: 'condemned'）沒有在希臘文聖經出現。

9 Collins 369 認為，這可能是此字首次在希臘文獻中出現，因此可能是作者（不是保羅）自鑄的。

10《新希》50*b*（s.v. αὐτοκατάκριτος）; LN §30.119: 'condemned by one's own actions'; H. Balz, *EDNT* 1.179*a-b* (s.v.): '[he] has brought about his own judgment through his behavior.' 咎由自取（當代）是不正確的意譯。**（1）** Vine 1.223 的解釋（'self-condemned . . . on account of doing himself what he condemns in others'）並不符合文理。**（2）** Blaiklock 91 理解為 '[s]elf-condemned . . . presumably by his own separation', 像約翰所嚴厲指責、從我們中間出去的那些人一樣（約壹二 19）。See also White 201*a*-1*b*: 'He is self-condemned because his separation from the Church is due to his own acknowledged act. He cannot deny that his views are antagonistic to those which he once accepted as true; he is condemned by his former, and, as St. Paul would say, his more enlightened self.'**（3）** Hanson III 195 認為，'he is self-condemned simply because his teaching when examined proves to be inconsistent with the official teaching of the church.'**（4）** Quinn 253 的解釋是，拒絕接受提多的 'apostolic admonition' 就是自己宣判自己有罪。

11 Fee 212. 特土良認為，異端者這樣定自己的罪 'takes place after the first admonition which was advocated in Titus 3:10'（Frisius, *Tertullian's Use* 54）。參三 10 註釋註 16（上面 444）。

給自己定了罪（新普），[12]「他被自己定罪為罪人」，[13]「他們自己的罪行把他們定罪」。[14]

12 See C&D 151*b*: 'such a person . . . has condemned himself through his sin.' 作者們認為 11b 節這句話的意思很清楚：'If the person being exhorted still does not listen, error becomes sin . . . Such a person has spoken his own judgment by his refusal to listen.' See also F. Büchsel, *TDNT* 3.952: '[he] has been admonished twice and . . . can have no doubts as to the wrongness of what he does'; Kelly 256: 'he . . . **stands condemned in his sin**'; 他既受到嚴重警告，一定知道自己不對，'and his own better judgment must therefore condemn him'; Hiebert 448: 'He knows that in his deliberate refusal to abandon his self-chosen views he is wrong and stands condemned by his own better judgement.'

13 NJB: 'is self-condemned as a sinner'. 參現修：他的罪行證明自己是錯誤的。

14 NLT: 'their own sins condemn them'. 參新譯：常常犯罪，定了自己的罪。（1）另一種翻譯將 ὢν 理解為「讓步（concessive）」分詞——自定己罪，還在犯罪（呂譯），自己明知不是，還是去做（新和）——彷彿 καὶ ἁμαρτάνει ὢν αὐτοκατάκριτος = 'and he sins though (or: in spite of) being self-condemned'. 照筆者所知，沒有其他中英譯本這樣理解原文子句。（2）Banker 116*a-b* 引用太二十七 4 來支持他的理解：

太二十七 4	ἥμαρτον	παραδοὺς αἷμα ἀθῷον
	'I have sinned	(by) betraying innocent blood'
多三 11b	ἁμαρτάνει	ὢν αὐτοκατάκριτος

班約翰指出，太二十七 4 的 παραδούς 是 'a supplementary participle indicating that in which the sin consists'. 多三 11 的 ὢν 可同樣理解為 'indicating that in which the divisive man's sin consists'. 可是，'I have sinned (by) betraying innocent blood'（即猶大的罪在於出賣了無辜人的血）這話的意思十分清晰，但是 'he sins by being self-condemned'（筆者語）這話卻很難明白，難怪班約翰沒有這樣說，而只能說 'indicating that in which the divisive man's sin consists, [namely] deliberately disobeying a command of a servant of God.' 他把原文分詞片語本身（ὢν αὐτοκατάκριτος）意譯為 '(since) he knows that he is doing what is wrong (yet he deliberately keeps on doing it)'（Banker 110, 115*b*）。筆者不認為班約翰的解釋具說服力。

丙部

結束的話

（三12～15）

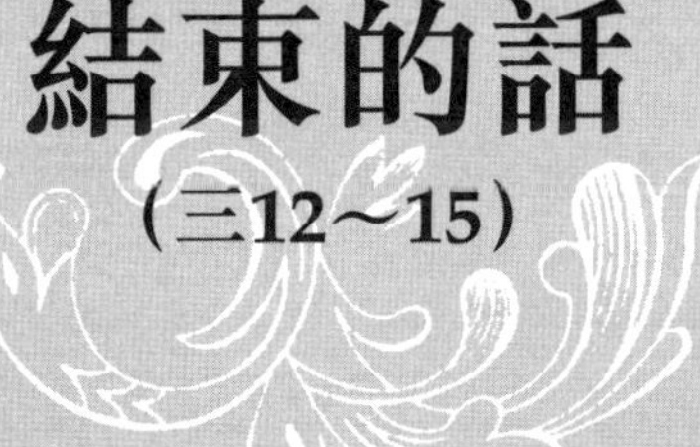

12a 我打發亞提馬或推基古到你那裏去的時候，

12b 你要趕緊往尼哥坡里來見我，

12c 因為我已經決定在那裏過冬。

13a 你要趕緊給西納律師和亞波羅送行，

13b 讓他們沒有缺乏。

14a 我們的人也該學習行善，幫助有迫切需要的人，

14b 這樣才不會不結果子。

15a 跟我同在一起的人都向你問安。

15b 請代向在信仰上愛我們的人問安。

15c 願恩惠與你們眾人同在！

（一）雖然並無連詞將頭兩節連起來，但第 12 節的動詞趕緊和第 13 節的副詞趕緊是同字根的，[1] 打發和下一節的給……送行也是同字根的，[2] 這種字詞上的重複將第 12 節和 13 節緊密地連在一起；儘管兩節談及的事並非彼此相關，但二者都涉及人員的移動。（二）第 14 節的形容詞我們的和第 15 節的代名詞我們[3] 則把這兩節緊密地連在一起。如此，這一連串重複的字詞將這四節劃為一個單元。[4] 另外，（三）第 14 節開首的也字將該節連於上一節：第 13 節要求提多給西納和亞波羅二人送行，讓他們沒有缺乏（這事需要信徒的參與），[5] 第 14 節隨即提出信徒也該學行善，幫助有迫切需要的人，[6] 這一點也加強了本段的合一性。

1 原文依次為 σπούδασον（12b 節），σπουδαίως（13a 節）。
2 原文依次為 πέμψω（12a 節），πρόπεμψον（13a 節）。
3 原文依次為 ἡμέτεροι（14a 節），ἡμᾶς（15b 節）。
4 See Quinn 260; Genade 108.
5 見三 13 註釋末段（下面 461-62）。
6 Cf. Banker 116*b*. 參三 14 註釋註 6、7 及所屬正文（下面 463-64）。

柒 個人的指示（三 12～14）

三 **12a** 我打發亞提馬或推基古到你那裏去的時候，

12b 你要趕緊往尼哥坡里來見我，

12c 因為我已經決定在那裏過冬。

打發意即差（現修）、派（新譯、新普）或「差遣」。[1] **亞提馬**這名字在新約不再出現，[2] 我們對這人的認識就只限於本節所提供的點滴；鑑於這名字和希臘女神亞底米有關連，亞提馬可能是從異教歸信基督的。[3] **推基古**的名字則在新約另外出現四次：（i）他來自亞細亞（徒二十 4），可能是以弗所人；保羅（ii）在以弗所書六章 21 節稱他為**在主裏的親愛弟兄、忠信的僕役**（呂譯），又（iii）在歌羅西書四章 7 節給他三重的描寫：**我親愛的弟兄、忠實助手**（新普），和**在主內的同僕**（思高）。[4] 推基古被保羅委託將這兩封書信（還有腓利門書）送交收信人（參：西四 8～9〔9 節提到阿尼西謀〕；弗六 22）。[5] 最後，（iv）保羅書寫提摩太後書時，透露他**已經打發推基古往以弗所去**（提後四 12）。保羅準備打發亞提馬或推基古到克里特，是要代替提多的

---

1 《新希》260*a*（s.v. I.1）。動詞 **πέμπω** 在保羅書信另外出現十四次（新約全部 79 次），詳見《帖後》236-37。See BDAG 794*a*-95*a* (s.v.);《新希》260*a*（s.v.）。

2 ’Αρτεμᾶς（Artemas）很可能是 ’Αρτεμίδωρος（Artemidoros, ‘Gift of Artemis’; Artemis 的拉丁名字是 Diana [Mounce 457]）的簡寫（BDF §125(1); BDAG 135*b* [s.v.]; Blaiklock 91; Quinn 254; Simpson 118. Marshall 341 和 Towner III 800 n.6〔唐 1170 註 6〕作 ’Αρτεμίδορος; Hendriksen 398, Kelly 257, Lock 158, Quinn 264 作 ‘Artemidorus’）。後一個字（’Αρτεμίδωρος）沒有在希臘文聖經裏出現。參三 13 註釋註 2（下面 459）。

3 Quinn 264.

4 詳參《西・門》724-26；《弗》1005-7。

5 詳參《西・門》727-32（另見 8-13）；《弗》1008-9。

地位（至少當提多不在克里特時），[6] 而保羅選擇這樣安排，而不是把領導教會的責任移交予長老，表示克里特教會的年日尚淺。[7] **我打發……到你那裏去的時候**其實隱含了「當他抵達時」的意思。[8]

或字表示，保羅寫信時尚未決定要打發誰接替提多在克里特的工作。一個可能是，鑑於保羅在提摩太後書（教牧書信的最後一卷）表示他**已經打發推基古往以弗所去**（四 12），提多則去了撻馬太（10 節），而撻馬太位於同一海岸的**尼哥坡里**（多三 12b）以北；故此可以推論，最後被差往克里特的是亞提馬。[9] 這就是說，亞提馬到了克里特接替提多的工作後，提多便前往尼哥坡里和保羅會合，其後又被差往撻馬太。[10]

趕緊（同新和）、**趕快**（思高、新譯）[11] 或**儘快**（新普）的另一

---

6 Guthrie I 209, Guthrie II 221（古特立 223）：'to replace Titus in Crete during the latter's absence'; Banker 11*a*: 'presumably to replace Titus'; Keegan II 104（Keegan I 66）其中一人要「遞補（replace）」提多。See Blaiklock 72: 'Paul speaks of replacing Titus by Artemas or Tychicus'. 但 'Artemas <u>and</u> Tychicus were to take over from Titus'（Blaiklock 92）或「提多是要……由亞提馬<u>及</u>推基古取替他的工作」（張 310 註 2）這種講法有欠準確。

7 Genade 109.

8 Banker 116, 117*a*: 'When I send either Artemas or Tychicus to you, (as soon as he arrives,)'; NLT: 'As soon as one of them arrives'; 新普：**他們一到**（嚴格地說，複數的**他們**是不對的；參上面註 6 末）。參思高：**當我打發……到你那裏<u>以後</u>**。Cf. BDAG 731*a* (s.v. ὅταν, 1 a β): '[used] w. the aor. subj. [here πέμψω], when the action of the subordinate clause precedes that of the main clause [here σπούδασον]'.

9 Fee 214; Keener 631*a*; Knight II 356; Montague 253; Mounce 457（460: 'From Nicopolis Titus eventually headed north to Dalmatia'）。不過 Laansma 294 認為，'There is too much we do not know about the timing of these letters to have any confidence of that.'

10 提多大抵趕及在冬天之前到尼哥坡里會見保羅（參 12b～c 節），然後或是（甲）和保羅一起過冬，次年<u>夏天</u>才前往撻馬太，或是（乙）隨即前往撻馬太；從尼哥坡里前往撻馬太並不涉及海上旅程，'so the trip could have been made <u>during the winter months</u>'（Mounce lx; cf. li: 'Possibly Titus arrived and either went on to Dalmatia <u>before winter set in</u> or stayed for winter and spring and then went on to Dalmatia'）。另一可能是，保羅在前往尼哥坡里途中被捕，然後被解往羅馬；提多則沒有在尼哥坡里留下來，而是繼續前往撻馬太，那是<u>夏末</u>（lxii, cf. 589）。孟威廉的最後選擇是：'Paul did reach Nicopolis for the winter, and Titus spent the winter with him, departing for Dalamatia <u>in the spring</u>'（Mounce lxii, cf. 589）。

11 See also Fairnbairn 57, 303, Lock 151, *Paraphrase* 295: 'make haste'; Witherington 164: 'come . . . with alacrity'; BDAG 939*a* (s.v. σπουδάζω, 1): 'to proceed quickly,

翻譯是**竭力設法**（呂譯）。[12] 大多數英譯本都採納後一個意思。[13]

第 12c 節解釋第 12b 節：為甚麼保羅要提多前往尼哥坡里[14]見他呢？因為保羅**已經決定在那裏過冬**。[15] **決定**意即「經過思考後得

---

hurry, hasten'. Marshall 341 認為動詞在這裏的意思顯然是 'to hasten, hurry', 但同時認為**你要趕緊**這命令也許只是書信方式（'epistolary style'），不必全然相信（'to be taken with a pinch of salt'）。Towner III 800（唐 1171）則認為，'the time frame probably suggests that, once relieved, Titus is to make his move without delay.'

12 原文動詞為 σπούδασον（σπούδασον ἐλθεῖν πρός με 此句亦見於提後四 9〔其後還有 ταχέως 一字〕）。留意 Himes（'Use' 86）的觀察：'It is difficult to see any significance here in the usage of the aorist, and it is somewhat odd that 4,9's request for Timothy to come to Paul has an aorist, while the request in 4,11 to bring Mark and the request in 4,13 to bring his coat are both present tenses (ἄγε and φέρε respectively).'

13 See **(i)** Oden 169 / RSV, NRSV, NIV, TNIV, NIV2011, NJB, ESV, NLT; Kelly 256, 257; Mounce 456, 457: 'Do/do your best'; **(ii)** NAU, Banker 116, 117*a*, Collins 370, 373, DC 152*a*, Fiore II 225, Griffin 331: 'make every effort'; **(iii)** KJV, NKJV: 'be diligent'.
(1) 動詞 **σπουδάζω** 在保羅書信另外出現六次，新約另外四次，意思也都是**竭力**（弗四 3；提後二 15；來四 11）、**努力**（彼後一 10；加二 10〔現修〕）、**想法子**（帖前二 17）、**竭力設法**（呂譯：提後四 9、21）、**盡心竭力**（彼後一 15）、**殷勤努力**（彼後三 14〔當代、新譯〕）。See BDAG 939*a-b* (s.v.);《新希》306*b*（s.v.）;《帖前》210。**(2)** 同字根的形容詞 σπουδαῖος 在新約出現三次（林後八 17、22a、22b：**熱心**），指提多「進行活動時是熱切的和費盡心血的」(《新希》306*b* [s.v.])。**(3)** 同字根的副詞 σπουδαίως 見三 13 註釋註 10 及所屬正文（下面 460-61）。

14 Νικόπολις = 'the city of victory / Victory City' (Ward 279 / Quinn 255), 'Victory/victory-town' (Kelly 257 / Hiebert 448), 'Victory Town' (Witherington 165), 'a city that overcomes' (Wall372); 馮譯作**大捷城**。這字在希臘文聖經出現僅此一次。**(1)** 釋經者一般認為，這尼哥坡里是希臘西（亞得里亞海）岸的 Nicopolis 'in Epirus'(e.g., Robert W. Smith, *ABD* 4.1108*a*; G. Schneider, *EDNT* 2.468*b* [s.v.]; Guthrie I 209; Guthrie II 221-22（古特立 223）; Hanson I 122; Lock 158; Quinn 264; Simpson 118-19）。這城是「亞該亞省伊庇魯地區最主要的城市，距東南方的雅典約 320 公里（200 英里）。從此處往西跨過亞得里亞海可達義大利半島東南角，之後循羅馬大道（亞比大道）前往羅馬。見 91 頁地圖」(彭編 108*a*〔筆者除去了原來的底線〕; see also Rogerson, *Atlas* 214）。此城由奧古斯都（路二 1）所建，以紀念他（原名渥大維：Gaius Octavius）早前在 the Battle of Actium（公元前 31 年）擊敗 Antony and Cleopatra 的聯軍（Collins 371-72; Kelly 257; Marshall 341-42）。**(2)**「這地點與保羅所說他的事工的範圍相符（直到以利哩古*〔羅十五 19〕，那就是在伊庇魯斯以北），也與後來所說提多在撻馬太*一致（提後四 10）」(唐書禮 1171〔方括號是原來的〕)。(*公元 9 年，羅馬將羅馬省分以利哩古的北部〔Pannonia〕與南部〔撻馬太〕分開，成為另一個省分，南部則繼續稱為以利哩古，但同時亦稱為撻馬太。參《羅》4.592 註 44。) See Rogerson, *Atlas* 214.

15 'Paul's intended visit to this city . . . implies a plan to establish a Christian mission on the west coast of Greece – a task that had not been accomplished during the journeys recorded in Acts'（G. L. Borchert, *ISBE* 3.535*a*）; cf. Hiebert 448: 'presumably making it a base of operation for work in Dalmatia'（參：提後四 10）。Laansma 232 認為保羅的

出結論，也因此可作決定」。[16] **在那裏**[17] 暗示保羅寫信時並非身在尼哥坡里，他將會前往該處**過冬**。[18] 通常在冬天（十一月中至三月中），在地中海旅行必須暫停，[19] 因此保羅要提多設法在冬天來臨之前到尼哥坡里和他會合。這表示保羅寫信時是夏末或秋天，[20] 但保羅寫信時身在何處則無從得知。[21] 無論如何，提多只有有限的時間去執行保羅交託給他的任務（一 5），他必須把握時間，努力作工！[22]

如費歌頓所指出，本節的一些細節對「教牧書信乃冒名之作」的理論十分不利：保羅對於要打發誰人接替提多猶豫不決；除了本節，

計劃是，春天來臨時，就從尼哥坡里西航，很可能前往意大利，亦可能往西班牙去（羅十五 24、28）。(**1**) Hinson 282 則對事情的先後有不同的理解：他認為保羅寫提後之前打發了提多到撻馬太（提後四 10），然後提多從撻馬太前往克里特。(**2**) Jeon II 37 聲稱，'Nicopolis was known for its harsh winters. By communicating his decision to stay the winter in a severe region, Paul contrasts himself again with the troublemakers who are gluttonous, lazy, and greedy for gain. The recipients of this letter, therefore, understand a stark contrast is being presented to them and are inspired to follow Paul's example of suffering for the gospel instead of using it as a means for personal gain.' 筆者十分懷疑，提多書的收信人（提多和克里特的信徒）會否同樣看見 Jeon 所看出來的「鮮明的對比」——更遑論受到激發去跟隨保羅受苦的榜樣——尤其因為他的第一句話（筆者加上底線的）未知有何根據。

16 《新希》193*a*（s.v. I.1）。動詞 **κρίνω** 在保羅書信另外出現四十次（新約全部 114 次），詳見《帖後》243-45。See also BDAG (s.v.) 567*b*-69*a*;《新希》193*a*（s.v.）。

17 副詞 **ἐκεῖ** 在保羅書信僅再出現兩次（羅九 26：**在那裏**；十五 24：**那裏**〔呂譯、新和〕），新約共 105 次。See BDAG (s.v.) 301*b*;《新希》103*b*（s.v.）。

18 See Banker 116, 117*a*: 'since it is there that I have decided to (go and) stay during the winter.' 因此，稱保羅、推基古和亞提馬為 'three [characters] in Nikopolis [*sic*] from which the Letter was sent'（Richards 71），或者說 'From Nicopolis . . . Paul requests his co-worker to come to him'（Conzelmann－Lindemann, *INT* 210），都是錯的。(**1**) Wallace 604 n.47 指出，不定詞 παραχειμάσαι 是間接引語，隱含了直接引語的未來時態動詞：'I have decided *to spend* the winter there' = 'I have decided, "I *will spend* the winter there"'. (**2**) 動詞 **παραχειμάζω** 在希臘文聖經僅再出現三次，意思也是**過冬**（徒二十七 12a，二十八 11；林前十六 6）。See BDAG 773*a* (s.v.);《新希》252*b*（s.v.）。(**3**) 同字根的名詞 παραχειμασία 在希臘文聖經僅出現一次（徒二十七 12b：**過冬**）。

19 Spencer 69.

20 Marshall 342; Laansma 294.

21 Witherington 164 則認為，尼哥坡里是從希臘出發前往意大利的海港，由此推論，保羅的計劃可能是由馬其頓橫過希臘到尼哥坡里，在那裏過冬，然後前往羅馬（提後就是寫於羅馬的）。

22 See Bouwman 157-59.

亞提馬不見經傳；保羅已把克里特的教會託付給提多，現在卻要他**竭力設法**（呂譯）離開克里特前往尼哥坡里；會合的地點是尼哥坡里。[23] 對於冒名的作者——據說他是以使徒行傳為起點的——而言，上述的細節是難以想像的，因為它們與使徒行傳的任何資料沒有半點相符。[24]

23 Keener 631*a*: 'Located near the coast and only about a century old, it was not a major city that would be likely to occur to a pseudepigrapher.'

24 Fee 214. Cf. Dunn, 'Titus' 276*b*: 'It is difficult to conceive of a later writer's having composed such passages [as Titus 3:1-2; 2 Tim. 4:6-21] except as an attempt to deceive his readers.' Gunther（*Paul* 114, 118）則以三 12～15 為 '[a] Pauline fragment', 並認為它是寫於 'not long before the writing of 2 Timothy 4:9-22'（118）。

三　**13a**　你要趕緊給西納律師和亞波羅送行，

13b　　讓他們沒有缺乏。

按原文次序，**西納律師和亞波羅**位於本節開首，表示他們就是本節的新題目。[1]（一）**西納**這名字（像上一節的**亞提馬**）在新約不再出現。[2] 經文並無表示，**西納**這位**律師**所專長的是摩西律法抑是其他的法律；但若是後者，很可能是羅馬法律。[3] 鑑於教牧書信對猶太律法的負面看法（一 14；提前一 6～7），加上一個猶太律法師不大可能會有**西納**這種異教名字，因此西納從事的工作很可能是與羅馬法律有關的。[4]（二）**亞波羅**的名字[5] 則在新約另外出現九次，有關的經文讓我

1　Banker 117*b*. νομικός（**律師**）這字已在三 9 出現過；參該節註釋註 29 之（1）= 上面 438。

2　Ζηνᾶς（Zenas）是 Ζηνόδωρος（= 'Gift of Zeus' [Lock 158; Quinn 257]; Marshall 343 作 Ζηνοδωρός）的簡稱。後一個字沒有在希臘文聖經裏出現。參三 12 註釋註 2（上面 454）。

3　So BDAG 676*a* (s.v. νομικός, 2);《新希》227*a*（s.v. I.2.b）：「民法專家」。See also Simpson 119: 'in the papyri it indicates one versed in Roman jurisprudence'; Baugh 509*b*: 'probably a Roman jurist'; Stott 211: 'a professional expert in Roman law'; 馮譯夾注：「精通羅馬法者。」
（1）LN §56.37 認為西納所專長的是「民事法律（civil）」，但亦有可能是「宗教法律（religious law）」，若是後者，便是指摩西的律法（§33.338）；參呂譯：**律法師**。（2）White 202*a* 認為，西納是摩西律法專家。Blaiklock 92 更認為，西納很可能是歸信了基督的拉比（'a converted rabbi'）。Keener 631*b* 也認為，也許西納和亞波羅 'were from the educated Jewish elite in Alexandria'; 若是這樣，西納較可能是個猶太律法的專家。Quinn 265 肯定地認為，νομικός 在這裏很可能指 'a Christian skilled in the Law par excellence, the Torah, even the whole OT.' 這樣，西納和亞波羅便是 'a pair of Jewish-Christian witnesses versed in the interpretation of the OT about Christ and for Christians', 他們構成律法所要求的**兩個證人**（申十七 6），他們的見證會對克里特的猶太基督徒（他們**輕看**由異教歸信基督的提多〔二 15〕）很有影響力（266）。馬唐納 569*a* 認為西納是律法師，「因為很可能他被召來是要幫助提多平息在摩西律法上（9 節）冗長的爭吵。」可是，沒有證據表示西納是保羅「召來」的；至於那些爭吵，保羅告訴提多要**遠避**而不是「平息」。

4　Fiore II 226; Kelly 258; Marshall 343; W. Gutbrod, *TDNT* 4.1088; 彭編 108*b*。Cf. Knight II 357: 'an expert in Roman law'; Towner III 801-2（唐 1173）：'His Greek name ("gift of Zeus") suggests that his expertise lay in Greek or Roman law and not in Jewish law.' 另見上註開首。（1）Keener 631*b* 則指出，'"Zenas" is attested as a name in Jewish funerary inscriptions, so his name cannot settle his ethnicity'.（2）**西納律師**（Ζηνᾶν τὸν νομικόν）與**醫生路加**（Λουκᾶς ὁ ἰατρός, 西四 14）和**城裏的財務官**以

們知道：他是**生在亞歷山大的猶太人**（徒十八 24），在以弗所時由百基拉、亞居拉夫婦引導而認識真道，繼而在亞該亞對猶太人力證耶穌是基督（十八 25～28）。他在哥林多的時候（十九 1），甚至被人視作教會的「亞波羅派」之首（林前一 12，三 4）；保羅就此譴責哥林多人，對他們解釋亞波羅（和保羅自己）在上帝的工作上的真正地位（三 5、6、22，四 6）。後來，亞波羅和保羅在以弗所一起（十六 12）。提多書本節則表示，亞波羅此刻和提多一起，但提多要給他（和西納）送行。[6] 經文並無表明亞波羅和西納是否從保羅那裏來到克里特，[7] 但他們似乎是這封書信的送信人之最佳人選。[8]

趕緊原文是副詞，與上一節的動詞**趕緊**同字根。副詞在這裏的意思可能是**趕緊**[9]（如在腓二 28：**盡快**），但它更可能的意思是**竭力設法**（呂譯），[10] 即是**盡力幫助〔二人〕上路**（新普），「盡力促成〔現修〕

拉都（Ἔραστος ὁ οἰκονόμος τῆς πόλεως，羅十六 23）在原文是同一模式（名字 + 稱號）。'It is a Pauline touch to identify a professional by his title' (Fee 215). (**3**) Wieland（'Crete' 353）指出，'it was common for lawyers to visit Crete in Roman times'. 此事實也稍微支持正文的立場。

5 Ἀπολλῶς，可能是 Ἀπολλόδωρος = 'Gift of Apollo' 的簡稱，或是 Ἀπολλώνιος（徒十八 24 異文）的簡稱（Lock 158; Quinn 257; see *TextC* 412）。Johnson（'Titus' 395*a*）說，如果這裏的亞波羅和林前三 1～6 的那一位是同一人的話，'it is perhaps a little strange to see him as a helper of Titus'. 但有甚麼線索表示，亞波羅是提多的助手呢？

6 Wieland（'Grace' 10*c*, with 11*c* n.5）認為，亞波羅（和西納*）曾對克里特的工作有所貢獻，如今要繼續前往別處；由於亞波羅是猶太人，他可能對於如何應付來自**那些奉割禮的人**的麻煩（一 10～16）給予提多十分寶貴的幫助（cf. idem, 'Crete' 353）。（*參上面註 4 之〔2〕。）

7 Harding I 130 認為他們大抵是 'delegates sent by Paul at some earlier date'. Jeon I 116 則把 13a 節理解為 'Titus and the Cretan community sending Zenas and Apollos to Paul.'

8 See Kelly 258: 'they are almost certainly the bearers of the letter'; Knight II 9: 'Zenas and Apollos . . . have probably been with Paul, since they are going through Crete, probably delivering Paul's letter'; Banker 12*b*: 'Paul may have specifically requested that they stop by Crete.' Arichea－Hatton 312 則認為，此理論純屬臆測（'it is at best speculative'）。

9 See also Witherington 164: 'with alacrity'.

10 參當代／新譯、新普：**盡量**／**盡力**；Kelly 256; Mounce 456, 458 / LN §68.65; Knight II 358: 'Do/do your best'; BDAG 939*b* (s.v. σπουδαίως, 2): 'pert. to being conscientious in discharging a duty or obligation, *diligently*, *earnestly*, *zealously*'; *EDNT* 3.267*a* (s.v.):

他們旅行的計劃」。[11] 這副詞被放在動詞給⋯⋯送行之前，表示它是受到強調的，[12] 它使本節的焦點落在提多應「如何」給兩人送行。[13]

送行原文動詞[14] 屬最早期基督教的宣教詞彙，幾乎是個專門用語，指教會對所支持的宣教士的供應，包括實質的幫助，例如：供應食物、金錢，安排旅伴、交通工具，提供旅途的指示和介紹信函。[15] 簡言之，送行的含意是幫助〔二人〕上路（新普），資助〔二人的〕旅程

'eagerly'; Fairnbairn 57, 304: 'Zealously'; Fiore II 225, Laansma 293, Spencer 70, 71: 'diligently'; Marshall 344: 'with diligence, zeal';《新希》306*b*（s.v. I.1）：「努力地；竭盡全力地」;《輔讀》530：「熱心地，勤奮地，懇切地」。

（**1**）這副詞（σπουδαίως）在新約僅再出現三次：路七 4（受百夫長所託的猶太人長老切切地求耶穌）；腓二 28（保羅更急著／越發急於〔新譯／新普〕要把以巴弗提打發回去〔參《腓》320〕）；提後一 17（阿尼色弗一到羅馬就千方百計／殷勤地／四處〔當代／新和／現修、新普〕尋找保羅）。參《新希》306*b*（s.v.）。（**2**）它在 LXX 只出現一次（次經《所羅門智訓》2.6），指「盡情（to the full）」（RSV, NRSV）享用世界。

11 《輔讀》531。Quinn 29, 253 兩次都翻譯為 'do your best / Do all you can' 之意；'the accent of the verb lies not on speed but on determination'（264）。

12 See MHT 3.227: 'An adverb <u>usually follows</u> the . . . verb which it determines, in NT.' 在 'Paul commands that these men <u>be</u> σπουδαίως <u>πρόπεμψον</u>'（Knight II 358）這句子裏，筆者加上底線的二字在文法上並不銜接，因 'be' 要求隨後的動詞為被動語態，但 πρόπεμψον 是（命令式語法）主動語態。

13 Banker 117*b*.

14 πρόπεμψον. Himes（'Use' 87）解釋，這裏使用過去不定時時態的動詞，'not because the aorist refers to a "once-for-all" kind of action, but rather because the concept of sending* somebody might (in Greek at least), [*sic*] be somewhat awkward in the imperative mood if expressed with a present imperative.'（*作者說：'Paul urges Titus to send (aorist) Zenas the lawyer <u>to him</u>.' 但並無任何線索表示西納和亞波羅正在前往保羅的所在地。另見下面註 19 所屬正文。）（**1**）動詞 **προπέμπω** 在新約另外出現八次：除了兩次指送人上船／送人到城外（徒二十 38／二十一 5），即是「在旅程的開頭部分與人同走一段短路程」（《新希》284*a* [s.v. I.2]），其餘六次皆指送行（徒十五 3；羅十五 24；林前十六 6、11〔送⋯⋯行〕；林後一 16；約叁 6），「有『提供援助』的含意」（同上 [s.v. I.1]）。See also BDAG 873*b* (s.v.). 'In Paul the vb. always has the meaning *equip for (further) journeys / send on one's way*' (*EDNT* 3.160*a* [s.v.]).（**2**）這動詞在 LXX 出現五次，分別指向人「提供安全通行（give safe conduct / provide . . . safe conduct）」（NRSV: 次經《以斯得拉一書》4.47／《馬加比一書》12.4）；有人會「送」猶滴到亞述軍隊的統帥那裏（《猶滴傳》10.15〔思高友弟德傳〕）；經師以利亞撒「告訴人快把他<u>送</u>到陰府裏去」（《馬加比二書》6.23〔思高瑪加伯下〕）；埃及人「匆忙地<u>送走</u>」以色列人（《所羅門智訓》19.2〔思高智慧篇〕[NRSV: 'hastily sent them out']）。

15 參《羅》4.618-19；Quinn 267.

（新譯）。這是接待基督徒客旅（一 8）[16] 的後續行動。按這種理解，雖然保羅對提多說**你要……給西納律師和亞波羅送行**，但這不等於提多要獨自一人供應他們的一切所需；送行的責任應該是由教會（尤其是有能力的成員）一起承擔的。給〔二人〕送行的目的[17] **是使他們不至於有甚麼缺乏**（現修）。[18] 他們很可能要從保羅所在地，並且帶著提多書來到克里特。[19]

---

16 參該節註釋第二段（上面 132-33）。

17 I.e., ἵνα 表達目的。See NKJV: 'that they <u>may</u> lack nothing'.（**1**）亦有將 ἵνα 視為表達結果的：'so that nothing is lacking for them / so that they lack nothing'（NAU / DC 152*a*）。（**2**）Zerwick §415 認為，13b 節開首的 ἵνα 是 "Ἵνα in independent wish or exhortation' 的例子。Cf. Lock 158: 'probably a new sentence, not dependent on πρόπεμψον'. 不少英譯本將 13b 節化為一項命令：'See that they are given / see that they have / and make sure they have everything they need'（NLT / NIV, TNIV, NIV2011 / NJB），'see that they lack nothing'（RSV, NRSV, ESV, *Paraphrase* 295）。

18 **缺乏**原文（λείπῃ）與一 5a 的**留**（ἀπέλιπον）和一 5b 的**未辦完**（λείποντα）是同字根（λειπ-）的。（**1**）Marshall（'Congregation' 116）認為，西納和亞波羅，像亞提馬和推基古一樣，都是 'evangelists whose task included the upbuilding of existing congregations'. 周 447, 448 稱亞波羅和西納為「旅行佈道家」。（**2**）Genade 120 聲稱，推基古、亞提馬（12a 節）、西納和亞波羅是獲得使徒授權作教會領袖的例子。（**3**）Keegan II 104 甚至認為，現在<u>提多</u>「要負起責任派遣一些人……去管理其它的地方教會」（Keegan I 66 原作 'Titus in [*sic*, is] now charged to send others . . . to exercise their ministries in other places'）。Collins 370 也認為，「保羅」（教牧書信作者，不是保羅本人）有效地將差派其他代表去宣教的責任交付給提多；如此，西納和亞波羅被確認為使徒的「第二代代表（second-generation delegates）」，「事奉承傳（succession in ministry）」的計劃就建立起來了。

19 Knight II 357.

三 **14a** 我們的人也該學習行善，幫助有迫切需要的人，

14b 這樣才不會不結果子。

也（同呂譯、思高、當代、新譯）或**並且**（新和）背後的原文其實是兩個小字；[1] **並且**似乎是翻譯了第一個，**也**則似乎翻譯了第二個。第一個小字表示，本節的指示延續了上兩節的兩個指示。[2] 在保羅書信裏，當這兩個小字按這裏的次序一起出現時，第二個小字常是**也**或**又**的意思。[3] 昆謝隆認為，這裏的兩個小字（他只翻譯為「也」[4]）暗示，**我們的人**要跟隨提多的引導（13 節）。[5] 不過，「跟隨引導」這種含意並不明顯，而本節與上一節的關係可另作解釋：上一節剛剛明確地提到西納和亞波羅二人的需要，這似乎給了保羅再一次機會，強調一般善行的重要性。[6] **也**字的含意似乎是，克里特的信徒不但要參與

1 δὲ καί: 'And . . . also' (KJV, NKJV). 一些英譯本只翻譯為（**i**）'And'（RSV, NRSV, ESV），另一些則只譯為（**ii**）'also'（NAU, NJB）。另有中英譯本（**iii**）完全不把二字譯出，只作 'Our people must learn . . .'（NIV, TNIV, NIV2011, NLT）；**我們自己的人必須學習**……（新普），**讓我們自己的人學習**……（現修）。

2 Wendland（'Discourse' 346）則認為，δέ 表達 'implicit contrast (i.e. to the false teachers / ungodly people)'. 但這種暗示的對比絕不明顯；這小字的意思較可能只是 'And'（KJV, NKJV）。

3 （**1**）例：（**也**）羅八 26（呂譯、思高、新譯；參《羅》2.691-95）；腓一 15（新和、新譯、現修）；門 22 節（思高；參《西・門》973 註 1 之〔1〕）；參：來七 2（現修；參《來》1.416-17）／（**又**）腓三 18（參思高：**再**；新普：**再次**；現修：**再一次**）；門 9 節（參《西・門》885）。（**2**）另參：腓四 15（參《腓》476）；弗五 11（參《弗》749 註 13、14 及所屬正文）。

4 Quinn 29, 253, 257, 267: 'too'.

5 Quinn 267-68: 'the Pauline congregations here in the PE are to follow the lead of Titus himself (again, note "too," *de kai*) as they "take the lead in fine deeds."' See also Lock 158: 'καί "as well as yourself"'; Hendriksen 399: 'Titus . . . should not try to shoulder the burden *alone*'; Towner III 802（唐 1173）：'Paul's intention was that this need be met not by Titus alone, but rather by the Cretan Christians themselves'; Jeon I 118: 'the sense is, "'our own' (the Cretan community) – alongside you personally (Titus)" must do the "good work" (3:1) of ensuring that "nothing is lacking for them"'; 周 447：「不僅提多本人要幫助西納和亞波羅之類的旅行佈道家，就連革哩底* 的信徒……也要學習行善」。（*和合；新和、和修：克里特。）

6 Banker 28*b*, 116*b*.（參三 12～15 註釋引言之〔三〕= 上面 453。）See also DC 152*a*: 'The clause [v. 14a] is . . . a generalization of the preceding verse'; Arichea – Hatton

給二人送行一事，[7] 也要學習在籠統的意義上行善。[8] 我們的人指克里特的信徒；[9] 另有譯為我們自己的人（現修、新譯、新普）。[10] 他們有別於異教徒和不信主的猶太人，亦有別於那些「反對陣營」中的猶太派基督徒（一 10）。[11]

學習原文動詞在這裏的意思不是「找出、確定」，[12] 也不是通過接受教導而獲得知識，[13] 而是透過經驗和實踐而學會。[14] 行善（同思

312-13: 'Paul takes this opportunity to once again inculcate into the minds of the Cretan Christians the overarching theme of the letter, which is to do good'; Montague 254.

7 參三 13 註釋末段（上面 461-62）。

8 Cf. Knight II 358-59: 'This is an obvious attempt to drive the general lesson home with this concrete case [v. 13]. Thus they are to learn "also" (καί) with reference to this pressing need as well as in the more normal routines of life.'

9 Arichea－Hatton 313: 'the Cretan Christians'; Saarinen 195: 'the Christians in Crete'; White 202*a*: '*those of our faith* in Crete'; Marshall 345: '[Cretan] Christians'（方括號是原來的）。Cf. Lock 122/158: 'our brothers and sisters' / '"the whole household of faith," "our brothers and sisters," in contrast to their pagan neighbours'; Leaney 131-32: 'Christians'; Scott 182: 'we Christians'; G. Schneider, *EDNT* 2.122*a* (s.v.): 'the Christians'; Keegan II 104（Keegan I 66）「是指全團體的成員（the entire community)」。**(1)** Collins 373 則認為，我們的人是指西納和亞波羅；本節是提多要給予他們二人的忠告：宣教士必須準備受苦，即使處境艱難，也要選擇行善。**(2)** οἱ ἡμέτεροι 是「名詞化用語」(《新希》149*a*（s.v. ἡμέτερος）；這形容詞（**ἡμέτερος**）在新約另外出現六次（徒二 11，二十六 5；羅十五 4；提後四 15；約壹一 3，二 2）。Quinn 257 說，此字「在新約出現八次」，這包括路十六 12 的異文（原來的讀文是 ὑμέτερον; see *TextC* 140）。

10 Genade 110 認為我們的人所指的就是那些正面回應保羅及其代表之教導的人。Fiore II 226 將 οἱ ἡμέτεροι 翻譯為 'our colleagues'.

11 See Quinn 267; 一 10 註釋末段（上面 160-64）。Cf. Knight II 358: 'Perhaps Paul uses this construction to distinguish those who follow him and Titus from the false teachers and their followers as well as from non-Christian neighbours.'

12 如在加三 2；參《加》626 註 2。

13 如在羅十六 17（你們所學的教義〔新譯〕＝你們已領受的教導〔新普〕）；弗四 20（學了基督〔呂譯、思高、新和〕；參《弗》639-40）。

14 如在腓四 11（我已經學會……知足〔參《腓》466〕）；提前五 4（寡婦的兒孫要在自己家中學習行孝，報答親恩），五 13（年輕的寡婦學了懶惰）。See BDAG 615*b* (s.v. μανθάνω, 3): 'to come to a realization, with implication of taking place less through instruction than through experience or practice'; Marshall 345: 'to learn through practice'; Quinn 267: 'It is learning charity by acting charitably'; Towner III 802: 'learning by doing' – '[a]s opposed to learning by means of formal instruction' (n.31)（唐 1174，註 31）。**(1)** 留意來五 8：基督因所受的苦難學了順從的意思不是「基督對上帝，起初不是或不常是順服的，後來不斷經歷苦難，結果學會完全順服」，而是「透過在苦難中順服上帝的經歷，了解到順服上帝實際上是怎樣的一回事」（詳參

高，新普同）重複了三章 8c 節的**留心行善**，二者在原文是完全相同的。[15]

幫助有迫切需要的人原文[16] 含有「生活所需」一詞，這詞在通

《來》1.324）。(**2**) 除了已提及的羅十六 17；加三 2；弗四 20；腓四 11；提前五 4、13；多三 14 本節（共七次）外，動詞 **μανθάνω** 在保羅書信另外出現九次，皆指不同方式的**學**（林前十四 35；提後三 14a、14b〔思高、新譯〕)、**學習**（林前十四 31；腓四 9；提前二 11；提後三 7）或**學到**（林前四 6；西一 7）。這字在新約另外出現九次（除了上述的來五 8，另見太九 13，十一 29，二十四 32；可十三 28；約六 45，七 15；徒二十三 27；啟十四 3）。詳見 BDAG 615*a-b* (s.v.);《新希》210*a*(s.v.)。

15 καλῶν ἔργων προΐστασθαι. (**1**) LN §68.67 將不定詞翻譯為 'strive to do'（參現修：努力行善）。但在這裏（如在 8 節），原文動詞的意思較可能只是 'Busy oneself with, engage in'（BDAG 870*b* [s.v. προΐστημι]）= **從事**（呂譯），「全情投入地參與一些事情」(《新希》283*a* [s.v. I.3]）。參以下英譯：'engage in'（NAU），'occupy themselves in'（NJB），'apply/devote themselves to'（RSV / NRSV, NIV, TNIV, NIV2011, ESV），'devote themselves (in concert) to' (B. Reicke, *TDNT* 6.703)。(**2**) KJV, NKJV 則翻譯為 'maintain'. Quinn 29, 253, 257, 262, 267 / Witherington 164 同樣翻譯為 'to take the lead in fine deeds / good works'; 參三 8b～d 註釋註 17 之（1）= 上面 427。See also Perkins 1445*a*: 動詞的意思是 'take the lead [in the activity of doing good]'
(**3**) 呂譯將行善理解為**從事正經的職業**（參新和：**學習正經事業**）。Cf. NEB: 'to engage in honest employment to produce the necessities of life'; Barrett 148: 'Productive (gainful) work was necessary in order to facilitate the Christian mission.' 但見三 8b～d 註釋註 17 之（3）= 上面 427。侯嘉文 167 則認為「這裏是勸勉信徒為公眾利益行事。」
(**4**) Wendland（'Discourse' 345）稱本節為 '*thematic summary* (corporate gospel consequence)', 與同樣稱為 '*thematic summary* (cosmic gospel core)' 的一 1b～3 首尾呼應。但兩段其實並不對稱，因本節的主要內容只有**學習行善**一樣，但一 1～3 則含有豐富得多的神學內容，因此筆者認為，作者視本節為全書的「主題總結」，這做法並不恰當。

16 εἰς τὰς ἀναγκαίας χρείας. Quinn 29, 253, 257, 262, 267 翻譯為 'with regard to the urgent necessities of life'（cf. A. Strobel, *EDNT* 1.79*b* [s.v. ἀνάγκη, 4]: '*urgent* necessities of life'）; DM 103-4 則把介系詞 εἰς 解釋為 'because of'. 但 εἰς 在這裏可能表達目的：MHT 3.266 視之為 'Purposive εἰς' 的例子；Fiore II 226 譯作 'to meet compelling needs that are lacking'; M. J. Harris（*DNTT* 3.1187）作 'to supply the necessities'. (**1**) 形容詞 **ἀναγκαῖος** 在新約另外出現七次，除了一次指親密的朋友（徒十 24，思高、新和），其餘六次的意思都是**必須的**（徒十三 46，呂譯〔現修、新普欠「的」字〕)、**必須有的**（林前十二 22，呂譯）= **不可缺少的**（當代、新譯）、**勉強的**（林後九 5，當代、新譯、新普〔新和、現修欠「的」字〕) =「不得不這樣做」、**必須的**（腓一 24〔呂譯〕，二 25；來八 3）。See BDAG 60*b* (s.v.); 在本節的意思是 'pressing needs'（also Marshall 345; Dunn 878 n.145）。亦參《新希》21*a*（s.v.）。
(**2**) 名詞 **χρεία** 在保羅書信另外出現十三次，其中五次也是指生活上的需要（羅十二 13；弗四 28；腓二 25，四 16、19〔參《腓》493-94〕)，其餘八次則指另一些方面的需要（林前十二 21a、21b、24；弗四 29〔參《弗》684-86〕；帖前一 8，四 9、

俗哲學常指生活上的物質需要。[17] 問題是，這裏所指的是自己的還是別人的生活所需？[18]（一）不少中譯本似乎將這裏的**需要**視為信徒自己的需要：**好應付必須的需用**（呂譯）、**為應付一切急需**（思高）、**預備所需用的**（新和）、**供給生活上的需要**（現修）、**供應日常的需要**（新譯）。[19] 但是上一節剛提到，提多要幫助西納和亞波羅上路、資助他們的旅程、供給他們所需，而本節隨即指示信徒**也該學習行善**，因此文理提示，（二）**幫助有需要的人**（新普）才是正確的理解：信徒要學習行善濟急（當代），**幫助有迫切需要的人**。[20]

不結果子[21] 是比喻講法，其意思（按上段第一種理解）是「過

12〔參《帖前》334-35〕，五 1）；新約另外 35 次（新約全部 49 次）。詳見 BDAG 1088*a*-*b* (s.v.);《新希》356*b*（s.v.）。

17 DC 152*a*-*b*. τὰς ἀναγκαίας χρείας = 'the necessities of life'.

18 White 202*a*-2*b* 和 Lock 159 認為是兩者：供給自己和家人的需要，以及幫助不能自助的弟兄。

19 See also NIV: 'in order that they may provide for daily necessities'; NJB: 'doing good works for their practical needs'; Köstenberger 625*b*: '"doing what is good" . . . so as not to be a burden to anyone'.

20 參以下英譯：'so as to help cases of urgent need' (RSV [endorsed by Guthrie I 210; Guthrie II 222；古特立 224], ESV); 'Our people must learn to do good by meeting the urgent needs of others' (NLT); 'Our people must learn to engage in good works by way of relieving the pressing needs of others' (*Paraphrase* 295).（**1**）Marshall 346 認為，**幫助有迫切需要的人**或是明確地指幫助基督徒客旅，或是籠統地指促進基督教的佈道工作。（**2**）另有翻譯為「為了必須的用途（for necessary uses）」，所指的就是為了像「基督的僕人在從事主的工作時，供給他們的需要」這種正當和重要的目的（Fairnbairn 304-5）。Cf. Bassler 214: 'to provide for the "necessary needs" . . . of the traveling Christian workers'; Towner III 803（唐 1175）：'in order to provide for urgent needs [of such Christian travelers]'（方括號是原來的）。Towner II 263 甚至認為是指 'the needs of <u>these</u> travelers'. So also Richards 92.（**3**）Johnson II 31 認為，'His [Titus's] duty in Crete may also have included some fund-raising (see Titus 3:14)'; cf. Johnson, 'Titus' 384*a*: 'His duty in Crete may well also have included fund raising (see Titus 3:14).'

21 **ἄκαρπος** 是複合形容詞（from καρπός + α-privative）；名詞 καρπός 見正文下文。（**1**）這複合形容詞在新約另外出現六次，分別指種子**結不出果實**（太十三 22 ‖ 可四 19），理智**沒有效果**（林前十四 14），黑暗的行為是**不結果實**（弗五 11，馮譯）= **無善果**（呂譯）的（參《弗》748），信徒**不結果子**（彼後一 8），以及假教師是**沒有果子的樹**（猶 12 節）。See BDAG 35*a* (s.v.);《新希》12*b*（s.v.）。（**2**）這形容詞在 LXX 僅出現三次，分別指「<u>不結果子的</u>地（γῇ . . . ἀκάρπῳ）」（耶二 6），畫家「<u>無結果的</u>辛勞工作（πόνος ἄκαρπος）」（次經《所羅門智訓》15.4），和 'fruitless nurturings

無生產的生活」，[22] 作閒散無用的人（現修），[23] 或（按上段第二種理解）是對人無所貢獻（當代）。名詞果子在新約一共出現 66 次，六分之一是在保羅書信裏。[24] 有兩次是字面意義的果子（林前九 7）或果實（提後二 6，呂譯、新譯），其餘九次是比喻用法。在此之下，保羅提到多種果子：**消極方面**，（**i**）信徒歸主之前所得的果子，無非是他們如今看為羞恥的事（羅六 21，參呂譯），那些事的結局就是永遠的死亡；[25] **積極方面**，（**ii**）信徒作了上帝的奴僕，其果子就是成聖過程的開始，而其結局就是永生（羅六 22）；[26]（**iii**）保羅計劃要在羅馬人當中得些宣教工作的果子（羅一 13）；[27] 他若繼續在肉身活著，就能讓他多結工作的果子（腓一 22，呂譯），即是為基督做多結果子的工作（新普）；[28]（**iv**）他要帶交耶路撒冷教會的果子（羅十五 28，呂譯），就是外邦教會給耶城教會中的窮人的捐款（思高、新普）；[29]（**v**）他不求腓立比人的饋贈，只求他們的果子不斷增多，歸在他們的賬上（腓四 17），即是有豐厚的利息歸入他們的賬內（思高）；[30]（**vi**）聖靈的果子（加五 22）是聖靈在信徒的生命中工作而產生的倫理品質；光的果子是在於一切的良善、正義、和真誠（弗五 9，呂譯）；仁義的果子（腓一 11）就是耶穌基督在〔信徒〕生命中孕育出來的（新普）品格與行為（基本上＝聖靈的果子）。[31] 在不結果子這字裏面，果子一定

[ἄκαρποι τιθηνίαι]'（偽經《馬加比四書》16.7 [RSV, NRSV]）。

22 NIV, TNIV, NIV2011: 'live unproductive lives'. Leaney 132 認為：'The sense is material and economic. Christians are not to be non-earning and unproductive.'

23 See also *Paraphrase* 295: 'they must not be useless'; Banker 118*b*: ὦσιν ἄκαρποι 'is a dead figure in New Testament Greek for "living uselessly."'

24 提後四 13 的 Κάρπος 不算在內，因那是個人名字（Carpus, 加布）。

25 詳見《羅》2.310-15。

26 詳見《羅》2.316-17。

27 詳見《羅》1.225-26。

28 詳見《腓》151。

29 詳見《羅》4.639-40。

30 詳見《腓》484-85。

31 詳見《腓》108-9。

不是消極意義的，而是積極意義的**好果子**（太三 10 || 路三 9；太七 17～19 || 路六 43）。文理提示，這裏所指的主要不是品格方面的果子（**vi**），而是造福別人的實際幫助。[32]

32 Dunn 878*b*.

捌　問安和祝福（三 15）

艾理斯給予本節的標題是「保羅親筆問候及祝禱」，[1] 這表示他認為，本書的其餘部分都是由抄寫員代筆。保羅在帖撒羅尼迦後書的信末問安這樣說：我保羅親筆問候你們。這是我每一封信的記號；我的筆跡就是這樣（帖後三 17，新譯）。這字所指的最可能是他親筆問候的事實，而重點不在問候，乃在親筆，因為隨後一句說，我的筆跡就是這樣，表示保羅要讀者特別留意的，乃是他親筆問候時的筆跡或字體是怎樣的。而他親筆問候時的筆跡就是他每一封信的記號。這話似乎有這樣的含意：連那些沒有明說保羅親筆問候（如在林前十六 21；西四 18；帖後三 17）或提到保羅親手／親筆寫（加六 11／門 19 節）或提及代筆人（如在羅十六 22：我這代筆寫信的德提）的書信，包括現已失傳的保羅書信，都有他親筆問候的部分，儘管他不一定指出此點來吸引讀者的注意。[2] 如果這推論正確，則「都有他親筆問候的部分」暗示，其餘的部分都是代筆人書寫的。如此，艾理斯給予本節的標題反映了正確的理解。

1　Ellis, 'Pastoral Letters' 665*b*: 'Greetings and Benediction in Paul's Hand'（《辭典》963*b*）。

2　參《帖後》378-80。

8.1 個人的問安（三 15a～b）

三 **15a** 跟我同在一起的人都向你問安。

15b 請代向在信仰上愛我們的人問安。

並無連詞將這兩句連接起來，這表示兩句是獨立於彼此的；雖然兩句都涉及問安，但兩句並非完全平行，第二句並不支持第一句，也不是由第一句衍生出來的。[1] 在保羅書信的信末問安裏，動詞問安（不管是直說式語法〔如在 15a 節〕，[2] 或是命令式語法〔如在 15b 節〕）[3] 總是居於句子的首位；若動詞是直說式語法，隨後的總是賓詞（被問候者），然後是主詞（問候者）。[4]

跟我／同我在一起的人（現修／呂譯、新譯）可能（一）籠統地指保羅所在地的教會信徒：**同我在一處的人**（新和）相當於**這裏的人**

---

1 Levinsohn, 'Constraints' 331. 本節是個例子，說明了「無連詞現象（asyndeton）」'is found . . . between individual propositions that are viewed as independent of each other' (ibid.); 'the second does not strengthen or develop from the first'（idem, *Discourse Features* 119）。

2 及羅十六16b、21、22、23a、23b（詳參《羅》4.752-54，786-803）；林前十六19a、19b、20a； 林後十三12b；腓四21b、22；西四10、12、14；提後四21；門 23 節。（以上十六次。）

3 及羅六3～16a 的十六次（詳參《羅》4.686-752）；林前十六20b；林後十三12a；腓四21a；西四15；帖前五26；提後四19。（以上 22 次。保羅書信一共四十次；參《腓》502；《帖前》476-77。）

4 動詞 **ἀσπάζομαι** 在新約另外出現十九次，即新約全部 59 次。See BDAG 144*a-b* (s.v. ἀσπάζομαι);《新希》48*a-b*（s.v.）。**(1)** 除了第三人稱的問候（例：多三15a）和第二人稱的問候（三15b），保羅書信還有第一人稱的問候，其中使用與這動詞同字根的名詞 ἀσπασμός：ὁ ἀσπασμὸς τῇ ἐμῇ χειρί（我保羅親筆問候你們〔新譯〕：林前十六21；西四18；帖後三17）實質上相當於 ἀσπάζομαι. 在這種親筆問安的形式裏，原文並無動詞，須補充寫（呂譯）字，直譯作「這問安是我保羅親手寫的」。**(2)** 名詞 ἀσπασμός 在保羅書信僅出現上述三次，在新約另外出現七次，分別指文士和法利賽人喜歡人們向他們問安（太二十三7 ‖ 可十二38 ‖ 路十一43；）、天使對馬利亞的問候（路一29、41、44），以及馬利亞對伊利莎白的問安（路一41、44）。See BDAG 144*b* (s.v.);《新希》48*b*（s.v.）。

（新普）；[5]（二）特指和保羅一起的同工；[6]（三）包括上述的所有人。在腓立比書的信末問安裏，保羅區別**跟我一起的眾弟兄**（腓四 21）[7] 和**眾聖徒**（四 22），這提示前者是數目較小的一班人，很可能就是保羅的同工。在這前提下，加拉太書一章 2 節**所有跟我一起的弟兄**[8] 可同樣理解為保羅的同工。[9] **那同我在一起的**（加二 3，呂譯）和**與我一同**（腓二 22，思高）這片語，[10] 分別指提多和提摩太，而提摩太是保羅的同工；提多雖然當時不是保羅的同工，但後來成為保羅親密的同工；[11] 這一點亦稍微支持腓立比書四章 21 節**跟我一起的眾弟兄**和加拉太書一章 2 節**所有跟我一起的弟兄**均可理解為保羅的同工。上述兩節（腓四 21；加一 2）一起提示，提多書本節**跟我在一起的人**（現修）很可能也是保羅的同工；[12] 雖然本節所用的介系詞與該兩節（和另外兩節）所用的都不同，[13] 但在如此相似的文理中，兩個介系詞是可以交換使用的。[14]

---

5 See NJB: 'Everybody here'.

6 **(i)** Kelly 256, 259: 'All my companions'; Marshall 348: 'the writer's companions . . . his colleagues'; Hendriksen 399: 'the fellow-workers who are in the company of . . . the apostle'; Hiebert 449: 'All the workers with Paul'; Knight II 359: 'his fellow workers'; Quinn 268: 'They are emphatically Paul's men, at his side . . . sharing his apostolic work'; **(ii)** Lock 159: 'perhaps "my *travelling* companions," as no place is mentioned'; Towner III 79: 'the team members travelling with him' =「跟他一起旅行的伙伴」（唐 109），804: 'those traveling with Paul' =「那些與保羅同行的人」（唐 1179）。黃編 230 則認為，「『同我在一處的人』指仍與坐監的保羅保持交通聯繫的同工和信徒」。可是，並無任何線索表示，保羅寫此信時是在牢獄中。

7 οἱ <u>σὺν ἐμοὶ</u> ἀδελφοί.

8 οἱ <u>σὺν ἐμοὶ</u> πάντες ἀδελφοί.

9 參《加》218 連註 3、4。

10 在原文依次為 ὁ <u>σὺν ἐμοί</u> 和 <u>σὺν ἐμοί</u>.

11 提多在當時（加二 3）是以「證物甲」的身分被保羅帶同前往耶路撒冷的，後來才成為得力的同工，參導論第貳節首段（上面 23-24）。

12 Jeon I 120 則認為，'it may also be a subtle way of expressing a sense of camaraderie between those who are of a "common faith" (1:4) in distinction to those "who turn away from the truth" (1:14).' 參註 22（Mounce）= 下面 473。

13 οἱ <u>μετ' ἐμοῦ</u> πάντες，其他四節則用 <u>σὺν ἐμοί</u>（見上面註 7、8、10）。

14 M. J. Harris, *DNTT* 3.1206: 'in Hel. Gk. they [σύν and μετά] are virtually synonymous'. 留意哈利斯隨即指出保羅用法上的重要區別（1206-7）：見《西》518-19 註 23 之（1）（2）的引述和應用。

這裏的動詞愛字不是與二章 2 節「在愛心上健全」那個名詞同字根的愛字，[15] 而是較弱的「喜愛」一字；[16] 信上數個複合形容詞就是以這個「愛」字為其前綴的：作監督的必須樂意接待外人（一 8），並且喜愛良善（同上，新譯、新普）；[17] 年輕的婦女要愛丈夫，愛兒女（二 4）。[18] 在信仰上和卷首的在我們共同的信仰上（一 4a，現修）前後呼應。在信仰上愛我們的人[19] 意即「那些因為與我們有同一信仰而愛我們的人」。[20] 一章 13 節在信仰上健全，哥林多前書十六章 13 節在

---

15 即不是與 ἀγάπη 同字根的 ἀγαπάω. 後者在保羅書信一共出現 34 次（新約全部 143 次）。

16 《新希》227*b*(s.v. φιλέω, I.1)。See also BDAG 1056*b* (s.v. 1 a): 'have affection for, like'. 這動詞 **φιλέω** 在保羅書信僅再出現一次（林前十六 22：若有人不愛主，這人該受詛咒），在新約另外 23 次；除了三次的意思是吻（當代：太二十六 48 ‖ 可十四 44 ‖ 路二十二 47），其餘二十次的意思都是（**i**）「愛」，其對象是人物（十五次：太十 37a、37b；約五 20，十一 3、36，十五 19，十六 27a、27b，二十 2，二十一 15、16、17a、17b、17c；啟三 19），或（**ii**）「喜歡」，其對象是事物（五次：太六 5；太二十三 6 ‖ 路二十 46；約十二 25；啟二十二 15）。See BDAG 1056*b*-57*a* (s.v.); 《新希》227*b*（s.v.）。

17 原文依次為 φιλόξενος, φιλάγαθος.

18 原文依次為 φίλανδρος, φιλότεκνος. Genade 111 聲稱：'The verb φιλέω is an instance of paronomasia at this late stage in the letter.' 可是，三 15 跟二 4（尤其跟一 8）相距甚遠，因而並不符合 paronomasia 的定義所要求的 'close proximity'（見二 12 註釋註 27〔上面 296〕）。

19 τοὺς φιλοῦντας ἡμᾶς ἐν πίστει = 'those who love us in the faith' (NKJV, RSV, NRSV, NAU, NIV, TNIV, NIV2011, NJB, ESV).（**1**）Arichea－Hatton 314 將此片語視為 'an idiom referring specifically to Christians in Crete; hence "our dear Christian friends"'; 但並無提供理據支持此說。（**2**）G. Stählin（*TDNT* 9.137）認為，'φιλέω ἐν πίστει corresponds materially to ἀγαπάω ἐν θεῷ, Jd. 1'. 不過，猶 1 節的用詞是被動語態的 ἐν θεῷ . . . ἠγαπημένοις, 而蒙愛所指的愛是上帝的愛（see, e.g., Bauckham, *Jude* 25; Kelly, *Peter* 243），不是作者或其他信徒對收信人的愛。換言之，分詞片語不應理解為 'beloved (by us) in the Father', 因為被召（κλητοῖς）、蒙愛（ἠγαπημένοις）、〔被〕保守（τετηρημένοις）三者平行，三者所隱含的行事者都是上帝（cf. Green, *2 Peter* 156）。（**3**）**ἐν πίστει** 這片語在保羅書信另外出現八次，除了一次（加二 20：<u>因信上帝的兒子而活</u>），其餘皆在教牧書信裏：提前一 2、4，二 7、15，三 13，四 12；提後一 13。See Marshall 213-17. G. Barth（*EDNT* 3.97*b*）認為，'ἐν πίστει is occasionally used formulaically (1 Tim 1:2, 4; Titus 3:15).'

20 Cf. Mounce, 'Titus' 107: 'those who love us as fellow believers.'（**1**）雖然 Quinn 29, 253, 259, 268（只）翻譯為 'those who <u>in faith</u> are <u>friends</u> of ours', 但是他也是將 πίστις 解釋為信仰：'This friendship and affection take their origin from the faith, the true faith as Paul teaches it.'（**2**）Marshall 214 把這裏的 πίστις 理解為 'a continual

信仰上要站穩，哥林多後書十三章 5 節在信仰中生活，信仰原文皆有冠詞，在本節則沒有冠詞。雖然如此，鑒於正確的教義在提多書是個重要的主題，這裏無冠詞的「信」字可能仍是指信仰。[21] 這問安語的對象只是同一信仰的朋友們（現修）或所有愛我們的信徒（新普），這似乎暗示在克里特島上有一些信徒不再忠於保羅和他的福音；[22] 他在信上重複提到的那些假教師（一 10～16，三 9～11）顯然不屬於同一信仰的朋友們或愛我們的信徒之列。

activity or process [of faith]'; cf. 215: 'for the writer faith is the key characteristic of the Christian (cf. . . . Tit 1.13; 3.15).' Hiebert 449 則解釋為 'the sphere where their affection was operative'. 參黃編 230：「『因有信心』〔新和〕原文作『在信心裏』，指信心乃是他們的愛心發生作用的範圍；『因有信心愛我們』〔新和〕指愛我們的愛，完全是在信心所產生的關係裏面而有的（參約壹五 1）。」**(3)** Barrett 148 認為 ἐν πίστει 表達雙重意思：'"Our faithful friends" might convey better the double sense, that the friends are Christians, and that they can be trusted.'

21 See Banker 120*a*. 辛普遜指出，'ἐν πίστει may doubtless be rendered *in the faith*, the article being dropped after a preposition'（Simpson 119; cf. TEV: 'our friends in the faith'）。不過，他把這片語翻譯為 'faithfully'（endorsed by Guthrie I 211, Guthrie II 223; cf. Aageson 52: 'who love us faithfully'），其理由是 τοὺς φιλοῦντας ἡμᾶς <u>ἐν</u> <u>πίστει</u> 跟弗六 24 的 τῶν ἀγαπώντων . . . <u>ἐν</u> <u>ἀφθαρσίᾳ</u> 十分相似。但後一個片語可能並不是動詞的修飾語；見《弗》1015-18 的討論。

22 Fee 216. Cf. Davies I 112: 'the greetings are sent . . . to *all who love us in the faith*, that is, to those who remain faithful to the Pauline mission rather than to those criticised in 1.10-15; 3.10-11'; Knight II 359: 'The recipients of this greeting are . . . distinguished by this designation from those who are disloyal to Paul and his gospel'; Saarinen 196: 'the group of orthodox Pauline Christians is meant.' Mounce 456（cf. 459）認為，'Hidden in v 14 [οἱ ἡμέτεροι] and v 15 [ἐν πίστει] is a final warning that not all the Cretans who call themselves Christian are truly Christian.' 參註 12（上面 471）。

8.2 最後的祝福（三 15c）

三 **15c** 願恩惠與你們眾人同在！

你們這複數第二人稱代名詞，在全書僅在此最後一節出現，指提多和克里特教會的信徒。每一封保羅書信都有信末的「恩典的祝福」，而祝福的對象幾乎全是複數的你們（惟一的例外是弗六 24）。[1] 有認為這裏的你們眾人不必表示保羅在上文是對整個克里特教會說話，而只是表示，保羅不但祝福收信人提多，也祝福信上所提到、保羅要提多牧養的那個教會。[2] 較可能的看法是，你們眾人「指出這祝福是給大家的，而且這整個書信是意欲寫給大家的，而……不是只給弟鐸，而是給全教會的。」[3]

這裏沒有指明恩惠的來源；[4] 這現象另見於四封保羅書信（弗六 24；西四 18；提前六 21；提後四 22）。在其餘八封保羅書信的信末祝福中，皆指明恩惠的來源是主耶穌（林前十六 23，呂譯、思高、現修、新普）、我們的主耶穌（羅十六 20，現修）、主耶穌基督（林後十三 13；腓四 23；門 25 節）或我們〔的〕主耶穌基督（加六 18〔思高、現修〕；帖前五 28；帖後三 18〔思高、現修〕）。[5]《當代福音》作願主恩常偕，

---

1 羅十六 20（十六 24 並不是原來的〔參《羅》4.803-6〕）；林前十六 23；林後十三 13；加六 18；腓四 23；西四 18；帖前五 28；帖後三 18；提前六 21；提後四 22；多三 15；門 25 節。在弗六 14，祝福的對象是複數第三人稱的所有……愛我們主耶穌基督的人。

2 Van Neste, 'Structure' 123. Aune 475*b* 則認為，'this may be an early universalizing interpolation', 意即有人在作者(不是保羅)的原句(三 15b)之後加上這句(三 15c)，'so that communities are also addressed'.

3 Keegan II 105（Keegan I 66）。參導論第貳節第二段（上面 24-25）。

4 有古卷在 ἡ χάρις 之後加上 τοῦ κυρίου(主的)或 θοῦ θεοῦ(上帝的)；see *TextC* 586.

5 參三 7 註釋註 20 的圖表之「主格（2）」(上面 408)。

似乎是以「主耶穌基督」為本節恩惠的來源；[6] 不過，鑑於恩惠原文不久之前用來指上帝的恩典（三 7），[7] 再上一次也是指上帝救眾人的恩典（二 11），因此，將這裏的恩惠理解為上帝的恩惠（新普）似乎更為可取。[8]

願恩惠與你們眾人同在這句話的原文[9] 雖然並無動詞，但是這處採用補充祈願式語法的動詞[10]（從而得出這種翻譯）是正確的做法。[11]《現代中文譯本修訂版》將本句翻譯為願上帝賜恩典給你們大家！前一種翻譯（和修）保持了原句的重點（在恩惠），後一種（現修）則把重點轉移到上帝賜之上。其實，上帝的恩典（新普）和賜恩典的上帝（現修）不可分割，前者不能離開後者而單獨存在。以下的事實支持這個看法：（i）在帖撒羅尼迦後書三章 16 節，頭一句祝願賜平安的主……賜給你們平安，第二句祝願主與你們眾人同在；羅馬書十五章 33 節則祝願賜平安的上帝與你們眾人同在。這兩點都提示，賜平安的

6 See also Banker 119, 120*a*: 'our(inc) Lord Jesus Christ'. Quinn 270 則從卷首的問安推論，本節恩惠的來源是父上帝和我們的救主基督耶穌（一 4），重點在基督（參：提前一 14）。

7 參三 7 註釋註 20 之（1）= 上面 407-8。

8 See NLT: 'May God's grace be with you all.' See also Hendriksen 396 n.211: 'Literally "the grace," that is, the grace of God.'（**1**）弗六 24 的恩惠可能同樣指上帝的恩惠（新普；參現修：願上帝賜恩典；見《弗》1014、1018）。西四 18c（原文比多三 15c 只少了眾人一字）的恩惠則可能指基督的恩典（參《西・門》780-81）。（**2**）來十三 25 的信末祝福與多三 15c 完全相同，該節的恩惠可能也是指上帝的恩惠（新普；參現修：願上帝賜恩典給你們各位），因作者在上文多次提到神的恩典（新譯：二 9，十二 15）、上帝恩典的寶座和恩典（四 16，現修；原文並無「上帝的」，但這裏的寶座確是上帝的〔參《來》1.293〕），以及施恩的聖靈（十 29；聖靈是上帝恩典的媒介〔參《來》2.204〕）。

9 ἡ χάρις μετὰ πάντων ὑμῶν. 有古卷作 ἡ χάρις μετὰ τοῦ πνεύματός σου（恩惠與你的靈同在），另有在 μετὰ πάντων ὑμῶν 之後加上 καὶ μετὰ τοῦ πνεύματός σου（亦與你的靈同在）；兩者都是受了提後四 22（ὁ κύριος μετὰ τοῦ πνεύματός σου. ἡ χάρις μεθ' ὑμῶν = 願主與你的靈同在！願恩惠與你們同在！）的影響所致（*TextC* 586）。

10 εἴη (optative). See also KJV, NKJV, RSV, NAU, NIV, TNIV, NIV2011, NJB, ESV, *Paraphrase* 295 / NRSV: 'Grace be with you all / with all of you'; Marshall 349: 'we should supply some such word as εἴη or πληθυνθείη [be multiplied to].'

11 詳細的討論請參《羅》4.784-85；《西・門》781-82。*Pace* Bouwman 169: '*Grace is with you all*!'

主和賜平安的上帝不能與所賜的平安分割，後者不能離開前者而單獨存在。(**ii**) 在提摩太後書四章 22 節，頭一句願主與你的靈同在和第二句願恩惠與你們同在（除了單數的你和複數的你們）幾乎是同義平行；這同樣提示，願上帝的恩惠與你們眾人同在（多三 15c，新普）和願主與你們眾人同在（帖後三 16b）是可以交換使用的祝福語，這表示上帝（或主）是在祂所賜的恩典中，祂在所賜的恩典中賜下自己。[12]

但若是這樣，為甚麼保羅書信的末尾對教會的祝福總是以「願恩惠與你們同在」這方式出現，[13] 卻沒有一次用「願主與你們同在」這方式呢？[14] 筆者不知道準確的答案，但這現象至少提示兩點：**第一**，信末祝福對恩典的著重，與卷首問安對恩典的著重[15] 同出一轍，前後

---

12 See W. Grundmann, *TDNT* 7.778;《腓》507。

13 (1) 願 恩惠與你們 同在（西四 18c；提前六 21b；提後四 22b）
願 恩惠與你們眾人同在（多三 15c）
(2) 願 主耶穌 的恩 與你們 同在（林前十六 23，呂譯）
願我們 主耶穌基督的恩 與你們 同在（羅十六 20b）
願我們的主耶穌基督的恩惠與你們 同在（帖前五 28）
願我們 主耶穌基督的恩惠與你們眾人同在（帖後三 18）
願 主耶穌基督的恩 與你們的靈同在（腓四 23；門 25 節）
願我們 主耶穌基督的恩 與你們的靈同在（加六 18）
(3) 願主耶穌基督的恩惠、上帝的慈愛，以及聖靈的相交，與你們眾人同在（林後十三 13，新普）
(4)「願（上帝的）恩典與所有愛我們主耶穌基督的人同在，恩典連同不朽」（弗六 24；參《弗》1015-18）。這祝福語基本上是 (2) 的形式，只是祝福的領受者以第三人稱表達（所有……愛我們主耶穌基督的人），且在末尾鬆散地加上「連同不朽」。

14 提後四 22 含有雙重祝福：願主與你〔提摩太〕的靈同在！願恩惠與你們〔眾信徒〕同在！留意「願主與你同在」這方式只是用於提摩太；對教會的祝福仍是願恩惠與你們同在！

15 (1) 願恩惠、平安 歸給你們（帖前一 1b）
(2) 願恩惠、平安從我們的父上帝 歸給你們（西一 2b）
(3) 願恩惠、平安從我們的父上帝和／並主耶穌基督歸給你們（羅一 7b；林後一 2；加一 3；弗一 2；腓一 2；帖後一 2；門 3 節／林前一 3）
(4) 願恩惠、憐憫、平安從父上帝和我們 主基督耶穌歸給你（提前一 2b；提後一 2b）
願恩惠、 平安從父上帝和我們的救主基督耶穌歸給你（多一 4b）

呼應。**第二**，保羅在信末不說「願主／上帝與你們同在」，而總是說「願恩典與你們同在」（弗六 24：「愛主的人」代替「你們」），彷彿要提醒信徒，在信徒與上帝（和／或與基督）的關係中，最重要和最顯著的一點就是，上帝是賜恩者，我們是受惠者。第二點可擴充如下：**(1)** 對保羅而言，信徒得以脫離罪惡歸向上帝，完全是由於恩典：保羅用那導致生命的豐盛恩典（羅五 15、17、20～21）來描寫信徒的被召（加一 6）、得救（弗二 5、8；提後一 9；多二 11）、[16] 救贖（弗一 7）、[17] 稱義（羅三 24；多三 7）等事實。**(2)** 在保羅看來，信徒的生命是被恩典包圍、被恩典推動的：他們站立在恩典中（羅五 2）；他們能夠慷慨捐輸，是上帝的恩典運行的結果（林後八 1）。**(3)** 保羅自己是上述「第二點」最完美的示範：舉例說，他以恩典來描述自己的事奉：他蒙上帝的恩典所召（加一 15），特別要在外邦人中傳揚基督的豐富（弗三 2、8）；他憑著所賜給他的恩典說話（羅十二 3）；他的一切都是上帝的恩典所帶來的結果（林前十五 10；提前一 14）；他一生的整個志向，就是要完成〔他〕從主耶穌所領受的職分，為上帝恩典的福音作見證（徒二十 24）。事實上，上帝的恩典這概念滲透了保羅的整個思想；難怪保羅是解釋及推薦上帝恩典的最卓越的新約作者。[18]

---

16 原文依次用動詞 σῴζω（頭三節）和形容詞 σωτήριος（後一節）。

17 原文用名詞 ἀπολύτρωσις.

18 名詞 **χάρις** 在新約一共出現 155 次（羅十六 24 不屬原著，因此不算在內），有 100 次（64.5%）在保羅書信裏，尤以羅（24 次）、林前後（10、18 次）和弗（12 次）（合共 64 次 = 64%）為最多，儘管並非每一次的意思都是神學意義的「恩典」；例如，這字在西四 6 的意思就是世俗意義的「美麗、可愛」（參《西・門》714-15）。See BDAG 1979*a*-81*a* (s.v.);《新希》354*a*（s.v.）。

參考書目

說明

1. 中文按楷體、英文按黑體部分引述。(若條目只有一字,不用黑體。若只有二至四字,則按情況或不用黑體,或按其中的一或二個黑體字引述。)
2. 同一作者的作品按出版日期排列;但若超過五項則按黑體部分的英文字母次序排列。
3. 在不會引起混淆的情形下,同一姓氏的不同作者只由所屬的條目自然區別。
4. 除了極少數的例外,所有書名的副題從略。
5. 為了節省篇幅,除了直接論及提多書的條目之外,本書目並不包括聖經辭典或百科全書內的文章,因其數目甚多;此等文章以「作者、辭典名稱、頁碼/卷數及頁碼」之形式引述(例如:A. B. Luter, Jr., *DPL* 869*a* / A. Weiser, *EDNT* 1.352*b*)。另見本書開首的簡寫表。

甲部:中文書刊(按姓氏之英文次序排列)

卡森(D. A. Carson)、穆爾(Douglas J. Moo):〈新約書信〉、〈教牧書信〉,《21 世紀新約導論》(香港:天道書樓,2007)309-331,539-572

張略(Cheung):《雅各書註釋》(聖經研究叢書;香港:基道出版社,2008)

馮蔭坤（Fung）：〈因信稱義、作神兒女與領受聖靈——從加拉太書三至四章看這三者的關係〉，《中國神學研究院期刊》3（1987 年 7 月）105-107[1]

李耀坤（Lee）：《至理至誠——如此加爾文》（中國神學研究院・普及神學叢書；香港：福音證主協會，2016）

梁薇（Leung）：〈聖經詮釋方向〉，載林榮洪、黎惠康合編：《守望新紀元》（新世紀講座文集；多倫多：天道神學院戴德生華人事工中心，2001）55-66[2]

盧玉音（Lo）：《小先知書》（聖經釋讀；香港：中國基督教播道會文字部，2014）

Marshall, I. Howard,〈提多書（Titus, Book of）〉，載《神學釋經詞典》（香港：漢語聖經協會，2014）*762b-765a*[3]

奧斯邦（Grant R. Osborne）著，劉良淑、李永明譯：《21 世紀基督教釋經學》（台北：校園書房出版社，2012 年 9 月增訂初版）[4]

鮑維均（Pao）著：《路加福音（卷上）》（天道聖經註釋；香港：天道書樓，2008）

辛惠蘭（Sun）：〈從命？抗命？——從新約聖經看順服掌權者〉，載雷競業、辛惠蘭編：《迎向政治的呼召》（香港：香港基督徒學生福音團契，2017）129-150

---

1 這是乙部 Fung, 'Sonship' 一文（見下面 487）的中文撮要，為時任執行編輯吳羅瑜女士所寫。（吳羅瑜博士現為美國基督工人神學院兼任資深教授〔Adjunct Senior Professor〕。）

2 英文版本見乙部之 Lai, 'Hermeneutical Prospects'（下面 492）。

3 這是乙部 Marshall, 'Book of Titus'（下面 494）之中譯。

4 英文原著見乙部之 Osborne（下面 497）。

施賴納（Thomas R. Schreiner）著，石彩燕、麥啟新譯：《詮釋保羅書信》（新約詮釋指南；香港：天道書樓，2000）[5]

黃錫木（Wong）：〈語言學、釋經、譯經〉，《中國神學研究院期刊》9（1990）71-104〔英文撮要 105-108〕

薛霞霞（Xue）：〈不可不知的上文下理——再思羅馬書十三章 1 至 7 節〉，載雷競業、辛惠蘭編：《迎向政治的呼召》（香港：香港基督徒學生福音團契，2017）061-080

乙部：外文書刊

A

Achtemeier, Paul J., Joel B. Green, & Marianne Meye Thompson, *Introducing the New Testament* (Grand Rapids, MI / Cambridge, U.K.: Eerdmans, 2001) [cited as **Achtemeier－Green－Thompson, *INT***] 447-464 [esp. 459-461]

Aitken, Ellen Bradshaw, '**Fragments**: A Sermon for the Feast of Saints Timothy and Titus', *Sewanee Theological Review* 50.1 (2006) 166-170

Akin, Daniel L., 'The **Mystery** of Godliness Is Great: Christology in the Pastoral Epistles', in Köstenberger－Wilder [2010] 137-152

Aune, David E., 'The **Pastoral Letters**: 1 and 2 Timothy and Titus', in David E. Aune (ed.), *The Blackwell Companion to the New Testament* (Chichester, West Sussex, U.K.: Wiley-Blackwell, 2010) 551-569

5　英文原著見乙部之 Schreiner, *Interpreting*（下面 500）。

B

Bailey, Mark L., 'A **Theology** of Paul's Pastoral Epistles', in Roy B. Zuck & Darrell L. Bock (ed.), *A Biblical Theology of the New Testament* (Chicago: Moody, 1994) 333-367

Barclay, John M. G., 'There is Neither Old Nor Young? Early Christianity and Ancient Ideologies of **Age**', *NTS* 53.2 (2007) 225-241

Barrett, C. K., Review of Collins [2002], *JTS* 55.2 (2004) 655-656

Bassler, Jouette M., 'A Plethora of **Epiphanies**: Christology in the Pastoral Letters', *Princeton Seminary Bulletin* NS 17.3 (1996) 310-325

----------, 'Epiphany **Christology** in the Pastoral Letters: Another Look', in Calvin J. Roetzel *FS* [2002] 194-214

----------, Review of Towner III [2006], *CBQ* 69.3 (2007) 598-599

Bauckham, Richard J., ***Jude**, 2 Peter* (WBC 50; Waco: Word, 1983)

Beale, G. K., *A New Testament Biblical **Theology*** (Grand Rapids: Baker Academic, 2011)

Belleville, Linda L., '**Christology**, the Pastoral Epistles, and Commentaries', in Grant R. Osborne *FS* [2013] 317-336

----------, 'Christology, Greco-Roman Religious **Piety**, and the Pseudonymity of the Pastoral Letters', in Stanley E. Porter & Gregory P. Fewster (ed.), *Paul and Pseudepigraphy* (Leiden: Brill, 2013) 221-243

Best, Ernst, 'Spiritual **Sacrifice**: General Priesthood in the New Testament', *Int* 14.3 (1960) 273-299

Blomberg, Craig L., '**Titus**: A Manual on Church Order', *From Pentecost to Patmos* (Nashville: B&H Academic, 2006) 351-357

Bockmuehl, Klaus, '"to live soberly, righteously, and godly in the present age." A **Meditation** on Titus 2:12', *Crux* 21.4 (1985) 2-5

Bowman Jr., Robert M., '**Jesus Christ**, God Manifest: Titus 2:13 Revisited', *JETS* 51.4 (2008) 733-752

Brauch, Manfred T., '**Titus**', in Walter C. Kaiser Jr., Peter H. Davids, F. F. Bruce, Manfred T. Brauch, *Hard Sayings of the Bible* (Downers Grove: IVP, 1996) 675*a*-676*b*

Brindle, Wayne A., '**Titus**', in Elmer L. Towns & Ben Gutierrez (ed.), *The Essence of the New Testament* (Nashville: B&H Academic, 2012) 247-254

Bruce, F. F., *The **Acts** of the Apostles* (2nd ed.; London: Tyndale, 1965 [1952])

----------, *The **Book of** the **Acts*** (NICNT; rev. ed.; Grand Rapids: Eerdmans,1988)

Burkett, Delbert, *An Introduction to the New Testament and the Origins of Christianity* [cited as ***INT***] (Cambridge and New York: CUP, 2002) 436-445

C

Campbell, R. Alastair, 'Identifying the Faithful **Sayings** in the Pastoral Epistles', *JSNT* 54 (1994) 73-86

Carson, D. A., Douglas J. Moo, and Leon Morris, *An Introduction to the New Testament* [cited as **Carson – Moo – Morris, *INT***] (Leicester, England: Apollos, 1992) 359-385

Carter, Warren, & Amy-Jill Levine [cited as **Carter—Levine**], 'The **Pastorals**: 1 and 2 Timothy, Titus', *The New Testament* (Nashville: Abingdon, 2013) 238-254

Clark, David J., 'Discourse **Structure** in Titus', *BibTr* 53.1 (2002) 101-117

Clarke, W. K. Lowther, *New Testament* ***Problems*** (London: SPCK, 1929)

Classen, Carl Joachim, 'A Rhetorical Reading of the Epistle to **Titus**', in Stanley E. Porter & Thomas H. Olbricht (ed.), *The Rhetorical Analysis of Scripture* (JSNTSS 146; Sheffield: SAP, 1997) 427-444

----------, 'A Rhetorical Reading of the **Epistle to Titus**', *Rhetorical Criticism of the New Testament* (Boston: Brill Academic, 2002) 45-67 [A revised version of the previous entry]

Collins, Raymond F., 'The **Theology** of the Epistle to Titus', *Ephemerides Theologicae Lovanienses* 76.1 (2000) 56-72

Conzelmann, Hans, & Andreas Lindemann, *Interpreting the New Testament* (E.T.; Peabody: Hendrickson, 1988) [cited as **Conzelmann—Lindemann,** ***INT***] 209-213

Couser, Greg A., Review of Collins [2002], *JETS* 46.3 (2003) 562-564

----------, 'The Sovereign **Savior** of 1 and 2 Timothy and Titus', in Köstenberger—Wilder [2010] 105-136

D

D'Angelo, Mary Rose, '*Εὐσέβεια*: Roman Imperial **Family Values** and the Sexual Politics of 4 Maccabees and the Pastorals', *BibInt* 11.2 (2003) 139-165

Denton, David R., 'The Biblical Basis of **Hope**', *Themelios* NS 5/3 (1979-80) 19-27

deSilva, David A., *An Introduction to the New Testament* [cited as ***INT***] (Downers Grove, IL: IVP / Leicester, England: Apollo, 2004) 733-775

Duff, Jeremy, 'A Reconsideration of **Pseudepigraphy** in Early Christianity', *TynB* 50.2 (1999) 306-309

Dunn, James D. G., '**Anti-Semitism** in the Deutero-Pauline Literature', in Craig A. Evans and Donald A. Hagner (ed.), *Anti-Semitism and Early Christianity* (Minneapolis: Fortress, 1993) 151-165

----------, ***Baptism*** *in the Holy Spirit* (Studies in Biblical Theology 2/15; Naperville, IL: Alec r. Allenson Inc., 1970)

----------, 'Deutero-Pauline letters [*sic*]', in Morna D. Hooker *FS* [1996] 139-144 [esp. 140-143]

----------, ***Romans*** *9-16* (WBC 38B; Dallas: Word, 1988)

----------, '**Romans 13.1-7**—A Charter for Political Quietism?' *Ex Auditu* 2 (1986) 55-68

----------, 'The First and Second Letters to Timothy and the Letter to **Titus**', in *The New Interpreter's Dictionary New Testament Survey* (Nashville: Abingdon, 2005) 274-282 [= Dunn (2000) 775-786][6]

E

Edwards, J. Christopher, 'Reading the Ransom Logion in 1 Tim 2,6 and

6 Dunn 780 n.19 第二行的 '997-1084' 是 '977-984' 之誤；這錯誤複製於 Dunn, 'Titus' 281*a* n.19.

Titus 2,14 with Isa 42,6-7; 49,6-8', *Biblica* 90.2 (2009) 264-266

----------, 'The **Christology** of Titus 2:13 and 1 Timothy 2:5', *TynB* 62.1 (2011) 141-147

Ehrman, Bart D., 'In the Wake of the Apostle: The Deutero-Pauline and **Pastoral Epistles**', *The New Testament* (6th ed.; New York, OUP, 2016) 434-459 [esp. 449-459]

Ellis, E. Earle, 'The **Authorship** of the Pastorals: A Résumé and Assessment of Recent Trends', *Paul and His Recent Interpreters* (Grand Rapids: Eerdmans, 1961) 49-57

----------, '**Traditions** in the Pastoral Epistles', in Craig A. Evans and William F. Stinespring (ed.), *Early Jewish and Christian Exegesis: Studies in Memory of William Hugh Brownlee* (Atlanta, GA: Scholars, 1987), 237-253

----------, 'The **Pastorals** and Paul', *ExpT* 104.2 (1992) 45*a*-47*a*

----------, 'Pastoral Letters', *DPL* [1993] 658*b*-666*b*（=《辭典》953*a*-965*a*）

Emerson, Matthew Y., 'Paul's Eschatological **Outlook** in the Pastoral Epistles', *CTR* n.s. 12.2 (2015) 83-98

F

Faber, Riemer, '"Evil Beasts, Lazy Gluttons": A Neglected Theme in the Epistle to **Titus**', *WTJ* 67.1 (2005) 135-145

Fanning, Buist M., III, **Review of Marshall [1999]** and Liefeld [1999], *BS* 159/634 (2002) 251-252

Fatum, Lone, '**Christ** Domesticated: The Household Theology of the Pastorals as Political Strategy', in Jostein Ådna (ed.), *The*

Formation of the Early Church (WUNT 183; Tübingen: Mohr Siebeck, 2005) 175-207

Fee, Gordon D., '**Reflections** on Church Order in the Pastoral Epistles', *JETS* 28.2 (1985) 141-151[7]

----------, *The* ***First*** *Epistle to the* ***Corinthians*** (NICNT; Grand Rapids: Eerdmans, 1987)

----------, *God's Empowering* ***Presence*** (Peabody: Hendrickson, 1999 [1994]) [esp. 776-784]

----------, *Pauline* ***Christology*** (Peabody: Hendrickson, 2007) [esp. 437-449]

Fellows, Richard G., 'Was **Titus** Timothy?' *JSNT* No. 81 (2001) 33-58

Fiore, Benjamin, 'The **Pastoral Epistles** in the Light of Philodemus' "On Frank Criticism"', in John T. Fitzgerald, Dirk Obbink, Gleen S. Holland (ed.), *Philodemus and the New Testament World* (NovTSup 111; Leiden: Brill, 2004) 271-293

Fitzmyer, Joseph A., 'The Structured **Ministry** of the Church in the Pastoral Epistles', *CBQ* 66.4 (2004) 582-596

Frisius, Mark A., ***Tertullian's Use*** *of the Pastoral Epistles, Hebrews, James, 1 and 2 Peter, and Jude* (Studies in Biblical Literature 143; New York: Peter Lang, 2011)

Fung, Ronald Y. K., '**Charismatic** versus Organized Ministry? An Examination of an Alleged Antithesis', *EQ* 52.4 (1980) 195-214

----------, 'Justification, **Sonship** and the Gift of the Spirit: Their Mutual Relationships as Seen in Galatians 3-4', *CGST Journal* No. 3 (July 1987) 73-104

7 Reprinted in Fee, *Listening to the Spirit in the Text* (Grand Rapids: Eerdmans / Vancouver: Regent College, 2000) 147-162.

G

Gannett, M. Lynn, 'Older Women / Younger Women: The Implementation of **Titus 2**', in Kenneth O. Gangel & James C. Wilhoit (ed.), *The Christian Educator's Handbook on Family Life Education* (Grand Rapids: Baker Books, 1996) 83-95

Gill, David W. J., 'A **Saviour** for the Cities of Crete: The Roman Background to the Epistle to Titus', in Bruce W. Winter *FS* [2004] 220-230

Glasscock, Ed, 'The Husband of One Wife **Requirement** in 1 Timothy 3:2', *BS* 140/559 (1983) 244-258

Goulder, Michael, 'The Pastor's **Wolves**: Jewish Christian Visionaries Behind the Pastoral Epistles', *NovT* 38.3 (1996) 242-256

Gray, Patrick, 'The Liar Paradox and the Letter to **Titus**', *CBQ* 69.2 (2007) 302-314

Green, Michael, ***2 Peter** and Jude* (TNTC; London: IVP, 1974 [1968])

Gunther, John J., ***Paul**: Messenger and Exile* (Valley Forge, PA: Judson, 1972)

Guthrie, Donald, *New Testament **Theology*** (Leicester, England / Downers Grove, IL: IVP, 1981)

----------, 'Pastoral Epistles', *ISBE* 3[1986].679*b*-687*a*

----------, *New Testament Introduction* [cited as ***NTI***] (4th rev. ed.; Leicester, England: Apollos / Downer Grove, IL: IVP, 1990)

H

Haenchen, Ernst, *The **Acts** of the Apostles* (E.T.; Oxford: Basil

Blackwell, 1971)

Hagner, Donald A., 'The **New Testament** and Criticism: Looking to the Twenty-first Century', *Theology, News & Notes* 45.2 (1998) 7-10, 23

----------, '**Titus** as a Pauline Letter', *Society of Biblical Literature 1998 Seminar Papers*, Part 2（No. 7; Atlanta, GA: Scholars, 1998）546-558

----------, *The **New Testament*** (Grand Rapids: Baker Academic, 2012) [esp. 614-642]

Hanson, Anthony Tyrell, 'The **Domestication of Paul**: A Study in the Development of Early Christian Doctrine', *BJRL* 63.2 (1981) 402-418

Harris, Murray J., 'Titus 2:13 and the **Deity** of Christ', in F. F. Bruce *FS*(2) [1980] 262-277

----------, ***Colossians** & Philemon* (Exegetical Guide to the Greek New Testament; Grand Rapids: Eerdmans, 1995 [1991])

----------, 'Our Great God and **Savior** (Titus 2:13), *Jesus as God* (Grand Rapids: Baker, 1992) 173-185

----------, 'A Brief **Response** to: "The Christology of Titus 2:13 and 1 Timothy 2:5" by J. Christopher Edwards', *TynB* 62.1 (2011) 149-150

Harrison, Everett F., *Introduction to the New Testament* [cited as ***INT***] (rev. ed.; Grand Rapids: Eerdmans, 1971 [1964]) 347-366

Haykin, Michael A. G., 'The Fading Vision? The **Spirit** and Freedom in the Pastoral Epistles', *EQ* 57.4 (1985) 291-305

Hempelmann, L. Dean, Review of Oden [1989], *Concordia Theological Quarterly* 68.2 (2004) 160-161

Herzer, Jens, 'Rearranging the "House of God": A New **Perspective** on the Pastoral Epistles', in Pieter Willem van der Horst *FS* [2008] 547-566

Himes, Paul, 'The **Use** of the Aorist Imperative in the Pastoral Epistles', *FilNeot* 23 (2010) 73-92

Ho, Chiao Ek, '**Mission** in the Pastoral Epistles', in Köstenberger—Wilder [2010] 241-267

Hodge, Charles, *A Commentary on **Romans*** (London: Banner of Truth, 1972)

Holman, Charles L., 'Titus 3.5-6: A **Window** on Worldwide Pentecost', *JPT* = *Journal of Pentecostal Theology* 4 (1996) 53-62

Hopkins, Anthony D., Review of Lea—Griffin [1992], *Perspectives in Religious Studies* 21.3 (1994) 261-263

Horrell, David, 'Converging **Ideologies**: Berger and Luckman and the Pastoral Epistles', in Stanley E. Porter & Craig A. Evans (ed.), *New Testament Interpretation and Methods* (Sheffield: SAP, 1997) 102-120 [Reprinted from *JSNT* 50 (1993) 85-103]

Howell Jr., Don N., 'God-Christ **Interchange** in Paul: Impressive Testimony to the Deity of Jesus', *JETS* 36.4 (1993) 467-479

Hultgren, Arland J., 'The **Pastoral Epistles**', in James D. G. Dunn (ed.), *The Cambridge Companion to St Paul* (Cambridge and New York: CUP, 2003) 141-155

Hunter, David G., '"A Man of One Wife": Patristic Interpretations of 1 Timothy 3:2, 3:12, and **Titus 1:6** and the Making of Christian Priesthood', *ASE* [*Annali di storia dell'esegesi*] 32.2 (2015) 333-352

J

Johnson, Luke Timothy, 'Pastoral Letters: 1 Timothy, 2 Timothy, **Titus**', *The Writings of the New Testament* (3rd ed.; Minneapolis: Fortress, 2010) 375-401 [esp. 395-398]

K

Kaestli, Jean-Daniel, '**Luke-Acts** and the Pastoral Epistles: The Thesis of a Common Authorship', in C. M. Tuckett (ed.), *Luke's Literary Achievement* (JSNTSS 116; Sheffield: SAP, 1995)110-126

Karris, Robert J., 'The Background and Significance of the **Polemic** of the Pastoral Epistles', *JBL* 92.4 (1973) 549-564

----------, *A **Symphony** of New Testament Hymns* (Collegeville: Liturgical, 1996)[8] [esp. 127-141]

Kee, Howard Clark, 'The **Pastoral Letters**: Structure and Order in the Churches', *The Beginnings of Christianity* (New York: TTC, 2005) 263-274, 334-336 [endnotes]

Kelly, J. N. D., *The Epistles of **Peter** and of Jude* (BNTC; London: Black, 1990 [1969])

Kidd, Reggie M., '**Titus** as *Apologia*: Grace for Liars, Beasts, and Bellies', *HBT* 21.2 (1999) 185-209

Kim, Hong Bom, 'The **Interpretation** of μάλιστα in 1 Timothy 5:17', *NovT* 46.4 (2004) 360-368

Klinker-De Klerck, Myriam, 'The **Pastoral Epistles**: authentic Pauline writings', *EurJTh* 17.2 (2008) 101-108

8 Review: Frederick W. Danker, *CBQ* 60.1 (1998) 161-162.

Koskenniemi, Erkki, 'The Famous **Liar** and the Apostolic Truth', *FilNeot* 24 (2011) 59-69

Köstenberger, Andreas J., 'Hermeneutical and Exegetical **Challenges** in Interpreting the Pastoral Epistles', *The Southern Baptist Journal of Theology* 7.3 (2003) 4-17

----------, 'Hermeneutical and Exegetical Challenges in Interpreting the **Pastoral Epistles**', in Köstenberger – Wilder [2010] 1-27

Köstenberger, Andreas J., L. Scott Kellum, & Charles L. Quarles [cited as **Köstenberger – Kellum – Quarles**], 'The Pastoral Epistles: 1-2 Timothy, **Titus**', *The Lion and the Lamb* (Nashville: B&H Academic, 2012) 266-285

Krentz, Edgar, Review of Taylor [1993], *CurTM* 21.4 (1994) 298-299

Kümmel, Werner Georg, *Introduction to the New Testament* [cited as ***INT***] (rev. ed.; London: SCM, 1982 [1975]) 366-387

L

Ladd, George Eldon, *A **Theology** of the New Testament* (Grand Rapids: Eerdmans, 1974)

----------, *A Commentary on the **Revelation** of John* (Grand Rapids: Eerdmans, 1978 [1972])

Lai, Barbara M. Leung, 'Hermeneutical Prospects', in Wing-hung Lam & Warren Lai (ed.), *Beacon For the New Century* (The Millenium Lecture Symposium; Toronto: The Hudson Taylor Center for Chinese Ministries, Tyndale College and Seminary, 2001)

141-154[9]

Lamp, Jeffrey S., '"Appearance" Language in **Titus**: A Semantics of Holiness', *Weslyan Theological Journal* 40.1 (2005) 93-109

Lane, William L., *The Gospel of **Mark*** (The New London Commentary on the New Testament; London: Marshall, Morgan & Scott, 1974)

Lappenga, Benjamin J., '"Zealous for Good Works": The Polemical **Repercussions** of the Word ζηλωτής in Titus 2:14', *CBQ* 75.4 (2013) 704-718

Lea, Thomas D., '**Pseudonymity** and the New Testament', in David Alan Black & David S. Dockery (ed.), *New Testament Criticism & Interpretation* (Grand Rapids: Zondervan, 1991) 535-559

Lee, G. M., '**Epimenides** in the Epistle to Titus (I 12)', *NovT* 22.1 (1980) 96

Levinsohn, Stephen H., 'Some **Constraints** on Discourse Development in the Pastoral Epistles', in *Discourse Analysis* [1999] 316-333

----------, ***Discourse Features** of New Testament Greek* (2nd ed.; Dallas, TX: Summer Institute of Linguistics, 2000)

Lightfoot, J. B., 'Additional Note on the **Heresy** Combated in the Pastoral Epistles', *Biblical Essays* (Peabody, MA: Hendrickson, 1994 reprint [1893, 1940]) 411-418

M

MacDonald, Margaret Y., *The **Pauline Churches*** (SNTSMS 60; Cambridge: CUP, 1988)

Madsen II, Thorvald B., 'The **Ethics** of the Pastoral Epistles', in

9 中文版本見甲部之梁薇：〈詮釋方向〉（上面 480）。

Köstenberger－Wilder [2010] 219-240

Malherbe, Abraham J., ***Social Aspects*** *of Early Christianity* (2nd ed.; Philadelphia: Fortress, 1983)

----------, '**Medical Imagery** in the Pastoral Epistles', *Paul and the Popular Philosophers* (Minneapolis: Fortress, 1989) 121-136

----------, 'Paulus Senex', *RestQ* 36.4 (1994) 197-207

----------, '**Paraenesis** in the Epistle to Titus', in James Starr & Troels Engberg-Pedersen (ed.), *Early Christian Paraenesis in Context* (BZNW 125; Berlin and New York: de Gruyter, 2004) 297-317

----------, '"Christ Jesus Came into the World to Save Sinners": **Soteriology** in the Pastoral Epistles', in Jan G. van der Watt (ed.), *Salvation in the New Testament* (NovTSup 121; Leiden and Boston: Brill 2005) 331-358

Mappes, David A., 'Moral **Virtues** Associated with Eldership', *BS* 160/638 (2003) 202-218

Marshall, I. Howard, 'Titus, Book of' [cited as '**Book of Titus**'], *DTIB* [2005] 806*b*-809*b*[10]

----------, 'The **Christology** of Acts and the Pastoral Epistles', in Michael D. Goulder *FS* [1994] 167-182

----------, '**Congregation** and Ministry in the Pastoral Epistles', in Richard N. Longenecker (ed.), *Community Formation in the Early Church and in the Church Today* (Peabody: Hendrickson, 2002) 105-125

----------, 'The **Holy Spirit** in the Pastoral Epistles and the Apostolic Fathers', in James D. G. Dunn *FS*(1) [2004] 257-269

10 中譯見甲部之 Marshall,〈提多書（Titus, Book of)〉（上面 480）。

----------, 'The Pastoral Epistles in **Recent Study**', in Köstenberger－Wilder [2010] 268-324

----------, Review of Wilson [1979], *JSNT* 10 (1981) 69-74

----------, '**Salvation**, Grace and Works in the Later Writings in the Pauline Corpus', *NTS* 42.3 (1996) 339-358

----------, *New Testament* ***Theology*** (Downers Grove: IVP, 2004)

----------, 'The Letters to **Timothy and Titus**', in I. Howard Marshall, Stephen Travis & Ian Paul, *Exploring the New Testament. Vol. 2: A Guide to the Letters & Revelation* (2nd ed.; Downers Grove: IVP Academic, 2011) 183-200

----------, 'Titus' in *TINT* [2008] 175-181

Marshall, John W., '"I Left You in Crete": Narrative **Deception** and Social Hierarchy in the Letter to Titus', *JBL* 127.4 (2008) 781-803

Martin, Ralph P., *New Testament* ***Foundations****. Vol. 2: Acts-Revelation* (Exeter: Paternoster, 1978) 298-307

Martin, Ralph P., & Julie L. Wu [cited as **Martin－Wu**], 'Galatians', in Clinton E. Arnold (ed.), *Zondervan Illustrated Bible Backgrounds Commentary*, Vol. 3 (Grand Rapids: Zondervan, 2002) 264-298

Martin, Troy W., 'Entextualized and Implied Rhetorical Situations: The Case of 1 Timothy and **Titus**', *Biblical Research* 45 (2000) 5-24

Massey, Preston T., '**Cicero**, the Pastoral Epistles, and the Issue of Pseudonymity', *RestQ* 56.2 (2014) 65-84

Matera, Frank J., 'Reliable **Moral Guides**: The Pastoral Epistles', *New Testament Ethics* (Louisville: WJK, 1996) 229-247, 299-301 [endnotes]

----------, 'The **Pastoral Epistles**', *New Testament Christology* (Louisville: WJK, 1999) 158-172, 279-282 [endnotes]

McDonald, Lee Martin, & Stanley E. Porter [cited as **McDonald－Porter**], 'The **Pastoral Epistles**', *Early Christianity and its Sacred Literature* (Peabody, MA 2000) 488*a*-498*b*

Meade, David G., '**Pseudonymity** in the New Testament', *Pseudonymity and Canon* (Grand Rapids: Eerdmans, 1987) 103-193 [esp. 118-139]

Merkle, Benjamin L., *The **Elder** and Overseer* (Studies in Biblical Literature 57; New York: Peter Lang, 2003) [esp. 121-161]

----------, '**Ecclesiology** in the Pastoral Epistles', in Köstenberger－Wilder [2010] 173-198

Merz, Annette, 'The Fictitious **Self-Exposition** of Paul: How Might Intertextual Theory Suggest a Reformulation of the Hermeneutics of Pseudepigraphy?' [Translated by Brian McNeil], in Thomas L. Brodie, Dennis R. MacDonald & Stanley E. Porter (ed.), *The Intertextuality of the Epistles* (New Testament Monographs 16; Sheffield: Sheffield Phoenix, 2006) 113-132

Metzger, Bruce M., 'A **Reconsideration** of Certain Arguments Against the Pauline Authorship of the Pastoral Epistles', *ExpT* 70.3 (1958) 91-94

Mitchell, Margaret M., 'New Testament **Envoys** in the Context of Greco-Roman Diplomatic and Epistolary Conventions: The Example of Timothy and Titus', *JBL* 111.4 (1992) 641-662

Mott, Stephen Charles, 'Greek **Ethics** and Christian Conversion: The Philonic Background of Titus ii 10-14 and iii 3-7', *NovT* 20.1

(1978) 22-48

Moule, C. F. D., 'The **Problem** of the Pastoral Epistles: A Reappraisal', *Essays in New Testament Interpretation* (Cambridge: CUP, 1982) 113-132 [first published in *BJRL* 47 (1965) 430-452]

Mounce, Robert H., *The Book of **Revelation*** (New London Commentaries; London: Marshall, Morgan & Scott, 1978 [first published in the NICNT series in 1977 by Eerdmans])

----------, 'Paul's Letter to **Titus**', *Dear Friends, This is Paul* (Eugene, OR: Cascade Books, 2016) 105-107

Munck, Johannes, *The **Acts** of the Apostles* (AB 31; Garden City: Doubleday, 1979 [1967])

Murphy-O'Connor, Jerome, '**2 Timothy** Contrasted with 1 Timothy and Titus', *RB* 98.3 (1991) 403-418

----------, 'Pastoral Epistles', *RB* 108.4 (2001) 630-635

N

Nardoni, Enrique, 'Introduction to the **Pastoral Epistles**', in *The International Bible Commentary*, ed. William R. Farmer et al. (Collegeville: Liturgical, 1998) 1730-1732

North, Stephen Richard, '***Presbuteroi** Christianoi*: Towards a Theory of Integrated Ministry', *TynB* 51.2 (2000) 317-320

O

Osborne, Grant R., *The Hermeneutical **Spiral*** (Downers Grove: IVP, 1991)[11]

11 中譯本見甲部之奧斯邦：《釋經學》（上面 480）。

P

Padgett, Alan, 'The Pauline Rationale for **Submission**: Biblical Feminism and the *hina* Clauses of Titus 2:1-10', *EQ* 59.1 (1987) 39-52

Page, Sydney, 'Marital **Expectations** of Church Leaders in the Pastoral Epistles', *JSNT* 50 (1993) 105-120

Pao, David W., 'Let No One Despise Your Youth: **Church** and the World in the Pastoral Epistles', *JETS* 57.4 (2014) 743-755

Pfleiderer, Otto, *Paulinism* (2 vols.; E.T.; 2nd ed.; London: Williams and Norgate, 1981)

Portefaix, Lilian, '"Good Citizenship" in the Household of God: **Women's Position** in the Pastorals Reconsidered in the Light of Roman Rule', in Amy-Jill Levine (ed., with Marianne Blickenstaff), *A Feminist Companion to the Deutero-Pauline Epistles* (London: TTCI, 2003) 147-158

Porter, Stanley E., 'Pauline Authorship and the Pastoral Epistles: **Implications** for Canon', *BBR* 5 (1995) 105-123[12]

----------, 'Pauline Authorship and the Pastoral Epistles: A **Response to R. W. Wall's Response**', *BBR* 6 (1996) 133-138

----------, 'Pauline **Chronology** and the Question of Pseudonymity of the Pastoral Epistles', in Stanley E. Porter & Gregory P. Fewster (ed.), *Paul and Pseudepigraphy* (Leiden: Brill, 2013) 65-88

----------, *Linguistic **Analysis** of the Greek New Testament* (Grand Rapids: Baker Academic, 2015)

12 See Wall, 'Response'（下面 503）。

Poythress, Vernon S., 'The **Meaning** of μάλιστα in 2 Timothy 4:13 and Related Verses', *JTS* 53.2 (2002) 523-532

R

Reicke, Bo, *Re-examining **Paul's Letters***, ed. David P. Moessner & Ingalisa Reicke (Harrisburg: TPI, 2001)

Richardson, Neil, '**Christ-Language** in the Deutero-Paulines', *Paul's Language about God* (JSNTSS 99; Sheffield: SAP, 1994) 330-334

Ridderbos, Herman, *Paul* (E.T.; Grand Rapids: Eerdmans, 1975)

Riesner, Rainer, '**Once More**: Luke-Acts and the Pastoral Epistles', in Sang-Won (Aaron) Son (ed.), *History and Exegesis* (E. Earle Ellis *FS*[2]; New York and London: TTC, 2006) 239-258

Robertson, A. T., *Word **Pictures** in the New Testament* (6 vols; 1930-33; reprinted Nashville: Broadman, no date)

Robertson, Michael Scott, 'Neophyte **Pastors**: Can Titus 1 Be Used to Justify Placing New Converts in the Office of Pastor?' *SWJT* 57.1 (2014) 77-86

Robinson, J. A. T., ***Redating** the New Testament* (London: SCM, 1976)

Rogerson, John, *The New **Atlas** of the Bible* (London: Macdonald, 1985)

Rowe, Galen O., 'Style', in Stanley E. Porter (ed.), *Handbook of Classical Rhetoric in the Hellenistic Period 330 B.C.-A.D. 400* (New York: Brill, 1997) 121-157

S

Saucy, Robert L., '**Husband** of One Wife', *BS* 131/523 (1974) 229-240

Schnelle, Udo, 'The **Pastoral Letters**', *The History and Theology of the New Testament Writings* (E.T.; London: SCM, 1998) 326-348

Schreiner, Thomas R., ***Interpreting** the Pauline Epistles* (Grand Rapids: Baker Academic, 1990)[13]

----------, '**Overseeing** and Serving the Church in the Pastoral and General Epistles', in Benjamin L. Merkle & Thomas R. Schreiner (ed.), *Shepherding God's Flock* (Grand Rapids: Kregel, 2014) 89-117 [esp. 89-112]

Scott, Jeff, 'The **Profit** of Our Purification: A Sermon on Titus 3:1-7 and Westminster Larger Catechism Q&A 167', *MAJT* = *Mid-America Journal of Theology* 24 (2013) 211-216

Sewakpo, Honore, 'An African's Perspective on Leadership in the Book of **Titus**', *IJOURELS* [*Ilorin Journal of Religious Studies*] 5.2 (2015) 1-22

Skeat, T. C., 'Especially the **Parchments**: A Note on 2 Timothy IV. 13', *JTS* n.s. 30.1 (1979) 173-177

Smedes, Lewis, 'The **Priority** of Grace', *Theology, News & Notes*, June 1973, 8, 9, 12

Smith, Kevin, & Arthur Song [cited as **Smith – Song**], 'Some Christological **Implications** in Titus 2:13', *Neotestamentica* 40.2 (2006) 284-294

Smith, Kevin Gary, 'The **Structure** of Titus: Criss-cross Chiasmus as Structural Marker', *Conspectus: The Journal of the South*

13 中譯本見甲部之施賴納：《詮釋》（上面 480）。

African Theological Seminary 3 (March 2007) 98-110

Stegemann, Wolfgang [David E. Orton, translator], 'Anti-Semitic and Racist **Prejudices** in Titus 1:10-16', in Mark G. Brett (ed.), *Ethnicity and the Bible* (Leiden: Brill, 1996) 271-294

Sterling, Gregory E., 'Hellenistic **Philosophy** and the New Testament', in Stanley E. Porter (ed.), *Handbook to Exegesis of the New Testament* (New Testament Tools and Studies 25; Leiden: Brill, 1997) 313-358

Strecker, Georg, '**Sound Doctrine**—The Pastoral Letters', *Theology of the New Testament* (E.T.; New York: W. de Gruyter / Louisville: WJK, 2000) 576-594

Streete, Gail Corrington, '***Askesis*** and Resistance in the Pastoral Letters', in Leif E. Vaage & Vincent L. Wimbush (ed.), *Asceticism and the New Testament* (New York: Routledge, 1999) 299-316

Sumney, Jerry L., *'Servants of Satan', 'False Brothers' and Other **Opponents** of Paul* (JSNTSS 188; Sheffield: SAP, 1999) [esp. 290-302]

T

Tamez, Elsa, '**Pastoral Epistles**', in Daniel Patte (ed.), *The Cambridge Dictionary of Christianity* (New York: CUP, 2010) 928*a*

Thatcher, Tom, 'The Relational **Matrix** of the Pastoral Epistles', *JETS* 38.1 (1995) 41-45

Thielman, Frank, '**Old Convictions** in New Settings: The Law of Moses in Paul's Later Letters', *Paul & the Law* (Downers Grove: IVP, 1994) 214-237 [esp. 230-237], 300-308 [endnotes]

Thiselton, Anthony C., 'The **Logical Role** of the Liar Paradox in Titus 1:12, 13: A Dissent from the Commentaries in the Light of Philosophical and Logical Analysis', *BibInt* 2.2 (1994) 207-223

Thornton, Dillon T., Review of Wall [2012], *JETS* 56.4 (2013) 882-884

Thurston, Bonnie Bowman, 'The Theology of **Titus**', *HBT* 21.2 (1999) 171-184

Tollefson, Kenneth D., '**Titus**: Epistle of Religious Revitalization', *Biblical Theology Bulletin* 30.4 (2000) 145-157

Tomlinson, F. Alan, 'The **Purpose** and Stewardship Theme within the Pastoral Epistles', in Köstenberger – Wilder [2010] 52-83

Towner, Philip H., 'Pauline Theology or Pauline Tradition in the Pastoral Epistles: The Question of **Method**', *TynB* 46.2 (1995) 287-314

----------, 'The **Pastoral Epistles**', *NDBT* [2000] 330*a*-336*b*

Trebilco, Paul, 'What Shall We Call Each Other? Part One: The Issue of **Self-designation** in the Pastoral Epistles', *TynB* 53.2 (2002) 239-258

----------, 'The **Significance** and Relevance of the Spirit in the Pastoral Epistles', in James D. G. Dunn *FS*(1) [2004] 241-256

V

Van Nes, Jermo, 'The **Problem** of the Pastoral Epistles: An Important Hypothesis Reconsidered', in Stanley E. Porter & Gregory P. Fewster (ed.), *Paul and Pseudepigraphy* (Leiden: Brill, 2013) 153-169

Van Neste, Ray, '**Structure** and Cohesion in Titus: Problems and Method', *BibTr* 53.1 (2002) 118-133

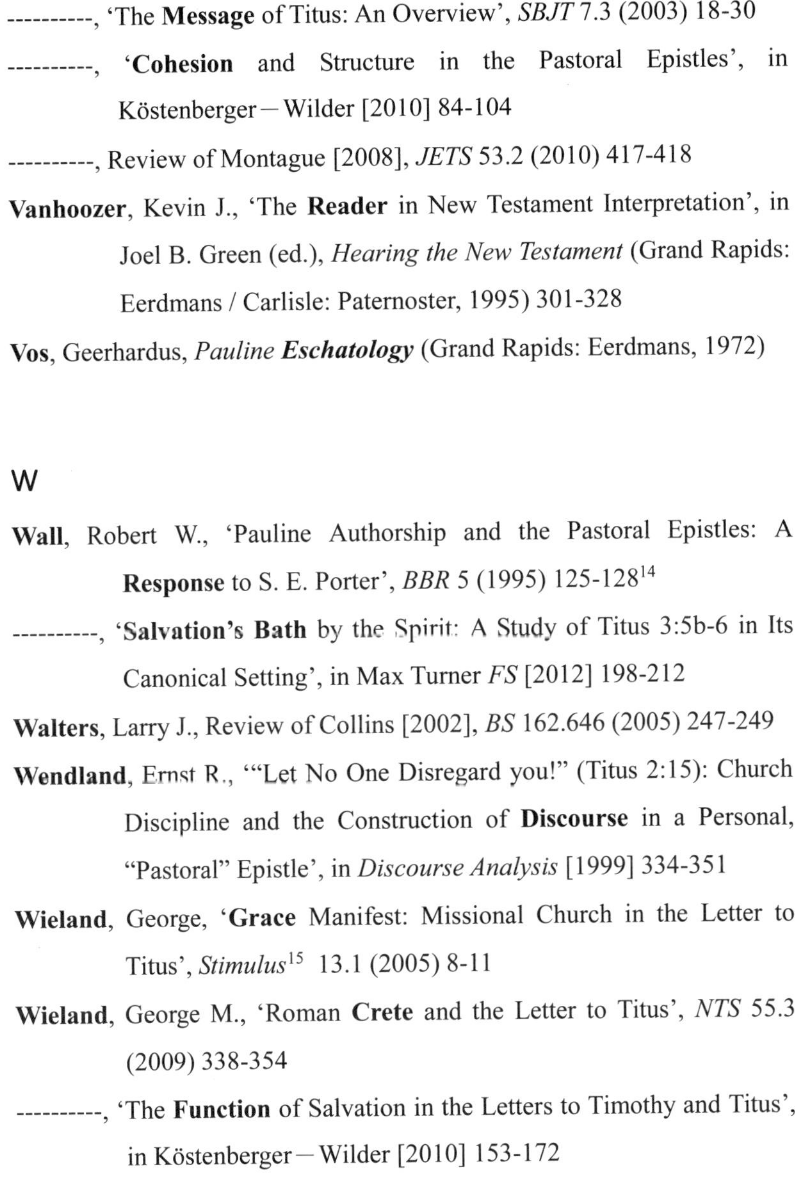

----------, 'The **Message** of Titus: An Overview', *SBJT* 7.3 (2003) 18-30

----------, '**Cohesion** and Structure in the Pastoral Epistles', in Köstenberger—Wilder [2010] 84-104

----------, Review of Montague [2008], *JETS* 53.2 (2010) 417-418

Vanhoozer, Kevin J., 'The **Reader** in New Testament Interpretation', in Joel B. Green (ed.), *Hearing the New Testament* (Grand Rapids: Eerdmans / Carlisle: Paternoster, 1995) 301-328

Vos, Geerhardus, *Pauline* ***Eschatology*** (Grand Rapids: Eerdmans, 1972)

W

Wall, Robert W., 'Pauline Authorship and the Pastoral Epistles: A **Response** to S. E. Porter', *BBR* 5 (1995) 125-128[14]

----------, '**Salvation's Bath** by the Spirit: A Study of Titus 3:5b-6 in Its Canonical Setting', in Max Turner *FS* [2012] 198-212

Walters, Larry J., Review of Collins [2002], *BS* 162.646 (2005) 247-249

Wendland, Ernst R., '"Let No One Disregard you!" (Titus 2:15): Church Discipline and the Construction of **Discourse** in a Personal, "Pastoral" Epistle', in *Discourse Analysis* [1999] 334-351

Wieland, George, '**Grace** Manifest: Missional Church in the Letter to Titus', *Stimulus*[15] 13.1 (2005) 8-11

Wieland, George M., 'Roman **Crete** and the Letter to Titus', *NTS* 55.3 (2009) 338-354

----------, 'The **Function** of Salvation in the Letters to Timothy and Titus', in Köstenberger—Wilder [2010] 153-172

14 See Porter, 'Response to R. W. Wall's Response'（上面 498）。

15 *The New Zealand Journal of Christian Thought & Practice*.

Wilder, Terry L., 'New Testament **Pseudonymity** and Deception', *TynB* 50.1 (1999) 156-158[16]

----------, ***Pseudonymity**, the New Testament, and Deception* (Lanham, MD: University Press of America, 2004)

----------, Review of Towner III [2006], *JETS* 51.3 (2008) 656-659

----------, 'Pseudonymity, the New Testament, and the **Pastoral Epistles**', in Köstenberger—Wilder [2010] 28-51

Williams, C. S. C., *The **Acts** of the Apostles* (BNTC; 2nd ed.; London: Adam & Charles Black, 1964 [1957])

Winter, Bruce W., ***Roman Wives**, Roman Widows* (Grand Rapids: Eerdmans, 2003)[17] [esp. 141-169]

Witherington III, Ben, *The Many Faces of the Christ: the **Christologies** of the New Testament and Beyond* (New York: Crossroad Publications, 1998)

----------, 'The **Pastoral Epistles** and the Problem of Pseudonymous Letters', *Invitation to the New Testament* (Oxford: OUP, 2013) 237-254

16 An abstract of the author's Ph.D. thesis (University of Aberdeen, 1988), which was subsequently published as *Pseudonymity, the New Testament, and Deception* (next entry).

17 Reviews: Edward Adams, *ExpT* 116.3 (**2004**) 95*b*-96*a*; Kathleen E. Corley, *Int* 58.3 (2004) 318; Kenneth D. Litwak, *The Covenant Quarterly* 63.1 (**2005**) 44-46; Shelly Matthews, *CBQ* 67.1 (2005) 162-163; Carl B. Smith II, *Journal of the American Oriental Society* 125.1 (2005) 152*a*-153*a*; Suzanne Dixson, *JTS* n.s. 56.2 (2005) 558-561; Christoph W. Stenschke, *Themelios* 30.2 (2005) 67-68; James R. Wicker, *SWJT* 47.2 (2005) 252; Peter Bolt, *Reformed Theological Review* 64.3 (2005) 172-173; Ron Clark, *RestQ* 47.3 (2005) 194; Mary Rose D'Angelo, *Journal of Religion* 85.3 (2005) 480-481; Susan A. Calef, *Theological Studies* 66.4 (2005) 930*b*-931*a*; Lynn McVay, *AshTJ* 37 (2005) 134-135; Darryl W. Palmer, *Australian Biblical Review* 53 (2005) 88-89; Robert Horst, *CJ* 32.2 (**2006**), 245-247; Edgar Krentz, *CurTM* 34.3 (**2007**) 217; I. Howard Marshall, *EQ* 80.1 (**2008**) 83*b*-85*a*.

Wolfe, B. Paul, 'The Sagacious **Use of Scripture**', in Köstenberger–Wilder [2010] 199-218

Y

Young, Frances M., 'The Pastoral Epistles and the **Ethics** of Reading', *JSNT* 45 (1992) 105-120 [18]

----------, '**On Ἐπίσκοπος** and Πρεσβύτερος', *JTS* 45.1 (1994) 142-148

Z

Ziesler, J. A., *The Meaning of **Righteousness** in Paul* (SNTSMS 20; Cambridge: CUP, 1972)

----------'Pastoral Epistles', *DBI* [1990] 518*b*-520*b*

18 Reprinted in Stanley E. Porter & Craig A. Evans (ed.), *The Pauline Writings* (The Biblical Seminar 34; Sheffield: SAP, 1995) 268-282, and in Porter & Evans (ed.), *New Testament Interpretation and Methods* (Sheffield: SAP, 1997) 293-307.

聖經研究叢書

探索與鑽研神的話語，傳承真理。

雅各書註釋

張略 著／HK$148

馬可福音：敍事鑑別與神學註釋
Mark: A Narrative-Theological Commentary

曾思瀚、鄧紹光 合著／曾景恒 譯（曾思瀚部分）／HK$168

列王紀神學註釋
1 & 2 Kings

利法特（Peter Leithart）著／李金好 譯／HK$158

馬太福音神學註釋
Matthew

侯活士（Stanley Hauerwas）著／李雋 譯／HK$153

壞鬼釋經——糾正新約金句的常見詮釋
Commonly Misinterpreted Texts: Exegetical Fallacies in the New Testament

曾思瀚 著／曾景恒 譯／HK$88

壞鬼釋經：舊約敍事篇——糾正舊約金句的常見詮釋
Commonly Misinterpreted Texts II: Exegetical Fallacies in the Old Testament Narratives

曾思瀚 著／李梅 譯／HK$83

壞鬼釋經：舊約詩歌篇——糾正舊約金句的常見詮釋
Commonly Misinterpreted Texts III: Exegetical Fallacies in the Old Testament Poetry

曾思瀚 著／李梅、倪勤生 譯／HK$93

壞鬼比喻：馬太福音篇——糾正新約比喻的常見詮釋
Right Kingdom, Wrong Stories: A Backward Reading of Matthew's Parables

曾思瀚 著／曾景恒 譯／HK$93

壞鬼比喻：馬可福音篇——糾正新約比喻的常見詮釋
Stories Telling Stories: A Study of Mark's Parables

曾思瀚 著／曾景恒 譯／HK$78

壞鬼比喻：路加福音篇——糾正新約比喻的常見詮釋
Right Parables, Wrong Perspectives: A Diverse Reading of Luke's Parables
曾思瀚 著／曾景恒 譯／ HK$98

士師記的刻劃研究——領袖、女性與家庭的故事
Judges Characterized: Stories of Leadership, Women and Family
曾思瀚、吳瑩宜 著／ HK$138

啟示錄的刻劃研究——英雄、女性與國度的故事
Revelation Characterized: Stories of Heroes, Women and Empires
曾思瀚、吳瑩宜 著／ HK$118

歷久常新的生命故事——約翰福音人物研究
Eternal Word Spoken: A Literary Study on Characterization in John's Gospel
曾思瀚、吳瑩宜 著／ HK$98

使命傳承的故事——路加—使徒行傳的人物研究
Embodying Jesus: Luke-Acts Characterization
曾思瀚 著／吳瑩宜 譯／ HK$98

天國就在我們中間——馬太福音登山寶訓解經研究
Wise Relationships for God's People: Reading the Sermon on the Mount as Wisdom Literature
曾思瀚 著／吳瑩宜 譯／ HK$78

傳到地極——羅馬書初探
To the Ends of the Earth: An Exposition on Romans
曾思瀚 著／吳瑩宜 譯／ HK$78

天國與福音——反思舊約天國觀
Gospel and Kingdom: A Christian Interpretation of the O.T.
高偉勳 (Graeme Goldsworthy) 著／陳克平、陳慕賢 譯／ HK$78

基道釋經手冊
Introduction to Biblical Interpretation
(Revised and Expanded)
威廉·克萊因 (William W. Klein)、克雷格·布魯姆伯格 (Craig L. Blomberg)、羅伯特·哈伯德 (Robert L. Hubbard, Jr.) 合著／邵樟平 學術顧問／蔡錦圖 主編／ HK$288

新約評經法導引
A Beginner's Guide to New Testament Exegesis: Taking the Fear Out of Critical Method
埃理克森 (Richard J. Erickson) 著／許子韻、吳國雄 譯／ HK$128

聖經導論叢書

一套高質素的原著作品，適合華人神學院和資深信徒使用的教材！

新約歷史與宗教文化導論

黃錫木、孫寶玲、張略 合撰／HK$108

在學習聖經的過程中，一般人都只專注於經卷的內容，而忽略了「聖經背景」的重要性，甚至認為它是可有可無的。然而，若要正確理解聖經經文所傳達的內容，我們必須從它們的處境出發。要成功地進入經文的世界，對經文的歷史和文化背景的認識是不可缺少的。全書分兩大部分：歷史篇遠溯至希羅文明的源頭，並介紹「兩約之間歷史」、「新約歷史」及「猶太散居地」。至於，宗教文化篇則分別介紹「新約世界的希羅宗教」和「猶太人的基本信念與實踐」，主要論及有關的宗教文化概念與神學思想。

福音書總論與馬可福音導論

黃錫木 編著／HK$98

使徒行傳導論

袁天佑 著／HK$83

加拉太書導論

郭漢成 著／HK$63

啟示錄導論

吳獻章 著／HK$88

讀者意見表

緊扣時代 服事教會

以文字傳揚基督真道

衷心多謝你購買本社書籍。本社一直致力以出版事工服事教會，幫助信徒扎根於神的話語，促進靈命增長。為使我們的出版更能滿足你的需要，請填寫下列各項資料，並寄回或傳真予本社。

所購書籍：＿＿＿＿＿＿＿＿＿＿＿＿＿＿＿＿

本書最吸引你的地方：

□作者　□適切性　□文筆　□設計　□實用性

□其他：＿＿＿＿＿＿＿＿＿＿＿＿＿＿＿＿

購買本書地點：

□基道書樓　□基督教書店　□非基督教書店

性別：□男　□女　職業：＿＿＿＿＿＿＿＿

信仰：□基督徒　□非基督徒

年齡：□ 16 歲或以下　□ 17～25 歲　□ 26～35 歲
□ 36～55 歲　□ 56 歲或以上

學歷：□中三或以下　□中五　□預科
□大學　□研究院

□我欲更多了解基道出版社的事工及考慮支持，請寄給我下列資料：

□機構簡介　□新書資料　□基道會員通訊

□《基道文字事工通訊》

姓名：＿＿＿＿＿＿＿＿＿＿＿＿電話：＿＿＿＿＿＿＿＿

地址：＿＿＿＿＿＿＿＿＿＿＿＿＿＿＿＿＿＿＿＿

＿＿＿＿＿＿＿＿＿＿＿＿＿＿＿＿＿＿＿＿＿＿＿

傳真：＿＿＿＿＿＿＿＿　電子郵件：＿＿＿＿＿＿＿＿

其他意見：＿＿＿＿＿＿＿＿＿＿＿＿＿＿＿＿＿＿

＿＿＿＿＿＿＿＿＿＿＿＿＿＿＿＿＿＿＿＿＿＿＿

多謝賜教！

基道出版社

意見表可以傳真（2687-0281）或直接郵寄以下地址：
香港沙田火炭坳背灣街26號富騰工業中心1011室
基道出版社編輯部收